On 25th November 1993, I wrote to HRH The Prince of Wales, begging his help to assist me in avoiding the premature death of 2,000 UK citizens every week and 2,500,000 worldwide every year. My pleadings were not for financial support, but merely for what would have amounted to the sacrifice of just one single day in his lifetime.

It is now 15th January 1994. To date I have received no reply to my letter. Since 25th November 1993, already over 15,000 UK citizens and 350,000 citizens worldwide have suffered needless and horrendous premature deaths and a like number of youngsters have been recruited to take their place.

I FIND THAT VERY SAD

OBVIOUSLY PRINCE CHARLES DOESN'T

A Letter to Prince Charles

.... or The Only Way to Stop Smoking

Allen Carr

Produced by Laws and Stimson Associates
31 Malden Way
New Malden
Surrey KT3 6EB

Printed and bound in Great Britain by
Biddles Ltd, Guildford and King's Lynn

CONTENTS

IMPORTANT

If drugs like nicotine, alcohol and heroin have such widely different properties and all drug addicts have their unique mental and physical characteristics, how can Allen Carr's method work for all drugs and for all drug addicts?

There are many differences between a house and a tree, but the same ladder will enable any individual to surmount either:

PROVIDED YOU UNDERSTAND HOW TO USE IT!

Allen Carr's method is the ladder that will enable any drug addict to escape from the pit of addiction to any drug:

IMMEDIATELY!

EASILY!

PERMANENTLY!

PROVIDED YOU UNDERSTAND HOW TO USE IT!

To do that it is essential to read the whole of this book and to be familiar with Allen Carr's previous best seller: THE EASY WAY TO STOP SMOKING, or the video or audio tapes of the same name. Details of how to obtain copies are given inside the back cover.

CHAPTER 1

Allen in Wonderland

"What on earth are you doing to yourself?"

"I'm enjoying a cigarette."

The inquisitor was my wife Joyce. One of those lucky people that try just one cigarette and find it so obnoxious that they are never tempted to light another. But how can a non-smoker possibly understand the great *joy and pleasure* to be obtained from smoking?

The cigarette was dangling from my lips 'Humphrey Bogart' style, and the *pleasure* was not in the slightest way diminished by the fact that it was saturated with my own blood! The cause was a nosebleed, the second within the space of an hour.

The first was a really bad one caused by the paroxysms of coughing brought on by those *very special* early morning cigarettes. These nosebleeds had recently become part of my daily routine. Joyce had already given me the usual lecture about what smoking was doing to my health. It went in one ear and, presumably because there was nothing to impede its flow, straight out of the other. I knew that smoking was killing me anyway, all the nagging did was to make me feel even more stupid than I already felt – it just seemed to increase my dependency on cigarettes. It wasn't that I didn't want to stop I knew that I couldn't stop! I accepted the fact and gave up even trying.

Eventually the first nosebleed ended. I changed my suit and went out to my car. I sat in my car depressed and miserable. I thought: "If this is life with my little crutch, there is no way that I could cope with life without it!" I was desperate for another cigarette, but I knew this would start the nosebleeding again. That first nosebleed had frightened me, I estimated that I had lost at least a pint of blood and was reluctant to lose more.

It was an extreme example of the tug of war of fear that all drug addicts suffer whilst they remain dependent on the drug. It was a

1

particularly dismal Monday morning I was terrified of what the smoking was doing to me and at one and the same time thinking: "If ever I really needed a cigarette, it's now!"

It didn't take long for my addicted brain to come up with a simple solution to the problem. One of the few subjects that I took any interest in at school was biology. I knew that the human body carries about 8 pints of blood, with one pint short, my blood level must have sunk below my nose. That's obviously why the first nosebleed had stopped, so I could safely smoke another cigarette. Needless to say, I did.

I regard myself as a reasonably intelligent man. I will forgive you at this stage for doubting my word. I remember well Tony Hancock's classic remark in 'The Blood Donor' and his look of horror and utter disbelief when informed that he was expected to donate a whole pint: **"A pint! That's almost an armful! I'm not going to walk about all day with a floppy arm just to satisfy some legalised vampire!"**

I was fully aware of how the circulatory system works and in particular, that the brain depends on a constant supply of blood; but isn't this another of the many anomalies of being a drug addict? All our smoking lives we have many powerful reasons not to smoke, but we work so hard to block out those reasons and devote all our ingenuity to finding any flimsy excuse which will allow us to smoke **JUST ONE MORE CIGARETTE!**

In no time at all I was smothered in blood again, oblivious to everything other than my own misery, I was suddenly aware that Joyce was staring at me through the car window. She had that haunted look on her face that I had come to dread. I gritted my teeth and waited for the usual lecture.

It never came. I believe it had finally dawned on Joyce that rationality and sound common sense are a complete waste of time when dealing with a drug addict. It was fortunate that she allowed natural emotion and feminine intuition to take over.

She had been watching a film about a couple whose child was slowly dying of leukemia. They were stoically trying to build a constructive life, not only for their child, but for themselves. Just watching such a film is a harrowing enough experience, but the actual trauma of the real situation must be infinitely worse.

Joyce said: "Do you think that you could handle a situation like that?" At the time, I confess to being so wrapped up in my own petty problems that I was oblivious to other people's. She continued: "It must be awful for that couple, but, at least they have the consolation of knowing that they are doing everything in their power and that the disease was not self-inflicted, how much worse do you think it is to have to watch someone you love slowly destroying himself and spending a fortune for the privilege, when you can see so clearly that he's getting no benefit whatsoever from smoking. Have you any idea of the pain that you are causing me and your children? Do you realise how incredibly selfish you are being? How would you like it if I started doing to my body what you are doing to yours?"

'OPEN SESAME'

Just as those words had magically opened the entrance to Ali Baba's cave, so Joyce had finally hit the key which would provide me with infinitely greater treasures than those revealed to Ali Baba: a release from the lifelong slavery to nicotine. At the time neither of us could have predicted that she had started a chain reaction which I believe will change the course of history. I dearly hope that we both live to see it happen.

There had been a dark, locked room in my brain that, like a giant clam, refused to be prised open. The key word was **SELFISH**. Up until that time I had always regarded smoking as my personal problem. I knew that it was killing me, but if I was prepared to run the risk of a shorter, and as I believed at the time, a sweeter life, what had that got to do with anyone else?

That closed door in my brain began to open, as the light began to penetrate, so those years of darkness, depression and futility began to disappear. Up to then, I had always regarded my smoking from an insular perspective. Previously, whenever I sensed that someone was trying to advise me against smoking, my defensive shields would go up. I might even adopt an aggressive attitude. It all depended upon the nature of the attack. But now it was almost as if I were suddenly released from the confines of my own mind and body and was able to observe myself as a non-smoker would see me. As you can imagine, the object of my observations did not exactly fill me with pride.

I tried to imagine that Joyce was the smoker and I the non-smoker. I pride myself on having a good imagination. I could see her as 'Fag Ash Lil'. I could see her wheezing and coughing whilst cooking a meal, fag dangling from the lips with an inch of ash about to drop into the saucepan. I could picture the nicotine stains on her fingers, teeth and lips. I could picture her dull eyes and grey complexion. I could imagine the foul smell of her breath, and because I love her dearly, I believe that I would have tolerated these things. I could have tolerated all the money that she was wasting. I even believe that I would have put up with all the phoney arguments that she would have made to justify her stupidity. I hope that I would have been as tolerant towards her as she had been to me all those dark years. But having to watch her go through the misery that I was going through, that I couldn't have stood!

I began to think about those people born with terrible disabilities like Downs Syndrome and Thalidomide, and how they seem to rise above such handicaps. What chance do you think you would have of obtaining a decent job if you were confined to a life in a wheelchair? That didn't stop Franklin D.Roosevelt from holding the No.1 job. There are people like Simon Weston, the soldier that suffered multiple burns in the Falklands. If you have ever brushed a lighted cigarette over your skin, you'll know the intense pain that just a slight burn would cause. It's almost inconceivable to imagine, the pain, the fear, the discomfort, the utter despair that he must have suffered, but did he let this defeat him? No way. He has since married and is already a television star and modern day folk hero.

Another classic example was Christopher Nolan, the young Irish boy who spent his first 15 years as a vegetable. His condition was such that he had no means of communication. The natural tendency was to treat him like an imbecile. But inside that broken body was an intelligent brain. Eventually he learned to communicate by typing with a stick attached to his forehead. He even wrote a bestselling book. Some of the critics were benevolent enough to knock it with comments like: "It's okay but he tends to be slightly excessive with the use of adjectives." His mother said: "If only they could see the effort that it took him to type one word, they'd know that every word was essential, the fact that they couldn't see his point, was their problem, not Christopher's."

Can you imagine being treated as a vegetable for 15 years, when you are in fact highly intelligent, but not able to communicate? You would have thought that once Christopher had learned to communicate, his first message would be: "Please put me quietly to sleep." But no, just like all other creatures on the planet, no matter how underprivileged, deformed or ugly they might appear in the eyes of other creatures, the first rule of nature is: **SURVIVAL!** Christopher wanted to live, because whether we like it or not, life is precious. Sadly, Christopher is not with us today, but I hope that wherever he is, he is able to appreciate the marvellous legacy that his example left to mankind.

The sheer stupidity of what I had been doing suddenly hit me. There were people like Christopher Nolan, born with massive disabilities, and yet able somehow to surmount them. Then there was me, not only privileged to be born, but lucky enough to be born with a complete and healthy mind and body. There I was, slapping the creator in the face, saying: "Thank you for my healthy body. But why didn't you give it to Christopher Nolan? I'm sure that he would have appreciated it. Why did you waste it on someone like me? **SOMEONE WHO DEVOTES MOST OF HIS LIFE TO DREAMING UP INGENIOUS EXCUSES IN ORDER TO JUSTIFY HIS OBSESSION TO SPEND A FORTUNE ON SELF-ADMINISTERED POISONS!**

For years I had stubbornly resisted Joyce's pleadings to seek help. I resisted, not because I was too proud to seek help, but because I knew

4

that if it were possible for me to stop, I would have already done so.

Now, I am aware that when I describe the depth of degradation that I had descended to, most readers, particularly younger smokers or casual smokers will be consoling themselves with the thought that: "I would never let it get to that stage, and even if I did, I would stop." I am also aware that you might be forming the impression that this book will be umpteen pages of blood and gore and that I am going to attempt to frighten you into quitting. Not so, if I thought that I could succeed by using such shock tactics, I wouldn't hesitate to use them. But they didn't help me to stop and if they were any use to you, you would already be a non-smoker. I promise you that I have nothing but good news for you. What I need you to know, is why smokers who are aware that they will die unless they stop, **STILL DON'T STOP!** Because unless you understand the true reason now, **NEITHER WILL YOU!**

You might also be forming the impression that the actual key that Joyce pressed to open my mind, was the sudden realisation that I was destroying my own body. Not so, I was fully aware that smoking was killing me. That had been blatantly obvious for years. I had merely closed my mind to the fact.

It might also have occurred to you that the decisive factor was the realisation I was being selfish, and that although I wasn't prepared to make the great sacrifice to save my own life, I would now unselfishly do so for the sake of my wife and children. I would like to take credit for being that noble and unselfish, but I'm afraid that the truth is that smokers cannot even force themselves to stop for selfish reasons and there is no way that they can do it for other people. Let me make it quite clear, at this stage the key word had done absolutely nothing to change my views about smoking, it had merely pricked my conscience which in turn lead to my agreeing to seek help.

I knew that the hypnotherapist would not be able to help me. But I thought that if I go through the ritual, I could come home, conscience completely clear, and say: "You see, it was a complete waste of time and money. Will you now just accept that, whether I like it or not:

I WILL NEVER BE ABLE TO STOP SMOKING!"

People that know Joyce will confirm that her name signifies her nature. She is a bundle of optimism and Joy. But I believe that she too was anticipating bad news.

I was hoping that it would be the end of the lectures, even so, I wasn't relishing the effect that my failure would have on her.

They say that fact is stranger than fiction. I believe it.

I'M GOING TO CURE THE WORLD OF SMOKING!

These were the actual words that I greeted Joyce with on my return. Her reaction disappointed me. She couldn't have looked more aghast if I had hit her on the knee with a hammer. The looks she used to give me when I was coughing and wheezing were bad enough, but this one was a quantum leap, "YOU'VE COMPLETELY GONE OFF YOUR ROCKER." No words were spoken, the look clearly conveyed the message. I was on such a high at the time that I couldn't understand her disbelief.

When I reflect on the facts, the miracle is that she didn't have me certified there and then. I think that she believed that the hypnotherapist had put me into some sort of trance and forgotten to take me out of it. For years after I had stopped smoking and had successfully helped to cure thousands of other smokers, I think she still feared that one day I would awake from that trance and that again she would see me with that awful fag in my mouth.

Her disbelief was understandable. She had witnessed umpteen previous failed attempts to stop. She remembered how I had once looked her straight in the eye and blatantly lied when I assured her that I had stopped but was secretly smoking. Bear in mind that my most recent attempt two years earlier had ended in tears after 6 months of black depression, bad temper and abject misery; I was crying because I knew that if I didn't succeed then, I would never have the willpower or strength to go through that misery again and, like my father before me, was doomed to die a smoker. Strangely it never particularly worried me that I would die because of my smoking. I suppose I believed that I chose to take the risk, but I hated the thought that I would never be able to stop:

THAT THE CIGARETTE WAS CONTROLLING ME

There I was, an hour earlier the worst nicotine addict I had ever known, (I've still yet to meet a worse case) returning, not only free, but going to cure the rest of the world? I'm sure that you can understand Joyce's scepticism.

What you will find difficult to believe is that before I extinguished that last cigarette, I was already a non-smoker and already knew that I would never have the need or desire to smoke again. Mind you, although I knew at that time that I would never need to smoke again, I wasn't expecting it to be easy. The incredible revelation was: not only was it ridiculously easy, but I actually enjoyed the whole process right from extinguishing that final cigarette. It didn't take any willpower, there weren't any bad withdrawal pangs and I haven't craved a cigarette since that day. An additional bonus was, far from gaining weight, 6 months after I extinguished that final cigarette, I was 28 pounds lighter.

What you will find even more difficult to believe, is that my discovery is equally effective for any smoker, including **YOU**. Indeed it is equally effective for any form of chemical dependency, including alcohol and heroin.

My visit to the hypnotherapist was on 15th. July 1983 and was the most important day in my life. From here on I will refer to it as Independence Day. You might well be tempted to rush off to the nearest hypnotherapist. Please don't! I am loathe to run down the man that I consulted, because I would be dead now if had not made that visit. But I succeeded in spite of and not because of that visit. Later I will explain more about the mysteries surrounding hypnosis which will enable you to decide whether or not it can be of service to you.

Although I did not fully comprehend everything that happened to me on that day, I was fully aware that I had made a discovery that every smoker was secretly searching for:

AN EASY WAY TO STOP SMOKING!

A few months spent testing the method out on friends and relatives confirmed my expectations. So much so that I took the momentous decision of quitting my job as a Chartered Accountant and set up a full time clinic helping others to escape from the slavery of nicotine.

We started off with a small ad in the local paper. Our first paying customer was Peter Murray, famous disc jockey and TV personality. It didn't dawn on me that he was *the* Pete Murray of 'The 6.5 Special' fame, and as I watched him walk up the drive I was shaking like a leaf. The whole experience was a nightmare, I had lost my voice and I was in a blue funk. I dread to think what he thought of that first session, and I never had the courage to phone him to find out. All I do know is that it is usually my job to relax the client, on this occasion it was the other way around. I didn't appreciate it at the time, but it turned out to be a blessing in disguise. I honestly believe that had he not been the pleasant personality that he is, I would never have had the courage to continue. If I didn't help him, I hope it is of some consolation to him to know that he has indirectly been the cause of helping me to help thousands of other smokers escape from this evil trap.

From that rather inauspicious start, my confidence grew and so did our success rate. We soon found that we had no need to advertise. Smokers were flying in from all over the world solely because of the recommendation they had received from successful clients.

I was the therapist and Joyce was typist, telephonist, receptionist and did all the other 1001 jobs that needed to be done. After 2 years we could no longer treat the number of smokers that sought our help, so I set out my method in a book:

THE EASY WAY TO STOP SMOKING

The book, published by PENGUIN, became a best seller, and has remained one every year since. I have always thought that a good title is an absolute essential for any book, yet I cannot even remember pondering about the title, it seemed obvious. I did however find the book very difficult to write, with the notable exception of the now legendary Chapter 21.

My only expectation of the book was that it would help smokers to escape from the nicotine trap. It came as a pleasant surprise when I started to receive hundreds of grateful letters from ex-smokers and their families. After all, although I attempted to make the book as interesting and amusing as possible, in effect it's an instruction manual, and I suspect that the only mail that writers of instruction manuals receive, are letters of complaint. I have received very few letters from smokers that failed to stop after reading the book. This is what you would expect, we all tend to throw tantrums when the instruction manual is incoherent, but how many of us take the trouble to write to complain about it? Surprisingly, even the letters received from failures are complimentary, the criticisms being mainly restricted to suggestions on how the book might be improved.

I find instruction manuals particularly annoying nowadays. I believe it's because they are usually translations from Japanese. The computer I am using at the moment is an 'Olivetti'. Great! It's not English, but it is Italian which must surely be the next best thing, after all, we're all Europeans now. But, stamped on the box is: MADE IN TAIWAN. I'm not being racist, the Japanese and Taiwanese are obviously more intelligent than we are, but why must the quality of their equipment be so incredibly high, and the quality of their translations so incredibly low? I'm sure the translator doesn't even speak English and just used a Japanese/English dictionary. 'The Easy Way to Stop Smoking' has already been translated into seven different languages. Although as a nation, the Japanese tend to be heavy smokers, the book has not yet been translated into Japanese. Perhaps I can get even by translating it myself.

This personal computer business is another pain. My friends and relatives that had one assured me how easy modern computers are. The jargon is 'user friendly'. They are about as user friendly as a four pound club hammer landing on your big toe!

"I don't know how I managed without one." They said.

"You're a Chartered Accountant, you'll find it a piece of cake."

User friendly! The instruction manual alone was larger than the complete works of Shakespere. It's taken me longer to learn to use the computer than it would have to write the book. If you think that Japanese is a complicated language, just wait until you start on

8

computer languages like RAM and FROGOL. The stupid thing was, that I sensed that I was being sucked in. They were all a tiny bit too enthusiastic about their computers. Of course they were! They'd spent hundreds of pounds and had to justify all that expense. They reminded me of teenage smokers that learn to get over the foul smell and taste, then realising that they are now hooked, try to convince their non-smoking friends of the great pleasure of being a smoker. Unfortunately, they all too often succeed!

Unwittingly, the computer operators' wives would join in the conspiracy:

"I've never known him to be so obsessed with anything. I never see him nowadays. He spends all night playing with it."

Of course he does! Endless, sleepless nights trying to understand the damn thing. Modern technology is a marvellous thing but it does have its drawbacks. I remember the good old days when there were only 2 warning lights on a car, and a radio only required 2 knobs. I heard the other day that less than 50% of adults know how to programme their video recorders. It was good news to me, I'm no longer ashamed to tell people that I rely on my seven year old grandson.

I think I'm beginning to get the hang of this computer now. It's really quite simple once you know how. Come to think of it, I can't think how I managed without it? I strongly recommend that you get one. They're tough little machines too. I've thrown this one through my study window 3 times, purely to test it out you understand, but it still works.

The letters that I have received have repaid, a thousand times over, the considerable time and effort it took me to write the book. Many people have asked me why I haven't written other books. It seemed a strange question to me. After all, I'm not a writer. I only wrote the book because I had important knowledge to communicate. Having completed my task, where was the need to write another book? There wasn't one.

So why am I writing one now? No, it's not for those massive royalties, I would gladly forfeit them and pay someone else to write the book if that were possible. There are several reasons, part good news part bad. Let's deal with the bad news first:

When I first discovered what I will now refer to as: 'The Magic Button', I thought that it would take about 5 minutes to persuade any reasonably intelligent smoker to quit, merely by explaining that the only pleasure or crutch that smokers receive when they light up, is trying to get back to the level of peace and tranquillity that non-smokers experience the whole of their lives, and that since each cigarette, far from relieving the withdrawal pangs from nicotine, is actually causing them, even that pleasure or crutch is illusory.

I estimated that it would take about 10 years to cure the world of smoking. No doubt, like Joyce, you also suspect that I need to be certified. But just reflect for a moment. Imagine that I had discovered a cure for lung cancer. Even if I were the world's leading expert on lung cancer, my cure would quite rightly be subjected to the most intensive and detailed scrutiny.

So how long would it take for me to prove that I had in fact found the magic button? This wasn't going to be easy, even my closest friends and relatives knew me as the most pathetic nicotine addict that had ever lived. How can I possibly convince them that overnight I had become the world's leading expert on how to quit? Perhaps you feel that it is impossible to be transformed overnight from confirmed chain-smoker to the world's leading expert? But imagine you had been imprisoned for nearly a third of a century, within an escape proof cell that had a combination lock, but no one knew the combination. Neither your jailors nor your fellow prisoners. Then suppose you hated that prison more than the other prisoners and that you had devoted most of your time trying to discover the combination. 'UREKA!' One day you discover the correct combination, you are free! Wouldn't you in the space of a few seconds have become not only the world's leading expert on escaping from that prison, but the only expert? That is virtually what happened to me.

Obviously I didn't expect people to believe me overnight, after all I'm not even a doctor. It would be like Columbus saying: "Look chaps, I've been giving this a lot of thought lately, I'm absolutely certain that the world isn't flat as we all thought, it's really a giant football. Perhaps you would be kind enough to spread the message and rewrite all the text books."

In any event, I knew from Joyce's initial reaction that I had a credibility problem. It was no real problem. Columbus proved his point by sailing around the world. I would prove my point by demonstrating to those smokers that consulted me, that it is ridiculously easy to stop smoking. They would then tell their friends, who would come rushing around for my magic cure.

I repeatedly refer to a 'magic button' or, a 'magic' cure. I should make it clear that I have no mystical powers. A telephone would be magic to stone age man. There is no such thing as magic. Magic is merely a word meaning: "I don't understand how it works". The 'magic' of my method is the same as the magic of being able to open a safe, provided you know the combination.

I thought it would take about 4 years to prove that my method was the magic cure that smokers had been praying for. I was over prudent. In fact we achieved that object to our satisfaction within 2 years. Even so, there were one or two shocks that I hadn't expected. When I decided to give the world the benefit of my knowledge by writing the book, I approached a famous publisher, explained to them that I had discovered a method that would enable any smoker to stop easily, that I wanted to put it into book form, and that I had selected them for the task. I didn't exactly say so, but my overall tone implied how lucky they were.

To my amazement they didn't jump at my offer over the phone, they didn't even offer to send the Managing Director around immediately. In fact they begrudgingly agreed to read the manuscript. I explained that I hadn't yet written the book, that there would be no point in their reading the manuscript anyway, after all it wasn't a novel or a work of art. It was merely an effective method to help smokers to quit, a method that I had already proved, and that since I was the world's leading expert on quitting smoking, they could just accept my word for it. As I put it to them, if Nick Faldo offered you his lifetimes' golfing secrets, would you be asking him these fatuous questions?

Needless to say I got nowhere, but I learned a lesson. Everyone knows that Nick Faldo is a great golfer. It hadn't occurred to me at that stage that I was the only person who knew that I was the world's leading expert on stopping smoking. Some of my converts might have suspected it, but I was the only one that *knew* it.

The experience with the publisher convinced me that I would be wasting my time trying to court others. I had heard stories about talented writers spending years trying to get their work published. So I decided to print the book myself. The problem was that at that stage, curing smokers was nothing like as lucrative as being a Chartered Accountant. The fact is, we were struggling to keep the wolf from the door. No problem, I had a successful and wealthy brother, the leading insurance broker in High Wycombe, who is always on the lookout for profitable schemes. I thought that I could kill 2 birds with one stone, provide him with a profitable investment and, because he knew that I was successfully curing smokers, and that I was of sound mind and body, it would save me the time and trouble of having to explain to financiers what a sound investment it was.

Unfortunately I failed to convince my brother that the book would be a sure-fire winner. There I was, convinced that I was writing the most significant book for mankind since the 'Origin Of The Species' and I couldn't even convince by own brother that he wouldn't lose his investment. His final body blow was: if you get any *good* ideas be sure to let me know!

Ironically, the situation reminded me of that classic monologue by Bob Newhart. It's not only the most amusing piece ever written about smoking, but it does help to get the whole thing into perspective. The theme is Sir Walter Raliegh. Having discovered tobacco in the 'New World', he is telephoning his agent in London, trying to persuade him to 'get in early' on a sure-fire winner. This is an edited extract:

11

"What's that Walt, you've bought a shipload of to-baaa-co. What's to-baaa-co Walt? It's a kind of leaf? You've bought 80 tons of leaves! This might come as a surprise to you Walt, but come autumn over here and we're up to our- Oh it's a special leaf. What do you do with it Walt? It has several uses? What are its uses Walt? You can take a pinch of tobacco and sniff it up your nose? Why would you do that Walt? It makes you sneeze! Yes I imagine it would. What else can you do with it Walt? You shred it, roll it up in a piece of paper and stick it—No! Don't tell me where you stick it Walt! Oh, you stick in your mouth. Why would you do that Walt? So you can set fire to it? Then you breathe the fumes into your lungs? It seems to me you could just stand over your fireplace and do that. Walt, we've been a bit worried about you, ever since you put your cape over that mud. I don't think to-baaa-co will catch on over here, but if you get any good ideas, be sure and let me in on it first! No, I'll ring you Walt!"

Ironic that Walt was regarded as an imbecile for believing that people could be persuaded to smoke, and I was being regarded with equal incredulity for believing they could be persuaded not to.

The experience with the publisher was merely a slight set back to my ego, however the incident with my brother was a real bone-crusher. It didn't shake my faith in my method, by this stage I had unshakable confidence in the the only two important facts:

1. All smokers secretly wanted to stop smoking, whether they or the rest of society realised it or not
2. I had the key to release them from their prison.

It was my credibility that was shaken. If I couldn't persuade my own brother, what possible chance would I have of persuading anyone else? I even questioned whether I had the right to ask anyone to risk their money. So I decided to drop the idea of the book. Then a wonderful thing happened, which more than restored my faith in human nature.

We were entertaining an old friend, Sid Sutton, who started life an orphan in a Dr. Barnados home and had risen to become a shrewd and successful businessman. His wealth emanated from the manufacture of the highest quality reproduction furniture sold at ridiculously low prices. Excuse the commercial, but this man deserves it and it's all true. Quite how the subject of the book came up I am not certain, I believe we were in conversation about our favourite subject – bank managers, and in particular, how they refuse to lend you money unless you can prove that you don't really need to borrow it. They are rather like publishers that will only risk backing you if you have already sold as many books as Babara Cartland. I can just remember Sid saying: "I'll give you the money for the book." I said: "Sid have you any idea of what it will cost? I'm very confident that it will be a success, but I cannot guarantee it."

It should be emphasized he said *give* not *lend*. If you are one of the thousands that benefited from The Easy Way to Stop Smoking, you are indebted to Sid. I am indeed a lucky man to have such a friend. I dedicated that book, in part to Sid. This book I dedicate to another very close friend, who also had unwavering faith in me and without whose help, I would have achieved nothing. They say that behind every *great* man is a woman. I suspect that in most cases the truth is – behind a rather mediocre man, is a *great* woman! I am not ashamed to admit to being in the latter category.

Now if I had discovered a simple and effective cure for lung cancer, which had been subjected to the most rigorous tests and those tests proved the cure to be genuine, how long do you think it would take for the news to spread throughout the civilised world? 10 years? It would be more like 10 hours! Yet smoking causes 10 times more premature deaths than lung cancer and is the leading cause of lung cancer. In fact smoking is easily the No.1 killer in western society and is currently killing about two and a half million people every year.

People often say to me: "You must get tremendous satisfaction from the work you do?" They are absolutely correct. I hated being an accountant I love helping smokers to escape from the nicotine trap. It's not only my profession and my vocation, it's my obsession. I cannot claim to do it for any noble, philanthropic motives. I do it for the purely selfish reason that, every time I hear that a smoker has escaped from the trap, it gives me tremendous pleasure, even when I have taken no part in that escape.

Nearly ten years have now elapsed since Independence Day. They have been the happiest years of my life and I am truly grateful for them. Hence the title of this chapter. I had considered it as the title of this book, but sadly, the last five of those years have been counter-balanced by an immense frustration. At times I feel I will explode. In the final paragraph of The Easy Way to Stop Smoking (To save your time and mine, henceforth I will refer to 'EASYWAY') I said: "There is a wind of change in society. A snowball has started that I hope this book will help turn into an avalanche. You can help too by spreading this message."

I know both from personal contact and from your letters, that thousands of you have been doing just that. I really appreciate your support and I am so grateful for it, but in the total context of the smoking problem, our combined efforts are no more than a 'spit in the ocean'.

13

If, as I claim, I had proved my method after two years, why hasn't the news of this cure spread like wildfire throughout the world? Why have some 20 million smokers had to have their lives ended prematurely and why have a similar number of youngsters been allowed to take their place?

There is one obvious answer: Allen Carr is a charlatan and a crank and that his system doesn't work in the way that he claims. If this is the answer, why did the presenter of 'Watchdog' successfully use Allen Carr's method? Why did several of the 'Panorama' team and several employees of TV-AM successfully use his method? If he is a charlatan and a crank, why haven't they exposed him as such? If he isn't, why do they deny the rest of society this simple cure? 'Panorama' recently televised what must have been a very costly expose on how The Council for Tobacco Research failed to publish evidence which implied a strong association between smoking and ill health. I should think that few members of the public are still naive enough to believe they would anyway, and since the medical experts have already informed us of the health risks, the programme wasn't much of a revelation. 'Panorama' would have better spent their time and money informing the public about what they didn't know – a simple and effective cure to the problem.

If Allen Carr doesn't advertise, why do smokers fly from all over the world to seek his help? After all, he's only one man, he hasn't got the massive resources of the BMA, ASH and QUIT. He's not even a doctor. There is one simple answer to that question:

HIS SYSTEM WORKS!

So what went wrong? When making my estimate of ten years, it didn't even occur to me that I would first have to convince the smokers themselves, let alone the rest of society, that they were not smoking because they chose to, but because they had fallen into a trap that they couldn't escape from. In fact the chief ingenuity of the trap, is that it can take years to realise that you are actually in it.

In my naivety, I thought that, like me, if there were a magic button that smokers could press to wake up the next morning as if they had never lit the first cigarette, all smokers would press it. But I soon learned that youngsters and casual smokers were convinced that they were in control.

It took me longer to learn that even smokers that realised that they were in a trap, would hesitate to press that button out of fear. Rather like people that have been institutionalised for most of their lives, hate it, but have become dependent on the institution, or like a prisoner that has planned an escape and dreamed about freedom for years but when freedom is finally granted, is at a complete loss. I am told that when released, many long term prisoners commit crimes, not because they believe that crime pays, but because it is the only way to get back to the security of the prison.

The latter is a good analogy in that it assists non-smokers, youngsters and casual smokers to understand why a smoker with a heavy cough that clearly gets no pleasure from smoking, continues to smoke. To such a smoker, the fear of remaining in the prison is less than the fear of being released. It is a bad analogy in that many institutionalised people may in fact be far better off within the institution. Let me make it clear: **EVERY SMOKER WILL FEEL FAR MORE HAPPY AND SECURE WHEN THEY LEAVE THE NICOTINE PRISON!**

In spite of the fact that we could no longer accommodate all the smokers that sought our help, the good news hadn't exactly spread like a forest fire. This was not only a surprise to me, but also to many of the smokers that we had helped to cure. Often they would ring up thanking us for our help and also say: "I've recommended you to hundreds of my relatives and colleagues, you must be absolutely inundated." Strangely, in some cases, only a few of those hundreds had sought our help. Now I could sense that the satisfied client had truly recommended the method. Perhaps the hundreds were really dozens. But why had so few taken advantage of the recommendation?

The reason is that although all smokers want to stop, part of the ingenuity of the trap is: "Yes I want to stop, and I will stop one day, but not today please, it just isn't the right time." I should have spotted it sooner. When we started the initial clinic at Raynes Park and found that we were getting more clients than we could handle, we would occasionally withdraw the ad from the local paper. Whenever we did this, the level of enquiries would increase. So much so that the local paper offered to run the advert free of charge because their telephones were inundated whenever we withdrew it.

I now know the reason for that anomaly. Readers would see our ad each week, secure in the knowledge that help was there when they needed it. The moment we withdrew it, panic set in. I think Emma Freud summed the situation up in the introduction to my video: "When 7 of my friends had consulted this man and stopped overnight, without the blowing of any trumpets, they hadn't even put on weight, I could no longer ignore him."

Earlier in the introduction she explained how much she hated being a smoker. So why was she even trying to ignore me? Why do smokers spend all their lives blocking their minds to the many powerful reasons that they have not to smoke and search for any flimsy excuse to have just one more cigarette? The answer is:

FEAR

Like all drug addiction, smoking is just a tug of war of fear. On one side of the rope is a very powerful team: "It's killing me, it's costing me a fortune, it's filthy and disgusting, it's controlling my life!" On the other side, an even more powerful team of fear: "How can I enjoy life or handle stress without my crutch? Have I the willpower and strength to go through this awful trauma of trying to give up smoking? Will I ever be completely free from the craving?"

To non-smokers and ironically, to smokers themselves, the first set of fears appear infinitely more powerful to their rational brains than do the second. So why do smokers allow the second set of fears to dominate them for the bulk of their lives?

It's because the first set of fears are fears of the future. It won't kill me today, I will have stopped before it does. It might cost the average smoker £30,000 in a lifetime, but I have no intention of smoking all my life and there is no way that I can recover the money that I have already spent. I accept that it dominates my life, but once I decide to stop that problem will be solved. But if I stop today, I'm going to have to cope with the misery of not being able to enjoy social occasions, not being able to cope with stress, unable to concentrate. I've got to go through the trauma, the black depression. I'm sorry, I will do it one day, but:

PLEASE DON'T LET IT BE TODAY!

Is it any wonder that we postpone the evil day for as long as possible? We do it for the same reason that we put off a visit to the dentist. What smokers fail to realise, is that both sets of fear are caused by the cigarette and that the greatest gain to be achieved from stopping is to be rid of that panic, insecure feeling that all drug addicts suffer when even the thought of being deprived of their drug enters their mind. Non-smokers don't suffer that feeling. The drug doesn't relieve it, quite the contrary the drug causes that feeling.

The real problem is society's attitude towards smoking. In spite of all the health scares, we still regard smoking as a rather distasteful habit, that might or might not injure the smokers' health and it is up to each individual smoker to choose whether the advantages justify the risks. Okay, even most smokers themselves regard it nowadays as anti-social, but that is really the only change in our general attitude.

Just consider these statistics published by Hansard 22nd July 1988. They relate solely to England & Wales during 1987:

CAUSE OF DEATH	NUMBER OF DEATHS	GOVERNMENT EXPENDITURE £
DRUGS	221	9,780,771
ALCOHOL	3,145	553,756
SMOKING	99,432	216,200

Now you probably suspect that I'm going on again about the harmful effects caused by smoking. I assure you that I am not. I am quoting these statistics merely to show society's warped attitude towards smoking.

What do these statistics really mean? They mean that our government is prepared to spend £44,000 to save the life of a heroin addict. An alcoholic's life is deemed to be worth £176. A smoker? £2.20! About the price of a packet of 20 cigarettes!These are quite remarkable statistics. When you further consider that a heroin addict is regarded as a criminal in law and that smokers contribute annually about £7,000,000,000 to the treasury coffers, the statistics are nothing less than **SCANDALOUS!!!**

Had I invented a cure for cancer, I would have been hailed overnight as an international hero. My name would be recorded in history with the likes of Madam Curie, Lister, Fleming and Pasteur. Yet effectively that is what I have done. No doubt you feel that I am exaggerating or over dramatising the situation. So let's try to look at the situation in hindsight by using a bit of foresight.

Imagine a conversation between a student of history and his teacher a hundred years from now, when the few smokers that remain will be regarded, rather like snuff-takers are regarded today:

"Please sir, my uncle is one of those secret smokers that you were telling us about. I tried one yesterday it was ghastly, it made me sick. Is it true that at one time 60% of adults in western society were addicted to nicotine?"

"Yes."

"And did it really kill one in four of them."

"Yes."

"Are you really saying that in just three generations it killed more people than all the wars of history combined, including the holocaust?"

"Yes."

"But didn't you also say sir that these people had to work hard to inflict the disease on themselves and that they received no benefits whatsoever?"

"That is true."

"And consumption of nicotine was still legal during the 1990's?"

"Not only legal but £100,000,000 were spent annually promoting it!"

17

"But sir only yesterday you were telling us that these same people were intelligent enough to put a man on the moon in the 1960's."

"That is also true."

"But how could the same people have been so intelligent in one way, yet so incredibly stupid in another? Surely they could have discovered a cure for the disease?"

"In fact a man called Allen Carr discovered a simple, effective cure for the disease in 1983."

"So why did it persist so long into the nineties?"

"That's very difficult to explain Smith minor, you see, although it was known that smoking could cause killer diseases, it wasn't generally regarded as a disease in itself. Most people didn't realise that it was just nicotine addiction. Even the majority of the smokers themselves believed that they were smoking out of choice because they got some form of crutch or pleasure from it. Whilst the effect on their health was not apparent they had no desire to stop. They didn't realise that they were hooked until they tried to stop. By then it was too late. Because their parents had warned them that they would become hooked, and because they failed to heed those warnings, they felt very stupid and would try to convince themselves and other people that they only smoked because they enjoyed smoking."

"But how could they have possibly fooled themselves, let alone try to convince other people that cigarettes are enjoyable? They must have been incredibly stupid."

"They thought so too. In fact they weren't. It was a very subtle trap. They only did one stupid thing."

"What was that sir?"

"They did what you did Smith minor. They tried one! Please don't be stupid enough to try another!"

"Don't worry sir, there's no way *I* could get hooked on cigarettes. So the real problem was that Allen Carr discovered a simple cure to a disease that most people didn't even realise existed."

This is my real problem, in spite of the statistics, society still generally regards smoking as a slightly distasteful habit, that probably can and does shorten smokers' lives, but smokers are aware of those risks, it's a free democracy, it's their choice.

You might question some of the statements that I have made above. The tobacco industry would argue that there are lies, damned lies and statistics. I know that the source of the statistics that I have quoted are subject to scrutiny. I also know that, far from being exaggerated, they are understated. But let us not get side tracked, even if you took a nought off of those statistics they would still be scandalous!

But probably the statements that I have made which you would feel justified in questioning, are:

1. That smokers get no genuine crutch or pleasure from smoking.
2. That smokers have no choice.

You might also question a finer point when I refer to smoking as a disease. You might interpret that as meaning the habit, crutch or pleasure of smoking, *can* be the cause, or be a contributory cause, of other diseases. You would be wrong. I'm saying that smoking itself is a disease. A disease called nicotine addiction. I am further saying that there is no such thing as smoking for smoking's sake, and that nicotine addiction is not just an unfortunate side effect of being a smoker, but is the only reason that people smoke. I am also saying that no smoker has ever got GENUINE pleasure or benefit whatsoever from smoking, and that once smokers have been tempted to sample nicotine, they've about as much choice as a fish that has been tempted to swallow the angler's bait.

I accept that you might question these facts. Before the end of this book I will prove to you, beyond any doubt whatsoever, that what I am saying is true. But if I could ask you to accept the truth of what I am saying for the moment. Smoking, apart from any other diseases it might contribute to, is not only a disease in itself, but is in fact the worst scourge that the human race has ever had to suffer, including war, famine and other diseases. Why is it that we still regard the black plague with fear and horror, when in terms of mortality, it wasn't even in the same league as smoking?

Why did we feel that the very existence of the human race was threatened when it was predicted that by 1990, 3,000 citizens of the UK will have died from AIDS, not per annum, but in total; when for years 2,000 UK citizens were dying every week, year in year out from smoking? Why is it that parents are terrified that their children will fall into the heroin trap, which kills less than 300 people annually in the UK yet seem oblivious to the fact that they themselves are in the No.1 killer trap?

If I had claimed a genuine cure for lung cancer, society would have shown immense interest. Even if I had been proved to be a 'quack' or a charlatan. Still some desperate individuals would have tried my cure in the same way that a drowning man will cling to a straw.

Why haven't organisations like the BMA, ASH and QUIT bothered to check me out? After all they spend millions of pounds telling smokers what they already know: that it's killing them. Why haven't the media allowed Allen Carr to give the public the benefit of his cure over national television? Why after over 9 years is my discovery still being treated like a closely guarded secret?

The real scandal of the Hansard statistics, is not the statistics themselves, but the fact that they went almost unnoticed. We sent copies of 'EASYWAY' to various influential individuals and

19

organisations that we thought might be interested in spreading the message. One such person was Edwina Currie, Junior Health Minister at that time. Now I do not think it was unreasonable to assume that a servant of the public, particularly a Minister of Health, would be just slightly interested in something that would save the lives of over 100,000 UK citizens every year!

We received this reply on 23rd. March 1987:

"Mrs Currie has asked me to thank you for sending her Allen Carr's book on smoking. It was a very kind thought and Mrs Currie is grateful to you – she hopes Mr Carr will continue to persuade further converts."

The letter was signed by Mary Grafton, Private Secretary. I suppose it was too much to expect that Edwina would answer the letter personally, perhaps I'm being unreasonable, she probably had at least ten other letters that day which offered a simple solution to save the lives of over 100,000 people a year. I admit that I was very disappointed, particularly as I felt that Edwina was one of the very few politicians that genuinely cared.

Probably the truth of the matter was that she received lots of letters from cranks and assumed I was just another crank. **BUT WOULDN'T THE LIVES OF 2,000 PEOPLE EVERY WEEK BE WORTH CHECKING ME OUT!**

But who was the concerned politician that informed the House of Commons of those scandalous statistics recorded in Hansard? You've guessed it, the same Edwina Currie! And those statistics related to the year 1987!

When I said: "I'm going to cure the world of smoking", I didn't mean completely. Snuff-taking, which was also just another form of nicotine addiction, became anti-social and died a natural death, yet there remains a secretive hard core of snuff-takers. Would you believe that the last bastion of snuff-taking is The House of Commons? I am informed that even in this enlightened age a barrel of free snuff is available to our Members of Parliament as they enter the debating chamber. I wonder who provides it? Why is it that our leaders always seem to be 100 years behind the rest of the population? No doubt they will be provided with free cigarettes a hundred years from now.

Now can you begin to imagine my frustration. I have discovered a cheap, simple, painless and almost instantaneous cure to a disease whose existence society denies. That's bad enough in itself. Can you now imagine how many times more frustrating it is when *you know* **THAT THE DISEASE NOT ONLY EXISTS, BUT THAT NO LESS THAN A THIRD OF THE WORLD'S POPULATION IS SUFFERING FROM IT!**

'EASYWAY' has been highly successful as an effective cure for smoking. But it has not solved the real problems. The truth is that the combined strength of people like myself, our disciples, converts and supporters have hardly scratched the surface.

One objective of this book is to enable society to see smoking in its true light. All smokers will then realise that they are suffering from a self-inflicted disease.

A second objective is to make all smokers aware that there exists a painless cure for that disease.

What do I estimate the time will be to achieve these objects? I make no estimate. Not because I got my fingers burnt the first time and have learned my lesson, but because the first time I was in control. I proved that my method was all that I claimed it would be, and I proved it within two years when I estimated four. I believed that having done so, the news would spread like wildfire around the globe!

You might feel that I was rather naive and underestimated the immense power and influence of the tobacco industry. I don't underestimate either its power or its scruples. The first two printers that I approached refused to print the book because they feared repercussions. I thought that they had been reading too many spy books. But it isn't hard to imagine, with an industry that spends 100 million pounds annually on promotion, the lengths that they might be prepared to go to, particularly when you consider that they are already killing two and a half million smokers every year. I must admit that the printers' attitude caused me to look over my shoulder for a few years. I don't think that I need have bothered.

The tobacco industry, once it realised that the connection between lung cancer and smoking, not only wouldn't destroy their industry, but would make its filthy poison appear to be even more desirable, are so convinced that the smoker cannot escape the insidious trap of nicotine addiction, they have become nothing less than arrogant. Benson & Hedges are actually using the Government Health warning to promote the sale of their filth. Such is their arrogance they even tell the hapless smokers that they have them hooked. If the combined forces of lung cancer, The BMA, ASH and Quit couldn't destroy them, why should they fear any threat from Allen Carr? I was merely an insignificant virus. Their arrogance will be their undoing. Their filthy products have spread cancer throughout the world, but just as the largest creature on the planet can be destroyed my the minutest virus, provided it grows and multiplies, so our combined efforts will spread like a huge terminal cancer on the tobacco industry to bring about its rapid and complete destruction.

Ironically, in my war against smoking, (I emphasize that it is not against smokers), the tobacco industry is the least of my problems. People often say to me: "I think you are so clever the way you present the case against smoking." But the real mystery is: **WHY SHOULD I NEED TO BE CLEVER?** After all, I have a marvellous product to sell:

THE LIFE OF A NON-SMOKER! I'm selling health, energy, wealth, freedom and happiness. I have only one competitor: the tobacco industry, selling disease, lethargy, slavery, poverty, misery and death! My product costs nothing and my rival's product costs a small fortune. It should be no contest. The problem is that my competitor has massive financial resources which enables it to maintain the very distorted impression that society has of its product.

Assume for a moment that I have already proved to you that society still sees smoking through highly-tinted, rose-coloured spectacles. Just think of it as it really is: The only reason that anyone starts in the first place is all the other people doing it. Yet every one of those smokers wish that they had never started, they even warn us not to be stupid. Eventually we try one. It tastes awful. All our lives smokers have been telling us that they smoke because they enjoy a cigarette. So we are fooled into thinking that while we don't enjoy them, we won't get hooked. We work so hard to get hooked, then spend the rest of our lives with our head buried in the sand trying to block our minds to the fact that we are smoking, or at odd times attempting to get free and telling our own children not to be stupid. The average 20 a day smoker now spends about £30,000 on smoking in a lifetime. An absolute fortune! Yet even smokers that can't afford to smoke say: "I'm not worried about the money." Why aren't we worried about the money? Why do we shop around to save a pound on essentials, yet write off that money almost as if it doesn't exist?

But it's what we do with that money that is so frightening. We actually use it to risk horrendous diseases. Okay, we console ourselves with the thought that it won't happen to us, or we'll stop long before it gets to that stage. Even if we do get away with it, we sentence ourselves to a lifetime of bad breath, stained teeth, misery and lethargy. Why does the sheer slavery never dawn on us? Most of our cigarettes, we smoke without even being aware that we are smoking. In fact the only times we are aware of it are those times when we are coughing and spluttering and wishing that we had never started, or when we are breathing smoke into the face of a non-smoker and feeling stupid and anti-social. The only other times that we are aware that we are smokers is when we are getting low on cigarettes and that panic feeling starts, or we are in situations where society will not allow us to smoke and we are feeling deprived and miserable.

WHAT SORT OF HOBBY OR PLEASURE IS IT THAT WHEN YOU ARE ALLOWED TO DO IT, YOU ARE EITHER NOT AWARE THAT YOU ARE DOING IT OR IF YOU ARE AWARE, WISH THAT YOU DIDN'T AND IT'S ONLY WHEN YOU ARE NOT ALLOWED TO DO IT THAT IT SEEMS SO PRECIOUS?

It's a lifetime of being pitied and despised by other people. But the very worst aspect of being a smoker is that it's a lifetime of otherwise

22

intelligent, happy, healthy, attractive human beings, having to go through life despising themselves, every budget day, every cancer scare, every time their family give them that haunted look, every time they are not allowed to smoke, or are the lone smoker in the presence of non-smokers, feeling unclean or out and out stupid. But do you know what is the most pathetic thing of all? The great prize that we obtain for our slavery, the loss of our health, money and self-respect, is just an illusion. Smoking does absolutely nothing for you at all!

I am aware that in all probability you will be questioning certain statements that I have made. However I will prove to your satisfaction that everything I have said is true. If for the moment you accept that to be the case, it is ludicrous to suggest that anyone would actually choose to become a smoker or that such a life style could be described as pleasurable. The real mystery is:

HOW DOES THE TOBACCO INDUSTRY CONTINUE TO PERSUADE GENERATION AFTER GENERATION TO START SMOKING?

As I will explain fully later:

IT DOESN'T!

The tobacco industry is no problem at all. My great mistake wasn't that I underestimated the tobacco industry, powerful and ingenious as it might be. My great mistake was in underestimating the sheer, incompetence, apathy, ignorance, ineptitude and plain stupidity of the very institutions that you would expect to be my strongest allies. Institutions that purport to care, like the BMA, ASH, QUIT, THE GOVERNMENT, THE CIVIL SERVICE, THE MEDIA and all their so-called experts who, far from assisting the poor smokers to get free, merely persist in giving them advice which is almost guaranteed to ensure their slavery for life! They merely perpetuate the myths that smoking is a habit, a pleasure or a crutch, that smokers smoke because they choose to smoke and because they enjoy it and the greatest myth of them all:

THAT IT IS DIFFICULT TO STOP!

The biggest irony is that the greatest stumbling block is the attitude of the smokers themselves. I know that all smokers feel stupid, I was more stupid than the rest of them for most of my life. But whilst we go on kidding ourselves and other people that we smoke because we choose to, or because we enjoy it, we merely play into the hands of the tobacco companies, the Treasury and any other vested interests that profit from the misery of smokers. Is it any real surprise that our children become hooked when we keep telling them **how much we enjoy it?**

Now for some of the good news. After about 3 years the reputation of the Raynes Park clinic was such that we could no longer treat individual smokers. We started running group clinics. I soon discovered that practically every group contained one or more ex-alcoholics. They would often refer to themselves as: a recovering alcoholic or just plain alcoholic, this in spite of the fact that, in some cases, they hadn't consumed one drop of alcohol for over 20 years! It came as a surprise to me that a few took offence to my use of the expression ex-alcoholic. Whether a person that hasn't touched alcohol for over 20 years is correctly described as an alcoholic, a recovering alcoholic or an ex-alcoholic, is debatable, and I will elaborate my views in a later chapter, in the meantime, I will continue to use the expression ex-alcoholic, please do not take offence, because absolutely none is intended.

Many of these ex-alcoholics had also been heroin addicts, in fact some of them had been through every sort of addiction that you could imagine. Moreover, they had kicked every one of their addictions. That is with one notable exception, their addiction to nicotine.

I found this very difficult to understand. Society had always lead me to believe that the really impossible one to kick, is heroin addiction. I had heard many stories to the effect that, once you were hooked on heroin, If you tried to kick it by going 'Cold Turkey', the attempt would kill you.

I would say to these people: "You've kicked the booze and the heroin and all these other things, what's so difficult about stopping smoking?" None of them could offer a logical explanation. I had always understood that the physical withdrawal pains from heroin were almost unbearable, when I asked them to describe those terrible pains, usually their answer would be something like: "Oh! It's terrible, it's like having flu!"

Now I am not trying to make out that having flu is pleasant, in fact it can feel as if you are dying. But most people seem to cope with a bout of flu without too many tears, or feeling that life is no longer worth living. It appeared to me that a bout of flu would be enjoyable if it released you from heroin addiction. In fact, if you said to a smoker: "You can have flu for 5 days, after which you will be a non-smoker" most smokers would jump at that opportunity.

The more I listened to these people, the more the symptoms that they described seemed to coincide with the black depression and irritability that I used to suffer when trying to stop smoking using the willpower method. I began to suspect that their real problem was identical to that of the smoker. It occurred to me that, if this was so, my method would enable alcoholics and heroin addicts to stop just as easily as it enabled smokers to stop. I began to test my method on alcoholics and heroin addicts. The good news is: that provided they hadn't already attended 'Alcoholics Anonymous' or 'Narcotics Anonymous', they were just as easy to cure as smokers!

Another objective of this book is to prove to you. That my method is equally effective for all forms of drug addiction and that the so-called experts of the establishment far from helping addicts to get free, actually make it harder for them. I expect you to be sceptical. I expect you to be saying to yourself: "What sort of moron is this man? Is he really expecting us to believe that all the millions of hours that have been spent by highly trained doctors, psychiatrists, social workers and drug experts, that all the millions of pounds that have been spent have been wasted? Do you seriously expect me to believe that one man, achieved overnight what those years of effort and research failed to achieve?"

The point is: I'm not a moron. I've already proved that. Bear in mind that the ex-heroin addicts and ex-alcoholics successfully kicked these drugs, and the majority of them succeeded without help from the established institutions. The man that started Alcoholics Anonymous died from cigarette smoking and Sigmund Freud, the father of modern psychology died from cigar smoking. They both spent years trying to fathom out nicotine addiction. So I think you should listen seriously to what I have to say. I admit that my claims are difficult to believe. But are they any more outrageous than Columbus suddenly declaring that the world was round, or Charles Darwin having the effrontery to declare that we descended from apes? They overnight turned up side down facts that had been common knowledge for centuries and before the end of this book I will prove to your satisfaction that I am right.

In any event, these things don't just happen overnight. Both Columbus and Darwin must have spent years questioning what they had been taught by the experts, aware that those teachings often seemed to contradict their own observations of the facts. Just as it usually takes years of blood sweat and tears to become a star overnight, so the vast majority of great discoveries were only made because of years of effort and research. Do you really believe that it is possible for an Eskimo to wake up one morning and say to his wife: "Nanook my darling, I think I've discovered how to split the atom." I spent most of my life trying to figure out an escape from the prison that I was in.

My frustration was greatly increased by the fact that for several years I had to keep the knowledge that my method would be equally effective for alcohol and other drug addiction to myself. I'd already learned the lesson from my difficulty in convincing society that I had the simple answer to smoking, and after nearly ten years of banging my head against the wall, I still haven't succeeded. But at that stage I believed that I was on the verge of succeeding. My plan was to cure the world of smoking first, then having successfully completed my task, perhaps the establishment might accept that I could also cure the world of other drug addictions.

The only nightmare that I remember vividly from childhood, is awakening from a nightmare, the details of which I cannot remember, then rushing down to my parents who were sitting in armchairs facing the fire. I called to them in my terror but they didn't seem to hear me. I shouted at the top of my voice. Very slowly their heads turned to my direction. Their faces had no features, they were just complete blanks. What was so frightening about that? I believed that I was awake!

The situation that I now found myself in was very similar. I had spent years in a nightmarish world of fantasy. A world of addiction and darkness. Joyce had helped me to escape to a 'Wonderland': a world of reality, freedom, sunshine and happiness. Now I felt that I was gradually slipping back into another nightmare, another fantasy world containing characters that would make the Mad Hatter and the Queen of Hearts appear normal, a nightmare far more frightening than the first because it isn't fantasy:

THESE CHARACTERS ARE REAL!

It takes me about 4 hours to convince the vast majority of the smokers that seek my help. Yet after over nine years of banging my head against the wall, I have failed to convince the educated and intelligent leaders of the establishment. These people are like the featureless parents of my dream.

Ken Livingstone summed it up: "Because they come from the best families, because they have been educated at the finest schools, because they are so eloquent, because they are so elegantly groomed and attired, because they actually occupy the exalted offices that they do, we are fooled into believing they are intelligent, imaginative, understanding human beings."

The reality is that most of them are mere robots. They just repeat the clichés and platitudes that they have been programmed to say. I have already referred to the complexities of computer languages and Japanese, however, these faceless bureaucrats have a language all of their own which is far more complicated than Japanese. If I ever write another book, it will be an English/Bureaucrat phrase book. I have already started to work on it. Let me give you a few examples:

"You have made a very valid point there. I shall certainly give it my fullest consideration."
TRANSLATION: "Look, I've sat for a good half an hour, patiently

listening to your jibberish, but after all old girl it is nearly lunch time."

"Hello Mrs. X, how lovely to see you again."

TRANSLATION: "I'm sure I've seen her before, can't for the life of me think what she was on about."

And after the fifth visit:

"Hello Mrs. X, we shall have to stop meeting like this, my wife is beginning to suspect we're having an affair!"

TRANSLATION: "Oh no! Not you again."

"Yes, I've read all of your letters. I assure you that I am treating this matter with the utmost urgency."

TRANSLATION: "Mrs. Smith, my waste paper basket is full again, you really must empty it more than 6 times a day!"

"Yes, I believe you, I'm sure you have a simple answer to the problem."

TRANSLATION: "Must I keep being pestered by these idiots?"

I am sure that you have experienced the type of thing I'm talking about. Apart from the Edwina Currie episode, I wrote to the editor of the Times. The reply I got was that they had recently commissioned a large article about stopping smoking. I replied to the effect that I had read the article and that it contained the same useless and fatuous information that the Media had been churning out for years. I pointed out that I had discovered the miracle cure! The 'Thunderer' wasn't interested.

I thought: "Good old Auntie BBC. They don't rely on tobacco advertising, they must be interested." I wrote to the Director General. "Your letter has been forwarded to the appropriate department." Needless to say, the appropriate department didn't appear to be interested. Neither were any of the other influential people that I approached. I might have got more response had I written to 'The Sphynx'.

The incident that finally convinced me that I was just wasting my time happened on a National No Smoking Day. Along with several other celebrities that were involved in the smoking war, I was invited to appear on the Kilroy television programme. I had appeared on several television programmes prior to this, but this was the first time that I had the chance to mingle with other people prominent in the smoking world.

Prior to the programme we were all assembled together. I was approached by a young doctor who explained that he had been commissioned, by no less an authority than The World Health Organisation, to write a booklet which was to be circulated to medical practitioners throughout the land, and possibly for all I know, throughout the world, suggesting the advice they should give to their patients that wished to stop smoking. Needless to say, the booklet contained the same platitudes that the medical profession had been propounding since the lung cancer connection.

However, this doctor, who incidentally was young enough to be a policeman, made two statements that to me were incredible. He said that they had advised doctors not to inform patients that smoking was merely addiction to nicotine. Did he really believe that such information would make it harder to stop? Surely the one essential you need to escape from a prison, is to realise that you are actually in one.

The other statement I found even more disturbing. He said: "I've heard about your book and how effective it is, I tried to get a copy of it before I wrote the booklet, but all the shops were sold out." (Thank you PENGUIN). What incredible dedication! Can you imagine a doctor being commissioned to advise all the worlds doctors about a cure for lung cancer, and having heard that someone had discovered one that actually worked, couldn't be bothered to pursue the matter?

Can you understand my frustration? There were people there representing FOREST and the tobacco industry. They were no problem. But what should have been my chief ally, the doctor representing The World Health Organisation, either couldn't be bothered, or hadn't got the gumption to obtain a copy of my book. We are all fully aware of the red tape and idiosyncrasies of the Brussels bureaucrats, but are all these institutions equally stupid?

I regret to say, that in my experience, yes they are.

There have been many remarkable achievements and discoveries that have been made over the years. How many can you think of that were made by committees or institutions? I can think of just one. I also believe that this one example is the greatest achievement of the human race. It wasn't a discovery. It was the directive of one of the greatest leaders in history. It was an achievement that I did not think would be even possible in my lifetime. It involved truly massive co-ordination and co-operation on a scale that hadn't been achieved since the construction of the pyramids. It demonstrated just what the human race is capable of achieving if it would only work in harmony and it happened almost a quarter of a century ago. I am talking about the placing of a man on the moon!

It took me over 30 years to escape from the nicotine prison. I thought that I had already achieved the difficult task and that now all that remained was the simple task of proving my method to the rest of the world. It had to be easy. All that I needed to do was to scatter seeds, one of them was bound to land on a person of vision, a person influential enough to spread the message.

After the Kilroy programme, it dawned on me that I still had just as big a problem as finding the cure itself. I openly admit that I have failed to solve that problem. But I'm not a quitter, I've been racking my brains, using what ever ingenuity that I possess to solve the problem.

To do so, I need access to the media. How did Bob Geldof gain entrance to the European Parliament? Who are the really influential people of today? Brilliant scholars and academics? Politicians? No, rightly or wrongly, the people that carry most influence today are pop stars and television personalities. People like the Beatles and Elvis Presley and it is probably the influence of such people that has enabled the drug pushers to proliferate.

"The meek shall inherit the earth." I hope they do, they deserve it. My parents taught me to respect authority, rules and regulations: "Be polite. Don't push yourself forward or make a fuss. Respect your elders and betters." Unfortunately it took me half a lifetime to realise that their advice was so much bunkum! How I wish that they were right. It should be that way, but the sad truth is that the more polite and considerate you are, the more society will abuse you. The more fuss you make, the more objectionable you become, the more people rush around to make sure that you are kept happy, or more relevant, that you are kept quiet.

Bob Geldof got access to the faceless bureaucrats of Europe because he saw what everyone else on the planet could plainly see, with the exception of those faceless wonders who had been blinded from the realities of life by the red tape. The difference was that Bob had the guts to bulldoze his way through all the red tape and make them realise that it is pointless to have mountains of surplus rotting food when there are people on the planet who are starving. Power to his elbow. We need more people like him that actually do something about problems rather than just keep talking about them.

I have a mission which I regard as equally important, and his example has inspired me to adopt similar tactics. So what's my ingenious solution? To become a pop star? I would if I thought that I could, but I have neither the time nor the talent. The reason that I give no estimate of the time it will take to achieve my object, is that I am incapable of achieving it alone. I make no apologies, I am reduced to begging, not for money, **BUT FOR HELP! I NEED YOUR HELP! I NEED ANYBODY'S HELP! I NEED EVERYBODY'S HELP!**

I have been spreading my net over a wide area with the hope of catching one large fish. I have failed. From now on I'm going to concentrate all my efforts on catching 'Moby Dick'.The trouble is that all the people that I had previously targeted, were wrapped up in their own problems. I wrote to Robert Maxwell. How was I to know that he had greater problems to worry about, like conning his employees out of their pensions. The other problem was, the sands kept shifting. No sooner did I feel that I was making progress with a particular official, than they would either retire, resign or be sacked. I wrote to Margaret Thatcher who was Prime Minister at the time. I obviously made a big impression on her. She has just accepted £50,000 to be political adviser to the tobacco industry. Why do they need a political adviser? They surely can't be going into politics? Or do they really need some strong individual to enable them to continue the decimation of the world's population?

So who of all the people on the planet, would be the ideal person to target? Bear in mind that the person that I am searching for should satisfy the following conditions

1. They should be a person of intelligence, influence and power.
2. They should be unemployed.

Sadly far too many millions satisfy the second requirement. Intelligent they may well be, but how many of them possess influence or power. These two factors alone would eliminate 99.99% of the world's population. If you further stipulate:

3. They should have unlimited access to the media.
4. They should be a caring, unbiassed person, and be so wealthy as to be above the suspicion of being suspected of bribery or corruption.

Any actuary will inform you that your chances of finding such a person are infinitesimal. Britain hasn't exactly surpassed itself in recent years, but I believe that it can boast the one man on the planet that fulfils all of the above requisites.

"A LETTER TO PRINCE CHARLES" a strange title for a book about drug addiction. But what are the British media interested in apart from celebrities, doom & gloom and sex? Only one thing – **ROYALTY!**

Let us see whether Prince Charles has the necessary requisites:

1. I do not claim to be a staunch royalist, but I would credit him with above average intelligence. Few people would dispute that he has immense influence and power.
2. Is he unemployed. Not exactly, but unfortunately he has been trained for just one job. Anyone that has been unemployed for any length of time will know what real fear and depression is. I'll wager that very few of us have had to wait for a vacancy for as long as he has. One senses that he tries to keep himself usefully occupied. One also senses that while he awaits the vacancy, he has nothing really worthwhile to get his teeth into.
3. Does he have unlimited access to the media? Stupid question. They won't leave the poor chap alone!
4. There is no doubt that he is wealthy, but is he caring, unbiassed and above suspicion of being suspect of bribery and corruption?

I believe he is. Experience has taught me to be cynical in my old age, but both my logic and my instinct tell me that he fulfils all the requirements. Either way it doesn't matter. He is the obvious choice. In theory he has no legal power, but I believe he has more effective power than The Prime Minister because he is above the temptations of the rat race and appears to be genuinely concerned about ordinary people and the serious problems that threaten our planet today.

I have important objectives to achieve but lack the power to make them happen. I sense that he too is concerned about the many needless ways that we're destroying our planet and the creatures that live on it. But I suspect that his problem is the complete opposite to mine. Because he is who he is, his hands are tied. In fact it wouldn't surprise me to learn that he is just as frustrated as I am. But between us and with your help we have the solution and the power to actually solve a major problem, instead of just talking and hoping that someone else will solve it.

In any event, I am no longer prepared to stand by and be aware that **EVERY DAY 7,000 HUMAN BEINGS** suffer premature and painful deaths from a disease for which there is a simple cure. I am no longer prepared, when I jog each morning, to watch 8 or 9 year old children puffing away as if smoking is the greatest gift to mankind.

I make no apology for making Your Royal Higness my target. On the contrary, I offer a marvellous opportunity, to assist me to end this blight. Wouldn't it be nice if Britain could restore some of it's former glory by releasing the world from the slavery of drug addiction?

If my appeal is turned down, I intend to keep a running total of the deaths and I will announce that total on every television or radio programme in which I take part and in every article that I write. I will tell the world who is directly responsible for those deaths, because if Your Royal Higness refuses his help:

HE WILL BE!

CHAPTER 2

Painting the Forth Bridge

An alarming fact I have discovered from writing this book is that young people have never even heard of so many expressions which I still regard as commonplace. In this context only, I define young people as under 40. Normally I define young people as under 60. In 2 years time I will up it to 70.

For the sake of those not familiar with the expression, 'Painting The Forth Bridge' means any job that, before you have completed it, the starting point is due to be done again. It doesn't have to be anything like as big as the Forth bridge. The average house owner has exactly the same problem.

I am afraid there is more bad news. You might think that setting out to cure the world of smoking is a fairly daunting task. But I was confident that I would achieve my goal well within the 10 years that I had allowed for. As a mathematician, I was well aware of the 'Snowball' or 'Domino' effect, or what mathematicians call geometrical progressions. The sort of things like:

> "If you put one grain of wheat on the first square of a chess board, 2 on the second, 4 on the third and so on. There aren't enough grains of wheat in the world to complete all 64 squares. Don't try it out. It will blow your mind. In any event, you would need a chess board the size of the United States."

> "If you started with just 2 mice that could breed so that they and their offspring died only of old age, within just one year, mice would outweigh the earth." If you try this one, make sure you start with a male and a female.

After 3 years The Raynes Park clinic was at full capacity even though by now we were conducting group therapy only, and we were successfully treating over 2,000 smokers each year. We knew from the letters that the book was also helping many smokers. There is no way of assessing accurate numbers, but you can be sure that for every convert that took the trouble to write, there would be dozens that didn't.

We also recorded the method on audio and video tapes. Again it's impossible to give accurate figures but the response has been similar to the book. In fact there were about 20 smokers in the production team that made the video, before its completion all 20 had stopped. The book and video were being interpreted into other languages. To my amazement I was becoming quite famous. Nearly everywhere I went I would be stopped and thanked by grateful ex-smokers. I was particularly honoured to learn recently, that my video was the subject of informal, stop smoking seminars at Oxford university.

Probably the greatest compliment that I have ever been paid was from Anthony Hopkins. I wasn't aware of the fact, but he had been advocating my method for a number of years. He agreed to do the introduction to my help line. For such a successful man, it was possibly not surprising that he did so free of charge. But when you consider that he was deeply involved with 'The Silence of The Lambs' it was a very generous offer of his time. When we recorded the help line, I was looking forward to meeting Anthony, he has always been one of my favourites, however when I arrived I was disappointed to be told by the producer that Anthony had already done his bit the previous day. He said: "Tony was very disappointed, he was looking forward to meeting you." I thought: "I think you've got it the wrong way round."

So there I was, going along all smug and happy and fully aware that apart from our direct successes, our converts themselves were helping to cure friends and relatives. I was also getting further successes from TV and radio appearances and from newspaper articles, added to which were the thousands that were stopping by the miseries of the willpower method. I had every reason to believe that the snowball, which had rapidly become a football, would soon start the avalanche.

When I first discovered the magic button, I knew that I would never have the need or desire to smoke again. I also had absolute confidence that the method would be equally effective for other smokers. As I put theory into practice, the results more than fulfilled my expectations. However two things happened which caused me to have doubts.

The first incident was when I was confident enough in my knowledge to write 'EASYWAY'. I was constantly trying to assess the ratio between the physical and mental effects of withdrawal symptoms. If you had asked me that question after a failed attempt on the willpower method, I think my reply would have been something like fifty/fifty. I say think, because when I failed after an attempt on the willpower method, it never even occurred to me to ask the question. All I knew was that I had failed. What difference did it make whether it was physical or mental? Anyway I was too wrapped up in finding excuses to cover up my failure.

Incidentally, I define the willpower method as any method other than Allen Carr's method. This would include Allen Carr's method if you don't follow all of his instructions. The point being, that unless you follow all my instructions, you are not actually using my method.

The question of the ratio between mental and physical only occurred to me after I had discovered the magic button. I couldn't understand why I wasn't having the terrible physical withdrawal symptoms that I had previously suffered. If you had asked me the question at that stage, I would have said 20% physical, 80% mental.

However, as I accumulated feedback from the clinic, at the time of writing the book, I would have said the correct ratio is more like 5% physical, 95% mental. However the experience of the various individuals varied enormously. Some would report that they had no withdrawal symptoms whatsoever. Others would say: "Like you said, It was bad for the first 5 days." Others would say that it was bad for the first 3 weeks. In fact I do not tell them that it will be bad for 5 days or 3 weeks. A few, usually the failures, would say: It was absolute murder. Strangely, when asked where it actually hurt, the details became vague.

One of the lessons that I had learned from my many failures when using the willpower method was that you must never have just one cigarette and when I hit the button, I vowed that I would never, ever take even a puff for the rest of my life. However, there had been about a 6 month delay between Independence Day and the opening of The Raynes Park clinic, and when clients told me that they had suffered noticeable physical withdrawal symptoms, I began to question my own memory.

Was it really as easy as I had remembered? Or, in my excitement in escaping from the trap, was I now looking back with rose-coloured spectacles? Before writing the book, I needed to know from personal experience just how bad the physical withdrawal symptoms were. So I started smoking again.

It shattered my little world. I had been saying that I knew more about smoking than anyone on the planet, that just one puff will get you hooked again, never mind a whole cigarette. But I couldn't get hooked! After about a month I had worked up to about 20 a day, and still couldn't feel any need or desire to smoke. It felt the same as when you start off as a youngster, you don't really want to smoke you're just going through the motions to feel adult, or part of the crowd.

Apart from shaking my beliefs, I began to get desperate for another reason. I had allotted time to write the book and that time was rapidly running out. Joyce expressed long and vehement protests about the stupidity of my tempting to start again. Her mildest comment was: "You call yourself an intelligent man. Why are you playing with fire?" I had to admit, not to Joyce of course, that I did have certain misgivings and the spectre that I might not be able to get free, loomed large and sinister at the back of my mind. However by this time, so confident was I in my method, that I was convinced that once hooked, I merely had to press the magic button in order to be released again.

Then suddenly the reason that I hadn't got hooked again hit me, and simultaneously, any doubts that I might have had about my beliefs, were not only eradicated, but replaced by even more confidence in the system. The beautiful truth was:

I COULD NEVER GET HOOKED AGAIN!

And neither could any other ex-smoker that understands my method completely and follows all the instructions!

So confident am I in my convictions, that I would be prepared to take heroin to prove that I couldn't get hooked on either heroin or any other drug. My wife cringes whenever I make that statement, and if up to now you suspect that you have been reading the ravings of a crazed lunatic, I have probably now confirmed your belief. But I assure you that I do not make that statement lightly.

Even the word **HEROIN** sends shivers down my spine. Like most heavy smokers, I have always had a morbid fear of drug addiction. I know thousands of people that have tried smoking 'pot' and many that still do. I've never met one that became hooked on it. I know a few that believe that they are, or were hooked on it, in fact it was really the nicotine content of the 'joint' that they were hooked on. I know that marihuana is not addictive in the same sense as nicotine or heroin. Yet I have never taken a puff of 'pot' in my life, because so strong and complete was my dependence on nicotine, I thought that if I tried what I then thought of as hard drugs, I would be dead in just a few months. Little did I realise that I was already hooked on the hardest of them all. If you still find that difficult to believe, take your head out of the sand. Do you know of another drug which at one time hooked 60% of the adult population and killed one in four of them? It's only the other little friend that we are trained to rely on from birth that even comes anywhere near, but even alcohol does not remotely challenge nicotine, and as I will prove to your satisfaction later, alcohol isn't physically addictive and in fact with most so-called alcoholics, their real problem is nicotine.

Let me make myself perfectly clear. I have no desire to take heroin or any other narcotic, neither do I wish to make flamboyant demonstrations. But if that is the only way that I can draw the attention of the faceless zombies that control our destinies, such is my confidence in my method, I am prepared to do so.

I need to issue a word of warning at this stage. It occurs to me that what I have written above might tempt youngsters, and particularly youngsters that are hooked on nicotine, or even adults for that matter to take the attitude that: "If I'm already on the hardest drug, I might as well switch to heroin." Please don't be stupid enough to do that! If you are a smoker you already have more problems than you realise. These other drugs will only make them worse. They are just as bad as our society makes them out to be, they will ruin the most precious gift that you will ever receive – your life! It's society's distorted view of smoking that needs changing.

It's all in the mind. How many times have we used that expression, knowing it to be true, yet somehow unable to solve our problem in spite of that knowledge. Why is it that before we start smoking we can enjoy social occasions and handle stress without cigarettes or any other outside props, but once hooked, we seem unable to return to that blissful state? You hear ex-smokers say: "I haven't smoked for 20 years, but I still miss one after a meal." It can only be in their minds, surely the body doesn't go on craving nicotine forever? I assure you that it doesn't. As I will explain in a later chapter, the body never craves nicotine, not even while you are addicted to it.

After the incident when I failed to get hooked again, I realised that the actual ratio between the physical withdrawal symptoms and the mental were more like 1% physical 99% mental. This is why I describe them in 'EASYWAY' as the little monster inside your body and the big monster inside your brain. In reality the problem is 100% mental. Oh the physical craving will be there for a few days after abstaining and it is absolutely essential that you are aware that the little monster will be trying to revive the big monster. But provided you have removed the brainwashing 100%, the little monster is so insignificant as to be hardly noticeable and it won't bother you any more than it did all the years you were smoking.

Now I am aware that some of you will still be thinking: "I don't care what Allen Carr says, I know I go through physical hell when I try to stop smoking." I do not doubt your sincerity. I too was convinced that I suffered severe physical withdrawal pains whenever I attempted to quit smoking using the willpower method. I did indeed suffer agony, but realise now that it was mental and not physical. It was irritability, bad temper, depression, deprivation, restlessness, emptiness, insecurity, fear and even panic. I believe this mental state did at times lead to problems that were indeed physical, like cold sweats and lethargy, but there was no physical pain. I will explain more about this later.

I have another word of warning against what I know to be a real threat. I have related the incident of how I tried and failed to get hooked when writing 'EASYWAY'. I know for a fact that certain ex-smokers that successfully adopted my method interpreted that incident to mean: "Great! Even if I try to get hooked again, I won't be able to." Let me make it quite clear if YOU try to get hooked again, you undoubtedly will get hooked again and what is more you won't be able to stop!

You might be tempted to adjust your stand point slightly by saying to yourself: "Okay! I'm not going to try to get hooked again. But if I'm using Allen Carr's method and he couldn't get hooked again even when he tried to, surely it will be quite safe for me to have just the occasional cigarette or cigar without getting hooked?"

I assure you that the result would be the same. Part of my brain resists relating the incident about when I tried to get hooked again, because I know that, in spite of the warning I have just given, many happy converts have fallen into the trap again. No doubt there are several others that feel too stupid and/or ashamed to tell me about it. In that case, why relate the incident? Because in order to remain a happy non-smoker for the rest of your life, you need to understand my method completely.

The reason that I couldn't get hooked again was because I had no real desire to smoke again. I was merely going through the process in order to be able to assess the actual physical pain caused by withdrawal from nicotine. No doubt you have already jumped ahead of me. It's not fair that I was allowed to do that and you can't. So why shouldn't you be allowed to go through the process of stopping again?

I had a reason, yours would merely be an excuse. Why should you even want or need to go through the process again. Would you plunge your hand into boiling water just to prove to yourself that you are better off with your hand removed? If you have successfully abstained but still feel a need or desire occasionally to light a cigarette, it means that you haven't understood my method completely. By the end of this book, I assure you that you will. To light a cigarette now would be like jumping out of an aeroplane without a parachute. If you are still in doubt, just ask yourself what advice you would give to another ex-smoker that had successfully kicked the weed but was tempted to smoke just one, particularly if that ex-smoker were your child or parent or spouse. Need I say more?

This now leads me to the really bad news. Having got over the slight hitch of not being able to understand why I couldn't get hooked again and coming out feeling more confident than ever, suddenly disaster struck. Several of my greater triumphs, heavy long-term smokers that had failed to stop by using the conventional methods and found it easy to stop with mine, people that had enjoyed several months, even years as happy non-smokers, that had recommended me to literally dozens of their friends and relatives, began arriving back at the clinic, heads bowed, full of remorse and shame. I emphasize that these were not weak, stupid people. In fact just the reverse.

Although I was relieved that not one of these people appeared to regard their recapture as the slightest blemish in my method, I was very disturbed for several reasons. One being that it had a serious effect on smokers that were planning to consult me when the time was right. I mentioned earlier that people that had been recommended to me would put off what they regarded as the 'evil' day for as long as they could. This gave them a guilt feeling because they now knew of a supposed 'magic cure'. Now they no longer had to search for excuses to put off the evil day. They now had the best possible excuse: the system doesn't work! We began to learn, when converts were recaptured because, the regular recommendations from that particular source dwindled rapidly, this in spite of the fact that the defaulter still continued to recommend the method as vehemently as ever. Strangely, the defaulters could never understand why their recommendations were ignored. But would you buy a hair restorer from a bald man?

I was also disturbed because when I tried to get hooked again but couldn't, I was certain that the method would be equally permanent for other ex-smokers. Although the incident had made me question my knowledge, the result was to increase my faith in the method. Now for the first time since Independence Day I began to doubt the system. Oh I knew right from the start that there would be failures and others that would succeed and get hooked again, either because they didn't understand the method completely, or because they were stupid enough not to follow all of the instructions. I thought these would tend to be the younger, casual smokers. But the disturbing thing was that it also happened with a few people that I was absolutely certain would never smoke again.

One case in particular shook my belief. A man telephoned me late at night. He was very distraught, in fact he was crying. He said "My doctor has told me that unless I stop smoking, I'll lose my legs. I'll pay you anything if you can stop me for a week. I know that if I can survive a week I'll be okay."

The man was convinced that we wouldn't be able to help him but nevertheless he attended a group session and found it easy to stop. He sent me a nice thank you letter and recommended me to several other smokers. Practically the last thing I say to ex-smokers leaving my clinic is: "Remember, you must never smoke another cigarette!" This particular man said: "Have no fear Allen, if I manage to stop, I will never smoke again."

It was obvious to me that my warning hadn't registered. I said: "I know you think that at the moment, but in 6 months time you will have forgotten."

"Allen, I'll never smoke again."

About a year later there was another phone call:

"Allen, I had just one small cigar at Christmas, I'm now back on 40 cigarettes a day."

"Do you remember when you first phoned? You were so miserable, you were going to pay me anything if you could stop for a week."

"I remember, haven't I been stupid?.

"Do you remember that letter you sent me? How much fitter you felt and how nice it was to be free?"

"I know, I know."

"Do you remember you promised me you'd never smoke again?"

"I know I'm a fool."

It's like finding someone up to their neck in a bog and about to go under. You help pull them out they are so grateful to you, then 6 months later, they dive straight back into the bog.

Ironically, when this man attended a subsequent session he said: "Can you believe it? I offered to pay my son £1000 if he hadn't smoked by his 21st birthday. I duly paid up, he's now 22 and puffing away like a chimney. Can you believe he could be so stupid when he's seen what smoking has done to me?"

I said: "You think he's stupid? At least he avoided the trap for 21 years, and he didn't know the misery he was in for. You were in the trap for over 40 years. You had personal experience of the misery of being a smoker, yet you only managed to stay free for a year!"

I should point out that I am well aware that at this stage many readers will be thinking: "But he wasn't free. Once you're a smoker, you are always a smoker. He was kidding himself." No, he was free. I am aware that smokers using the willpower method to quit, are never completely free. They are happy to be non-smokers, but they still have the occasional craving for a cigarette and as such, they always remain vulnerable. Come a trauma in their lives or just one drunken moment, they have just one cigarette or cigar, it tastes awful. They think: "I won't get hooked again." They are already hooked again.

I gave this matter much thought and realised that there was no basic flaw in my system. One of my instructions is never to smoke another cigarette, and if you do smoke one, you haven't followed all the instructions. Big Deal! What sort of system is that? That's the only instruction you need anyway to stop smoking. If it were that simple any smoker could stop at any time. However, all the other instructions are designed to make you happy to follow that simple instruction. With other systems you are struggling and miserable, you still crave for cigarettes, no matter how occasional those cravings are and you are not completely free. Follow my system and you won't even get occasional cravings. You'll be a happy non-smoker the moment you extinguish that last cigarette, and I assure you that you will remain that way for the rest of your life:

PROVIDED YOU FOLLOW ALL THE INSTRUCTIONS!

You might argue that there is a flaw in my system, in that because it is so effective and makes the whole process of stopping so easy, converts are more likely to lose their fear of getting hooked again, in the knowledge that they can always come back to Allen Carr if they do. That I believe is the case, but it is not a flaw in my system.

A man visits a brothel and contracts what is politely known as a 'social disease'. The establishment specialists offer him a variety of cures which are lengthy, partial and painful. He learns of a non-establishment doctor who claims a cure that is immediate, painless, complete and permanent. But the doctor gives no guarantee that the disease cannot be caught again if the man repeats his stupidity. On the contrary, the last thing he does is to warn the man to stay away from brothels from now on. **ARE YOU GOING TO BLAME THE DOCTOR IF THE MAN FAILS TO HEED THAT ADVICE?**

The truth is that no matter what system smokers use to get free, whether it be assisted, sheer willpower, or a combination of both, they are always liable to fall into the trap again. The reality is, that only too often they do!

Consider this situation. Your local council decide that in order to save costs, they will no longer put covers on manholes. After all, we are intelligent human beings, with due care and attention, surely most of us would avoid falling into a manhole. But would we? Hopefully we are all on this planet a very long time. I wonder how many, or more correctly how few of us would get through life without ever falling into a manhole? I suggest that most of us would undergo the experience several times. How many times have you got wet paint over your clothes in spite of the fact that adequate signs were displayed?

Now suppose those manholes were designed like lobster pots, so that if you did fall into one, it took immense willpower to get out. Every manhole that you passed would be occupied. To make matters worse, the council charge exorbitant rents for living in them. Your friends would see you looking cold and miserable, and shout out: "You surely haven't fallen into another manhole?" **"OF COURSE NOT! I'M HERE BECAUSE I ENJOY LIVING IN MANHOLES! THEY ARE VERY RELAXING! THERE IS NO STRESS DOWN HERE EITHER! THERE'S SO MUCH TO SEE THAT YOU NEVER GET BORED!**

Perhaps you feel that I am exaggerating the situation and that most of them would actually admit that they had fallen into a trap. I have no doubt that many of them would, just as all smokers will admit that they would love to be non-smokers when discussing the subject with their children. No one likes to appear stupid or to admit that they are weak-willed. Use your imagination. What's the first thing you do when you fall over in public? You jump up as quickly as you can hoping against hope that no one spotted you. You should be so lucky! Everyone within four square miles comes rushing over to help pick you up. You assure them that you haven't even scratched yourself. You are so embarrassed that you don't notice that your right leg is now double-jointed. You can't see it because of the blood that's pouring into your eyes from the gash in your head.

It would be exactly the same with manholes. They would feel even more stupid if they deliberately jumped back into a manhole that had once imprisoned them for years. Particularly if they had fallen into it for the sixth time!

I was naturally very relieved that my method withstood the scrutiny. However it was still shattering news. I suddenly realised that I had been painting the Forth bridge. I wasn't one tenth of the way through and the first part had begun to rust. But there was nothing wrong with the paint or the painter, my efforts were being sabotaged by sinister forces.

Smokers who stop for reasonable periods and then get recaptured present a special problem. One of the main objectives of this book is to enable such smokers to get free again and to remain free permanently. I have also taken this opportunity to update 'EASYWAY' with knowledge accumulated over the years since its first publication. Anyone that failed to stop with 'EASYWAY' cannot fail to succeed after reading 'A Letter to Prince Charles', unless of course they are stupid enough not to follow **ALL** OF THE INSTRUCTIONS!

There is one additional objective which could be more valuable than the rest combined. At one stage in my battle against the faceless zombies, I felt that I was completely alone in this nightmarish fantasy world. But the more I tried to get through to them, the more it occurred to me that literally dozens of other people were having the same problems, all banging their heads against the wall to alter an injustice that was obvious to a five year old, but not to the leaders of our society. I propose to refer to this matter in greater detail in the concluding chapter. Meanwhile, we will discuss:

WHAT TYPE OF SMOKERS FAIL?

CHAPTER 3

What Type of Smokers Fail?

Fortunately, there is only one type, the type that doesn't follow the instructions. They might not have followed because of stupidity, or because they didn't believe or understand them. I always hesitate before I say it, but in the early days of the clinics it soon became apparent that, the greater the intelligence of the smoker, the greater the chances of success.

Many non-smokers would claim that there can be no such thing as an intelligent smoker. Many smokers and ex-smokers alike would tend to agree with them. However, they overlook the fact that smokers do not choose to smoke. Many intelligent people have been imprisoned, they are not necessarily less intelligent because they failed to escape from the prison. It cannot be denied that many smokers, such as Bertrand Russell, are in fact highly intelligent people.

So why do I hesitate to say the greater the intelligence, the greater the chances of success? There are several reasons. One is that it makes me feel rather pompous and patronising. I detest both characteristics. Another reason is that I do not wish to destroy the confidence of anyone reading this book that doesn't consider themselves to be intelligent.

A third reason is that my motives for making the statement might be misunderstood. You might believe that it is just a ploy to trick you into stopping, rather like 'The king is in his altogether'. For those too young to have heard the famous Danny Kaye song based on the story by Hans Christian Anderson, about a suit made for the king, the tailor had informed the king and the rest of the population, that the more intelligent you were, the more stupendous the suit would appear to you, but a complete idiot wouldn't see it at all. In fact the suit didn't exist, but who amongst us is prepared to admit that we are a complete idiot? My worry is that you think my reason for making such a statement, is to kid you into stopping so that you can prove how intelligent you are. If I thought that such tactics would succeed, I would use them. The fact is that all smokers permanently feel stupid anyway, and if the threat of having their limbs removed doesn't stop them, there is no way that I could trick them into doing so.

I make the statement because I need you to understand how my system works. Some time ago a woman arrived at the clinic saying: "If only you could do for me what you did for my friend, she smoked 40 a day, she was grey, miserable and had a permanent smokers cough. When she left she was laughing and happy. You should see her now, she looks 10 years younger. From the day she left she hasn't had the slightest craving. I've blown smoke in her face, I've even tried offering her cigarettes, but it doesn't seem to bother her."

The stupid thing was, that smoker was envying her friend, just as every smoker envies non-smokers and wishes that they had never started. Yet all any smoker actually needs to do, is to extinguish the next cigarette and say to themselves:

ISN'T IT GREAT! I'M A NON-SMOKER!

It is basically just as simple as that. Of course it takes me 4 hours to make a smoker realise that it's just as simple as that. Unfortunately, that woman failed. She spent most of the 4 hours telling me and the other clients about the magic I had performed on her friend and waiting for me to wave my magic wand. It didn't occur to her that the magic was in the information I was imparting so that she too could understand the nature of the trap.

If we return to the prisoner in the cell analogy, it wouldn't matter if the prisoner were intelligent or otherwise. If I gave them the key to the cell, they would use it. However, one of the subtle strengths of the smoking trap, is that it takes some imagination to realise that you are actually in a trap. Intelligent people will question the powerful brainwashing that they have been subjected to from birth. They don't have to worry about who's telling the truth. Is it Allen Carr, or is it all the other experts? They use their brains. They are in a position to judge for themselves the merits of my arguments.

THAT IS THE MAGIC! THAT IS WHY THEY SUCCEED!

Now I don't want you to start worrying whether you are intelligent enough to succeed. The term is merely relative. Any human brain that hasn't been damaged is incredibly intelligent. If you are intelligent enough to read this book, you are intelligent enough to understand it. But your brain is only any good to you if you use it. That's what I need you to do. I don't care if you don't understand or agree with everything I say the first time you read it. I don't care if you have to discuss it with other people, or if you have to read it a dozen times. I need you to believe what I am saying, not because you trust me and hope that I will help you to get free, but because you understand what I am saying and know it to be the truth. I need you to:

OPEN YOUR MIND!

When I first estimated that it would take 5 minutes to help cure a reasonably intelligent smoker, I didn't realise that, although addiction to nicotine is what hooks smokers, it is not what keeps them hooked. The actual physical addiction is so slight we don't even realise that it exists. What keeps them hooked is the belief that they get some *genuine* crutch or pleasure from smoking, or, what it really amounts to, that they will never be able to enjoy life, or handle stress again without a cigarette, combined with the belief that it's essential to go through a terrible trauma in order to get free.

I emphasize that, throughout this book the term 'CIGARETTE' should include any form of tobacco, no matter how imbibed, or any product which contains nicotine.

Many of the so called experts on smoking try to classify smokers into different categories, such as:

The habitual smoker
The heavy smoker.
The chain smoker.
The casual smoker.
The occasional smoker.
The social smoker.
The stress smoker.

In fact there is only one type of smoker – the type that has fallen for the nicotine confidence trick. But every smoker is different, because what hooks the smoker is the brainwashing, and all smokers have their own individual brainwashing.

We get very few genuine failures at our clinics. Most of our failures are teenagers whose parents are forcing them to stop, or husbands or wives that arrive in an attempt to dispel the constant nagging from their spouses. Such smokers arrive with the wrong motivation and are convinced that they will not be able to succeed. Surprisingly, most of them do succeed.

A classic case, which caused me considerable embarrassment, involved a smoking husband who brought his wife to the clinic. He had no intention of stopping, but out of sheer boredom, whilst waiting for his wife, he read 'EASYWAY' and duly stopped. As you've already surmised, his wife failed. Needless to say she was irate. It wasn't easy to explain to her why she, whose need to stop was a matter of life and death, had paid to see 'The Maestro' in person and failed and her husband, who had no intention of stopping had paid nothing yet stopped.

However if you understand the smoking trap it's obvious. Imagine two prisoners. The jailer gives each of them a puzzle. To the first prisoner he says "Try to solve this for amusement, I bet you don't succeed within 24 hours." To the second prisoner he says "Unless you solve it within 24 hours, we'll chop off your head." Because it's a mental problem, the second prisoner would be in a state of panic and less likely to solve it.

It's on this point that smokers, and incidentally non-smokers get so confused. They think that because they know that smoking is killing them, they should be able to stop. All that does is to give smokers a strong desire to escape from the trap. What actually keeps them in the trap is the illusory belief that they enjoy smoking or need to smoke, or that they will find it difficult or impossible to stop. The real problem is to remove these illusions.

Another classic case was the only lady that has ever walked out of one of my sessions. It was in the early days when I only treated smokers on a one to one basis. She was one of the most impressive people that I have ever met; tall, elegant, with beautiful features, and nice complexion. Most smokers that arrive at the clinic are in varying stages of panic. This woman had tried everything to stop. She had already consulted other hypnotherapists, acupuncturists, Habitbreakers and had tried willpower and nicorette chewing gum. Usually when smokers have tried 'the lot' it is visually obvious. But this particular lady sat calm and composed with a permanent half-smile on her face. It was worrying me because she didn't fit into the normal pattern, I actually began to suspect that she was a plant from the tobacco industry.

About halfway through the session, the smile was suddenly replaced by a look of horror. She just stood up and said: "I'm sorry, but I must go." I couldn't understand it. I hadn't been talking about lung cancer or losing limbs. In fact it was the complete opposite, I'd just been saying how nice it was to be free of the slavery of the weed. What made it more frustrating, was that when I first started treating smokers, I would eagerly ring them up to find out how they were doing. To my consternation, I soon found out that occasionally they would lie to me. It dawned on me that, although I encourage clients to ring me if they need to, I soon learnt that I must never ring them, because if I did my role in the smoker's eyes would switch from life saver to persecutor, the giant clam would shut tight. However back to the story, as I said, what made it more frustrating was that I couldn't ring her up to find out what had happened. I assumed that she had suddenly remembered that she had left the gas on, or had to pick up a child.

Fortunately she telephoned me a few days later with the explanation: "I'm terribly sorry. Every other month my husband sends me to some quack or other to help me to stop smoking. When I came to see you I had no intention of stopping and I knew you wouldn't be able to stop me. But you began to get through to me. It suddenly dawned on me that I was going to have to stop. I panicked, I wasn't ready for it." I'd love a pound for every time I've heard a smoker say: "Oh I'll stop alright, when I'm ready, maybe tomorrow." Tomorrow never comes.

The lady visited me again and found it easy after the second visit. So much so, that she became one of my greatest advocates. But as I said, with mental problems, and the problem of stopping smoking is 99% mental, all the powerful reasons for stopping merely create panic and increase the sense of sacrifice and so make it harder. With physical problems, it's the complete opposite. The joke about the two drunks amply illustrates my point:

The first drunk took a short cut across a grave yard and fell into an unoccupied open grave. After several futile attempts to escape, he was exhausted and collapsed into a paralytic stupor. Shortly afterwards the second drunk made the same mistake and fell into what he thought was a grave occupied by a corpse. Needless to say, his efforts to escape were far more inspired and lasted much longer than the first. However, eventually exhaustion overcame the second drunk. He too came to the conclusion that escape was physically impossible. At this point the first drunk awoke and said: "What are you doing here?" The second drunk left with consummate ease.

We get very few genuine failures. When we do get one, I often have a few sleepless nights. Because I know that any smoker can find it easy to stop. I am fully aware that most people dispute this but I can assure you that it is true. If I ask you: "Is it easy to cross the road?" Yes, providing you have good eyesight, a sound pair of legs, use due precaution and use a crossing, it is ridiculously easy. Unless of course you do it at midnight, standing on your hands, half-cut, going backwards, during a snow storm with a convoy going by. Then you'll turn something that ought to be ridiculously easy into an impossibility, all because you went about it the wrong way.

You might consider that to be a silly and a flippant analogy because it's so obvious. In fact it's a very good analogy. Just think, why should it be difficult to stop smoking? No one forces us to smoke. In fact you don't even have to do anything. All you have to do is not light the next cigarette. But what about the terrible physical withdrawal pangs? Let us lay this bogey once and for all!

The actual physical withdrawal pain from nicotine is so slight as to be almost imperceptible. Just look back at the times you've tried to stop. I don't dispute that you were miserable and irritable, but where was the actual pain? Which part of your body actually hurt? If I hit you on your elbow with a hammer when you were 5 years old, you would remember exactly where I had hit you until your dying day. Terrible physical withdrawal pains are merely something that smokers have to dream up in order to excuse their failure.

But let us for a moment assume that severe physical pain is involved. We are equipped to handle pain. A man will suffer more physical pain during one rugby match than all his life from the withdrawal from nicotine. A woman suffers a thousand times more pain and fear from a single pregnancy than from a lifetime's physical withdrawal from nicotine. Yet many women will enter that state voluntarily on several occasions and not even become weepy or irritable. Some even enjoy the process.

Why can the same woman suffer the fear and pain of pregnancy and childbirth on several occasions, yet be a shaking, tearful wreck at the thought of life without a cigarette? The difference is this. The woman knows that pregnancy is a natural state, whereas we know even before we light our first cigarette that there is something evil and unnatural about smoking, and our first cigarette confirms that belief. The woman knows that, all being well, there's a reward at the end of her 9 months of fear and suffering, whereas as smokers we know that we are slowly being dragged down a bottomless pit. But the real difference is this, in the case of pregnancy, the woman knows that there is a definite limit to her pain and suffering, after 9 months whether the news be good or bad, it has an end. The terrible torture that smokers, heroin addicts, alcoholics and other drug addicts suffer, is not physical withdrawal pains, but the worst thing we ever suffer from – **FEAR**. The fear that they will never be able to enjoy life or handle stress without their little crutch or pleasure. The fear that they will have to endure a traumatic period in order to get free and worst of all, the fear that they can never be free. That there is some flaw in their physical or mental chemistry or some magic in the drug to which they are addicted that they cannot survive without.

Failures will often attempt to cover up their embarrassment:

"Do you know, I didn't even realise I was smoking the cigarette. I just lit up without thinking."

"But where did this cigarette suddenly appear from?"

This is usually followed by a short pause. The smoker looks to the ceiling and either has the sense to shut up, or continues with the tortuous process of 'Oh what a twisted web we weave, when first we practice to deceive.' If they continue with something like: "I had too much to drink, someone offered me one, I lit up without thinking." I say: "That's understandable. I sometimes immerse my hands in boiling water subconsciously, but as soon as I realise it, I take them out. Once you realised you had smoked a cigarette, why did you continue to smoke?" The answer is usually I was already hooked, or if the smoker is more honest – I don't know.

Although the number of smokers that fail to stop smoking after trying my method are comparatively few, every one of such failures causes me consternation for various reasons, not least of which is that I am aware that before they seek my help there is an element of – ignorance is bliss. They are well aware that they will be far better off as non-smokers, however they do believe that they get some genuine crutch or pleasure from their smoking. My programme removes these illusions. That's fine if they stop smoking, but if they continue to smoke they are left with nothing and feel even more wretched than they did before they sought my help.

However, the main reason that such failures cause me so much frustration, is that I know they can find it easy to stop, therefore it is not their failure but mine. I've failed to make them see just how easy it is to stop and just how nice it is to be a non-smoker. It is true that some smokers are not easy to convince. That might be because they are panic stricken and panic is not conducive to good communication. It might be that they are not particularly bright. Ironically, it's often due to the complete opposite, they are often very intelligent people that are so convinced by the lifetime's brainwashing, they think it is really me doing the brainwashing, by providing a clever philosophy, a sort of aid, an alternative way of looking at smoking which, provided they follow all the instructions, will help them to escape. After all, I'm asking them to accept some pretty drastic changes to facts that have been established for years. Can the millions of smokers over the years have all been so easily duped? Let's just consider a few of the facts that I am asking you to believe:

1. That smokers don't choose to smoke!
2. That smokers do not enjoy smoking!
3. That smoking neither relieves stress or boredom, nor assists relaxation or concentration!
4. That smoking is not a habit!
5. That the only reason any smoker continues to smoke is fear!
6. That it requires no willpower whatsoever to stop!
7. That the actual physical withdrawal symptoms from nicotine are almost imperceptible!
8. That smoking far from helping to reduce weight, actually causes weight problems!
9. That the following make it more difficult for all smokers to quit:
    A. The Media, the medical profession, the government, ASH and QUIT.
    B. Health scares and anti-social campaigns.
    C. Smoking bans in public places or anywhere else.
    D. The banning of smoking advertising.
    E. Substitutes particularly those containing nicotine.
    F. National No Smoking Days.
10. That smoking is the main cause of alcoholism, heroin and other drug addiction!

11. That younger, casual smokers are more addicted than long term heavier smokers!
12. That the dicta of: once a smoker always a smoker, or: the craving never goes; are complete nonsense!
13. That it is ridiculously easy for any smoker to quit!
14. That all smokers want to stop!
15. That all smokers want to continue smoking!

Surely the last two points contradict each other? They do! But the fact is that every smoker's brain is a contradiction. Even so, apart from smokers that have successfully followed my method, I do not suppose there is another person on the planet that would accept all of the above fifteen points. Can it really be true that all these people are wrong, including all the other experts and that it is only Allen Carr that is right? Nevertheless, **I AM RIGHT!** But until I can convince you of that and you in turn can help me to convince other people of those facts; smoking, alcoholism and other drug addiction will thrive.

The main problem isn't the powerful, vested interests, but ignorance of the facts by society generally. The real problem that we have to overcome is: **THE CLOSED MIND.** Even highly intelligent people can find it difficult to open their minds and to question what for a lifetime they have regarded as established facts.

The greatest evil on the planet and the real cause of all our problems is the closed mind, the entrenched point of view, the inability to observe any situation other than from a subjective point of view. I have made many mistakes in my life, but whoever said "The person that never made a mistake never made anything" was absolutely right. I have no regrets about the mistakes that I have made. On the contrary, with most of them I can convince myself that they were to my advantage. I don't even blame myself for lighting that first cigarette. I realise that such is the ingenuity of the trap, sooner or later I was bound to fall into it.

There is just one mistake I cannot forgive myself for. Because I was convinced, that if I couldn't quit by the use of my own willpower I could never quit, I became too stubborn and pig-headed to seek help, even though Joyce pleaded with me to do so. When I think of the quality of my life before I started smoking and how marvellous it has been since I stopped, and when I look back at the fear, misery and utter stupidity of those smoking years, I think: "You stupid idiot! Why didn't you seek help?"

I truly believe that I blighted over 30 years of what would probably have been the most pleasant and constructive years of my life. All because of this stupid attitude of: "You're a man, you've got to be tough and able to stand on your own two feet!"

Many smokers, usually the men, have this hang up about seeking help. If you are troubled by this factor, bear two things in mind: your sense of achievement will not be diminished by the fact that you sought help. Escapers from Colditz were not too proud to seek help. On the contrary, the sense of achievement is more satisfying. It is true that a trouble shared is a trouble halved, but a triumph shared is a triumph doubled. Any sportsman will confirm that there is far more pleasure in winning a team event than an individual event. However the important thing to bear in mind is that prisoners in Colditz who failed to seek help, also failed to escape.

"Let him without blame cast the first stone." I was guilty of a closed mind but I hope I have learned from my mistake. I hope the rest of the addicted world can benefit from that mistake and then I will feel completely exonerated. But I make no apology for casting either the first stone, or all the rocks that I have already hurled and will continue to hurl at the closed minds of our society in general and our institutions in particular.

It's hard enough to alter an entrenched position when the person has no axe to grind. But if it's a professional expert? It would take not only a very honest person, but a very brave person to admit that the advice and information that they have been giving all their lives is back to front. It's hard enough to persuade one individual, but you try convincing a whole profession. However, as far as alcohol and drugs are concerned, that is exactly what the BMA, ASH and QUIT have been doing and those facts have been available to them for nearly eight years now.

Since setting up the Raynes Park clinic, I now have nearly 9 years feedback, plus 7 years feedback from publishing 'EASYWAY'. Penguin recently asked me to review the book and to update it if necessary. This caused me some concern, because after I had been running smoking clinics for about a year, I thought I had heard everything that there was to hear about smoking. Yet 9 years later, I learn something new about smoking practically every day of my life. I was only too pleased to be able to pass on the additional knowledge. At the same time this would imply that the original book was outdated and that I would have the embarrassment of having to reverse advice which I had categorically stated as sound.

As I reviewed the original, I was very relieved to realise that I would not have to admit to any U turns. In fact it surprised me just how sound the basic structure was. The only chapter that I had serious doubts about was the one on timing. I still have some doubts about timing which I will cover later. The extra knowledge that I had acquired and continue to acquire, did not conflict with the basic principles of my method and was not necessarily relevant in helping smokers to quit, although much of it did enable me to get through to a greater variety of individual smokers.

I received three main criticisms about the book. One of the three criticisms I would like to apologise for now. My son Richard reviewed the original. He made various criticisms and suggestions, but the main one was "The style is incredibly male chauvinist." I blush at the truth of his statement. I've made an effort to mend my ways in this book. However there are times when I find it impractical, eg: when referring to the creator, or the creators, should the gender be he, she, it or they? I don't know and have used the traditional he. I gather that in the United States nowadays, 'manhole covers' should strictly be referred to as 'personhole' covers. I think this is going too far.

The other two main criticisms that I received from smokers that read 'EASYWAY' were:

1. You tend to be repetitive
2. Your method didn't work for me.

Ironically, the same people made both criticisms, and there lies the nub of my main problem. Although it is easy for any smoker to stop smoking, it is incredibly difficult to make some smokers realise this. My original clinics lasted about 40 minutes. Every time I got a failure, I would try to find out why and to think of other ways to get through to that smoker.

The sessions gradually lengthened to an hour then 2 hours. Our current sessions last 4 hours. At each noticeable increase my wife would say: "You can't keep people that long you'll bore them." This was a constant source of worry to me. I was well aware that if people are bored they lose concentration and fail. We go to a great deal of trouble to make the sessions as enjoyable and as interesting as possible.

There has to be an element of repetition in order to reverse the lifetime's brainwashing that we've been subjected to by the tobacco companies:

"PLAYERS PLEASE."

"HAPPINESS IS A CIGAR CALLED HAMLET."

"YOU CAN'T ENJOY A PINT WITHOUT A CASTELLA."

But the most prolific and effective brainwashing is supplied, not by the tobacco industry, but by its victims:

"What would life be without our little crutch?"

"It's the only pleasure left in life."

"What would a meal or a drink be without a cigarette?"

And to negate the bad side:

"Oh! You've got to die of something. Anyway they tell you everything gives you cancer nowadays."

"I think I would have ulcers if I didn't smoke."

"My doctor smokes more than I do. If there were any truth in these health rumours, he wouldn't smoke."

"I'd feel really stupid if I stopped smoking and stepped under a bus tomorrow."

"It's expensive, but I can afford it and it's worth it for the pleasure. In any case, it stops me squandering my money on other things."

Like food and clothes for the children. If ex-smokers are going through a bad patch at the time, is it any real surprise that they get recaptured? Especially if they are surrounded by 6 other smokers at the time all nodding their agreement to the above remarks.

I try to avoid being obviously repetitive by presenting the same point in a different way. Some smokers don't need the repetition, either because they are highly intelligent, or because they have good imaginations or, because like me, they have already reached rock bottom and no longer suffer the illusions of smokers being happy, cheerful people. Some smokers, before we even reach the hypnotherapy stage say: "You needn't say another word, you have helped me to see it so clearly, I know I shall never smoke again." If you do find a repetition annoying, please bear with me, many lives might be saved because of it, also bear in mind, it could even be your life!

At the other end of the scale, some say: "Your method didn't work for me." I say to them: "That isn't true. My method will work for any smoker. If you failed, you could not have used my method". "Oh I did, I understood everything you said. In fact I already knew everything you told me". This is followed by a short question and answer session which usually goes something like this:

Q: How did you feel after you left the clinic?
A: I felt great for a couple of days, then I had a row with my girlfriend and had to have a cigarette.
Q: Did that cure the row?
A: No, I felt worse, but after the row I couldn't stop thinking about smoking.
Q: I did tell you that the greatest mistake that smokers make using the willpower method is to try not to think about it. But anyway, if the cigarette made you feel worse, why did you continue to smoke?
A: I was so miserable, I wanted a cigarette.
Q: Do you know why you wanted a cigarette?
A: It's just a habit! (Or a crutch, or I enjoy them, depending on the reason, or rather, the excuse for failure) But there's one consolation, I'm only smoking 5 a day. But I have put on weight, I couldn't stop eating.

The truth is that the smoker has no more idea of the true reason that they smoke, than before they attended that 4 hour session. They might have been listening intently to everything that I said but they certainly didn't understand it. On at least 3 separate occasions during the first session, I state that smokers don't enjoy smoking and that smoking doesn't relieve stress or boredom, or help you to relax or concentrate.

The point is further reinforced several times by implication from statements like:

SMOKING DOES ABSOLUTELY NOTHING FOR YOU AT ALL!

I also go into great detail to explain why cutting down, or any attempts to control your intake will virtually guarantee failure, and why using substitutes makes it harder to stop. The fact is, those smokers neither understand all that I say, nor do they follow all the instructions. Effectively they do just the opposite. Not surprisingly they remain in the trap.

Before smokers attend the session we say to them: "Between now and the date of your appointment, whilst you are smoking the cigarette, but not when you are waiting for one, just ask yourself what it is you are actually enjoying, particularly those special ones, like the one after a meal." When they arrive at the session often those smokers say: "I did what you said, do you know I didn't enjoy any of them." Surprise, surprise!

Other smokers, even after 3 sessions, will say: "You keep saying we don't enjoy the taste, but I do!" I say: "I must have said this to you at least a dozen times now. At the beginning of each session I say to you – if you don't agree with what I am saying, you must say so, how can you possibly be a happy non-smoker if you feel that you are being deprived of a pleasure? But let's find out one way or the other, light one up now, take 6 deep puffs, concentrate on the smoke going into your lungs. Now tell me about the marvellous sensations that you are receiving. Describe the wonderful experience that I am being deprived of. Try to make me feel that I am missing out.

Usually the smoker refuses to light up, with some comment like:

"I wouldn't enjoy this one. It's the one after a meal I enjoy."

"But I'm not talking about the occasion, just the taste. Why should a cigarette taste any different after a meal?"

Later I will explain why a cigarette after a meal appears to taste better. If I can persuade the luckless victim to light up, they immediately begin to feel silly. The feeling is increased by the fact that the other members of the group are now staring with some amusement at the victim. At this point I should hasten to explain that my object is not to humiliate smokers that seek my help. On the contrary I deplore society's attitude of treating smokers like morons, but to achieve success, it is essential that smokers lose the illusion that smoking is pleasurable. Normally it is only light or casual smokers that believe they enjoy the taste. After 6 puffs the victim, in addition to feeling stupid, begins to feel giddy or sick.

It began to dawn on me that, no matter how many different ways you try to explain something, no matter how simple you try to make it, some people just cannot grasp it, not because they are simple, or unimaginative, but because, for whatever reason their mind is closed.

I learned to spot most of these people in the first few minutes of the first session. They would be staring around the room or at the other smokers. I would be in the middle of some point that should have been of vital importance to them and they would start up a separate conversation with another member of the group. The point is they hadn't really come to stop smoking. They had come because a relative or friend had persuaded them to. There's a money back guarantee, what have they got to lose?

The point is they hadn't yet received a trigger. The trigger might be a health scare, a social snub, a shortage of money, pregnancy or an office ban. Triggers should not be confused with reasons for stopping. All of the above might also be reasons for stopping. Health is by far the most common reason for stopping given by smokers at our clinics. But by far the most common trigger for their attendance at the clinic, is that they know a friend, colleague or relative that stopped easily after attending the clinic which inspired the smoker to think: "If it worked for them, it will work for me." All smokers intend to stop at sometime in the future, the trigger is the event, or combination of events that actually inspires them to make an attempt to stop.

Naturally unless the smoker has already received the trigger they don't have the correct motivation. Imagine building an MFI kit, even if you are desperately keen to build the kit, the instructions are a bore, all you want to do is to get on with the building of the kit. Now just think how it would be if you had no desire or intention of building the kit, the instructions would not only be boring but meaningless.

At one stage I considered not allowing such smokers to attend the clinic, or asking them to leave once their lack of interest became apparent, because they can cause distraction and lack of confidence in the rest of the group and in the early days they made a large dent in my success rate. Proud of our success rate as we are, we have not been forced to adopt such tactics, because the first session itself usually creates the trigger.

Many smokers have the trigger the day they fix the appointment, but have already changed their minds by the time the appointment comes. They need to be re-triggered and to have those triggers reinforced so that they are never reversed by the massive brainwashing which our society still permits. We had a classic example a few months ago. A lady arrived with her friend. The friend clearly had no intention of stopping and was taking absolutely no notice of what I was saying. About half way through the session I happened to mention that when I wrote 'EASYWAY', I tried to get hooked again and couldn't succeed in doing so. Suddenly the friends eyes lit up. She said:

"Does that mean you could smoke just 3 cigarettes a day if you wanted to?"

"Of course it doesn't. If I had the need or desire to smoke 1 a day, I'd have the need or desire to smoke 100 a day. I have no more need or desire to put those filthy things in my mouth and set light to them than I would to inject myself with heroin."

From that point on the lady began to listen and needless to say, she succeeded.

I am pleased to say that in spite of the fact that many smokers arrive untriggered and/or sceptical, the success rate at the Raynes Park Clinic during 1990, on the basis of the money-back guarantee, was 96%. We don't expect to improve on that, but we'll keep trying, because we know that any smoker can find it easy to stop. As far as we are concerned, there is no such thing as a failure, just smokers that have yet to succeed.

Another criticism I received was that I used too many analogies. I sympathise, it irritates me when a politician says: "We must grasp the nettle firmly." Or a marketing man says: "Lets hoist the flag up the flagpole and see if anybody salutes." I think why can't they just say what they mean. However, I found the use of analogies and anecdotes absolutely vital in helping smokers to get free.

If you cannot see the point of a particular analogy, or anecdote, BEWARE! The object of the analogy or anecdote is to help you to see smoking as it really is. Perhaps you are not following one of the absolutely essential instructions: **TO OPEN YOUR MIND!** Think over the point again. It might be a vital one.

If you say to a smoker: "The health scares actually make it harder for smokers to quit." I know most of those smokers just sit there thinking: "Well why do you think I have paid this money to come and see you?" If they already have emphysema they will probably say it out loud with a few added expletives. But if you then say: "But why hasn't it stopped you?" Then follow up with: "Does dieting make food less precious, or more so?" People can relate to that and although that doesn't enable them to stop smoking. It does get them to start opening their minds and to start questioning their entrenched views on the facts about smoking.

Similarly, for smokers who are convinced that they smoke because they enjoy the taste or smell. If you say: "Cigarettes are filthy disgusting objects that taste and smell awful." They'll merely put their blinkers on and write you off as one of these supercilious non-smokers or holier than thou ex-smokers. If instead you say "I didn't realise that you ate them. Where does taste come into it?" Or: "I love the smell of roses, but I would feel pretty stupid smoking one." Or: "Those special ones, like the one after a meal, if you can't get your brand and can only get a brand that you find distasteful, do you stop smoking?" "Are you serious? A smoker will smoke camel dung rather than nothing!" Then smokers start to open their minds.

CHAPTER 4

Why Didn't it Work the Second Time?

Imagine winning a whole year's holiday on a paradise island. Your every whim is catered for. During the holiday you are lucky enough to win another holiday then another. It gradually dawns on you that the other occupants of the island also keep winning holidays. Some of them have lived there 40 years and continually complain about the conditions. You wonder why they stay there if they don't like it. The thought disturbs you, but not too much, after all you can always leave when you choose to.

As the time goes by the discipline on the island becomes imperceptibly stricter. When you first arrived you could lay around on the beautiful sandy beaches for as long as you wanted to. Now you are compelled to lie in the sun 6 hours each day whether you want to or not and imperceptibly, the 6 hours become seven then eight. It gradually dawns on you that you're not on a holiday island, you're on a prison colony. So what? The life's still pretty good and the stretch of water between the island and the mainland only seems about a mile wide. You're still young and strong, you'll make your escape whenever you feel ready. The next thing you know, your a wizened old man that spends your days trying to persuade the new arrivals to leave whilst they can. But why should they take any notice of an old fool like you?

Heavy smoking parents can never understand why their children start smoking in the first place and having started, why they don't stop. Why should they? They enjoy their cigarettes, or rather suffer the illusion that they do, they have no reason to stop, so why stop? Try to picture smoking like life on that island. Even when it eventually dawns on youngsters that they are hooked, the nature of the trap is to postpone the evil day for as long as possible. That mile of water now looks five miles, and the tides are strong, and the water is cold and what will life be like if I do escape?

A common misconception about smoking, is that it's easier for youngsters and casual smokers to stop than for heavy smokers. The reverse is the case because younger, casual smokers have less reason to stop, or more correctly, are better able to block their minds to the reasons. Therefore most of them encounter fewer triggers to stop. Heavy lifelong smokers can no longer kid themselves that they enjoy smoking, they are fully aware that they are in a concentration camp and are desperately searching for some means of escape.

My method is really a key that will release smokers from the prison they are in, or to continue with the holiday island analogy, a safe 4 hour boat trip off the island. But if you still believe it is a holiday island, why would you even take the trip? Even if I persuaded you to, you would take the first boat back.

Many smokers that attend our clinics have umpteen years of accumulated gunge inside their bodies. They have grey complexions, are wheezing and coughing, short of breath, miserable and lethargic. Many of them have tried some or all of the other methods of stopping, including the use of their own willpower. Many are already in the early stages of diseases which will shortly kill them if they don't stop. They are nervous, often panic-stricken and convinced that we won't be able to help them.

A 60 year old that has already had multiple bypass operations will start to lecture a 20 year old that is concentrating on the quality of his smoke rings. The youngster says nothing, but his expression clearly says: "You silly old fool, you lecture me? I should be lecturing you. Fancy letting it get to that stage." This is another of the many anomalies about smoking. I have a friend with emphysema, his wife has a lump on her breast, their friend has one of those really hacking smokers coughs, the type that makes you think that they'll throw up. Each cannot understand why the other two continue to smoke and each appears to be completely oblivious to their own situation. Why is it that every smoker can see good, valid reasons for all other smokers to stop, the only exception to the rule is themselves? All will be revealed.

So the heavy long-term smokers have a tremendous desire for the key that will release them from their prison. They listen intently and follow all of the instructions. The gunge rapidly starts to leave their bodies, they soon have more energy and they realise that the impossible has happened: **THEY ARE FREE! WHAT'S MORE IT WAS EASY!** They achieve a wonderful experience: **THE MOMENT OF REVELATION!**

I recently watched John McCarthy experience it when released after 9 years as a hostage. But at what point did he experience it? When he was first informed that he was to be released? I doubt it. When he was handed over to friendly officials? I doubt it. When he boarded the plane? Even then there must have been doubts in his mind. Was he dreaming? Was it just a cruel hoax? Even if it were genuine, would

Sod's Law apply and the plane crash? He probably wouldn't even allow himself to accept it until the plane had landed safely and he was amongst his family and friends. Even then it might not have registered.

The moment of revelation is a wonderful experience, it is the moment when you realise that you have in fact escaped from the prison. I've been a very lucky man. I've had many memorable experiences in my life. When I passed my final accountancy exam I remember dancing around the room thinking: "Thank goodness I no longer have to spend night after night studying these monotonous subjects!"

When my first son was born my wife was 3 weeks overdue. Each day I would ring the hospital with excited anticipation, which gradually turned to gloom and doom as I became convinced that the baby would be still born. Finally after the usual question: "This is Mr Carr, is there any news yet?" I had almost replaced the receiver when I heard this voice say:

"You've got a beautiful baby boy!"

"Are you sure you got the right name? This is Mr. Carr."

"I've got the right name, you've got a lovely baby boy."

"What's wrong with him?"

"Nothing! He's perfect."

"What's wrong with my wife?"

"She's tired, but she's fine. You can visit now if you want to. They're both waiting to see you."

I was phoning from a call box in the City. When I stepped outside there were literally hundreds of people walking by. Suddenly all the fear and tension of the past few months lifted. I felt ten feet tall. I wanted to stop someone, hug them and tell them: "I'm a father!" But I was also British, to show emotion would have been a sin, to talk to a stranger would have been no less than sacrilege.

I remember clearly my excitement that day, as I do with many other highlights in my life. However, no matter how clearly I remember the details of these events, I find that I cannot recapture the feeling of excitement, except that is, with the moment of revelation. Even ten years after I first experienced it, it is a constant source of elation to me. If I have a bad day nowadays, I don't think of people less fortunate than myself, I just look back at those awful days when I was the slave of nicotine and think: "Today you might not feel so great, but boy are you a lucky man, you're no longer one of those pathetic people that have to go through life paying through the nose to choke themselves." It has been a constant source of joy and inspiration to me ever since.

I received the moment of revelation before I actually extinguished my final cigarette. In the previous chapter I described how it regularly happens to other smokers at our clinics. The majority of smokers that use my method experience that moment, if not immediately, then within a few days. Some ex-smokers never achieve it, particularly if they are using the willpower method. They are happy to be non-smokers, but they still feel vulnerable and spend the rest of their lives trying to resist the odd craving. Many of them succumb even after several years of abstinence. In fact occasionally ex-smokers that haven't smoked for ten years attend our clinics just to get rid of that feeling of vulnerability.

But why should the moment of revelation be such a marvellous experience. After all, what is so great about being a non-smoker? The truth is that there is nothing particularly great about being a non-smoker. Our creator never intended us to smoke, any more than he intended us to bang our heads against the wall every hour. We get no real exhilaration from not having to bang our heads against the wall. Non-smokers (people that have never smoked as opposed to ex-smokers) might well be puzzled as to why anyone should even bother to smoke, and they are no doubt pleased that they don't smoke, but they don't get all excited about it.

So why the great joy to be free? The joy is genuine. It's the same high or pleasure that hostages receive when they are finally released. This is a very important point to appreciate and to remember the rest of your life: **YOU DIDN'T ENJOY BEING A SMOKER. YOU NEVER CAN AND YOU NEVER WILL.** The immense pleasure of the moment of revelation, is not the joy of being a non-smoker, but:

THE ENDING OF THE MISERY OF BEING A SMOKER

The problem is, once smokers get free from the weed, they think: "Okay, I've solved that problem, now what do I do?" Life goes back to normal. They are still being hit with massive daily brainwashing from the tobacco companies and by equally powerful brainwashing from existing smokers. They are quite happy to be non-smokers, but come a change in their lives, boy meets girl, or a new job, or they find themselves in the company of smokers on holiday. The smokers are happy and cheerful, the ex-smoker thinks: "This isn't right, it's me that should be happy and cheerful not them." The ex-smoker forgets that they are not happy and cheerful because they are smoking, but because they are on holiday. Non-smokers are happy on holiday. In fact those smokers are probably not even aware that they are smoking and if they were aware of it they would become uncomfortable and apologetic. They would love to be like the ex-smoker, free from the whole filthy nightmare.

Would you envy a blind person? Obviously not. But don't be hasty, such a person might have certain advantages over you. For example, they might not have to sweat it out at the office every day as you do. Of course, I'm being stupid, it would be ludicrous to make such a sacrifice for the sake of a few comparatively superficial benefits. However, supposing you were stupid enough to wish that you were blind, in order to gain those advantages? If you were that stupid, you'd be in a very unenviable state, because while you still had your sight you'd be miserable because your wish hadn't been granted. If you were then unfortunate enough to have your wish granted, you would be even more miserable, because then you would realise how lucky you were when you had your sight.

It is quite possible that a sighted person might envy a blind person because of qualities or assets they possess, but it is inconceivable that they would envy them their blindness. Yet ex-smokers that envy smokers, or mope for odd cigarettes, put themselves in a very similar position. Every smoker wishes that they had never lit the first cigarette. Every smoker envies non-smokers. The ex-smokers forget this. They forget that the smokers will be envying them. Why is it so easy to see with blindness, and so difficult to see with smoking? Because with blindness it is quite obvious that for the superficial benefits you have to pay a price that is unthinkable. In other words you look at the total situation, you cannot have the good without the bad. But with smoking you can. You can just have the occasional, so-called special cigarettes. You can control it. You can split the good from the bad, or more accurately:

SMOKERS THINK THEY CAN

That is the myth that gets smokers back into the pit, the belief that they can enjoy an occasional cigarette and moreover that they can do so without becoming hooked again. I will explain later just why this isn't possible. But now the ex-smokers find themselves in an impossible position, they are in fact moping for a myth, a situation that is impossible, they are miserable because they can't have a cigarette, and even more miserable if they do. They feel deprived because they are not allowed to smoke. Like a dripping tap, it gradually wears their resistance down. They have just one cigarette. It tastes awful. But they have now put nicotine into their body. When they put that cigarette out, the nicotine starts to leave. A little voice is saying: "It tasted awful, but I'd like another one." Another little voice is saying: "You can't have another one, you'll get hooked again." So you allow a safe period to pass. Having allowed a safe period to pass, the next time you are tempted, you are able to say to yourself: "I didn't get hooked again, so I can safely have another cigarette."

You are already hooked again. You've fallen for the identical trap you did as a youngster. You either slowly get hooked again, or you precipitate back to the bottom of the pit.

It's usually not very long before they realise how stupid they have been. In fact they are not really as stupid as they think they are. The design of the trap is so subtle and clever, far more so than manholes without covers, to me the mystery is how anybody manages to avoid falling into the nicotine trap at least once in their life. After a few half-hearted attempts to stop on their own, and provided they don't feel too embarrassed, they eventually arrive back at the clinic.

However, when those smokers arrive back at the clinic, they do not have umpteen years of gunge inside their body. Neither do they have the panic feeling that they won't be able to stop. Allen can wave his magic wand and 'Hey Presto' they'll be non-smokers again. I can wave my magic wand again, but do they really want me to wave it? They are now in the same position as a youngster on the paradise island. My boat is there, but do they really want to board it? This is why the method doesn't appear to be so effective the second time.

Many so-called experts on drug addiction maintain that it is pointless even to attempt to persuade an addict to give up until they have reached rock bottom or close to it. Much as I understand why they hold that view, and sympathise with their reasoning, nevertheless it is not only unsound but highly dangerous. Ignore my method for a moment. Who would you say that society generally regarded as being more hooked, the long term chain-smoker, or the young casual smoker? Heavy smokers say to the teenager:

"You fool! Do you want to end up like me? Stop while you can!"

"It's you that needs to stop. Can't you see it's killing you? I'd stop before I reached the stage that you've descended to."

They both regard the chain-smoker as being more hooked. If that is true, why do these so-called experts maintain that you have to reach rock bottom before you attempt to quit? What is the real difference between the chain-smokers and the youngsters? Chain-smokers know that they are in a prison and believe that escape is impossible. Youngsters don't even realise that they are in the same prison. Which of the two is more hooked? Or to put it another way, which has the greater chance of escaping from the prison? If you know you are in a prison and want to escape, you might succeed. But if you are not aware that you are in a prison, or even if you suspect that you might be but have no intention of escaping until some time in the future, your chances of escaping today are zero.

The nearest thing to the nicotine trap in nature is the process by which a fly is lured into a pitcher plant. So named because it is shaped like a pitcher – the jug not the baseball player. Insects are attracted to the smell of the sticky goo with which the rim and internal surfaces of the plant are liberally coated. The hairs on the plant grow in one direction only – downwards, which combined with the effects of gravity, ensures that the fly travels in the same direction. This is of no concern to the fly because it can fly off whenever it chooses. But why should it even want to fly off? After all the nectar is delicious. Not until it is being digested by the juices in the base of the plant does the fly realise that it's being eaten by the plant, rather than the other way around, does the fly have any desire to leave. Too late! By then it is so saturated by the goo it can no longer move let alone fly.

Whether they be young, old, casual or heavy, all smokers are like flies at different stages of descent down the same pitcher plant. Obviously, the main aim is to prevent them from falling into the trap. But our society is a miserable failure in that respect. Having failed, do we just wait until they reach rock bottom, remembering that 2,500,000 of them go past rock bottom every year and die? Must we really sentence the lucky ones to the 30 odd years of misery that I went through?

My method will enable any smoker alive to escape easily from that pitcher plant. In an attempt to prevent youngsters from becoming hooked, our society wastes massive resources by informing them that smoking can damage their health. Then when they duly become hooked, we accuse them of being stupid. It's we who are stupid. Why should the health risks deter them from smoking just one cigarette? One cigarette won't kill them. Neither will two. But if they smoke that second cigarette, they've about as much chance of escaping as a fly from a pitcher plant!

Our children are as intelligent as we are. If we explained to them how a pitcher plant worked, they would understand and avoid the trap. Okay, so the nicotine trap is much more subtle, but shouldn't we try to make our children understand the ingenuity of the trap before they fall into it? If they have already fallen into it, shouldn't we explain at every possible opportunity, that with drug addiction, the more it destroys you, the greater your illusion of needing the drug. Oughtn't we try to make them realise that those chain-smokers that they despise so much, were once young like they are, and that if they don't stop now, what will prevent them from becoming chain-smokers themselves? Shouldn't we attempt to get through to them, that the more the drug destroys you mentally and physically, the more you block your mind to the facts and desperately search for any flimsy excuse to smoke:

JUST ONE MORE CIGARETTE!

On phone-ins with Brian Hayes, at least one caller says: "Why should I stop smoking? I enjoy it! I know the risks that I run and if I am prepared to accept those risks it is nobody's business but mine." Brian says: "Nobody is trying to make you stop. Allen is merely giving helpful advice to smokers that want to stop." Brian is wrong. I know that all smokers want to stop. In the early days of my clinics we would ask smokers "Do you want to stop?" I soon realised that it was a stupid question. If there were a magic button that smokers could press and wake up the next morning as if they had never lit that first cigarette, the only smokers tomorrow morning would be the youngsters just starting out convinced that they won't get hooked, just like you and I were at one time. This is why all parents hate the thought of their children smoking and all children hate the thought of their parents smoking. It is also why all smokers instinctively feel stupid. If at any time in your life you were to take your head out of the sand and weigh up the pros and cons of smoking, the answer is always a dozen times over:

YOU ARE A FOOL!

At the same time all smokers want to go on smoking, after all nobody forces them to smoke. The fact that they don't understand why they do it, or wish they didn't have to do it, doesn't alter the fact. All smokers are schizophrenic.

As I said, all smokers want to stop, but not today please, let it be tomorrow. Herein lies one of the great subtleties of the trap. We don't stop until we have a good reason to stop. At odd times in our lives something will trigger off an attempt to stop. However more times than not the trigger is poor health, or an office ban, or a social snub, or a shortage of money. But these are also the times when we feel insecure, depressed and vulnerable. The times when we most need our little crutch and are least likely to succeed. The schizophrenia is still there. At one and the same time, our desire to stop has increased and so has our desire to postpone the evil day.

I remember in the early days of therapy when I would only treat one to one. A man arrived. He said "Let me make it clear right from the start. I really resent having to seek your help. I know I am a very strong-willed person. I run my own business, with everything else in my life I'm in control. Why is it that all these other people are stopping. Why can't I do it?" He went on to say: "I think I could do it if I were allowed to smoke while I was doing it."

It sounds a contradiction, but I know what he meant. We think of stopping as a terribly difficult thing to do. What do we rely on when we have something difficult to do? Our little crutch. It never occurred to me at the time that this was one of the beauties of my method. You can actually continue to smoke while you go through the process of stopping. You get rid of all the fear and doubt before you extinguish the final cigarette, so that when you do extinguish the final cigarette, you are already a non-smoker and enjoy being a non-smoker for the rest of your life:

PROVIDING YOU FOLLOW THE SIMPLE INSTRUCTIONS

I emphasise, it is just fear that keeps smokers hooked. Smokers cannot force themselves to stop smoking any more than you could force a sufferer from claustrophobia into a confined space. They believe that they will suffocate. They won't, but if you believe you will it is the same thing. They would kill rather than allow you to force them. Similarly you cannot force a smoker to stop. What you can do is touch the correct trigger that will make them want to stop. But if you try to do this by telling them smoking is killing them, or costing them a fortune, or is a filthy, disgusting habit controlling their lives, you are merely telling them what they already know. They'll just keep their heads in the sand. What you have to do is to remove the fear, the illusion that they will never enjoy life or be able to handle stress without a cigarette and the fear that it is difficult to stop. Now I will explain:

WHY I COULD NEVER GET HOOKED AGAIN

CHAPTER 5

Why I Could Never Get Hooked Again

Any trapper or angler will tell you that there are two vital essentials to achieve success, one is to set a clever trap. However, it is not possible to do this without the other: a complete understanding of the nature of the creature you are trying to catch.

On the presumption that it is generally intelligent, strong-willed people that accumulate wealth, an efficient confidence trickster will design his campaign specifically to trap such people. He will actually use the intelligence of his victim to spring the trap. His trap also depends on another human trait that his potential victims all too often possess: GREED.

The nicotine trap is far and away the most ingenious trap devised by the combination of man and nature. The nicotine part of the trap, the equipment, is simplicity itself. What makes the trap so ingenious, is the nature of its victims, in particular, the incredible complexity of their brains.

'EASYWAY' explains how nicotine creates an illusion that cigarettes give a genuine crutch or pleasure.

Any smoker that wants to stop can do so easily by strictly following the instructions, including youngsters and casual smokers. From my earlier comments, I fear that I might have left younger, casual smokers with the impression that it must be difficult for them to stop. Not so! I emphasize that the key that will release any smoker from the prison is the same. The difficulty with young or casual smokers is whether they really want to use that key.

In pondering over the matter of why I could never get hooked again, whereas several smokers that appear to have understood my method completely have done so, it dawned on me that it was because of my deep understanding, not only of the nicotine trap itself, but of the nature and psychology of the smoker. 'EASYWAY' does not cover this aspect sufficiently. We are about to correct that situation. If to set a trap you need to understand the equipment and the victim, you need to be just as knowledgeable in order to escape from it and to remain free **PERMANENTLY!**

I knew right from Independence Day that my method would work for other smokers, without having to test it out, because I completely understood the nature of the trap. But how could I have known that I couldn't get hooked again? I obviously didn't. Otherwise why would I have made the attempt? I only found that out when I tried to get hooked again. So we now have two distinct and separate problems:

1. How to find it easy to stop?
2. How not to get hooked again.

The first problem is solved. Fine so why even worry about the second one? Why not just use the solution to the first one again. I've already explained that part of the ingenuity of the trap is that when you do get hooked again, there is a time lapse before you even want to stop again. In any event I also want to help those that have already got hooked again and to prevent youngsters or adults for that matter from falling into the trap.

That isn't quite so easy. The nicotine trap is the same for every smoker, but no two smokers possess the identical brainwashing, and it's the brainwashing that hooks the smoker. So in order for you to be certain of remaining free like me, you not only need to understand my philosophy, but you need to adopt it.

One of the vital clues as to why highly intelligent, strong-willed people who appear to understand my method completely yet still get hooked again, was provided by one such lady, who arrived back at the clinic in tears. I remember her well because she had also left the clinic two years earlier also in tears. I hasten to explain that they were tears of relief and joy. This is not an uncommon occurrence at our clinics for those smokers that understand immediately that they are already free. I am not ashamed to admit that I find it difficult not to shed a tear myself on such occasions.

This was a particularly intelligent lady, who like me had enjoyed the process of stopping right from extinguishing the final cigarette. Naturally she was very embarrassed and apologetic about her failure. Incidentally, failure was her word not mine. The more discerning amongst you will already have noticed that I do not refer to such people as failures, but as 'recaptured' simply because that is exactly what they are. I should explain that I do not judge success or failure by the period that a person abstains from smoking. A smoker can have abstained for 30 years, but if they still feel deprived and have occasional cravings for a cigarette, much as I admire their willpower, I still regard them as failures. In order to be successful, an ex-smoker must fulfil the following conditions:

1. Understand the nature of the smoking trap.

2. Realise that smoking provides no crutch or pleasure whatsoever!
3. Realise that it creates rather than fills a void.
4. Know that whether you be going through good times or bad, you will never have the need, desire or temptation to light a cigarette and will be happy to remain a non-smoker the rest of your life.

Perhaps you feel that I have overlooked one obvious condition i.e. not to smoke. I haven't overlooked it, but unfortunately many ex-smokers that fulfil all of the above conditions do. I regard them not as failures but as recaptured. But they couldn't possibly have known that they would be happy to remain non-smokers for the rest of their lives, otherwise they wouldn't have smoked again. When as a youngster I watched my father coughing and spluttering, I knew that I would never become a smoker. It didn't prevent me from falling into the trap. People make successful escapes from prison, that doesn't necessarily prevent them from being recaptured again.

ISN'T THIS WHAT THIS BOOK IS ALL ABOUT?

Back to the lady, I asked her what had gone wrong and she explained that she had lost her husband in tragic circumstances. I said did the cigarette eliminate your grief? She said: "Of course it didn't and the stupid thing was that I knew it wouldn't, in fact I can remember you warning me of such situations, you told me I would feel worse and I did, but I knew I would!" I said "And I suppose there was a helpful smoker there offering one to you?" She said: "Allen I begged for a cigarette, I knew it wouldn't do me the slightest bit of good, I suppose I just thought of it as a placebo. **I NEEDED SOMETHING!**"

That was the clue. I remember having exactly the same fear when I finally saw the light. I knew that I would never have the need or desire to smoke again, but I wondered what would happen if some great trauma occurred in my life. Would I turn to a cigarette?

It happened about 6 months after I stopped smoking. When I was a smoker, I was grossly overweight but could do nothing about it. The ironic thing was that I wouldn't touch food all day. After a few days of freedom from the 'weed' I had a feeling of energy, a strong desire to be fit and healthy again. My wife bought me a track suit and I started jogging each morning. When I think about it now, I don't know how I had the nerve to do it. I would come out of the house in this brand new track suit, jog about 10 paces and then collapse into a paroxysm of coughing. What the neighbours thought of me, I dread to think. But I was determined, I persevered. I can remember the first time that I succeeded in completing the trip round the block back to my house, it was as if I had just won the gold medal for the Olympic Marathon. Two years ago, I did 2 half-marathons during the same week. I don't particularly like running now. The truth is I find it boring, but I love that exhilarating feeling that running provides, the adrenalin starts to flow and you are set up for the day, that's a real high. Just feeling great to be alive!

After about 6 months I lost 2 stone, but I had a lump in the middle of my chest. I thought, typical Sod's law. I've spent a lifetime trying to kick smoking, I've finally succeeded, but I've left it too late. I had watched my father die from lung cancer and decided that if ever I got lung cancer, I wouldn't go into one of those hospitals like the Royal Marsden. I thought, if I'm in pain, I'll commit suicide. If I'm not in pain, I'll continue to enjoy life whilst I can.

Far from being in pain, I felt like a young boy again, but my wife sensed that something was worrying me. She asked me what the problem was:

"I've got this lump on my chest."

"You need to see a doctor."

"I'll see a doctor if you insist, but I can tell you, if he tells me it's lung cancer, it will destroy my life. All I will be doing is planning my death. If it isn't lung cancer why worry?"

"Fine if you can block your mind to it, that's up to you."

Unbeknown to me, she told my brother. He mentioned it to a doctor friend of his, and described the symptoms third hand. The news came back to me that the doctor didn't think that it was lung cancer and that he would be pleased to check me out. It had now reached the stage where I was being treated like 'Does he take sugar?' Every time the phone rang the door was gently closed on me and conversations were being held in reverential whispers.

Eventually I realised that, whether I wanted to or not, I'd have to face up to it, because everyone else was getting so uptight.

It was a week before the doctor was able to see me. During that week, I do not remember even thinking about smoking, so obviously it didn't bother me. On the day of the appointment, Joyce and I travelled to the doctor's practice in Princes Risborough. We arrived an hour early and I can remember sitting in his waiting room still convinced that I had lung cancer. I admit to being terrified, but I had no desire to light a cigarette. On the contrary, I thought: "Thank heavens I've kicked the smoking, at least I feel strong enough to handle the situation." I didn't mean physically strong, I meant mentally strong.

If I needed any final proof that cigarettes don't give you courage or confidence, that incident was it. The subsequent experience from running the clinics has reinforced this evidence a thousand times over.

Incidentally, in case you are the slightest bit interested, to my great relief it wasn't lung cancer, and to my great embarrassment, it wasn't even a disease. Now you'll say: "So it wasn't really a great trauma." Take my word for it, coward I may be, but I was terrified. People often say that the doubt is worse than the certainty. I've been fortunate not to have suffered from lung cancer or anything similar, the doubt is bad enough, I hope I am never qualified to comment on the certainty.

Back to the lady who *needed something*, I realised that what smokers miss when they stop smoking, is not the cigarette itself, but the void that it appears to leave in their lives. At those genuinely stressful times when the ex-smoker desperately needs a prop, the cigarette appears to be the least of alternative evils. Perhaps like some experts you would suggest a substitute. I will explain later why all substitutes merely make the situation worse.

The point is, I never have that void. Just as the pleasures of smoking are an illusion, so is that void. It is a cunning illusion that is merely a small part of the overall subtlety of nicotine addiction. So how do I cope with the stresses of life? Fortunately, since I escaped the trap, most of the things that I previously regarded as major traumas, I now take in my stride. I will explain more about these matters in later chapters. You will more readily appreciate them after we have dealt with:

THE INCREDIBLE MACHINE

CHAPTER 6

The Incredible Machine

Many smokers that have consulted other therapists prior to seeking my help, complain that they are questioned about their early childhood. They find this rather annoying because they cannot see the significance of the questions. They are absolutely correct. In order to understand the nicotine trap fully, you need to go back a little further – about 3 billion years, when life on this planet first developed. The human body is the result of 3 billion years of trial and error and is by far the most sophisticated object on the planet.

There are various levels of species on the planet, but our capacity to deduce and to communicate knowledge, not only from one generation to the next, but from one race, culture or language to the next, has put the human species way ahead of its rivals. So much so that many people believe that we are on a completely different plane to other animals in that, unlike us, they have no soul. We tend to regard the life of another human being as absolutely sacrosanct, and at the same time we permit lesser creatures to be tortured, mutilated and destroyed not because we need to eat them to survive, but purely for cosmetic reasons.

As in the old days, the leader of the tribe thought of themselves as a 'God' rather than just the mentally or physically strongest member of the tribe, so today human beings tend to treat the planet as if it were there purely for their sole convenience, to be abused, exploited, polluted and destroyed regardless of the needs or rights of lesser creatures.

Some species had to be at the top of the tree. It happens to be us. But if we were on a different plane to other animals, we wouldn't still have claws on our hands and feet, we wouldn't have created bombs that can destroy the planet a thousand times over, we wouldn't be systematically destroying the planet that all living creatures, including ourselves, are dependent upon. In evolutionary terms, we have been out of the jungle for less than a micro-second!

The main reason that I couldn't get hooked again is because I discovered this incredibly powerful machine – **THE HUMAN BODY** – and in particular **A HUMAN BRAIN!**

I have absolute belief that this machine is equipped to handle any situation without the need of drugs or similar aids. The good news is that you also possess one of these incredible machines. We all do, even people like Christopher Nolan. So his body wasn't as physically strong as mine, any more than mine is compared to Arnold Schwarzenegger's, but that is mere detail. Every human body possesses enormous physical and mental potential.

It wasn't the machine itself that I had discovered. That had been there all my life, but like most of the really important things in life like air, food, freedom, security, good health, employment, love and friendship, when we have them we tend either to take them for granted, or to complain about their quality. It's only when we are deprived of them that we truly appreciate them. When I was a teenager I was aware of the physical power and strength of that body, but at the age of 48 it had become physically and mentally weak and frail. I was aware that my heavy smoking wasn't helping the physical side, but in my mind that was purely incidental, society had also prepared me to believe that old age was a sort of terminal disease.

The discovery was how incredibly physically and mentally strong the human body really is, and it wasn't only because of the improved health and vitality resulting from not smoking, but more an extension of the mind opening process. I have no intention of getting into any religious debates. I'm referring in particular to the old dispute between religion and science. To be precise, are we the product of a creator or just the result of a coincidental, cosmic, chemical reaction followed by a process of natural selection?

I believe that most honest, thinking people nowadays see no conflict in the two scenarios. However, in case you still do, consider this hypothetical conversation between two ants gazing in awe at the Taj Mahal:

"The creations of man are truly wonders to behold Fred."

"You surely don't believe in all that claptrap about man do you Bill? If man really existed, why would he allow natural calamities like insecticides?"

It would be ludicrous to suggest that the Taj Mahal is just a coincidence, it is clearly the product of applied intelligence. The universe is a billion times more sophisticated than the Taj Mahal. To suggest that it resulted from mere coincidence and not as the result of applied intelligence is a billion times more ludicrous.

It would be equally ludicrous to suggest that natural selection doesn't exist. Thankfully, the creator gave us eyes, ears and brains to be able to behold the wonders of his creations, one of which is the marvels of nature including the incredibly efficient process of natural selection. There is no contradiction. Natural selection is just one of the systems that our creator uses to achieve his objectives.

71

Our creator obviously exists, or at least did so at one time, otherwise we wouldn't exist. The exact form or nature of the creator is a matter of personal faith, speculation, deduction or opinion. Is he male or female? A study of his methods would indicate that there is more than just one. For convenience I will use the traditional single male gender. Is he shaped like a human being? If so where does he live? And who created him? After all, you can't create yourself, you wouldn't be there to do it.

I believe that it is pointless to speculate on the form or motives of an intelligence a million times greater than our own, it would be like our hypothetical ants discussing man's motives for creating the hydrogen bomb. We can observe, analyse, dissect and study his creations. But do we understand how an acorn can fall at random onto the ground, and without any outside assistance or interference, can grow into a magnificent oak tree?

Our knowledge of the human body has improved a thousand fold in the last hundred years. We can transplant organs, and achieve mind-bogling results with genetic engineering. However, the greatest experts on these subjects admit that all their increased insight into the functioning of the human body does, is to make them realise how little we understand about the workings of that incredible machine. All too often it has been shown that our limited knowledge, in the long run, causes many more problems than it cures. If your highly sophisticated computer developed a fault, would you let your pet gorilla try to cure it?

The whole process of creation, whether it be by a superior intelligence, a process of natural selection, or a combination of the two, has instilled certain guiding forces within us. Whether we like it or not, the most powerful guiding force for any creature is **SURVIVAL**. Usually this is for the survival of the individual. At times the survival of the individual is superseded by the survival of the species. Ants and bees will instinctively sacrifice their lives when the colony is threatened. With certain species of spider, the male might be inhibited by the fact that he is likely to be devoured by the object of his affections, but that doesn't stop him mating with her. In both human and lower creatures, parents will often sacrifice their own lives to save the lives of their children.

Narrators of nature films often describe the extent to which creatures will go in order to pass on their own genes at the expense of a rival. They describe it as if the animal goes through a mental thought process: "Unless I'm very careful here, Fred will be passing on his genes instead of me." As human beings, we are better equipped than animals in assessing what it's all about, but when we have sex, isn't it either because we wish to satisfy a desire within us, or because we wish to produce a baby? Do you believe that any human being has ever thought: "I wish to pass on my genes?" It's only the last few generations that realised they had any genes to pass on.

What the narrator never explains is why we find it necessary to pass on our genes. What good does it do us? What's so special about our own individual genes anyway? It's quite obvious that Fred is bigger, stronger, better looking, more intelligent and a much nicer person than I am. That being the case, wouldn't I be doing the world a big favour if I stood aside and let Fred do the passing on? I have no doubt that I would, but it doesn't work like that. Our creator instilled a sexual drive within all healthy creatures to ensure that they procreate whether they like it or not. I do not know the creator's motives for so doing, all I do know is that lesser creatures can enjoy this natural function without guilt; it is only the *intelligent* human being that creates problems about it.

We are equipped with several guiding forces to ensure that we survive, whether we like it or not. One of those guiding forces is fear. Many people think of fear as a form of weakness or cowardice. But without a fear of fire, of heights, of drowning, of being attacked, we would not survive.

At the clinics, the times that I have heard smokers say: "I suffer with my nerves." As if feeling nervous were some form of disease. The door slams. You jump two feet in the air. That isn't bad nerves. That's good nerves. Watch starlings feeding, they appear oblivious to what's happening around them, but the slightest sound will cause them to fly off as one. That sound signified: 'CAT' and it's the one that doesn't jump that gets eaten by the cat.

We think of tiredness and pain as evils. On the contrary, they are red warning lights. Tiredness is your body telling you that you need to rest. Pain is telling you that part of your body is being attacked and that remedial action is necessary. There are people born without pain, nerves or fear, they find it very difficult to survive. Should they rest their arm on a hot stove, it's not until they can smell their flesh burning or until they see blood spurting from their arm, that they become aware of the problem.

So much of established modern medicine nowadays is obsessed with treating the symptoms of the disease rather than the cause. Take my own case, typical Sod's law. I spent half of my life ruining my throat because I smoked, and the rest of my life ruining my throat because I spend so much time talking about smoking. I get regular sore throats because I talk too much. Joyce gets me those anaesthetic sprays or tablets. The pain goes almost immediately. I think: "What marvellous stuff." It isn't! The sore throat wasn't the problem, that was my body telling me: "Give your voice a rest! If you don't you are going to cause bigger problems."

By anaesthetising the pain, all I really achieved was to remove the oil warning light instead of topping up the oil. I then do the one thing

73

that I shouldn't do, I go on talking. In fact, I've done much worse than that, by removing the symptoms, I have also removed the signals to my brain which would have triggered off my immune system. I have effectively negated the most powerful and efficient healing force on the planet: **OUR IMMUNE SYSTEM.**

Wild animals do not have the great variety of diseases that we do. They die mainly because they get eaten, either by us, or by other animals, or because of the massive pollution of the planet perpetrated by the superior species. Wild animals also manage to give birth and to survive without the assistance of doctors.

Many doctors are now discovering that drugs like valium and librium cause more problems than they solve. These drugs have a similar effect to alcohol, they take the persons mind off of their problems, but they don't cure them When the effect of the drug has worn off, another dose is required. Because the drugs themselves are poisons, they have physical and mental side effects and the body builds an immunity to the drug. The addict now has the original stress plus the additional physical and mental stress caused by being dependent on the drug that is supposed to be relieving the stress.

Eventually the body builds such an immunity to the drug that it ceases even to give the illusion of relieving stress. All too often the remedy is now either to administer larger and more frequent doses of the drug, or to up grade the patient to an even more powerful and more lethal drug. The whole process is an ever accelerating plunge down a bottomless pit.

Many doctors try to justify the use of such drugs by maintaining that they prevent the patient from having a nervous breakdown. Again they try to remove the symptoms. A nervous breakdown isn't a disease, on the contrary, it's a partial cure and another red warning light. It's nature's way of saying: "I can't cope with any more stress, responsibility or problems. I've had it up to here. I need a rest. I need a break!"

The problem is, strong-willed, dominant people tend to take on too much responsibility. Everything is fine whilst they are in control and can handle it. In fact they thrive on it. However, everyone has phases in their life when a series of problems coincide. Observe politicians when the are campaigning to become President or Prime Minister. They are strong, rational, decisive and positive. They have simple solutions to all of our problems. But if and when they achieve their ambition, you can hardly recognize them as the same person. Now they have the actual responsibility of office, they have become negative and hesitant.

Take a top sportsman like John MacEnroe. Forget the tantrums. He is clearly a superb athlete, and while he was the world's No.1 tennis player, it was equally obvious that he was also mentally very strong and brimming with confidence. Then, for whatever reasons, he slipped to No.2 or No.3. Suddenly the confidence began to drain from the man. He became a wimp. If you had not witnessed his former glory, you would have formed the impression of a rather weak individual. However, No.3 in the world is some considerable achievement in itself. Most of us normal mortals wouldn't dare even to dream of achieving such heights. MacEnroe was still basically a very, very strong individual who was just going through a very bad patch.

No matter how weak or strong we are, we all have bad patches in our lives. What is the natural tendency at such times? It is to seek solace through our traditional crutches: ALCOHOL or TOBACCO. I said *natural* tendency. There's absolutely nothing *natural* about it! We've been brainwashed from birth to believe it. With many fallen idols, like 'Hurricane' Higgins and George Best, it is blatantly obvious that the chemical dependence has not only not helped their problems, but is in itself the cause of their downfall. So it was with me, but I couldn't see it either.

The only answer to stress is to remove the cause of the stress. It's pointless trying to pretend that the stress doesn't exist. Whether the stress is real or mainly illusory, drugs will make the reality and the illusion worse. Another problem is that we are also being brainwashed into believing that we lead very stressful lives. The truth is that the so-called civilised human species, has already successfully removed most of the causes of genuine stress. We no longer have the fear of being attacked by wild animals every time that we leave our homes, and the vast majority of us don't have to worry about where our next meal will come from or whether we'll have a roof over our heads.

How would you like to be a rabbit? Every time you popped your head out of the burrow, you not only had the problem of searching for food for yourself and your family, but you had to avoid becoming the next meal of another creature. Even back in your burrow you cannot relax or feel secure, you are at risk from floods, ferrets and a myriad of other hazards. The stress of serving in the Vietnam war understandably caused many servicemen to turn to drugs. But they served for a comparatively short period. How does a rabbit survive 'Vietnam' its whole life yet still manage to procreate at a prolific rate and to feed its family? The average rabbit even looks happier than the average human being.

The reason that rabbits can daily take in their stride traumas that would cripple the average human, is because rabbits have adrenalin and other drugs ocurring naturally. The creator has equipped them with sight, smell, hearing, touch and instinct. In fact with everything that they need to survive. Rabbits are wonderful survival machines.

SO ARE HUMANS

Fortunately the creator did not neglect us. On the contrary, the human body is the most sophisticated survival machine on the planet. We have reached a stage of evolution whereby we can even partly control the elements themselves. Properly organised, we could eliminate the effects of drought, flood or earthquake. We really have just one substantial enemy to conquer:

OUR OWN STUPIDITY

We lay down standards that we try to achieve. A select few seem to achieve them all. The Richard Burtons, the Elizabeth Taylors of this world appear to have everything going for them. They are physically and mentally strong people. What destroys them? Their jobs? Old age? The normal stresses of life? None of these. What destroys them are the illusory crutches that they turn to: Nicotine, Alcohol and similar poisons.

We teach young boys not to cry. Again, we try to remove the symptoms rather than the cause of their sorrow. Crying is nature's way of relieving anxiety. No one has ever cried and not felt better for the experience. The boy desperately tries to fight back the tears. He might succeed in holding back his tears, but his twitching jaw confirms that his problem, far from being solved, is worse.

As Britains we are taught not to show our emotions: "Keep the stiff upper lip." So we bottle up those emotions. They merely fester and multiply until they eventually erupt into a trauma the size of a mountain as opposed to the original molehill. We are meant to display emotions. They are a vital and instinctive means of communication when we fail to communicate by other means. Which has the greater effect on you? The lucid words of the accomplished orator who tells you that he is so grateful words cannot describe his gratitude, or someone that is so grateful that they are genuinely rendered speechless?

At our clinics we ask smokers: "Do you have a smoker's cough?" Often the reply is: "I would stop smoking if I did." A cough isn't a disease. On the contrary, it is another of nature's survival techniques to eject harmful materials from the lungs. Just as vomiting is another survival technique to eject poisons from our stomachs. For years I thought that my smoker's cough would eventually kill me. I realise now that it was merely trying to save my life. It's in the lungs that the poisons cause the damage. One of the bad things that we do as smokers is, because we relate the cough to illness, we get into the habit of shallow breathing and avoiding physical activity in order not to cough. It's the smokers that don't cough that end up with lung cancer!

The human body is the result of 3 billion years of experimentation by a creator that is millions of times more intelligent than we are. It is a truly incredible machine whose every natural function is to make sure that we survive, whether we like it or not. To interfere with the natural functioning of that machine by introducing drugs and poisons without fully comprehending their total short and long term effects, would be equivalent to allowing a gorilla to meddle with the functions of a sophisticated computer. Even an imbecile wouldn't permit a gorilla to do that. It would be like saying that a gorilla is more intelligent than human beings. Every time we interfere with the natural functioning of the human body without understanding the full long term effects, we are really saying: "I know better than the person that created me." We are playing at being God!

If you did let a gorilla play with that computer, it would be irreparable within a half hour. So why haven't we destroyed ourselves by playing at being God? It's no thanks to us. As I'll explain in the next chapter, we're hellbent on destroying ourselves. A man made computer is indeed a frail and sensitive machine, which a gorilla could destroy it in ten seconds. However, such is the strength and ingenuity of the human body, that even when some misguided person like me, spends a small fortune systematically poisoning it for a period of over a third of a century, that incredible machine survived **in spite of my efforts.**

Just take smoking as an example: the first cigarettes taste awful. That is a warning from your body. It is telling you: "POISON! DON'T TOUCH!" Lesser unintelligent creatures would heed that warning, but the human species has been brainwashed to ignore it. Does your body just leave you to your fate? No way! Other alarms start to operate, you begin to cough, to feel nauseous, you might actually vomit.

Even if you fail to heed all of the warnings and continue to smoke, your body will begin to build an immunity to the poisonous effects. Rasputin was eventually able to survive a dose of arsenic 20 times greater than the dose that would kill an average human being all because he built an immunity to the poison. Rats and mice could survive 'Warfarine' after just 3 generations.

So sophisticated is the system, that your body, suspecting that you have no choice but to continue taking the poison, even arranges for you to become oblivious to the unpleasant smell and taste. It's rather like working on a pig farm, after a while your brain and body become immune to the smell. Could you conceive of a beautiful woman that has spent time and money to cleanse, perfume, groom and dress herself to perfection, finishing the whole thing off by rubbing 'Essence of horse manure' all over her body? That is the effect that smokers have on non-smokers. Fortunately most non-smokers are far too polite to appear to notice.

Then, if and when the systematic poisoning ceases, within just a few days that incredible machine will sense the fact and begin to eject the accumulated toxins from the the ex-smokers' bodies leaving them as strong as ever. **PROVIDED THEY HAVEN'T LEFT IT TOO LATE!** In spite of the overwhelming evidence to the contrary, there are still smokers today that refuse to believe that smoking affects their health. To me the mystery is how my body was able to survive the truly massive punishment that I inflicted upon it for so many years.

There are people who believe that there exists just one all-powerful God who created each and every one of us with a preordained purpose in life. As I look back on my life, my whole existence would seem to confirm that point of view. In hindsight, each pertinent stage of my life appears to have been a preparation to achieve just one object: to solve the smoking riddle. Abraham Lincoln said that you can't fool all the people all of the time. As far as smoking is concerned, I believe that is exactly what happened until I saw the light and that I was the first person to understand fully the true nature of the smoking trap. I would like to claim that it was due to my incredible powers of deduction, the truth is that it was really due to the peculiar circumstances of my life, most of which were completely outside my control, or appeared to be. There is no doubt that one of the contributory factors for the success of natural selection, is that nature sends millions of seeds into the atmosphere, in the expectation that some of them will find the correct conditions. I believe that I just happened to be the seed with the necessary experiences in life to solve the mystery of the nicotine trap.

I do not presume to know what the creator's motives were for creating us. I am however convinced that he has provided each of us with the necessary talents, tools and equipment to enable us not only to survive, but to enjoy that life to the full. They are contained within each human body and brain, a truly

INCREDIBLE MACHINE!

Whether we take full advantage of those provisions is up to us. One of the reasons that I could never get hooked again is because I now realise that I am not devoid, deficient or incomplete, and that it was only the brainwashing I received from modern society combined with the illusory crutch created by nicotine addiction that made me believe that I was.

As I look back over my life, equipped as I was, I find it difficult to understand how I could have remained deceived for so long. It was because, despite of its incredible sophistication and ingenuity, there is:

A FLAW IN THE MACHINE

CHAPTER 7

The Flaw in the Machine

The reason that the human species has progressed so far above other species is that we have learned to store and to communicate knowledge, not only from one generation to the next, but from one language, race or culture to the next. Other animals rely mainly on instinct. Part of our brain also works on instinct, but in addition we have another part which is capable of deduction. It can draw on experiences from the past and by the use of memory, imagination and experimentation, can solve new problems.

This so-called 'intelligent' part of our brain gives us tremendous advantages over other species, and enabled us to achieve mind-boggling advances in technology over the last 200 years. Ironically, it is this intelligent brain that is the flaw in the machine. It has enabled us to create bombs that are capable of destroying ourselves and every other living creature on the planet thousands of times over at the same hair-raising pace. Does it really matter that we've failed to solve petty problems like unemployment, pollution, disease, starvation and war? We were clever enough to create the bombs, but apparently not clever enough to control them or get rid of them. So clever are we, that the the most precious gift any of us have – just to be alive, and the 3 billion years it took to reach our stage of progression, we can wipe out in seconds!

IS THAT INTELLIGENCE?

I have always tended to rely on logic and rationality rather than faith and whenever the two are in conflict, I still do. In the past whenever my logic and my instinct were in conflict, I would back my logic. Today I back my instinct every time. Why? Because I know that my instinctive brain is many times more intelligent than my intelligent brain. This might appear to be contradictory, nevertheless, it is true.

Instinct isn't just a matter of hit or miss. It is the product of three billion years of experimentation, not of theories, but of actual trial and error. It enables birds to build complicated nests and spiders to spin exotic webs. Did you know that, pro rata to its thickness and weight, a spiders silk thread is stronger than anything that man has created? Instinct enables all creatures to breed, feed and to know the difference between food and poison. Wild animals can produce offspring without the great hassle that we have to go through, without the assistance of doctors. The fact that they cannot read or write and have no academic qualifications affects them not the slightest.

Take our cat as an example. Our previous cat had been killed by a lorry, so upset were we that we vowed never to have another. The new cat just turned up one day, whence we still do not know. Like most cats, she probably has two or three owners each of whom is convinced that she is loyal only to them. At the time we thought that we were adopting a stray, in hindsight, we realise that it really had nothing to do with us, she had merely decided that our house would be suitable for her purposes.

We provided her with a cat door so that she could come and go as she pleases. She sits on Joyce's lap in the evenings. I am asked to change the television programme because the cat looks so comfortable it would be a shame to disturb her. Meekly I comply, but shouldn't my comfort be more important than the cat's? She doesn't work hard all day to feed me. All she ever does is exactly what she wants to do. Those cold winter mornings when bed is so lovely, just one thing can make me leave it. I can hear the cat crying outside the front door. Bear in mind she has her cat door at the rear, but the cry is irresistible. I rush down the stairs, open the door and stand there shivering. Does she rush in full of gratitude? No way! She strolls past me in her own good time, tail stuck up in the air as if my sole purpose in life were to attend to her every whim. I close the door and rush back to that lovely warm bed only to find that she has already beaten me to the ideal spot, and of course her purring conveys such utter contentment that I don't have the heart to throw her out. I ask you, who is the more intelligent, me or the cat?

We have gained incredible benefits from that three billion years of experimentation. Watch a child learning to throw a ball. The first efforts are completely uncoordinated. It's even worse when trying to catch the ball. Now watch an ordinary cricket match. Forget the really spectacular catches or run-outs. I'm talking about where the fielder just lobs the ball to the bowler after each delivery and the bowler effortlessly reaches out a hand and catches it. The thrower rarely misses his target and the catcher rarely drops the ball. This happens ball after ball without any conscious action either from thrower or catcher.

Now imagine that you had to design a robot to simulate this mundane process. You possibly think that this has already been achieved. There are machines that will bowl a cricket ball at an exact speed at an exact spot or will serve a tennis ball in like manner, with a consistency far greater than any human being. That is true, but they cannot do it alone, they need man to line them up and to set the correct dials, even with man's help, their range of activities is very limited.

Our robot must be able to move independently from one spot to another. It must be able to see. A miracle in itself. Not only must it be able to see, but it must have some method of communicating that knowledge to the various parts of the body which need to take action. It would have to deduce the size, weight, shape and consistency of the ball, together with the effect of the force of gravity on the falling rate. It would have to deduce how far the thrower would need to take his arm back, the velocity and rate of acceleration to bring it forward, the arc, the direction, the shape of the movement of the various muscles, the timing and order of releasing each finger from the ball, the effect of wind, atmosphere and the speed and direction that the catcher is moving.

That simple operation in fact involves a process of acquiring, communicating and co-ordinating information which involves literally thousands of individual messages and a similar process has to be duplicated by the catcher each time. Yet the process is carried out time and time again without a single conscious thought by either thrower or catcher. At the same time that incredible machine is automatically breathing, pumping blood, oxygen and other essential chemicals around the body, digesting food, extracting wastes and toxins, constantly adjusting your temperature to the correct level and thousands of other necessary functions without a conscious thought.

You could argue that the throwing and catching of the cricket ball did not require a conscious thought. Practice makes perfect, and it was the child's practice that achieved the proficiency. True, but the child didn't have to make any conscious decisions while it was practising, its brain merely said: "Throw Ball." The rest was automatic, it just practised using the sophisticated equipment with which it had already been supplied.

The human species has produced marvellous machines and robots, however, none of them can work independently. They all require human programmers or operators to make them function efficiently. The computer that is helping me to write this book is an incredible machine. It enables me to calculate a thousand times quicker than I normally could. It can spell far better than I can. So what. The wheel and the internal combustion engine enabled man to travel many times faster, but they are mere tools that we use. So is this computer. It cannot operate without my help. Even with my help it makes unbelievably stupid errors.

The accumulated knowledge of those three billion years was designed to achieve one object: SURVIVAL. Over the last few hundred years, by using the instinctive and intelligent parts of its brain, the human species has basically conquered the problems of survival. We had time to turn our attention and ingenuity to other things, like leisure, art, music, business and other substitutes for survival against the elements, like sport, science and war on a truly massive scale.

While this process is under way and the lesser species are still concerned with basic survival, and accordingly are teaching their offspring how to cope with the real hazards of life, we are desperately trying to cocoon our children from the harsh realities of life. We create for them a fantasy world of Father Christmas, genies, fairies and magic lamps. We tell them that there is someone up there that is constantly watching over them, that will protect them and provide for all their needs. They merely have to pray. Even if they sin God will forgive them.

As very young children we believe what we are told. But we soon learn that there are many different religious faiths and the leaders of them all speak with such absolute conviction. To begin with we believe that the teachings of our own particular faith are correct. Then we learn of diabolical atrocities which are even to this day being perpetrated in the name of religion. At the same time we discover that there are no such things as genies or magic lamps. The pity is that the creator has provided us with the necessary equipment and tools, but we don't realise it, the deceit and confusion having caused many of us to lose faith in establishment religions.

The loss of that faith has left a void in our lives. We now believe that we need someone to protect and to provide. So we create characters like Superman, Batman and Spiderman. We soon learn that they are also deceptions, but already we have been programmed to believe that we cannot survive without some outside crutch. The void is already there. The truth is that up to now, the main tower of strength has been our parents. It is they that have provided sustenance, warmth, love, protection and anything else that we need.

However as we reach adolescence and, hopefully maturity, it begins to dawn on us that our parents are not the unshakable pillars of strength that we had always imagined them to be. We realise that dad can't lick any man on the block. If we examine our parents closely, cracks begin to appear. It gradually dawns on us that our parents are just grown up children, with the same frailties and fears that we have. Often they appear to be more neurotic and insecure than we do ourselves at that stage.

The tendency is to switch our allegiance to the heros and heroins of the real world. We start to idolise pop stars, film stars, television personalities or top sports personalities. We now start to create our own fantasies. We make gods out of these people and start to attribute to them qualities and skills far in excess of those that they actually possess. We should have been using those years to develop our own skills and strength. Instead of using those people as role models to show us what heights we can achieve, we cop out. We try to bask in their reflected glory. Instead of becoming complete, strong, secure and unique individuals in our own right, we become mere vassals, fans. Just FANATICS.

All this is happening during the most stressful period of our lives, from birth through childhood and adolescence. While the *lesser* species are being educated by their parents to cope with the real, practical problems of life, the human species at a very early age, delegates that responsibility to schools.

What's wrong with that? In theory, nothing. In fact it seems to be a perfectly logical process. If you want your son to play good tennis, don't teach him all your bad habits, send him to a professional. The problem is that school doesn't prepare children for the outside world. It's merely a sort of hangover from the monastic past. The stupid thing is that most of these teachers to whom we entrust our children's education have never even seen the outside world. They spend the whole of their lives in school. Would you send your son to a professional that had never *played* tennis?

I perceived school as a constant game or contest. The rules were quite clear. On one side were the poor teachers whose object it was to instil knowledge into our heads. On the other side were the pupils, whose sole duty was to resist this unwanted contamination of their minds by any means that they could devise.

Some pupils develop the art of day dreaming while giving the appearance of being fascinated by the abolition of the corn laws. The more adventurous would play truant, liar dice or battleships and cruisers. However, in those days to be caught meant a caning. A ludicrous affair in which the teacher struggled desperately, and sometimes unsuccessfully, to keep the smile off his face and maintain a rather austere 'this will hurt me more than it hurts you' expression, while the pupil struggled with equal desperation to replace his 'you must be kidding, do you have to hurt yourself quite so much expression' with a smile. Had the contest been a boxing match, the referee would have stopped the bout in the first round on the grounds of a mismatch. The poor teachers didn't stand a chance. Not only were they hopelessly outnumbered, but, as I have learned from my smoking clinics, it is impossible to force knowledge and understanding onto someone that has no desire to receive it.

However, the *experts* have helped to balance the scales nowadays. They've worked out that violence breeds violence, so teachers aren't allowed to cane pupils nowadays. Ironically, it's now the pupils that occasionally beat up the teachers. This is obviously why violence is completely absent from our society today and why our educational standards are so high.

The problem was that at no stage did anyone bother to explain why

I was at school. I was convinced that school was really some sort of penance that vindictive parents inflicted upon their children. The parents had to work all day, so why should the children be allowed to play? Not until the fourth year at grammar school did it dawn on me that I was being prepared for future life.

Some pupils were luckier than I and had a thirst for knowledge. However, when I look back at the curicula, I'm not so sure they didn't waste their time more than I did. The only justification for the hours spent learning algebra was that it's an exercise in intelligence. Are our educators so unintelligent, that after hundreds of years they have not been able to come up with a subject that is both an exercise in intelligence and has some practical value? We're taught a language that has been dead for over a thousand years. Why? Because doctors need to know Latin? Wouldn't it be more practical if the medical profession joined the 20th century and learned to write in English, or would that remove their excuse for their illegible writing?

What are the monumental turning points in history that stand out in my memory? King Alfred burnt the cakes. King Canute thought he could hold back the tide. King Harold was stupid enough to look up when it was raining arrows. Sir Francis Drake regarded a game of bowls as more important than defeating the Spanish Armada and Sir Walter Raleigh put his cape over a puddle.

When I finally left school, I didn't even know how to wire an electric plug or mend a fuse, let alone understand the electrical wiring of a house or car. However, I could recite Ohms law or Boyles law word perfect, together with hundreds of other facts that were absolutely meaningless to me, other than to enable me to pass examinations. While other species were being educated to understand what life, survival and enjoyment is all about, I wasted ten of the most valuable and informative years of my life doing the complete opposite.

While at school, we are not only being misguided, but we are also in a sense cucooned from the harsh realities of life. We leave school. A metamorphosis takes place. It might not be as obvious or as dramatic as the butterfly emerging from the chrysalis, but that does not detract from the effect. Overnight the youngster is expected to leave the fantasy world of being protected, to become independent and just a few years later, protector.

The void is already there. Now there is something else that we intelligent human beings have been programming our children to do since birth. We've taught them that when you grow up and become adult, the best thing you can do if you need a little crutch or boost is to drink alcohol or smoke. You might well have told them that it is stupid and that you wish you hadn't started, but you and millions of other smokers are still doing it: WHY?

Is it really surprising that youngsters will try just one to help fill that void? After all you did. Why should they be any different? Our society is programming future generations to become drug addicts.

We need to remove that void. I have heard recovering alcoholics say: "It took me 20 years to sink this low, I can't expect to be free in a couple of months." That is nonsense. It took me nearly a third of a century to reach the depths of degradation that I obtained. I was released in one second, just the time it takes to turn a key in a lock. It will take you a little longer, but only the time it takes for you to finish and to absorb the contents of this book. I will show you how to find that key. It is there hidden somewhere in your brain. I find the prospects of helping you to find it exhilarating. Has it yet dawned on you how much more exciting it should be for you, or are you still consumed with the greatest ally of addiction:

FEAR

If you were to take up say, hang-gliding. You are a highly intelligent person, but you know absolutely nothing about hang-gliding. So because you are intelligent and because you also happen to be very wealthy, you wisely seek the advice of the leading expert on the subject, a man who has been obsessed with the subject for 30 odd years. Having paid to receive this expert advice, would you lightly ignore it, particularly if your life depended on it? Of course not, or if you did, you would make sure that you had a very sound reason for doing so.

Now you probably think that I'm leading up to another repetition of: "YOU MUST FOLLOW ALL OF THE INSTRUCTIONS!" In fact I am not. But if you would hesitate to contradict the advice based on 30 years experience given by a person who might be much less intelligent than you are, how much more stupid would it be to ignore the advice of an expert whose intelligence is a million times greater than yours. That ability of human beings to communicate knowledge on any subject which they choose means that we don't have to learn by our own mistakes, we don't have to build our own houses or cars. It virtually means that a single human being has easy access to the total knowledge of all human beings throughout history. That's really something to think about and gives us incredible advantages,

IF THE KNOWLEDGE THAT WE COMMUNICATE IS CORRECT

This is the flaw. Often the information that we receive is not only contradictory, but the complete opposite to the correct information. We have progressed too quickly. We make vital changes in our life style without fully appreciating the long term effects. It doesn't matter too much if the wrong information is about music, art or your golf swing, but when the misconceptions are about survival, the result can only be disaster. We already have the correct information about survival. The fact that it is instinctive or subconscious doesn't detract from that knowledge. It too was stored and communicated from one generation to the next and, through the process of natural selection, from one species to another, not for a few thousand years, but for millions of years. Perhaps we have only recently become aware that this information has been passed down from our ancestors through aeons of time by means of our genes. You don't have to be aware of it. It is a classic case of a little knowledge being a bad thing. Lesser creatures do not have the intelligence or imagination to question their instincts. Lucky them! They have no choice but to act on them.

I have described our intelligent brain as a flaw in the machine. I mean no disrespect to the creator of the machine. Strictly speaking the flaw is our inability to use the machine properly. It's equivalent to a pieceworker removing the safety guard. The intention is to increase the size of the bonus. The outcome is to shorten the length of the arm.

There is no reason why our intelligent brains and our instinctive brains should be in dispute, they should run in harmony. However, if they are in dispute, you need to be very certain of what you are doing, because it would be rather unintelligent of you if you let your intelligent brain overrule that expert and those 3 billion years!

The intelligence that released the human race from the jungle in such a comparatively short period, is now plunging us into a nightmare far worse than our ancestors had to face in the jungle. After all, they were fully equipped to cope with that life. There have been red warning lights for generations. Why is it that human beings are the only mammals that have to learn to swim? All other mammals swim instinctively. Snakes can swim even though they have no limbs. Why can a fox drink daily from my fish pond and suffer no harmful effects, whereas in certain countries, I can't have ice in my drink? Why can the babies of other large mammals walk within hours of being born, whereas human babies take months? Is it really intelligent to create bombs that can destroy the whole planet and every living creature on it a thousand times over? The only justification for doing so was to prevent war. Couldn't our intelligent brains have come up with a more rational solution? We spent a fortune developing and creating these bombs, now we are spending another fortune trying to get rid of them. But will the knowledge of how to make them ever be lost? Have we sentenced all future generations to live permanently in the fear of being blackmailed or made extinct by the act of a single madman? Is it intelligent to destroy in just a few generations, rain forests that took millions of years to develop their incredible variety of trees, fauna and the creatures that depend on them, or to exhaust the whole planet's stock of fossil fuels, minerals, metals, chemicals and other nutrients in a comparative micro-second of the time it took to produce them?

As John Wayne said: "A gun is just a tool that can be used for good or evil, it is no better or worse than the man that totes it." Some would question whether a gun could ever be used for good, but the principle certainly applies to our intelligent brain. It is up to us to use it wisely. It isn't wise to play at being God. It is crass stupidity to think that we are wiser than our creator. I have already dwelt on the tendency of modern medicine to treat symptoms rather than causes. This tendency has been likened to a motorist steering one-handed, the wrong way down a one way street, at a hundred miles an hour and trying to shoot out the oil warning light with the other hand. Perhaps this is an exaggeration, but our tendency to search for some magical drug to solve all our problems needs to be examined. It is highly questionable whether an outside drug should be used to adjust what is thought to be a purely physical problem. However, to use drugs to upset the natural functioning of the human body in order to solve problems which are purely mental, cannot be right.

In fact there is no such thing as a purely physical problem. All our feelings or emotions, whether it be pain or happiness can only be transmitted through the brain. I recently appeared on a television programme with a Dr. Chris Steele who claims to be an expert on nicotine addiction. He was advocating the use of products which contained nicotine to help smokers to quit. At one stage he was explaining what a pleasant drug nicotine was. I was conscious of the disastrous effects this information would have on youngsters watching the programme, particularly as the information was not only incorrect, but coming from a doctor. I attacked Dr. Steele for advocating a powerful poison. He looked at me as if I were a madman. He said:

"Don't you use 'Paracetamol'?" Fortunately, I've never suffered with headaches and was able to answer honestly that I never had used 'Paracetamol'. However, had I have suffered from headaches, I might well have been tempted to use 'Paracetamol', thinking that it was a painkiller and doing me some good. I wonder how many other people that regularly use 'Paracetamol' and similar products, realise that they are taking poisons. We now make the suppliers of food declare the contents of their products. In an ideal world we shouldn't have to do this, they wouldn't sell products that could actually cause us harm. Would they? In fact they've been doing it for generations! But doctors are different, they have no commercial bias, they cure people they don't kill them. Why do you think that every medicine that you have ever been prescribed carries a warning: **DO NOT EXCEED THE RECOMMENDED DOSE OR, DO NOT ALLOW ACCESS TO CHILDREN? BECAUSE THEY ARE POISONS!**

Okay, perhaps on occasions we do need to poison our bodies in order to kill a virus, but don't you think we ought to be informed about it? After all the words medicine and poison would appear to be opposites. One cures, the other kills. I wonder how many people actually realise that, every time they take an aspirin, they are actually taking a poison! I think that we have the right to know!

What has all this got to do with stopping smoking? It is very important. I'm telling you to rely on your instinct. But isn't it now instinct if you have a headache to take an aspirin? Princess Diana was the first to break the custom of having royal babies born at home. How many other mothers now *instinctively* feel that it is wiser to have their babies in a hospital? The point is, once you have contaminated your instinctive brain with incorrect information, it becomes part of the programming. We don't need to smoke before we fall for the nicotine trap, but once we have fallen for the trap we seem to be contaminated for life. Years after we have stopped smoking we can suddenly have the feeling: "I fancy a cigarette." We are fully aware that it is illogical, that there is no rational reason why we should want a cigarette, it's instinctive, so eventually we back our instinct and light a cigarette.

So how can we tell what are our beneficial instincts, those that are the result of 3 billion years of accumulated knowledge, and the instincts which are false and are there solely from the contamination of our intelligent brains? In other words, how can we get back to that blissful state of never wanting or needing a cigarette? How do you find your way out of a complicated labyrinth? It's easy, provided you can remember the way into it. You need to understand the distinction between the instinctive (subconscious) mind, and the intelligent (conscious) mind. If they contradict you need to find out which one is wrong.

This isn't always easy. My logical brain tells me that there is no rational reason that I should fear spiders. But I do. It is possible by a process of thought and analysis to transfer information from the subconscious to the conscious mind. I have failed to understand why I dislike spiders so much. It probably relates back to my ancestors. It might be that someone else could rationally explain this fear. Freud's theory was that spiders were visually similar to the pubic hairs of a woman. I admire his imagination, but cannot agree with his logic. Why should the pubic hairs of a woman hold terrors for a man? Even if they did, why do women appear to be generally more terrified of spiders than men? I think Freud was just obsessed with sex.

To this day I do not know why I hate spiders and I've stopped worrying about it, I just accept the fact. Lot's of other people admit to being frightened of spiders, and I've long suspected that many of those that deny it are being somewhat untruthful. Why else would they need to hold a huge, hairy monster in their hands? I'm not afraid of lumps of sugar, but I don't find it necessary to hold one for several seconds in order to prove the fact. If there's a spider on the ceiling, I won't walk directly beneath it. If it's on the floor, I will without conscience step on it. Problems are only problems if you worry about them. If you have a valid reason for worrying, like the ill effects of smoking, remedy the situation. If you are unable to remedy the situation, you are merely causing yourself needless aggravation by worrying about it.

No doubt you have jumped on this advice to convince yourself that, as you can't stop smoking, you will stop worrying about it and continue to smoke. No you won't! I don't know the answer to the spider anomaly, but I do know the answer to the smoking anomaly, because it happened in my living memory. I can remember when I had no need or desire to smoke and so can you. Like me you too can return to that blissful state. It is possible to distinguish between beneficial and false instincts, although nature provides many subtle traps. Part of the ingenuity of natural selection and survival are these traps. Insects that look like flowers and vice versa. The most subtle trap of all is nicotine addiction. However, addiction only exists in the subconscious mind. Once you transfer it to the conscious mind and understand its nature, it loses its power over you. In fact it ceases to exist, just as the magical effect of a conjuror disappears once you understand the illusion.

You need to open your mind. Even when you have done that it is sometimes difficult to know:

IS IT FACT OR ILLUSION?

CHAPTER 8

Is it Fact or Illusion?

There is all the difference in the world between knowledge, understanding and believing. We all know the world is round. But at one time, everyone believed that it was flat. Yet today, we have no greater proof that the world is round than our forbears had for believing it was flat. All any us actually know is what we have been taught to know. You might question that statement. You might say: "But I've sailed around the world, or I've flown around the world." How do you know that? How do you know that you didn't sail/fly out and then return to where you started from? It's common knowledge that if you walk in the desert with no means of navigation, you merely walk in a huge circle. Do you conclude that you have walked round the world when you arrive back at your starting point?

The truth is, although we know the world is round, we still think of it as flat. You doubt me? Have you been abroad to America or Spain. Think of those people there now, do you see them standing on their sides. Do you see the Statue of Liberty upright, or like the Leaning Tower of Pisa. When you think of a test match being played in Australia, do you really see them running around upside down? Yet if you are in England, that is exactly what they are doing. When I point this out to some people they say: "But you are ignoring gravity." No I'm not ignoring gravity. It's only because of gravity, that they are standing on their sides. Now imagine the world the size of your house. Would you see the Spaniards standing upright?

If you are still not convinced, try looking at it another way, when I drive from London to Scotland, ignoring the intermediate twists and curves, ups and downs that I make, I imagine that overall I am gradually going uphill. Yet when I drive to Wales, I sense that overall, the journey is flat. Now is this because the Highlands are in Scotland, or because our knowledge of geography comes mainly from maps and atlases. North is depicted at the top of the page. Is that why we talk about going up North and down South. If you drive from London to either Scotland or Wales, if you ignore the intermediate twists and turns or ups and downs, you are merely completing a gentle arc around the earth's circumference, but do you see it that way?

Let's use a different example. We are standing on the roof of the

Empire State Building. I am your father you trust me implicitly, I say look over the side, look down to the concrete below. What I am about to ask you to do, you will find very difficult, but I promise you that no harm will come to you. I want you to jump off the roof I promise you that you will merely float on air. Would you jump off the roof? Of course you wouldn't. But why wouldn't you jump? Because you didn't trust me or have complete faith in me? This must be partly true, or perhaps the reason you didn't jump was that you were a coward and frightened to jump. Alternatively, your reason might have been you are not a fool, why should you jump? You had little to gain and your life to lose.

Now even if you saw 20 other people jump and just float in air, it would still take enormous faith in your father, or courage, or stupidity to make you jump and given those circumstances not one person in a million would actually jump.

But how would you know which of the factors prevented you from jumping? You would probably say: "Because I'm not a fool I had nothing to gain and everything to lose." But if you had complete faith in your father, you had nothing to lose and an exhilarating experience to gain. The point I am making is this, your brain won't be capable of assessing whether it was lack of faith, or fear, or whether it was because you were just not stupid enough to jump that prevented you from jumping. In truth, it was probably a combination of all of these factors. Even so, if you accept this, your brain will not be capable of assessing the exact extent each factor bore in arriving at your decision not to jump. The point is you didn't need to go through a logical thought process. The reason that you refused to jump was 'instinct'. The correct decision had already been made for you by your ancestors millions of years earlier. You had no more need to make a decision than you do to blink your eye when a fly hovers near it.

What do you make of the hieroglyphics below? Just let your imagination run wild. See if you can make anything of it:

X	AB	AB	SOS	X
X	AB	AB	SOS	X
AB	SOS SOS	STOP	TODAY	AB
AB	ILLUSION	TODAY	NOW	NOW
AB	TODAY	TIMING		STOP
AB	TODAY	PITCHER		PLANT
AB	ILLUSION	ESSENTIAL		PITCHER
AB	ILLUSION	STOP NOW		PITCHER
X	TIMING	AB		TIMING
X	TIMING	AB		TIMING

91

If you couldn't see the wood from the trees, place the book on the table and gradually move further away from it. You will see the word **FLY** stand out and hit you. If you slowly move back towards the book, it will be just as clear. Why couldn't you see it before? Was it an optical illusion? In a way it was, but it wasn't your eyes that were fooled, it was your brain. It was trying to make some sense out of the X's instead of the gaps in between. You saw the picture as black painted on a white background. You should have been looking for the reverse. Your eyes are just one of the tools that your brain uses. We only see what we are conditioned to see.

In fact this is another ingenious aspect of the incredible machine. You can be looking at a huge panorama and yet have the ability to focus on one small bird within it. For the few moments that you concentrate on that bird, you have effectively wiped out the rest of the world. The ears also have this incredible ability. There can be a cocophany of noises yet we have the ability to concentrate on just one and wipe the rest out. Again, incredibly complex and sophisticated tools that they both are, it isn't really the ears or the eyes that have the ability, it is your brain that controls them, and your brain can deceive.

When I was a teenager most girls seemed to me to be ugly, nowadays all women appear to be beautiful. Ah, that's just a sign of getting old. Perhaps, but I think there's more to it than that. I think that Hollywood films taught me to look for physical perfection in a woman. I was always concentrating on the faults of the girls, nowadays I see their assets, it is purely my choice but it makes life more enjoyable to be in a world full of beautiful woman and my main philosophy in life is that it should be enjoyed.

What one person sees as beautiful another sees as ugly, neither is right nor wrong. We must all have gone through the experience, at least once in our lives, of being completely infatuated by another person, oblivious to any defect in their physique or character; then at some later period, we are left wondering what could possibly have attracted us to that person in the first place.

In Chapter 13 I describe a film in which the jury enter the jury room all convinced that the accused is guilty, and leave two hours later convinced that he is innocent. Our complex brains give us the ability to see a half-filled bottle as half full or half empty. We can even be deluded, or delude ourselves, into believing that a full bottle is empty or vice versa.

Aren't we lucky. We have the ability to make the world appear exactly as we want it to. What a wonderful asset this is, to be able to have an empty bottle and to believe that it's full, or as Bob Hope says: "You don't need to be a millionaire, provided you live like one." Does it really matter if smoking does absolutely nothing for us at all, providing we believe it relaxes us, gives us courage, helps us to concentrate and relieves stress and boredom?

Are you finding this somewhat confusing? I sympathise. The fact is that our brains are incredibly complex and the subject is very confusing. But are we really so lucky? Do we really have this ability to see things exactly as we choose to? To find out, we need to remove the confusion, and to do so we need to distinguish clearly between perception and deception. Let us delve a little deeper into some of the examples.

I have the choice to concentrate on the good points rather than the flaws of women, friends, relatives or colleagues. I have learned to do so for the selfish reason that it makes life more enjoyable. I am able to apply perception. But what about the idyllic love affair that goes wrong. These things are heart-rending enough when they are just brief childhood infatuations, but supposing a long-term marriage, home, children and the stability and happiness of many people are involved? Why do we not exercise our perception and continue to see the previously loved one as all virtue and no fault, instead of as we now see them, as all fault and no virtue?

Some people explain it by: "The person changed." Or: "I matured or progressed but they didn't." Which really means that you changed. Strange how our perception enables us always to put the other party in the wrong rather than ourselves, we never see them as maturing or progressing.

Other people put it down to: "Familiarity breeds contempt." If so, how does it often work in reverse? Why is it that with some people, you intitially find them physically repulsive, insignificant or even offensive, yet the more you get to know them, the more attractive and interesting they become?

Isn't the truth of the situation that intitially we used our perception to delude ourselves into believing that person was perfect because it suited us at the time to see them as such, and all that familiarity did was to shatter our delusions, and as a consequence it now suits our purpose to perceive only their faults?

For 500 years our genes have been programmed to make us believe that the world is round. This belief is confirmed and reinforced from birth by instruction about the law of gravity, the solar system and astronomy. Yet for everyday practical purposes, we still regard the world as flat? There is no real self-delusion or deception here. The fact is that because of our size in relation to the earth, unless we are going on a very long journey, and since we cannot fall off the edge, it is of no practical advantage to regard the world as round and to do so would merely confuse the issue.

Why did the jury all change their minds? The evidence didn't change one iota. Was it because they were fickle or easily persuaded? No, they were 12 conscientious people, with no axe to grind, all attempting to make the correct decision from the evidence given. It was the greater familiarity and insight that allowed them to see the same evidence in its true light. This is the problem with delusion, self-inflicted or otherwise, once you have seen through the deception you can no longer delude yourself whether you choose to or not.

So how can you tell when you are being deceived? Which is correct, the picture about smoking that the tobacco companies and society generally see about smoking, or the picture that Allen Carr is painting for us? Some smokers see themselves as pathetic junkies, others still have the Humphrey Bogart/Marlene Dietrich image. Most smokers nowadays are about midway between these images. Surely that is a matter of personal choice, whether you see another person as ugly or not, is purely aesthetic. But there is reality and illusion. Take the **FLY** example. Did I brainwash you into seeing FLY? If I did, then I should have the power to reverse the process so that you can no longer see it. But I know of no way of doing that. All I did was to clear the confusion and enable you see what was there all the time. From today you will always be able to see **FLY**.

With the jury you couldn't persuade those men to revert back to guilty in a million years, unless you introduced new evidence or pointed out the flaws in the existing evidence.

What's wrong with seeing the bottle half full rather than half empty. Absolutely nothing! It will make you happy and you won't be deluding yourself. What's wrong with living like a millionaire even if you aren't one? Ask Robert Maxwell. It made him so happy that he sacrificed his most precious possession, his life. Ah, but why the delusion persisted he was happy. Was he? Did he ever give you the impression of being happy? Mr. Micawber had the true answer to that one. I know several people that try to live above their means. I know most of them are miserable because they do so. I don't know of one person that is happy because they do so. In my experience, it is better to be a millionaire and live like a pauper.

What's wrong with seeing the bottle as full when it's empty? Just this, while you have no need to drink from it, what possible advantage does it give you? Once you have need to drink from it, the delusion will be gone. With luck you won't be crossing the desert at the time too late to discover that your life-saver is just an illusion.

What's wrong with believing that smoking is pleasurable and relaxing, that it relieves stress and boredom, and that it helps you to concentrate? Just this:

IT DOESN'T DO ANY OF THOSE THINGS. IT'S DELUSION.

IT DOES THE COMPLETE OPPOSITE!

But does that matter? While you are deluded into believing that smoking has those advantages, isn't that effectively the same as having them? No! If I'm ugly and you delude me into believing that I am handsome, that might not bring me the girlfriends, but at least that particular illusion will make me feel happier. However, if you delude me into believing that I am handsome, but in spite of that, I still feel ugly, I don't even get the psychological boost.

That is the reality of the smoking trap. It's the same as the empty bottle that you think is full. If you don't need to drink it's no advantage whatsoever. If you need to drink, the delusion is shattered. It's only when you are not smoking that you suffer the delusion that the cigarette has any advantages. What can that possibly do other than to make you feel unnecessarily deprived?

When you are actually smoking the cigarette, the delusion is gone. You have nothing but the reality. The congestion, the foul smell and taste, the wheezing and coughing, the lack of energy, the depression, the slavery and the self-despising. This is why 99% of our smoking is subconscious. Being lethargic and miserable isn't very nice, neither is wasting your money, or cancer or having your legs removed. The actual illusion with nicotine is that smokers are deluded into believing that the bottle is full of sustenance and pleasure. The truth is, the bottle is full:

FULL OF POISON! THAT IS THE REALITY!

Delusion can only be bad because the addict is not in control. At any time the bubble can be burst, and that is the worst aspect of smoking: **THE SLAVERY.** Smokers don't have a choice, if they did they wouldn't be smoking.

It wouldn't be so bad if the delusion that smoking provides some sort of crutch or pleasure, actually made smokers feel happier. The fact is that it doesn't. In spite of the delusions, smokers remain miserable, irritable, self-despising and frightened. That is the reality. That's why they hate the thought of their children becoming hooked. In fact the situation is far worse than believing that an empty bottle is full, not only is it full of poison, but smoking actually creates the void. It converts a feeling of confidence and completeness into a feeling of insecurity and emptiness.

Some of my initial failures say: "I followed all of your instructions. I understood everything that you said. I kept telling myself that cigarettes did absolutely nothing for me whatsoever. I kept telling myself that I neither needed nor wanted a cigarette. So why did I fail?"

Why indeed? They claimed they had followed my instructions. But they hadn't fully understood them. They hadn't fully appreciated the subtle differences between knowledge, understanding and belief. Why

95

did they need to keep telling themselves that cigarettes did nothing for them and that they neither needed nor wanted one? I know that heroin will do absolutely nothing for me and that I neither need or want it, but I don't have to keep telling myself that. The mere fact that they had to keep telling themselves meant that there was some doubt in their minds and that they didn't fully believe it. You could spend the rest of your life telling yourself that red was black, but do you think that would make you believe it?

No it wouldn't, because red isn't black, and to delude you that it was, you have to do more than just try to brainwash yourself that it is. There has to be some sort of trick or illusion to delude you. However, it's absolutely essential not only to know and to understand why smoking does absolutely nothing for you at all, why you won't miss it and will enjoy life more and be better able to cope with stress and why it is easy to stop, it is also essential:

THAT YOU BELIEVE IT

It will enable you to understand better if we answer the question:

WHERE DID IT ALL GO WRONG?

CHAPTER 9

Where Did it All go Wrong?

Queen Bee wants to mate. So why does she fly off and make the drones chase after her? Because the creator programmed her to ensure that she mates with the strongest.

A million male sperms race to the egg. The strongest achieves penetration and the miracle of another human life is conceived. The cells begin to multiply and to change. Some become skin, muscle or bone, some form delicate organs each a miracle in itself. Man has achieved medical marvels, but they really amount to experimentation with organs that already exist. The simplest of living cells is more complex than anything that man has yet to produce. Some so-called experts would dispute that statement. Call their bluff, ask them to create a living cell.

After 9 months the pinnacle of creation is ready to be born. Up to now the only part that man has played is to carry out the natural function of copulation. Things have gone pretty well. But now man's intelligence starts to interfere with nature.

Why is it that Aborigine women, when about to give birth, drop behind the rest of the tribe, do so and have caught up with the rest of the tribe within 20 minutes? Because they are primitive savages and know no better? They know and do what the creator taught them to. Do you not think that their method is much simpler than the one that western man has created? Do you not find it incredible that it is mainly men that have decided the best way that women should have their babies? What arrogance to purport to be an expert on something that you have never done and can never be capable of ever doing.

Anyway, lets ignore the women's problem for the moment at least she has the choice to have a natural birth or otherwise. But what about the poor baby who has no choice. Our creator never intended birth to be a disease. I'm not even convinced that it was intended to involve pain or stress. I must admit that when watching films of wild animals giving birth, on occasions the poor mother looks exhausted. But exhaustion in itself isn't painful in fact it's sometimes nice to get exhausted, it makes relaxation afterwards so pleasurable. But all mothers, whether they've been through a long and stressful labour or otherwise, seem to have this marvellous contented glow about them.

A natural birth involves an incredibly complicated and co-ordinated mental and physical reaction between mother and baby. If man starts to interfere with a natural process designed by our creator, things are bound to go wrong. So we try to introduce drugs to rectify the situation. These drugs themselves interfere with the natural chemical reactions and the situation gets worse.

Have you ever been in a completely dark room and suddenly been subjected to bright sunlight. Can you imagine the shock on that poor little creature whose only existence up to now has been cuddled up in its mother's womb, suspended in a comforting warm liquid, listening to the steady, reassuring beat of its mother's heart as it pumps oxygen and nutrients into the baby.

Then suddenly a huge alarm goes off, the liquid disappears, the heart beats become faster, the baby is suddenly being ejected from the warmth and security of the only home it knows. The baby instinctively senses that it has to leave. It tries to fight its way down this incredibly tight tunnel, it uses all its reserves of strength and energy and finally emerges into what? A world of blinding neon lights. Can you imagine the shock to that poor little creature? How much worse if mother and baby cannot manage the trauma on their own. A natural birth must be quite an ordeal to the new baby, but can you imagine the additional shock of being dragged into that bright asylum by means of clamps attached to your head?

What's the next thing that happens? They turn off your supply of oxygen. Whilst you are connected to the umbilical cord, you don't have to breathe, you could be born in water you wouldn't drown. Try holding your breathe for a minute. Not easy is it? But it isn't so bad, you can start breathing whenever you want to. Now imagine having someone else's hand clamped over your face so that you cannot breathe and have no way of telling whether you will ever breathe again. And how do we make them breathe? We turn them upside down and slap them on the bottom. When they bellow, we have the gall to say: "He's got a strong pair of lungs."

Assuming the baby survives, all it now wants is the comfort of its mother's breast, the warmth of her body and to be near those reassuring heart beats. The baby needs a transitional period to get over the shock of being born. Many primitive women keep their babies close to their bodies for several months, they even work with the baby strapped to their body. What does intelligent, modern man do? We separate them, wash them, weigh them, examine them, stick a hypodermic syringe into them and tab them. Then we deposit them with other equally terrified and screaming babies. All because mother needs a rest. Even when the baby leaves the hospital, all too often it isn't allowed to sleep in the same room as the mother let alone the same bed, and if the poor little beggar cries all night: "You musn't give in to him, show him who's boss, give in once and you'll always have to give in." I wonder who suffers the most on those occasions, the frightened little wretch that is crying out for comfort, or the poor mother whose every natural instinct is to pick him up and comfort him, but instead has to listen to the torture of those cries. All because some psychiatrist, who has probably never even had a child, thinks he knows better than God.

People don't cry just for the sake of it whether they be babies, children or adults. People cry because they are suffering some aggravation. They are crying for help. Perhaps the baby is crying for attention if so, give it some. Another curious anomaly is that our superior, intelligent brains have brought us so much happiness that we are the only species that needs to cry!

If you consider the shock a baby goes through with a natural healthy birth, is it surprising that with the additional trauma that we inflict upon it, the baby is crying the first few weeks or months because of the shock of the birth? Why do we find cot deaths such a mystery? To me the real mystery is how any baby can survive that ordeal. I know many adults that would wilt in such a situation. But how on earth do we expect a new born baby to survive it **AND NOT BE ALLOWED TO CRY!**

Now I expect you are wondering what all this has to do with smoking and drug addiction. It has everything to do with it. I've said that nicotine addiction, far from filling a void, actually creates one. The reality is that smoking increases a void that already exists. I'm referring to the empty, insecure feeling of childhood and adolescence, already enlarged by the pressures of modern day society.

Imagine a headache pill that gave the illusion of curing headaches but actually caused them. Imagine that it was being used on a similar scale to smoking. There are 3 basic ways to solve the problem:

1. What I refer to as 'The King Canute' approach. You attempt to prevent all the nasty people that become multi-millionaires by producing the pills to see the error of their ways. The lesson of prohibition and the complete failure of the authorities to even check the increase in hard drugs has shown this approach to be totally ineffective.
2. By removing all headaches so that the need to take the pill in the first place is removed.
3. By mass education of the population explaining why the pill causes rather than cures headaches.

Solution 3. is the only practical way to solve the problem completely, and that's how I've been attempting to solve the smoking problem for nearly ten years. It is also what much of this book is about.

Unfortunately, we have yet to discover how to create a headacheless society, so solution No: 2 is impractical. However that would be the ideal solution. It would not only solve the problem of the pill, but also solve the problem of headaches. The smoking equivalent would be to remove the stress and strain of childhood and adolescence, and to remove the enormous anxieties created by modern society. Some hope of doing that. Anyway even if that were possible, wouldn't that be rather like using a sledge-hammer to crack a nut. Perhaps you feel that there is no practical solution to the problem? BUT THERE IS!

What's more, it is not dependent on the discovery of incredibly sophisticated technology such as was necessary in order to put a man on the moon. Civilisations have lived in peace and harmony for thousands of years. Why should childhood and adolescence be so stressful? The other major problems that threaten our existence have been created by us. We already know the solutions. They are ridiculously simple. It's merely a question of organising ourselves. In any event, quite apart from removing the void that creates the need for youngsters to smoke or dabble in other drugs, it would be a very worthwhile exercise in its own right. Even if we didn't succeed in removing the bulk of the anxiety from our lives, the removal of any of it would be its own reward. This is also what this book is about.

Supposing your problem were that you didn't want weeds to grow in your garden. You hunt down all the weed seeds in the world and destroy them. That's clearly impossible. The only practical solution is to so prepare your soil or plant other crops so that weed seeds find it difficult or impossible to germinate. The same applies to cigarettes and drugs. It will help greatly to negate the attempts of the tobacco industry, other smokers and society generally to brainwash you again. But what we can also do is to remove the void. Perhaps I have given the impression that to remove that void, we need first to solve all of these other problems. Not so, all you need to do is to make sure that you realise the physical and mental strength of the incredible machine that you possess, so that in spite of the fact that these problems are not yet solved, you feel as I do, and those seeds don't just fall by the wayside, or on stony soil, or even on concrete but on:

BRIGHT, SHINING, STAINLESS STEEL!

Once you have escaped from the pit, even if you made no attempt to help others to experience your joy, they will sense it and be only too pleased to follow your example.

I have already dealt with ways in which, rather than eliminate this void, we in fact worsen the situation by being over protective to our children. Another bad tendency is that we get them into the habit of eating sweets. Forget the fact that we are going to make them loose their teeth about 30 years before they have to, but we are also introducing into their minds that you have to have little rewards to punctuate the day. That's fine, but life always provides sufficient real rewards to punctuate each day, that is if you are fit and healthy and in a happy frame of mind, so why introduce phoney substitutes?

Adolescence has always been a very stressful period. Up to now we've been programmed to believe that the really important things in life are academic achievements, exams, sports, music, whatever, depending on the particular bias of our parents. But now they move the goal posts. It matters little that you were king on the rugby field, the important thing now is: can you make it with the girls? Do the opposite sex find you attractive? You then have to start learning what you had previously considered as rather cissy pastimes, like dancing. It's not long before you are being programmed to worry about whether you will be an adequate breadwinner or nest-builder.

Today's youngsters have numerous additional stresses looming in the background, the 'bomb', pollution on a massive scale, holes in the ozone layer, global warming, melting of the glaciers, overpopulation, overfishing, overfarming, exhaustion of our natural resources, AIDS and unemployment, to name but a few. At the same time, the standards, stability and feeling of security that religious faith and stable marriages provided are gradually being eroded. What have we given them in their place? An obsession with material wealth. Fast cars, colour televisions, labour saving devices and automation. What's wrong with that? Nothing, unless you are one of the millions that have become redundant and cannot afford these dubious pleasures, perhaps you then resort to the other evil that we have left them – VIOLENCE!

You must admit, we haven't exactly created paradise for future generations. They might not be daily conscious of all these things, but they are there like an ever-increasing fallout cloud hanging over their heads. The real miracle is that so many of them grow up to be pleasant, compassionate, well-balanced human beings. I believe this to be in spite of our efforts and not because of them. While all the above is happening, they have been bombarded daily with brainwashing on a truly massive scale telling them that cigarettes relax, relieve stress, give confidence and help concentration. We have programmed them to rely on another legacy that we have left them:

DRUG ADDICTION

Eventually most youngsters will light a cigarette. The nicotine leaves the body and the second cigarette replaces that nicotine. It's followed by a secure, satisfying sensation which the teenager probably isn't even aware of at that stage. However, his subconscious mind will be. It is saying: "This tastes awful, but it is relaxing." Already the subconscious brain is being deceived and it won't be long before the conscious brain catches up with it.

THE NICOTINE TRAP HAS CLAIMED YET ANOTHER VICTIM

CHAPTER 10

Inside the Pitcher Plant

The fish knows that it is hooked the moment the angler makes a successful strike. After the second cigarette the smoker is just as firmly hooked, but the nicotine trap is far too subtle to allow the youngster to realise the fact at this stage.

That second cigarette is the start of a lifetime's deceit and lying, not only to other people, but to oneself. We have already broken one vow. The vow that all youngsters make to themselves, whether it be conscious or subconscious: **"I'LL NEVER BE ONE OF THOSE IDIOTS THAT GET HOOKED ON CIGARETTES."**

It's not very long before we break the second vow: **"SURE I ACCEPT THE OCCASIONAL ONE FROM A FRIEND, JUST TO BE SOCIABLE, BUT I WOULD NEVER DREAM OF PAYING GOOD MONEY FOR THEM!"**

Youngsters believe that you don't get hooked until you learn to enjoy the taste and smell of tobacco. Rather like heroin, the first cigarettes are pushed on them by their friends. The youngster has no guilty conscience about accepting these hand-outs, because at that stage they are unsolicited and unwanted. The youngster senses that they are doing the friend a favour, that like all drug addiction, the friend feels stupid and uncomfortable partaking alone. But the youngster soon reaches the stage when they start asking the friend for a cigarette. Understandably, the friend takes umbrage: **"IT'S TIME YOU BOUGHT A PACKET."**

The youngster sheepishly buys a packet. But was it really because of the reason he gave?

"I only bought the packet, not because I needed them, but to repay the ones that I had borrowed."

Or was it because the youngster now needed a cigarette, and the only way to get one was to pay good money for them. How do you know? By asking pertinent questions. For example: why wasn't that youngster's conscience pricked while the friend was prepared to continue the supply of cigarettes? Would he have repeatedly accepted hand-outs of money, food or drinks without feeling obligated to return the favour? If the youngster bought the packet not because he needed a cigarette, but to fulfil his obligation, why didn't he just buy a packet for his friend and then stop smoking?

The nearest thing to the nicotine trap in nature is the process of a fly being lured into a pitcher plant. To begin with the fly eats the nectar. Why should it fear the plant? The fly has wings, it can fly off whenever it wants to. But why should the fly even want to fly off? After all the nectar is delicious. Not until it dawns on the fly that it is actually being eaten by the plant, rather than the other way around, does the fly have any desire to leave, but now it's too late.

The nicotine trap is far more subtle than a pitcher plant. There is no lure! Those first cigarettes taste awful, any latent fear that we might become hooked is immediately removed. The fly in the pitcher plant knows it's trapped once it tries to escape but cannot. So subtle and clever is the nicotine trap, that even when the victim tries to escape but cannot, it still doesn't realise that it is actually trapped. Indeed, it would appear that many smokers have lived and died without even realising that they are actually hooked. They believe that they are in full control and smoking purely because they enjoy it.

I said it would appear that many smokers do not believe that they are hooked. In fact I have serious doubts about this. In my endeavours to understand smoking completely, I find it very frustrating that when I look back on my life, I am unable to assess my exact feelings about smoking at any particular stage. The problem is exacerbated by the fact that you not only need to have a good memory, but you need to know that your opinions were warped at the time. How can you assess to what extent they were warped? My own case is particularly confusing. I was a chain-smoker and as such I must have believed that I got more pleasure or crutch from smoking than casual smokers. At the same time I cannot ever remember actually enjoying smoking a cigarette.

If within a few days after I had finally stopped, you had asked me at what age did I realise that I was really hooked on nicotine? I believe that my answer would have been late twenties, early thirties when I was struggling to bring up a young family and had a really responsible job. Yet when I look back at indisputable, isolated facts that I can remember, I was clearly hooked at a much earlier date.

I can remember seeing a film in Biggleswade with two other teenage audit clerks. It was about the boxer Rocky Graziano and in particular how, after being treated with morphine in hospital, he became addicted to the drug. The horrendous withdrawal symptoms got the usual 'Hollywood' treatment. A feeling of silent gloom hung over us as we left the cinema, each engrossed in his own thoughts. Eventually the silence was broken by one isolated remark: "I'm going to stop smoking!" There was no discussion, disagreement or protestation from the other two, merely silent nods of approval. I was the eldest of the three. At 17 I had been smoking regularly for less than 2 years. Why did all three of us relate those highly exaggerated withdrawal symptoms to smoking? I emphasise that this was at a time before cancer scares and before any of us even realised that there was such a thing as nicotine addiction. There can be only one correct answer to that question: WE ALREADY KNEW THAT WE WERE HOOKED! whether it was conscious or subconscious at that stage, I still do not know.

An even earlier incident occurred at the age of 15. My best friend, Desmond Jones, was suffering from what I initially considered to be a very serious affliction. For some time he had lost all interest in sports or poker. Eventually his lack of interest became so accute that I was obliged to broach the subject. It transpired that he had discovered an exciting new pastime and persuaded me that it was I who was missing out. No doubt you've already guessed that the new craze was girls. Having accumulated nearly two months knowledge on the subject, he was obligingly giving me the benefit of his considerable expertise. I soon learned the essentials. This was no great academic feat because there were only two to learn. They were both designed to make us appear older and more suave than we really were. The trouble was they both cost money, which neither of us had at that time. One was a trilby hat and the other essential was a cigarette dangling from the side of your mouth. Humphrey Bogart, you have much to answer for.

I really resented the cost of the trilby. I can remember trying to adapt an old scouts cap, but it made me feel more like Baden-Powell than Humphrey Bogart and it had the same effect on girls. We solved the smoking problem by taking it in turns to buy a packet of 5 'Players Weights' each Saturday night. We would smoke two whole cigarettes each during the evenings revelries, not in one go, in fact we somehow managed to make them last the whole evening. I lived in Putney, Desmond lived across the river in Fulham. It became an established custom that whichever of us had bought the packet would break the fifth cigarette in two and we would smoke the two halves while overlooking the river discussing our conquests, or to be factual, our near misses.

On this particular occasion, Desmond had bought the cigarettes. Instead of breaking the final cigarette in half, he lit it, commented that as he had bought the packet, he was under no obligation to share it and threw the empty packet onto the towpath. I immediately saw red and aimed a mighty kick at the packet. Desmond let out a yell that must have registered 9.3 on the Richter scale. Too late! My foot was only 6 inches from the packet and it went soaring into the mighty Thames. The packet, not my foot.

It transpired that there was a whole cigarette left in the packet. Now I've always thought of myself as being as open-minded as the next person in the sick humour area, but really, some subjects are just too

105

sacred to joke about. However, the packet merely floated on the surface. We started to lob various missiles in a vain attempt to direct that packet to within our reach. Putney bridge eventually forced us to terminate our efforts. We stood despondent with wet and cold feet.

There is a moral to this story. If you are ever tempted to play a practical joke on someone, no matter how harmless it might appear, just think what disasters might ensue. DISASTERS? This is the real point of the story. We were only 15 at the time and would quite happily go to the following weekend without even thinking about smoking. Where was the great disaster? Why did we regard the ruining of two pairs of socks, shoes and trousers as insignificant details? Why were we behaving as if the very survival of the human race depended on our retrieving that cigarette?

Smokers that tell you that they only smoke because they enjoy smoking can be very convincing. They are often intelligent, strong-willed, dominant people that only smoke a few cigarettes a day. They assure you that they can go days without cigarettes if they have a mind to. Now why do they feel the need to impress that upon you? If they had been explaining to you how much they enjoyed playing golf, would they feel the need to terminate the conversation with: "Mind you, I can go days without playing if I've a mind to." Do they really know themselves that they are hooked and are merely trying to deceive you, or are they genuinely deceived themselves? I am absolutely certain that I had no idea that I was hooked before or after the floating packet incident, yet I was clearly already hooked. I must have known that I was hooked by the time of the Rocky Graziano film, but the exact stage that I knew I cannot tell. It was obviously always there in my subconscious mind, perhaps it was the film itself that triggered the transfer from subconscious to conscious mind.

There are clues to help you decide whether these 'in control' smokers are really as 'in control' as they make out to be. Strangely, they never seem to want to smoke in my presence. You might think that the reason for that is obvious. But is it? I don't object to people smoking in my presence. On the contrary I go out of my way to point out that I am surrounded by smokers all day and that it doesn't bother me in the slightest. If we are having a meal I even say that I have no objection to them smoking between courses, or even during them if they want to. Even so, the tendency is for them not to smoke. Their hands start to fidget, I begin to feel uncomfortable, I know they are dying for a cigarette. In desperation I say: "There is only one thing that annoys me about smokers and that's when they refuse to smoke in my presence, you'll be making me feel uncomfortable if you don't smoke." Even so, often they still persist in not smoking. Why? These are pleasant, rational, sociable people. One minute they are telling me how much they enjoy a cigarette after a meal, I am telling them that it will offend me if they don't light up, and still they don't. Now why would an otherwise pleasant sociable person deliberately offend me and at the same time deny themselves a pleasure? Why do those smokers go out of their way to prove, whether it be to me or to themselves, that they are in control? All they succeed in proving is the complete opposite. The moment they leave my presence, they light a cigarette and how relaxing that cigarette is, just like removing tight shoes that you've been forced to wear for hours.

However, the above is no real proof, perhaps these smokers are really just being cantankerous. For real proof just ask these smokers the following questions:

"You tell me you smoke because you enjoy smoking, do you encourage your children to smoke?"

"I don't have any children."

"If you did, would you encourage them to smoke?"

I have asked this question thousands of times. On not one single occasion has the answer been yes. It is either no, or an attempt to avoid the question, such as:

"I believe they should have the right to choose."

"Naturally, but would you please answer the question that I asked you, would you encourage them or not?"

Invariably, they continue to waffle and sooner or later decide to sit on the fence:

"I wouldn't encourage them one way or the other, I would merely make them aware of the advantages and dangers of being a smoker and allow them to choose."

"Now suppose your children decided that they would rather like to play in the road or to inject themselves with heroin. Would you merely point out the pros and cons, or would you implore them not to be stupid?"

This question is usually followed by more waffling, but the point is that it is not only the duty but the desire of every parent, human or otherwise to educate and prepare an offspring to cope with the dangers of life. The truth is that no parents encourage their children to smoke. The only reason that some of them find difficulty in answering the above question, is because they continue to smoke themselves. If they did so because they truly believed that the pleasure or crutch outweighed the dangers, why do they wish to deny their children these pleasures? Because of the dangers? There are dangers in driving, do we persuade our children not to drive? Believe me, there is only one reason that no parent encourages their children not to smoke and that is because every smoker knows logically and instinctively that they are not smoking because they choose to, but because they've fallen into a trap. Naturally, they don't want their children to fall into the same trap. If that's true, why don't they stop smoking themselves? For the simple reason that they are not in control as they say they are:

THEY ARE WELL AND TRULY HOOKED!

Some parents explain the anomaly away by saying: "Of course I don't want my children to smoke. It's filthy, unhealthy and expensive and what you've never had, you don't miss. It's different for me, I know what I'll be missing." To begin with, I do not believe it is true that what you've never had you never miss. I had a tremendous desire to play golf years before I succeeded in doing so. To say what you never had you never miss is to deny the existence of ambition, imagination or sexual drive. In fact all too often the anticipation of a pleasure can exceed the reality. The real problem is the latter half of the statement: "I know what I'll be missing." I tend to agree. Once denied a real pleasure, life goes on, but you never completely lose the feeling of deprivation.

This is the real subtlety and strength of the nicotine trap, the greatest allies of the trap are the victims themselves. It is so designed to make the smokers think that they are not hooked and that, no matter what depth of degradation they have reached, they are smoking because they choose to smoke. They create their own imaginary pitcher plant and the deeper they sink into the abyss, the greater becomes their desire to remain trapped.

Before we fall into the trap, we are already aware that there are powerful reasons not to smoke, but the trap is so designed that eventually practically everyone tries one. I'll wager that there is not one person in a million that never, ever tried one. Even the millions that never became hooked, very few of them never tried just one. Ask a youngster that has just started smoking:

"Why do you smoke?"

They will lie and say something like:

"I enjoy smoking."

They don't enjoy it. It's blatantly obvious they don't know what to do with it. They daren't inhale lest they have a coughing fit or begin to feel sick. Ask the same question a few weeks later and they can now genuinely say:

"I enjoy the taste and smell".

What they are really saying is they no longer find the taste and smell offensive. Ask the same question a few weeks later and they will say:

"It relaxes me. It helps me to concentrate. It gives me confidence".

Now in the space of just a few weeks, the cigarette has changed from something that tastes foul and disgusting, into something that, not only tastes and smells pleasant, but is also a prop or crutch. It's blatantly obvious that the cigarette itself hasn't changed, merely the youngster's perception of it. Ask the same question a few years later and the answer is likely to be:

"It's just a habit I got into".

Now why do we start saying it's a habit I got into? Why don't we continue to say "Because I enjoy it, or it's a crutch." It's because we have lost the illusion of enjoying it. We wish we had never started, but we now sense that we are hooked and cannot stop. Ask the same question another couple of years later, and if you have reached the stage that I once reached, when every cigarette physically hurts you, when you are just waiting for it to kill you, when you lie in bed every night hoping you'll wake up the next morning, either with no desire to smoke, or with sufficient willpower to fight the temptation, then you know the only honest reply is:

I'M A JUNKY!

All our lives, our excuses for smoking keep changing. The actual reason never does. It is merely to try to end that empty, insecure feeling that the first cigarette created. But of course each cigarette doesn't end that feeling, it merely guarantees that you suffer it again and again for the rest of your life.

I'm telling you that once you have been deprived of a pleasure, you can never completely lose that feeling of deprivation. I'm also telling you that the nicotine trap is far more subtle and clever than the pitcher plant, but once the fly realises it's trapped, there is still no escape. So how can you ever completely escape the nicotine trap? Even if you could:

HOW COULD IT POSSIBLY BE EASY?

I promise you that it is. The fly cannot escape from the pitcher plant because it does not possess the physical strength to escape from the glue that entraps it. But no physical bars restrain smokers. The smoking prison only exists in the smoker's mind. Smokers are conned into becoming their own jailors. With sufficient desire, ingenuity and help, a few found it was possible to escape from 'Colditz', but how do you escape from a prison that doesn't physically exist, a prison in which you became your own jailor, a prison in which your desire to escape will always eventually be overcome by your desire to remain imprisoned?

The strength of the trap is also its weakness, because you are your own jailor, and because the reasons that you became your own jailor are false, once we have removed the illusions that kept you wanting to remain a smoker, you will already be free. Ex-smokers can never be completely free while they believe that they are being deprived of some pleasure or crutch. But the beautiful truth is:

THERE IS NO PLEASURE OR CRUTCH IN SMOKING!

Once you can understand and accept this beautiful truth:

YOU WILL SUFFER NO FEELING OF DEPRIVATION!

Do you still find this difficult to believe? If so, do you think you would ever greatly miss banging your thumb with a hammer? Or does the thought that you will never be allowed to inject yourself with heroin unduly concern you? Of course in doesn't! In fact the thought probably fills you with horror. But why do you think heroin addicts have this great desire? Do you envy them? Of course you don't! On the contrary, you pity them. Why do non-heroin addicts see heroin addicts with such a completely different perspective to that with which the heroin addicts perceive themselves? Could it be because one perspective has been grossly distorted by the effects of a drug? Non-smokers see smokers with a completely different perspective to that with which smokers see themselves. I wonder why? Start trying to perceive yourself:

AS A NON-SMOKER SEES YOU!

After four hours counter-brainwashing at our clinics some highly intelligent, strong-willed, dominant business person will say something like:

"I know what you are telling me is true, because, before I started smoking I didn't need a cigarette, my life was complete. I remember looking at my father and thinking what a ridiculous, filthy, disgusting habit smoking is. I remember well how foul those first cigarettes tasted and how hard I had to practice to inhale and look like a tough guy. I know that non-smokers aren't missing out that, like all other smokers, I've fallen into a clever, subtle trap. The point is, I have fallen into the trap and I've been in it umpteen years. I just cannot visualise a meal or drink without a cigarette or cigar, or being able to cope with a difficult phone call without a cigarette."

Isn't it amazing how a powerful, strong, business executive regards a phone call? The phone won't blow up or bite you. It's the craving for nicotine that causes the stress not the phone call. I'm not saying that a phone call of itself cannot be distressing. Neither am I saying that, if you don't particularly enjoy your work, most phone calls will distress you, but this applies whether you are a smoker or a non-smoker. The point is: the cigarette far from relieving any genuine stress, actually increases it. I say to these people: "Does it bother you that you can't inject yourself with heroin after a meal or before you answer the phone?"

"Now you are just being facetious."

"Explain the difference to me."

"Heroin is a killer."

"That's right, it kills less than 300 a year in the U.K. compared with over 100,000 killed by nicotine."

"But heroin kills quickly."

"In fact it doesn't. It is far less poisonous than nicotine which is used as an insecticide. The nicotine content of one cigar injected directly into a vein will kill you. Heroin addicts usually die from the substitutes included with the heroin. Anyway, don't we usually say that we'd prefer a quick death rather than a slow tortuous one? In any event, who wants to die? The most powerful guiding force for any creature on this planet is survival, whether we like it or not. Smokers often say to me: 'I think I've got a self-destruct button'. I say: 'If you really believe that, try jumping off the roof before you light your next cigarette, see whether it's a genuine self-destruct button."

"Ah, but the withdrawal pangs from heroin are so severe, heroin addicts will kill to get the drug".

"I don't deny that. However the expression 'I could murder for a cigarette' isn't pure dramatisation. It's happened on more than one occasion. Fortunately, because they are relatively cheap compared with heroin, and because they are legal and readily available, the necessity to commit murder for them is rather rare. I cannot visualise killing another human being for them. Nevertheless, I'm truly grateful that I was never put to the test. The point is, to claim that smokers who are prepared to have their legs amputated rather than stop smoking, aren't killing themselves is ludicrous. The truth is, every smoker on the planet is killing the most important person on the planet, they are killing themselves. The fact that we try to block our minds to it doesn't mean that it isn't happening. Even the authorities that allow it to remain legal and extract about 5 billion pounds annually from smokers concede that 1 in 4 smokers die prematurely as a direct result of their smoking".

The conversation invariably ends up with the smoker saying: "The real difference is, I've never been a heroin addict. I have been a nicotine addict and I know what I'm missing." This is the most important point of all. I've never been a heroin addict and I thank my lucky stars that I never will be. However I have been a nicotine addict. Both smokers and ex-smokers often say to me: "I cannot believe that you never, ever crave the occasional cigarette." I never do for the simple reason that I remember smoking, not through the rose-coloured spectacles that society had created for me, but as it actually was when I was a smoker.

I remember the effort it took to get out of bed each morning and that depressed, lethargic feeling. I remember the greeny brown fur on my tongue, which made it feel like a rasp. I remember the suffocating feeling of the first cigarette of the day and the wheezing, coughing and nose-blowing that always ensued. I used to say: "I never get colds. Because I smoke so much, germs cannot survive within my lungs." The truth was, I used to cough up so much phlegm each morning, I never knew whether I had a cold or not. I thought that every one had a runny nose and coughed up phlegm in the winter, it wasn't until I stopped smoking that I realised the truth. I'm still in the habit of making sure that I have more than one handkerchIef in my pocket, but I now only use them when I have a cold. Nowadays I detest getting a cold as I know the difference between feeling ill and well. When I do get a cold it makes me marvel at the fact that I used to inflict that congested, depressed feeling of having a cold on myself permanently and thought of it as normal.

I can remember the brown stain that I had on my upper lip each morning. In my attempts to remove it, I merely succeeded in scrubbing it into a red one. After an all night card session a friend once asked me if I was growing a moustache? He was very embarrassed when on closer inspection he realised that it was a nicotine stain. Needless to say, there was one person in the room that was even more embarrassed, but the incident didn't stop me smoking.

For years I would only smile or laugh with my lips closed, because I was ashamed of the stains on my teeth. I hated visiting the dentist. I thought it was because I was a coward and afraid of the pain. I realise now it was really because I was ashamed of the nicotine stains on my teeth and of the inevitable lecture that I would receive from the dentist.

I remember the haunted looks that my wife and children gave me during those particularly severe bouts of coughing, the mental anguish that I was causing them when they were forced to watch this pathetic creature that was their father, systematically killing himself, to say nothing of the mental anguish I had, being aware that I was the cause of their discomfort, yet incapable of doing anything about it.

At Christmas and birthdays, my family would ask me what present I would like. I would reply: "I don't want anything, I already have all that I need." In silence I would add: "I spend so much money on cigarettes, money that I could have spent on necessities or luxuries, I don't deserve anything else." It didn't occur to me until years after I had stopped smoking that the last thing that I had purchased for myself, for purely selfish reasons, was a gleaming new bicycle, acquired at the age of 15 from the earnings of a paper-round. One of the things I really enjoy today, is to buy things for myself, to indulge myself outrageously, without the slightest feeling of guilt. It was long after I had stopped smoking that I realised that such luxury had been denied to me for over a third of a century, not only because my heavy smoking absorbed so much of my money, but, even if I could afford the luxury, my guilt complex prevented me from indulging myself.

I used to feel uncomfortable if another human being, even my close family, got within 3 feet of me. I thought I had a phobia about close personal contact. I did, but I didn't realise that it was caused by the fact that I was forever conscious of whether or not that person could smell the nicotine on my breath. Even as a late teenager, I never had the pleasure of kissing a woman on the lips without wondering whether she could smell my breath.

However, the thing that I remember most about being a smoker, was despising myself for being dependent on something that I secretly loathed. With everything else in my life, I was in control. I hated the the slavery and the knowledge that other people knew that I was a slave. I hated worrying about whether I had sufficient cigarettes, whether the plane would be delayed on the runway, whether the next person that I met would be a smoker or a non-smoker. Do I ever have cravings for the occasional cigarette? Don't be stupid! Why should I, or any one else for that matter?

Why do I never crave to smoke the occasional cigarette? For exactly the same reason that I don't crave to wear tight shoes, or to bang my head against the wall, or to immerse my hand in boiling water, or to inject myself with heroin. All of them are very unpleasant things to do. I'm sure that you'll agree that it would be stupid to punish yourself by craving for a pleasant thing that you cannot have, but how much more stupid is it to crave for something unpleasant that you don't even need. The only point of contention between us at this stage can only be whether or not there is some crutch or pleasure to be gained from smoking. Probably your rational brain already believes that there isn't. However, to be completely free, we must also remove any last vestiges from your subconscious mind. Remember, while part of your brain is saying: "I need or want a cigarette," it doesn't matter that you don't understand why you want that cigarette, or that the thought is illogical. If you want a cigarette and can't have one, you will be miserable.

I expect that by now I am beginning to try your patience. Why don't I stop talking about what we have to do and just get on and do it? The more discerning reader will realise that I have already been doing this. Trainee pilots are always impatient to fly. However, they will not survive long without a knowledge of mathematics, navigation, aeronautics, radio, mechanics and other subjects some of which would seem to have little bearing on being able to fly. Their patience brings its own reward and so will yours. Anyway, I'm probably more anxious than you are to get on with it. I'm happy to inform you that we have prepared the ground work and can now get on with the business of:

HOW TO BE A HAPPY NON-SMOKER FOR THE REST OF YOUR LIFE

113

CHAPTER 11

How to be a Happy Non-Smoker for the Rest of Your Life

Smokers that have successfully used Allen Carr's Easy Way to Stop Smoking, whether it be via clinic, video, book or audio cassette, and get recaptured, cannot understand why the 'magic' cure sometimes appears to be less effective on the second occasion. It is because they now have a completely different problem. It's easier explained with the use of the manhole analogy:

If a man has been trapped in a manhole for several days, between us we have the two necessary ingredients to effect his escape. He contributes a strong desire to leave the trap and I provide him with the tool that will release him. All he now has to do is to follow the correct instructions for the use of that tool to escape. However, having successfully escaped, we both now have a completely separate problem: to make sure that he never falls into another manhole. That's a pretty tall order. How can I help him other than by following him around the rest of his life?

I could help him by ensuring all manholes had covers. The smoking equivalent would be remove all products that contain nicotine. Clearly impractical. So how can Allen Carr prevent one individual from ever smoking one cigarette, let alone 99% of the world's population?

It is possible. Remember the manhole is a physical trap, smoking is a purely mental trap: an illusion. Like all confidence tricks, once you see through the trick, you will never fall for it again. Also remember, millions of people have already lived their lives without falling for the nicotine trap, and this in spite of the massive brainwashing to which they have been subjected, and in spite of not understanding the true nature of the trap or the true facts about smoking.

What is it that we are actually trying to achieve? That's obvious: to be a non-smoker. Then your problem is already solved and you don't even have to do anything, just never light another cigarette. Come on, it can't be as simple as that, what about the terrible craving, the misery and depression? Exactly! There's more to it than that.

What is the real difference between a smoker and a non-smoker? Obvious: one smokes the other doesn't. True, but we are trying to alter that situation, we need to know why one smokes and the other doesn't? Who forces the smokers to light up each cigarette? The smokers themselves. The fact that part of their brain wishes that they didn't have to smoke, or that they don't understand why they smoke, doesn't affect the situation one iota. The real difference between smokers and non-smokers is that the latter never have a desire to smoke.

However, I have no doubt that like me, you have probably known some non-smokers, and certainly many ex-smokers that have an occasional desire for a cigarette. It would be surprising if they didn't, after all, they have also been subjected to the brainwashing since birth. Smokers tend to overlook the fact that non-smokers suffer exactly the same schizophrenia about smoking as they themselves do. The real difference between a smoker and a non-smoker, is that in the case of non-smokers, the schizophrenic scales are weighted so heavily in favour of not smoking, that any temptation to smoke is so slight as not to be a problem.

So is that what we are trying to achieve in order to become a non-smoker, to make sure the temptation is so slight that it ceases to be a problem? No! While the slightest desire or temptation to smoke exists in your mind, you'll suffer a feeling of deprivation and be compelled to exercise willpower and discipline for the rest of your life. Furthermore, you will be vulnerable to falling into the trap the whole of your life. I am aware that non-smokers find the odds against the risk of becoming hooked, so momentous, as not to be worth worrying about. I would remind them and you, that approximately 60% of the population felt exactly the same way, until:

THEY WERE HOOKED!

In any event, whether they be non-smokers, smokers or ex-smokers, it is essential that no one goes through life feeling deprived, vulnerable or of having to resist temptation, no matter how slight that feeling might be. The rest of your life is an awful long time to be vulnerable. So what we are really trying to achieve, is for everyone, not only never to smoke a single cigarette, but never to have the need or desire to smoke during the rest of their lives. In other words what we are trying to achieve is for everyone:

TO BE HAPPY TO BE NON-SMOKERS FOR THE REST OF THEIR LIVES

The more discerning of you will have noticed that I have not only grouped smokers with ex-smokers, but have actually included non-smokers. Am I suggesting that non-smokers need to read this book? That is exactly what I'm implying. Is that so surprising? Would you wait until your child was drowning before teaching it to swim?

How can I possibly imply that smokers suffer from exactly the same problem as ex-smokers, let alone non-smokers? I don't! Smokers suffer the problem of already being in the trap. Both ex-smokers and non-smokers suffer the problem of being vulnerable to fall for the trap. Their problem is different, but the solution to their problems are identical: to have no need or desire to light a cigarette, not today or tomorrow, or next year but:

FOR THE REST OF THEIR LIVES!

All we have to do is to ensure that no one ever has the need or desire to light a cigarette. Perhaps you feel that is an impossibility. But that's just because of the distorted way we see smoking. Supposing our task were to make sure no one ever had a need or desire to stick their hand in boiling water, would it still seem insurmountable?

Anyway, it's my task to ensure that no one ever wants to, all you need to do is to make sure that you never have the need or desire to light another cigarette. I promise you it's easy!

EASY! ABOUT AS EASY AS CLIMBING EVEREST!

CHAPTER 12

Climbing Everest

Suppose you woke up one morning and decided it would be quite an achievement to climb Everest. Would you book the next flight to the Himalayas, remembering to take your overcoat, your thermal underwear and a good pair of walking shoes? What would be your chances of success? **ZILCH!**

Everest is a bad analogy to use in a way, because all along I've been saying it's ridiculously easy to stop smoking, when everyone knows how difficult it is. I'm now implying it's like climbing Everest. No the point I'm making is that Everest is very difficult to climb. To have any chance of success you would need considerable physical and mental preparation together with extensive finance, equipment, backup and planning. You'd probably also need a fair slice of luck. Even with extensive preparation and planning, it is still difficult and the climbers experience physical and mental hardship, but do you think they are miserable? No way! They are exhilarated by the experience. Misery only enters into it if disaster, bad luck or, most of all, failure rears its ugly head.

Richard Branson described his attempt to break the transatlantic power boat record. I can't imagine a more uncomfortable experience. He nearly drowned in the Irish sea. Yet a few months later, he is back again doing the same thing in a hot air balloon. The balloon touched down in Ireland and the pilot jumped out. The balloon cleared England completely with Richard still aboard. He eventually landed safely in France. Both events must have been hair-raising experiences, but as he describes them, even in his modest, laid-back manner, it's quite obvious that he actually enjoyed them.

Fortunately, it is easy to stop smoking. The physical craving is so slight as to be insignificant. The problem is mental. You can open a safe within seconds provided you have the correct combination. You can be a happy non-smoker immediately, but only if you have the correct frame of mind and keep it for the rest of your life. The vast majority of attempts to stop smoking fail because they are initiated by a short-term, haphazard situation, like too much smoking at Christmas, or a bad chest, or shortage of money. The problem is, once the smoker stops, so does the bad chest and shortage of cash. Now the reasons that initiated the attempt to stop in the first place have disappeared. But the desire to smoke hasn't. On the contrary our temporary abstinence has made the cigarette appear even more precious and eventually we find a plausible excuse to have just one cigarette.

STOPPING SMOKING IS ONLY EASY IF YOU FIRST PREPARE YOURSELF MENTALLY. If you don't, your chances of success will be not much greater than climbing Everest. Again, you think I exaggerate. After all half the adult smokers have already kicked it. That's true, but did they find it easy? Do they still have cravings for the occasional cigarette? How many of them have fallen back into the pit again? Do you really want to be like them? Or would you like to be a happy non-smoker the rest of your life?

Now a warning. You'll no doubt be receiving advice from so-called experts or well-wishers given with the best possible intentions. It might appear to be logical. But if it contradicts the instructions I give you, **IGNORE IT.** Sometimes my strongest advocates, smokers that like me, found it ridiculously easy to stop, in their desire to help their friends, will cause their failure by misinterpreting, not fully understanding or even placing the wrong emphasis on something that I say. A classic example is:

"He told me that smokers never actually enjoy smoking any cigarettes, even the one after a meal. I checked it out and to my amazement he was absolutely right!"

Say that to a friend who is convinced that they enjoy a cigarette after a meal and the probability is that they won't even bother to check it out. They just think: "No point in me going to an Allen Carr clinic because I definitely enjoy one after a meal." Ironically, it will also prevent smokers that already realise that they don't enjoy one after a meal from seeking my help. Their attitude is: "What's new? I don't need Allen Carr to tell me what I already know." Another classic example is:

"I didn't think about smoking after I left that session."

One of the really important instructions I give is: "It is fatal even to attempt *not* to think about smoking." In fact that smoker was probably constantly thinking about smoking for a few days. Thinking how lovely it was that they no longer had a need or desire to light a cigarette. What they really meant was: "From the day I left that clinic, it never occurred to me to light a cigarette." The friend leaves the clinic his mind obsessed with the subject of smoking. How could it possibly be otherwise? For four hours we've been discussing smoking. He *should* be pondering the subject, questioning the things that have been discussed, absorbing the information and contemplating the joy of being a non-smoker. Then he thinks: "Wait a minute, Fred told me that he never even thought about smoking when he left. Obviously something has gone wrong."

The above two cases are examples of misguided statements made inadvertently. However, sometimes the ex-smoker will actually advise the friend to ignore one or more of the instructions. Something like: "He tells you not to, but I kept a packet with me." The friend follows that advice and can't understand why he fails.

But why is it that I say it is essential to follow ALL of the instructions, yet some people follow only half of them and still find it easy to stop? It is partly for the same reason that you might omit one of your preparations to climb Everest, but still succeed, provided you are lucky and partly, because every smoker has his or her own individual state of brainwashing.

Imagine a fence 12 feet high which you have to climb over. You have no aids or equipment or outside assistance. The only way is to jump over it. You wouldn't succeed. Now suppose the fence were made up of twelve one foot slats. The bottom slat is solid mahogany. But the other eleven slats don't really exist: they are subtle illusions. This is the problem that I am trying to solve with each smoker. The real difficulties in stopping smoking are the illusions. Each instruction I give is equivalent to removing one of those illusory blocks. Each one that you remove will make it easier for you to stop. The bottom slat, the mahogany slat, is represented by the few days that your body will suffer the slight aggravation of feeling deprived of nicotine. How can I help you over that? Do you really need my help to climb over a one foot fence? **IT'S EASY!**

Think of each one of the instructions I give you to make it easy to stop smoking as removing one of those imaginary slats. Even if I only remove 6 of them, a normal, healthy adult would still find it comparatively easy to surmount that fence. 'EASYWAY' gives all the instructions in addition to extensive detailed explanation, surely all that you need to do is to follow them? True, and if you are a long term smoker and have a powerful desire to stop, you'll follow them and be successful. But if you are a non-smoker or recently recaptured, you have no need or desire even to read the instructions let alone follow them, but you are still being subjected to the massive daily brainwashing that's enticing you to try:

JUST ONE CIGARETTE

CHAPTER 13

Twelve Angry Men

Have you seen the film 'Twelve Angry Men'? It must be the best film ever made in ratio of quality to cost. I should make it clear that there was absolutely no stinting in the quality of the cast. All twelve acted superbly. The film is so absorbing that it is difficult to believe that 99% of it is shot in just one room. A teenager has been tried for murdering his father. The case is a fait accompli. He threatened to do it, he was seen doing it, he was heard doing it, he had no effective alibi and was caught with the murder weapon on him.

Almost the entire film consists of the discussions between the various jurors, followed by a series of ballots. The result of the first ballot was 11 guilty 1 not sure. The doubter, played by Henry Fonda, was not able to give any logical reason for his doubts, he even agreed that all the evidence pointed to GUILTY. There was just something which didn't add up. One of those cases where the logic is in conflict with instinct. However this prompted another juror to point out a slight anomaly in the evidence that didn't quite add up in his mind. It was an insignificant point but prompted further discussion. Cheap budget the film might have been, but it is also one of the most fascinating films that I have ever seen. Now the detective work is actually done by the jury and at each ballot the guilty votes become less and less, until eventually they prove that the boy was not guilty and could not possibly have committed the murder.

Many clients say: "I was sceptical before the session, during the session and after the session, yet I've never had the slightest urge to light a cigarette since the day I left your clinic and it was ridiculously easy. Most of the things you said I already knew. Why did I find it so difficult and impossible on my previous attempts?" Interviewers say to me: "What is it you say to smokers that makes it so easy for them to stop?"

Both ex-smoker and interviewer expect some ingenious and snappy one-liner. When I fail to come up with it, the ex-smokers think that I am trying to keep my 'magic' secret and the interviewers think that I haven't got one. It would be like saying to the twelve jurors: "What particular point convinced you that the boy was innocent?" A juror might in all sincerity quote the decisive point which made him change his opinion from guilty to innocent, but this was only after hearing and processing the preceding discussions. Each juror didn't come to the same conclusion at the same time. Each was an individual. Certain points weighed more heavily with some jurors than with others.

What actually happened in that jury room? Just one significant thing: all twelve entered it with a picture of that boy in their minds, a frame of mind that said: MURDERER! GUILTY! All twelve left knowing that he was innocent. This is what we do at my clinics. Smokers arrive in various states of panic. Some are visibly nervous. Others appear to be cool and assured, they are similar to the swan gliding across the lake all grace and serenity, but beneath the surface, turmoil!

Apart from being nervous, they are often incredibly confused:

> "I'd love to be free, but I enjoy it so much, but it's killing me, but will I be able to cope without them, but think of the money I'll save, but what about those awful withdrawal pangs, but how pleased my family will be and I'll be so proud, but have I got the willpower and will I ever enjoy a meal again, is it really possible ever to be completely free and is it really the right time to try?"

It's little wonder that most smokers are nervous wrecks. They suffer permanent schizophrenia. When they leave the jury room, I mean the clinic, all those doubts and fears have been removed. They arrive in a frame of mind of panic and confusion, they leave in the frame of mind: ISN'T IT GREAT TO BE A NON-SMOKER! I don't mean that is what they are telling themselves, I mean that's how they actually feel and that's what we are trying to achieve:

THE RIGHT FRAME OF MIND

CHAPTER 14

The Right Frame of Mind

Imagine that I am going to persuade you to try another drug. I'll be completely fair and warn you in advance that it is a rather sinister drug, very similar to heroin. I deal in this drug and I make a fortune out of it. If I can get you hooked as well I'll make a lot more money. However, I said I would be fair so I'll first provide you with all the relevant facts:

It is highly addictive and the odds are that you will not only become hooked immediately, but will remain hooked the rest of your life. It is very expensive. The average addict spends about £30,000 in a lifetime. I will provide the first shot free, but from then on, I will make you pay through the nose and again I warn you that whatever I choose to charge you, or how much you might resent it, you will somehow *cough up* the money. It happens to be a powerful poison. In countries where it is established, it quickly becomes the No.1 killer. It causes the premature death of 1 in 4 of its victims. As soon as you start to take it you will become increasingly lethargic, short of breath and less resistant to disease. However, worst of all, imperceptibly it will destroy your nervous system, your courage, your confidence and your concentration, and the more it ruins them, the more you'll feel dependent upon the drug. It will taste awful. Those are the disadvantages. The advantages? What will the drug do for you?

ABSOLUTELY NOTHING!

No doubt you have correctly surmised that I have just listed the actual clinical facts about our old, friendly, sociable habit of smoking. Perhaps you believe that I have exaggerated the facts. I assure you that if anything the reverse is the case. The medical authorities now inform us that smoking causes the premature death of about one in four smokers. They are wrong! What they really mean is that one in four smokers die of a terminal disease caused by smoking. The truth is because smoking reduces the effectiveness of our immune system, it causes the premature death of all smokers, provided they continue to smoke and that some even more premature cause, like stepping under a bus, doesn't kill them even more prematurely.

Expressions used by the medical profession can also cause confusion. The word 'TERMINAL' induces a feeling of finality and hopelessness. The fact that there are people that have lived fifty years with a terminal disease doesn't alleviate the effect. Yet life itself is a terminal disease, from the moment we are conceived, we not only begin to live, we begin to die. For some reason the expression 'premature death' doesn't induce the same feeling of panic. To a smoker the expression doesn't even mean death. It means: "I won't live as long as I would have done. But, who cares! I'd rather have the shorter, sweeter life anyway."

Let's get back to the drug I was describing. Imagine that you are not a user of the drug, but a pusher. You have a concession from the tobacco companies to develop smoking in a country that knows nothing about it. Ignore the moral aspect, you merely want to make money and you know you will become a millionaire several times over. I am a banker in that country, you need to raise finance, but I know nothing about smoking. You arrive very excited. I say:

"Calm down and tell me about this exciting idea of yours."

"No, it's not my idea, but it's been proved a million times over. All we do is to grow this special plant. We dry the leaves in the sun, shred them and add chemicals to make them burn easier. It doesn't matter how foul they taste. We then roll them up into little tubes of paper and put them in very attractive packages. We'll make a fortune!"

Could you imagine thousands of people wandering around with burning cigarettes in their ears? You would see them as clowns. Try to picture your pet dog or cat smoking. Non-smokers and smokers alike see smoking as a stupid pastime, but the only reason we don't double up in convulsions of laughter whenever a smoker lights up, is because we've been brainwashed from birth to see it as perfectly normal behaviour. Don't just accept this image. Start looking at smokers in the context of nature, and seeing them as they really are. Can you conceive of anything more unnatural than to inhale doses of poison into your lungs, all day, every day? Open your mind and smokers soon appear as, not just objects worthy of your pity, but as objects of ridicule. I'm not suggesting that you should point at them and raw with laughter every time one of them lights up. Though come to think of it, that might be the quickest way to end the slaughter. Anyway, back to my role as banker, from the description that you have given me, I'd be thinking that we were discussing fireworks:

"No, these aren't fireworks. You put these into your mouth and set light to them."

"Why would you want to do that? Does it have to be your mouth what about your ear or your backside?"

"No it has to be the mouth because you need to breathe the fumes into your lungs."

"That doesn't sound very pleasant."

"It isn't to begin with. In fact many people find it so foul and obnoxious they cannot physically cope with it. However provided they have the willpower to persevere, their bodies become immune to the poisons and they can actually believe that they enjoy the taste. But the important point is they can't stop. Some have to smoke 2 or 3 packets a day, every day for the rest of their lives and no matter how much they learn to loathe it, they have to go on doing it. Some will have their legs removed rather than stop!"

By now, I would be having serious doubts about your credibility.

"But surely they must get some enormous compensating benefits from going through the learning process. I assume there are substantial health benefits?"

"Well, actually not. As a matter of fact it kills one in four. As soon as they start they will become more lethargic, short of breath and less resistant to other diseases. It also gradually destroys their nervous system. But the beauty is, the more it drags them down, the more they are fooled into believing that it helps them."

I am now certain about your credibility. It is now your sanity I'm beginning to question.

"I assume then that you plan to mount a massive advertising campaign that will persuade people that it would make them healthier?"

"I'd like to do that, but unfortunately I'm not allowed to. The thing is that your government insists that we put a warning on each packet advising users that it will actually kill them!"

"Yes, I can quite see their point Mr. er...what I don't quite see is how you possibly hope to sell this stuff, but I tell you what, why don't I give you a ring in a few days time?"

How have we reached a stage in society in which, about 5 people die from salmonella, so the whole of our egg production is brought to a standstill and Edwina Currie is forced to resign? Why are we up in arms because a couple of cats died from mad cow disease? Yet the real evil, that kills over two thousand week in week out on this little island alone, is not only legal, but our own treasury is the biggest vested interest and we even allow the tobacco industry to spend £100,000,000 annually on promoting its filth. How can we get our priorities so distorted?

I have repeatedly related nicotine to heroin and used the expression: "Do you need to inject yourself with heroin?" You might suspect that this is a ruse that I employ to make you dislike being a smoker. I hope that it is having that effect. But the real reason is to make you open your mind and to ask yourself why the thought of one of your children becoming a heroin addict fills you with horror, yet your smoking problem appears insignificant by comparison? Why do the actual facts of the drug that I described above sound more like heroin than nicotine? It is because we've been brainwashed into having a distorted view. Not about heroin, but about smoking. We must rectify this distortion.

I have said that stopping smoking isn't the problem. The real difference between a smoker and a non-smoker is that a smoker feels a need or desire to smoke a cigarette and a non-smoker doesn't, but why? Because non-smokers see smoking with a different frame of mind. Their view of smokers will range from: You pathetic addict, spending a fortune to choke yourself and kill yourself with that poison, to: I just cannot see why he needs to keep putting those filthy, smelly things into his mouth and setting light to them.

Many smokers have the same frame of mind, but they have the additional feeling of: I want or need a cigarette. Now think of the heroin addict, or the ex-heroin addict that is still craving heroin. Which would you rather be: them or you? Who do you think has the correct conception of heroin addiction: the addict or you? Do you see them as people in full control, enjoying the delirious dreams that heroin induces, or do you see them as pathetic drug addicts, descending deeper and deeper into a bottomless pit that they cannot escape from?

Provided that you are not a heroin, or ex-heroin addict, you have a considerable advantage, because your brain isn't warped by the effects of the drug, you are able to see heroin addiction in its true light. Now start seeing yourself in the same light. Non-smokers view you just as you would view a heroin addict. They are just as correct about you as you are about the heroin addict. Accept the fact that you are already descending down this bottomless pit. Fortunately you can escape from it, but the first essential is to realise that you are in it.

So what we are really trying to achieve is to change your frame of mind, so that you see smoking as it really is without the slightest need or desire to light one. In fact to go one stage further, so that, like me, you get a thrill every time that you realise that you no longer want or need to light one. But what is your frame of mind at the moment? Do you see it as a filthy, disgusting, killer disease that costs you a fortune and enslaves you, or do you still have the Humphrey Bogart/ Marlene Dietrich image? This is the real problem, when you think of heroin you get a certain picture in your mind: ADDICTION! SLAVERY! POVERTY! MISERY! DEGRADATION! DEATH! and if you're not an addict or ex-addict, that picture remains constant, it's not affected by changes in your mood, location or prosperity. The same picture is presented by the media and society generally, your eyes are not being bombarded hourly with pictures of happy, laughing heroin addicts.

The trouble with smoking, is the picture keeps changing, one day we are seeing the social prop the next day the killer disease, or both at the same time. Smokers have a myriad of memories and situations both good and evil closely associated with a cigarette. They suffer from chronic schizophrenia. Even non-smokers have it. They have also been bombarded since birth with this two-sided image about smoking. The difference is that they don't suffer from it unless and until they too fall into the pit.

Fortunately one side of the face is pure illusion. The implication is that the smokers are laughing and happy *because they are smoking*. Not true! They might well have been miserable if they hadn't been smoking, but that's not the same thing. Non-smokers don't suffer from this problem. We need to remove the illusions from our brain, the part that sees smoking as some form of crutch or pleasure so that, as with heroin, we have the same constant picture. We need to get you into the frame of mind so that whenever you think about smoking, the thought is always:

YIPPEE! I DON'T NEED OR WANT A CIGARETTE!

But we have to keep you in that frame of mind for the rest of your life. That might seem a tall order to you, after all, what about this lifetime's brainwashing and all these associations, surely it's not possible to wipe the slate clean just like that? No it isn't, but you don't have to wipe the slate clean, all you have to do is to prepare your brain in advance so that no matter what the situation might be, you are never even tempted to light a cigarette.

Basically we have just two things to do. One we have already dealt with. That is to remove this feeling of frailty and insecurity that modern society has programmed within us, and to appreciate the truly immense potential and strength provided by the incredible machine. In other words to remove the void that makes us search for illusory solutions in the first place. You might well not be feeling anything like the full benefit from this at the moment. However, once your physical health improves and you no longer have this insecure feeling that nicotine withdrawal creates, and I emphasize that it's what smokers suffer while they are smokers – **NOT WHEN THEY STOP** – you will understand fully what I mean.

Apart from removing the belief that you *need* some chemical crutch to fill the void, you also need to realise that, far from filling the void, nicotine, alcohol, heroin and similar drugs, create a void.

Now let's go back to our lady in Chapter 5, the lady who just *needed something*. Why did she turn to a cigarette? As she said she knew that she was being stupid. In fact she wasn't being as stupid as she thought she was. Her rational mind knew it was stupid, but all smokers know that the whole of their lives. So why do they spend a lifetime doing it? It is because the true reasons we smoke are subconscious.

Most smokers confess that they only enjoy about two of the

cigarettes that they smoke each day. Ask them why they ruin their health and pockets by smoking the remainder if they don't really enjoy them, and the only answer they can come up with is: "It's just HABIT." Ask them why they got into the habit of smoking cigarettes that they don't enjoy and, if they don't enjoy them, why they don't break the habit and restrict their smoking to the ones that they do enjoy? After all it shouldn't be any hassle not to smoke the ones that they don't enjoy. Some will then explain it by saying: "But I don't realise that I'm lighting them."

Now I can understand how you can scratch an itch without being aware of it, but to light a cigarette you have to take the packet and matches out of your pocket, extract a cigarette from the packet, put it into your mouth and light it. I'll accept that it is conceivable that you could do this inadvertently 20 times a day, but would an intelligent person not find a simple solution to this problem, like leaving the cigarettes in the car or in a locked drawer, so that when you reached for that cigarette that you won't enjoy, you weren't able to light it, and as a consequence only smoked the ones that you actually enjoyed?

Perhaps you think I've just given you the ideal answer to your problem. Before you rush to try it, I can tell you that millions of smokers have already tried it, or something similar, the probability is that you have done so yourself. It doesn't work. Why doesn't it work? Because you weren't smoking those cigarettes out of habit. There was a subconscious reason that you reached for every one of them. In fact the reason that you reached for the two that you did enjoy was also subconscious. The conscious reason that you gave, no matter how logical it might have appeared to you, was just an excuse. The subconscious reasons themselves are illusions. But if we aren't even aware of them, how can we remove them? Only by first transferring them to the conscious mind.

The only reason any smoker ever lights any cigarette is because their brain says:

I WANT A CIGARETTE

There can be a myriad of things that could trigger off the feeling of: "I want or need a cigarette" in ex-smokers lives, whether it be when their guard is up during the few hours or days after they have extinguished that final cigarette, or ten years later when they cannot even conceive how they were ever hooked on cigarettes, and their defences are down. We have to remove every one of those triggers. Some people follow half the instructions and still find it easy to stop. You might conclude that you can safely ignore some of them. Not so! It is just those smokers that get hooked again.

You can't ignore any of them. Let's use the Everest analogy again.

127

One climber might anticipate and prepare for every conceivable contingency, overlook just one and if he is unlucky, it could be the difference, not only between success and failure, but between life and death. Another might not have prepared half as well, be lucky and succeed. Whether you realise it or not, you are playing for exactly the same high stakes. I've spent years perfecting my system so that your life doesn't depend on luck. This book is guaranteed to make it not only easy, but enjoyable to stop, and to make you a happy non-smoker the rest of your life, provided you follow ALL THE INSTRUCTIONS.

'EASYWAY' fully explains the logical reasons that you shouldn't smoke. In the next few chapters I will explain why subconscious, illusions overrule your logic. But it will take both of us to achieve success. You are the smoker – it's your mind that we need to alter and part of that mind doesn't want to stop. To succeed both of us need to be sceptical on one hand and open-minded on the other. Ostriches stick their heads in the sand when frightened, smokers just light a cigarette, neither solves their problem, in fact they both make it worse. In order to understand the other illusions we must first understand the chief ally of drug addiction:

THE TUG OF WAR OF FEAR

CHAPTER 15

The Tug of War of Fear

I believe that most ex-smokers share with me a tremendous sense of achievement. There have been other moments in my life when I have had cause to be pleased with myself, but none remotely compares with my escape from the nicotine trap. I imagine the Count of Monte Christo felt a similar sense of achievement. The successful climbers of Everest or Olympic Gold medal winners must get a similar feeling. They must also suffer a considerable fear of failure before they achieve success. I wonder whether the fear of success ever enters their minds?

One of the many curious anomalies about smoking is that it reverses normal patterns. Usually it is the fear of failure that achieves success. With smoking it is often the fear of success that causes failure. Many smokers that attend the clinic say: "I never tried before for fear of failure." I suspect that the true reason was fear of success. However both fears need to be dealt with. As it's the easier, let's dispel the fear of failure first.

The fear of failure itself is probably mainly caused by all the other fears associated with smoking which we shall be removing in later chapters. However, let us assume for the moment that it is just what it appears to be: "I'm the sort of chap that, if I set my mind on doing something, I do it. If I fail to stop smoking, it will make me feel weak-willed."

Isn't this attitude a bit like the famous Jewish joke where, every year the Rabbi complains to the Lord that he never wins a prize in the lottery? Eventually, The Lord booms down: "Will you meet me half way? Buy a ticket!"A fear of failure is the most illogical fear of all. You are in effect, postponing the possibility of a calamity that's already happened: **YOU ARE ALREADY A FAILURE!** You might be kidding yourself that you continue to smoke because you enjoy it and are in control, but don't fool yourself into believing that you are deceiving anyone else. Everyone nowadays knows that smokers smoke, not because they enjoy it, but because they are hooked and have either failed to stop or are just too frightened to make the attempt.

This is the other completely illogical fact about the fear of failure. It is really the fear to make an attempt to stop. You can only suffer that

129

fear all the years that you fail to make the attempt. Ironically, the only thing to remove the fear of making an attempt **IS TO MAKE IT.**

THE BEAUTIFUL TRUTH IS YOU HAVE ABSOLUTELY NOTHING TO LOSE

The worst thing that can happen to you is that you fail. In which case you are no worse off than you are now. But just think about the marvellous advantages you have to gain. The other beauty is, that your family, friends and colleagues will expect you to fail anyway. They've also been programmed to believe that successfully stopping smoking is equivalent to climbing Everest. Just think how proud of you they will be when you actually succeed, and most important, how marvellous you will feel yourself!

Perhaps your fear of failure is due to the fact that you have tried so many times and so many different systems that you are already convinced that failure is inevitable. Don't worry, so did I, my reputation was built on smokers just like you. Or, perhaps you are still worried that if you make the attempt and fail, you might remove one fear: the risk of failure, and replace it with an even greater fear: the certainty of failure. Forget yourself for the moment. Ask yourself who you would despise the most, the person who hadn't got the guts to make the attempt, or the person that tried and failed. My guess is that you would despise the former and respect the latter. There's really no decision to make. If you make the attempt, you risk failure. If you don't make the attempt:

YOU GUARANTEE FAILURE!

Now let us deal with the real fear that stops smokers from making the attempt: **THE FEAR OF SUCCESS!**

When I first saw the light, I couldn't help but try to convince my family and friends how easy it was and how nice it was to become a non-smoker. Joyce would say: "Allen, can't you see that they don't want to stop? You are only making yourself unpopular." The problem is that I picture all smokers as believing themselves to be having a mud bath when in reality they are sinking imperceptibly deeper into a bog. I had been in up to my neck in that bog, about to go under and was lucky enough to escape in the nick of time.

It was a typical 'Catch 22' situation, and of course, as usual, Joyce was quite right. My attempts got the head in the sand treatment and I believe that I have actually lost close friends because of those vain attempts. I've learned my lesson now and I no longer try to influence them, not because it makes me unpopular, but because I soon learned that if I tried to force the issue the clam would shut tight, but it takes immense self-restraint on my part to stand in silence. The situation is even more frustrating when you later see that person crippled or disfigured through smoking. I can only put my predicament to you. If you saw someone that you loved, up to their neck in mud, and about to go under, would you watch them suffocate, or would you try to save them knowing that you'll lose their friendship if you did? Logic doesn't even come into it, either way you lose a friend, but take my word for it you wouldn't be able to help yourself, you'd do exactly as I did.

I thought 'EASYWAY' would solve my problem. I gave a copy to each of my friends and relatives. I worked on the theory that if my friend had written a book, I would read it even if it were the worst book ever written. To my delight some read the book and stopped smoking. To my chagrin, some didn't. Later I learned that they hadn't even bothered to read the book. I admit I was somewhat piqued, particularly when I heard that my best friend, to whom I had given the original signed copy, had actually given it away!

It did not take me long to realise that it wasn't lack of loyalty that prevented them from reading it. I had overlooked the dreadful fear that smokers undergo when even contemplating stopping. My mother once said to Joyce: "Why don't you just threaten to leave him if he doesn't stop?" The unhesitating reply: "Because he would let me leave if I did." I'm ashamed to admit it, but much as I love her, I believe that she was right, such was the state that *my little friend* had reduced me to.

As I gradually got feedback from the book, some readers made the criticism: "You shouldn't advise smokers to continue smoking until they've completed the book. Because of this I would only read one line a day." It never occurred to those readers that if I had advised them to smoke their last cigarette before they read the book, that's the last line they would have read.

In Chapter 1, I referred to the lady that walked out of my clinic in a panic, the same applies to the book, many readers reach the stage where panic sets in. They think: "If I go on reading this, I'll have to stop smoking." No doubt many other smokers that have attended my clinics were tempted to walk out but were too embarrassed to do so. In fact some have mentioned the fact and how pleased they were that they stayed, but how much easier to close a book.

I used to advise people to buy 'EASYWAY' as a Christmas or birthday present for their smoking friends. What nicer present could you buy a smoker? How naive I was, it was like a golfing fanatic weighing up the size and shape of his christmas present, anticipating unwrapping a box of twelve shining golf balls and finding instead a book on how to give up golf.

As I said, it's 'Catch 22'. If only smokers could see that the panic feeling which makes them frightened to finish the book, is actually caused by nicotine and not relieved by it, that the greatest benefit they'll receive from stopping, is to be rid of that panic feeling and that if only they finish the book, that fear will already be gone.

So how do we get over this problem of: "I've bought him the book. Now tell me how I get him to read it." Don't buy the book as a present for your smoking friend or relative, do it the other way around. When it's Christmas or your birthday, say to the smoker: "I'd like you to give me a very special present, one that will give me more pleasure than anything else that I could possibly imagine. I would like you to read this book. I am not asking you to stop smoking, just to read the book. If after you've read it you choose to continue to smoke, I will respect your decision."

If only there were a way to transfer every smoker immediately into a non-smoker so that they could get a direct comparison. They'd think: "Will I really feel this good?" I don't mean just health and energy, but confidence and courage. What it really amounts to is: "Have I really sunk *this* low?"

Fortunately, there is a way: OPEN YOUR MIND. At the moment it might be difficult for you to imagine life without cigarettes. All smokers think that way until they actually succeed. You didn't need cigarettes before you became addicted to nicotine. Okay, perhaps you did stop previously for weeks, months even years and still missed smoking, but I promise that you won't miss them this time. I need you to trust me. All that keeps any smoker smoking is the fear that they won't be able to enjoy life or cope with stress without smoking, or that they'll have to go through a terrible ordeal in order to succeed. I promise you that if you finish the book and follow the simple instructions that I will give you, you will enjoy life more, be better able to handle stress and you will even enjoy the process of your escape. By the end of the book, you won't need to trust me.

If this book has been purchased for you by a loved one, you are obligated to read it. If you purchased it for yourself, you are no less obligated, you owe it to yourself. A true gift should cause equal pleasure to both giver and receiver, so your success will give you double the pleasure. You have so much to gain! What have you to lose?

ABSOLUTELY NOTHING!

Now let us start removing these fears, doubts and uncertainties. Your first instruction is to follow all the others. What is your frame of mind at the moment? Doom and gloom? Panic? Fear? These are the disciples of failure. So your next instruction is to change that frame of mind **NOW**. Remember you have nothing to lose, so whether you succeed or fail you might as well enjoy the process. But let us now stop talking about failure. You are about to make a great escape, something that every smoker would love to achieve. Something really exciting is happening! Let us enjoy the planning and preparation because:

ABSOLUTELY NOTHING CAN PREVENT YOUR ESCAPE

CHAPTER 16

But I Do Enjoy a Cigarette

At the clinics most smokers seem to grasp quickly the concept that the only pleasure you get from a cigarette is trying to end the craving for nicotine and that since each cigarette, far from relieving that craving, is actually causing it, the pleasure or crutch is purely illusory. However the same smokers seem unable to relate that concept to their everyday smoking, they are still convinced that they do enjoy certain cigarettes.

It is absolutely essential that you understand that no smoker ever has and no one can ever enjoy imbibing nicotine in any form, whether it be by smoking it, sniffing it, chewing it or by absorbing it through the skin. That is quite a sweeping statement to make. I will explain it to you with logical argument, but the only way you can *prove* it to yourself is while you are still smoking. You cannot prove it once you've stopped and if you quit, still believing that you got genuine pleasure from certain cigarettes, you will feel deprived. Absence of a pleasure makes the heart grow fonder. You will be vulnerable for the rest of your life, or worse you'll be in the pit again.

So how would it be possible to create an illusion on such a massive scale? All the billions of cigarettes, cigars, and pipes that have been smoked through the generations, no one enjoyed a single one of them? It seems hardly credible! Nevertheless it's true. Let's test it out.

Try asking smokers what it is that they are actually enjoying when they smoke. Make sure you ask the question when they are about half way through a cigarette. There are a variety of standard replies, but the most common one is:

"I enjoy the taste and smell."

"I didn't realise that you actually ate them."

"Of course I don't."

"So where does taste enter into it?"

"Well, you do get a taste of the tobacco in your mouth."

"If that's all you do it for, wouldn't it be wiser not to inhale?"

"Well it doesn't taste quite the same if you don't inhale."

"Why is that, your lungs don't have taste buds, and surely the experts would have discovered something by now which gave the taste without having to risk these horrendous diseases?"

They have done. It's called nicotine chewing gum. It tastes just as foul as the first cigarettes, but persevere with it and, just like cigarettes, you'll soon learn to *enjoy* it. If you are one of those smokers that think they don't inhale, I'm afraid you're kidding yourself. It's just that you don't consciously take deep drags like some smokers do. To say: "I don't inhale," is like saying: "I don't breathe." We are seldom consciously aware that we are breathing, but we still do it. For years I convinced myself that I couldn't come to any harm because I didn't inhale. So where did my hacking smokers cough come from? I didn't ask myself that question. Smokers only hear what they want to.

So why do we suffer the illusion that we enjoy the taste of tobacco? Because we've been brainwashed from birth to believe that we do. You would think that the first few cigarettes would dispel that belief. The truth is that we are either, consciously or subconsciously, secretly relieved to discover that the first cigarettes taste awful. This means we won't get hooked like all these other idiots that are paying through the nose to destroy themselves. So why do we smoke the second and third cigarettes? Certainly not because we enjoy the taste. Some people argue that they knew they had to persevere to obtain the acquired taste. But that is equivalent to believing that even before addicts smoked their first cigarette, or had their first shot of heroin, or drank their first alcohol:

THEY DELIBERATELY PLANNED TO GET HOOKED!

Do you honestly believe that a single drug addict or alcoholic, living or dead, actually set out to become one before they even had a need for the drug or had *acquired a taste for it*? Frankly that just isn't logical. With drugs, you don't acquire the taste and then get hooked. It works the other way around, you get hooked then acquire the taste, or more accurately, learn to block your mind to the taste. The great subtlety is that you don't realise that you are already hooked. Even if you believed that you had a genuine need for the drug, that fact alone would prevent you from taking it. You would have feared that you might have become hooked and never been able to get free. This is why a few very shrewd people never even try an experimental puff.

Another reason that we believe we enjoy the taste of tobacco, is that taste is very closely associated with smell and it *is* possible to enjoy the smell of tobacco. Ah! I hear you say, so you can get a genuine pleasure from smoking! If you enjoy the smell, that is surely a genuine pleasure. It is, but if you examine the facts you'll find that you'll only enjoy the smell when you are not smoking. A pipe smoker will sniff into his pouch with great pleasure when anticipating a smoke, but he doesn't do it after he lights up. You'll find that those occasions when you get the gorgeous whiff of tobacco only occur when someone else is smoking and you are not.

Because I sit all day in a room filled with smokers and my body suffers nicotine withdrawal as a result, I occasionally get the whiff of a burning cigarette and it smells gorgeous, particularly in the open air. This worries some people. They say: "Doesn't that tempt you to smoke?" No way! I love the smell of a rose, but I haven't the slightest desire to smoke it? I'm only too pleased to be able to enjoy that smell knowing that it is no longer my poor lungs or pocket that are having to cope with the punishment. That pleasure is somewhat tempered by pity for the smoker. Some non-smokers occasionally experience pleasure from the smell of tobacco. I will explain exactly why they do in a later chapter.

The main reason that we believe we enjoy the taste of tobacco is that because in the first few years of smoking we do not realise that we are actually hooked. The feeling of dependence, of not being able to relax, or concentrate or cope with stress without it, is already there, but we haven't yet accepted it, therefore we must enjoy the taste, why else would we do it? Anyway, it's common knowledge that once you've learned to smoke, they do taste pleasant, why even question it? Common knowledge it might be, it is still a misconception.

Another reason that we think we enjoy certain cigarettes is because certain cigarettes seem to taste so much better than others. By certain cigarettes, I don't mean different brands, I mean different occasions when smoking the same brand. Even smokers themselves will admit that there's nothing particularly pleasant about the taste of the first cigarette on a winter morning, but they still have to smoke it. Incidentally, the reason that the first cigarette in the morning makes you cough, is not only have you gone all night without nicotine, but you've lost some of your immunity to the poison, you have to smoke one or two before you get it back again.

Some smokers argue that if they couldn't get their own brand they wouldn't smoke at all. In that case why did they bother to learn to enjoy the taste of their own brand. Whether those smokers really believe it themselves, or whether it is part of the self-deceit that all drug addicts have to adopt in order to maintain some semblance of self-respect is disputable, but one thing's for sure, they don't fool other smokers. Any smoker worth his or her salt will smoke camel dung rather than not at all!

So, why does your own brand of tobacco appear to taste so much better on certain occasions than on others? Imagine that when you extinguish that very first cigarette and the nicotine is leaving your body, that you have created a feeling of hunger, not for food, but for a particular poison – NICOTINE. Although that feeling doesn't involve any pain, it is physical, but because it is hardly perceptible most smokers have lived and died without even realising that it is there. It is merely a feeling of emptiness, restlessness, insecurity, smokers only know the feeling as: "I want or need a cigarette."

When the smoker lights up, the nicotine is immediately replaced, the empty, insecure feeling goes and the smoker gets an immediate boost. That is the feeling that smokers describe as relaxing, comforting or, as the tobacco advertisers used to plug: "GIVES MAXIMUM SATISFACTION." However, in order for a cigarette, or anything else for that matter, to be able to relax, comfort or satisfy you, you must of necessity first be unrelaxed, discomforted or dissatisfied. So why is it that one of the favourite cigarettes is the one after a meal at a restaurant? Surely smokers would already be relaxed and satisfied at such times. Non-smokers are.

It is therefore quite obvious that smoking, far from giving satisfaction, actually creates the feeling of dissatisfaction. However, the situation is confused because that empty, insecure feeling is identical to that caused by normal hunger, anxiety or stress. The nicotine withdrawal, which from now on I will refer to as the 'itch', merely increases the level. Most people start smoking at a time when they're already going through a period of anxiety, whether it be adolescence, starting university, or work, whatever, they have already accepted that state as normal. Because they suffer the 'itch' when they are not smoking and partially relieve it when they light up, they understandably regard the cigarette as a crutch or friend rather than an enemy.

The other problem is that most smokers tend to be casual smokers to begin with. Therefore, for most of their lives they're suffering the itch rather than relieving it, and because the increased tension caused by the 'itch' is so imperceptible, smokers regard that state as normal, just part of the stress of modern living.

But the real problem is that nicotine is a drug and a poison and our bodies build an immunity to it. So subconsciously we start to increase the dose. We do this in one or all of the following ways: inhaling deeper and more frequently on the same cigarette, reducing the gap between cigarettes, switching to larger and stronger cigarettes and increasing the types of occasion that we smoke. Of course the process is progressive, the more nicotine you imbibe, the more your body resists and you soon reach a state in which, even when you are smoking the cigarette, you are only partially relieving the 'itch'!

Assume that the highest high is 100 points above par and the lowest depression is 100 points below par. Assume you have reached the stage in your descent down the pit, whereby the itch causes you to be permanently 10 points below par. I emphasise that you would not be aware that you were 10 points down because you would regard that state as normal. Assume that you recover 5 of those points when you light up. You will receive a slight boost. Most smokers have lived and died without ever being consciously aware of that boost. However it is there and it is physical. Our subconscious brains are aware of it and that's the reason that we light the cigarette. I've used the word boost. This might imply some form or crutch or pleasure. I will explain later why even the boost itself is illusory.

You are having 'one of those days'. It's Monday morning. The postman's cheerful "good morning" seemed a little bit too cheerful. You realise that it's because he's delivered double the normal quota of bills that you cannot pay. You are already late for work and it's the first heavy frost of the year. You lose half an hour trying to get into the car and another half hour trying to see out of it. Then the second most excruciating sound in the world (the first is the noise of a dentist's drill) Uhrrrr, Uhrrr, Uh! A dead battery that could have used its last bit of energy to start your car, instead uses it to dramatise its death!

Assume that the result of the above events has caused a non-smoker to be suffering a 40 point below depression. You'll be suffering a 50 point below depression. Naturally, you'll light up and get the immediate 5 point boost, but will you be happy and cheerful? Will you be relishing the pleasure of smoking that cigarette? Will it start your car or pay your bills? To a smoker the cigarette at times of extreme anxiety might taste awful but is still essential. It's rather like when you suffer a prolonged, severe pain, anything that will relieve the pain slightly is a welcome relief, even though you are still in severe pain.

I have been talking about a 5 point boost. In fact you will still be 5 points lower than you would have been were you a non-smoker. So what? Say you, even if it is illusion won't that 5 point relief make me feel better? Use the physical pain analogy. If you had a physical pain at the level of 40, would you increase it to 50 in order to bring it back to 45? If so why stop at 50? That 5 point boost will appear much more effective if you can increase the level to 100, then bring it back to 95. This is what drug addicts effectively do, but only because they don't understand it.

I would also emphasize that the 10 points below par that you would be suffering has nothing to do with the effect that smoking has on your health, freedom, pocket or self-respect. It relates purely to the empty, insecure feeling of the 'itch'. In reality a smoker would be many additional points below par because of these other factors. However, because the decline is so gradual, smokers aren't aware of that further depressed state. Just like the itch, they've come to regard the total depressed state as normal.

Even with none of the usual traumas that smokers and non-smokers alike suffer throughout their lives, such smokers have reached a state in which they suffer permanent stress, caused purely by their smoking. The mere thought of being low on cigarettes will be sufficient to create panic, let alone the reality. Now they are not just 5 points below how they would have felt as non-smokers, but many points below. This is the great evil of all these drugs. You reach the stage where you don't need to have one of those days. The effects of the drug turns your whole life into one of those days. But of course, the more stressful your life becomes, the greater your need for that 5 point boost. Why else do you think someone would rather have their legs removed than stop smoking?

Assume the health and other side effects of being a smoker causes them to be an additional 30 points below par. They will actually be 35 points below par even when smoking, because none of those points are recouped when the smoker lights up. In fact the situation gets worse when they light up. Fortunately, all the points are recoverable if you quit, provided of course:

THAT YOU HAVEN'T LEFT IT TOO LATE!

The point is this, the taste of cigarettes at times of stress is unimportant, even if they did taste good, you would still be miserable at such times and so get the illusion of only a 5 point boost. Now let us look at the other end of the scale, the cigarettes that smokers believe taste so good. Don't those really special tasting cigarettes tend to be after a meal? With a drink? With a coffee? Home from shopping? After exercise? After sex?

Different smokers have different priorities. However, the occasions when cigarettes appear to taste better, tend to have two common conditions: a period of abstinence and a period when we tend to be relaxing and enjoying ourselves anyway. Let's use the one after a meal as an example. Particularly the evening meal when work for the day is over. Even better, a meal on holiday, when we have completely forgotton about mundane things like work, bills and decorating. If the restaurant has a pleasant ambiance, decor and a panoramic view, so much the better, and the situation is further enhanced, if you are in the company of people who are as equally pleasant, cheerful, attentive and broad-minded as you are yourself. Why can't those petty minded miseries at home be the same? Even the waiter is smiling and happy. He actually hugs you, and kisses your wife on both cheeks. He has never met you before, but acts as if Frank Sinatra has just walked in. He treats his next customers exactly the same. But what does it matter? The meal is quite the best you've ever tasted. The drinks are exotic. You are tanned, wearing your best holiday clothes and, providing it's the beginning of your holiday, you have thousands of units worth of the local currency in your pocket. The background music starts to get through to you. You start to sing. The locals join in. You later discover that they are also shy, inhibited Brits. To your amazement you actually sound better than Frank Sinatra, even he could never have felt better than this. You are on a complete and utter **100% HIGH**!!! (Actually 90% but you won't know that)

You reach for another cigarette: "What! Packet empty already! Can't be! I only opened it a few minutes ago. Mind, I have been a bit liberal handing them around. No panic, I've got two full packets in my jacket."

You start to search systematically through the pockets of your jacket. All completely empty. Then it hits you: that idiot of a woman that you call your wife – the very same woman that you were dancing with just a few moments earlier, into whose beautiful eyes you were gazing as you serenaded her with your arrangement of 'Lady In Red', tune and lyrics a definite improvement on Chris de Burghs, telling her that the song must have been written with her in mind, you believing every word of it, her believing you've had too much to drink – the stupid, interfering, busybody made you change your jacket at the last moment. Still no panic. You can buy a packet of the local brand, they taste like stale tea leaves but who cares at this stage of the evening. But Guiseppe the smiling waiter informs you that they don't stock cigarettes or cigars.

Genuine panic now begins to creep in. But wait a minute, there's your fellow Brits! They won't mind you asking. You'd do the same for them. They've been smoking your cigarettes all evening anyway. Amazingly, all but two of them claim that they are non-smokers. Of the other two, one has run out and the other only has enough left for his own consumption, selfish *******!

The panic begins to take a hold. Back to Guiseppe, he's been crawling round you all evening and if he's expecting a big tip, he's going to damn well have to earn it. Surely one of the waiters smoke? "Ima soree." You know that the chef does, because earlier you were worried that his ash would fall into the local 'Specialty of the House'. "Ima soree sir, no can elp." For the first time you notice the nicotine stains on Guiseppe's fingers. You get angry, suddenly Guiseppe, who earlier was explaining how he'd spent 16 years living in Soho, "Dusenta understand eenglish." All foreigners ought to me made to learn English!

Now panic of the size last experienced on the Titanic has set in. They've built this stupid restaurant perched on top of a cliff, surrounded by a 100 miles of stinking ocean on one side and a 100 miles of barren desert on the other. There is absolutely no way of getting a packet of cigarettes, other than tipping Guiseppe upside down and shaking him. You flirt with the idea but soon discard it, you can now visualise a pretty tough hombre lurking beneath that smile.

Meanwhile there's this awful, raucous noise going on in the background. You've been unlucky enough to share a restaurant with a bunch of singing lager louts. Why don't they confiscate their passports? And why do they have to put so much garlic in the food, and what's this muck I'm drinking, whoever heard of a purple drink and if I'd wanted a pound of fruit in my drink, I'd have ordered the fruit salad. How ridiculous! It's got its own little umbrella. Are they worried that it will be ruined if it rains? And why does that stupid, grinning, idiot Guiseppe keep asking me "Ifa everything's alla right." He's a smoker, can't he see that Ima dying? Why did we come to this godforsaken country anyway? I wanted to go to Blackpool again!

Perhaps I have exaggerated ever so slightly, but I'm sure that you can identify with the situation. Smokers that aren't allowed to smoke after a meal aren't on a high at all. On the contrary, they are feeling deprived and miserable. They are depressed. If it's a 50 point below depression, the difference between having that cigarette and being deprived of it isn't just 5 points, it's 150 points. That's why cigarettes appear to taste better at sometimes rather than others. After all one cigarette is going to taste exactly the same as another cigarette out of the same packet. The cigarette doesn't change! It's the concept of the smoker that keeps changing.

We've already established that most smokers admit that they only enjoy a couple of the cigarettes that they smoke each day. The truth is that they never enjoy the taste of any of them. If you smoke subconsciously you are not aware of it and therefore cannot enjoy it. If you smoke consciously, the cigarette will taste awful, for the simple reason that they do taste awful! That is the reason that the bulk of our smoking is subconscious. It is also why we go through life as smokers, trying to ignore the massive powerful reasons that we should stop and desperately trying to cling to any flimsy excuse that will allow us to smoke just one more. If every time you lit up, you were forced to to be conscious of the foul smell and taste, the f30,000 you were going to waste, your slavery and the thought that this cigarette, might just be the one to trigger off cancer in your lungs, do you think you would enjoy it? Take your head out of the sand! It will be the one to trigger off cancer in your lungs, because if you smoke it, what will stop you from smoking the one after and the one after that? You either smoke:

OR YOU DON'T!

The majority of smokers can remember how foul those first cigarettes tasted. When I was a youngster, you weren't considered to be really tough unless you could dangle the cigarette permanently between your lips Humprey Bogart style. It isn't easy to do. I spent hours perfecting the process and it was a very painful affair. Occasionally the smoke would drift into my eyes with the same effect as tear gas. Sometimes I would remove the cigarette from my mouth together with a chunk of my lip that had stuck to it. Even more embarrassing and more painful was when the tip of the cigarette remained firmly stuck on my lips, but the rest of the cigarette would disintegrate and burn my fingers as I tried to extract it. Some smokers do believe they actually enjoyed the taste of those first cigarettes. Unfortunately the memory dims. They might well have got some indirect pleasure from smoking that first cigarette, like satisfying their curiosity, or feeling grown up or like a rebel. But the actual process of smoking it could not accurately be described as enjoyable. In any event, it certainly had nothing to do with taste. No non-smoker, no matter what age, is able to inhale tobacco without coughing, or to smoke three consecutive cigarettes without feeling sick.

Clearly, taste has nothing to do with it. In truth, the only time that we are ever aware of the taste, is when it is so foul that we are unable to ignore it. However, even on those occasions, we still smoke it. Ironically, it is after one of those all-night parties when the cigarettes are supposed to taste so good, that the state of our mouths is so foul, it triggers off an attempt to stop. I enjoy the taste and smell is the reason that smokers prefer to justify their smoking, because this means that they are fully in control, smoking purely because they choose to. To have to admit that they need it to concentrate or to relieve stress, is virtually saying: "I am incomplete! I am weak! I cannot cope with life without my crutch!" The next stage is to have to admit that they are hooked. But ask such smokers to explain how breathing poisonous, vegetable matter into their lungs can help them to concentrate or relieve stress and they will be at a loss.

Concentration and stress were my chief excuses. Concentration rates a chapter all of its own. But where was all this great stress that I was suffering as a young accountant? I was well trained, well paid, had the best qualifications and was competent and oozing with confidence. In fact the job was a piece of cake. Any real stress that I was suffering was caused by my heavy smoking, the remaining stress seemed real at the time, I now realise that it was the cunning invention of my addicted brain to justify my smoking.

I was 5 years old when the second world war started. For two years I was evacuated to a couple that were cruel to me. It was a very stressful period in my life. We were branded as bomb-dodgers and resented by the locals. I had a daily two mile walk to school and I can remember varying the route each day in an attempt to avoid being beaten up by the local bullies. Being separated from my parents at that tender age, and under those stressful circumstances, was quite an ordeal. However, like the rabbit, I was equipped to survive it without cigarettes. I don't believe that it has left irreparable scars. On the contrary, I believe it's left me street-wise and stronger.

Another classic excuse is: "I smoke out of sheer boredom." This is an intermediate stage excuse. It's dawned on you that you don't actually enjoy them, but you still can't admit that you are hooked. You are not being flattering to your own intelligence. Are you really telling me that you spend a fortune to risk horrendous diseases, not because you get a crutch or pleasure from smoking but because you can think of no better way of relieving boredom than breathing poisonous fumes into your lungs? That doesn't strike me as providing much to occupy your brain. In fact I'd have thought that you could do that without even thinking about it. Anyway, if you're the type that suffers from boredom, I should have thought you would have soon got bored with smoking, after all the process of smoking a cigarette isn't exactly a great mind-absorbing intellectual, feat. After the first 100,000 cigarettes, I should have thought you could smoke them subconsciously!

This is of course what we actually do. Even the ritual of lighting up tends to be automatic. So how can smoking possibly relieve boredom? The truth is, it actually causes boredom, because it often prevents the smoker from finding a genuine relief from boredom, even if the smokers have the desire, they often haven't got the mental or physical energy to find an alternative. Smokers smoke when they are bored because they have nothing to take their minds off the 'ITCH'.

Another in between excuse is: "It relaxes me." Again if you enquire exactly how it manages to do that you are merely greeted with blank stares.

A few years ago the adoption authorities threatened not to allow smokers to adopt children. Their motives were understandable, but is it really necessary to keep persecuting the poor smoker? Surely they have a hard enough time of it already. A man protested strongly. He said "They are completely wrong. I remember when I was a child and had to raise some contentious matter with my mother, I would wait until she lit a cigarette, knowing that she would be more relaxed then." It didn't occur to that man to wonder why he couldn't talk to his mother when she wasn't smoking? Why are smokers so **UNRELAXED** when they are not smoking, even after a meal when they should be completely relaxed. The next time you are in a supermarket and you see a young housewife screaming at a child out of all proportion to its crime, just observe, the moment she leaves she'll light a cigarette.

Some smokers are able to analyse that they get no genuine pleasure or crutch other than the ritual itself: the glossy packets, the gold cigarette lighters and cases, the opening of the packet, the offering of the packet to a close friend, even the handling of the cigarettes themselves, the lighting up, that gorgeous buzz as the first inhalation hits your lungs."

Arguments like this can be difficult to dispel. However if we search a little deeper they prove to be fatuous. We tend to ritualise many things in life, such as courtship, weddings, mating and wakes; but there is always a purpose to the ritual. Can you think of a single ritual, other than smoking, that we undertake purely for the ritual's sake? If it is the ritual that's so pleasant, why don't we alter it ever so slightly, by not actually lighting the cigarette, thereby still retaining the pleasure of the ritual, and at the same time avoiding the nasty part of that ritual that we tend to overlook: the filth, the poverty, the lethargy, the slavery, the degradation? Because the ritual wouldn't be quite the same? Why not?

We can best explain why by examining the ritual that is the most comparable to smoking: the ritual of eating. For special meals or banquets we dress up in our finery. We bring out the silver, the best china, the cut glasses and the candelabra. They all enhance the pleasure of that meal, but would you enjoy any of that ritual if you knew that you would not be allowed to eat the meal?

If it's the ritual that's so important, why do we smoke the other 99 out of the hundred cigarettes that we smoke without even going through that ritual? That gorgeous 'buzz' has nothing to do with the ritual, it is merely you trying to feel for a few moments how you would feel the whole of your life if you quit smoking. The gold, silver, cut glass and glossy paraphernalia connected with the smoking ritual are merely to assist you to blind yourself and other people to the fact it is merely a filthy, disgusting, anti-social, expensive and highly dangerous addiction.

Over the years thousands of excuses have been given to justify smoking. I'm just dealing with the more common ones. Some require chapters of their own:

"I just smoke to be sociable." It is difficult to imagine a more anti-social pastime than smoking.

"I just do it to keep the weight down." Strange, have you thought of not eating so much? I assume that when you want to cut down on your smoking, you eat! Illogical, but that's exactly what most smokers do.

"It's my best friend." Now we enter the realms of fantasy. Yet so many smokers believe it and I did for a third of a century.

If I tried to sell you a magic elixir that would help you to concentrate and a half hour later, would help to relieve boredom, two complete opposites; that would assist both in moments of stress and relaxation, two more opposites, that tasted and smelt marvellous, that would reduce your weight and be a social prop, I would readily accept that it would be your best friend. **BUT WOULD YOU BELIEVE ME?** Of course you wouldn't! You would quite rightly have me safely locked away. Yet this is what the tobacco companies and smokers themselves claim that smoking does for them.

Perhaps you feel that I have forgotten three other classic excuses that smokers rely on to justify their smoking:

"I just cannot stop." You have my sympathy. At least you are being honest with yourself, which means you will stop when you finish this book.

"I'm going to stop but the time isn't right." We'll discuss that later.

And the biggest cop out of all:

"IT'S JUST A HABIT"

With this one smokers don't get trapped into the pitfalls of having to explain their arguments. It's almost as if it is no longer their problem: it's just a habit that's impossible to break, what can they do about it?

Along with: "I *do* enjoy a cigarette." The belief that smoking is a habit is the illusion that smokers, even those that appear to have understood everything that I have said, find most difficult to shatter. They might well believe that it is also addiction, but they still think of it as habit.

In order to remain free permanently, it is imperative that you understand smoking completely, and in order to understand it completely, you need to realise that

SMOKING IS NOT A HABIT

I've been referring to the 'itch'. It will help you to understand the difference between habit and addiction by first contemplating:

WHY DO WE SCRATCH AN ITCH?

145

CHAPTER 17

Why Do We Scratch an Itch?

"Because it relieves the itch."

"How does it relieve the itch?

"By creating a greater pain which takes your mind off of the itch?

"Why on earth would you want a greater pain, and since the greater pain doesn't actually cure the itch, but merely distracts your mind, the itch would still remain once the greater pain had subsided. So, why scratch an itch?"

"I don't know."

The scratching of itches is a constant point of contention between Joyce and I. If I get an insect bite, I scratch it. Joyce says:

"Scratching will only make it worse."

"You can't prove that unless you have two identical bites, one you scratch, the other you don't."

I suspect that she is correct. She usually is. I have theories on why it helps to scratch an itch, but I don't know the reason. I don't need to know the reason. I don't know why when I press the light switch, the bulb lights up. Oh I can wire it up, but I still don't understand how it works. The point is, I don't need to understand it. Scratching the bite might make it worse, but I don't care. Providing I am allowed to scratch the itch, it doesn't bother me, even if I prolong the process for a month by so doing. I can cope with the situation. But to suffer the irritation without being allowed to scratch? That would be intolerable. If you find that you are scratching yourself at this moment, don't worry, so am I. Scratching is even more contagious than yawning.

So how does this help to understand smoking? I'm merely giving an example of how our subconscious or instinctive mind works. My wife gives logical reasons for not scratching an itch. At times her logic becomes visually obvious when I scratch so hard that I make the bite bleed. Yet my instinct tells me to scratch and I do, just like the lady who *needed* a cigarette knew that it was illogical but still lit one. However, whenever I get a cold sore, I find it irritates. My initial tendency is to scratch it, but I have learned that if you tamper with a cold sore it just gets bigger and bigger. Nowadays, if I get a cold sore both my instinctive brain and my intelligent brain say: "Don't scratch

146

it." So I don't.

For thirty odd years my logical brain said: "Don't smoke cigarettes." But that little 'itch' inside me kept saying: "Smoke a cigarette." And I would scratch the 'itch'. I still do not know the true reason that I scratch insect bites and leave cold sores alone, but I do know the reason that I scratched the little nicotine itch for thirty odd years and why that itch is now gone, permanently never to return! Scratching a cold sore doesn't cause the sore, but merely makes it worse. Smoking the first cigarette creates the nicotine itch each subsequent cigarette makes it bigger and bigger ad infinitum, until:

IT DESTROYS YOU PHYSICALLY AND MENTALLY!

CHAPTER 18

Is it Habit or Addiction?

Perhaps it's a combination of both, but who cares anyway, we all know it's difficult to stop. It isn't if you understand completely the nature of the trap and the victim. It is absolutely essential to know the difference between habit and addiction. It's no good rushing to your dictionary, it won't help you. Unfortunately our society makes it more difficult nowadays by often using the words synonymously. We even talk about a heroin 'habit'.

I used to refer to myself as a nicotine addict. I didn't really believe that I was a drug addict. I thought that I had merely got into the habit of smoking. So this was an example of a situation in which I referred to myself as an addict, believed it was merely habit, but was in fact an addict. Little wonder our brains get so confused. I now know that if only my elders had taught me the true implication of the difference between habit and addiction, instead of trying to convince me how unhealthy, filthy and expensive smoking was, I never would have become hooked and neither would you, or your children and grandchildren.

For many years I referred to myself as a golf addict. I loved playing golf and would take every opportunity to do so. I would spend most of my working day planning my next round of golf. I really believed that I was addicted to golf. This was an example of a habit, or rather, a true pleasure that I had got into the habit of indulging myself in as often as I could, which I thought was a true addiction.

Why is the difference so important? Because to believe that smoking is a habit or part habit would lead to the following wrong conclusions:

1. That there's some genuine pleasure or crutch in smoking. Why else would anyone have got into the habit? It does not matter that their conscious minds cannot see any rational reason why there should be a genuine crutch or pleasure, their subconscious minds will tell them that there is. This will lead to the second problem:
2. Even if they never smoke again, their subconscious mind will continue to believe that there is a genuine crutch or pleasure, and

they will remain feeling deprived and be vulnerable to recapture for the rest of their lives.

3. They will believe that provided they don't make a regular habit of it, they can have an occasional cigarette or cigar without getting hooked again. From past experience, their rational brain will know that they will, but their subconscious brain will be contradicting their rational brain.

When I question a failure or smoker that has been recaptured, the question and answer routine always ends with: "Why did you light the cigarette?"

"I DON'T KNOW"

The most important reason of all that you need to know the difference between habit and addiction is because unless you do, you won't understand either the complete nature of the victim or of the trap and you will always be vulnerable.

So how do you tell the difference between habit and addiction? There are two very useful guides. Have you noticed how heavy smokers always seem to envy casual smokers, the type that only smokes five a day, or just on social occasions? Can you imagine a fanatical golfer, one that plays 5 times a week, envying one that only plays once a month? So the first guide is: with a habit, you are doing it because you genuinely want to do it. With addiction, you wish you didn't have to do it. If that is so, why do so many smokers insist that they enjoy it? Because they have been brainwashed into believing that they do! However, if heavy smokers envy casual smokers so much, logically, they should envy non-smokers even more, why don't they? Because of this misconception that casual smokers are in control, and get the best of both worlds. In fact, they get the worst of both!

Ironically, on the rare occasions that I now play golf, I wander around the course planning how I can improve my techniques to help smokers to stop, but when I lost interest in golf, I just stopped playing. I didn't have to spend years trying to break the habit and I didn't need the assistance of an expert to help me to stop! "Habits are difficult to break." The only reason that particular cliché came into being, is because when 60% of the population was addicted to nicotine, they thought that it was just habit and because they generally found it almost impossible to break the habit, it was naturally assumed that all habits are difficult to break.

You have probably heard of many smokers that just got bored with smoking, decided not to do it any more and found it ridiculously easy to stop. I was one of them, but please don't forget, that I actually got bored with smoking 30 years before I found it easy to stop and if you care to probe, you'll find the other examples went through a similar experience. If you are hoping that you will one day just get bored with smoking and stop, just like that, you are kidding yourself.

This is the second guide: with addiction the more you learn to dislike the drug, the greater becomes your illusory dependence on it, and the greater your intake.

THE DRUG CONTROLS YOU!

With habits, you are in control. They might be filthy, disgusting habits in the eyes of other people, or even in your own eyes, but you do them only because you want to. Habits are easy to break provided you want to break them.

You might well argue that nail-biting is a habit and that many people fail to break the habit even though they want to. I'm sure there is a sound, underlying reason for nail-biting. Not so long ago nails were claws that needed sharpening. Now the fact that you or I don't understand the reason that some of us continue to bite our nails, doesn't mean that a valid reason doesn't exist. It has to, why else would we get into the *habit* in the first place? Nail-biting isn't just habit.

'It's a habit' doesn't explain the reason for any habitual behaviour, be it smoking or otherwise. It only became 'a habit' because the behaviour was repeated on a regular basis. 'It's a habit' has no purposeful meaning in itself. The important thing is the underlying reason that certain behaviour becomes habitual. That reason might be beneficial. If so, why break the habit? It is very unlikely anyone would deliberately get into the habit of repeating behaviour that provided them with no benefit whatsoever. Unless of course they were deluded into believing that an evil was beneficial:

AS IN THE CASE OF DRUG ADDICTION

Some so-called experts on smoking say that in order to stop you really must want to. That's pretty obvious. When they make statements like that, they are really admitting that they haven't a clue about smoking. It's like saying: "If you want to get onto a bus, you must first want to get onto a bus." Brilliant! Why would anybody decide to stop smoking unless they wanted to stop? The same experts will then reverse their logic: "It's reasonably easy to stop providing you really want to." **BALDERDASH!** Why do they ignore the thousands of smokers that like me hated it and tried desperately to get free for years? I couldn't do it even though my very life depended on it.

Many smokers believe that they choose to smoke because they enjoy smoking. However, if at any time in the smoker's life, they were to take their head out of the sand and list all the advantages and disadvantages of being a smoker, and allocate points out of 10 the result would be a dozen times over: **"YOU ARE A MUG. STOP DOING IT."** This is why all smokers, and incidentally, all alcoholics and other drug addicts instinctively feel stupid. In fact they are not stupid. There is a powerful force that more than balances the scales. The word that we use to describe that force is:

ADDICTION

But the word addiction doesn't explain our predicament. All it really means is: "Some unknown force makes me go on doing it against my better judgement. The fact that I now have a name for the situation I'm in doesn't help me one iota!" In fact it makes it worse, because addiction in itself doesn't actually exist. It is merely a certain state of mental misunderstanding. Remove the misunderstanding and you remove the addiction. But by actually giving this misconception a name, you reinforce the addict's belief that he suffers from an actual physical state. The same thing has happened with alcohol. Many *alcoholics* believe that they have a different chemical make up to non-alcoholics. Effectively, it places them in a prison that doesn't physically exist. With great luck and ingenuity, they might escape from Alcatraz, but how can they escape from a prison that doesn't exist?

This is why it is essential to understand that smoking is not a habit but drug addiction. Whilst you believe it's just habit, what you are really saying is "I don't understand why I smoke. I don't believe that I get any genuine pleasure from it. It's just a habit I've got into and providing I can survive long enough without a cigarette, time will solve the problem and my craving for tobacco will eventually go." But you will be kidding yourself. You were not smoking out of habit. There was a genuine reason why you lit up those cigarettes during good or bad times. The fact that you didn't understand the reason doesn't mean that it didn't exist. The fact that the reason was a subtle illusion won't alter the situation while you remain deluded. Therefore, even though you may have kicked the weed for many years, at stressful times your brain will remember for some unknown reason cigarettes seem to help and you will be tempted to try one. If you understand it completely as I do, you will never be tempted. I don't mean you will resist the temptation. I mean you won't have any need or desire to smoke.

This unknown force that makes drug addicts continue to destroy themselves and lead lives of misery, this unknown, mysterious force that we call addiction isn't unknown. On the contrary, it's a very common force and one of the worst experiences we ever suffer from. It's called **FEAR!** The real problem is, it works back to front. It's when you are not smoking and the nicotine is leaving your body that you suffer the empty, insecure feeling. When you light up it partially relieves it and your brain is fooled into believing that the cigarette is your crutch or friend. The more it drags you down the greater your need for the crutch.

Like all confidence tricks, intelligent people fall for them. But once they know it's a confidence trick, it's only idiots that go on deceiving themselves. Fortunately most smokers aren't idiots, they only think they are and this is why we get the high success rate that we do. Once you understand the smoking trap completely, you will have no more need or desire to light a cigarette than to bang your head against a wall in order to get the pleasure of stopping.

As I repeatedly say. It is easy for all smokers to stop once they understand the nature of the two beasts, the nicotine trap and the smokers themselves. I also believe that the potency of the trap is due to two of the powerful forces that nature has equipped us with in order to survive. Fear we have already dealt with. The other is:

HUNGER

Hunger and thirst are two more ingenious devices that the creator has equipped us with to ensure we survive whether we like it or not. We tend to take them for granted. But just think what a clever device hunger is. We are intelligent human beings. We know that if we don't eat we will die. But other animals don't know that, you might dispute this, but other animals eat for exactly the same reason that we do: that we're hungry! Do you think a worm knows it will die if it doesn't eat? All living creatures are vested with this incredibly powerful and sophisticated force called hunger.

Aren't we lucky that we don't have to remember to breathe, we wouldn't survive more than a few hours if we did. Animals, we included, don't have to remember to eat, our bodies send automatic signals to the brain. We have also been equipped with the miracles of smell and taste to enable us to distinguish between food and poison and to tell us which foods are the most suitable for our particular species. When you buy a new car you don't have to experiment with putting different types of liquid into the petrol tank to make it go. The manufacturer of that car knows better than you do. They will tell you whether to use petrol or diesel and they will even tell you the grades to use. If you wonder why all dietary experts seem to vary in their opinions and why the general trends seem to change as the years go by, it's because they are trying to play at being God. Wild animals don't need dieticians. They've already been programmed to know instinctively what's best for them by the creator. **SO HAVE WE.**

The really ingenious thing about hunger is that it involves no great physical pain. We can go all day without eating and without physical pain. Our stomachs may be rumbling, but that isn't physical pain. In fact hunger strikers can go weeks without food purely on a matter of principle. I well remember when a boy, Sunday lunch was always two hours later than on other days but my stomach didn't know this. It was agony being able to smell that delicious roast without being able to satisfy my hunger, but there was no physical pain.

My eating habits are similar today as when I smoked. I do eat breakfast nowadays, but I don't touch food again until about 7 o'clock in the evening. I go 12 hours without food and I'm not even aware of it. Not only doesn't it bother me, but it would annoy me to have to interrupt a clinic to eat. However, if I am running late and I get a preview whiff of Joyce's culinary delights, I suddenly feel hungry. But it isn't actually the smell of the food that made me feel hungry, the wiff was merely a signal to my brain to make me aware of the chemical reaction that had been gradually building inside my body throughout those 12 hours.

Now I'm not saying that hunger is a pleasant thing. It isn't. It's an empty, insecure feeling that, if not satisfied, will lead progressively through depression, irritability and fear to panic!

Do those symptoms sound familiar to you? Aren't they identical to those you suffer during an attempt to stop smoking using the willpower method? This is another ingenious aspect of the nicotine trap. The actual physical withdrawal symptoms from nicotine are identical to hunger for food.

In western society we build a ritual into eating as if there were a genuine pleasure in eating purely for eating's sake. In fact the only genuine pleasure we get from eating is the ending of the aggravation called hunger. The word breakfast used to mean break your fast, not have a great blow out. This is why wild animals don't have the same problems of overeating that we do. When they are hungry they eat. When they stop feeling hungry they stop eating. Sadly we have inflicted our eating habits upon domestic animals with the result that many of them suffer the same dietary problems that we do.

Some people find it difficult to accept that the only genuine pleasure in eating is the ending of the aggravation of hunger. Look at it from the creator's point of view. He creates this incredible variety of life. How can he ensure that all these creature don't poison themselves? Yes it's fine for human beings, our parents go to a lot of trouble to make sure we don't eat poisons. They keep them out of our reach and put a security cap on the bottle. But what about all these other creatures, how would you make sure that they didn't poison themselves?

There is a simple and ingenious way: make the poisons smell and taste awful and make food smell and taste delicious. That is in fact what the creator did. You will find that all the food and drinks that doctors and nutritionists are now telling us are drugs and poisons, are the things that we found offensive as children, and had to learn to acquire a taste for, like nicotine, alcohol and coffee. " Ah what about chocolate?" I hear you say: "That tastes nice." No it doesn't. Try eating plain cocoa. It's the sugar additives that taste nice. By now you are also probably wondering: "Why is it all the good things in life are harmful? Are there no genuine pleasures?" This is just the point, they aren't good things, we're merely brainwashed into believing that they are. The greatest pleasure in life is just feeling great to be alive! There's no substitute for that and the beautiful truth is, you don't need one!

It is true that we would rather end our hunger with some foods than others, just as we would rather end our craving for nicotine with our favourite brand. However, the system is so ingenious that it has an inbuilt failsafe device against overeating. Even our favourite foods only smell and taste good if we are hungry. Eat too much of them and nausea and vomiting will ensue.

I love curries. If I'm really hungry and the service is slow, I'm being tortured by the gorgeous smell. Once I have eaten far more than I should have done and the remains are still on the table, and particularly if I'm sat by the kitchen and my nose is being continually bombarded by other people's curries, the same smell becomes nauseous. I once ate half a chinese takeaway in bed and awoke to the smell of the other half. I didn't eat another chinese meal for 3 years.

The system has two other ingenious failsafe devices. One is that if genuine food becomes putrid, no matter how hungry you might be, it too will smell and taste awful. Smokers will smoke stale cigarettes rather than not at all, no matter how foul they might taste. This is because they have trained themselves to be oblivious to a substance that is already poisonous. But have you ever been hungry enough to eat a rotten egg if fresh ones were not available? The second failsafe device is that, if you go long enough without food, even a rat will become a delicacy. It's all designed to make sure that you survive, whether you want to or not.

The similarity between hunger and the withdrawal pangs from nicotine is one of the main reasons why our society cannot see smoking as it really is. It causes the following main problems: I should make it clear, I'm not talking about the discomfort that smokers suffer when making an attempt to stop smoking. I'm talking about the withdrawal symptoms that they undergo throughout their smoking lives. The empty feeling we know as: "I want a cigarette."

1. Because we believe that eating is habitual, we are lead to believe that smoking is habitual.
2. Because we know that food is good for us and we tend to eat our favourite foods, our logical minds assume that we would only

crave for something that was enjoyable. This reinforces the illusion that cigarettes **MUST** be enjoyable why else would we crave them?

To understand smoking we need to understand eating. Some people believe that eating is a habit. I ask them: "What would happen to you if you broke the habit?" It doesn't take them long to work out that they would die. Eating is not a habit. It is an absolute essential to survival. People are in the habit of satisfying their hunger at different times, with varying types of food and rituals. Doctors often ask their patients if they open their bowels regularly, but surely no one would suggest that defecating is a habit. Eating is no more a habit than defecating is.

Addiction is the hunger, not for food, but for poison. It is the illusion of a need. I have said: "The only *genuine* pleasure in eating is the ending of the aggravation called hunger." It would follow that smokers must get genuine pleasure from ending the aggravation of craving nicotine. In fact they do not. Craving in itself, whether it be for something pleasant and beneficial like food, or for something foul and destructive like nicotine, is decidedly unpleasant. It means that you are feeling unsatisfied and deprived. The longer the craving lasts, the more miserable and insecure you become!

Ending a hunger for food, is a wonderful feeling and a *genuine* pleasure. Partly because, providing it is good food and you are genuinely hungry, it does actually taste good and partly becauses it truly satisfies that empty, insecure feeling. It doesn't satisfy it forever. But that's an even greater bonus. We can go on enjoying the pleasures of eating the whole of our lives. This is one of the reasons that I believe that our creator intended us to enjoy life, because the system is so ingenious, in that hunger is no real hassle, but ending it is such a joy. When I say hunger is no real hassle, I am not of course referring to starvation, that is quite another matter.

To end your craving for nicotine, you have to poison your own body and to suffocate yourself. There's no pleasure in that! But surely the relief of the craving gives some *genuine pleasure*? It would do if it actually relieved the craving. But it does the complete opposite! The first cigarette starts it. The others merely perpetuate the process. Far from relieve the craving, **EACH CIGARETTE CREATES THAT EMPTY INSECURE FEELING! NON-SMOKERS DON'T SUFFER IT!**

This is why smokers and other drug addicts can never win. When they are smoking they wish they didn't have to. It's only when they can't have one that the cigarette appears to be precious. They mope for something that doesn't exist. Oh cigarettes exist, it's the smokers perception of a crutch or pleasure that doesn't. This feeling that the other mans grass is always greener doesn't only apply when we try to stop. It lasts the whole of our smoking lives, unless we remove all the brainwashing.

This is the terrible dilemma that all drug addicts suffer. The drug only appears to be precious when they aren't allowed to take it. Don't take my word for it. If you are not already smoking, light a cigarette now, inhale 6 deep glorious lung-fulls of the cancerous filth, ask yourself what it is that is so precious about it?

Let us remove some more of these blocks that either frighten smokers from making an attempt to stop, or defeat them if they pluck up enough courage to have a go. One of the classics is:

I HAVEN'T GOT THE WILLPOWER

CHAPTER 19

I Haven't Got The Willpower

Nonsense! You only think that because you have failed to stop so far. The fear of lack of willpower is really a form of fear of failure, but it warrants a special chapter.

This will appear to be a contradiction, but it is probably because you are strong-willed that you are still smoking. Perhaps you think this is nonsense, but before I explain the apparent anomaly, just look at the facts. When you were young, which of your friends first got on to smoking? Didn't it tend to be the boys who were tough and leaders and girls who matured quicker? Who tend to be the really heavy smokers you know? Don't they tend to be the managers, the executives, the directors, the foremen, the self-employed. Who were the idols that sold us the image in the first place? Wasn't it the Humphrey Bogarts the John Waynes, the Bette Davies the Marlene Dietrichs? You still have the modern day equivalents like Hurricane Higgins, Eric Bristow and Jimmy White. The traditionally heavy smoking professions are crime prevention, acting, teaching, jounalism, professional sports and ironically, firemen and miners. The last two go to great lengths to keep smoke and dust out of their lungs, and what do they do when the days work is done? Spend the extra money that they deservedly earn for running such risks to choke themselves. Ask them why? "You've got to have some pleasure in life." Why pay for the pleasure? Why don't they just do overtime and get paid for it?

Again ironically, we have more doctors and nurses at our clinics than any other single profession. Now you have to be strong-willed to survive the training or intense competition in many of these professions. We get a complete range of the population at our clinics, 90% of them are dominant, intelligent people.

I had a classic case a few years ago which illustrates many important facts about smoking. This man is Managing Director of a huge conglomerate. He said:

> "I never wanted to be a smoker, I was a good athlete at school, but you know what it was like in the old days, if you were a man and didn't smoke, you were regarded as a cissy. But having

spent all this money and ruined my health, I really resent society suddenly turning around and treating me like some sort of social leper and have resisted all the attempts of my family, friends and colleagues, either to frighten me, or to humiliate me into stopping smoking. My attitude to smoking is this: I don't kid myself that I get any advantages at all from smoking. I know I was missing nothing before I started and I can remember how hard I had to work to learn to smoke. As far as I am concerned, smoking is a disease that society inflicted on me as a youngster, but at my time in life, society is damn well stuck with me. If I want to smoke, I smoke, whether it be in the theatre or in the home of a non-smoker." He continued:

"But I was recently on holiday on the Mediterranean. I met another businessman who was head of an equally large firm. He offered to take me out deep-sea fishing. We started out at about 7am, just the two of us on the boat. We'd been going for about an hour. I was feeling really great. The sun had begun to rise and I was standing in my shorts breathing in the briny. I reached for a cigarette. I'd forgotten to bring any. In panic I turned to the other man and to my horror realised that he was not only a non-smoker, but one of those supercilious types that have to make their views known. I thought: 'I'll just have to suffer.' Half an hour later, I was my pulling hair out. I thought: 'This is ridiculous. I'm supposed to be enjoying myself.' I sauntered up to man and said: 'Look old chap, I've forgotten my cigarettes. If you don't have any on the boat, we'll have to go back."

Just think of the wording. If you don't have any on the boat, as if it was the other man's fault. Why should he have any? He wasn't a smoker. The conversation continued:
"Go on, you're pulling my leg, you surely don't want to smoke out here?"
"I assure you I'm serious."
"Oh come on, just breathe this air into your lungs. Can't you really go a few hours without one?"
"Look, if you want me to enjoy this trip, I need those cigarettes."
"I can't understand it myself, but you are my guest and, if you really are serious then we'll go back."
"It took an hour and a half to get back. I felt so embarrassed. I couldn't look at this other chap. I was just staring straight out to sea. But every now and again, out of the corner of my eye, I could see him staring up at me, wondering what sort of halfwit I was. I'm about 6'4" and the other chap must have been about 5'8". But every moment I was feeling shorter and shorter and more and more miserable. Then it

suddenly hit me. Here I was, Managing Director of this conglomerate, no one pushes me around. Here I am resisting all the efforts of my family and friends to make me stop, being made to look a fool in front of this man. It finally dawned on me that it was the cigarettes that were controlling my life. It was as if all of my life I had been obsessed with turning a rusty tap to no avail, then suddenly realising that it had a left-handed thread. I'd heard about your reputation, and I decided there and then that after the holiday, I would fix an appointment to see you. But the nub of the story was, it took us an hour and a half to get back. I got the cigarettes, in fact 4 packs. It took another hour and a half to get back to where we were. I was so pleased with myself, I didn't smoke a single cigarette the whole of the trip! It didn't even bother me. At the end of the trip I thanked my host, but he refused to shake my hand. I said:

"Are you annoyed that we went back?"

"Not in the least. You told me that you needed them, we wasted 3 hours getting them, and I've been watching you, you haven't smoked a single cigarette!"

Now how do you explain that to a non-smoker? Every smoker on the planet knows the panic that man felt when he suddenly discovered that he was in the middle of the ocean with no cigarettes, and every smoker knows how proud he felt because he didn't have to smoke them once he had them. You've probably already guessed the first thing he did when he left the non-smoker, was to light a cigarette!

This 'YACHT' story illustrates several important aspects about smoking which I will refer to later. The point I wish to make now is that he wasn't a weak-willed person. On the contrary, it has been my privilege and pleasure to be consulted by many exceedingly physically strong and mentally strong-willed people over the years, including Kerry Packer and a former chief of the SAS, whose name I omit for obvious reasons. The man on the yacht was in the same category.

I recall a classic case of a man living in Wiltshire during one of those rare years when the south of England was hit badly by snow blizzards. He risked life and limb battling to get home from work. When he finally reached the comfort of a roaring fire in his living room, he said to his wife: "It's atrocious out there!" He switched on the television and saw pictures of snow ploughs and stranded cars. At the end of the item, the narrator, in typical BBC style said: "We would strongly advise motorists not to use their cars unless it is absolutely essential." The man turned to his wife and said: "Listen to this idiot. Can you imagine anyone going out in weather like that unless they were forced to?"

He then went to light a cigarette and found that he had only 3 left. In his battle to get home, he had forgotten to buy any. What did he do? He did exactly what I would have done when I was the slave of that filthy weed. He risked life and limb to drive 2 miles to the nearest pub to buy something that was going to slowly kill him anyway. There is no way that shortage of a *non-essential*, such as food, would have dragged him from that roaring fire on such a night. It is often incidents like this that can trigger off an attempt to stop. That panic feeling can make smokers realise just how dependent they have become on nicotine.

Having had umpteen failed attempts to stop myself when using the willpower method, I found it difficult to understand why many long-term, heavy smokers who attended our clinics, had never even attempted to stop. It never occurred to me that such incidents, will not only trigger a smoker to want to stop, but will at the same time create such panic in the minds of some smokers that they are frightened even to make the attempt. The thought process is: "If I have to risk serious injury or even death, because I can't face the thought of spending just one evening of my life with only three cigarettes, how can I possibly expect to survive the rest of my life without any?"

The panic created by the mere thoughts of quitting can be so great, as to cause smokers who are making an attempt to quit, to actually smoke their next cigarette sooner that if they hadn't decided to quit. There are smokers who lie in bed every night and vow that they will never smoke again, hoping and praying that they will wake the next morning, either with no desire to smoke, or with the willpower to resist that desire. For many years I was one of those smokers, and like the others, within ten minutes of waking, I would be puffing away.

I say to smokers that think that they are weak-willed. If you ran out of cigarettes late at night, how far would you walk for a packet, a mile, two miles? A smoker would swim the channel for a packet of cigarettes. On National No Smoking Days you'll hear on the media: "This is the day that all smokers attempt to quit." The truth is that for most smokers, it is the one day in the year that they refuse point blank to quit. Many will smoke twice as many and twice as blatantly. Like the man on the yacht, strong-willed people don't like being told what they can or cannot do, particularly by people who have no understanding whatsoever of smoking.

However, I assure you that it is not lack of willpower that prevents smokers from stopping. Quite the reverse, it is their strong will that keeps them smoking. You might well conclude that it is incredibly stupid people that block their minds to the forces that have made millions of smokers decide to quit: the serious health risks, the money, the filth and slavery, combined with the intense social pressures. However, don't overlook the fact that it also takes some considerable strength of character to continue to smoke, in spite of these enormous risks and disadvantages and to be able to resist these immense social pressures.

Ask yourself if you are weak-willed in other ways? Or is it purely the inability to stop smoking that makes you think you are? Perhaps you also eat and drink too much. I'll explain later why these are really part of your smoking problem.

Whether you understand why you do it or not, it is only you that lights each cigarette, it is not lack of willpower but a conflict of will. In the opening chapter, l described how I once survived 6 months using the willpower method and how at the end of the 6 months I was crying like a baby because I had failed yet again. I couldn't understand my mixed emotions. I understand them completely now. I had gone through 6 months of black depression. Ironically the longer you go through that depression, the more precious it becomes. You are in a similar position to a marathon runner that has survived 25 miles of torture. He will kill himself to finish that last mile. However, if he had got cramp in the first mile he would have given in.

Each day I would say to myself: "It would be stupid to give in now, just keep going, eventually the craving must go." But the depression was like a dripping tap gradually dragging my resistance down, each day getting heavier and heavier. Eventually I was bound to crack and when I did, I was so disappointed with myself, because all that misery and depression was wasted. I'd failed yet again. If only I had possessed the willpower to last out a little longer, perhaps I would have succeeded. That's why I cried.

I realise now that it was only my willpower that allowed me to suffer that 6 months, and even if I'd had a stronger will, I would only have used it to prolong the depression and misery. In the end I would still eventually have given in. No matter how severe the marathon runner's agony might be, at least he knows that there is a definite end in sight. The worst agony the drug addict using the willpower method to quit suffers, is that he does not know how long his ordeal will last and while he continues to crave for cigarettes that he will not allow himself to smoke, the answer is never. The ex-smoker begins to suspect that it will be never. It doesn't matter how strong-willed that smoker might be, eventually he will give in.

In reality, I made a perfectly rational decision. I would have gone to my grave still feeling miserable and depressed, far better to have the shorter, sweeter life of the addict, than the longer miserable, deprived life of the ex-addict. I accept that. I would even support that attitude if it were true. I would still be a smoker if it were true. Correction, I'd be dead now, but I would have died a smoker. The beautiful truth is, it isn't true, but if you believe it is, it might just as well be!

Whenever I do phone-ins, I am haunted by a man who I call uncle Fred. He is in his late 70's or early 80's, and describes with intricate detail how he took up smoking during the war. How it was his life-saver during those awful years in the trenches and how, when he retired on a limited pension, it was the only real pleasure that he had left in life. He then describes that awful day when the government decided to increase the price of a packet of cigarettes by tuppence. No longer was he prepared to be blackmailed by the government. He decided to quit.

Uncle Fred placed his last packet of cigarettes above the fireplace and placed himself in his favourite armchair opposite. For six months Fred and the packet stared at each other, the packet determined to tempt Fred, and Fred equally determined not to give in. Happily the story has the desired ending, with justified pride Fred explains that after six months, his willpower prevailed and he successfully quit.

Bear in mind that the object of the phone-in including Fred's call, was to give listeners pointers on how to quit. So what? Say you, Fred's story is one of triumph of good over evil, an example to other smokers that it is possible to quit. That is true. But also bear in mind that I've spent half the programme telling these smokers that it doesn't take immense willpower to quit. What's more, Fred always ends his discourse with: "Don't try to tell me it doesn't take willpower, I know for a fact that it does."

What were the real messages that Fred was giving to other smokers? That during stressful periods, cigarettes can actually save your life? That they were the only pleasure in life? That the only reason he stopped was because he couldn't afford them anyway? What was exorbitant about tuppence a packet? Most smokers would regard such an increase as a reprieve. Fred had watched cigarettes rise from under 5p to over a pound a packet during his smoking lifetime, why hadn't he got on his high horse before?

However, the worst message that Fred's story gave, was that you'll never stop without the use of immense willpower. Unfortunately, Fred has already taken up the other half of the programme, in the few seconds that I have left, I only have time to say: "Fred, how come it took you 50 odd years to find all this willpower?"

It is the willpower method itself that makes smokers believe that they are weak-willed. They force themselves into a self-imposed tantrum like a child being deprived of its chocolates. Think of the analogy for a moment, which child will continue the tantrum longer, the weak-willed child or the strong-willed child? This is why weak-willed smokers find it easier to stop when using the willpower method, they soon accept the new situation and stop moping, strong willed-smokers just prolong their agony.

"I haven't got the willpower" was an excuse that I was never able to use. From other events in my life I knew I was a very strong-willed person. I know many other smokers that cannot understand why they are so strong-willed in other areas, and see less strong-willed people stop without any hassle, yet themselves find it impossible to do so.

You only require willpower to stop if part of your brain is tempted to smoke a cigarette. The schizophrenia is causing parts of your brain to pull against each other, once we remove the need or desire to smoke, the whole of your brain, be it conscious or subconscious will be pulling in the same direction and you will have no need to exercise willpower. Whether you be the weakest or strongest-willed smoker on the planet:

MY METHOD WILL STILL WORK FOR YOU!

Now let's deal with another influence that can either boost an attempt to stop or destroy it:

EX-SMOKERS

CHAPTER 20

Ex-Smokers

Ex-smokers can be grouped into two main categories, those that have 'kicked it' completely and, by far the larger group, those that on occasions have to resist temptation. The latter group can be subdivided into the 'holier-than-thous' and the 'whingers'. It is difficult to know which of the sub-groups has the greatest effect on keeping smokers in the pit. I have to admit that both groups had a profound effect on keeping me in it for thirty odd years. Let us deal with the 'holier-than-thous' first.

HTTs are the ones that, no sooner have they extinguished what they hope will be their final cigarette, put up no smoking signs in their homes, cars, offices and anywhere else that society will allow them to. They invite smokers into their homes, not because they want their company, but with the sole purpose of forbidding them to smoke so that they can gloat over them. If a smoker is stupid enough to accept an invitation and even more stupid enough to ask for an ashtray, an HTT will adopt an expression of such utter disbelief that, were they a silent movie actor and had just been informed that the Martians had landed, would have been chastised by the director for overacting. As if their look of horror was not sufficient, they then find it necessary to follow up with a comment like "If you have to smoke could you do it in the garden?" Their mercy is not tempered by the force 10 blizzard that happens to be blowing at the time.

HTTs will keep reminding you that smoking ruins your health and pocket and find it incomprehensible that an intelligent person like you finds it necessary to repeatedly put those filthy things into your mouth and set light to them. They appear to have forgotten completely that they did exactly the same thing for 30 odd years and have now stopped for 2 days four hours and twenty minutes.

I don't know why I'm telling you all this. I haven't had to suffer HTTs for nearly 10 years now, and you probably know more about them than I do. You can't fail to have noticed that most ex-smokers are more intolerant than non-smokers towards smokers? In restaurants non-smokers will wait until you actually blow smoke in their faces before they politely request you to refrain. But just reach in your pocket and you'll get: "I hope you are not going to smoke!" from the nearest HTT. A good plan is to keep in the same pocket as your cigarettes, one of those things that you pull out of christmas crackers that, when you blow on it, unfurls and makes a sound like a duck. One blast on that is far quicker and more effective than the arguments that usually follow those situations.

However, you would expect ex-smokers to be more tolerant than non-smokers on such occasions, after all, having once been smokers themselves, you'd think they would show a bit more compassion. Ironically, smokers themselves adopt a similar attitude if one of their number switches to a certain brand of herbal cigarettes. They are remorseless in their complaints and have no hesitation in letting the herbal smokers know about the stink that they are causing. It never seems to occur to smokers that they have exactly the same effect on non-smokers, yet many smokers get annoyed if a non-smoker dares to complain. I recently overheard this comment:

"I asked the girl on the next table if she minded me smoking. I couldn't believe it, she said she'd prefer that I didn't, in spite of the fact that she had finished her meal."

Clearly many smokers think that non-smokers complain, just to be awkward. Because smokers are immune to the foul smell themselves, they cannot appreciate the effect it has on non-smokers. Picture someone that worked in a sewer or on a pig farm, immune to the smell themselves, entering a smart restaurant in their working clothes, can you imagine the reaction they would receive from smokers and non-smokers alike?

In the presence of non-smokers, some smokers have enough imagination and consideration not to smoke until the meal is over. It is pure torture for me to watch the poor smokers on such occasions. I know the great effort they have made not to smoke during the meal. But their great sacrifice has been made in vain. Non-smokers find the smell of exhaled tobacco just as offensive after the meal as they do during it. Always last to finish is a non-smoker, with the last forkful of his crepe suzette hovering about an inch from his mouth, where it's been hovering for the previous 20 minutes while he relates what is actually a very amusing anecdote. The smoker laughs when the others laugh, but isn't hearing a word, he's visibly trying to will that last morsel down the bore's throat. Then he realises that the bore is an HTT and is doing it deliberately. He whips off to the rest room for a crafty one, knowing that the HTT can't go on forever, but his ploy only backfires on him, he returns, only to find that HTT found the crepe suzette quite the best he has ever tasted and, has not only ordered a second helping, but has persuaded all the other non-smokers to do the same.

Do you know *why* ex-smokers tend to be more vociferous in their attacks than people that have never smoked? It is because the worst thing that smokers do to ex-smokers, is not to pollute the atmosphere, but to put nicotine into it. The problem is, that when smokers quit by using the willpower method, although they are pleased to be non-smokers, they still believe that they've made a genuine sacrifice. Social functions are one of the occasions that most ex-smokers believe that they enjoyed smoking. The smokers light up, often it doesn't worry the ex-smoker if the smokers are smoking haphazardly throughout the meal. But if it's an official function, and for some reason the royal toast has been unduly delayed, the ex-smokers feel one-up. It isn't bothering them and they know that the smokers are climbing up the wall by this stage.

The ex-smokers are secretly congratulating themselves on how sensible they were to *give up*. Then comes the announcement: "LADIES AND GENTLEMEN, YOU MAY NOW SMOKE." The fact that the words: "IF YOU MUST" are often added nowadays doesn't affect the situation. The sense of relief is like an electric vibration that spreads throughout the room. Suddenly the situation is reversed, the smokers are all happy and cheerful as they light up. It doesn't occur to the ex-smoker that what they are really enjoying, is not the cigarette or cigar, but the ending of their misery. It's almost as if there is another course after the desert which will top the whole evening off. But non-smokers aren't allowed to share in the pleasure. It has the same effect as a 'Ladies Invitation Dance' when you are the only man present that doesn't get an invitation. The smokers are positively doing something. The ex-smokers are negatively watching them *enjoy* their cigarettes. The situation isn't enhanced when non-smokers will also *enjoy a cigar* on such occasions, but the poor ex-smoker dare not take that risk.

In no time at all, the atmosphere is filled with nicotine. The ex-smokers have no choice but to breathe it in. It starts to leave. Now in addition to the mental feeling of deprivation, the ex-smokers have actual physical withdrawal from nicotine. The ex-smokers think: "After all this time, the 'itch' is still there." In fact it had gone, but is now re-kindled. Naturally there is a temptation to scratch. But there's no way they want to get hooked again. They know that they are far better off than these pathetic smokers, but the smokers don't seem to realise this and at this particular point in time, neither do the ex-smokers. They feel one-down.

How do they resolve the situation? They've 2 choices. The first is to light up. But they have probably already been down that slippery path before. Hopefully they are sensible enough not to fall into the pit again. However, they are still feeling deprived, miserable and one-down on the smokers. The only other way they can see to resolve the situation, is to humiliate the smokers.

I'm talking about HTTs as if they are a particularly obnoxious breed of individual. Every smoker that has ever attempted to stop has been an HTT to a lesser or greater extent, including me and including you. It's not the individual character that is obnoxious. It's the effect that this insidious weed has on us. The HTTs feel insecure and vulnerable, their defences start to disintegrate. All aggression is based on fear. They are not really being hypocritical, they lash out in self-defence. They don't consciously set out to annoy smokers. It's instinctive, a self-protect button to stay out of the pit. They are not so much trying to convince the smokers that ex-smokers are better off as to reassure themselves. They really have no need to do that. Smokers know it already! In fact they know that, not only aren't non-smokers one down, but dozens of points up. Ex-smokers knew it when they were smokers. That is why they stopped! But the passing of time and the social occasion help to distort their perception.

This regular pollution of the atmosphere with nicotine, is not only a strong influence in getting ex-smokers hooked again, but is a strong influence in getting non-smokers hooked in the first place. At the clinics, many smokers who got hooked relatively late in life have described how they worked in a heavily smoke-filled atmosphere, looked upon their smoking colleagues with pity, had not the slightest desire to smoke, yet eventually ended up as smokers themselves. They were actually partially hooked before they smoked their first cigarette. In all probability every smoker was assisted into the pit by passive smoking. This is why many non-smokers occasionally like the smell of tobacco. If they live or work in a smoky atmosphere, they are partially addicted to nicotine. I've heard of several cases where, a non-smoking wife, when her heavy smoking husband is working away for a few days, has actually found herself sniffing his clothing, just to get that *comforting* smell of tobacco. Non-smokers that are not regularly subjected to passive smoking, invariably detest the smell!

HTTs have two disastrous influences on smokers which makes it almost impossible for smokers to stop. One is that even when HTTs do make their remarks with the best of intentions, smokers are so antagonised by them, and become so absorbed in resisting all the influences that are trying to force them to stop, that they lose sight of the real enemy. This is one of the messages to be drawn from the 'YACHT' story.

But the *really* destructive damage caused by HTTs is to ingrain into smokers minds: **"ONCE A SMOKER ALWAYS A SMOKER. YOU MIGHT STOP SMOKING, BUT YOU CAN NEVER BE COMPLETELY FREE!"** They might not be consciously aware of it, but they suspect that HTTS are only as antagonistic as they are, because they still secretly crave cigarettes. It wouldn't be quite so bad if it remained just a suspicion, unfortunately, ever present to confirm the smoker's doubts are the other breed:

THE WHINGERS

The whingers are those ex-smokers who, the moment you completed the ritual of singing Auld Lang Syne, wished all your friends a happy new year and cast that last cigarette packet into the fire with a wonderful feeling of having finally exorcised an evil spirit from your body, will shake you by the hand, wish you success, tell you how much healthier and wealthier you will be, assure you that you've made the right decision and will never regret it, then go on to describe how they smoked their final cigarette 30 years ago, but still miss them badly at times like these. The effect is immediate and devastating. You burn your fingers trying to get the packet out of the fire, and while your friends are still busy kissing each other, you are sneaking over to the cigarette machine assuring your family that you meant that you would stop in the morning.

It happened to me once on one of my more determined efforts to stop by using the willpower method. I had reached the stage where I knew that my real problem in trying to get free was the apparent inability to concentrate without a cigarette. I could put up with the bad temper and irritability. I thought, what I need is a springboard, a period when I didn't need to concentrate. I decided to devote my 3 weeks annual holiday to stop smoking. I just sat in an armchair all day in a state of black depression. Knowing what I know now, it appears ludicrous to me, but at that time it appeared to be logical. I thought if I sat there long enough, eventually my craving would go and I would be free.

The experiment appeared a complete failure. Each day, far from feeling better, the depression just got worse and worse. Near the end of the holiday, something marvellous happened. I awoke that morning, with a wonderful feeling of euphoria. I thought: "I've kicked it, I'm free!" I had what I now call the 'Three week syndrome' and I was free. For the first time I felt able to function again. I decided to decorate our living room. The next two days were exactly the same. I was on cloud nine without the slightest hint of doubt or temptation. On the third day I listened to a play on the radio about a salesman that had decided to stop smoking. He was was going through absolute misery. In a funny way it helped me. I thought: "Thank heavens I've got through that stage. I'm free!"

Eventually the salesman sought the help of his doctor, one of those typical, curt Scottish types.

"What's your problem?."

"I want to stop smoking."

"Use your willpower."

"It's not as easy as that. You're a doctor, how could you possibly understand it?"

"Och! I understand it alright, I used to smoke 60 a day!"

"Really, when did you stop?"

"Twenty years ago, when they proved the connection between smoking and lung cancer."

"But I thought they still hadn't proved that."

"That's only to the tobacco companies and to smokers that cannot face up to the facts."

"You are probably right. But after twenty years, you've forgotten all about it, how could you possibly know the misery that I'm going through?"

"Listen laddie. Never a day goes by that I don't yearn for a cigarette!"

What effect that had on the salesman, I cannot tell you, but I felt that I had just been kicked in the stomach. I was immediately back in black depression. The play was purely fictional. It didn't matter, I went straight out and bought a packet of cigarettes. It was another two years before I built up enough courage to make another attempt.

Another classic example happened a few years ago. I was at a dinner party. There was a girl there that I had met once before, but she had got embarrassed smoking in front of me. People know what I do for my living and assume that I'm bound to be the worst HTT that they are ever likely to meet. They assume that I'll lecture them about the evils of smoking. It so happened that on this second occasion, she was the only smoker there, but even though the meal had finished, she wasn't smoking. I don't think she was worried about offending anyone, I think she just felt self-conscious because she was the only smoker. But she had 'The smokers twitch'.

Everyone else was chatting away. This girl sat fiddling with her lighter and cigarettes. I cannot bear to see smokers in that position. I said: "Margaret, the meal is over, no one will complain, have a cigarette if you need one." She said: "I don't need one, but I would like one." I should have shut up really, but it was like waving a red rag under my nose, I just couldn't resist it, I said: "If you don't need one, leave it. There's no point in choking yourself if you don't need to." She was about to light up. Instead she just said: "Fine, I'll leave it." I continued conversing with the girl next to me, who I hadn't met before, but my attention remained with Margaret. I wanted to see how she would get over the situation and of course now the twitching became unbearable. No doubt your sympathies will be with Margaret. As smokers, I'm sure you've no doubt suffered many similar situations in your life as I did, but get it clearly into your mind, I wasn't the real villain. That filthy weed was the real villain. Non-smokers don't have this problem of being miserable when they are not allowed to smoke. At one time

Margaret got up to go to the toilet. She picked up her lighter and cigarettes, glanced across at me and immediately sat down. I can only assume that she thought that I would have made some facetious remark. I was now beginning to feel petty. Far from easing the situation, I had made it worse. I was trying to think of a way to get over the impasse, when the girl that I had been chatting to suddenly said: "I'd murder for a cigarette now."

I was truly shaken, because I knew the girl was a non-smoker. In fact, I was convinced that she had never been a smoker. She was one of these delicate types like Dresden china. She had a beautiful complexion. But I think what actually fooled me was that she was a vicar's wife. Why a vicar's wife shouldn't smoke I don't know.

Most of them probably do. But you get preconceived ideas about people. As I said earlier, in our clinics there are usually one or more ex-alcoholics, heroin addicts, whatever. People who have been through the lot and kicked the lot except smoking. You imagine them to be twitching, nervous wrecks. Instead, they always appear to be the calmest, healthiest and strongest members in the group. One of my chief supporters in the fight against the weed tells me that he is an ex-heroin addict and had so little control over his personal life that he had to attend Weight Watchers at the age of thirteen. Yet today he is one of the fittest, most confident of young men that I have yet to meet.

I cannot visualise nuns smoking, yet I am assured that some in fact do. We recently had a Rabbi in a group. It disturbed me, I kept thinking: "What are you doing here! Rabbis don't smoke." A few years ago we had a whole run of ballerinas from the Royal Ballet. Even now, when I watch Swan Lake, I can't visualise those ballerinas with a fag stuck in their mouths. In fact they are the world's worst. We think of smokers as mentally and physically weak people. In truth it's the complete opposite.

Back to the dinner party. I said to this girl: "I'm sorry, I didn't realise that you were a smoker, and if you are not smoking because of me, you will offend me, I was the world's worst." She said: "No way! I haven't smoked for eight years, and I will never smoke again. But I used to love a cigarette after a meal and I really would enjoy one now." Meanwhile Margaret, who believed I was now genuinely occupied with the vicar's wife, had lit up and was taking a crafty drag.

The incident amply illustrates the total futility of being a smoker. There was Margaret, looking decidedly guilty and uncomfortable, snatching crafty puffs on her cigarette, hoping that no one had noticed that she had lit up and wishing she were free like everyone else in the room, and there was the other girl, who hadn't had a cigarette for 8 years, actually moping for something that she herself hoped she would never have!

It was a ridiculous situation and typical of smoking. It's a bit stupid to envy the other man even if you believe his grass is greener than yours and there is nothing you can do about it, but here you had a situation where both girls envied each other, yet each had the choice to be smoker or non-smoker. The annoying thing for me was, that I had spent half an hour before the meal chatting to Margaret, not HTT talk you understand, but gently persuading her just how nice it was to be free and that she could do it. I had a rope around her waist and was gradually easing her out of the pit. Margaret was one of those smokers that had never managed to survive a whole day without a cigarette. Can you imagine the effect it had on her when she heard the other girl was still craving after 8 years?

A national daily recently devoted a whole page article about another woman that had decided to start smoking again after 8 years of abstinence. She went into elaborate detail about the depressive misery of those years and how she had gained pounds in weight. She described how wonderful she felt when she made the positive decision to smoke again, but most of all she waxed lyrical about how gorgeous that first cigarette tasted.

Now I have every sympathy with that lady. I have referred to my miseries when attempting to stop by use of the willpower method. I am also very aware that I greatly exaggerated the trauma. I have no doubt that she wasn't a happy non-smoker, but let's examine her statements more closely. If she thought smoking was so great, why did she stop in the first place? If her 8 years was so bad, why did she not abandon her attempt much earlier? The fact that she didn't would imply that she really hated being a smoker. If she really suffered so badly during that 8 years, I cannot believe that she felt any feeling of pleasure when she finally had to admit to herself that her 8 years penance had been a complete and utter waste of time!

I can remember an enormous feeling of relief when I finally allowed myself to give up the struggle during those failed attempts to quit when using the willpower method, but I cannot remember ever thinking: "Great! You're a smoker again. Doesn't this cigarette taste absolutely gorgeous!" On the contrary, that feeling of relief was always tempered by a feeling of failure and foreboding, and the first few cigarettes always tasted weird. Diarrhoea is unpleasant to most people, but to someone that has been constipated for 8 years it would appear to be utter bliss. I've no doubt that if you've waited 8 years for a cigarette, the relief would be immense, but not the taste! As I have said: "All drug addicts are liars. They have to be." The dinner party girl's remark was quite innocuous, even so, its effect on Margaret was obvious. Can you imagine the effect of that article had on someone that had recently stopped who was going through the miseries of the willpower method? Can you imagine its effect on any smoker that was contemplating an attempt to stop?

171

There is a debate currently in progress about the media only being interested in bad news. A famous journalist defended the policy by saying that if they were compelled to include good news, it would be tantamount to propaganda. But aren't they being propagandist by excluding it? Wide publicity was recently given to a catholic church desecrated by protestant louts. No publicity was given to the far more constructive and pleasant sequel to the story, that several protestant families came to clean up the mess.

I can understand and even forgive that lady. The natural reaction of all drug addicts that have failed to escape the pit is to ensure that they have plenty of company in it, especially after the tremendous effort she went through to escape. Such is the evil of the drug. What I cannot forgive, is the utter irresponsibility of that newspaper to publish the article. After all it could hardly even be regarded as news. Why won't they let me write an article on what would be world shattering news:

HOW EASY IT IS AND HOW NICE IT IS TO BECOME A NON-SMOKER!

You will shortly become a non-smoker. The thought that you may become an HTT or a whinger might deter you. What might deter you even more is that like them you can never be free. I promise you that you need have neither fear. Let's take a look at another category: the ex-smokers that are completely free. A breed that I never realised existed until shortly before I saw the light. I was certain that all ex-smokers craved the occasional cigarette. It never dawned upon me until after I had stopped smoking, that I never asked ex-smokers whether they missed cigarettes or not. This was because, whatever the answer was, I didn't want to hear it. If they did still miss them, it confirmed my belief that you could never be completely free. If they didn't miss them, it meant you could be free and I would have to go through those months or even years of tortuous withdrawal pangs again. It was a typical example of the tug of war of fear that causes smokers to close their minds.

The first of the breed that I met, is a man called Patrick, a giant of a man, good-natured and, as the name suggests, an Irishman. I am very grateful to Patrick. The incident that I am about to relate was one of several that happened in close proximity and enabled me to escape from the pit. We would meet once a year through mutual friends on the occasion of Royal Goodwood. I had just survived a particularly severe bout of coughing and Patrick was giving me one of those quizzical 'what possible pleasure can you be getting?' looks that non-smokers have on such occasions. In an attempt to cover my embarrassment I said: "Patrick you don't know how lucky you are not to have been a smoker." He said: "What are you talking about, I used to smoke 40 a day!"

I stared at him in disbelief. I'd known him for 5 years and I was convinced that he had never been a smoker. Why I was convinced, I don't know, but you can sense these things. In hindsight it was probably because he was neither HTT nor whinger. I must have sensed that he didn't miss them, because he was the first ex-smoker to whom I put the question. The reply was a revelation to me:

MISS THEM? YOU'VE GOT TO BE JOKING!!!

I started asking other non-smokers that I had known for years and was amazed how many of them were in fact ex-smokers. Then I started asking people that I knew were ex-smokers whether they ever missed them and was relieved to learn that Patrick wasn't an isolated case.

THERE ARE THOUSANDS OF PATRICKS!

In truth Patrick was not the first of the breed I had met, but the first that I had recognized. I also said that the HTTS and whingers are a much larger group than the Patricks. I'm not sure that is true either. The real problem is that we only ever hear the complaints of the HTTs or the whinings of the whingers. The Patricks don't sit at social functions telling everyone how nice it is to be free.

THEY SHOULD

You will soon be a Patrick. It will help you to remind yourself during the first few days just how nice it is to be free. When you receive the Moment of Revelation you'll have no need to remind yourself. But keep shouting it from the roof-tops, the greatest fear that keeps smokers in the pit is the fear that you can never be free and you will help other smokers to remove that fear. I'll deal with that particular fear in a later chapter, meanwhile let us remove another classic block:

I'VE GOT AN ADDICTIVE PERSONALITY

CHAPTER 21

I've Got an Addictive Personality

Or: "In this world there are non-smokers, people that play at being smokers and people like me – The genuine confirmed smoker, **THE REAL McCOY.**" I can quite understand why you think you are. I believe that this was the main reason that prevented my escape. I didn't enjoy them. I knew that they were killing me. True, I thought that they gave me confidence and helped me to concentrate, but I couldn't see why or how. Like me, most of my family were chain-smokers. They seemed to be reasonably intelligent human beings. The only logical explanation was that either there was some genuine crutch or pleasure in smoking, or that there was some weakness in our metabolism, character, personality or even in our chemical make-up.

Like the feeling of lack of willpower, this is another extension of the fear of failure. You start off by believing that you are attempting the impossible. The feeling is merely reinforced by your previous failed attempts. This is further reinforced when you learn that alcoholics and heroin addicts also tend to be very heavy smokers. The fact that doctors tend to be more vulnerable than ordinary people just adds to the overall confusion. The whingers that I described in the last chapter would also tend to support the theory that there is such a thing as a 'Smokaholic' or 'Addictive Personality'. After all, if someone has abstained for over 30 years and is still craving cigarettes, they must surely be over the physical effects of withdrawal, the only possible explanation must be that they have some chemical flaw in their make up.

In fact: 'I've got an addictive personality' is just another cop out. My favourite author is Conan Doyle. My favourite character is Sherlock Holmes. My favourite quote is: "If you've exhausted all the other possibilities, the one that remains, no matter how improbable it may seem, must be the solution." I forget which particular case Mr. Holmes was undertaking at the time, and I apologise in advance to avid members of the Sherlock Holmes society, no doubt I have misquoted, but the gist is the same.

There is quite a bit of snobbery in the expressions we use. The working class man that downs 16 pints over the weekend is merely a heavy drinking oaf that knows no better. The professional man who partakes of a bottle of whisky each day is an alcoholic. It's not really his fault, he's intelligent enough to recognize the futility of it, but what choice does he have, he's exhausted all the logical reasons, so the only possible remaining explanation is that there is something in his genetic make-up that he has no control over. He's an alcoholic.

I've got an addictive personality is the professional man's equivalent to: "I smoke out of boredom." Professional men cannot use that excuse, so they have to think up some other excuse. Again their logical brains cannot understand why they are stupid enough to be smokers. They could use 'Habit' but to do so would be to admit that they hadn't got the willpower to break the habit. So they cop out: "It's not my fault! I just happen to have an addictive personality."

It might appear that I imply that such smokers are consciously going through a logical thought process, deliberately making up lies to fool themselves and their families. No, what I am describing is the result of the total confusion of contradictory facts, misinformation, anomalies and general ignorance about smoking that all smokers are confronted with throughout their lives. I am not belittling smokers, how could I? I have yet to meet a smoker that sunk lower than I did, or lied more to hide the fact.

One of the fascinating things about running the clinics is the incredible variety of excuses that smokers give to justify the fact that they continue to smoke. One of the most bizarre was given by a barrister, she said:

"I was born with a silver spoon in my mouth. At school I was not only academically top at most subjects, but I was also the best at sports for my year. I also happen to be No.1 in my particular branch of the legal profession."

Again, as I relate this story, you might form the impression that the lady's real problem was that she needed a stronger neck to support the weight of her head. I am also very conscious that when I relate personal stories, I might also give the impression of being a very arrogant person. Whether I give that impression or not is irrelevant. I merely relate the facts of my life, whether during the dark ages in the pit, or subsequent to my escape, as honestly and as factually as I am able, in order to help you out of the pit. You will already have noticed that I am prone to exaggeration. I make no apologies for this. It is a technique that I have learned from the tobacco companies. You'll know when I exaggerate because I'll either exaggerate outrageously, or start the sentence with imagine. The other anecdotes that I relate are factual, the names have often been omitted to protect the innocent or embarrassed. This lady did not give the impression of being arrogant, she was desperately seeking my help and merely being honest. She continued:

> "The other girls hated me. I was known as Miss goody goody. It left its mark on me. I didn't let them know it, but I didn't like being isolated. I felt that I was perfect and that they resented it. I'd listened to all the reasons that other smokers use to justify their smoking, and satisfied myself that they were all phoney. But I needed some flaw in my make-up and I believe that I deliberately started to smoke in order to provide that flaw."

That lady had an IQ far higher than mine and she had quite correctly surmised that all the other smokers reasons for continuing to smoke were mere excuses. She had used all of her intelligence to provide her own reason but that still didn't explain the real reason that the other countless millions continued to smoke and neither did it explain hers. Her real reason for starting was exactly the same as millions of other smokers, she just wanted to be part of the crowd. But let us assume that her true reason for starting was the one that she claimed, then why, when she decided that she no longer wanted to be a smoker, did she need my help?

BECAUSE SHE WAS HOOKED LIKE THE REST OF US!

We recently had a 91 year young lady attend the clinic with her 65 year old son. Her reason for stopping was that she wanted to set an example to her boy. I wonder why it took her 65 years?

It is essential to realise that there is no such thing as an addictive personality or confirmed smoker, because if you do believe it, you will be vulnerable the rest of your life. I promise you:

YOU ARE COMPLETE WITHOUT NICOTINE ALCOHOL OR SIMILAR DRUGS

It's a chicken and egg situation. Did you become an addict because you had an addictive personality? Or do you think that you have an addictive personality, because you became addicted to a drug? Let us examine the evidence on both sides. There is considerable evidence that would support the addictive personality theory:

1. Heavy smokers seem to be a certain type, physically and mentally strong people, that work hard, play hard and live their lives to the full. True, but don't you have to be physically strong to be a

heavy smoker, and mentally strong to be able to block your mind from the terrible risks that you run?
2. Most alcoholics, recovering or otherwise, tend to be heavy smokers. Nearly all heroin addicts have been or still are smokers and drinkers. This would suggest that there is such a thing as an addictive personality.

True, but such evidence is circumstantial. A gambler might regularly lose his money on dogs, horses, cards and roulette. That would suggest that he was born with 'a gambling personality'. However there is another simpler explanation. Perhaps he didn't listen to his maths teacher and learn that the odds are so stacked against him that even Lady Luck becomes his enemy. There is a rational explanation why most heroin addicts and alcoholics are also smokers. In fact, as I will explain later, I believe most of them became heroin addicts or alcoholics, as a natural consequence of first falling into the nicotine trap.

I should make it clear that the reverse situation doesn't necessarily apply. Practically all heroin addicts and alcoholics are smokers, but not all smokers become alcoholics or heroin addicts. Surely if they had addictive personalities, they would do?

I'm prepared to let you decide whether there is such a thing as an addictive personality. Supposing I said to you that I have learned that thousands of more Egyptians drown in the Nile each year than Russians. There is a million pounds, investigate it for me, find out why? Would you waste my money delving into the physical make-up or mentality of a Russian compared to an Egyptian to find out if Egyptians had an 'In the Nile drowning' personality? Or would you say: "Allen why waste your money? Of course more Egyptians drown in the Nile than Russians, they live near the Nile!"

To say addicts become addicted because they have addictive personalities, is like saying skiers break their legs because they have 'broken leg' personalities. They break their legs for no other reason than that they ski. Drug addicts become drug addicts for no other reason than they take the damned drugs. Can it be sheer coincidence that anyone that you ever met that had an addictive personality, also just happened to be addicted, or was at one time addicted to a drug?

I believe that one of the strong influences that made me feel that I had an addictive personality, was that smokers seemed to be a different breed to non-smokers.

Some people split the world between black and white, east or west, rich or poor, catholic or protestant, upper or working class. To me such distinctions were no more significant than whether you broke your eggs at the small end or the large. The only important distinction was: are you a smoker? If you were, it didn't matter whether you were

Mother Theresa, Hitler or an eskimo, I could relate to you!

Smokers had interesting personalities, whereas non-smokers appeared to be supercilious killjoys. Or was it really that I felt more comfortable in the company of smokers? I could pollute the atmosphere as much as I wanted without the guilty conscience. I could cough and splutter as much as I wanted to without the feeling: "This man thinks I'm an idiot." Why didn't it dawn on me until after I had stopped smoking that most of my friends were actually non-smokers or ex-smokers? My wife is a non-smoker!

One of the influences which tends to support this belief that smokers, alcoholics etc. are a different breed and have addictive personalities, is because they do possess certain physical characteristics which non-smokers and teetotallers do not. However, just as the addictive personality is caused by becoming addicted to a drug rather than by some inherent flaw in the make-up of the victim, so the grey complexion of the heavy smoker and the high blood pressure appearance of the heavy drinker, are a direct result of systematically poisoning the body. The reason that I couldn't visualise Patrick or the girl at the dinner party that had stopped for 8 years as smokers, wasn't just because I had never seen them smoke, but because neither had the debilitated complexion, the lethargic appearance or the haunted look of a person dependent on nicotine. Fortunately, shortly after you quit, you recover both physically and mentally.

At one time 60% of the adult population were hooked on nicotine. That's an awful lot of addictive personalities! The only reason the other 40% didn't have addictive personalities, was that they couldn't physically cope with the poison. In those days cigarettes were mainly non-tipped and very strong, the learning process was not easy and many had neither the willpower nor the desire to go through it. Many others just didn't have enough money to be able to afford an addictive personality!

Ah! Yes say you, but just as 90 odd per cent of the adult population drink alcohol, the vast majority of them can take it or leave it, there is a special breed of drinker: alcoholics, that because of their chemical make-up, or addictive personalities cannot control their drinking. They will scrape, borrow, beg or steal if they haven't got the money, so there are confirmed, heavy smokers that cannot control their smoking.

I assure you that you are wrong. Take the flies in the pitcher plant. Some are still hovering gaily on the surface, others are in the deep recesses of the pit already part-digested, the remainder are somewhere in between, but they are all travelling in the same direction:

DOWN!

So it is when you smoke your first cigarette you hover on the rim of a pitcher plant. If you smoke your second you have stepped onto a slippery slope that goes one way only. The slope is so slight that it is imperceptible for miles and miles. Some people hover in that area the whole of their lives without ever realising that they are in a trap. Some smokers, like me, plunge headlong down that slope and become chain-smokers almost overnight. The rate at which each individual smoker plunges down the slope is affected by 1001 different factors. Your personality might be one of them, if you like to socialise, or be one of the crowd. But your *addictive* personality isn't one of them!

To say: "I have an addictive personality", is to say: "I have the type of personality that likes to fall for a confidence trick." Surely nobody would want to fall for a confidence trick? The biggest fools on earth might keep falling for confidence tricks, but they don't *want* to!

It is true that having become addicted, some people would appear to become more addicted than others. The reason that I became a chain-smoker almost overnight was that I had a strong pair of lungs which could cope with the poisons, I could afford to chain-smoke and I had a job which allowed me to chain-smoke. These are three of the main factors which decide our rate down the slippery slope. It never even occurred to me that some smokers restrict their intake to 10 a day because they physically cannot cope with more, or because they couldn't afford to smoke more, or because their hatred of the slavery is so great as to make them restrict their intake throughout their lives. Another important factor is the rate at which your friends and colleagues tend to smoke.

It is exactly the same with alcohol. There are differences between nicotine and alcohol, just as there are different types of pitcher plant, but the principle is exactly the same.

You didn't become a smoker, alcoholic or any other sort of addict because of your addictive personality. You only think that you have an addictive personality because you started taking an addictive drug. This is the awful effect these drugs have on you. They make you feel that you are dependent on them, that there is some weakness in your make-up. That's how nicotine made me feel for a third of a century. I have an advantage over you. I'm now out of that pit and am able to compare the two situations. Believe me, there is no contest. You also have a great advantage, you have an intelligent brain and you have the imagination to know that what I am saying to you is true.

At least give yourself the opportunity to savour life outside that pit. After all, what have you to lose? If I've lied to you, you can always jump back in. But I promise you, you won't even want to. The only mystery will be why you once thought it necessary to be in the pit and for so long!

We believe we have addictive personalities because, like Mr. Holmes, we've exhausted all the other possible explanations of why we continue to smoke. That's because we don't understand the true reason that we smoke. Just like Dr. Miller, whose case I will describe in the next chapter, we are searching for terribly complicated answers, when the simple solution has been staring us in the face. The incredible confusion created by that imperceptible itch and the massive brainwashing that ensues from it.

Do you really believe that our creator programmed us to depend on nicotine? If so, why do you think it is only in the last few generations, since we learned to mass produce cigarettes and developed communication techniques that can brainwash the whole wide world on a massive scale, that smoking has become such a dominant part of our lives? Do you really believe that smoking is vital to our survival or even our happiness? If so, and you still believe that you have an addictive personality, perhaps you can explain to me:

WHY YOU DIDN'T NEED THE DRUG *BEFORE* YOU STARTED TO TAKE IT?

Imagine applying a bandage to a finger that has no cut, only to find that when you removed the bandage a cut has miraculously appeared. You now have to apply another bandage, the process continues for the rest of your life. Would an intelligent person argue that there was something in their personality that made them apply the original bandage even though no cut existed? Or would they be more likely to think: "Why was I stupid enough to apply the bandage when there was no cut." How on earth the bandage created the cut in the first place, I don't know. But what I do know is that I would never have got that cut unless I had applied the bandage. One things for sure, even if the bandage didn't cause the cut:

IT CERTAINLY HASN'T CURED IT!

I've explained how nicotine withdrawal from your first cigarette created the need for the second:

DID YOUR SECOND CIGARETTE CURE IT?

It's not your personality or your genetic make-up that addicts you:

IT'S THE DRUG!!!

Now let's dispel another myth that causes smokers to feel that they are a breed apart:

HOW I WISH I WERE A NON-SMOKER

180

CHAPTER 22

How I Wish I Were a Non Smoker

What is a non-smoker? Every time any smoker extinguishes a cigarette, they become a non-smoker, until they light the next one. However no one would describe such a person as other than a smoker. I'm a non-smoker means different things to different people. Let's use the example of Ron Stokes, a close friend that I couldn't get through to for years. We were visiting on the occasion of an important wedding. I should point out that this is not an uncommon event in the Stokes family, half the population of Ramsgate are Stokes. I had subtly got onto the subject of smoking. Ron's defences were down. I was explaining just how much more pleasant life was as a non-smoker. I had him nibbling, could I get him to bite? Suddenly a look of sheer panic appeared on his face. He said: "Please don't stop me now, wait until after the wedding." The shutters came down, and needless to say, the wedding came and went and with it went Ron's desire to stop.

Eventually Ron read 'EASYWAY', threw his cigarettes and lighter into the dustbin and announced to all and sundry: **"I'M A NON-SMOKER"** and was as good as his word. Since that time I have heard him say to his smoking friends and relatives: "Just throw the cigarettes away and say I'm a non-smoker!" Of course it didn't work for them. No matter how often you repeat it, you don't become a non-smoker by calling yourself one. You don't become a non-smoker by *saying*: "I feel like a non-smoker" any more than you would become an elephant merely by calling yourself one or *saying* you feel like one. Fortunately you can become a non-smoker, not by *saying* you feel like one, but by *actually* feeling like one. By the time Ron had finished reading 'EASYWAY', he *FELT* like a non-smoker and *KNEW* that he was already one. For the purposes of this book, let us agree to apply the following definitions:

> **NON-SMOKER:** A person who has never smoked. This includes someone that tried those experimental cigarettes but never smoked since. It would not include casual smokers, no matter

how infrequently they imbibe. Many casual smokers don't regard themselves as hooked. I met one recently that smoked 10 small cigars a day, but regarded himself as a non-smoker. He was smoking the equivalent of 30 cigarettes a day.

EX-SMOKER: A smoker who has stopped smoking completely. If you have an occasional cigar after a meal, you are still a smoker, and in all probability you will soon be a heavy smoker.

SMOKER: Any other person.

I have frequently used the word non-smoker, when according to the above definitions, I should have referred to an ex-smoker. I do this because many smokers believe that once hooked, it's impossible ever to regain the blissful state of mind of a non-smoker. The term ex-smoker tends to support this belief. For example Ron's statement: "I'm a non-smoker" would not have had any impact whatsoever had he said: "I'm an ex-smoker." I trust that you will understand why I continue to adopt this practice, and that it will not cause you confusion.

Smokers and ex-smokers envy non-smokers. They think: "What you've never had, you don't miss." They are wrong. I know that I am now better off and less likely to get hooked than a non-smoker. You find that difficult to believe? I assure you it is true. In fact I know that I could never get hooked again. Let me make it quite clear, I don't mean that I'm pleased that I smoked. On the contrary, like all other smokers, I envy people that never fell for the trap. What I mean is: I haven't the slightest desire or temptation to smoke, whereas many non-smokers do.

You probably find this difficult to accept. But just think about it. Why do any of us light the first cigarette? After all we are not addicted to nicotine until after we light it. So the need or desire was created before we lit that first cigarette. But non-smokers are also subjected to passive smoking and the massive brainwashing from birth. They too believe that cigarettes relax you. But because, for whatever reason, they don't fall into the trap, any slight feeling of deprivation that they might have is far outweighed by the disadvantages of being a smoker. But many still believe that they are missing out. However, most of them will no more admit to it, than smokers will admit that they wish they were non-smokers.

Incidentally, I should at this stage dispel another common misconception. When I explain that the only reason that the smokers block their minds to the health, the money, the slavery, the social stigma, etc. is to replace the nicotine, many smokers assume from this that, although nicotine is a powerful poison, the body does get some pleasure or crutch from imbibing it. No, there is no pleasure whatsoever in craving nicotine or anything else. The pleasure you get is ending the aggravation of the craving. But it is an illusion. Each cigarette far from ending the craving, causes it.

Let us look at some examples of these happy, non-smokers. A classic case was that of Dr. Miller and his wife. It sticks in my memory for two important reasons. The first was that I believe he was one of the very few people to consult me that failed because he was too intelligent. He just couldn't bring himself to believe that an accountant had discovered a simple solution to a problem that had confounded the medical experts for years. I believe he came to see me because some of his patients had recommended me to him. They had told him that I used hypnotherapy. I like smokers to be sceptical but I couldn't get him to listen to what I was saying because he kept asking me what mystical powers I possessed. Even when I explained to him that I claimed no mystical powers but just special knowledge, he was still obsessed with the hypnotherapy.

Dr. Miller had obviously given smoking considerable thought. Like many highly intelligent smokers that fail to quit even though they know they'll die shortly unless they do, he was at a loss to understand why. He came to the conclusion that it was the elegant packaging. There was this highly intelligent, scientific brain, so convinced that I was some sort of charlatan, that he completely blocked his mind to what I was saying, yet believed himself to be simple-minded enough to be fooled into imbibing a substance, that he *knew* to be poison, just because it was elegantly packaged. Incidentally, if you believe it is the clever packaging that fools you, switch to roll-ups, there's no clever packaging involved there. However, roll-your-own smokers are just as hooked on nicotine as the rest. I should know, when I switched to roll-ups, I was soon consuming 2 ounces of tobacco per day.

However the other reason that I remember Dr. Miller so vividly was he came with his wife. Dr. Miller had already had a heart attack but was still smoking sixty cigarettes a day. Mrs. Miller was terrified that he would shortly die if he didn't stop. I strongly suspect that he only came to see me under her duress. Like all non-smokers, she had little understanding of what smoking is about, incidentally nor do smokers. But such was her concern for her husband, every time I said something, she would nod her head vigourously and on occasions give me verbal support as well. At the end of the session I asked her if she had ever been a smoker. She said: "No I keep trying, but I just can't learn to enjoy them!"

I managed to avoid laughing aloud, but the terrible irony of the situation struck me. There she was terrified that the cigarettes were going to kill her husband and at the same time complaining because she couldn't enjoy them herself! Anyway, what right had I to laugh at Mrs. Miller aloud or otherwise? I could clearly see what smoking was doing to my father, but that didn't stop me from becoming hooked. I'm grateful to Mrs. Miller, she made me realise for the first time that it's not only ex-smokers that feel that they are missing out, obviously so do many non-smokers.

Most parents believe that if they can help their children to avoid falling into the pit before they reach maturity, they will be immune for life, and like Mrs. Miller, all non-smokers no matter what their age, are convinced that they could never become hooked:

SO WAS EVERY SMOKER UNTIL THEY FELL INTO THE TRAP!

While there are manholes without covers, anyone is capable of falling into one. Again, some of the most amusing and tragic stories are those of smokers who fell for the trap comparatively late in life, like the non-smoker who had her first holiday abroad at the age of thirty, discovered that Spanish cigarettes were only a quarter of the price of English cigarettes, and just couldn't resist the bargain. That bargain cost her about £10,000!

An unbelievably unlucky case was that of the non-smoking national serviceman who actually successfully avoided falling into the trap until the week before his demob. That wasn't an easy thing to do. If you managed to resist the temptation of 'duty frees' or cheap cigarettes, there was always the constant pitfall of: "Now we'll have a break for a smoke." In the services you never had a break purely for the sake of one, it was always for a fag. Little wonder non-smoking servicemen felt they were missing out and that so many of them eventually succumbed.

However, this particular serviceman was not bereft of all the vices. In fact his favourite pastime was poker. That was unfortunate, because he wasn't very good at it, or as he put it: "I'm the unluckiest card player there ever was." However in that fatal last week he had one of those nights that all gamblers dream about. Unfortunately, at that time in the services, cigarettes were regarded as legal tender. In addition to winning a lot of money, he also won a lot of cigarettes. What else was there to do with them but smoke them. Which he duly did. He described it as the luckiest night of his life. I didn't have the heart to tell him that his luckiest night cost him about £30,000.

As a youngster, did you ever try to win something in an amusement arcade on one of those machines whereby you could guide a miniature crane? You'd spend all your pocket money trying to hook what looked like a solid gold watch. Finally, you guided the crane to perfection, you held your breath as the crane prised the watch clear of the surrounding objects, jerked its way across to the winning chute and then dropped the watch about an inch short. I began to suspect that there was someone inside such machines whose sole purpose in life was to hit the 'nobble' button. Did you ever win anything worth more than a piece of bubble gum on one of those machines? Do you know of anyone that was lucky enough to win anything valuable? I do, I met him just a few days ago. At the age of 20, he was lucky enough to extract a packet of five Weights. It started him smoking. At the age of 54 he was still smoking 40 a day. That piece of luck cost him about £40,000.

The most pathetic case that I know was of the lady who nursed her father through a tortuous and painful death from lung cancer. His last act was to make her promise that she would never become a smoker. When he finally passed away, she lit her first cigarette ever. She was 35 at the time, became hooked from that day and sought my help 15 years later. I think I have more understanding than anyone about the subtlety and ingenuity of the smoking trap, even so I found it difficult to understand her action. I said: "Was it your father's influence that had prevented you from smoking prior to his death, or did the fact that he made you vow never to smoke make you rebel against him?" She said: "It was neither of those things. I always loathed smoking and had not the slightest desire ever to do so. It was just that, in spite of all that he suffered because of the smoking, he continued to smoke right to the end, even though he was gasping for breath. I thought he must be getting some tremendous comfort from those cigarettes. When he finally passed away, I got a strange feeling of relief, partly because his suffering was now over and partly because my ordeal of having to nurse him and to watch him suffer was also over. This sense of relief was immediately followed by a feeling of utter despair as it dawned on me that I would never see my father again, that I was completely alone in the world and, onerous as my existence had been, suddenly with no purpose in life. I desperately needed a prop, anything! My father's cigarettes were there. He didn't need them any more. I did. I had no intention of smoking more than one and I've hated being a smoker all these years."

That lady had tears in her eyes throughout that story, and by the end of it, so did everyone else in the group. Before the end of the clinic, she made another statement that really affected me. She said:

"I read your book two years ago and It's taken me that long to pluck up enough courage to come and see you. I know I shall never smoke again, but something is worrying me. In the book you described that nicotine monster inside the smoker's body. I knew that there wasn't an actual living being inside my body and that you were just helping me to focus my hatred. But when I used to watch my father coughing and spluttering, yet still smoking, I just couldn't understand it. It was as if some evil demon had possessed his body. When he died he looked so peaceful and contented. It seemed as if the parasitic demon needed a new host and found me. I have children of my own now and I'm terrified that if I purge that monster from body, it will prey on one of my children."

185

I sympathise with that lady. Her fear might appear irrational to you or me, but not if we had undergone the experience that she had. At times it has appeared to me like a living monster. The fact that it isn't, that the trap is mainly mental, doesn't detract from the evil. The truth is the smoking disease is far more contagious just because it is mainly mental.

A few years ago a top actress, I think it was Judy Dench, was playing the part of a very heavy smoker, and being a true professional, she had observed that when non-smokers try to smoke, they never quite look the part. So she was teaching herself to smoke properly. I can remember the interviewer's look of horror. He said: "Aren't you worried that you'll become hooked?" She said: "No, they are absolutely disgusting. I could never become hooked on them." I could imagine every smoker viewing saying to themselves: "I don't believe it. How do you think everyone else got hooked?"

Another case was of a youngster that I had helped to cure. He was made redundant and started smoking again. He came back to see me. I asked:

"Did smoking get you another job? Did it improve your financial situation?"

"It wasn't that. I didn't even want to smoke again. But I was miserable. My mother said: 'You haven't got any pleasures in life.' So she bought me a packet."

"I didn't realise your mother was a smoker."

"She isn't!"

Even non-smokers believe that smokers get some sort of pleasure from smoking. After all, why shouldn't they? Smokers keep telling them, that they do. This is why I'm better off than non-smokers. They know that overall they are far better off than smokers, but they have also been subjected to the brainwashing. Like most ex-smokers, they still believe that they are missing out. What's worse, they are still vulnerable. Whereas I know:

I'M MISSING NOTHING! I COULD NEVER GET HOOKED AGAIN!

Now let us examine another group of people that can have a strong influence on your continued success:

OTHER SMOKERS

CHAPTER 23

Other Smokers

The bulk of the authorities and so-called experts believe that youngsters still get hooked in this enlightened age because of massive cigarette advertising. The tobacco companies refute this claim, and much as it hurts me to do so, I agree with them.

If you study individual cases including your own, 99% of smokers get hooked because of the influence of their smoking friends, colleagues and relatives, probably in that order. If you do manage to escape from the pit and get hooked again, it is usually for exactly the same reason or because whenever you suffer a severe crisis in the future, there is always a smoker present only too ready to tempt you. There isn't a car accident in history at which a smoker hasn't been first on the scene to offer the shocked victim a cigarette. For every samaratan trying desperately to extract you from the burning wreckage, there are at least three more attempting to shove cigarettes down your throat.

As adolescents our parents give us grave and serious lectures about the dangers of sex, drinking and smoking. It appears to be basically sound advise, completely negated by the fact that they hypocritically spend most of their lives participating in all three. Why should we be surprised when our children act like dogs straining on the leash to get launched?

There are many pathetic aspects to smoking, not least of which is that every smoker is a Jekyl and Hyde. Dr. Jekyl is the friend and colleague that works next to you. For the last three months he has been continually complaining that he can no longer concentrate because of the noise of your chest. For the few moments that he isn't doing that, he is reminding you exactly how much you are now spending each year on cigarettes and cannot believe that you are unaware of what a filthy disgusting habit it really is. No, he's not an HTT, he's a smoker. Not only that but he smokes twice as many as you do. In fact it was him that persuaded you that there couldn't be any harm in having just one at the firm's last Christmas party. That helpful piece of advice ended five years of freedom from the 'weed'.

You assume that Dr. Jekyl has a guilty conscience about getting you hooked again and is now trying to make ammends. You assume wrongly. He is lecturing you because he really wants to stop himself, but doesn't believe that he'll succeed with you puffing away all day beside him. But he begins to get through to you. You have a particularly heavy bout of socialising over the weekend, your mouth feels like a cesspit and you decide that's it.

You arrive at work and can't wait to tell Dr. Jekyl the good news. But Dr. Jekyl no longer works there. His place has been taken by this man called Hyde. His physical resemblance to Jekyl is quite uncanny. He even smokes just as heavily as Jekyl did. But it can't be Jekyl. Jekyl only offered his cigarettes to non-smokers. If you went down on bended knee and begged him for one he would never relent. But Hyde keeps leaving his open packet within arm's reach of you and telling you that in no way does he want to tempt you, but if the withdrawal gets too bad, feel quite free to help yourself. Hyde is obviously a much nicer type than Jekyl but you wish he didn't always seem to be breathing the smoke in your direction. You also wish that he didn't keep on about what pleasures are there left in life and what's the point of being healthier and having more money if you are going to be miserable and as he continually points out, have they actually proved the connection with lung cancer, and even if they have, you've got to die from something, you could step under a bus tomorrow. Yes there's no doubt he's a much nicer type than Jekyl. All the same you wish that Jekyl was back!

This is an extension of the schizophrenia. Be the smoker your best friend or worst enemy, part of his brain wants you to fail. As more and more smokers leave the sinking ship, those remaining are terrified that they will be the sole remaining smoker in the group. Another part of that smoker's brain wants you to succeed, because if you can do it, perhaps he can as well. Unfortunately his efforts almost guarantee your failure.

One of the most pathetic incidents that happened to me after I had successfully stopped for several years, was that a very good friend would offer me cigarettes at social occasions. He really couldn't believe that I had no need or desire to smoke whether socialising or not. Now if you consider that I had once reached the stage that I almost died from smoking, you might think that it was not a very friendly thing to do. If you further consider that my profession, indeed my whole purpose in life is to help other smokers to get free, and the effect it would have on them if I were to start smoking again, you would be excused for thinking that far from being a friend, he was a very evil man. You would be wrong. He is one of the nicest people I have ever met. It wasn't really him acting, it's what this insidious weed does to otherwise pleasant, honest people of integrity.

This particular friend was one of those smokers that never smoked before lunch. When the connection between lung cancer and smoking was first established, the medical authorities said it was the early morning cigarettes that did the real damage and many smokers decided not to smoke either before breakfast or lunch. It's quite amazing how we just accept what doctors tell us without question. After all, a cigarette is a cigarette, why should it be more harmful first thing in the morning than at any other time? I presume it was because the early morning cigarettes were the ones that made us cough. This would actually make them less harmful. In any case the coughing was not because it's early morning, but because when smokers go 8 hours without smoking, they lose part of their immunity to the poisonous effects.

In any event, this friend decided that he would not smoke the first cigarette of the day until after lunch. I failed to make him understand that if you go all night without a cigarette, when you wake up you have gone 8 hours without nicotine, and that first cigarette, even though it makes you cough will appear to be very precious. If you don't smoke before lunch, you have now gone 14 hours without nicotine and the illusion of pleasure will be even greater. However, on holidays I noticed that he would light up immediately after breakfast. I said:

"I thought you didn't smoke until after lunch?"

"Normally I don't eat breakfast, so this is really lunch."

Such is the poetic licence of the drug addict. The other thing which didn't seem to occur to that smoker was that lunch used to start at 1 o'clock, over the years it gradually crept forward to 11 o'clock. In fact that friend was in danger of becoming an alcoholic in order to start smoking, and in consequence drinking, at 11 o'clock.

His wife claimed to be a casual smoker. She would only smoke to keep her husband company at social events, or so she said. Eventually she contracted a smoking related disease and decided to quit. Naturally I offered my help. She explained that she was only a casual smoker and wouldn't need help. It was torture for me to watch her attempting to quit by using the willpower method. It's like watching someone drown when all you have to do is to reach out and pull them out of the water, but they won't let you.

Anyway, to her credit, after 3 months she had more or less kicked it. It was just the one after a meal that continued to worry her. Her husband would light up and she would say: "I could murder for a cigarette now." He would tell her not to be stupid, and congratulate her on how well she had done. I would sit there thinking: "It would help her if you didn't light that cigarette." But I know what it's like when your a smoker, particularly the one after a meal. After about 6 months he had just lit up and his wife said: "I've kicked it completely now. I haven't got the slightest urge to smoke a cigarette, in fact you look ridiculous with that thing stuck in your mouth." Joyce and I congratulated her. I said: "You've gone the wrong way about it, but all credit to you, the important thing is that you kicked it. You're free!" To my surprise her husband was silent. I knew that they were both very worried that the disease that she had been afflicted with might recur.

Occasionally in old black and white films, the hero would light two cigarettes simultaneously and pass one to the heroine. There's a very famous shot of Paul Henreid doing it. As a teenager I used to practice doing it. It looks easy, but believe me it's not as simple as it appears. You tend to light one cigarette half way up. The first time I accomplished the feat with any semblance of panache, I handed the girl the cigarette and she said she didn't fancy one. Just being a smoker can make you feel ridiculous. But I assure you that the most ridiculous object on this planet, is a smoker that has a burning cigarette in each hand and doesn't know what to do with either of them. I've heard many bizarre stories about incidents that caused smokers to become hooked, but I once asked Danny Baker, who was presenting a programme about smoking on TV, why he had never been a smoker? No sooner were the words out of my mouth than I could have bitten off my tongue. It wasn't a stupid question to me, because he was clearly both mentally and physically a very strong man and in a profession in which the temptation to smoke is almost irresistible, and I found it hard to believe he had never been hooked. However, it immediately struck me as being an incredibly stupid thing to ask of a non-smoker. I must just as well asked him why he never became a heroin addict? To my surprise, instead of coming back with some sort of facetious reply, he said: "When I was a youngster, I fancied this girl at a dance. She smoked so I bought a packet of cigarettes, went over to offer her one and they all fell out onto the floor. My friends guffawed and I felt so stupid that I never tried again." Now that's what I call lucky!

Anyway back to my friend at the restaurant. To my amazement, a few minutes later he was doing a 'Paul Henried' and handing a lighted cigarette to his wife. I couldn't believe what I was seeing. It looks corny enough when Paul Henried does it, but to watch a 50 year old man whose wife had just completed the trauma of quitting using the willpower method, to be actually handing her a lighted cigarette. I said:

"What are you doing?"

"She's done so well, she deserves a reward!"

By now you must be convinced that he was either evil, selfish or just plain stupid. I assure you he is none of these things. That's just the effect that this awful drug has on us. Just consider the psychology. When his wife was moping for cigarettes, he was still able to smoke. He wasn't being deprived. But suddenly the situation has changed.

Three people on the table have no need or desire to smoke. They see it as it really is: ridiculous and stupid. The lone smoker also begins to feel ridiculous and stupid. So what does he do? He does what all drug addicts try to do. He feels embarrassed and his warped mind induces him to try to drag some other soul into the pit. The extent of the fear and panic that this insidious drug creates, is such as to block his mind to the fact that the person he is trying to persuade, is someone he loves dearly and that his action might actually kill them.

In Chapter 10 I described how youngsters get hooked by accepting hand-outs from friends and then feel obligated to buy cigarettes. To me the most nauseating aspect of all about smoking is watching an adult who had been quite happily free for a number of years, going through the same procedure. A friend warns them:

"You'll get hooked again."

"No way! I'd never buy them."

Already the insidious 'weed' has blocked their mind to any sense of decency or manners. Would we borrow, food, clothing or money from our friends and be rude enough to declare at the same time that we haven't the slightest intention of returning the favour? Are we so rude because we sense that, far from being offended by our bad manners, the friend is secretly enjoying the fact that we *needed a cigarette*?

I loathe watching these situations. The one person that cannot see that they are already hooked again is the ex-addict who, like a dog awaiting a titbit from its master, dutifully clings to the *friend* that is pushing the filth, awaiting the next hand-out. I cannot stand the phoney, patronising attitude of that friend who is saying: "I really feel bad about this. You were doing so well." At the same time struggling to keep the grin off of his face, relishing the power that he holds as his victim squirms and thinking: "You never really got free. You just went through a penance for a few years. Welcome back into the pit." Momentarily forgetting that he is also a prisoner of the insidious 'weed'!

Eventually, the pusher will pull up the drawbridge. He absolutely refuses point blank to supply you with any more cigarettes, not because he begrudges the cost, but because he suspects that you are getting hooked again. This is shortly followed by the moment I hate most of all, when the person who a few days earlier was actually free, the person who swore that they would never buy cigarettes again has the choice of going without, or buying a packet and being humiliated in front of their family and friends. By this stage there is only one winner:

NICOTINE

We try to mitigate our humiliation with the excuse that we only bought the packet to replace the cigarettes that we had borrowed. We don't even kid ourselves let alone anyone else. Then comes that awful moment, you've sneaked off to buy that first packet, you eagerly light up that first cigarette, it tastes absolutely foul, you are suddenly hit with a feeling of remorse and horror:

YOU ARE BACK IN THE PIT AGAIN!

You throw the cigarette down in disgust and stamp on it as if it's a deadly snake. You flush the packet down the toilet. A few hours later you go through exactly the same routine, then again and again, until you accept that you are indeed the slave of the 'weed'; and smokers say to me in tones ranging from surprise to disbelief: "Do you really not miss smoking and never crave cigarettes?" Miss them? I still cannot get over the joy of being free!

Anyway, back to my friend doing his 'Paul Henreid' act. To her credit, his wife never uttered a word, but the look that she gave him spoke volumes. He realised that he had done something very stupid and tried to pass the whole incident off as a joke. The trouble was each of us knew that it was no joke. Each of us sat there wishing the floor would open up and swallow us. The incident itself was embarrassing enough, even worse is that I am occasionally haunted by the stupid look that my friend had on his face. How much worse must it have been for his wife? But the real torture must be with my friend. To have to go through the rest of his life remembering the misery and effort his wife went through during the 6 months and at the end of it, when she had finally got free, he actually tried to get her hooked again! Such is the awful fear that the weed instils in its victims.

A typical example of the demoralising effect that other smokers can have on people attempting to quit, was the case of a mother, one of the first visitors to our Birmingham clinic. She arrived in tears about as depressed as it is possible for a smoker to be. She also left in tears, and I hasten to add, tears of joy, which spread to the remainder of the clinic, including me. She gave me a big kiss as she departed in a state of euphoria, already a happy non-smoker. She visited her daughter and son-in-law the same evening to inform them of the good news. Her son-in-law had decided to quit at the same time, but of course, he was using the willpower method and his mother-in-law's obvious delight only served to increase his feeling of deprivation. He said: "Why are you getting so excited? You haven't even stopped for a day!" The effect was catastrophic. The four hours that I had spent helping that lady out of the pit were destroyed in 2 seconds. She didn't smoke in their presence, but the seed of doubt had been sewn. It germinated, festered and grew. Fortunately she came back to me and learned the lesson to ignore other smokers.

In Chapter 19 I spoke about uncle Fred, the character that haunts every phone-in that I do. In fact there are two versions of uncle Fred. I Have already dealt with the version that eventually quits. But by far the most despicable version is the variety that smoked 40 a day of the strongest brand of non-tipped cigarettes since the age of 14 and enjoyed every one of them, point blank refused to quit, lived until he was 80 and what's more, never had a day's illness in his life. Incidentally, I call him uncle Fred purely because every smoker seems to have one, and if they haven't, they unashamedly adopt someone else's uncle Fred.

The point is every smoker has to have an uncle Fred, we need him to counteract these awful statistics which society insists on pestering us with whether we wish to hear them or not. We also cling just as doggedly to his wife auntie Jane, who never smoked a cigarette in her life yet died from lung cancer at the age of forty. Isn't it incredible how otherwise logical, scientific, intelligent people happily accept results of a pole based on just one person yet refuse to accept the evidence of statistics based on thousands of people? Such is the warped mind of the drug addict.

The uncle Fred that phoned during the last programme that I was involved in was from a particularly virulent strain. Honesty forces me to credit him because he did declare that he was involved in the tobacco industry. He also claimed that he was in his seventies, had smoked 40 cigarettes a day for over 50 years and had never had a day's illness in his life. Pause for a moment. Why have none of these uncle Fred's ever had a day's illness in their lives? Why do we just accept these clichés without question? Do you really believe that any human being on this planet, be they smoker or non-smoker, has never had a day's illness? That means that they have never had a cold, flu, diarrhoea, measles or chicken pox, not even a headache? I think that we would be justified in believing that anyone that claims that he has never had a day's illness in his life, is someone that is prepared to bend the truth.

This particular uncle Fred had one attempt to stop smoking. Shortly after stopping he began to feel unwell (already he confirms his lie). His doctor could find nothing wrong with him. The man claimed he saw 3 separate Harley St. specialists (I'll leave you to judge whether he exaggerated) none of whom could find anything wrong with him. The third specialist asked him if he had changed his life style recently and being informed that he had stopped smoking, advised uncle Fred that was the sole reason for his problems. Needless to say, uncle Fred started smoking again and lived happily ever after.

Now I appeal to you, can anyone be naive enough to believe that story. I'm not disputing that he was miserable when he stopped smoking. So was I whenever I tried to stop by using the willpower method. But I didn't need my doctor and 3 Harley St. specialists to tell me why I was miserable. But wasn't he proving my point? They couldn't find anything wrong with him. That's because there wasn't anything wrong with him other than he thought he couldn't enjoy life or handle life without cigarettes.

I am not denying that uncle Freds exist even though their lives are not quite the bliss that they and we try to imagine. They are strong people, they have to be in order to develop an immunity to the poisons. This is why non-smokers are more affected by passive smoking, they haven't any resistance to the poison. Auntie Jane probably contracted lung cancer from the filth that uncle Fred had been belching forth for 30 years.

The other aspect that distorts the uncle Fred syndrome is this: if you blindfold 1,000 people and told them to keep crossing the M1 all day, at the end of the day you might have one survivor. The survivor would be very relieved to be alive and convinced they were indestructible. Now if they had some special reason for actually wanting other people to cross the road blindfold, they might well argue: "See I've proved my point! There is really no danger in crossing the road without looking." Unfortunately, you will not be able to hear the opinion of the remaining 999.

Uncle Fred exists, but bear in mind, he was a very lucky man. He was also a very strong man. He had to be. The reason that he spends his whole life ringing up phone-in programmes is because he no longer has any friends. They all died premature deaths due to their smoking. That is very unfortunate for Fred. It is even more unfortunate for the rest of us. If they had been able to ring up and give the other side of the story, we might not have been so hoodwinked by all the uncle Freds!

My father was a strong man, my sister was a strong woman. They both died in their early fifties due to smoking. I am convinced that they would both be alive today had they never smoked. I was a strong man. I know that I wouldn't have reached 50 had I continued to smoke and it is only through the grace of God that I live to tell the tale.

It is not tobacco advertising, but the influence of other smokers, that the tobacco industry manipulates to recruit new smokers and to drag ex-smokers back into the pit. It is a mistake to ignore the effect that peer pressure has on us. Unfortunately smokers do tend to be dominant people, not because they smoke, but because the trap is designed to catch that type of person. There is also the negative effect of being a non-smoker. When you are smoking you are positively doing something. It's easy to kid yourself into believing that you are receiving some genuine crutch or pleasure. But how can you sit there thinking: "I'm enjoying a non-smoke?"

IN FACT YOU CAN! I DO EVERY DAY OF MY LIFE!

It's simply a matter of seeing smoking as it actually is. Just as we are brainwashed from birth to see smoking through rose-coloured spectacles, so we have been brainwashed to see smokers in exactly the same way. We assume that they are all in control, enjoying their crutch or pleasure. Any weapon can be used for good or evil and just as other smokers can be a powerful weapon in getting and keeping us hooked, they can be an even more powerful influence in helping us to get free, and more importantly, to stay free.

The problem is that all smokers lie, not only to other people but also to themselves. They have to! We feel stupid enough being smokers even when we try to block our minds to the filth, the poison, the wheezing, the coughing, the slavery, the waste of money, the sheer idiocy of the whole business. If we had to face up to it, the whole thing would become unbearable. The problem is, we not only begin to believe our own lies, we believe the lies of other smokers. All that keeps us moping for cigarettes when we try to stop is the feeling that we are missing out, that we are being deprived.

You would expect smokers to change their tune once they had contracted one of the killer diseases caused by smoking, but usually it's the opposite. A few years ago a famous disc jockey contracted lung cancer. He bravely did not whinge about the fact, on the contrary, he said: "I enjoyed every one of those precious cigarettes!" But if you think more deeply about it, this would be the natural reaction. If we have to lie to ourselves when we only suffer the stupidity of risking horrendous diseases, how much more necessary is it to keep up the pretence when:

WE'VE LEFT IT TOO LATE TO DO ANYTHING ABOUT IT!

Have you ever heard a smoker that hasn't yet contracted lung cancer say: "I've enjoyed every precious cigarette that I have smoked!" If you feel stupid being a smoker now, just think how much more stupid you will feel if you left it too late. You'd have to exaggerate the pleasures of smoking even more in order to live with yourself. I'm sorry, I meant in order to die with yourself!

Perhaps you believe that smokers are like racing drivers, in that they weigh up the rewards and are prepared to accept the risks? If a driver were able to know in advance that he would die if he entered a particular race, do you believe that he would still enter it? Be honest with yourself. If you knew for certain that the next cigarette you smoked would be the one to trigger off cancer in your lungs, would you smoke it? Most people that accept these risks don't really accept them at all, they just think:

"IT WON'T HAPPEN TO ME"

Do you really believe that there is a smoker living, that before they smoked that first cigarette, actually weighed up the one in four chance that it would kill them and consciously accepted that risk before lighting it? If not why are there millions of smokers consciously accepting that risk now? There's only one logical reason, not only don't they accept the risks, they can't contemplate even to think about them. They are not smoking because they choose to smoke, but because like the flies trapped in a pitcher plant, they believe they cannot escape

The effect that the disc jockey's statement might have had on existing smokers, or youngsters that might have been contemplating smoking that first cigarette is very unfortunate. The message really was: "Even if they do kill you, the pleasure is well worth it." I'm sure that he wasn't consciously trying to broadcast that message, but merely trying to cope with death as bravely as he could. I admire his bravery, but he was really just another extreme example of the depths to which this insidious weed will reduce its victims.

However, I admire even more the bravery of the few exceptional smokers that have not only been able to die bravely from deaths which they knew were caused through smoking, but had the additional courage to admit that for most of their lives they were stupid. It takes real courage to admit that you are stupid, particularly when you know that stupidity has cost you your life. Yul Brynner had the guts to admit it after he knew that it would kill him. I gather that the 'Marlboro' cowboy has also contracted lung cancer and is now an active anti-smoking campaigner – power to his elbow! If only all smokers would stop trying to justify their stupidity by trying to kid themselves and other people that they get some genuine pleasure or crutch from smoking, they would all soon realise that they won't be missing out or feel deprived if they quit.

Perhaps you are not convinced. If so just consider this piece of market research:

1. How many non-smokers would you say that there are in the world that wish they were smokers?
2. How many ex-smokers do you think that there are in the world that wish they were still smokers? I'll grant that you know several ex-smokers that still crave the occasional cigarette, but why don't they smoke it? Is it because they are terrified that they will become a smoker again? After all, they have the choice they could become smokers again if they really wanted to!
3. How many smokers do you know that, if they now had the choice to go back to the time when they lit that first fatal cigarette, would choose not to have lit it?

If you have been honest, I think you will find that the result of your market research is:

NUMBER THAT WANT TO BE NON-SMOKERS: TOTAL WORLD
POPULATION!
NUMBER THAT WANT TO BE SMOKERS: ZILCH!
That's a fairly conclusive result. But if you *still* do not believe me,
consider this: for years I have been making an offer to so-called
confirmed smokers. I'm talking about a smoker that isn't worried
about the health scares, the money, the slavery or the social stigma. I
have not met one of these smokers for years, and frankly, I don't
believe that there are any left in the UK. A few years ago, there were
many. I was one of them.

I used to get into arguments with such smokers, or perhaps I should
say heated discussions. If it were a wealthy person, I would say: "I
can't believe that you aren't worried about the money?" Their eyes
would light up. If I had attacked them on the grounds of health or
social stigma, they would have been in trouble. But on money they
were on secure ground, it was worth it for their crutch or pleasure.
Curiously, even smokers that can't afford to smoke don't appear to be
worried about the money.

I would then say: "I don't believe you. As a 20 a day smoker you
will spend about £30,000 in your life on cigarettes. What will you do
with that money? You won't even just set light to it. You will use it to
suffer a lifetime of bad breath, stained teeth, wheezing and coughing,
slavery and deprivation. You'll only be aware of the vast majority of
cigarettes that you smoke when you are either choking yourself, or
getting into a panic because you are running low, and you will spend a
large part of your life feeling deprived because you are not allowed to
smoke. You'll spend that money to risk horrendous diseases, to go
through life being despised by other people and, worst of all, to go
through life despising yourself. I do not believe that you think that
£30,000 is worth it!"

It soon becomes obvious that the smoker had never even considered
it as a lifetime's expense. For most smokers, the price of a packet is bad
enough. Occasionally, we work out what it costs us a day, or even a
week, or a year, and we only do that when we are trying to quit. Over
a lifetime the cost is unthinkable.

At this stage the smoker tends to become aggressive, and say
something like: "The money is nothing to me. I can afford it. It's worth
it for the pleasure." I say: "Okay, I accept what you say, but you are an
intelligent person, I'll make you an offer that you cannot refuse. You
pay me a year's smoking money in advance, and I will provide you
with free cigarettes for the rest of your life!"

Now this is a very generous offer. Bear in mind that I am not talking
to smokers expressing a desire to stop, but to those who say they have
no intention to quit, that *enjoy* being smokers and intend to go on
enjoying being smokers for the rest of their lives. Now supposing I had

I said: "Give me a year's electricity money in advance and I will provide you with free electricity for the rest of your life!" Obviously they wouldn't believe me. But supposing it were a genuine offer? If it were, I would be inundated with acceptances. Yet I have been making the smoking offer for years on Radio and TV programmes. It was included in 'EASYWAY'. When PENGUIN took the book over, I thought that they would ask me to omit the offer. But they didn't. I've lost count of the number of copies of the book that PENGUIN have sold. All I do know is, not one single smoker has ever taken me up on the offer. Not one single smoker has even taken the offer a stage further to say: "How do I know that I can trust you?" Several smokers have said: "I might take you up on that." Not a single smoker ever has!

Do you not find that surprising? After all, even if they only continued to smoke for a year, they would be no worse off. A longer period would accrue considerable financial benefits. The truth is, even confirmed smokers that try to convince themselves that they are in control and enjoying their 'habit', when the gauntlet's thrown down, they cannot even face up to smoking for only one more year, let alone the rest of their lives!

Whenever we have to make a decision, we weigh up the pros and cons, sometimes it is very difficult to arrive at the correct decision, particularly in trying to compare, one refrigerator or washing machine with another. However, If you go through the same exercise with whether you would rather be a smoker or a non-smoker, the answer is a dozen times over:

NON-SMOKER!!

No smoker smokes because they choose to or want to, just one thing keeps us smoking:

FEAR!

It doesn't dawn on us that non-smokers don't have that fear and that the cigarette, far from relieving that fear, actually causes it. So great is that fear that, for most of our lives it blocks our minds to the other fears created by the weed. The fear of early death and bad health, the fear of slavery, and the fear of squandering hard earned money.

Have you heard of **FOREST**? It stands for the Freedom Organisation For the Right to Enjoy Smoking Tobacco. It was an organisation formed by really hard core smokers in an attempt to resist the tremendous pressure our society has been subjecting the poor smoker to in recent years. It is an organisation that I had much sympathy with when I was a confirmed smoker. It is an organisation that I would still have sympathy with if I believed it was organised by genuine confirmed smokers. In reality it is merely a front for the tobacco industry.

I thought the real test for my PENGUIN offer would be to make it to members of FOREST. Surely, if they really were the happy smoking community that they claimed to be, they would jump at the opportunity. The problem was, in spite of the fact that a representative of FOREST appears on practically every programme about smoking, I couldn't find one member of FOREST. None of my acquaintances had ever met one and I couldn't find them in the telephone directory. Then chance took a hand. About 4 National No Smoking Days ago, I was invited to appear on national TV . Anyone that was in any way remotely connected with smoking was there and before the programme commenced, I was introduced to the Managing Director of FOREST. I thought: "Let's find out how sincere this man is." I put the offer to him. He took the wind out of my sails by replying: "I would love to take you up on the offer, however I'm a non-smoker!" The penny dropped. How clever to have a non-smoker as leader of the group. Someone who is completely unbiased and solely interested in the right of individuals to freedom. It seemed very strange to me for an organisation like FOREST to have a salaried managing director, but not so strange when you have experience of how the tobacco industry works.

On National No Smoking Day 1992, I was interviewed on LBC by Michael Parkinson. His previous guest was the current managing director of FOREST. Although I was appalled by his comments, I could not help but admire the ingenious manner in which he manipulated the arguments. I have learnt much from these techniques, and if only I were as clever in putting the case against smoking as they are in promoting what appears to be a completely lost cause, I'm sure I would already have achieved my ambition. He was a very glib young man and started off by explaining that Hitler was the first person to attempt to ban smoking. Can you see the sinister implications? It's the thin edge of the wedge. Today institutions like ASH and QUIT are trying to remove our right to smoke, if we let them get away with it tomorrow they'll be exterminating millions of innocent people.

I am extremely grateful to Michael for allowing me to question the man. The strange thing is that we were in fact in complete agreement. I believe in freedom of choice, providing it does not reduce the quality of life of other people. I'm against this comparatively recent trend to persecute smokers, partly in principle and partly because it makes it harder for them to quit. The only point on which I disagree with the managing director of FOREST is that his motives have nothing to do with freedom of choice. He is merely a paid vassal of the tobacco industry. Whether it be inadvertantly, or as I strongly suspect deliberately, he overlooks the following points:

1. Smokers have no freedom anyway. They do not choose to become hooked any more than a fish chooses to become hooked. They are lured into taking the bait! Would anyone dream of forming an organisation for the rights of fish to remain on the hook?
2. Smokers do not enjoy smoking tobacco. They only think they do because they are miserable when they are not allowed to smoke.
3. The only real connection between Hitler and smoking is that smoking now brings about the premature death of two and a half million innocent people on this planet every year. The 'Holocaust' is undoubtedly generally regarded as the greatest crime against the human race in history and quite rightly. But the perpetrators have where possible, been tried and punished. But the tobacco companies are now killing people at an even greater rate. They have already killed more people on this planet than all the wars of history combined, including the 'Holocaust'. Bear in mind, it is from but the last few generations, since mass production of cigarettes, that this deadly toll has been exacted. But not only are the tobacco companies not treated as criminals, not only are they legal, even respectable, they are actually allowed to advertise their lethal filth!
4. What right does the managing director of FOREST, who has never smoked in his life, have to advertise the No.1 killer disease in western society? When I asked him whether he thought heroin should be made legal, he refused to answer. Why had his great principles for the freedom of the individual been suddenly so fragile. After all, injecting heroin doesn't affect innocent people. What about the rights of non-smokers to be able to breathe air free of pollutants contained in tobacco excrement?
5. Most important of all, why was this man only interested in the rights of smokers to shorten their lives? Surely there are thousands of far more worthwhile causes that he could have used his considerable talents to protect. After all, he isn't even a smoker himself. I will let you decide whether you think his motives are genuine, or whether you think he is merely doing the job that he is paid to do. Perhaps I judge him harshly. His job is the equivalent to persuading people to stay in a holiday camp which is in fact a concentration camp. As he has never visited the camp himself, it is possible that he is more ignorant than evil. I hope he sleeps well at night. I hated being an accountant, I realise now how lucky I was compared to him.

Now, just as you need to start seeing the cigarettes themselves, not as society has brainwashed you to see them, but as they actually are, so you need to start seeing smokers themselves, not as the chic, sophisticated adults, in complete control, but as they actually are:

MISERABLE, PATHETIC, PANIC-STRICKEN, DRUG ADDICTS!

Now let us discuss a special class of other smokers. Smokers that can have an enormous effect, be it conscious or subconscious, on getting us hooked and keeping us hooked.

OUR HEROES & HEROINES

CHAPTER 24

Our Heroes & Heroines

I don't suppose a single youngster has been tempted to light that first cigarette after watching a tramp picking up a dog-end from the gutter, watching an old boy coughing and spluttering or a typical 'Fag Ash Lil'. These are all smokers near the bottom of the pit, why on earth should we expect teenagers to relate to them, particularly when they are being bombarded with the other side of the picture: young, strong, sophisticated, wealthy, successful and attractive people that are smoking? I'm not talking about cigarette adverts. I'm talking about real, live, intelligent people: TV & film stars, pop stars and sporting personalities. Obviously youngsters will be influenced by this side of the picture, but they don't realise that it is phoney. **COMPLETE ILLUSION!**

Look at one of those typical pictures that depicts a beautiful, elegant, sophisticated lady, or a macho square-jawed, successful man smoking a cigarette. Now place your finger over the cigarette. Does that lady look any less sophisticated? Does the man appear to be less macho? The cigarette wasn't providing sophistication, a sophisticated woman:

WAS SELLING YOU POISON!

The coughing, spluttering old man and the 'Fag Ash Lil' are the **REALITY** – created by the cigarette.

What possible sense can there be in imposing TV bans on adverts which no one watched any way, when the actual programmes seem to be dominated by smokers? It wouldn't be quite so bad if it were just the old Bogart type films, but when an incredibly attractive and sophisticated woman like Joanna Lumley smokes on TV, just one shot must do more damage than a thousand adverts.

Who actually insists that the cigarette is essential to every scene? The writer, the producer, the director? Or is it that the stars themselves are so hooked that they are unable to act without smoking? Or might the tobacco companies have some influence here. After all, if we keep banning more and more of their ineffective adverts, the more money they have to promote their filth in more subtle and more effective ways. Perhaps you think they wouldn't stoop to such levels. Don't be naive! I wasn't the greatest fan of Mrs. Thatcher, but even I didn't believe that she would sell her soul to the tobacco industry for £50,000!

There is no doubt that Hollywood has a lot to answer for, not only for getting millions of individuals hooked, but for creating and perpetuating the illusory image about smoking. I have no doubt that its indoctrination was responsible not only for my capture, but for most of my friends. Many ladies attending our clinics have confessed to spending hours in front of the mirror, practising the Marlene Dietrich or Lauren Bacall effect.

No doubt the Bogart image helped to entrap me. But we rapidly mature out of the influence of those early celebrities. It was not long before I began to despise smokers that had a permanent cigarette dangling from their lips. However, that didn't prevent me from remaining one of them. The problem is that there are always an ample supply of equally influential role models in the stage of maturity that we've moved into. I eventually reached the stage where I had exhausted all the possible excuses to justify my continuing to smoke. I then used Bertrand Russell as my excuse. Lest you suspect that I'm trying to give the impression that I'm an intellectual, let me make it quite clear, I have never read a single word that he has written – in fact I'm not even sure what his profession was. I knew only two things about him: that he was a genius and that he had a permanent dog-end dangling from his lips. He provided me with the excuse that I needed: "I don't understand why I smoke, but this man's a genius. There must be a justifiable reason, otherwise he wouldn't smoke."

Genius or not, I now realise that he did it for the same reason that every other smoker does it: **HE WAS CONNED!** My hero Sherlock Holmes also had a great influence on me. Although Conan Doyle was himself a doctor, I related him not to Dr. Watson in the stories, but, because he had conceived the plots, I attributed to him an intellect and deductive powers equal to those of Holmes himself. He talks of: "A THREE PIPE PROBLEM!" Absolute proof to me that smoking assisted concentration.

Another curious irony. I'm convinced that I became a chain-smoker because I hated being an accountant. In case you have formed the impression that I am running the profession down, let me assure you I am not. I can conceive of no finer training to enable a young person to obtain early insight into what business and life generally are about. With most instruction, you are trained to accept what your elders and betters tell you. Accountancy training teaches you to be sceptical about everything. You learn to read the relevance of the way people say things as opposed to the actual meaning of their words. If someone says: "I'm almost 100% certain." Those words imply that they are 99%

certain. What they are actually telling you is: "I should have checked this out, but I don't want to give the impression that I neglected to do so." They've used the word certain to tell you that they are uncertain. You also learn that what people omit to say can tell you more than what they actually say. Holmes obviously had a great influence in keeping me hooked, but without the influence of those fascinating stories combined with my accountancy training, I could never have solved the mystery of the world's biggest confidence trick. Pupils should have the option to read Sherlock Holmes instead of algebra. Not only would it be far more interesting, but an infinitely better training to improve their intelligence and to prepare them adequately to cope with the realities of life.

I'm not sure that I was consciously aware of the exact effect that Bogart, Russell, Holmes, Dennis Compton and the thousands of other exceptional people had on my life. This is the point: you don't have to be consciously aware of it, your subconscious brain will do the work for you. It's saying: "I can't be that stupid, all these other people are doing it, they are top of their professions. Smoking must help them. It certainly can't hinder them, otherwise they wouldn't do it."

I've said that it is not tobacco advertising that gets youngsters hooked. I believe the real damage that the advertising does is to negate the influences that might help to prevent youngsters from getting hooked. How many lives have been saved per annum by the introduction of compulsory seat belts? It might be three or three thousand who knows? It doesn't matter. Our leaders are caring people. They make sure that we don't kill ourselves whether we are prepared to take the risk or not. Total egg production was banned after only about five people died from salmonella. So these statistics that the medical profession perpetually bombards smokers with cannot possibly be true. If they were, our caring government would surely ban not only advertising, but the sale of tobacco products?

We need to be aware of the influence that role models have not only on our children and grandchildren, but on ourselves. There's good old Jimmy Saville. As nice a man as you could wish to meet, always at the forefront of charitable work, marathon runner, kiddies friend. Jim'll fix it! Can't someone fix it so that he isn't always portrayed with that stupid cigar stuck in his face? What sort of example is that to kiddies? Can we really expect children to see smoking as the killer it really is, when a cartoon character like Popeye has a pipe permanently stuck in his mouth, and does that pipe serve any purpose whatsoever, other than to perpetuate the myth that there is something normal or natural about smoking?

There is this constant argument that the proliferation of drugs, sex and violence depicted on TV does not affect the behaviour of youngsters. The programme merely reflects what is happening in modern society. If you believe that, you must also believe that all communication is completely ineffective, that all adverts are a waste of the advertiser's money, and that it was sheer coincidence that thousands of teenagers started having 'beatle' haircuts during the sixties. Such thinking is clearly ludicrous. It would mean that our environment or upbringing had no effect on us whatsoever, that all our knowledge, views and actions were purely instinctive. It would also mean that a baby born to an English couple in England, that was adopted from birth by a Russian couple living in Russia, would grow up speaking perfect English and not understand Russian. The conclusions are mind-boggling. It would mean that all those years at school were a complete waste of time. It would also mean that we could all instinctively build a Rolls Royce or even a rocket to the moon.

The truth is the bulk of our knowledge, views and actions, whether they be true or false, good or evil, are a direct result of information which has been communicated to us from birth, no matter what form of communication was involved. Do you really believe that it's natural to smoke? That our creator intended us to smoke? Of course not! You only smoke now because you were subjected to false information. Indeed, correcting that situation is what this book is all about.

As a child, I remember before the days of television, whatever happened to be the current film at the local cinema would dominate our lives until the next week. If it were Arabian Nights, we would be Arabs with blankets and swords. Robin Hood would bring out the bows and arrows. A western would create swarms of cowboys and indians.

Nowadays, with the bans on regular TV advertising, the tobacco companies have taken to the association between glamorous sporting functions and even the sportsmen themselves with smoking. Do you really deny that youngsters are influenced by the fact that top dart players like Eric Bristow, or top snooker players like 'Hurricane' Higgins and Jimmy White smoke?

You not only need to be aware of the influence that these role models have on you, but you need to start looking a bit deeper. You need to do what you did to the picture of the sophisticated woman or macho man.

Visualise them without the cigarette. Would Joanna Lumley be less attractive? Would Jimmy White lose his charisma? Your smoking heroes and heroines became top of their profession, not because they smoked, but in spite of that fact. A few years ago, in sports like snooker or darts, the world champion was nearly always a smoker. Was this so surprising when 90% of them were smokers anyway? However things have now changed. Let us use snooker as an example. Who would you say were the most *naturally* talented snooker players of recent years? Many would say 'Hurricane' Higgins. I believe most would say Jimmy White. He would be my choice. Perhaps you don't agree. But what is unquestionable is that both possess immense talent and charisma and would no doubt have a strong influence on up and coming snooker players. Both are smokers!

However, who are the two players that have dominated the sport for over a decade? Steve Davis and Stephen Hendry, both non-smokers. It is difficult to argue whether talent is *natural* or acquired through practice and/or common sense. If I had to choose, I would say that both Higgins and White had more natural ability than Davis or Hendry, and that Davis and Hendry are better players mainly because they don't smoke!

If you question my judgement, all I can say is, observe the actual players. For years we have watched Higgins on television. He is the classic example of an advanced nicotine addict. He can no longer keep still. His face is permanently twitching. He drags on the cigarette so deeply that he almost swallows it. You can see him visibly trying to extract the nicotine. For years I watched him and formed the impression: "There's a nervous young man that the cigarette is helping to relax." I realise now that just as it was destroying my nerves, so it was gradually turning a world champion into a physical and mental wreck! Perhaps you know better, that in fact alcohol or stronger drugs were the cause of his demise. As I will explain later, they are all birds of the same feather. I still admire Higgins' talent, but his sportsmanship is at a level that will be difficult to emulate in any sport: he is the pits. Whether the weed had the same effect on his character as on his talent, I cannot say, but I know that it adversely affected mine.

For years I have had the pleasure of being entertained by Jimmy White. A few years ago, Jimmy was 'The Rock of Gibraltar'. There is always immense competition at the top level of any sport, but Jimmy's greatest attribute is probably the esteem in which he is held by his fellow professionals, not just for his skill but for sportsmanship. For years I have had the displeasure of watching Jimmy slip down the same slide as Higgins. To his credit, there is no evidence that it has affected his sportsmanship, but he now has the obvious permanent state of restlessness, the twitch in the facial expressions, the frequent jerk in the cueing action and the permanent grey complexion of the confirmed nicotine addict!

Why has such an obvious talent never won the world championship? Draw your own conclusions. He makes no secret of the fact that he is deeply concerned that he will go down in history as the greatest player never to do so. He even cut out the booze one year in an attempt to win it and almost succeeded. Time is running out Jimmy, come and see me, we are almost neighbours, I'll help you to remove the real block that stands between you and that title!

The other problem with smoking heroes and heroines is that again it's positive, you only have to see them light up on one single occasion and your brain, conscious or otherwise, registers: "Ah! A smoker!" Whereas the reverse doesn't apply, when you see someone not smoking, your brain doesn't register: "Ah! A non-smoker!" In that sense smokers are a far greater influence on youngsters than non-smokers. Would you say that Clint Eastwood is a smoker or a non-smoker? I have been assured that he is in fact a non-smoker. I still find it difficult to believe. I wonder how many youths have been tempted to smoke because of that permanent cigar butt stuck between his teeth in those spaghetti westerns. He doesn't even remove it to take a bath!

You need to be aware of the influence that your smoking heroes and heroines have on you. They might well be intelligent, attractive, charismatic, sophisticated, successful, strong and dominant people, but they are those things, not because they smoke, but in spite of them. See them and recognize them for the qualities that they possess, but in so doing, don't blind yourself to the fact that they are also:

MISERABLE, PATHETIC DRUG ADDICTS!

Perhaps you think that only simple-minded people would be influenced by the famous? If so I can do no better than conclude this chapter with the comments of Robin Hayley, about a recent TV series called 'Hooked' which attempted to shed light on all drug addictions including nicotine. Robin is himself a success of the Allen Carr method and an Oxford graduate. I've yet to meet a brighter man. He is senior therapist at our Birmingham clinic, which was featured in one of the programmes.

The programme itself was a nonsense. Indeed the series was the usual media hotchpotch of so-called experts perpetuating society's misconceptions about drug addiction. The series featured an Oxford don, Norman Stone who is a famous academic. A man who has reached the pinnacle of his profession. He made the following statement in his broad Scottish accent:

"There is no doubt about it. Smoking definitely helps with the concentration."

Let's assume it to be true. Can you in your wildest imagination conceive of the following conversation between interviewer and applicant for a job that involves a great deal of concentration:

"Do you smoke?"

"No."

"Are you prepared to take up smoking?"

"No."

"We would only insist that you smoke during actual periods of concentration, at other times you would be perfectly free not to smoke."

"The answer is still no!"

"Pity, in other ways you seem just the person we're looking for, but I'm afraid we can't use you."

The thought of such a conversation actually happening would be ludicrous even to Norman Stone who is obviously a highly intelligent man. I don't for one moment suppose that he encourages non-smoking students to smoke. On the contrary, like most intelligent people that have fallen into the nicotine trap, I assume that he advises smoking students to quit. Yet the logical consequence of Norman Stone's statement is the above conversation, and although such a conversation never has, or is likely to happen, nevertheless his influence must have directly or indirectly been the cause of disastrous consequences.

Try to imagine the effect that a person of the stature of Norman has on non-smoking undergraduates, merely because of his physical example of being a smoker. Imagine the tenfold effect it has when he actually justifies his action with logical reason. All very well you might say, but that won't influence students to smoke, what about the health risks? But Norman Stone is an intelligent man, he knows about the health risks. He must have weighed up the pros and cons and come to the conclusion that the advantages outweigh the disadvantages. Why else would he do it?

Why else indeed? Because, like me, Norman Stone wasn't really saying: "Smoking aids concentration." What he was really saying was: "Here I am, Norman Stone, a successful, intelligent academic. I'm a Scot, and we Scot's have a reputation of being down to earth, practical human beings that don't beat about the bush. I am responsible for the future and education of thousands of students. I'm very lucky, I have the opportunity to help shape the minds of the cream of British youth. However, I have a basic flaw in my make up: I'm one of these stupid, illogical smokers. How can I justify my stupidity to these youngsters that look up to me?" Only one way Norman, use the same excuse you've been using to justify it to yourself all these years, convince them that smoking helps you to concentrate.

I dread to think how many thousands of students Noman Stone has helped to trap, and then the sheer irresponsibility of perpetuating his misconceptions a million times over on national TV. I'll forgive Norman Stone. His statement arose from ignorance and fear rather than from malice. Fortunately, many undergraduates that were subjected to Norman Stone's example will have avoided the trap. But imagine the effect on them, here they are at Oxford, aspiring academics, future leaders of our land, in intense competition with each other during a very stressful period in their lives, being told by their mentor, possibly their idol:

SMOKING ASSISTS CONCENTRATION!

It would be a stupid statement to make even if were true, but since it isn't true,

IT'S NOTHING LESS THAN CRIMINAL!

Now consider the effect of Norman Stone's statement on undergraduates that have already fallen for the trap before they even came under his influence. Up to that point it had probably not even occurred to those students that smoking had anything to do with concentration. They were probably still at the stage where they thought that they were smoking just to appear adult or sophisticated. Many of them had probably already decided that they would stop smoking if they were lucky enough to be accepted at Oxford. They might have felt that they were already a financial drain on their parents or the state, or both without adding the cost of cigarettes. Imagine a father advising his child:

"Stop smoking now, while you can."

"But dad, Norman Stone smokes. He is one of the greatest brains in the country. Don't you realise that smoking helps concentration? Stop worrying dad. I'll stop, but it would be silly to do it now. I need to concentrate now more that at any time in my life. But once I've graduated and passed my exams and achieved the promotions that I need, then I'll stop."

As I said, I forgive Norman Stone. But what about the TV company that allowed him to perpetuate his misconceptions to millions of TV viewers? They spent 3 hours at our Birmingham clinic. They heard perfectly logical explanations to explain why smoking not only doesn't aid concentration, but actually impedes it. Why did they allow only one side of the argument to be presented, and if they were prepared to allow only one side to be presented, why did they only give the opinion of a layman, a person that knows nothing about smoking, no matter how eminent that person might be in other fields? Why did they choose to ignore the comments of the world's leading expert in that field? If their reason is that they only had time to present one point of view, then why, oh why must they always present the side that favours the tobacco industry even when that view is false?

WHY DID THEY DELIBERATELY MISLEAD THEIR VIEWERS?

Their reasons are immaterial, their actions are:

CRIMINAL NEGLIGENCE!

In 'EASYWAY' I briefly describe why smoking, far from assisting concentration, actually impedes it. However several highly intelligent ex-smokers that have understood and used my method successfully, still found concentration difficult without a cigarette. The subject requires some elaboration. Let us once and for ever lay this bogey of:

HOW CAN I CONCENTRATE WITHOUT A CIGARETTE?

CHAPTER 25

How Can I Concentrate Without a Cigarette?

I had reached the stage in my decline down the abyss in which I had come to the conclusion that it was only the inability to concentrate without a cigarette which actually prevented me stopping successfully. I could put up with the bad temper and misery. In fact I used to get a masochistic pleasure from the feeling of martyrdom. The social ones didn't bother me one iota. On the contrary, for someone so completely dependent on the weed, I got a great feeling of self-esteem at social events to be able to stand there completely naked, not literally of course, basking in the combination of admiration and disbelief in which my family and friends beheld me, as I proved that I wasn't the lilly-livered weakling that they thought I was.

Their admiration didn't last long and their disbelief proved fully justified. It was never long before I was chain-smoking again. But my undoing was my job. I earned a relatively high salary for using my brain, but without cigarettes my brain was about as effective as a blob of putty. I have already described an occasion when I used my annual holiday as a springboard. On another occasion I toyed with the idea of asking my boss if he would excuse me from any concentrated work for about a month. But he was a non-smoker and I knew he wouldn't understand, so I decided to do it anyway.

However there was one 10 minute job that I could neither delegate nor put off. It was the preparation of the monthly payroll. For the whole month I played naughts and crosses with myself, whatever. At odd times I would attempt to do the payroll, but each time the brain would switch off and I would leave it until the next day, until I could delay no longer. On the fatal day I sat gazing at the payroll for two hours in a cold sweat. It was ridiculous. I sneaked out, bought ten cigarettes, returned and completed the 10 minute job in 8 minutes flat! That incident proved to my satisfaction that I was unable to concentrate without smoking. Exactly why I couldn't, I did not know, any more than I knew why I scratched an itch.

There was another explanation. However, my ingenious, addicted, subconscious brain didn't want to know about it. Perhaps it had worked out that if I could suffer the misery of abstaining for a month, providing I didn't complete that 10 minute job, I would be able to say, with an absolutely clear conscience, to my family and to myself: "Bad luck old chap. It's not really your fault. It's just that you cannot function without cigarettes."

Obviously I didn't start the attempt with that frame of mind. Like all smokers that make a genuine attempt to stop by using the willpower method, I hoped that time would solve the problem. It didn't. The craving got worse as each day went by. But that 10 minute job was my lifeline. Had I completed it, I would have had no excuse to give in without ignominy.

Whether I truly believed that I genuinely was incapable of concentrating without smoking at that time, I cannot tell. It doesn't really matter one way or the other. The point was that I was miserable without the cigarettes and believed that I would always be miserable without smoking. That misconception was the true reason that I bought those cigarettes, but lack of concentration seemed a more logical scapegoat.

So, how can we prove one way or the other whether smoking helps concentration or otherwise? It is absolutely vital to do so because, if you have the slightest doubt about it, the doubt will guarantee that you cannot concentrate without smoking.

There are clues to help us decide. One was another incident involving smoking and concentration. I hated being an accountant. The only reason that I became one was that in a 10 minute interview at school, the careers master, who had never actually taught me during the whole 5 years that I attended the school, said: "Yes, er Carr, you appear to be good at mathematics, I suggest you become an accountant."

People wonder why we cannot compete with the Germans or the Japanese. The miracle is how we survive at all. So much for the British education system. Five years work, or lack of it, and my whole future is decided in 10 minutes by a person who neither understood me, nor had the remotest idea of what an accountant actually does. The only practical use a knowledge of maths has for an accountant, is not to appear stupid when delegated by your friends to take the 'chalks' during a game of darts. What you do need is a detailed knowledge of a variety of unbelievably boring subjects, which neither you nor anyone else on the planet is the slightest bit interested in.

I didn't find out what an accountant was until I'd been working for the firm for about three years. The only reason I became one was because my parents were so proud of me that I didn't have the heart or the courage to tell them that I would rather sweep the motorway than be an accountant.

Anyway, after three years of studying I had to sit the intermediate examination. My employers generously granted me 6 weeks study leave. After 3 weeks I learned that it was forbidden to smoke during the exam. Can you imagine my fury? I was already a chain-smoker and the times when those cigarettes were absolutely essential, were the times that I needed to concentrate. No way could I pass those exams without smoking. I had just found out that I'd spent three years studying subjects that I loathed and was doomed to fail, all because some idiot neglected to inform me at the start, that you can't smoke during the exam.

I began to consider alternative employment. However, I'm not the type to surrender easily. Perhaps it was possible to go three hours without a cigarette? I got a copy of examination questions from a previous year, set an alarm clock, tried to reproduce in my mind the tension of the actual exam, and succeeded so well that I couldn't stop my hand shaking sufficiently even to write, let alone think! Surely absolute proof that you cannot concentrate without cigarettes?

That incident, now over a third of a century ago, will forever remain vivid in my memory. Curious that I have no recollection whatsoever of an incident that happened shortly after which proved that my conclusion was wrong. An incident which, even though I have no recollection of it, must have indeed happened. An incident which didn't occur to me until I had successfully escaped from the prison: I not only passed those exams, but during them the thought of smoking never even entered my head. When it came to the crunch, even when I was physically addicted to nicotine and during what must have been one of the most tense, stressful and highly concentrated three hours of my life:

I *DIDN'T* NEED THEM! IT WAS PURELY PSYCHOLOGICAL!

Now let us go back to that ten minute job that I couldn't complete without smoking. There was nothing complicated about that job. It was purely routine. The only reason that I hadn't delegated it was not because of its complexity, but because of its confidential nature. Now I am not denying that I couldn't concentrate without the cigarette at that time, but that was because I *genuinely believed* that cigarettes helped me to concentrate, and if you believe that, then it's impossible to concentrate without them.

Let us forget smoking for a moment and consider concentration. In order to concentrate you first remove distractions. The children are making a noise, you can't concentrate. You have the choice of moving to another room or of yelling: "Could you please keep the noise down, I'm trying to concentrate!" It is within your power to remove the distraction and if you don't do so, you will get uptight and irritable.

Now you have a bad cold. You have to blow your nose every minute which makes it difficult for you to concentrate. But can you ever remember thinking: "When will this cold go so that I can concentrate properly?"

The difference is, if there is something that you can do to remove a distraction, you are distracted and irritable until you have removed it. If there is nothing you can do about it, you accept it and get on with it. A concert pianist will be distracted by the drop of a pin, yet stock brokers, commodity brokers, currency brokers and the like, are able to apply intense concentration during an atmosphere of sonic chaos. Has one ever suddenly shouted out: "**WILL YOU ALL JUST SHUT UP! I'M TRYING TO CONCENTRATE!**"

So why the difference? Just this: a concert pianist expects perfect silence and will be distracted by anything less. The broker expects, and has no choice but to accept, sonic chaos. The non-smoker expects and accepts that they will have mental blocks. What do they do when they have mental blocks? They either do a Dave Brubeck and hope that the break solves their problem, or they damn well get on with it. What do smokers do when they have mental blocks? They light a cigarette. The probability was that they were already smoking when they had those mental blocks. In fact people in professions which depend on concentration or inspiration tend to chain-smoke at such times. I admit that many smokers find it impossible to concentrate without smoking, but that's only because they have the permanent 'itch' and their inability to scratch it will distract them from the problem of their mental block. In fact it will supersede that problem. Why else do smokers drive around in the small hours searching for an all night garage? Now when you are a smoker with a mental block, can you honestly say that the moment you light that cigarette, the mental block mysteriously evaporates? If so it would mean that smokers **NEVER EVER HAD MENTAL BLOCKS**. That is obviously nonsense!

So how did you solve the problem of your mental blocks? You did it in exactly the same way that non-smokers do:

YOU JOLLY WELL GOT ON WITH IT!

What is certain is this: when I extinguished my final cigarette, I was neither aware of not being able to concentrate, nor of any of the other unpleasant symptoms that I had suffered on previous attempts. So if other smokers are made aware that smoking in fact doesn't help concentration but impedes it, why do they suffer lack of concentration when they attempt to stop?

Some believe that it is due to the actual physical withdrawal from nicotine, but that is so slight as to be imperceptible. The real problem is that the ex-smokers brain has now been programmed to believe that when you get a mental block, there is a simple solution. Obviously for a few days after the final cigarette, the little monster will be nagging away, even if there were no little monster to remind you physically, for a period whenever you had a mental block your brain will automatically set off a trigger: "Reach for a cigarette." This is the crunch. You are taken unawares. The natural tendency is to think: "At times like this I would have lit a cigarette, now what have I got?" Yes, you would have lit a cigarette, but it wouldn't have done the slightest bit of good. But the problem is that you are no longer even trying to solve the problem of the mental block, you are thinking about smoking, while you are thinking about smoking, you'll obviously lose concentration. That loss of concentration will in turn cause you to question whether smoking does in fact aid concentration, doubt will creep in, you will begin to feel deprived, now you will be thinking: "Perhaps I should try one cigarette, just to test it out?" If you do light one you no longer have to go through the thought process of should I? Now all that remains is to get on with solving the mental block and now that your brain isn't being distracted by whether or not you should smoke, in all probability you solve your problem and so perpetuate the illusion that smoking helps concentration. On the other hand, if you hadn't lit that cigarette, the doubt would have continued in your mind, thus guaranteeing:

THAT YOU WON'T BE ABLE TO CONCENTRATE!

Why is it, that from whichever angle you look at it, the cigarette always seems to end up the winner? It's because it's an incredibly ingenious trap. But I remind you that provided you understand it, it's easy to quit. So how do we avoid these triggers, not only for the few days after the final cigarette, but for the rest of our lives? You cannot avoid them. Even to attempt to avoid them is to court disaster and misery. Remember this whole book is about changing our frame of mind. Why was it that during the trial run for that exam, I couldn't even write let alone concentrate, yet during the actual exam the lack of cigarettes didn't bother me, in spite of the fact that I believed that I was completely and utterly dependent on cigarettes? It was because I had no doubt. I *knew* that I couldn't smoke.

I said that I never even thought about smoking during that exam. Perhaps I did think about it at odd times and just don't remember. If so, the reason that I don't remember was because I didn't waste time thinking about it, I knew I couldn't smoke, so I got on with the matter in hand. Ah! Say you, but that was forced on you, you didn't have to use any willpower, but what about the poor ex-smokers that haven't got someone to force them to stop?

It wasn't the forcing that did it, we've already established that the more you try to force smokers to stop, the greater will be their resistance. It was the **CERTAINTY! THAT WAS THE KEY! THE LACK OF DOUBT!** That's another thing that this book is doing, to prepare you, to get it so certain in your mind, that if or when these triggers come: **YOU NEVER DOUBT!**

It's just a question of preparation. One of the important things they teach at golf is to shout 'FORE' as loudly as you can whenever you hit a ball that might be in danger of hitting another golfer. Unfortunately they omit to tell you the correct action to take when you hear the shout. The natural tendency is to peer in the direction of the shout in order to pick up the flight of the ball. Your chance of succeeding is marginally better than picking up the flight of a bullet. However, one day you do manage to see it. In fact it's very difficult to miss it. It has landed in the spot where your front teeth used to be. It's not only the golf ball that hits you. The lesson that they omitted also hits you: when you hear 'FORE' you face the complete opposite direction, cover as many vital parts as you can and make yourself as small a target as you are able. It might feel undignified, but believe me, it's better than the alternative.

Training your brain to reverse instinctive reactions occurs in many aspects of life. If you are pushed, the instinctive reaction is to push back. There are now two equal forces negating each other. Study Judo and when pushed you instinctively pull. Now you control the combined weight of both yourself and your adversary.

For a few days after you extinguish that final cigarette, if you get a mental block, your brain might well say: "Light a cigarette." There's no great problem. Two choices are open to you. You can either ponder the matter and go through the process that I described above, in which case, whether you light a cigarette or not, you will be both distracted and miserable and guarantee:

PERMANENT LACK OF CONCENTRATION!

The alternative at such times, is merely to remind yourself that smoking actually impedes concentration and benefits you in no way whatsoever, that you *know* that you've made the correct decision and that no purpose will be served by delving into the subject. That thought process might not solve your mental block, but it will enable you to concentrate on the matter in hand, instead of moping about a solution that doesn't exist, then at least you give yourself a chance to clear the block. You might find that you cannot get your mind off the subject of smoking. If so, there's still no problem, just indulge yourself in self-satisfaction and self-congratulation. Then, whether you solve your mental block or not, you'll feel happy rather than miserable.

Like every other aspect of smoking, it's not so much the cigarette

216

itself that ex-smokers miss, but the void that it appears to leave and the lack of a suitable substitute to fill that void, this is another subject that many ex-smokers cannot seem to grasp and I'll deal with it next. In the meantime what you need to get clear in your mind is that smoking didn't help you to concentrate, it made it harder for you to concentrate. It didn't fill the void, on the contrary:

SMOKING CREATED THE VOID!

But if you spend the rest of your life either bemoaning the fact or just pondering it whenever you have a mental block:

YOU WILL BE *CREATING* A VOID!

CHAPTER 26

If Only There Were a Suitable Substitute

I have often been asked the question: if there were a clean cigarette, completely harmless, which cost nothing, would you smoke again? I can answer without the slightest blush: definitely NO!

Ask me if I would have stopped smoking had there been such a cigarette and I can answer with equal honesty: NO WAY! So why do I have a diametrically opposed reaction to the same thing: A CLEAN, FREE CIGARETTE?

Millions of pounds have been spent searching for a clean substitute for tobacco. By clean, I don't mean one that has no filthy smell or taste, I mean one that does not kill you. Older smokers might remember that a few years ago, some tobacco companies themselves tried to introduce substitute tobaccos. They spent a fortune in research and promotion, then dropped them with not so much as a whisper. Why do you think that was?

Just think what a fortune you would make if you could invent a clean cigarette. If the tobacco industry can make billions of pounds from western society's number one killer, just think what smokers would be prepared to pay for a cigarette that didn't kill them, and how many non-smokers and ex-smokers would start smoking?

I have good news for you. A clean cigarette has been discovered. Now before you rush out to buy some, I need to inform you that you have in all probability already tried them. They are called herbal cigarettes. "What! Those foul, smelly, stinky things that give no satisfaction?" Yes but your brand of tobacco once tasted foul. Nicotine chewing gum tastes awful, however, it gives satisfaction. Persevere with your brand, or any other brand, or anything containing nicotine, eventually you'll learn to *enjoy the feeling of satisfaction*. However, if you smoke herbal cigarettes for the rest of your life:

YOU'LL NEVER SUFFER THE ILLUSION OF ENJOYING THEM

Do you enjoy injections? If you are anything like me, you hate them.

218

Can you imagine anyone actually enjoying injections? Heroin addicts do. Perhaps, also like me, you are under the impression that they inject themselves in order to obtain those marvellous highs that drug addicts talk about. Try to picture a heroin addict that cannot get a fix. Do you really believe they need that heroin to obtain a marvellous high, or to end the feeling of panic and misery that they are suffering? Non-heroin addicts don't suffer that panic feeling. If you are a smoker, like the man on the yacht, you can relate to a heroin addict that's deprived of the drug. You know the panic feeling caused by being low on cigarettes, or even worse, of having none. Heroin addicts don't really enjoy injecting themselves. That is merely the ritual they go through to end that awful panic feeling. Smoking is purely the ritual that smokers go through to do exactly the same thing.

Perhaps you find it hard to compare the smoking of a cigarette with the injecting of heroin. If so, put the same question to a non-smoker, they won't be able to understand why anyone would want to do either. This is why smoking is so much more subtle than heroin addiction. Heroin addicts know that they only inject themselves to get the heroin, whereas smokers believe that they smoke, not to obtain nicotine, but because they enjoy smoking.

If you knew a heroin addict that wanted to quit, would you say to them: "Look, if you get some pleasure from injecting yourself, why don't you leave the heroin out of the syringe?" Obviously, that would be ludicrous. It is equally ludicrous to say to a smoker: "Look, if you get some pleasure from smoking, why don't you smoke a cigarette that contains no nicotine?" The only reason that heroin addicts inject themselves is to get the heroin. The only reason a smoker smokes is to get the nicotine! The fact that smokers don't realise this might confuse the situation, but doesn't alter it!

This is also why, if you switch to a low tar brand, to begin with, you get no satisfaction. You have to puff twice as hard and usually end up smoking twice as many. What does this phrase: 'IT GIVES ME SATISFACTION' mean? To be satisfied, you first need a state of dissatisfaction. Why doesn't smoking satisfy non-smokers? There can only be one reason, they do not have the state of dissatisfaction. The logical conclusion is that smoking, far from satisfying, causes dissatisfaction. The experts have discovered that it is the nicotine in tobacco which creates the feeling of dissatisfaction. So if it is nicotine that is causing our problems, what is the sense in chewing it or absorbing it through patches on our arms?

The thing I want you to get into your mind is this: we believe that there is some basic pleasure in smoking, purely for smoking's sake. We regard the filth, the health risks, the expense and the slavery as annoying side effects which interfere with our smoking pleasure. If only we could find a safe substitute to smoke so that we could get the pleasure without the risk. There is no pleasure in smoking purely for smoking's sake. It is very unpleasant to breathe poisonous fumes into your lungs. The only reason that any of us believe that smoking for its own sake could be pleasurable, is because that is the method we used to end that dissatisfied feeling of our bodies craving nicotine.

If I had been writing this book 200 years ago, I would have been saying: "Look, there really is no pleasure in sniffing dust up your nose, the snuff is just tobacco, which contains nicotine, it's just your way of obtaining nicotine, but it's the nicotine that is causing your problem."

There are already thousands of ex-smokers hooked on nicotine chewing gum, many of them are still smoking cigarettes. Ex-smokers attend our clinics just to get off the chewing gum. There has recently been immense publicity about nicotine patches. We've already had a lady at the Raynes park clinic that said: "I take my patch off about three times a day so that I can have a cigarette with my husband and stick it back on with sticky tape." Are we really going to have to ask clients in a few years time: "Now be honest, how many patches a day are you on?" Will nicotine addicts in 20 years time be bragging:

"I'm down to two patches a day!" or,

"I only wear them when I'm socialising." or

"I don't need them, I enjoy them, what could be more relaxing than wearing a nice patch after a meal?"

If you think such comments are stretching the imagination, try to imagine the same comments about sniffing dust up your nose. That's the sort of comments that snuff-takers actually made to justify their stupidity. So why not patch wearers?

The reason that the tobacco companies dropped substitute tobaccos without a murmur, was because it dawned on them, that nicotine addiction isn't one of the hazards of smoking, it is the **ONLY REASON** for smoking. The reason that I wouldn't smoke a clean cigarette be it free or otherwise, is exactly the same reason that I wouldn't stick a burning cigarette in my ear: **I WOULD FEEL VERY, VERY STUPID AND GET ABSOLUTELY NO PLEASURE FROM IT AT ALL.**

I've just said that the **ONLY** reason that we smoke is nicotine addiction. Now there is a great danger here, particularly when eminent members of the medical profession are condoning these massive campaigns to find alternative methods of administering nicotine to the body. Having perfected the 'patch' technique, I hear that they are now working on nasal sprays. Surely the next stage is a powder that you can sniff and so complete the cycle. Anyway, why will we need nasal sprays? Are they telling us they don't believe the patches will work? Have you noticed that the reaction of smokers that have tried the patches tends to be: "They help with the physical withdrawal, but they don't seem to help with the psychological aspect." It doesn't even occur to such smokers that there is no physical problem. The problem is purely mental. The only way patches could help, would be to put one over each eye and hope you couldn't find your cigarettes.

The so-called experts argue that, even if you do get hooked on the substitute, by not smoking you avoid all the other harmful compounds associated with smoking tobaccos. The argument is a fallacy. Just like cutting down should make smoking less harmful, but because it keeps you hooked and causes you to eventually smoke more, it is actually more harmful; so substitutes keep you hooked and eventually you end up smoking again.

In any event, nicotine is a powerful poison in its own right. It took the medical profession many years to discover the harmful effects of *smoking* tobaccos. Nearly every month smoking is being related to some new disease. It's bad enough breathing an insecticide into your lungs. Already many smokers have suffered adverse symptoms merely from having a nicotine-impregnated patch in contact with their skin. I would advise you to consider very carefully before you decide to put it into your stomach or on any other part of your body. Anyway, nicotine gum has been on the market for over a quarter of a century backed by massive advertising. If it worked all smokers would now be cured. If the gum didn't work, why should the patch?

In practice ex-smokers that become dependent on the nicotine substitute sooner or later end up back on smoking. There is little illusion of pleasure in chewing gum which contains nicotine and there is no illusion of pleasure in wearing a patch. Eventually, the nicotine addicts are forced to accept themselves as what they actually are: PATHETIC NICOTINE ADDICTS! It's so much easier to revert to the cigarette. At least they can now kid themselves that they are smoking because they enjoy it. Now they can group together with other smokers, you don't get the same feeling of camaraderie when passing round the gum or the patches, but it could happen, remember it was once considered very sociable to pass the snuff around.

Logically, there are two reasons for using substitutes:

1. To find a permanent pleasure or crutch to fill or part fill the void left by no longer being able to smoke.
2. To find a temporary aid during the period the ex-smoker is suffering severe physical withdrawal pangs.

Obviously, an alternative product that contains nicotine, would be an ideal substitute to satisfy the second reason. The great danger is, the way these products are being marketed. Aided and abetted by Dr. Steele's statement that nicotine is a very pleasant drug, ex-smokers are beginning to regard these products as also providing a permanent substitute. Another eminent doctor recently stated on national television that he thought that some heavy smokers would have to take nicotine substitutes for the rest of their lives.

A few years ago the general attitude was: "There would be nothing wrong with smoking if it didn't harm your health and cause some smokers to become addicted to nicotine." The latest impression appears to be: "There is nothing particularly wrong with nicotine addiction, provided you don't smoke." There is everything wrong with nicotine addiction in whatever form. You don't need to take my word for it, look it up. Collins New National Dictionary, 1971 reprint: 'An alkaloid present in the tobacco plant; colourless and highly poisonous when pure, it is used in the manufacture of insecticides for fruit trees'. In fact our *friendly* tobacco plant is in the same genus as deadly nightshade! Strangely Collins have made slight amendments in their 1988 Dictionary: 'A colourless oily acrid toxic liquid that turns yellowish-brown in air and light: the principle alkaloid in tobacco'.

The changes might appear to be subtle and insignificant. Perhaps you feel I have a vivid imagination. But I have experience of how the tobacco industry operates and I can sense its influence here. 'Powerful poison' has been substituted by 'toxic'. What's the difference? Well what would cause you most alarm, the fact that you have been partaking of a powerful poison or a substance that was merely toxic? The word liquid has been included. Why? For greater accuracy, or to leave smokers with the impression that, provided you don't drink it, it's harmless? Why has the connection between nicotine and tobacco been transferred from the beginning to the end of the definition, and why has the reference to its use as an insecticide been dropped. Can it be because we might form the impression that nicotine actually kills living creatures?

The medical profession might argue that, in certain circumstances, it is justifiable to use poisons to help cure a disease, but to actually prescribe a powerful poison to cure a disease that only exists because the victim is already taking the powerful poison, a disease from which the **ONLY** cure is to stop taking the poison, is not just stupidity on a massive scale, it is nothing less than:

SHEER LUNACY!

Why does the BMA sit on the fence? Why do they concentrate on the evils of the tars and underplay the real problem: NICOTINE? Is it because they receive large hand-outs from the tobacco industry?

The point is, the two reasons for taking substitutes only appear logical if you don't understand the smoking trap. In fact, like everything else about smoking, if you work out what seems logical and do the opposite, you will invariably be right. It is essential not to use any form of substitute. It is just as essential to know why, if you do use substitutes, you will not only make it harder to stop, but impossible to be permanently free.

If we go back to the analogy of the 12 foot fence that I described in Chapter 12. There is something that I didn't tell you about those imaginary slats. They are not completely independent of each other. For example, if you fail to follow the instruction of never, ever smoking another cigarette, it won't matter that you meticulously followed the other ten instructions, whether you realise it or not, you will not have got over the fence. If you fail to follow the instruction: DO NOT USE ANY SUBSTITUTES, you will not only fail to remove that particular slat, but you will automatically have failed to remove other slats. You'll believe that you are making a sacrifice. You will believe that there is a void in your life. You will be waiting for something to happen and you will probably put on weight. Sooner or later the cumulative effect will be misery shortly followed by **FAILURE!**

Let us examine the *"logical"* reasons for substitutes separately, starting with the search for a permanent substitute. When searching for a substitute, we are usually trying to find something as near to the original as possible. So let's first establish exactly what we are searching for. We are looking for something that we didn't need or want before we started taking it, but that once we start taking it, we won't be able to enjoy life or cope with life without. Ideally it should be something that is filthy and disgusting, that'll destroy us mentally and physically, will cost us a fortune and enslave us for life. It must appear very precious to us when we are not using it, but at the same time make us feel irritable and insecure. When we are using it, it must congest and poison our lungs, but at the same time give the illusion of relaxing us.

Why on earth would anyone want a substitute for such a product? Anyway the nicotine substitutes will fulfil all of the above specifications except the poisoning and congestion of your lungs, but why bother with them? You don't really need a substitute at all, why not stick to the original?

So smokers search for a substitute, not because the original is no longer available, but because you like the original, but it has certain aspects that you would like to change. You would like a substitute that has all the advantages without any of the disadvantages. Obviously you don't want the deterioration of your health, mental or physical, or the cost, slavery, filth or stigma. So you want something that will make you feel insecure and irritable when you are not taking it, that will partially relieve that feeling for a few moments, before it makes you feel insecure and irritable again.

What, you don't want that either? So what do you want? You want something, that you only need to take every now and again, that you don't eat but will improve the taste of food, that you don't drink but will make a drink taste better, that will help you when you feel both relaxed and distressed, will relieve boredom and at the same time help you to concentrate. What's more, you would like it to be inexpensive? I can well understand you wanting something like that, and if you ever find it, please let me know about it! The beautiful truth is: such a product not only exists, but is absolutely free! But it's not a substitute. In fact it's what you had before you started smoking and will have again after you've quit. A healthy mind and body will provide all the advantages stipulated above with not one of the disadvantages! But you have mislead me. You told me that you needed a substitute, yet the product you have described:

IS THE COMPLETE OPPOSITE TO THE ONE YOU HAVE BEEN USING!

Why on earth would you want or need a substitute for something:

THAT DOES ABSOLUTELY NOTHING FOR YOU AT ALL?

This is the great danger of substitutes, if you search for one, you are searching for something that cannot possibly exist and you will be miserable because the substitute that you are using won't work and you won't be able to find one that will. But merely by searching for one you perpetuate the myth that you are making a sacrifice. In other words, you create a void that doesn't actually exist.

When you get over a bout of flu, do you search for a similar disease to substitute for it? Of course you don't! On the contrary you rejoice in the fact that you are now free of it. The point is: you don't need a substitute for flu. Moreover:

YOU DON'T NEED A SUBSTITUTE FOR NICOTINE

THERE IS NO SUBSTITUTE FOR A HEALTHY MIND AND BODY

The beautiful truth is:

YOU DON'T NEED A SUBSTITUTE FOR THOSE EITHER!

I hope that I have convinced you that you do not need a substitute. However, if you insist on trying to use one, I have in fact perfected a pill that is as near to the original as it is possible to get. I admit it tastes awful, but don't worry about that. You chew this pill for about ten minutes. About an hour later, you will begin to feel restless and insecure. No problem, just take another pill. It too will taste awful, but it will immediately remove that empty feeling. About an hour after you finish it, the empty feeling will return, but the beauty is another pill will remove it immediately. Yes that pill will also taste awful, but I promise you that will be no problem.

After a while you won't even notice the foul taste, in fact most people actually learn to enjoy the taste, and you need never be without them. I guarantee you'll always be able to buy them. Just look at this attractive bottle, it holds about 20 of them. No need to take my word for it, half the adult population are regularly taking these pills. They wouldn't do that if they didn't get enormous benefits from them. Yes, they are expensive, they'll cost you about £30,000. But that works out at only £2 a day, you won't even notice the cost. Yes there are rumours of side effects. the medical profession say that one in four users die from these pills, but everyone knows what scaremongers they are.

Look, what are you worried about, no one can force you to take them, you'll only go on taking them if you want to. **WHY DON'T YOU JUST TRY ONE?**

Does my pill remind you of something? Are you going to try one? If you were already taking them:

WOULD YOU CONTINUE TO TAKE THEM?

Obviously there is no point in searching for a permanent substitute for nicotine. But surely the second reason for taking substitutes is valid? It must be helpful to take a nicotine substitute to gradually ease the physical dependence on nicotine during the period of severe physical withdrawal? It might appear that way. The so-called experts believe that it is the combination of two powerful forces that make it difficult to kick. One is to break the habit. The other is to withstand those awful withdrawal pains. Why even attempt to defeat two powerful adversaries at the same time? It's much more sensible to defeat them one at a time. While you are breaking the habit, keep the body supplied with nicotine. Once you have broken the habit, gradually starve that little monster by weaning yourself off of the nicotine substitute.

It all sounds very logical, and so it would be if it were not for the fact that the criteria that it is based on is false:

SMOKING IS NOT HABIT IT IS DRUG ADDICTION

THE PHYSICAL WITHDRAWAL PAINS ARE ALMOST IMPERCEPTIBLE

To stop smoking successfully, you need to kill two monsters. The little nicotine monster inside your body which is so slight you don't need a weaning process. The only significance of the little monster is to trigger the real problem, which is the big monster inside your brain, the one that interprets the little monsters message as: "I NEED OR WANT A CIGARETTE" which will cause you to feel progressively deprived and miserable if you can't have one. By continuing to provide nicotine, you merely prolong the life of both monsters.

If a weaning process actually works, why even bother with a nicotine substitute? Why not ease both the breaking of the *habit* and those *terrible* withdrawal symptoms by progressively cutting down on your smoking? Any smoker knows from experience that cutting down doesn't work. In Chapter 35 I will explain why it cannot possibly work and why any attempt to control your nicotine intake, whether by smoking or by substitutes, will make cigarettes appear to be infinitely more precious. However the greatest evil that substitutes cause is, far from removing the real problem, which is the belief that you are making a sacrifice, they actually perpetuate it, make the illusion of sacrifice even greater and thus prolong the life of the big monster indefinitely.

The worst substitutes are those that contain nicotine. Apart from possessing most of the disadvantages of other substitutes, they contain the additional disadvantage of keeping you physically and psychologically addicted. To advise a smoker that wants to quit smoking to use a nicotine substitute, would be like saying to a heroin addict that wants to quit heroin: "Don't smoke it! Smoking is dangerous! Just inject it directly into your vein!" If you even tried to do that with nicotine:

IT WILL KILL YOU!

However, surely there can be no harm in chewing gum or sucking a peppermint during that transitional period between extinguishing the last cigarette and becoming a happy non-smoker? There is immense harm. I will explain it in the next chapter when we explode:

THE WEIGHT MYTH

CHAPTER 27

The Weight Myth

There's a popular misconception that smoking helps to reduce weight or prevents you from gaining weight. How can I possibly call it a misconception when every smoker knows that if you stop smoking you are almost certain to gain weight. What's more the gain is usually permanent. You probably know several examples. In all probability it has already happened to you. It certainly did to me. Every time I attempted to stop I would put on stones rather than pounds. There was one notable exception. The last time I stopped I lost two stones within 6 months of extinguishing that final cigarette.

I do not deny that most smokers gain weight either temporarily or permanently when they attempt to quit. Nevertheless I still maintain that, far from helping you to reduce weight, smoking actually encourages you to become overweight. In 'EASYWAY' I explain why even a chain-smoker like me, that only ate one meal a day, was permanently two stones overweight for his height, or as I used to put it: "I'm not overweight, I'm just 6 inches shorter than I should be."

When we awake each morning, both smokers and non-smokers relieve a series of aggravations. We relieve our bladders, we relieve our thirst. Non-smokers will also relieve their hunger. However, smokers are more likely to light a cigarette. The empty feeling caused by craving nicotine is almost indistinguishable from the empty feeling caused by a hunger for food. This is why there is a close association between eating and smoking. The problem is that although the empty feeling is the same, food will not satisfy the craving for nicotine and nicotine will not satisfy a hunger for food.

The problem is exacerbated when the smoker reaches the stage when the body becomes partially immune to the effects of nicotine, so that even when smoking the cigarette, the smoker cannot relieve the withdrawal pangs completely. Those smokers are now in a position of feeling permanently hungry. They are therefore permanently trying to either eat or smoke. The number of cigarettes that they can smoke each day will vary with each individual and is limited by a combination of their pockets, their jobs, the strength of their lungs and their willpower. (Not a contradiction, it takes no willpower to stop smoking, but immense willpower to control it) When they are not smoking, they will be eating. This is why most heavy smokers, far from being slim as you would expect them to be if smoking actually helped to reduce weight, are often in fact just like I was:

GROSSLY OVERWEIGHT

So why do smokers always seem to put on weight when they stop smoking? Because the natural tendency for the few days after extinguishing that final cigarette, while the craving for nicotine is accumulating inside your body, is to satisfy that empty feeling by chewing gum or sucking peppermints. What's so bad about that? Just this:

IT WON'T SATISFY THAT EMPTY FEELING

So you will get no benefit at all from doing it. But what it will do is this:

1. It will make you feel irritable and frustrated because it has not satisfied that empty feeling.
2. The first few peppermints might taste okay, but soon you will become sick of them. If you've ever chewed gum for any period, you will know that the first few chews are fine, but soon your jaw begins to ache and you cannot wait to get rid of the gum. I do not dispute that unrelaxed people feel a need to chew. However, I do dispute the suggestion that chewing helps to relax them. Observe them. They still look tense and unrelaxed when they are chewing! Aren't they really just finding an excuse for doing what they were already doing – GRINDING THEIR JAW! Chewing tends to perpetuate rather than solve the problem. Both peppermints and gum will ruin your teeth. They will also ruin your appetite and you will lose the pleasure of enjoying your meals. Eating is a wonderful pleasure, but overeating is just another frustrating disease.
3. Worst of all, you will now be training your body and your brain to expect little rewards. By now both body and brain will be utterly sick of the gum, peppermints or whatever substance you are substituting and every time you take the substitute you will remind yourself that what you really want is not a substitute but the cigarette. You only took the substitute to fill a void. All the substitute has actually done is to perpetuate that void and the feeling of sacrifice.

I'm merely explaining why, although it might appear that substitutes will help you to stop, in fact they make it harder. You don't need to take my word for it. In all probability you've already tried substituting with gum or peppermints. Did they help you to stop? Or did they make you feel fat and miserable, and give you a valid excuse to start smoking again? The fact is: **SUBSTITUTES DON'T WORK.**

The myth that smoking helps to reduce weight arose purely because smokers tend to start substituting food for nicotine when they stop smoking. So what? Say you, that only happened because they stopped smoking. You are wrong! Like every other problem caused by smoking, it happened:

BECAUSE THEY STARTED SMOKING!

No doubt you have heard of people that only started smoking to reduce weight. Do not overlook the fact that they must have had a weight problem *before* they started smoking. I've heard that reason given many times, plus a variety of equally valid reasons for starting, but of all the thousands of smokers I have helped to quit, not one ever convinced me that they made an actual decision to become a smoker for life. They all tried, just one cigarette and became trapped, their logical reason for starting comes at a later date and is really an excuse for being stupid enough to fall for the trap. What they don't realise is that they look more stupid when they make these phoney excuses:

"I started smoking to lose weight."

"You mean you actually *deliberately* addicted yourself to the No.1 killer disease? Wasn't that like chopping off your fingers in order to stop biting your nails. You must have given it very considerable thought before deciding upon such a drastic action."

"Oh I did."

"I see. You worked out that you were overweight because you were a non-smoker. Do you not feel that your weight problem was more likely caused by the fact that you ate or drank too much?"

"Yes I realised that, but I couldn't control my weight and I heard that smoking helps to reduce weight."

"No, what you probably heard was that smokers put on weight when they try to stop. It's not really the same thing. In fact wouldn't it indicate that smoking makes you put on weight?"

"Perhaps you are right but I still thought it worth a try and I had no idea that I would get hooked."

"Oh come on, if you heard that smoking reduces weight, you must also have heard that smokers get hooked and find it almost impossible to quit. Now if you had thought it through as you claim, and couldn't control your eating, how could you have hoped to control a highly addictive drug like nicotine? Are you telling me that you were prepared to accept the health risks, the cost, the filth and the slavery for the rest of your life? Even if you thought you could have stopped, wouldn't you have just regained the weight?

Ironically, smoking does actually assist some smokers to lose weight: **THEY LOSE THEIR LIMBS!** It might be logical *deliberately to* put on weight if you thought that would help you to stop smoking, but to start smoking deliberately to help you to reduce weight? That would be lunacy! There are stupid people on the planet, but the biggest idiot of all wouldn't be stupid enough *deliberately* to fall for the smoking trap.

There are experts that will tell you that the reason that you put on weight when you stop smoking is because it alters your metabolism. How do they explain why it didn't alter my metabolism when I finally stopped and that instead of gaining stones, I actually lost stones? Why do the so-called experts keep searching for incredibly complicated solutions, when the obvious solution keeps jumping up and biting them on the nose?

It is ridiculously easy to stop smoking. All smokers wish that they had never lit that first cigarette. All you have to do to be a happy non-smoker the rest of your life is to extinguish your next cigarette and from that point on, whenever you think about smoking, whether you be undergoing stress or socialising, say to yourself: "Aren't I lucky I'm a non-smoker!"

So why isn't it as simple as that? Because the whole subject is confused by mythology, misconception and brainwashing. The object of 'EASYWAY' and this book is to clarify the myths, the mists and the illusions that make smoking appear to be a very complicated and mysterious subject, so that you see it as simply and clearly as I do.

If you find smoking and overeating difficult problems to solve, by merging them you merely confuse the situation and make them even more difficult. In fact they are both easy to solve, provided you understand them. The two problems are associated. Whether the association is physical, psychological, actual or merely illusion is completely irrelevant. The fact is that one problem, far from curing the other, merely exacerbates the other, but in order to understand them you need to treat them separately.

Let us for the moment assume your metabolic rate did slow down when you quit, and that because you ate exactly the same amount of food as you did before, you gained weight and are now concerned about your weight. You're now a non-smoker that is worried about being overweight and wants to do something about it. Because you genuinely believe that your excess weight is due to the fact that you've quit, you contemplate starting smoking again. But you are in exactly the same position as a non-smoker that took up smoking to reduce weight. The cause of your excess weight is immaterial. It would be just as ludicrous for you to take up smoking again as it would for someone that had never smoked!

However, like them you have 2 alternatives: you can either accept the weight gain as the lesser of the two evils, or you can take the attitude: "Okay, I've stopped smoking, my metabolic rate has dropped. Great! Not only will I save money on tobacco but I now don't need to eat as much as I used to, I'll also save money on food."

I assure you that smoking is a prime cause of obesity, not just because it creates this permanent hunger, but because the lack of energy causes smokers to quit active sports years before they should do. The other evil about smoking is that as you become more and more dependent on the drug, you subconsciously avoid any activity which doesn't allow you to smoke. Smokers tend to drop sports like tennis and swimming. I wonder whether part of my fascination for golf was that I could chain-smoke whilst playing?

The main reason that smokers put on weight when they stop smoking, is not because smoking helps them to reduce weight, but because they start substituting food for nicotine. Frankly I do not know whether or not the metabolic rate slows down when deprived of the stimulant provided by nicotine. As I have explained above, it's irrelevant, just one of the many red herrings that confuse both problems. I realise that I have introduced another red herring. Some of you will now be saying: "Ah! Nicotine is a stimulant! That's why it helps me to concentrate." Even if it is a stimulant, you don't need it! Your body is already equipped with ample non-toxic stimulants, which your brain will automatically supply to your body, in the correct quantity and at exactly the right time that you need them.

In any event, any stimulating effect that nicotine might possess is more than counteracted by the lethargic effect created by progressively gunging up the body with poisons. Both ill-effects will decline rapidly from the moment you extinguish your final cigarette. If in fact the metabolic rate does decline when stopping smoking, I believe that it is not because the ex-smoker is being deprived of nicotine, but because if you attempt to stop by using the willpower method, you tend to lounge around bemoaning the fact that you are not allowed to smoke any more. You're miserable and irritable. You are disoriented and feel like a zombie. At one and the same time you feel both restless yet listless. You wish you could do a Rip Van Winkle for a few weeks and hope to wake up free.

That's why I didn't put on weight when I extinguished that final cigarette. I wasn't feeling deprived or miserable. On the contrary, I felt elated! A dark shadow that had been dominating my life had suddenly evaporated. It was the same feeling of elation that I felt when the doctor told me that I hadn't got lung cancer. I could respect myself again. No longer was I the pathetic slave to nicotine.

I WAS FREE!!!

Forget about your metabolic rate – it's just another red herring. Remember, every reaction of your body, whether it be physical or mental, is controlled by your brain. Perhaps nicotine is a stimulant. But deliberately to take nicotine as a stimulant is equivalent to taking cyanide because you like the taste of almonds! Later I will explain why it is imperative not to alter your life style because you stop smoking. I make one exception to that rule: if ever you feel the need of a stimulant, use the greatest stimulant of all: **EXERCISE!** Start exercising straight away, not because you've stopped smoking, but because it will start the adrenalin running and make you feel great. That's the real high, just feeling great to be alive!

One of the evils of smoking is that smokers tend to take less exercise than they would otherwise do so. You need to exercise for the purely selfish reason that you will enjoy life so much more. A fit and healthy body will help to produce a fit and healthy mind. If you are out of condition, start slowly. Do not extend yourself. It doesn't matter how little you do to begin with. As your strength and energy gradually increase, so you will automatically obtain the strength and energy to increase the level of your activity and at the same time improve the quality of your life. If you have any worries about the type or extent of exercise that you should take, consult your doctor first.

Some clients claim they gained weight even though they didn't use substitutes or increase their intake of food. I don't dispute this. Dieticians will tell you that dieters will stake their lives on the fact that they stuck rigidly to the prescribed diet and still gained weight. Yet strangely when exactly the same diet is used under controlled conditions, they mysteriously lose weight.

The extra energy and zest for life after quitting makes food infinitely more appetising and there is a tendency to eat larger meals. This is no problem, it is merely one of the many joys that you will achieve when you quit. Follow the instructions and any weight gain will be small and only temporary.

I promise that when you get 'The Moment of Revelation' you'll have such a feeling of confidence and wellbeing you'll be able to control any mental problem, be it be weight or otherwise. You'll find it enjoyable to be exactly the weight that you want to be. However what you must not do is to start picking between main meals. If you do that, not only will you put on weight, but you will not receive the 'Moment of Revelation'.

In fact stopping smoking and reducing weight are very similar problems, they are both easy to solve provided you understand them. If you find that you still have a weight problem after you have successfully kicked the 'weed', obtain Allen Carr's 'EASYWEIGH TO LOSE WEIGHT'. (see inside back cover)

For years I was convinced that smoking helped to keep my weight

232

down. I am fortunate to still have several friends that date back to my school days and several others that I acquired shortly after. Without exception the ones that never fell for the trap have roughly the same outline as they did when they left school. By that, I mean that they are not pot-bellied. Not all the smokers or ex-smokers have potbellies, but many of them like me, were either grossly overweight, or still are.

I am not trying to imply that no non-smokers are overweight and that all ex-smokers and smokers are. All I am asking is that you open your mind. Neither take my word for it nor just accept the brainwashing that you have been subjected to for years. Do your own research. Check whether the people you know are non-smokers, smokers or ex-smokers. Find out for yourself whether it tends to be non-smokers that are overweight or vice versa.

The important point is this: smokers only put on weight when they stop smoking because they go about it the wrong way. So, if substitutes don't help, how do you cope with the period between extinguishing your final cigarette and the time when your body stops craving for nicotine? Let us take a closer look at:

THOSE TERRIBLE WITHDRAWAL PANGS

CHAPTER 28

Those Terrible Withdrawal Pangs

How can I possibly say that the only reason that a smoker lights a cigarette is to relieve the physical withdrawal pangs from nicotine, and at the same time say that the actual physical withdrawal pangs from nicotine, are so slight, as to be almost imperceptible? I admit that it does appear to be a contradiction, nevertheless, like many other anomalies about smoking, it is true.

Let's go back to our man on the yacht. All smokers have been in a similar position more than once in their lives, it is every drug addict's nightmare. When he had no cigarettes, he was in a panic. However, once he had them, not only was the panic gone, but strangely, he had neither need nor *desire* to smoke while he was on the yacht, or more accurately, while in the company of a non-smoker? Even more strangely, he was actually pleased that he didn't smoke. Obviously his problem was purely mental.

Why, when I conducted my mock exam was I a shaking wreck within seconds of extinguishing the cigarette, yet sat 3 hours during the real thing without being aware of not smoking? Why can smokers sleep through eight hours of abstinence then wake up and not have the screaming habdabs? Is it because they are asleep and not aware of it? That might be so, but if the physical withdrawal pain was so bad, it would surely awaken smokers throughout the night. Many smokers do wake up regularly during the night, and if they do, it is quite natural that they might light up and scratch the itch. It wouldn't surprise me if withdrawal pangs were the main cause of their restlessness, even so, there is no physical *pain*! In fact most smokers nowadays get out of bed before lighting up. Many will not smoke in the bedroom. Others will complete their ablutions, eat breakfast, leave the house, even wait until they arrive at work, before they light that first cigarette. Not only are they not suffering physical pain in the meantime, they are not aware of any discomfort:

PHYSICAL OR MENTAL!

Naturally, they will be anticipating that first cigarette with relish, just as much as they would be anticipating the first cup of tea or coffee if they hadn't relieved their thirst shortly after awakening. However, if when they went to light that cigarette, you had snatched it from their lips and taken their packet, they would have broken your arm to get those cigarettes.

That panic feeling isn't physical. It starts before you even run out of cigarettes. You must often have been in those situations when it's late at night, you do a mental calculation: "I reckon I'll be up about another four hours, but I've only got about an hour's supply left in the packet!" The seeds of panic are already sewn. It's not quite so bad when you are being entertained, you can always feign a headache and leave early. However if you are the host you are trapped. The panic reaches its height when you are actually smoking your last cigarette. Or even worse, when you have meticulously rationed those last few cigarettes.

Your guests finally take the hints that you have been blatantly broadcasting for the last two hours. You have two cigarettes left. One to smoke before you go to bed and that really essential one for the morning on which will depend whether you settle for a sleepless night, or spend two hours searching for an all-night garage. There is one other smoker in the company, one whose only contribution to the conversation throughout the evening, has been to draw everyone else's attention to the number of cigarettes that you smoke, and to repeatedly enquire why you can't be like them and only smoke a few cigarettes a day?

All others present are gravely and silently nodding their agreement, except your non-smoking spouse, who finds it necessary to make regular interruptions of: "That's what I've been saying for years!" Why are they all oblivious to the fact that the so-called casual smoker has matched you cigarette for cigarette throughout the evening. Even more frustrating is that they are also oblivious to the fact that, although that smoker generously arrived with two bottles of wine, they omitted to bring any cigarettes, and it's your cigarettes that they have been chain-smoking ever since the meal finished; and that's why you only have two left and are beginning to panic. Then they drop a bombshell: "Do you mind if I have one of those?"

"Mind! Of course I mind! You can have a pint of my blood! You can even have one of my kidneys! But there is no way you are having one of those cigarettes!" That is what we are thinking, but what do we do? We meekly hand over one of those precious cigarettes with: "Of course you can," desperately hoping that our tone or expression didn't betray our true feelings. In case I'm now helping to bring on that panic feeling, let me remind you, the drug creates that feeling, non-smokers don't suffer it. Soon you'll be able to watch other smokers squirming, and I don't just mean the smoker that was down to two cigarettes, I mean the so-called casual smoker, who could supposedly take them or leave them, having to rely on hand-outs all evening and then having the ultimate indignity of having to beg for one! As a smoker you will have suffered similar experiences, and in all probability you will have occupied at various times in your life, both the role of the smoker running low and of the casual smoker.

Most smokers get that panic feeling when they get down to the last few cigarettes in the packet. I got in when I got down to the last few packets! I wasn't happy playing a round of golf unless I had 5 full packets in my golf bag. Bear in mind, that even on the windiest of days I could only chain-smoke 40 cigarettes in a round. Why on earth did I need 5 packets? Because in the days when I only carried 2 packets, on a particularly dewy day one packet got completely saturated. I like to feel that I am a man that learns from his mistakes, henceforth I carried 3 packets.

On a subsequent occasion, a golfing friend approached me in the middle of a round, explaining that he had run out and could I spare any? Without thinking, I blurted out: "Sorry, but I've only got 3 packets." I leave you to imagine his reply. From then on it was 5 packets. Why five? Surely your friend would be satisfied with a whole packet? I told you, I learn by my mistakes. Twice in 30 years I'd been caught out, perhaps there was some other eventuality that I had not anticipated.

Older smokers may remember the 'Kensitas' packet with a tiny extension containing: 'Four for your friends'. I thought it was an incredibly ridiculous gimmick. Can you visualise a situation in which you offered your open packet to a friend, only to find that although you still have ample supply in the main packet, the four have been used up: "Sorry old chap, I'm so embarrassed, but those are all mine." Can you visualise an even more ridiculous situation of waking up in the morning, finding the main packet empty but one left in the friends' compartment: "No, much as I need that cigarette, I will not stoop to robbing my friends. Then again, I'm sure they wouldn't mind me borrowing one."

Surely a cigarette's a cigarette. If you want to offer your friend one, why not just give him one of yours? Or was it such a ridiculous gimmick? Were the marketing executives in those days astute enough to realise that smokers hate parting with their own precious supply of the drug, unless it's to get someone else hooked?

When I refer to 'that panic feeling' at group sessions, most smokers will be nodding in sympathy. Occasionally a heavy smoker will say: "I'm sorry, but I don't know what you mean." The rest of the group would look at that person with raised eyebrows. When later on in the session I remark that smokers will smoke camel dung rather than nothing, and the same smoker says: "I can't agree with you. If I couldn't get my own brand, I wouldn't smoke anything." The former inquisitive looks become positively hostile.

This situation threw me to begin with. I know that all drug addicts have to lie to themselves. But most of that self-deception is to convince themselves that they have no need to stop. Once they have decided to seek my help, they no longer need to continue the deception. In fact they get obvious pleasure in being able to purge their consciences, and from realising that other members of the group also indulged in the same self-deceptions.

I was aware that many younger, casual smokers might not be aware of the panic feeling, or if they were, were too proud to admit to it. But such smokers are usually not too worried about what brand they smoke. They don't particularly enjoy any of them, so what difference does it make? Usually it is only heavy, confirmed smokers that specialise in one brand only.

I was also aware that many heavy, confirmed smokers arrived at the clinic with no intention of stopping. But to us such smokers stand out like a bishop in a brothel, and the smokers I am talking about appeared to be both genuinely wanting to stop and speaking honestly. In fact the rest of the group, though sceptical, were somewhat impressed by these people that didn't get that panic feeling when they got low on cigarettes and if they couldn't get their own brand, had no need to smoke at all.

Impressed as I was, nevertheless it worried me. I like to think that I understand the nicotine trap completely, and such smokers didn't conform to the usual pattern. Eventually the penny dropped. Why it took so long, I do not know, because for years I had been one of those smokers myself. The reason they don't get the panic feeling, is because they are too frightened to get it. Just as I used to, they make damned sure they never get low on cigarettes. They might well believe that if they couldn't get their own brand they wouldn't smoke at all. But they never have to put it to the test, because they are too frightened to run out of their own brand.

There are two essential aspects about the withdrawal pangs from nicotine that must be firmly implanted in your mind. One is:

THEY INVOLVE NO PHYSICAL PAIN

In Chapter 3 I gave the example of how a man receives more physical pain in one rugby match yet enjoys the process, and of how many women can adequately cope with the pain of pregnancy. I'm sorry ladies if you think that I am being either flippant or arrogant by comparing the pain of 80 minutes of rugby with 9 months of pregnancy, I assure you that I am not. There is a common cliché: 'If the wife had the first baby and the husband the second, there would be no third!' A more suitable cliché would be: 'If the husband had to have the first, there would be no babies at all!" I cannot imagine a more terrifying experience, and having racked my brains to search for an equally terrifying experience that the male of the species has to endure, apart from hemorrhoids accompanied by permanent constipation, which I would be far too polite to mention, the nearest comparison I can think of is a boxing or rugby match.

In fact there are endless examples to draw from. If you break a limb you suffer tremendous physical pain. You also suffer fear. You are anticipating the further pain that you will suffer. However, once the medics have done their job and the plaster's on, the bulk of the fear has gone. You are still in severe pain and know you'll have more to come, but now you can handle the situation, you'll start joking with the nurses and allow your friends to scribble on the plaster.

The point is that even if physical pain were involved, we can handle physical pain. Test it out for yourself. Pinch your thigh and dig your nails in gradually increasing the pressure. It is possible to endure quite a severe level of pain and discomfort without any accompanying feeling of fear or panic. That's because you are in control. You not only know the cause of the pain, but can eliminate it whenever you choose to. Now repeat the exercise, and when the pain has reached the highest level that you can bear, try to imagine that it wasn't you causing the pain and that it had just suddenly appeared and that you knew neither the cause, nor how long it would last. Now imagine that pain, not in your thigh, but in your head, ears or chest. You would be in an instant state of panic. Pain isn't the great evil in life. We are equipped to deal with pain. The great evil is: **IGNORANCE! Which leads to FEAR AND PANIC!**

Marathon runners can endure long periods of physical torture and yet at the same time enjoy themselves. Another classic example is the annual varsity boat race. The losers sit head and shoulders bent in abject misery. Yet the winners, who are just as physically exhausted, sit upright and smiling. Physically exhausted they might be, but at the same time they are on a high. Why is one team on a high and the other in deep depression? That's pretty obvious, both teams have expended hours in preparation, training and physical and mental hardship to achieve just one object: TO WIN. Just one inch might separate the two crews at the end of the race. Even so that inch makes the difference between elation and misery. However, it has absolutely nothing to do with their physical state, it is purely mental. The winning crew could immediately row the complete course again, just as olympic runners that have expended their last ounce of energy in winning the gold medal, will immediately complete a lap of honour without even being aware of tiredness.

Mention withdrawal pangs from nicotine and smokers and non-smokers alike immediately associate them with the terrible trauma that smokers undergo whenever they try to quit. This is the second essential point that you need to get firmly implanted in your mind: **WITHDRAWAL PANGS ARE WHAT SMOKERS SUFFER: THROUGHOUT THEIR SMOKING LIVES!** I've referred previously to the smokers' 'Twitch'. Observe smokers, particularly when they are not allowed to smoke, they will either be fidgeting with their hands, or one hand will be near their mouths, or if everything else is still, they will be grinding their jaw. I believe that I ruined my teeth with this continual grinding, I didn't relate it to my smoking and thought it was caused by the normal stresses and strains of life.

Because each cigarette only partially relieves the physical aggravation, smokers suffer physical aggravation even when smoking a cigarette. Many heavy smokers will have their free hand near their mouths when not actually puffing on it.

I said smokers *suffer* withdrawal pangs. In fact this is incorrect, because the true physical withdrawal pain from nicotine is so slight as to be imperceptible, it is merely an empty, insecure feeling. Smokers never *suffer* withdrawal pangs! What they do suffer when they attempt to quit, is a feeling of misery, fear even panic, whenever they are deprived of the crutch that they believe will end the empty feeling. Two other essentials to get clearly into your mind:

1. Smokers don't need to suffer that feeling of deprivation when they quit, provided they realise that, far from relieving it, cigarettes actually cause it.
2. If you don't realise this and continue to smoke, you'll suffer that empty insecure feeling the rest of your life, every time you are not allowed to smoke, or run out of cigarettes, even when you merely suspect that you are running low.

Do not misunderstand me. Because I say that the physical withdrawal pain from nicotine is almost imperceptible, in way am I implying that smokers do not suffer when using the willpower method to stop. They might well exaggerate their physical suffering. If they do, it is because the mental misery and depression that they undergo is very real. I know. It reduced me to tears on more than one occasion. If you were thrown from a skyscraper unaware that there was a secure safety net to catch you, your level of fear would be exactly the same as if there were no safety net. If it were me, I don't think the level of fear would be reduced even if I knew there was a safety net.

That fear is such that smokers have limbs amputated rather than stop. I once sat in a car moving at 60mph from which a woman threatened to jump because her husband refused to stop to let her buy cigarettes. No doubt she would not have jumped, but she had the door open!

A detective was once explaining about the difficulty of obtaining signed confessions from criminals. I said:

"If he's a smoker, just deprive him of tobacco, he'll sell his mother within half an hour."

"We aren't allowed to do that, and even if we were, I couldn't do that to him even if he were public enemy No:1. I'd rather give him my own cigarettes."

Strange that the fear of deprivation is so great that a smoker couldn't inflict it on a fellow smoker, no matter what his crime. Even stranger that our laws do not permit public enemy No:1 to be deprived of the public's No:1 killer.

Nevertheless, real as that fear and panic might be, it is purely mental and caused by ignorance and illusion. Fortunately, it can be removed before smoking your final cigarette. In Chapter 17 I asked: "Why do we scratch an itch?" Imagine having an itch that you are not allowed to scratch that lasts, not for a few seconds, but for 6 months. Imagine the state that you would be in after 6 months and the tremendous willpower you would have had to use in order not to scratch that itch just once during those 6 months. Furthermore, imagine that you truly believed that the itch would last the remainder of your life unless you scratched it. How many hours, days, weeks, months or years do you think that you would survive before you scratched that itch? And if you did manage to survive 6 months without scratching it, try to imagine the sense of relief and elation you would obtain when you finally relented.

That's the torture that smoker's suffer when using the willpower method. Long after the body no longer suffers any aggravation from physical withdrawal, every time those smokers finish a meal, or are bored, or suffer stress, or need to concentrate, they still believe that they are being deprived of a genuine pleasure or crutch. The fact that it is illusion doesn't prevent them from now having a little mental itch that they can no longer scratch. It's the feeling that addicts so aptly describe as: 'The monkey on my back'. Just as the almost inaudible aggravation of a dripping tap will gradually accumulate and drive the victim to madness, so the resistance of the ex-smoker is gradually worn down. At the same time they are gradually forgetting the powerful reasons that made them quit and losing their fear of getting hooked again. Eventually the scales tip and they light a cigarette. They are either dragged slowly and imperceptibly back into the pit or rush helter-skelter to the bottom.

So how do you remove that monkey from your back? Fortunately that monkey isn't real. It is only a figment of your imagination, or more correctly, a leftover from the brainwashing. Why is it that I cannot resist scratching bites and yet am quite able to resist scratching cold sores? Simply because I know that if I scratch a cold sore, It will never disappear. Why did I find it so easy to stop when I extinguished my final cigarette? Because I realised that the empty, insecure feeling of wanting a cigarette was caused by the last cigarette and that the one thing that would ensure that I would suffer that awful feeling the rest of my life, would be:

THE NEXT CIGARETTE

Why didn't I suffer the awful withdrawal pangs that I had suffered previously when I tried to stop? Because I hadn't suffered awful withdrawal pangs previously. The torture and misery that I had suffered previously was the belief that a cigarette gave me some form of crutch or pleasure of which I was now being deprived. Since I now realised that the crutch or pleasure was just illusion, there was no sense of deprivation and consequently, there was no feeling of misery or torture. On the contrary, there was just a feeling of:

I'M FREE!

Okay, perhaps I have convinced you that the actual physical withdrawal pangs from nicotine are almost imperceptible, even so, there will be a period after extinguishing that final cigarette, during which your body will continue to crave nicotine, how do you handle that period? Supposing it is purely mental, how do you get rid of the craving and most important of all, how do you *know* when you have truly escaped?

I promise you that all will be revealed, but there are two aspects about the easiest way to stop smoking about which I still possess certain doubts. Let me make it quite clear, I understand both aspects completely. My doubt is purely the advice I should give to any particular smoker wishing to stop. One aspect is timing, which I will cover later. The other is when you should receive the 'Moment of Revelation'. You need first to understand:

THE 'FIVE DAY' AND 'THREE WEEK SYNDROMES'

241

CHAPTER 29

The 'Five Day' and 'Three Week Syndromes'

Because the physical withdrawal pangs from nicotine involve no pain and are so slight as to be almost imperceptible, you could be excused for believing that they can be safely ignored. Excused, you might be, but:

FREE YOU NEVER WILL BE

It is essential that you are aware that when you lit your first cigarette, you created an evil monster inside your body, rather like a tape worm, except that this little monster depends upon and thrives on one substance only: a powerful poison called NICOTINE! The moment you cut off the supply of nicotine you have already taken the only action that you needed to take in order to purge that evil from your body. Nothing can now prevent that monster from dying of starvation. Have you seen these films in which the hero says to the heroine: lock the door. On no account open it to anyone but me." No sooner has the hero left the scene than his best friend is knocking on the door. At that point every one of the millions that have ever watched the film now realise, without any doubt whatsoever, that the best friend is the werewolf. They also know with equal certainty, that the one person on the planet that won't realise it, is the heroine, and that having just been instructed not to open the door to anyone, the stupid bitch will open it!

You will be in exactly the same situation for a few days. That nicotine monster will be physically there. By comparing it to a tape worm I am not trying to imply the nicotine monster is an actual living parasite. However, its effect is exactly the same! It is real and it is physical, just as a hunger for food is real and physical. But whereas a hunger for food will never go, the craving for nicotine will begin to die the moment you cut off its supply. It will try to entice you to feed it and it will help you to think of it as an actual living parasite.

There are two aspects about that monster that many ex-smokers find difficult to grasp. The analogy of the cold sore can help to explain both of them:

1. If I cannot suffer the irritation of an insect bite for a few seconds, surely it must take enormous willpower to resist scratching a cold sore for several days? In fact it doesn't. Remember I choose to scratch insect bites and have no reason to resist the temptation. Anyway, cold sores are nowhere near as irritable as insect bites, it needs very little willpower to resist them. Ah! Say you, so it must take some willpower to resist the little nicotine monster for a few days. No, because the physical withdrawal from nicotine is so slight as to be imperceptible, the problem is purely mental. However because it's purely mental, if you start off by believing that you'll suffer terrible withdrawal pangs, that fact alone will guarantee that you do.
2. You can physically see a cold sore, observe its gradual demise and know exactly when it's gone. Because the physical withdrawal from nicotine is imperceptible, you can neither see it, nor feel it. There is a danger therefore that you won't realise it is there at all. But it will be there for a few days. You will only know that feeling as: "I want a cigarette." This will worry you, because after all the counter-brainwashing, you shouldn't be wanting a cigarette. Doubt will creep in. The dripping tap will start.

This is why it is essential to know that the little physical monster is actually there. Some ex-smokers are so effectively counter-brainwashed that they aren't even aware of it. I was aware of it when I extinguished my final cigarette, but I no longer interpreted the feeling as: "I want a cigarette." I could see it so clearly for what it actually was: an empty, insecure feeling created by the last cigarette. The feeling itself wasn't pleasant, yet at the same time I was elated because I understood the cause of that feeling and knew that little monster inside me was dying. I took sadistic delight in every one of those death throes and it took no willpower whatsoever, because I wasn't the slightest bit tempted to light a cigarette.

So, even if you do get that feeling of: "I want a cigarette" for a few days, don't worry about it. See it for what it is, a little monster trying to make you open the door. Are you going to be as stupid as that heroine? Or are you going to gloat over the reversed situation: it now holds no power whatsoever over you. On the contrary you now have complete control over it. It is no longer killing you:

YOU ARE DESTROYING IT

The moment that you extinguish that final cigarette, your body will begin to crave nicotine. Imagine a graph in your mind whereby the cumulative effect of that craving tends to build up until it reaches a peak. That peak arrives after about 5 days after extinguishing the final cigarette. I call that peak: 'The 5 day syndrome'. After that peak the physical craving begins to decline, until after about 3 weeks, it disappears completely.

The medical experts will tell you that nicotine is a very fast acting drug and that the nicotine actually leaves your body in a matter of hours. I do not dispute this: In fact my own observations and deductions would support it. However, the speed with which nicotine leaves the body is irrelevant. What is relevant is after what period does a body that has become dependent on nicotine stop suffering aggravation after being deprived of it? I would submit that since the physical aggravation is so slight in the first place and that the real problem is mainly mental, it is impossible to answer that question exactly. So where does my 'five day syndrome' come from? It comes from my personal experiences when I tried to stop by using the willpower method supported by the experience of thousands of other smokers that I have helped to cure.

Smokers using the willpower method tend to find that for about the first five days their minds are completely obsessed with smoking, or more accurately, no longer being allowed to smoke. Then comes a period, it might only be a couple of hours, when ex-smokers suddenly realise that they have forgotten about smoking. That realisation can be a revelation, in that the belief that life would always be miserable without smoking, is now replaced with the belief that time will solve the problem. That moment can also be a great danger. The ex-smokers sense that they are over the hump, congratulate themselves on surviving the awful trauma, feel they are entitled to a little reward and what possible harm could there be if they just had one cigarette?

The 'three week syndrome' presents an even greater danger. This is the moment when you sense that you really have kicked it. You no longer look at other smokers with envy. On the contrary, you wonder why they need to keep sticking those stupid things in their mouths and setting light to them. It's a greater danger because, at that time you feel physically and mentally free. There is an enormous temptation now to light a cigarette, not as a reward or because you genuinely want one, but to prove to yourself that you are free. If you are stupid enough to light it, it will taste weird and give you no sense of crutch or pleasure whatsoever, except to prove your point: THAT YOU ARE FREE!

And you were! Until you lit that cigarette. However that cigarette has put nicotine into your body. The moment you extinguish it the nicotine will start to leave and doubt will enter your mind. One little voice will be saying: "That tasted awful." Another little voice will be saying: "Maybe, but I'd like another one." If you follow the usual trend you will resist having another one immediately.

There is no way that you want to get hooked again, so you allow a safe period to pass. The next time you are tempted, you can now say to yourself: "I smoked one last week and didn't get hooked, so what danger in trying just one more?" You might not realise it at the time, but you have already fallen for the identical trap that you did as a youngster.

The 'three week syndrome' is about the nearest that a smoker using the willpower method gets to 'The Moment of Revelation', and I emphasize that the above observations relate purely to the willpower method. So if Allen Carr's method makes it so easy the moment that you extinguish the final cigarette, why go into such detail about the willpower method?

This is my quandary about the advice that I should give you. If you both understand and follow all of the instructions, I can tell you categorically, that you'll get 'The Moment of Revelation' either before or immediately after you extinguish the final cigarette, and never be tempted to smoke again. I would like to be able to assure you that it will definitely happen for you. However, you might well believe that you have understood everything, but how will you *know*? From the feedback I have acquired over the years, I am aware that most smokers misunderstand several of the points that I make yet still find it easy to stop.

Often smokers will say to me: "It was just as you said it would be, it was hard for the first 5 days (or 3 weeks), then it was ridiculously easy." In fact I never say that. But did they find it hard because they had misunderstood that particular point and the mere suggestion that it would be hard had caused it to be, or did they find it hard because they misunderstood a different point? I cannot answer that question. Even if they did find it hard for a period, they still succeeded. Bear in mind, even when using the willpower method many of smokers have successfully stopped, therefore do not despair if you do not receive 'The Moment of Revelation' immediately.

So how will you know when you are over the hump, or when your body no longer craves nicotine? It's a 'Catch 22' situation. If I don't give you a time limit, you could spend the rest of your life waiting for it to happen, just as many smokers that stop when using the willpower method actually do. If I give you a time limit like 5 days or three weeks, you'll expect it to happen, and if for some reason it doesn't, you'll lose faith, become miserable and so guarantee that it never happens.

The five days and three weeks are factual, but the periods are not exact. The problem is that they are affected and distorted by so many other influences. It might be that the 5 days following your final cigarette were good days for other reasons. You think: "What's so difficult about this?" Then the sixth day you have one of those days that both non-smokers and smokers occasionally have, when absolutely everything that can go wrong does. It really has nothing to do with the fact that you have stopped smoking, but the little monster inside your body has reached its peak, at the very time you thought that you would be over the hump, you are suddenly at rock bottom.

There is another important factor that you need to understand. The physical craving for nicotine is identical to normal hunger, normal stress and panic. It just increases the intensity of the empty, insecure feeling. However, it is at times of normal hunger or stress that you are most likely to light up, and of course when you do, you get a slight relief, your brain is fooled into believing that this relief is genuine.

This is one of the reasons why smokers using the willpower method are never quite sure when they've kicked it. Like the woman at the dinner party who was still craving cigarettes 8 years after she had quit, long after their bodies have ceased to suffer the empty feeling that nicotine withdrawal creates, when they suffer a normal hunger or stress situation, their brains still relate that feeling to: "I need a cigarette!" In reality a cigarette wouldn't even give the illusion of partially relieving the stress, but how are they to know that? They don't. On the contrary, they are still convinced that a cigarette will help the situation. The genuine stress is now increased because they believe that they are being deprived of a crutch that will ease the situation.

They are now in a 'Catch 22' situation. They either go through the rest of their lives believing they are missing out, or they can check it out. Unfortunately, the only way they can do that is to light a cigarette. If they do, they will obtain slight relief; not from any genuine stress, nor from the stress caused by nicotine withdrawal, but from the extra stress caused by feeling deprived of a crutch that is in fact an illusion.

There is of course a knock-on effect. They have now put nicotine into their bodies. The moment they extinguish that cigarette, it will start to leave. This will increase the level of stress caused by any genuine stress situation. It will be further increased because they have broken their vow never to smoke again. What's the solution? Might as well be shot for a sheep as a lamb: light another cigarette. This cigarette will also give them a slight boost. It will partially relieve the withdrawal stress caused by the previous one. All they have now done is to convince themselves that cigarettes do give genuine relief. They don't realise it's just illusion. At that stage they don't even realise that they are back in the pitcher plant and that there is only one direction to travel:

DOWN!

How do we break this 'Catch 22' situation? Why should you believe me when you've probably heard of dozens of ex-smokers that suffer the same problem as that woman? If the actual physical withdrawal from nicotine is so slight as to be almost imperceptible, and if it cannot be distinguished from normal hunger and stress, how can I prove that it even exists? Because smokers also suffer it when there is no genuine stress. Remember the man who ran out of cigarettes in the Spanish restaurant and the man on the yacht. They were in very relaxing situations, their only stress was that they had no cigarettes. Picture the fear and panic of a heroin addict deprived of their heroin, and the marvellous relief when they obtain it. Non-heroin addicts don't suffer that agony. Non-smokers don't suffer it either, and neither did smokers and heroin addicts until they started taking the drug. The drug doesn't relieve the panic:

IT CAUSES IT!

Okay, it's pretty obvious that the problem is caused by the drug, but if the physical withdrawal is imperceptible, how will you know when it's gone? You won't! That's just the point, because it's so imperceptible, you don't need to know. Whether you suffer it before you decide to stop smoking like the man on the yacht, or after you stop smoking like smokers using the willpower method, the problem is mental. Based purely on an illusion that you are being deprived. Once that illusion is removed, so is the problem.

The lady at the dinner party was clearly not suffering from any *physical* withdrawal after 8 years of abstinence. Her problem was obviously purely mental. She started her attempt to stop by believing that she did in fact enjoy a cigarette after a meal. If she believed that when she stopped, why should she not believe it after 8 years, or indeed, for the rest of her life? However, had she first proved to herself that cigarettes are as disgusting after meals as at any other time, would she have perpetuated her illusion?

You solve the 'Catch 22' situation by simply putting it to the test. Shortly, that is exactly what you are going to be doing, so don't worry about it. Perhaps this thought still creates panic in your mind? Remember, the tobacco companies depend on that fear and panic to keep you hooked. Also remember, nicotine doesn't relieve fear and panic, it causes it. Pause for a moment. Is there really any need to panic? If I *have* lied to you, you can always light a cigarette. Now I don't want you to commence your attempt in that frame of mind. I'm merely pointing out that there is no reason to panic, and even if you did, what's so bad about that? What terrible things would happen to you if you never lit another cigarette?

TERRIBLE THINGS WILL HAPPEN IF YOU DO!

I shall merely be asking you to do something that you have already done thousands of times before: to extinguish a cigarette. But this particular cigarette will be a very, very special cigarette. It will probably be the only cigarette that you will genuinely enjoy in the whole of your life, for the simple reason that it will be your last cigarette. But if you extinguish it with a feeling of gloom or sacrifice, you will be miserable.

If when you extinguish it, you wait for 5 days or 3 weeks to pass, what will you actually be waiting for?

For the physical craving to go? I've already explained that it is impossible to tell when the physical craving goes.

For the mental craving to go? If you are still craving cigarettes for 5 days or 3 weeks, why on earth will you stop craving after 5 days or 3 weeks?

To see whether or not you have succeeded? Why should you be wiser after 5 days or 3 weeks?

Supposing you planted grass seed. Would you just sit around for 7 to 10 days waiting for the grass to appear. That would be a stupid thing to do, and you would be pretty bored and miserable if you did. Much better to get on with your life and to wake up one morning and have the excitement of seeing a magnificent green lawn. Even so, if you were stupid enough to sit and watch it each day, that wouldn't stop that grass from eventually growing. It's a physical thing, it is not affected by how miserable or happy you are in the meantime. However, suppose that you are waiting, not for grass to grow, but to stop being miserable. Do you think it would help your cause to start off by being miserable for 5 days or 3 weeks or the rest of your life?

This was another aspect about stopping smoking that didn't even occur to me and I have to thank another old Wandsworthian, Dennis Bray, for enlightening me. I was three weeks into one of my many failed attempts to stop when using the willpower method. As I remember, I wasn't feeling too bad. Dennis, who was also an ex-smoker asked me how I was doing.

"I've survived three weeks."

"What do you mean, you've *survived* three weeks?"

"I've gone three weeks without a cigarette!"

"Well what are you waiting for? Are you going to *survive* the rest of your life? You've done it! You're already a non-smoker!"

He got through to me. I thought: "What am I waiting for? To spend the rest of my life wondering whether I'll ever smoke again?" I had a mini 'Moment of Revelation' and for a few days I was fine. I say mini, because I still didn't understand the smoking trap completely and although it was magic for a few days, eventually something went wrong and I was back in the trap. But the point was noted for the future.

Some smokers ask: "When will I feel like a non-smoker?" Or "What does it feel like to be a non-smoker?" Would you dream of asking someone: "What does it feel like not to eat oranges?" If you re-phrase the question "What does it feel like to want an orange but not be allowed to have one?" The answer is: "Lousy." If you don't want an orange, it won't bother you. On the contrary, it will annoy you if you have to have one. The same thing happens when you say: "I don't want a cigarette." Try to remove this image of smokers and non-smokers as if they are separate breeds. A smoker isn't smoking all of the time. During the interval between cigarettes they are actually non-smokers. Do you feel a different person the moment you extinguish each cigarette? Of course you don't! In fact most of your life you weren't even aware that you were lighting up, smoking and extinguishing cigarettes. All that really happened when you extinguished each cigarette was that you stopped choking yourself for a few moments. In a few days time you will feel like you have always felt: **LIKE YOU!** It'll be a physically and mentally stronger you with more money, more energy more confidence and more self-respect, but it will still be **YOU!**

It is essential not to wait 5 days, 3 weeks or even 5 seconds to become a non-smoker. This is one of the main reasons why smokers using the willpower method find it so difficult. What are they actually waiting for? To find out if they'll ever smoke again? If so, they are waiting not to do something, and will have to continue to wait not to do it:

FOR THE REST OF THEIR LIVES!

You become a non-smoker the moment you extinguish your final cigarette. Remember what we are trying to achieve is **A FRAME OF MIND!** It is equally essential to start off with a feeling of elation, confidence and victory. If the thought of those physical withdrawal pangs still cause you apprehension, remember you have been suffering them all your smoking life and were not even aware of them, so you'll be absolutely no worse off right from the start. Think of the boat race. One team is elated because it won, the other is in deep depression because it lost. That's the only fact which caused their differing frames of mind. Their chances were only fifty/fifty, you are very lucky, you've a 100% chance of defeating your adversary provided:

YOU FOLLOW ALL THE INSTRUCTIONS

Are you still worried that you won't get the 'Moment of Revelation'? Stop worrying, if you follow all the instructions, you'll be a happy non-smoker the moment you extinguish the final cigarette and you won't even need the 'Moment of Revelation'. That will guarantee that you get it. All you need to worry about is to ensure that you understand and follow all of the instructions. What can prevent you from following all of the instructions?

Unfortunately there are powerful influences that can either deceive or distract you. Just as you need to understand my method, so you need to understand and negate the effects of these other influences. Let us start with:

OTHER EXPERTS AND OTHER METHODS

CHAPTER 30

Other Experts and Other Methods

The massive launch of nicotine patches is now over. The media gave tremendous free publicity to the manufacturers, and convinced many smokers that the patch would be the answer to their prayers. Having assisted in persuading them to part up with their hard-earned money by giving them false hopes, the media is now going through its normal routine of knocking the patch.

I recently appeared on television with the managing director of the company that markets nicorette patches in the UK. Apparently he already knew my views on nicotine substitutes and threatened not to appear if I attacked the product. He was a non-smoker and as such had not the slightest understanding of the problem that smokers face. His attitude was: "The real enemy is the tobacco industry, let us not waste time attacking each other. After all a method that will work for one smoker might not work for another." I have every sympathy with his attitude. In fact Brian Hayes who has given me more media support than any other individual, would introduce me as: "Allen Carr, who has a method of stopping that you might find helpful."

In Chapter 3 I asked what chance of success you'd be likely to have if you attempted to cross a road at midnight, standing on your hands, half cut, going backwards, during a snowstorm with a convoy going by. The nicorette man thought that was a bad analogy because obviously not even an idiot would attempt to do it that way. It would be making something that is ridiculously easy into an impossibility.

In fact it's an excellent analogy because that is what these other methods do. They make stopping smoking, which should be ridiculously easy, range between difficult to impossible. The reason the nicorette man and other so-called experts cannot see it, is because it isn't obvious. For years society has been brainwashed by incorrect information.

Nicorette purport to be experts on helping smokers to quit. The brochure which introduces their new patch gives eight tips to help you stop smoking. Let us closely examine their eight little gems:

1. **PICK THE RIGHT DAY:** This is a classic example of the usual platitudes given by people who purport to be experts, but in fact know no more than the average layman. They therefore resort to making meaningless or obvious clichés. They give no guide whatsoever on how to select the right day. Do we really need to be told to pick the right day? Would anyone deliberately pick the wrong day? If your friend had a ticket for the cup final, would you insult his intelligence by saying: "I've got a useful tip for you, make sure you go to Wembley on the right day?"

2. **QUIT WITH A FRIEND:** This is also obvious advice, but has the added disadvantage of being incorrect. The theory is that like mountaineers roped together, if one slips the others will save them. Unfortunately with smoking, it works on the principle that the chain is no stronger than the weakest link. The friend has usually been inveigled to join the attempt anyway, and is not so much a weak link as a missing link, whose sole object is to drag the other smoker down with them. There are several reasons why it is far easier to quit alone and the greater the number in the group that is quitting, the less chance there is of success, because:

   A. Usually just one person in the group has made the decision to stop, and if so, only one person is fully committed. The remainder, although they would like to be non-smokers, are really just going through the motions to support the prime mover. Even when two smokers are both fully committed, one will always find it harder, or think they are suffering more than the other. They begin to lose heart and start saying things like: "Surely just one cigarette can't do any harm?" Or: "Let's just smoke on special occasions." The other suspects them of having crafty puffs and feels cheated and deprived. Suddenly the battle is no longer against the 'weed' but against each other.
   B. Even using the Allen Carr method, ex-smokers might not be aware of it, but their bodies are being subjected to additional tension for a few days. This tension can be quite oppressive when using the willpower method. If several members of an office or family are undergoing that tension at the same time, they will all be searching for and needing compassion and understanding. They will all be expecting it, but none will be eager to give it. Again, it soon becomes a battle against each other.
   C. With group attempts you rely on each other for support. You also tend to be dependent upon one another for failure. If one member of the group fails, they all tend to. Your chances of

success when using the willpower method alone are about one in ten. If your success depends on just one other smoker succeeding, they become less than ONE IN A HUNDRED!

D. When you quit alone, you are the Prima Donna, the centre of attention. You will have the support and sympathy of family, friends and colleagues. This can be a tremendous boost, particularly over the first few days. They will be expecting you to be undergoing terrible traumas and a little bit of exaggeration on your part can't possibly cause any harm, after all, you are achieving something marvellous. Don't misunderstand me, I am not advising you to refuse help and support, I am merely explaining why it is better to have nine people safely at the top of the mountain, all helping to pull the tenth one to safety, than to have ten people all tied up together, slipping and sliding half way up the mountain.

3. **REMOVE ANY TEMPTATION:** Sensible advice. However, is it practical? To do so would involve: never going to a pub, restaurant, football match or any other event or place where smokers might be. You could never buy a newspaper or petrol. You would have to drop all your smoking friends, change your job unless there were a non-smoking policy in the workplace. You would even have to divorce your smoking partner. In fact you could never leave the house and if you stayed at home, you couldn't even watch television. You'd be making enormous genuine sacrifices without any need to do so whatsoever. Sorry nicorette, so far you've come up with 3 duds out of 3. I wonder what comes next?

4. **TAKE ONE DAY AT A TIME:** I suppose they just couldn't resist it. This is the most common yet ridiculous of all the platitudes made by so-called experts on drug addiction. What choice does anyone have in life but to take one day at a time? The expression is completely meaningless, yet conveys a strong implication of misery to come. If they are merely trying to convey that time will heal the wound, why don't they say so? Is it because, like me when I used the willpower method, far from healing the wound, time just made it fester?

5. **KEEP YOURSELF BUSY:** Why? They don't tell us why! I assume it's because they think the answer is obvious. If so, why do they bother to give the advice? I assume the idea is that if you keep yourself busy, you won't sit around all day bemoaning the fact that you are not allowed to smoke. Again, before you even start your attempt, you are being brainwashed into believing that you

must undergo a terrible trauma. Are they really saying that because you stop smoking, you have to keep busy all day every day, never being allowed to sit Down and relax? I'm only halfway through their useful tips and if I were still a smoker, I'm sure that I would have already gone off the idea of quitting. Have they forgotten that they have already advised us to avoid temptation. To do that we would need to live like a hermit. So how would we keep ourselves busy? I suppose we could play patience all day. But that's one of the times that I needed to smoke. Surely that would tempt me? Anyway, most of us cannot sit around all day doing what we choose to do, even in these days of mass unemployment the majority of us still have to work, and even if the unemployed wanted to squander their money on nicotine patches, they probably couldn't afford them. Perhaps they've left the best until last:

6. **CASH NOT ASH:** The man that drafted the brochure was obviously a frustrated poet. Even so, let us be fair to him. It is a very useful tip. I don't suppose there's a smoker in the country that realises that cigarettes cost money.

7. **AVOID PUTTING ON WEIGHT:** Finally they have come up with a really useful tip. This is a genuine worry that many smokers have when they attempt to quit. But let us not be blinded, they don't actually give us any tips on how to avoid putting on weight. Up to now all seven of their tips are either obvious, impractical, unhelpful, meaningless, or incorrect.

8. THE NICORETTE EFFECT:

As the first seven tips are so pathetic, I wouldn't even consider the eighth, even if I understood what it meant. Having read the brochure closely, I believe that what they are actually saying is: "You can break nicotine addiction by taking nicotine." That's about as logical as saying: "You can escape the heat of the frying pan by jumping into the fire." An earlier Nicorette leaflet would say: "The longer you can go without a cigarette, the greater your chance of success." Again, on face value it sounds perfectly logical. It is logical. It is also obvious and meaningless. Take it to its logical conclusion. It's really saying: "If you can go the rest of your life without a cigarette, you have a reasonable chance of becoming a non-smoker. Whereas, if you smoke one within ten minutes, or a week, or a year, you will have failed." Smokers must be so grateful for that sort of advice. I don't suppose there is any way that they would have worked it out for themselves? Mind you, if we act like complete imbeciles, we can't really complain about being treated like them.

It wouldn't be so bad if such statements, although meaningless, gave some sort of psychological boost. In fact they do the exact opposite. If you are trying to go as long as you can without a cigarette, you are either waiting until you give in, **OR UNTIL YOU DIE.** Either way:

YOU NEVER ACHIEVE FREEDOM

What I would really have liked Nicorette to explain is: if the patches work on the same principle as the gum, how on earth will they help to cure smokers if the gum failed to cure them?

I agree that the tobacco industry is the main enemy. My method will successfully defeat the tobacco industry, but every time anybody advertises or advocates a method that makes it harder to stop, it might not be their intention, but effectively they are assisting the tobacco industry. My method isn't just another method that smokers might try, it is the method that will enable any smoker to stop. If smokers fail to stop by using my method, they have about the same chance of succeeding when using another, as a runner who couldn't complete a mile with his legs free would have of completing it with his legs tied together.

It *is* easy to stop smoking if you go about it the right way. Imagine you have spent your life trying to escape from a maze. I have a map of the maze. I know exactly where you are. I know where the exit is. You will come to eight junctions. At each junction I will tell you whether you need to take the left fork or the right. All you have to do is to follow those instructions exactly and you will be free. However there are many rival maps, like the nicorette map, that will be giving you contradictory instructions. At certain junctions it will not give you an instruction to go right or left, instead it will merely advise you to: "Avoid taking the wrong fork." Or: "It will help you to take the correct fork." At certain junctions it will even tell you to take a left fork when you should take a right.

What chance do you think you would have of escaping from that maze if you followed the instructions of those rival maps? Oh you might still do it. Just as many smokers have succeeded in stopping smoking in spite of the bad advice they have received. I've not only tried most of these other methods, but I've studied them. I understand how they work. They all make it harder, not just for certain types of smokers, but for all smokers. Any useful qualities that they might possess, like hypnotherapy, I've already incorporated into my method.

IT IS EASY TO STOP SMOKING!

That is a fact. Smokers think I perform miracles to make something that is extremely difficult, ridiculously easy. I don't! What I actually do is to prevent them from making great difficulties in achieving something that *is* ridiculously easy. If it's really as simple as I maintain, why is it that only Allen Carr discovered the fact? To answer that we need to go back to the hieroglyphics in Chapter 8. Supposing they had been printed so:

XSTOPXTODAY	PITCHER	PITCHER	PITCHER
XSTOPXTODAY	PITCHER	PITCHER	PITCHER
TODAY AB	PLANT	PLANT	PLANT
TODAY	TODAY	TODAY	TODAY
ILLUSION	TODAY	TODAY	TODAY
ILLUSION	TODAY	ILLUSIONX	
TODAY	TODAY	TODAY	
PLANT	PLANT AB	PLANT	
PITCHER	XSTOPXTODAY	PITCHER	
PITCHER	XSTOPXTODAY	PITCHER	

There would have been no riddle. Apart from the fact that it was printed in relief, the diagram is exactly the same. Just one small illusion confused the issue. Yet that one illusion was sufficient to prevent most people from solving the puzzle, myself included. In fact that one small illusion prevents many people from seeing the word FLY, even when the illusion is explained to them.

The smoking trap is confused by many illusions. I've listed fifteen of them in Chapter 3. If you take into account that we have all been brainwashed into believing these illusions from birth, the miracle is not why no one else could see the wood from the trees, but how on earth Allen Carr did, particularly as he couldn't even solve the **FLY** puzzle.

I have often been asked how I did. It's not an easy question to answer. Can you imagine an archeologist specialising in ancient Egyptian hieroglyphics. Someone that has spent a lifetime fascinated and obsessed by the subject, yet unable to crack the code. Then discovering the clue that suddenly makes everything make sense, that explains all the illusions and mysteries?

I was obviously greatly assisted by the fact that, because of the peculiar circumstances of my life, my view of smoking wasn't clouded by many of the illusions that affect most smokers. My father was a chain-smoker. It was blatantly obvious to me that he smoked, not because he enjoyed it, but because he was the slave of something evil. I can remember how foul those first cigarettes tasted, and because I became a chain-smoker so rapidly, I never suffered the illusion that I smoked to enjoy the delicious taste as so many smokers believe.

Many smokers genuinely believe that they smoke because they are weak-willed. I knew from other aspects in my life that I was a very strong-willed person. Many smokers believe that they smoke for social reasons or just to be part of the crowd. I can remember as a teenager doing things for no other reason than being different from the crowd. At dances I despised how most of the boys were like bees round a pot of honey, pandering to the prettiest girls. I would make a beeline for the ugliest. All my friends would rave about Sinatra and his clan. I would maintain that Fred Munge was a far better crooner than Frank Sinatra. They couldn't deny it because they'd never heard of him. Not really surprising, he didn't exist.

Apart from not having many of the illusions that most smokers suffer from, my accountancy training helped me to see through those that I did have. However, unlike the Egyptologist who eventually discovered the key because of his obsession, with me it happened the other way around. I became obsessed because I had discovered the key. It is true that I had spent many hours pondering the smoking problem, not because I had any particular fascination in the subject, but because I hated it and couldn't understand why I couldn't kick it.

Ironically, the vital information that enabled me to solve all the mysteries, had been common knowledge for years. It was that cigarettes contained an addictive drug: nicotine, and that when you stopped taking the drug you suffered withdrawal pangs. What the peculiar circumstances of my life enabled me to see clearly, was just one important aspect of that knowledge which hadn't occurred to anyone previously. Other experts, including smokers themselves, believed that withdrawal pangs from nicotine are what smokers suffer when they try to quit, and that nicotine addiction is some unfortunate side effect to being a smoker which makes it rather difficult to break the habit. They also believed, and many still believe that there is some genuine crutch or pleasure in smoking purely for smoking's sake.

What I could see clearly was that it was only the withdrawal pangs from nicotine that made any smoker light the next cigarette. Once I realised this, it became obvious to me that all the other illusions arose from this one basic illusion. The next logical step was to realise that each cigarette, far from satisfying, was actually causing the dissatisfaction, and the most pathetic and ironic conclusion, that the only reason that any smoker goes through the lifetime of misery and slavery, is to try to get rid of that itch. In other words:

TO TRY TO FEEL LIKE A NON-SMOKER!

Two other important facts eventually occurred to me:

1. There is no such thing as physical addiction to a drug!
2. Exactly the same principles apply to alcohol, heroin and any similar addictive drug.

If it is really as simple as Allen Carr suggests, why isn't it immediately obvious to other intelligent people? Don't underestimate the subtlety of the trap. In spite of the fact that I had spent years puzzling the problem, it wasn't all obvious to me immediately, any more than the relatively simple illusion of the **FLY** puzzle.

Why should it be obvious? We've been brainwashed from birth to believe that smoking does provide some crutch or pleasure. Once we become hooked ourselves, should it be any great surprise to us when it appears to be true? After all, when we light up we do actually feel less nervous, more confident, more relaxed or however we like to interpret the feeling. This is why all drugs seem difficult to kick. When you aren't taking them you feel empty and insecure. The moment partake you get partial relief. Because the whole thing has happened so slowly and gradually, you were completely unaware of what was happening to you. You regard that empty, insecure feeling as normal. For you it is normal you know no different.

That's true, but we are intelligent human beings, when we drink too much and get a hangover the next day, we aren't drinking at the time, but it doesn't take a genius to relate the hangover to the previous night's excess drinking. Are you certain of that? Have you noticed that since so many people have quit smoking, those terrible headaches don't seem quite so severe as they used to be, and even the nausea and mouth feeling like a cesspit doesn't appear quite so bad? Could it be that a major part of that hangover was due to the smoking?

Even if it were all caused by the excess of alcohol, that's a physical effect that we can easily relate to the alcohol. We can do exactly the same thing with the adverse physical effects that we suffer from smoking, the wheezing and coughing, the congestion. However we are now talking about that empty, insecure feeling caused by withdrawal from nicotine. In the previous chapter we established that it is identical to the empty, insecure feeling caused by many other things in life, such as hunger, poverty, disease, unemployment, and that it is just at those times when you are having 'one of those days' that you are most likely to light up. However, your brain isn't capable of discriminating exactly between the various causes. It can't say:

> "I'm suffering a 100 point below depression today. I reckon 10 points is because my wife keeps nagging me to ask for a raise. How do I tell her that in the excitement of getting the sack, I forgot to ask for it? It's not going to be easy to get another job at my age, that accounts for another 40 points. I've got this dental appointment looming on Thursday and the MOT's due on the car, it only just scraped through last year. That must account for another 20 points. Now that all adds up to 70 points. I wonder what's causing the other 30 points? Of course, how could I forget?

I'm a long term heavy smoker, my current level of mental and physical debilitation leaves me permanently 30 points below."

All you will know is that you feel utterly miserable. You will light a cigarette and feel slightly less miserable. The more miserable you felt, the more precious that slight relief will appear. We also discussed in the previous chapter the confusion of the 'Catch 22' situation created if smokers make an attempt to quit still believing that they are making a genuine sacrifice. If they don't smoke the illusion is perpetuated, if they do smoke the illusion is perpetuated. Is it so surprising that the trap isn't immediately obvious even to highly intelligent people? That it fooled all of the people, all of the time for so many years?

Now let's return to that day when you were suffering a 100 point below depression. When you lit that cigarette, and the one after, and the one after that, did it solve your problems, were you laughing and happy? However, there is no doubt that you would solve the bulk of them if you stopped smoking. You would have a 30 point bonus for starters. Perhaps you wouldn't need a raise if you stopped smoking and your wife might not nag you so much. Perhaps you wouldn't need so many visits to the dentists, and you might find that, like me, the visits you do need don't create the same terror. Perhaps you could afford a car that didn't need an MOT and certainly the cost wouldn't worry you so much if it did. You might not even have lost your job had you been a non-smoker. In any event you'll be 100% better equipped to find another. If that doesn't convince you, just think how guilty you'll feel if you have to waste money on cigarettes if you're unemployed. Or perhaps you feel I'm just painting a rosy picture?

I AM! FORTUNATELY THAT'S THE REALITY!

Smoking is a very simple and easy trap to escape from, made difficult by the brainwashing and numerous misconceptions and illusions. My method is to to remove the brainwashing, the misconceptions, the illusions. Many of the other popular methods actually increase the mystique. They merely succeed in making it even harder for smokers to quit. In case you might be tempted to try them, I will go through some of the more popular ones to explain why they make it harder to stop. Let's start with a very popular one:

ACUPUNCTURE:
I never tried acupuncture myself. I used to think it was because I was more frightened of the needle than I was of dying from smoking. However, at the dentist I insist on an injection for the smallest of fillings, so I think my true reason for not trying acupuncture, was because I have a logical brain. I could see the logic of: "Unless you stop smoking, I'm

going to stick needles into you!" But I could see no logic in: "After I've stuck needles into you, you will have no desire to smoke again."

I know many smokers claim that acupuncture did actually help them to stop. This didn't surprise me. I took the view that any smokers so desperate to stop that they were prepared to pay a lot of money to have needles stuck into them, would probably have stopped without the acupuncture. The large number of smokers who attended our clinics that had tried acupuncture and failed confirmed this theory. There was however one notable exception. This man said:

"I found acupuncture very successful."

"In that case why are you here?"

"I found that if I wanted an occasional cigarette, I could remove the bead from my ear. But I now find that I am removing it about 40 times a day!"

It's amazing just how confused some smokers get. When acupuncturists themselves started to attend the clinic, I lost faith completely. Let me make it quite clear, I am not trying to imply that acupuncture will not aid other diseases. My experience with smoking has taught me to keep a completely open mind. It has also taught me to be sceptical without being cynical. I was recently invited to lecture at Yeovil hospital. Another lecturer was an acupuncturist who also happened to be a qualified doctor. I looked forward with great anticipation to hearing a scientific explanation of how acupuncture worked. I can seldom remember being so deflated. It was unbelievably corny. He actually concluded his lecture by saying that it was difficult to assess to what extent acupuncture was just a placebo! Conveniently, this leads me into the most common method of all:

SHOCK TREATMENT:

Is understandably the main tool employed by the medical profession to help smokers to quit. I was brought up to believe that doctors were just one step below God. My knowledge about smoking has shaken my faith in the medical profession. After all, there can be few more common diseases than smoking, yet doctors seem to possess less understanding about it than the average smoker. Let me make it quite clear, I bow to the medical profession's superior knowledge about the diseases that smoking causes, I am referring only to the disease itself, i.e. nicotine addiction and how to cure it.

The frightening thing about the acupuncture lecture, was not only did the doctor himself admit he was dabbling in something which he didn't appear to comprehend, but that the audience, which apart from myself and my colleagues, consisted entirely of the medical profession, seemed so impressed with the lecture and were promising to refer smokers to this doctor. Bearing in mind that they too were dabbling in helping smokers to quit, it didn't exactly inspire confidence in their techniques.

You might well have formed the impression that I'm biased against the medical profession. If so, you are wrong. My youngest son is a doctor. I could not be more proud. I know of no finer profession than devoting your life in order to improve the length and quality of other people's lives. In my opinion most doctors and nurses are outrageously overworked and underpaid. However, this must not blind us to the fact that they are also human.

In Chapter 5 I described a visit to a doctor when I suspected that I had lung cancer. It was Dr. Maisey of Princes Risborough. I could not have been in his presence for more than 10 minutes, but even during that short period I couldn't help but be impressed. I suppose the most important asset of a doctor is to inspire confidence, yet so many that do also give you the impression that you walked under the door rather than through it. Dr. Maisey has this wonderful gift of inspiring confidence, yet at the same time exuding compassion and not talking down to you. If the BMA ever do a training manual on the ideal bedside manner, they should use Dr. Maisey as their role model.

Often at our clinics the atmosphere in the waiting room, is one of lambs being lead to the slaughter, rather than being set free. Such an atmosphere in itself can cause failure, and our receptionists are trained to reverse it before the actual therapy commences. It amazes me that so many doctors and dentists make no attempt to remedy the situation, particularly as the waiting period is all too often longer and more stressful than the treatment.

The day I visited Dr. Maisey was typical. Each patient sat head and shoulders bent staring silently at the floor. I confess that, far from helping to remove the overall atmosphere of doom and gloom, I was probably the chief cause of it. I was still convinced that I had lung cancer and admit to being terrified. Dr. Maisey had just finished examining what was obviously a very wealthy patient who must have been in her nineties. He watched her leave as her chauffeur escorted her at a snail's pace across the waiting room. He must have sensed the atmosphere, as she reached the exit he called out: "Next week I want you back for a pregnancy test." Her body might have slowed down with the years, but her brain was sharp enough: "No need, I'm on the pill!" If a picture can speak a thousand words, there are times when a few words can paint a thousand pictures.

How can I possibly be arrogant enough to believe that I know more about stopping smoking than the whole of the medical profession? Have you heard the expression: 'The majority is always wrong'. How can that possibly be? If nine intelligent people vote one way, the tenth person must be an idiot if he contradicts them. But that isn't the natural reaction of a simple-minded person. Simple-minded people tend to be only too pleased for someone else to make their decisions for them. Simple-minded people tend to fall in with the majority. So let us assume that the dissenter is a reasonably intelligent person. Why does he contradict the other nine? After all, he knows why they have drawn the conclusion that they have. It might be that he has a biased reason. In which case his arguments will appear illogical and betray his bias. On the other hand he might be playing devil's advocate. In which case he will either convince the other nine that he is right, or they will convince him that he is wrong.

Now assume that the dissenter is neither stupid, biased nor playing devil's advocate. Such a person must be pretty sure of his convictions if he continues to contradict the majority. The principle applies if one person is contradicting just nine other people. If he is contradicting the rest of the world, he must be convinced that he is right.

All organised professions have an inbuilt flaw. Students are taught en masse the accepted practices of their elders and betters. They are all reading the same text books, who are they to argue with the combined knowledge and experience of generations of experts? So if there was a mistake in the system, that mistake is passed on from generation to generation, and because all these intelligent, learned people advocate the error, it tends to be accepted.

At the same Yeovil lecture an official from QUIT played a very graphic video made by a young Australian doctor. It was incredibly effective. It showed pictures of smokers that had their legs removed as a direct result of smoking. Again the medical audience were in raptures. Why don't we show that video to every teenager in the country, that would surely prevent them from becoming hooked. The remainder of the audience applauded in agreement.

It's understandable that the medical profession should be obsessed with the health aspects of smoking, after all, that is their expertise, but why are they and parents so surprised when their children get hooked:

"I can't believe that Jane has started smoking, she used to hide my cigarettes she hated it so much."

Everyone does until they become hooked!

"We didn't know about the cancer scares, I really cannot understand how youngsters can start smoking with that knowledge."

If cancer scares don't stop you from smoking, why should they prevent you from starting? Do you think seeing gory pictures of road accidents would prevent youngsters from driving cars or motor cycles? It might do, but only for a couple of weeks. Have you never seen a gory road accident? Did it stop you from driving? Usually it doesn't even stop the people that are involved in them from driving.

At the Kilroy show that I referred to in Chapter 1, he had reached his usual objective whereby half the audience was trying to shout the other half down, so much so that he was beginning to lose control. He cleverly switched the attention to a pretty 10 year old girl and asked her what she thought about smoking:

"I think it's incredibly stupid to spend lots of money and risk awful diseases just to stick those smelly things in your mouth and set light to them."

The statement was made succinctly and with the air of a head mistress that had just entered a room full of 6th formers who were acting like 1st formers. There was a magical moment of complete silence while smokers, ex-smokers and non-smokers alike, absorbed the simple truth of what she had said. However, the little spell that she had cast over us was brief. We were soon shouting at each other again. It was hard to picture that little girl puffing away in just a few years time. I used to regard my father's smoking as pathetic. It didn't prevent me from becoming even more pathetic. Sadly, the odds are that she is already hooked. Too many parents who thought that it was impossible for their children to get hooked have been forced to change their opinions. It's time we stopped it happening.

Another common misconception about smoking is that we weren't aware that smoking did adversely affect health before the lung cancer announcement. That just isn't true. I clearly remember the rest of the school boxing team lecturing a 13 year old on how he had no chance of being a champion if he smoked. Cigarettes were nicknamed 'Gaspers' because they made you gasp and 'Fags' because they fagged you out. All creatures on this planet instinctively know the difference between food and poison. A bird knows from an insects colouration whether it is poisonous.

The lung cancer announcement was shocking news to me, but I cannot say that it was a surprise. I knew smoking was killing me and was expecting some such announcement. To me the only surprise is why the connection took so long to be established. However, the point is that teenagers know that one, two or three cigarettes, won't cause them any harm whatsoever. Therefore shock treatment won't prevent them from experimenting. The trap is identical today as it was before the cancer scares, when youngsters try those first experimental cigarettes, they have no more intention of getting hooked than you or I did.

Be they children, teenagers, centenarians, ex-smokers or people that have never touched a cigarette in their lives, in order to prevent them from lighting that first cigarette, there is no point in trying to frighten them, any more than there would be any point in trying to prevent a fly from sampling the nectar of a pitcher plant when it knows that it can fly away whenever it wants to. To prevent anyone from falling for the trap, you must educate them to understand the nature of the trap. You must make them realise that if they light the next cigarette, they will be compelled to light the one after and the one after until they also reach the stage when they would rather have their legs removed than stop smoking.

The problem is, that society in general and the media in particular, assume that doctors are experts on stopping smoking. They might be experts on the details of exactly how smoking ruins your body, but smokers don't smoke because it kills them, they smoke because they are in a prison that they cannot escape from. Shock treatment appears logical, it ought to work. In fact it has worked for many smokers. However once you know that smoking kills you, if that knowledge hasn't enabled you to stop, repeating that knowledge merely frightens the life out of smokers and makes their need for the next cigarette even greater. If shock treatment works, why do Benson & Hedges spend millions of pounds using exactly the same tactics to sell their poison?

The Kilroy programme was previewed by three smokers. One had lung cancer, another had advanced emphysema and the third had just had a leg removed. They were in tears pleading with other smokers to quit before they suffered a similar fate. Before they had even finished their pleas a Yorkshire coal miner was shouting them down: "Who are you to tell me not to smoke? I smoke a hundred a day and have never had a day's illness in my life." (Another one) Kilroy said: "But they were probably like you a year ago, aren't you worried that you'll be like them next year?" "I'll meet that problem when I come to it." How do you solve the problem of losing a leg? Such is the stupidity, or more accurately, the fear that nicotine addiction creates in its victims.

It was a situation of immense pathos and drama. As Kilroy programmes go, it was a tremendous success in that he had smokers and non-smokers hurling the same sort of non-constructive abuse at each other as they have done on the media since the cancer connection. I sat there as I sit through all of these charades thinking: "If only they would give me a couple of hours on national television, I could cure the whole country!" Kilroy couldn't hide his immense satisfaction. After the programme he asked me what I thought of it. I said: "If the object of the programme was to help smokers to quit, you lost most of your audience before it even started. Smokers don't want to hear about lung cancer, they spend most of their lives avoiding health warnings.

On one National No Smoking Day I was invited to attend a radio phone-in at Nottingham. Also in attendance was a doctor from ASH, some local health workers and a local doctor that ran a stop smoking clinic. In fact the presenter of the programme had successfully stopped after attending his clinic. I say, successfully stopped, I mean he hadn't smoked since. During the programme it became quite obvious that he had found the whole process very difficult and that he hadn't completely got rid of the craving. As each call came in I was getting very frustrated. The Ash 'Expert' would recommend 'Nicorette'. I would say: "Don't touch it with a bargepole." He would advise cutting down, I would absolutely forbid it. Any smoker listening to that programme must have been utterly confused.

Towards the end of the programme the presenter asked various medical experts about their plans for the big day. To me it was both frustrating and pathetic to realise the immense effort that these kind-hearted people were going through, not just one year, but every National No Smoking Day and that the same effort was being repeated all over the country by equally well meaning people, merely to perpetuate illusions about smoking and make it harder to stop.

The presenter then turned to me and asked my opinion of National No Smoking Day. I said it's the one day in the year that any self-respecting smoker will refuse to stop. Most of them will not only smoke more on that day, but more blatantly. I was immediately and understandably subjected to a verbal attack by the doctor from ASH. He accused me of undermining their considerable efforts.

Now just consider the situation. The doctor that ran the clinic claimed a 20% success rate. One of his successes was presenting the programme, but he was certainly no advert for the doctor. All of our clinics currently achieve a success rate in the nineties. Suppose I suddenly decided that there was quite a good living to be made from removing appendixes. I'm not a qualified doctor, but I'm willing to have a go. And suppose I was successful in 20% of the cases. Unfortunately I kill the other 80%. But I figure that they would have died anyway, so I'm still doing some good in the world. That sounds fine. But if the established medical procedures achieve a 96% success rate, I would quite rightly be treated as a butcher and would be imprisoned if I continued to practice.

I said to the representative from ASH "Why are you condoning a method that boasts an 80% failure rate and criticising a method that boasts a 4% failure rate? Ash purport to help smokers to quit. You've known about my method and claims for over 5 years now, not only from me but from several other sources. Why have you not bothered to establish whether the claims are true?" Two more years have passed, and they still haven't! Perhaps you are thinking: "But they are doctors, they are qualified men. Allen Carr isn't." True, but their expertise is purely in the damage that smoking causes to the human body, as far as helping you to stop is concerned, they are no more qualified than you are! The problem with doctors is that because they are qualified people of integrity, we tend to believe the statements they make without questioning them. That is a mistake. Even more dangerous is for doctors themselves to make the same mistake. To assume that their qualifications automatically endow them with specialised knowledge.

Robin Hayley had a similar experience when attending a stop smoking conference at the NEC. A women who had conducted stop smoking courses for 21 years, achieving a 9% success rate, became aggressive when she heard of ours. "How could you possibly achieve such a high success rate after only 3 years, when mine is so low after 21 years?" When Robin suggested that it might just have something to do with her method, she became even more annoyed. Apparently she had stopped smoking herself for health reasons, but admitted that she still had a desire to smoke.

I believed that the medical profession would be my greatest ally. Naively I thought the first doctor that consulted me and found it easy to quit would write to the BMA and insist that they at least investigate the method. Unbelievably after nine years of helping hundreds of doctors and nurses to quit, they still haven't done so. Yet many doctors regularly recommend me to their patients. I have received many compliments over the years, the two that gave me most satisfaction were from doctors. One was from a doctor whose son had quit smoking with the aid of 'EASYWAY'. He merely said: "How I wish I had written that book." The other was from a doctor Myriam, regrettably, I don't know her surname, but she had a distinct Scottish accent. I was doing a phone-in with Robbie Vincent on LBC. Doctor Miriam said: "Allen Carr, your method helped me to quit smoking and I've been using it to help cure other smokers. You have probably saved more lives than I have, more power to your elbow."

I suppose the case of Dr. Miller referred to in Chapter 22 should have forewarned me of what to expect. However what really brought it home was the doctor who was mainly responsible for the introduction of National No Smoking Day in the UK. He is an eminent physician and runs stop smoking clinics at one of the major London hospitals. Derek Jameson, having failed to quit with the usual methods had read 'EASYWAY' and stopped. He invited me to talk about my method on BBC Radio 2. The doctor heard the interview and telephoned me the following day. I was very flattered when he complimented me on the content of the interview and invited me to attend one of his clinics. I confess to being somewhat piqued when he explained that he thought I might pick up a few useful pointers. I was naive enough to believe that perhaps he thought that I might be able to give him a few pointers. However, piqued as I was I had every intention of accepting his invitation, on the basis that, although I might gain nothing, I had nothing to lose.

Unfortunately the doctor went on to explain how they had divided smokers into nine basic categories, and then began to enthuse about the dummy cigarette that they had almost perfected. I realised that, in quitting smoking technology, I had discovered the Rolls Royce while he was still trying to discover the wheel. Perhaps you think I was being stupid, callous and arrogant to believe that I knew more about quitting smoking than a doctor who had probably devoted much of his life to the problem. But that was the actual situation. The man on the yacht summed it up: "It was as if all my life I had been trying to turn on a rusty tap then realised that the tap had a left-handed thread."

Who would be more likely to succeed in turning on a rusty tap? An expert in rust, penetrating oils, mechanics, engineering or leverage that believed the tap had the usual right-handed thread, or a person that had no special expertise, but knew that the tap had a left-handed thread? Shock treatment, or the doctors' method merely reinforces your desire to escape from the prison, but it doesn't give you:

THE KEY TO THE PRISON

I have already explained exactly why smokers cannot force themselves to quit and the more you try to force smokers to quit by the use of shock treatment, the harder you make it for them. Regrettably in recent months, far from understanding the smoker's predicament, certain members of the medical profession have actually increased the persecution of smokers with what is tantamount to blackmail. I am referring to the current trend of some doctors refusing treatment to smokers unless they quit.

A doctor's motive for adopting such a policy might be one of the following:

"Why waste valuable time and facilities trying to prolong your life when you deliberately negate my efforts."

"With limited time and resources, there's no point in giving preference to a smoker, he is killing himself anyway."

"If I refuse to treat him, that will make him stop. I'm really doing him a great favour."

Whichever of those motives might apply, I can only sympathise with the doctor's attitude. However, they overlook one basic and all important fact:

THOSE SMOKERS HAVE NO CHOICE! THEY ARE NOT SMOKING BECAUSE THEY WANT TO OR BECAUSE THEY CHOOSE TO. THEY ARE SUFFERING FROM A DEADLY DISEASE THROUGH NO FAULT OF THEIR OWN. ONE THAT SOCIETY INFLICTED UPON THEM. A DISEASE THAT'S ALREADY DESTROYED THEIR COURAGE. THEY ARE ALREADY TERRIFIED AT WHAT IT HAS DONE TO THEIR BODIES. THEY ALREADY FEEL STUPID AND GUILTY. THE VERY LAST THING THEY NEED IS TO BE MADE TO FEEL MORE TERRIFIED, MORE STUPID AND MORE GUILTY! WHAT THEY DESPERATELY NEED FROM THE MEDICAL PROFESSION IS SYMPATHY, UNDERSTANDING AND MOST OF ALL CONSTRUCTIVE HELP TO ENABLE THEM TO ESCAPE FROM THAT PRISON. IF THE MEDICAL PROFESSION FAILS TO PROVIDE THAT ASSISTANCE, IT SHOULD STOP VILIFYING ITS PATIENTS AND AT LEAST REFER THEM TO SOMEONE THAT CAN!

AVERSION THERAPY:
Is another popular method which most smokers try themselves in one form or another at some time during their smoking lives. It should not be confused with shock treatment which is designed to frighten smokers into stopping by use of such ploys as, showing them what smokers' lungs look like. Aversion therapy is designed, not so much to frighten smokers, but more to make them utterly sick of smoking. The basic tactics involve either drastically increasing the intake of nicotine so that the smoker finds each cigarette physically offensive, or to imbibe other substances, or add other substances to the tobacco in order to achieve the same object.

I never deliberately tried aversion therapy. I had no need to. Chain-smokers suffer permanent aversion therapy and even that doesn't stop them. Most smokers have tried some form of aversion therapy in their lives, either by switching to a brand that they find offensive, or to a pipe or cigars. A common example of aversion therapy is to retain a bottle filled with dog-ends. The idea being that if you are tempted to smoke a cigarette, you merely sniff the foul contents and are reminded of how your breath smelt to a non-smoker.

Aversion therapy is rarely effective for other than relatively short periods, because like all methods other than mine, it does not remove the reason that we smoke. Cigarettes do taste and smell awful, even after we become hooked, we only close our minds to that foul smell and taste, because we believe we need to smoke. Aversion therapy is only effective to help further tip the scales during the period that our reasons for quitting exceed our illusory reasons to smoke. Unless you remove the illusions, sooner or later the scales tip back in favour of smoking. When that happens, we merely block our minds again and stop sniffing the bottle. In fact it soon ends up in the dustbin, because its only purpose now serves to make us feel even more stupid than we already do.

HYPNOTHERAPY:
Another very popular method. Some mystical character, usually with a 'goatee' beard and dressed in a red waistcoat sends you into a trance and appeals to your subconscious, psychic, transcendental mind or whatever. When you come out of the trance, like magic, your craving to smoke, or whatever particular phobia you had, has gone forever. If only life were as simple as that. However, as many smokers have found to their cost when consulting hypnotherapists, it didn't work. Now how can I be knocking hypnosis when I use it myself? I'm not knocking hypnosis. What I am knocking is the popular media-created image of hypnosis. A Svengali type figure controlling his victim's mind. Unfortunately many practitioners are ex-stage hypnotherapists and encourage this image and most of the books written on the subject tend to perpetuate it. Just as society has a distorted conception of

smoking, so it has about hypnosis. But if these delusion techniques help someone get rid of a disease, why explode the myth, doesn't the illusion justify the result?

If in fact it achieved the result, I would agree. But as I said, the hypnotherapist I consulted used these gimmicks and delusion techniques. They served only to embarrass me and to make me lose faith in the process. He did help me, but it was in spite of his efforts not because of them. In fact his gimmicks so distracted me, I almost missed the important message that he was trying to get into my mind.

Hypnotherapy is a powerful and scientific method of communication which is definitely more powerful and effective devoid of the mystique, aids and gimmicks that most hypnotherapists find it necessary to employ. I will explain how it works.

In western society we tend to rush from one panic to another. Our brains are being daily bombarded with a mass of information, but we seldom give ourselves an opportunity to absorb that information. Smoking is a classic example of this panic. All our lives as smokers, we know we shouldn't be smoking, but fear blocks our minds, it's easier to keep our heads in the sand. We'll tackle the problem tomorrow and with a bit of luck the problem may have solved itself by then. This is why it is always easier to solve another person's problem than your own. If you have a problem, the fact that you have one, creates fear and panic. Fear and panic are the enemies of constructive thought.

So the technique is to remove the problem from the subject's mind initially, and to help them achieve a relaxed state and a feeling of warmth and security. The desired state can be simply and effectively self-induced I play an imaginary round of golf at my favourite golf club. The weather and conditions are perfect and I'm playing what looks like turning out to be the finest round of golf that's ever been played. I'm now in a state of bliss, and having achieved the correct state, I can now forget about golf and concentrate on the particular problem that I had to solve in a relaxed and constructive manner.

Obviously it needn't be golf. Anglers will tend to choose an idyllic fishing spot. It doesn't even have to be an actual place, it can be a complete fantasy, or a situation in your childhood. In the group sessions at our clinics we describe a walk around a beautiful garden. "You are nearer to God in a garden than anywhere else on earth." Many people believe that, myself included.

Hypnosis does not stop people smoking! In fact hypnosis doesn't cure any disease or phobia! In medical terms it is the equivalent of a hypodermic syringe. It is the drug contained in the syringe that cures or kills the patient. It's the message that stops you smoking or cures your phobia! Hypnosis is purely a relaxed state in which the subject becomes more receptive to the message.

Sometimes our failures write to us and say: "Hypnosis just didn't work for me." That's like saying: "Hypodermic syringes don't work for me." Often people will say: "I didn't go under." Or "I wasn't hypnotised." We say to them: "What do you mean, you didn't go under?" This is the damage that the Svengali type protagonists engender, an expectation in the subject that they will undergo some weird or mystical experience. The problem is that many subjects do, even with my method. We do not use any gimmicks or illusory techniques, even so often people say things like: "I couldn't open my eyes." Or: "I felt so heavy." Or: "I felt as if I was floating on air."

A famous hypnotherapist has demonstrated on TV how it is possible to push a needle through the skin between the thumb and forefinger of a smoker under hypnosis, without the subject being aware of it. The feat is greeted with gasps of admiration from the audience, mind you, what bearing it has on helping the smoker to quit is never explained. Neither is it explained why the subject remains unaware of it after being brought out of the 'hypnotic trance'. Could this be because it was purely a gimmick? I can remember as a schoolboy sticking pins in my skin. If you do it in the right place there is no pain.

On the other hand, some people say: "I went under really deeply." What actually happened was that they were so relaxed that they fell asleep. You might think that would prevent the message from getting through. In fact it doesn't. Your ears don't stop working just because you are asleep. Neither does your brain.

There are various methods of communication. The written word, the spoken word. The most powerful of all and consequently the greatest form of hypnosis, is the combination of the spoken word with the visual image. I am of course talking about television. Fashion and advertising experts have been aware of it for years.

When watching a fascinating programme on TV or reading a good book, you are so absorbed that you are no no longer aware of your immediate surroundings. You haven't lost consciousness, but you are in a trance. However, are you aware that you are in a trance? Of course not. If you were, you would no longer be in one. However, there is nothing sinister or even mystical about the situation that I have described. In fact it's an everyday occurrence known as being in a shell of concentration. An observer could see that you were in that trance and would have the power to bring you out of it merely by breaking your concentration. The trance is not only capable of being self-induced, but subconsciously is so practically every day of our lives. It's called daydreaming. However in that hypnotic state, whether it be consciously or subconsciously self-induced, or induced by an author, playwright, orator or hypnotist, the communicator has direct and unhindered access to your mind. That doesn't mean that the communicator controls your mind. It's up to you to assess the information and suggestions, and to accept or reject them.

Recently another hypnotherapist telephoned me and said: "I think you have done more for hypnosis than anyone past or present." I was extremely flattered but I am not convinced that this is true. In fact I know that I have annoyed many practitioners by removing, or rather trying to remove the mystique from the subject. I hope in the long term this will help to advance what is an extremely useful technique.

Let me make it quite clear, we achieve the high success rate that we do at our clinics, not because Allen Carr is the greatest hypnotist in the world, but because Allen Carr understands the mysteries of the smoking trap better than any one else in the world. Hypnosis is just one of the tools that I use to help me to remove the fear that blocks smokers' minds and so enable them to receive my message and the key to their prison. There are many similar examples. The one that influences, or hypnotises me more than any other, is Alistair Cooke, the 'Letter from America' man. He doesn't shout or rant and rave. He has the quietist, softest voice imaginable. But I listen to his voice in raptures. The particular fact that he is stating, I'm often already aware of, but he has this marvellous ability of opening my eyes, of making me see the same facts in a completely different light.

Barbara Woodhouse had the same gift with dogs and horses. Sir Patrick Moore has done the same for astronomy. These people are often eccentrics, but their knowledge and enthusiasm for their subject transcends all. Perhaps the greatest living example is David Bellamy. I am sure he would excuse me for pointing out that he is not the greatest physical example that ever lived. He even has a slight speech impediment. That must be quite a handicap for someone that depends so much on communication. Can you imagine a more boring subject than botany? Yet he reigns supreme, apparently oblivious to these handicaps, when he talks about botany, you cannot help but be hypnotised by his knowledge and enthusiasm for his subject, he compels you to feel as excited as he does.

Suggestion is an exceedingly powerful tool, but only if the listener is relaxed enough, not only to hear the message, but to absorb it. Hypnotherapy is the power of suggestion. Some people believe, including many hypnotists themselves, that some people are bad subjects for hypnosis, or even cannot be hypnotised at all. That is nonsense, from the moment we are born we are all subjected to suggestion, how else would we learn anything?

Other people believe that the only hypnosis is self-induced hypnosis. In a sense that is true. You can neither induce a subject that doesn't want to be hypnotised into an hypnotic state, nor can you force a subject in such a state to do something that they do not wish to do. One of the essentials to achieve a truly hypnotic state is for the subject to feel calm and relaxed. It automatically follows that, if the subject has no wish to be hypnotised, or should the hypnotist make a suggestion which the subject finds improper or frightening, the subject would no longer be relaxed.

You might well question that. Possibly you have seen or heard of stage hypnotists that force people to act like chickens or to striptease. Don't be fooled. These people are volunteers, they know full well what they are volunteering for, why else would they volunteer? The showman doesn't force them to do what they do, like the effects of alcohol, he gives them the excuse to make an exhibition of themselves. You don't have to hypnotise people to do that. Visit any rugby clubhouse after the match, there are people who just cannot wait to make a fool of themselves.

If it were possible to control the minds of people by the use of hypnosis, the world would be controlled by criminals. Come to think of it, it probably is. But they do it without the use of hypnosis.

Obviously the hypnotist must have the cooperation of his subjects, and will not get it unless he also has their confidence and trust. Subjects can induce themselves into the desired relaxed state of mind and body. This effectively removes any feeling of fear or panic, thus enabling them to think clearly and objectively. However, what good is that if the subject does not have the requisite knowledge or understanding to solve the problem? In such cases, the support of the therapist is essential. Not only to assist the subject to achieve the relaxed state, but to replace the illusions with reality.

This does not mean that hypnosis cannot cause damage. It can and all too often does. Smoking is a classic example. Hypnotherapists that attempt to cure smokers have the same misconceptions about smoking as the rest of society. The better hypnotists they are, the more effectively will they ingrain the wrong and damaging facts into the minds of their victims.

Hypnosis is a powerful tool that should only be used, not just by an expert hypnotist, but by an expert on the particular problem or phobia that the afflicted person suffers from. No matter how impressive the premises, the qualifications and the diplomas might appear, on no account should you consult a hypnotist that purports to treat a wide variety of problems, unless you have received a personal recommendation from someone that you know you can trust.

The point is that all these other methods have been around in one form or another for years, if they worked, smoking would already be dead. You could say that the same applies to Allen Carr's method. But Allen Carr doesn't possess the mass financial and marketing strength of the BMA, ASH, QUIT or the Acupuncturist, or Hypnotherapy professions, he is a lone individual. There is only one reason that he has achieved the fame that he has, it's the same reason that smokers fly from all over the world to consult him:

HIS SYSTEM WORKS!

But surely, people are different, some methods must suit some smokers more than others. There are many top golfers, but their swings and techniques vary quite considerably to accommodate their varying shapes and sizes and there really isn't so much difference between the scores of the top professionals. That is true, but you will find there are certain basic principles in the techniques of all top golfers, without which, they would not be top golfers. For example, supposing they literally got the wrong end of the stick. If Nick Faldo tried holding the club by the head and tried to hit the ball with the shaft, he couldn't beat the worst player in the country.

Perhaps you think that I exaggerate. Take the case of George Howard, the recently retired professional from my golf club. A more canny customer you will not be likely to come across. Any man that can make his living from the most difficult game ever devised must command respect.

For over thirty years, every time I've driven off from the first tee at Malden, I have been aware of George watching me and thinking: "How on earth does he expect to hit a golf ball with a swing like that?" To his eternal credit, he kept his thoughts to himself and I admire him for the incredible feat of self-restraint that must have necessitated. Even so, he could not resist dropping a few subtle hints like: "You hit the ball very well for a man with a broken arm." But I forgive him.

However, everything comes to he who waits. For health reasons, George recently made an attempt to stop smoking. The tables had suddenly turned. Since I had never sought his help as a professional, I cannot blame him for not seeking mine. Nevertheless, I was both very interested and supportive of his attempt, and George was aware of my interest. George decided to keep a packet of his favourite cigars with him. I said: "George, why are you doing that if you are not going to smoke again?" He ignored my advice but every time we met he would proudly open the packet of cigars and prove to me that he hadn't smoked one. However, one day he didn't. So I asked to see the packet. One cigar was missing. Only one mind you, that was until the next time I saw him.

Now if I had a lesson from George and had tried to hold the club the wrong way around, he would have thought me an imbecile. But by keeping a packet of cigars with him, George was also holding the wrong end of the stick. The only real difference was that in one case it was blatantly obvious. If we translated these so-called smoking experts advice into golfing terms, they are saying:

"You'll get a firmer grip on the club if you hold it with the head."

"Keep your eyes closed. It will prevent you from being distracted."

"You'll generate much more distance if you pivot like a hammer thrower before you strike the ball."

There have been numerous technical advances in recent years which have contradicted what the experts had been teaching for years. The 'Fosbury' flip in high jumping and the 'V' position in ski jumping. However, although these techniques proved the established experts to be wrong, they were merely refinements to established techniques. My method is a complete reversal to the established techniques. The problem is that every smoker that has ever successfully quit automatically becomes an expert. Now I am not saying that no smokers have ever found it easy to stop, either by using other methods or, by using their own willpower. Thousands have, in fact it was a very famous ex-smoker that first implanted the idea into my mind that it might be easy to stop. When I was a smoker I would spend every evening half asleep, half awake watching television. On this particular evening I woke up and could hear Dennis Norden speaking in that calm matter of fact manner that he has. I never even opened my eyes and to this day I cannot tell you which programme it was, but he was saying something like: "I woke up in the morning and my mouth was like a cesspit. I decided there and then to stop smoking, and you know, I'm ashamed to say, but I never had the slightest craving. It was easy."

I immediately dozed off again without even giving it a thought. But his words must have been playing on my subconscious mind while I slept. When I woke up in the morning I found myself thinking about smoking. In particular I was thinking: "Why should it be so difficult?" I decided there and then to have another try at stopping, but instead of building up feelings of doom and gloom I thought: "I'll pretend that it's easy to stop." To my utter amazement, it was. For a few days I was floating on cloud nine. I really believed that the problem was solved. However something happened and because I still didn't understand smoking at that time, the magic bubble burst and I found myself back in the trap, but it was another important piece in the jigsaw puzzle.

When shock treatment does work, it can be very effective. A client at the Birmingham clinic said:

"I wish I could be like my husband. He smoked 3 times as many as I did. Three years ago he woke up one morning and said that he would never smoke again. He did not suffer any withdrawal pangs and has never had the slightest urge to smoke since." I said:

"I waited over a third of a century listening to similar stories and hoping that one day it would 'just happen to me'. It never did. Nowadays I always probe these stories and invariably there is more to it."

"I assure you it happened just as I have said."

"But if I could talk to your husband there must have been something to trigger the attempt."

"He had visited his friend in hospital the previous day."

"What was the friend suffering from?"

"Lung cancer."

"You have already given the explanation. Your husband was just like the rest of us – It won't happen to me. Then he saw it happen to his friend. It was no longer just a statistic. He saw the misery and fear that his friend was going through. He probably thought – that could be me lying there. It was the trigger he needed to see smoking as it really is, not through rose-coloured spectacles."

Another common situation is when smokers are forced to abstain for a period because of bad health or some other reason. Many smokers nowadays find it too much hassle to smoke on long distance flights. Providing they survive the initial panic, they usually soon forget about smoking and, like the man on the yacht, are quite pleased to learn that they can actually endure quite long periods of not smoking without any discomfort. Nine times out of ten, once the reason for the abstinence has gone the smoker will light up, and just as a meal tastes so much better after a fast, so that cigarette will appear extra special.

However, occasionally smokers will use that period of enforced abstinence as a springboard. Sometimes they don't even make a conscious decision to quit. They merely delay lighting the next cigarette, and providing they continue to delay, it eventually dawns on them that they are now non-smokers. They almost drift out of smoking as they drifted into it, and because they don't get all uptight and into a panic, they find it relatively easy.

A few years ago I was enjoying a meal at my golf club. After the meal, a young girl engaged me in conversation:

"I don't want to stop smoking, I enjoy it too much, but I've heard you used to smoke 100 a day. You must have really enjoyed smoking?"

"I hated it!"

"But you must have enjoyed the one after a meal?"

"Not really, I couldn't enjoy meals without smoking, but that's not really the same thing. The truth is, meals used to interfere with my smoking and I stopped eating breakfast and lunch because of it."

"I can't believe you've enjoyed this meal without smoking."

"I know. While you're still a smoker, it's hard to believe it's possible to enjoy a meal without one, or anything else for that matter. But you've been smoking while we were talking, and you haven't given me the impression that you are getting any particular pleasure from it, in fact you didn't appear to be conscious of it until now. Just take a couple of deep drags on that cigarette and tell me what marvellous sensations you are experiencing that I am missing. Make me feel I'm being deprived."

There was a pregnant pause at this stage. I think the girl was expecting me to tell her about the harm it was causing her health and about all the money she was wasting and how disgusting smoking is. But after her brain had ticked over a few seconds she took a couple of drags. The conversation continued:"I'm not even enjoying it."

"Then why do you find it so difficult to believe that I don't miss them?"

"I believe you now. Obviously you don't miss them."

"But you've just told me that you are not even enjoying that cigarette, so why are you smoking it?"

"I don't know. But I'm going to try to stop."

About a month later I received a phone call from the girl. She said:

"Mr.Carr, I must know what you did to me. I wasn't aware of being hypnotised or of going into a trance, but when I've tried to stop before, I can't even go an hour without screaming at my baby, I haven't even had the slightest urge to smoke. I've had no withdrawal pangs and I feel absolutely great! What did you do to me?"

"I just helped you to see the truth, nobody actually enjoys being a smoker."

I invited her to attend my clinic to get the full Allen Carr treatment. She said: "No need, I'm a happy non-smoker." I understand her attitude, but the tragedy is, that in all probability, she will get get hooked again. It's nice to hear stories about smokers that found it easy to stop. I am convinced I would now be dead had I not been lucky enough to hear Dennis Norden's words. Such stories do much to counter the morale destroying effects of the whinging stoppers. Unfortunately stories of smokers that found it easy to stop can do almost as much damage. They do boost morale, but they also create several dangers:

1. They give other smokers false hopes. You are lead to believe: "If I wait long enough, I too will wake up one morning and have no desire to smoke." I waited over 30 years for it to happen to me. Ah say you, but it did eventually happen. That's true, but it wasn't just the Dennis Norden incident, it involved a combination of factors. I was just incredibly lucky. Don't forget that every year two and a half million smokers aren't.

2. The smokers that found it easy to stop do not understand why they found it easy to stop. If they happened to be using nicotine gum or patches, or acupuncture, shock treatment, aversion therapy or hypnosis, they might well believe it was the gimmick or expert whose help they sought that made it easy to stop. Naturally, they will recommend that particular method to their friends and

perpetuate the myth that these methods do assist some smokers to stop. **THEY DON'T! SMOKERS STOP IN SPITE OF THEM AND NOT BECAUSE OF THEM!** If the smoker doesn't seek help, they will often attribute their success to the wrong factors. The smokers that drift out of it tend to keep a packet of cigarettes in their pocket or handbag. They will advise their friends to adopt the same procedure.

3. Because they stopped, but didn't actually remove the reason that they smoked, they are always vulnerable. Eventually they are tempted to try just one cigarette and get hooked again. Sooner or later it dawns on them that they have been incredibly stupid. They then try to repeat the formula that worked so successfully before. What they don't realise is that the formula only worked because of the particular circumstances that prevailed at the time. Now the situation has altered. They think: "Before, I never even thought about smoking." So they try to block it from their minds. But they did think about smoking on the previous attempt. They thought: "Isn't it marvellous, I don't need to smoke." Whereas now they are thinking: "I'd love a cigarette, but I'm not allowed to have one. I'll try not to think about it." Is it really surprising they can think of nothing else?

There are just two essential ingredients to ensure that it is easy to stop: **A HAPPY FRAME OF MIND** and **CERTAINTY!** They are dependent on each other. No way will you achieve a genuinely happy frame of mind unless you are certain that you have stopped permanently. You might stop for a period with just a happy frame of mind as I did after the Dennis Norden incident. Similarly, it isn't possible to be certain that you have stopped, unless you are happy about it.

The reason that shock treatment is effective when it works, is because it is certain. The smoker's usual panic of: "How can I possibly function without cigarettes?" is completely obliterated by the greater panic of: "Unless I stop, I'll die!" The man whose friend contracted lung cancer was lucky. His friend provided the necessary shock. Unfortunately his friend wasn't so lucky. Usually, it is the smoker's own health that provides the shock. Sometimes they are lucky, the shock is a warning signal. All too often however, it is too late. Ironically, such smokers often ignore the warning signal and stop when it's too late.

The problem is, that although shocks can be sufficient to prevent the ex-smokers from moping about the fact that they can't smoke, they aren't particularly happy about it. As time passes the effect of the shock diminishes and at the same time the feeling of deprivation increases. Sooner or later they are tempted to try just one cigarette.

The type of smoker that just drifts out of it does the complete opposite. They remove the panic and are quite happy to be non-smokers, but there is no certainty. They are like a leaf being blown in the wind. They have no real control. They hope that they'll remain non-smokers, but retain the belief that they've made a genuine sacrifice. As the gunge gradually leaves their bodies, they also tend to forget the evils of being a smoker. Sooner or later the massive temptation to which ex-smokers and non-smokers are being daily subjected to takes its toll.

The point that I want you to get firmly into your mind is this: **IT IS EASY TO STOP SMOKING!** You don't have to rely on doubt, chance or luck to stop smoking. If you experiment with other methods or heed the advice of other experts, that is exactly what you will be doing. You might be lucky enough to get out of the maze, but why rely on luck when my method will guarantee your freedom? I don't care if you think: "How can Allen Carr be so arrogant as to think he knows more about stopping smoking than anyone else on the planet?" I don't think it:

I KNOW IT!

Now let's deal with the so-called experts that cause the most damage of all:

THE MEDIA

CHAPTER 31

The Media

My loss of faith in the medical profession is insignificant compared to my disillutionment with the media. I knew that I had to prove my method, but just as I thought the first doctor that understood the method would spread the word, so I thought the first TV producer or celebrity would do the same.

The following celebrities have actually attended our clinics: Johnny Cash, Susannah York, Julie Christie, Ruby Wax, Dennis Waterman, Rula Lenska, Emma Freud, Mathew Kelly, Tony Anholt, Lady Astor, Lord & Lady Bonham-Carter, Marti Caine, Patrick Cargill, Tracy Childs, Christopher Cazenove, Quentin Crewe, Frederick Forsyth, Fish, Mark Knopfler, Dave Stewart, Leslie Grantham, Marie Helvin, Mike Reid, Jane Irvine, Robin Jackman, Ian Maxwell, Jenny Murray, Pete Murray, John Sessions, Pamela Salem, Nina Simone, Dudley Sutton and Kerry Packer. We do not advertise. All came because of a personal recommendation from one or more ex-smokers that found my method successful.

We have also helped to free many TV and radio producers, journalists and ex-smokers in similar positions of power and influence within the media. I cannot claim to have cured them all, but I know that many of them found it easy to stop having failed by using the usual methods.

Even the most loyal of my supporters will tell you that I am not the most patient of individuals and that, in spite of the fact that I really do try, I find it difficult to suffer fools lightly. However, it has taken an almost unbelievable amount of restraint on my part to sit in silence and on occasions to suck up to some jumped up impresario, repeating the same sort of dull sludge that the media has been churning out about stopping smoking for over 30 years. The stupidity, the inefficiency, the criminal waste of labour and materials, the lack of organisation, the tantrums, the petty jealousies, the sheer arrogance and pomposity of the whole profession.

Half the programmes nowadays are taken up by the credits. Is anyone really interested in who did the dubbing or vision mixing? Can you imagine the chaos if every business felt it necessary to adopt the same procedure? When you go out for a meal, it's nice to know the name of the waiter or the owner, but do you really need to know who chopped the carrots? The media's obsession with its own self-importance might be excusable if it produced the goods. All too often imagination is rife in news and documentary programmes, when all we really need is truth, and completely lacking in fictional entertainment where it would be most welcome.

I have a choice of 41 television programmes. You would think my main problem would be in deciding which programme to watch. In fact it's the complete opposite. I used to spend an evening watching television. Nowadays I spend an evening flipping through the channels in a vain search to find just one interesting programme.

So why have I sat in silence and sucked up to the media? Because I know that I cannot possibly win the war without the help of the media. Why don't I continue to grovel? Because that policy hasn't worked. There is good and bad in every profession, I'm relying on the fact that there must be members of the media that are both big enough and powerful enough to accept, or even reject my criticisms, yet still have enough imagination and guts to assist me in my cause.

Ironically, it was an incident involving one of the giants of the media that has opened my eyes. I'm referring to the Robert Maxwell scandal. After his death and the revelation that he had been conning his employees out of their hard-earned pensions, several of these fearless knights of the press confirmed that they knew or suspected what had been going on, but were frightened to talk for fear of being sued by the great man. It's pathetic how often the press will print inuendoes or even blatant lies about some defenceless individual, yet with the likes of Maxwell, they hadn't the guts to print the truth. That is of course until he was dead. How even more pathetic that our legal system, which was surely designed to protect the innocent and punish the guilty, usually does the complete opposite.

I have already referred to the pathetic attempts of the media over the years to assist smokers to quit. If I had to judge them on sheer incompetence, the BBC effort a few National No Smoking Days ago would get the oscar. Their expert on this particular occasion was Anne Robinson. Anne spoke with such authority and confidence, that it didn't even occur to me for a while that she hadn't actually stopped smoking at the time. Can you imagine the BBC doing a programme about 'How To Play Golf', and instead of having Nick Faldo to give the expert advice, to have a person that had **NEVER ACTUALLY PLAYED GOLF?**

Anne came out with all the usual meaningless or incorrect clichés and platitudes like: "Take one day at a time." "Avoid smoking situations." However, she did come out with a new one, at least it was one that I hadn't heard before: "You must have more than one reason to stop." I have heard many stupid statements about smoking over the years, but this one struck me as reaching new heights of idiocy, and as a smoker herself, even Anne must have exercised incredible self-control to make such a statement without blushing.

In one of my vain attempts to stop when using the willpower method, I listed 30 valid reasons not to smoke. The idea is that every time you are tempted to smoke, you take out the list and by the time you've got to the fifth item the temptation has gone. It sounds very sensible, but like the other variations of the willpower method, it ignores the real problem, which is to remove your desire to smoke. Eventually that desire becomes so great that you don't bother to take the list out of your pocket. The point is: that list didn't change anything, I'd merely recorded what I already knew: **SMOKERS ARE MUGS!**

One client at Raynes Park with a much better imagination than mine once listed 60 valid reasons. It did not work for him either. Anne wasn't being very flattering to herself, and like most of these so-called experts, was insulting the intelligence of her viewers. I should imagine that most smokers nowadays are aware that smoking is a killer, costs a fortune, is filthy and enslaves its victims. I should have thought that any one of those reasons was sufficient to make any smoker want to stop. The combination of all four gives every smoker on the planet sufficient reason to stop, add on the other 56 valid reasons and there ceases to be any argument. If smokers can block their minds to the threat of losing a limb, they can just as easily close their minds to comparatively insignificant reasons like £30,000 or a lifetime's slavery. The point is: it does not matter one iota that smokers have umpteen, powerful reasons to stop, if they want a cigarette and believe that they will always be miserable without one, they will block their minds to all the powerful reasons to stop and apply all their efforts to find an excuse to smoke a cigarette. It doesn't matter how feeble or illusory the excuse is.

Admittedly Anne did preface each pearl of wisdom with: 'They say'. Unfortunately she didn't say who 'they' were, but I can assure her and the BBC that 'they' were wrong! This is the terrible damage that such programmes do. Anne Robinson is a journalist. I've admired and enjoyed her comments over the years on 'Points Of View'. She is an attractive, intelligent, constructive, pleasant, objective and broad-minded lady. Because she is so impressive, had I been listening to a subject other than smoking, I would have accepted her *expert* advice lock, stock and barrel. But because I am an expert, I was aware that she was talking absolute nonsense. However, how many millions of viewers accepted what the BBC offered as expert advice and remained in the trap as a result?

Every one of the dozens of programmes and so-called experts that I have listened to over the years, which attempted to help smokers quit, actually make it harder. Fortunately most smokers themselves have sensed this and have learnt not to watch them. In fact there is only one person that I have heard talk sense about smoking. That is Dr. Bobbie Jacobson, a very pleasant and attractive lady with a quiet and rather laid back manner, but positive and convincing. She was explaining that once you got it certain in your mind that you really wanted to stop, it wasn't really so difficult. I remember thinking: "That's good. If I were still a smoker, I would have been encouraged by those remarks."

Unfortunately Bobbie only spoke for a few moments and was immediately followed by an actress who had successfully kicked the weed. Nothing wrong with that, good positive back up to what Bobbie had been saying. The actress described how the first 3 weeks had been absolute misery. However, she was determined not to give in because millions of viewers were charting her progress. The tone of the programme was beginning to change, but I suppose many smokers watching might have been prepared to suffer 3 weeks of misery in order to get free. The interviewer said:

"After 3 weeks you were okay?"

"Oh no, the next 6 weeks were even worse!"

I'm not doubting the sincerity of that lady. Obviously she exaggerated as we all do when using the willpower method. I think it would also have been apparent to most viewers, that being an actress, she probably poured on the agony. But can you imagine the effect she had on the many smokers that don't believe they could survive a day without cigarettes. All Dr. Jacobson's efforts were wiped out with one fell swoop.

Very few of the smokers that attend our clinics understand the method completely. Most of the smokers that have already tried all the other methods are very grateful. They needn't necessarily understand why the method works, but are aware that they wouldn't have stopped without it. Many believe that I have some special mystical power. What I do have is specialised knowledge, a map of the maze. I have often heard it said that a genuine giver needs no thanks for the gift, the mere act of giving is reward enough. I wish I were that noble. It is sometimes extremely difficult to talk for eight hours, practically nonstop, in a smoke-filled room and at the same time maintain the level of enthusiasm and concentration that is required. It is always mentally exhausting. If you happen to have a cold or throat infection, it can also be physically painful. I don't search for sympathy or praise. I do what I do for the purely selfish reason that I thrive on it. However that praise is my life-blood. I could not carry on without it. It is as essential to me as laughter is to a comedian.

It is very frustrating when our clients succeed but give no credit whatsoever to us. The man who had tried everything, succeeded with my method but wanted his money back because, 'he had done it himself', was the extreme. However, there have been several similar cases like, 'I think I only did it because I had to pay you money and I didn't want to waste that money'. Even when you ask why the £30,000 that they would have saved anyway didn't seem to help them to stop, the penny still doesn't seem to drop. However we have learned to be philosophical about these things. We know that these smokers were unlikely to succeed without our help and the praise and gratitude that we receive from the others more than compensates. Except when the ex-smoker is a person of fame or influence.

There are two such people that have given me more sleepless nights than all other smokers combined. Ironically, they were both successes and I believe them both to be men of intelligence and integrity.

The first is Paul Reisen of TV-AM fame. They had decided to do a big anti-smoking campaign during the week leading up to National No Smoking Day. Paul was the man in charge of the campaign. I was delighted. It was the opportunity I had been waiting for. Not only had I helped at least a dozen employees of TV-AM to quit successfully, but Paul Reisen happened to be one of them. He explained that each day they would be featuring different methods of quitting and that he would like to feature my clinic on the final day. I said: "Paul, you have personal proof that my system makes it easy to stop, why don't you give me the whole week? I'll start a campaign that will get the whole world off of smoking." He said: "But your way is the easy way. Some people can't do it the easy way, they have to do it the hard way. In any case, part of the campaign will be to go to the States to study their methods, they are always fifteen years ahead of us over there."

He'd just given me a quick left and right to the solar plexus which he eventually followed up later with a knife in my back. I'm not often lost for words, but how do you explain to an intelligent man, that if people find it difficult to achieve their objective by doing it the easy way, they cannot possibly improve their chances by making it harder? Perhaps I misjudged him. It seemed to me as if he had had just one golf lesson from Nick Faldo and now looked upon himself as the world's leading expert on golf.

It is quite amazing how people that have never helped one single smoker to quit, including themselves suddenly become experts on the subject. Once when doing a phone-in with Robbie Vincent, I had spent fully 10 minutes explaining why substitutes make it more difficult to stop. Robbie immediately followed it by saying some character on a soap opera had used chopped carrots. I thought: "I wonder if Robbie were interviewing a leading brain surgeon, would he be advising the surgeon how to do his job?"

The other belly blow was that during my lifetime I've been forced to observe the gradual decline of Britain's influence in the world. We were led to believe that we were the victors of World War Two. What happened to the vanquished? No one would dispute that Germany is the most influential nation in Europe. When I was a boy 'Made in Japan' was a code phrase for: 'It is inexpensive, but if you buy it, it won't last a day.' 'Made in Britain' meant: 'It might be more expensive, but you have bought the best that money can buy'. It wouldn't be quite so bad if we had merely reversed roles with Japan, but all too often the Japanese product is now the best but still the cheapest. The British equivalent is still the most expensive but now the worst quality.

I don't begrudge the Americans from taking over from Britain the role of the most influential nation in the world today. The Americans aren't perfect, but if the world has to have one dominant nation, I for one am grateful that it's the Americans. I don't begrudge the Germans or the Japanese, while Britain has been busy being owed a living, these countries have been busy earning theirs. However, like many of my generation, I find it difficult to accept that the land of hope and glory has deteriorated so rapidly into a fourth rate power. A land of depression, bureaucracy, unemployment, defeatism, doom and gloom. A land that lead the industrial revolution, whose industrial base has now been destroyed.

Paul Reisen was right. The United States has been fifteen years ahead of us in most things, but there was at least one area in which they weren't. An area in which smokers were flying to Britain from all over the world, including the United States, because a Britain was 15 years ahead. I can understand Paul Reisen believing that the Americans might have had something better to offer, but when he went over there and investigated the crap that they had to offer, how could he have been so blind as not to see what was dangling on the end of his nose?

The stab in the back was the programme. Paul described how he had visited Raynes Park, paid £85 and found it easy to stop. It didn't matter that Paul didn't find it necessary to thank me for my help, but did he really need to finish the item with: "But you don't really need to pay £85, if you really want to stop, you can do it yourself."

Advice like that makes me puke. I made many attempts to stop and squandered over £100,000 on cigarettes. If only there had been someone that I could have paid £85 to with a money-back guarantee!

Many smokers are grateful to Paul Reisen because they phoned the clinic after watching the programme, but I wonder how many millions of smokers watching the programme interpreted his remarks as I would have done: "If I want to stop, I can do it without Allen Carr's help. If I don't want to stop, why on earth should I seek Allen Carr's help?" I wonder how many of those smokers are still in the trap five years later because of his advice. The £85 they would have spent must seem very insignificant compared with the £4,000 that on average they would have saved. Even more significant, I wonder how many of them are now crippled or dead because they heeded his advice? Paul Reisen, you have much to answer for.

If Paul Reisen advised people to pull their own teeth, or extract their own appendixes, society would lock him up. Yet something that society generally believes is difficult, if not impossible to achieve, something on which those people's very lives might depend on, to say nothing of the thousands of pounds they would have saved, he advises them to do it themselves. Paul, didn't you even have enough imagination to realise that, if they were capable of doing it themselves, **THEY WOULD HAVE ALREADY DONE IT?** And if you felt it was so easy to do it yourself: **WHY DID YOU SEEK MY HELP? AND WHY HAVE YOU PERSONALLY RECOMMENDED ME TO SO MANY OF YOUR ACQUAINTANCES?**

The TV-AM campaign provided the usual fact-sheet which turned out to be completely useless. It did however contain one ingenious gimmick to help smokers to quit: the 'Wrist-Flicker'. It consisted of a small piece of circular cardboard attached to an elastic band which you wore around your wrist. The idea was that every time you were tempted to smoke a cigarette, instead of lighting up, you would stretch the cardboard then let go thus causing pain to your wrist. It terrifies me that such a powerful influence as television can be entrusted to such idiots. If you are quitting by using the willpower method, you are desperately trying to forget the fact that you are no longer allowed to smoke. It would be bad enough to be constantly reminded of the fact by the childish and irritating gimmick on your wrist. But then to have to endure the additional pain and humiliation of flicking a piece of cardboard onto your wrist must be almost unbearable. I bet the Americans loved that one.

Another counter-productive statement that the media tend to make on National No Smoking Days is: "50,000 smokers have quit since the previous NNSD, and most of them managed it without any help whatsoever." There are two incorrect conclusions that are often drawn from this statement. The first misconception is the assumption that those ex-smokers didn't seek help. At the clinics we ask smokers if they have already tried other methods. There are many times when the smoker says no, and then during the therapy it transpires that they have previously consulted not just one, but several other so-called experts. We also know for a fact that many ex-smokers that successfully attended our clinics do not recommend us purely because they do not wish it known that they sought help.

Nowadays there is an awful stigma about smoking. Society believes that it takes willpower to stop. Nobody likes to admit that they are weak-willed. Therefore smokers are tempted to deny that they sought help. The other common misconception, is that the 50,000 stop purely because of NNSD. Over two thousand of them attended my clinic. I cannot tell how many stopped with the help of my book, audio or video tapes, but from feedback, I would estimate about 4,000 a year. This means that over a tenth of the fifty thousand were assisted by my method.

Ironically it was Paul Reisen that brought me into contact with the ex-smoker that has caused me even more frustration. The occasion was NNSD 1992. Paul invited me to appear in a programme that his company was producing called 'The Last Cigarette', a ninety minute extravaganza on how to quit. I was excited. At last I was about to achieve my ambition of obtaining over five minutes national TV time.

I should have known better. The bulk of the programme was taken up by musicians, comedians and other celebrities. It turned out to be merely a hotchpotch of gags, gimmicks and gore, just a conglomeration of the crap that the media has been churning out about smoking since the connection with lung cancer was established.

As requested, I dutifully arrived at 8pm and eventually appeared for about one minute at twelve o'clock midnight. That minute was shared with two other so-called experts. One was Dr. Steele who spent his time explaining what a pleasant drug nicotine was, and the other a very pleasant lady who was explaining that when you stop, you go on craving cigarettes the rest of your life and how best to cope with that craving.

During the superfluous four hours, I met John Stapleton of 'Watchdog' fame. Now I'm a great fan of 'Watchdog'. It always amused me how, with all the legalised atrocities in the world today, the BBC could devote almost an entire programme persecuting some poor wretch that was trying his best to avoid the dole queue by selling second hand gas ovens. John or his wife Lynn Faulds-Wood, would look at the man in utter disbelief because he hadn't subjected each appliance to the required safety tests. They would then point out that a faulty appliance might seriously injure or even kill one of his customers. It didn't seem to occur to them that he was only charging £10 for the gas oven and that if he did apply the safety tests he would have to charge £50, and that the type of person he was selling to couldn't afford £50. They would then buy, not from him but from his competitor who only charged £10. The truth is that most people would have looked at him with disbelief if he had applied all the safety checks.

Don't misunderstand me, I'm not condoning that man, it was just that I knew the programme wouldn't remedy that situation, it was so frustrating watching that valuable national television time being wasted when I could have used it to actually save the lives of 2,000 Britains every week. I thought: "Watchdog could avoid that carnage by giving me one of their programmes. However they don't know about me. Never mind, they soon will."

John informed me that he had consulted Roy Sheehan at Raynes Park 9 months earlier and hadn't smoked since. I thought: "Great! John is bound to mention the fact on the programme and no doubt 'Watchdog' will inform the rest of the country of our 'miracle' cure." However, as the conversation proceeded I got the impression that John hadn't been particularly impressed. In fact he was quoted in a national daily as saying: "The hypnotherapy was Mumbo Jumbo." It's incredible. We don't use any Mumbo Jumbo. In fact we go to a lot of trouble to warn clients in advance that there will be no Mumbo Jumbo!

The trigger that inspired John to consult us was that his wife had contracted cancer and that he wanted to give her as much support as he could. He had explained to me that he had made an earlier attempt to stop as part of a television campaign. Apparently umpteen million viewers were charting his progress. I would have thought that was a pretty strong incentive for success. But not only didn't he succeed, but this honest, strong-willed Yorkshireman delayed informing those viewers of his failure until that failure became obvious.

John used his valuable time on 'The Last Cigarette' to explain that his success was due to his wife's cancer. I'm sure the smoking viewers found that a useful tip: "Don't even attempt to stop smoking until your spouse contracts cancer." So the difference between success and failure is: "You musn't let down your wife, but it doesn't really matter if you let down umpteen million viewers." Obviously the fact that he succeeded when using Allen Carr's method but failed when he didn't had no bearing on the situation whatsoever. However, it's a shame that John did not find it necessary to tell the viewers that he had sought help and let them judge the true reason that he succeeded. I have no doubt that John's reason to stop was to support Lynn, but if that was what made him stop, why did he need to seek our help? We don't provide reasons for smokers to escape from the prison, they already have them. We do show them how to do it.

It's ironic that John in his role to warn millions of viewers of 'Watchdog' to avoid dangers and snares that might entrap them, didn't have the imagination or integrity to advise them of a service that could have helped them escape from the No.1 killer trap, a service that he himself had taken advantage of. Recently, I had occasion to think that John had had second thoughts. I was invited to appear on a TV programme: 'The Time The Place'. John was the presenter and the subject was smoking. The particular theme of the programme was the role that smoking parents play in influencing their children to smoke.

I could have told John straight away that whether the parent smokes or not has absolutely no bearing whatsoever on whether the child will smoke. Because my father was a chain-smoker and most of my siblings were heavy smokers, I thought it must be hereditary. Why did I discount completely, the influence of my mother, who was not only a non-smoker, but the dominant character in our family? When I started the clinics I would ask smokers if their parents smoked. If they did, the smoker would say: "I obviously smoked because my parents did." If the parents didn't smoke, they would say: "I only started smoking to rebel against my parents."

Like Paul Reisen, John hadn't even succeeded stopping himself without seeking help, but felt that he was now an expert on quitting, even worse, he had become one of those holier-than-thou ex-smokers. I presume his thought process was: "If I can make the great sacrifice for Lynn, surely parents will stop to set a good example to their children. There was a 21 year old pregnant girl in the programme. I had an opportunity to talk to her before the programme. She was a really lovely girl. She already had a guilty conscience because she hadn't stopped smoking and it must have taken a great deal of courage for her to appear on the programme. She was made to feel even more guilty: " How could she possibly risk the health of her unborn child?" The poor girl was still virtually a child herself. She did not choose to fall for the trap. She wasn't smoking to kill her baby. She was smoking because she didn't know how to stop.

I had an opportunity to talk to several of the smoking parents before the programme. They were not ignorant, uncaring people. Like most smoking parents, they openly admitted feeling guilty about the example they were setting their children. It wasn't that they didn't want to stop, they didn't know how. During the commercial break one couple said to me: "We've taken in what you said before the programme and we've made up our minds to stop." They told John of their decision. John said:

"We have some excellent news, Terry and Steve having, heard what they heard on this programme, said: 'That's it, we are going to give up.' You heard it here first folks. Millions of you heard it on this programme. They don't smoke any more. Note particularly people of Broughton, Salford and North West England."

I'll overlook the fact that John attributed their decision to the programme, but why did he feel it necessary to add the final sentence? Did he feel it would help the couple to know that their progress would be closely observed by their neighbours? Did he not realise the more you try to pressurise smokers to stop, the more difficult you make their task? You might think that he would have learned that lesson when he failed to stop himself when umpteen millions of viewers were charting his progress. He certainly should have realised it after attending the Raynes Park clinic, it's one of the essentials that we emphasize. I would also repeat another point that we emphasize, try to get out of this habit of referring to 'giving up' smoking John. Apart from being inaccurate, it is dangerous. The mere expression implies a loss or sacrifice. It is far more truthful and helpful to use expressions like: 'STOPPING', 'QUITTING' or better still: **'ESCAPING'!**

There was John advising all these people how to stop, but didn't feel it necessary to tell them that the only way he had actually achieved it was by using the Allen Carr method. The final back stab was that he finished the programme by saying: "If you need help the doctor has all the information you need." Needless to say the doctor was advocating nicotine gum!

Perhaps you write off my attacks on Paul Reisen and John Stapleton as the ravings of a bitter old man. I admit to feeling let down at the time and I probably did feel bitter. If so it was because I felt that their lack of support was due to their own egotism. I realise now that it was merely due to lack of understanding. I hold no bitterness towards them now. In fact they will probably be thinking that I have stabbed them in the back. Perhaps I have, because they are not isolated examples. They do however encapsulate the attitude that society in general, and the media in particular, regard smoking and my method. I have not pinpointed them because I regard them as the dregs of their profession, on the contrary, I regard them as the cream. The only reason I even mention the incidents is out of the sheer frustration caused by my inability to get my message across. If I can't get through to intelligent men of integrity like John and Paul, who have proof that my system works, am I merely banging my head against a brick wall in vain by trying to convince the rest of the world? I hope not, because my head is getting very sore!

To be fair to John, he did say before the programme that he could not advertise my clinic because we actually make a charge for helping smokers to get free. This was a point that had never occurred to me. After my TV confrontation with Dr. Steele, he said: "You charge a fee to help smokers stop." In my pique I said: "That's right, I'm a professional, you're an amateur and amateurs oughtn't to dabble in things that they don't fully understand." I've since learned that Dr. Steele receives fees at the rate of £100 per hour when plugging nicotine substitues. Perhaps he isn't just the *pure* amateur that I thought he was.

I recently appeared on another TV programme with the leading light of the tobacco advisory council. He attacked me by saying: "You've made a lot of money out of smoking." It was an incredible situation. Here was a man that was also making a lot of money out of smoking. He made his money by helping to persuade two and a half million people to commit suicide the slow and painful way each year. I made my money by saving lives, yet he, Dr. Steele and the media seem to think of this as some sort of crime.

Is it me that has a distorted view? Far from being ashamed of it, I'm really proud of the way that I make my living. Do people despise doctors because they make their living from curing disease? Is that really the level of stupidity that we have reached? That John Stapleton and his ilk cannot tell you of a method that saves thousands of pounds and will save millions of lives because the inventor makes his living from it? The logical conclusion is that if someone discovered a genuine cure for AIDS and charged you for it, John Stapleton would feel duty bound not to tell you about it.

Perhaps I'm still being naive, but I do not believe that is the true reason that my method has not received the attention from the media that it should have. Perhaps you still believe that it's because I overestimate its effect. I have not overlooked that possibility. My greatest critic by far, is me! If no one else had seen the possibilities, I would have accepted that fact, however practically every week I get a letter from an ex-smoker that can see the situation as clearly as I can. Often that person is a part of the media. I could quote several examples. The following is part of a memo from Mick McGovern to Roger Bolton both employees of Thames Television:

THAMES TELEVISION
Re: STOPPING BRITAIN SMOKING.

I wish to propose the television event of the decade, if not the century.

If the programme which I will outline below were to be broadcast I believe that the lives of thousands, if not millions, of British people could be transformed in the time it takes to watch it.

The good publicity that could be generated for Thames Television is enormous, yet the film would cost next to nothing to produce.

In a nutshell my proposal is for a programme that will get a large proportion of the nation's smokers to stop smoking permanently, without using scare tactics, dubious psychological pressures or gimmicks. The programme I have in mind already exists in video form. Thames masterstroke will be to revamp it for broadcasting nationwide.

It is called Allen Carr's Easy Way to Stop Smoking! It is an 80 minute video which consists of former 100 a day smoker Allen Carr talking about the insights that led him painlessly to give up smoking overnight, and how smokers can emulate his achievement.

Below I shall outline in more detail the gist of his method. All I wish to stress at this point is that it works purely by appealing to common sense. Indeed, its remarkable effectiveness springs from its simplicity. Its power to destroy the urge to smoke lies in its ability to make the smoker look at smoking in a completely different light.

I gave up two months ago using this method, as did a close friend. The video is introduced by Richard Branson who talks about how he and many of his friends have stopped smoking thanks to it, and the actor Anthony Hopkins has also been used to vouch for it. Allen Carr himself claims a 90% success rate.

I think the reason why no one has ever approached Allen Carr before about doing what I propose is because he is seen as someone who earns his living by selling his method. And to those unfamiliar with that method, particularly non-smoking commissioning editors, it might seem as simply one among many. The thought would tend to be: why give a financial advantage to one product over another when there's no real difference in the final achievement?

My contention is that this method is qualitatively different in its approach and in its success rate. What is more, Allen Carr is a man with a mission. His mission is in a lifetime to see smoking go the same way as snuff taking: to disappear as a human habit.

I believe him when he says that making money from this method has always been incidental to his mission. When I contacted him to say I wanted to propose this idea he said that he would not want any money for his help. He said: "I don't want any more money. I have got enough money. All I want is to help rid the world of smoking." It is highly likely that this programme would destroy his lucrative video business.

But wouldn't it be ethically dubious to give air time to a man whose explicit aim is to change behaviour which he finds offensive? Couldn't it set a dangerous precedent? I would argue that the behaviour the programme would be trying to change merits the special treatment. After all, almost all smokers say they want to stop. Hundreds of thousands die through smoke-related diseases every year. The government itself, with cross-party support, spend millions of pounds annually trying to get people to give up smoking.

THE METHOD:

A written description of what the video contains does not do justice to its peculiarly powerful appeal to smokers. What follows is an attempt to explain the intellectual essence of the method.

When I first sent off for this video it was with extreme scepticism and with a determination to take advantage of the 'money-back guarantee'. Having tried unsuccessfully to give up smoking I could not believe that, as the advert assured me, I could stop smoking instantly without using willpower and without the usual agonies.

I was even more incredulous when the video arrived. It said: "If you follow my instructions you will be happy to be a non-smoker for the rest of your life. While you are still a smoker, you will find it easier to concentrate on the video if you continue to smoke while you watch. At the end I will ask you to smoke your final cigarette and at last you will be free from the weed".

Allen Carr is totally opposed to the use of the usual 'willpower method' for stopping smoking. He believes that this method forces the brain through a self-imposed tantrum. The smoker hopes that if the tantrum continues long enough the brain will reach the stage where it says: "EUREKA, I've kicked it, I'm free". But while a small minority of smokers may give up by this method, most will return to smoking because they never deal head on with the reasons for smoking, rather than the craving.

What Allen Carr does is to make you look at smoking in a completely different light. He destroys the various 'illusions of pleasure' and in a cogent and incisive manner goes straight to the heart of why people smoke: they are addicted to the drug nicotine.

Now all smokers are vaguely aware that nicotine helps keep them hooked but most believe that their attachment is to cigarettes: the nicotine is simply an unwanted aspect of their loved one – the cigarette. After all, they enjoy smoking; it relaxes them; it relieves stress and boredom; it is just a habit. Carr says that the habit does not exist – it is drug addiction.

He makes you distinguish between the cigarette and the nicotine. He makes you see that the cigarette is simply the syringe with which you inject the nicotine into your body. His objective is to change your frame of mind so that when you think of smoking you have no more desire to light up than you would to inject heroin.

Carr's objective is to get you to get rid of the craving first. He says it is not pleasure that keeps you smoking it is fear, and he describes the 'tug of war' of fear that takes place inside every smoker: on one hand is the fear that cigarettes are killing you, on the other is the fear of not being able to enjoy life without cigarettes. Yet both fears are caused by the cigarette. Carr's aim is to remove the reasons for smoking because until you remove the reasons for smoking, all reasons for stopping (e.g. health worries) make you want to stop but don't actually help you.

Smoking is a confidence trick which is obvious once you start to understand it. It's like scratching an itch. Cigarettes don't get rid of the itch, they cause the itch and ensure you continue scratching. He talks about smokers being 'slaves of the weed'. "If you find the prospect of never ever smoking another cigarette difficult, then look at the alternative, which is accepting life in which you're never ever allowed to stop. All non-smokers are happy to be non-smokers and all smokers would like to be non-smokers."

He gets you to accept that there is nothing to give up. Once you accept that all you are curbing is your desire to inject nicotine into yourself, then denying your body nicotine is easy. The symptoms of nicotine withdrawal are no worse than a bad cold and last for only a few days.

On the back of his video are testimonials from articles written by journalists from the Sun, The Independent and the Evening Standard. And there is a quote which sums up the power of this method: "If there was a magic button that you could press to wake up in the morning a non-smoker, and happy to be a non-smoker for the rest of your life, would you press it?"

There are millions of smokers out there (30% of the adult population) who would jump at the chance to press the button."

-0-0-0-0-0-0-

I emphasise the words are Mr. McGovern's, not mine. In fact I did not meet him until after it was written. The memo does contain a few slight inaccuracies but he has grasped the essence of my method and, apart from the use of certain expressions like: 'giving up' and 'habit' rather than 'stopping' and 'addiction', he has expressed my case better than I could have done. However, let us examine the content of Mr. McGovern's letter more closely.

The television event of the decade, if not the century? I agree with him, but aren't we both being a little over dramatic? Are we in fact? Consider the massive media coverage of the Gulf war and of the terrible things that are now happening in what was Yugoslavia. Yet in terms of total deaths and misery, they are hardly significant compared to smoking.

I found the amount of coverage devoted to tragedies like the Kings Cross tube and Bradford football stadium fires so incredibly frustrating. They flog the last ounce out of every aspect of these tragedies. Quite right say you, it is important to draw attention to them, if only to make sure they never happen again. However, the real point is that the media coverage, massive as it was, served merely to report those situations and has done little or nothing to cure them. They could do, merely by giving me just one tenth of national TV time devoted to either one of those events. Both tragedies, like thousands of similar deaths each year, were caused by discarded dog-ends. In fact the death toll caused by smoking, in the UK alone, is equivalent to 3 combined Kings Cross and Bradford disasters:

EVERY DAY OF THE YEAR!

Needless to say, Mr. McGovern got no joy from Mr. Bolton. He was however undaunted convinced that he would have no problem finding a producer with the necessary modicum of imagination. Like all the others both before and since, so far he hasn't been lucky. I know it was not for lack of trying and you all have my sincere thanks.

I would also like to thank many other members of the media that have given me tremendous support over the years, in particular: Derek Jameson, who did have the courage to plug 'Easyway' on BBC, Patrick Cargill, Ruby Wax, Pamela Salem, Emma Freud, Anthony Hopkins, Richard Branson, and Michael Balfour who telephoned today to thank

293

me having successfully stopped after consulting me just one year ago. Congratulations Michael!

The news has just reached me that LBC are about to lose their licence. Is this another incredibly stupid decision of the faceless zombies? Why do they cancel the franchise of what is clearly the best commercial radio company broadcasting to London, which means it's one of the best in the world? It is particularly sad for me, because LBC gave me more support than any other branch of the media. I would like to give them my special thanks and in particular to their presenters Brian Hayes, Robbie Vincent, Michael Parkinson and Peter Murray.

I have little faith in either the integrity or the imagination of the featureless wonders that control our lives, but I do not believe that my failure to obtain the national television coverage that I require is due to the fact that I make my living from helping smokers to quit.

Even my advocate Mr. McGovern distorts the situation. I do not make my living from 'selling' my method, any more than a doctor or dentist does. Like them I make my living from applying my specialised knowledge and skills to help cure people. Perhaps you see no distinction, if so I would prefer that you regard me in the same light as you would your doctor.

However, let us assume that I am the most mercenary, money-grabbing individual on earth. Is that just reason to deprive millions of smokers from the benefit of my method? Doctors get paid, but we don't denigrate them for it. I make no apologies because I charge smokers, I have no choice, like everyone else I have to survive. Nick Faldo makes millions from playing golf. I envy him his success, but I don't envy him his rewards. He has worked hard for them and still does. Good luck to him, he has earned and deserves his success and has enabled every Britain to share in part of that success. If Nick offered to give the secrets of his golfing success free on television, would they refuse the offer because he was a professional? Of course not, so what sort of a system would refuse the free assistance of a professional that would save lives?

I have concentrated on TV and radio and must not ignore the very powerful medium of the press. Grateful as I am for the many articles that have been written about me in the national press. The majority of these articles have been supportive, reasonably accurate and with the best intentions. Even so, every one of those articles causes me consternation. I'm being somewhat unfair in that I am expecting the journalist to be as expert as I am about the intricate complexities of helping smokers to quit. The article that most encapsulated the essence of my method, was headed:

THE EVANGELIST WHO SMOKED THROUGH MOUTHFULS OF BLOOD!

What would be the reaction of most smokers to such a title?
"Mouthfuls of Blood? No wonder he stopped smoking so would I have done! Anyway, I'm sick of hearing about the bad health effects caused by smoking."
"Evangelist? He must be one of those holier-than-thou ex-smokers. Just because he's had to stop, he has to start preaching to everyone else."
The article itself was excellent. However, had I still been a smoker, the heading would have prevented me from reading it. I cannot accuse the journalist of being untruthful and fully understand her motives: let's create some interest here, build up the drama. But wouldn't it have been just as truthful, and so much more effective, if the title had been:

HOW TO BECOME A PERMANENT, HAPPY NON- SMOKER, OVERNIGHT

Not quite so dramatic I agree, but which heading is more likely to tempt smokers to read the article? Let me emphasize, there is no deceit involved, both titles are true. However, just as the tobacco industry is adept into luring its victims into a trap by selecting the right choice of lies, I have to be even more adept at helping them to escape by selecting the right choice of truths.

One essential instruction that you must follow to achieve success, is to ignore the advice of other so-called experts when it conflicts with mine. I am the world's leading expert on helping smokers to quit. However, there is one expert that you cannot ignore. An expert who has infinitely more finance and influence than I have, whose methods are just as ingenious as mine. Unfortunately this expert is dedicated to keeping you in the smoking trap. I'm referring of course to my adversary, the combined brains, power and influence of the tobacco companies.

I truly believe that tobacco advertising has little or no effect on getting youngsters hooked. But it would be a great mistake to underestimate the influence of the tobacco industry. It is like an insidious, giant octopus that spreads invisible tentacles throughout the world, designed to perpetuate the myths and illusions about its filthy product and to keep its victims hooked.

I can't prove it's this influence that has prevented me from obtaining the coverage I need. At the same time, there is absolutely no doubt in my mind that this is the real cause. To understand your adversary is to defeat him. When you extinguish that final cigarette, you too will be subjected to the influence of these invisible tentacles. You will be better equipped to avoid them if you're aware of them. Let's learn more about the techniques of:

THE INSIDIOUS, GIANT OCTOPUS

CHAPTER 32

The Insidious, Giant Octopus

In Chapter 23 I referred to my confrontation with the managing director of FOREST. If you apply for membership of FOREST they send you, free of charge, a very sophisticated, glossy folder containing about 20 equally professional documents which expound some fascinating misinformation. To me the most interesting was a picture of Hitler the anti-smoking campaigner with several leading Nazis. In the corner of the picture is the head of good old 'Winnie', defender of freedom, complete with huge cigar.

Never in the history of human conflict was so much owed by so many to so few. It is indeed sad that so few of those Battle of Britain fighter pilots survived the war. Very few of them could have still been alive about 40 years later when FOREST was founded. Yet amazingly we are informed that FOREST was actually founded by one. How nicely it all fits into the pattern.

The Chairman, Supporters Council & Advisory Council, include six Lords, two Knights, an Earl, five MPs, nine doctors, eight professors and, to ensure that the church also condones smoking, a Reverend Canon. Again, I'm sure that it must be just sheer coincidence, but one of the professors just happens to be our old friend Norman Stone. Now I wonder how Norman Stone managed to get so much TV coverage expounding the virtues of smoking on a programme that was intended to help people off drugs?

Dr. Goebbels might have been an expert on propaganda, but he wasn't in the same league as the tobacco industry! The campaign manager of FOREST has admitted to me that two thirds of their revenue comes from the tobacco industry, I suspect that is an understatement. It is public knowledge that Margaret Thatcher has sold her soul to the tobacco industry. I wonder how many other pillars of our society are merely paid vassals of the killer 'weed'.

Do you not find it strange that Norman Stone, who after all is just another smoker can get TV time about smoking, yet someone like me that could help every smoker to get free cannot? Is it possible that some of these articles or programmes that on the surface are meant to help you stop smoking are in fact financed and controlled by the tobacco industry? Even if this is not the case, it certainly produces the same effect. The tobacco industry donates vast sums to the medical profession. Is this why the medical profession always seems to emphasize the evils of the tar, to the exclusion of the real problem, the nicotine, either ignoring it, or like Dr. Chris Steele, actually praising it? So effective is this campaign of the right of smokers to *choose*, that it is very easy to overlook the fact that the tobacco industry is campaigning for a right that smokers already have: **THEY ARE ALLOWED TO SMOKE AND ALWAYS HAVE BEEN.** Any restrictions that have been placed on them have been purely to prevent smokers from denying non-smokers of their right to breathe air free from the foul excrement contained in tobacco fumes.

I anticipated opposition from the commercial media, after all the tobacco industry is their biggest customer, however I thought the BBC would welcome me with open arms. Strangely they didn't, even though many of their executives personally took advantage of my services. Apart from the personal initiative of Derek Jameson, the attitude has been one of either complete indifference, or on certain occasions, open hostility.

There is one other notable exception at the BBC to whom I would like to offer special thanks. It is "The Way Out" programme on Radio 5 presented by Samantha Meah. She may not be as famous as the Parkinsons or Jamesons, but she will be soon.

It doesn't take a Sherlock Holmes to deduce that as an organisation to protect freedom loving people, FOREST is just a sham. A cursory investigation reveals that its real object is to protect the tobacco industry. But for years I believed that FOREST was a genuine organisation, after all, it has the support of many influential and eminent people for a freedom that it already possesses. If the tobacco industry is prepared to adopt such underhand tactics, and at the same time is prepared to conscript the likes of Margaret Thatcher, am I being harsh in suspecting that the invisible tentacles apply influential pressure at key positions within the media, the Houses of Parliament, the legal profession and any other area which might help to prolong the legalised carnage that the tobacco industry is allowed to perpetuate in this *civilised and enlightened* age? On the contrary, it would be ridiculously naive not to have such suspicions.

I had always admired Kerry Packer, the larger than life Australian who had the guts to take on the stuffiest and most archaic of all sporting authorities. Some years ago the wonderful game of cricket was slowly dying due to the lack of imagination of the controlling bodies. I believe Kerry Packer to be the main reason for the restoration to its present day glory. Kerry was a very heavy smoker and sought my help. The problem was that he is an incredibly dominant character. He reminded me of a real life John Wayne.

I found it very difficult to get him off the health aspect, or as he kept putting it: "I don't want to be crook!" I said: "Look, you've sought my help because you are worried about your health, you haven't consulted me to tell you what you already know." In an attempt to distract him from the theme, and aware that he had been a media magnate, I said: "Have you noticed how for the few days after new year, budget and NNS Days, there's a preponderance of pro-smoking films on TV?"

I should explain that pro-smoking films are not films that openly advocate smoking, but films in which the great pleasure or crutch provided by cigarettes, are visually displayed to far greater effect than any tobacco advert could possibly achieve. I suppose the classic example is 'All Quiet On The Western Front', a film about trench warfare during WW1. Every few minutes a soldier is wounded, takes a deep drag on a cigarette and the obvious pleasure makes him oblivious to the fact that he is about to die.

The most poignant and visually effective episode in such a film, was one in which three allied soldiers were stranded in North Africa behind enemy lines. First their food ran out, followed a few days later by their water, both events depicted by their obvious consternation. What worse event could possibly happen to them? You've guessed it, a few days later they were down to their last cigarette. They sit passing it around, inhaling deeply as they drag the maximum succour from that final cigarette. The scene is more exaggerated than from any silent movie. Can you imagine even wanting to smoke in the desert after going days without water? Any smoker can identify with that panic feeling of being without cigarettes, and any smoker watching that film five days into their New Year's resolution has had more than enough food and drink, but what wouldn't they give for just one puff of nicotine? Such films have terminated literally thousands of attempts to quit. The episode that I have just described terminated one of mine.

Kerry Packer went berserk: "I used to schedule programmes myself, I can tell you that such things just don't happen." I admit to being somewhat flustered by the ferocity of Kerry's defence. It wasn't until later that it occurred to me that it was rather OTT. I'm a Chartered Accountant. It so happens that I was honest. However, I am not naive. I am fully aware that there are many crooked accountants. If someone informs me of that fact, I don't get annoyed, I agree with them. So why did Kerry get so angry? I should make it clear that I wasn't accusing Kerry of manipulating programmes. In no way could he have possibly thought that I was. Now Kerry is probably just as aware as I am of the many malpractices in this world that operate under the cloak of respectable business. So why did he get so uptight? He couldn't possibly have known all the television programmers in the world. Why wasn't he interested to hear the evidence I had? I leave you to wonder why?

If I had a large stake in the tobacco industry, and was able to close my eyes to the fact that I was making millions out of the misery and death of other people, I would feel that I was being negligent if I didn't bribe a few programmers, controllers, producers, editors, dubbers and mixers, perhaps this is the reason that so many programmes appear on the media which purport to help smokers quit, but in fact make it harder.

There was a sequel to the Kerry Packer incident which I would have found amusing were it not so pathetic. A few days later it was announced on the news that he was attempting to take over a large tobacco company, his reasoning being that he didn't think that smoking had been fully exploited in the third world. You would think that a man that had more millions than he could possibly need, would try to do some good in the world. Hasn't the third world population got enough to contend with without Mr. Packer trying to kill them. You'd think he would have more understanding and compassion especially as he was so anxious not to be 'CROOK' himself.

While we are on the subject of hypocrisy, what else can explain this incredible, double standard in our society whereby genuine medicinal drugs, designed to improve and prolong lives, are subjected to the most stringent tests before they are allowed to be sold to the public, and woe betide the company that produced the drug should it turn out to have harmful side effects. At the same time the tobacco industry can advertise and sell a product that affords no benefit to the consumer whatsoever, whose sole effect is to impoverish, harm and shorten lives, that actually contains a warning to that effect, and yet, until very recently, has enjoyed the almost complete protection of the law?

Some people attempt to excuse this absurdity on the grounds that smokers having been acquainted with the facts are able to exercise their choice. Ironically it is the complete reverse. Most partakers of medicinal drugs are not addicted to those drugs and are therefore in a position to make a rational choice. Because the only genuine reason to smoke more than one cigarette is addiction to nicotine, all smokers are nicotine addicts. The fact that they are not aware that they are addicts, or refuse to accept that they are addicts, doesn't alter that situation. On the contrary, it makes it worse. If you are aware that you're in a prison you can at least attempt to escape; while you remain unaware you have neither the need nor the desire to escape. It is ludicrous for society to keep maintaining that smokers have a choice. It is a contradiction in terms.

'ADDICT' MEANS I CAN'T CONTROL! I HAVE NO CHOICE!

Have you seen this new brand of cigarettes called 'DEATH'? What an ingenious idea that was. They are contained in a black packet with a conspicuous, large, white skull & crossbones displayed on it. Robin Hayley recently met their managing director at a social gathering. They had a rational and friendly discussion about the questionable ethics of the company. The 'Death' man argued that because they emphasise the health risks, tell smokers that nicotine is addictive and actually advise smokers to quit, they are not being unethical, after all smokers have a choice. Robin was about to leave the party. The 'DEATH' man asked Robin if he thought he could help him to quit, explaining that he had a punctured lung, had to quit, but couldn't do it. So much for the smoker's choice. Knowing that he had no choice himself, how could he possibly close his mind to the fact that his customers had none either. Does he really believe that they:

ACTUALLY CHOOSE DEATH?

The moment smokers realise that they have a genuine choice, they cease to be addicted, at the same time they will also cease to be smokers. As I will explain later, addiction to any drug is not dependent on the physical withdrawal effects of the drug.

Often the very codes that are designed to safeguard the public can be used to harm them. Recently a TV company did a programme on the Raynes Park clinic. Under the code they were obliged to interview a couple of successes and a couple of failures. I pointed out that one of the reasons that smokers found it so difficult to quit, was that for years they have been bombarded continuously by the media with information confirming that it is indeed difficult. I further explained, that if the object of their programme was to help smokers to quit, they would do much better if they ignored failures and concentrated on successes.

Perhaps you feel that I was being deceitful. Assume for one moment that I was. Would that be such a great tragedy? There are numerous examples where the code allows deceit to be used for the purposes of evil. It is common medical practice to 'sweeten the pill' for humane motives, wouldn't it be even more excusable if the outcome was to actually help someone to be cured of a killer disease?

I wouldn't hesitate to be deceitful if I thought it would help smokers to quit, but the truth is that I wasn't being deceitful. I daren't. One of the powerful weapons that will enable me to defeat the power of the tobacco industry, is that they tell lies and smokers are aware that they lie. I tell the truth and it is essential that smokers are aware that I tell the truth. My success and reputation is built on the fact that smokers can trust me and have confidence in my method. If I were to be caught out in just one lie, it would cast doubt on everything else that I say and my method would collapse like a house of cards. I do not lie about our success rate. In his first full year as therapist at Raynes Park, on the basis of the money-back guarantee, Roy Sheehan achieved a success rate in excess of 96%. That is fact and the records are there for anyone to check. When I first discovered the method, I would have been delighted with a success rate of 50%. Nowadays we quote a success rate of over 90% The reason that we do not quote 96% is because we believe that smokers would question our credibility.

However the company insisted that they were duty bound by the television code to give a balanced view. Now can you imagine the effect on smokers watching that programme. They see two successes and two failures. This would form an impression of 50% failure and 50% success. Smokers watching would think: "What's so special about that? The successes would probably have stopped anyway." That view might be balanced, it would also be highly distorted. Now imagine the effect if the viewers sat listening to the stories of 96 ex-smokers that attended the clinic and found it easy to stop, interspersed with just 4 people that had failed.

Exactly the same distortion follows on practically every TV or radio programme about smoking. On one side you have two highly-paid, highly-trained, media-seasoned professionals representing the tobacco industry, and on the other, a doctor plus a non-smoker complaining about passive smoking who are probably making their one and only television appearance.

Other organisations that I suspect are under the influence of the invisible tentacles are the Advertising Standards Authority (ASA) and The Independent Television Commission (ITC). They purport to protect the public. As far as smoking is concerned, they achieve the complete opposite.

They inform me that they are financed by a levy from the advertisers. If so, how can they possibly describe themselves as independent? They are surely breaking their own rules and standards. Who spends more on promotion than the tobacco industry? The only thing they appear to be independent of is any form of logic or common sense.

When we initially opened the Birmingham clinic, we tried to advertise the fact. We were informed that the adverts did not conform to their regulations. Are you aware that one of their regulations is that you cannot advertise a quit-smoking aid that claims to work without the use of the smoker's own willpower? That might well appear to be very sensible to you. It did to me. It would prevent a disreputable firm from making claims which they could not substantiate.

I explained that whilst I could understand the reason for their rule, I had in fact discovered a method that didn't require the use of willpower and that since over 100,000 UK citizens had their lives shortened every year because of smoking, weren't they participating in this decimation by not allowing the public to be acquainted with my method?

They also wouldn't allow me to quote my success rate. They wanted to know what field trials I had done. I said: "Look, I think you have got the wrong end of the stick. I'm not selling a poison, I'm providing a cure for the No.1 killer poison. I use no aids or gimmicks. It cannot possibly cause smokers any harm. The worst thing that can happen is that it doesn't work. In which case we give them their money back. Now if you are worried about the validity of the guarantee, I can give references or I'm even prepared to deposit a substantial bond with you. If you are worried about the validity of the success rate, you are welcome to inspect and to investigate my records."

They were sorry but they had their rules which were laid down by experts and it was more than their jobs were worth etc. etc. I pointed out that their rules were now obsolete and that their so-called experts clearly knew little about helping smokers to quit. I asked if I could be allowed to discuss the matter with these so-called experts. I wasn't even allowed to know their names. It was like talking to a brick wall. No it was worse than that, you don't expect to get a sensible response from a brick wall. But these people purport to be intelligent, caring human beings occupying positions of responsibility. Now you would think that someone whose profession is protecting the public would jump at the opportunity to help save the lives of over 2,000 Britains every week.

At first these people appear to be very helpful, they suggest that you reword the advert to fit in with their stupid regulations. When you point out that if you advertised a method that would only work with the use of willpower but actually didn't need such willpower, you would be telling lies. Surely the ASA didn't want me to deceive the public *deliberately?* Strangely, that didn't seem to bother them, but on principle I refused to bend to their stupid rules. The effect was that smokers weren't allowed to know about my method.

How can we reach a state where our society will allow £100,000,000 to be spent annually promoting a poison that kills 2,500,000 smokers every year and at the same time prevent an isolated individual from spending a pittance to promote an effective cure for that disease?

I got nowhere by using reason, so I tried ridicule:

"This panel of anonymous experts that you rely upon seems to understand little about smoking. Would you rely on a panel of expert ping-pong players to judge whether Nick Faldo was competent to write a book on how to play golf?

This argument had no effect. I tried another tack: imagine a child drowning in a boating lake. You are about to dive in to rescue it. The park-keeper prevents you:

"Sorry sir, you're not allowed to swim in the lake."

"But there's a child drowning!"

"I can see that sir, but rules are rules. It's more than my job's..."

"Don't be stupid! The rules weren't meant for a situation like this."
"Believe me sir, the rules were drawn up by experts. They know far better than you or I sir."
I'm not trying to denigrate park-keepers. Such a situation could never arise. The most unimaginative, regimented, obstinate park-keeper in the world would be in that lake trying to rescue the child himself. Yet when 2,000 people are drowning in the lake every week, these intelligent executives, who are highly paid to protect the public, actually use all their imagination, energy and authority to prevent me from saving them.

Can they really be that thick or is there a more sinister reason for their apparent lack of initiative, imagination or common sense? How unbelievably convenient it is for the tobacco companies that the ASA have a rule that you cannot advertise a quit-smoking aid that doesn't require the aid of willpower. Perhaps it's really the influence of one of those hidden tentacles? Reason and ridicule got me nowhere. I would ask for the matter to be passed up to someone that had either the authority to alter or at least question their stupid rules, or the common sense to use the 'Nelson' touch. Eventually I resorted to abuse with exactly the same effect. Their final word would always be: "I see no point in continuing this conversation."

Strangely the members of the ASA council also includes an impressive list of Dames, JPs, Knights and Professors, all of whom appear to take no active part in the running of the association, other than appearing on the council.

You cannot fail to have noticed the massive publicity involved in the introduction of 'The Nicotine Patch'. There has been nothing to compare with it since cigarette advertising itself was banned on television. I can do no better than include a complaint that I sent to the ITC:

13.3.93

Dear Sirs,

ADVERT: NICORETTE PATCHES AND GUM

Have I misunderstood the purpose of your organisation? I was under the impression that its object is to protect the public. The above campaign, ironically centred around National No Smoking Day, would appear only to benefit the tobacco industry, or to use a more accurate title, the nicotine addiction industry.

It would be blatantly obvious to a 5 year old child, that the specific advert to which I refer, is the archetype of adverts that you should be banning. Surely the advert is intended to help smokers to quit, yet it starts off:

"If you've tried to give up smoking, you know how difficult it can be." No! It is ridiculously easy, but one of the things that can make it difficult, is being brainwashed by massive advertising campaigns telling you just how difficult it is.

"The craving just won't go away." What never? This is a blatant lie! The body doesn't crave cigarettes. The body doesn't even crave nicotine. The body is not capable of craving anything. It is only the brain that craves and if you keep telling the brain that the craving never goes, then it *will* never go.

"You can't concentrate. You are irritable. Your fingers have little to do. You may put on some weight, socially you feel awkward." Again the advert is ingraining into the smoker's brain that it is impossible to give up.

"If you are determined to quit, Nicorette will help you to beat the craving, leaving you free to give up smoking."

If I were still a smoker and determined to quit, that advert would convince me I was wasting my time. If the craving never goes, surely a nicotine substitute will not do the slightest bit of good. This would imply that the real intention of the advert is to persuade the nicotine addict to switch from smoking nicotine to chewing it, or to wearing patches permanently.

If you think that is far-fetched, do you think that heroin addicts inject heroin because they enjoy injections? Do you think that cocaine addicts sniff coke because there is a genuine pleasure in sniffing dust up their noses, or because they are addicted to cocaine? Why do you think that snuff-takers sniffed dried tobacco up their nostrils? There *is* only one logical explanation: **THEY WERE ADDICTED TO NICOTINE!** There is only one logical explanation why smokers breathe cancerous fumes into their lungs: **THEY ARE ADDICTED TO NICOTINE!**

Are we going to reach the stage in another 100 years when we hear patchers saying: I'm down to just three patches a day, but I just cannot face the thought of not having that really delicious patch after a meal? You still think that is far-fetched? For years my clinics have been consulted by ex-smokers that are now hooked on the gum. There are literally thousands of nicotine addicts hooked on the gum, many of them actually smoke and chew at the same time. You are still not convinced, you can already buy a nice leather case to contain your Nicorette gum, how long do you think it will be before a nice silver or gold case is on the market?

In any event, Nicorette themselves claim no other benefit for their products than a 'weaning' process. Any smoker will tell you that cutting down makes it 10 times more difficult. If the gum didn't work, then why should the patches? If you cannot see what is obvious, I'll be pleased to supply you with logical proof to show exactly why it is easier to go 'cold turkey'.

Nicorette neither explain how nor even claim that their products remove the lack of concentration or irritability. They certainly do not give you something to do with your hands, or prevent you from putting on weight. They say socially you feel awkward. That is another blatant lie! It is the complete reverse, it is smokers that suffer the feeling of being anti-social nowadays and that is one of the main reasons they were determined to stop, that is, until they saw the nicorette advert. In any event, does anyone really believe that chewing that poisonous gum, or wearing one of those ridiculous patches could by any stretch of the imagination be regarded as sociable behaviour?

So, apart from ingraining into your mind just how difficult or impossible it is to stop, the only aid or help the advert offers, is not to relieve any of these symptoms, all of which are psychological illusions anyway, but to prolong the cause of them, i.e. your addiction to nicotine.

This would all be forgivable if the product did actually help smokers to quit. I have no doubt that the manufacturers have produced field trials to prove their point. But if someone produced field trials to prove that you can run a mile faster with a 30lb weight on your back, would you believe them? Only if you were incredibly gullible or if it suited your purpose to believe them. I don't know who sits on your advisory panel. I would love the chance to discuss the matter with them. I cannot believe that they are as gullible as they make out. Either way, I don't expect to get that opportunity because neither idiots nor rogues like to justify their actions.

Replay the advert. I don't suppose the tobacco companies could have dreamed up a better advert themselves to keep smokers hooked. I suspect that this is not just coincidence. At one time the manufacturers of Nicorette was owned by the same company that owned Swedish Tobacco. Even the word 'nicorette' is synonymous with cigarette. In fact a UK director of Nicorette informed me personally that nicotine substitutes were developed originally, not to help smokers to quit, but to assist Swedish submariners by bridging the gap during periods when they weren't allowed to smoke.

My main objection to the advert is: having ingrained into the smoker's mind just how difficult it is to stop, the advert gives no claim or explanation of how Nicorette will relieve any of these symptoms. However, they do claim that Nicorette will help you to beat the craving, leaving you free to give up smoking. How can Nicorette help you to beat the craving if it keeps you craving nicotine? Even if you are stupid enough to believe that a 'weaning' process is easier than 'cold turkey', how can you permit the outrageous claim that: 'Nicorette leaves you free to give up smoking', when far from removing any withdrawal symptoms, it actually increases and prolongs them? How can it possibly free you **IF IT KEEPS YOU ADDICTED TO NICOTINE?** And how ironic that, in spite of Nicorette's massive campaign, when other companies are struggling to avoid liquidation, BAT shove their fingers up and announce a substantial increase in profits the day after National No Smoking Day. With your help Nicorette will probably be doing exactly the same thing for the next hundred years.

No doubt Nicorette have eminent members of the medical profession to support their claims. However, if they are so expert on helping smokers to quit, why are the eight tips they give in support of their products so pathetic?

Yours faithfully,

I have protested about other advertisements that made exaggerated claims about helping smokers to quit. So far the appropriate authority has upheld my objections. Yet, in spite of the fact that these adverts were nothing like as offensive or misleading as the Nicorette advert, I have an intuition that on this occasion, I will not be successful. I cannot put my finger on the reason for my foreboding, just as I've learned to sense when there's a spider in the room, I've learned to detect the influence of one of those sinister, invisible tentacles.

Swedish Tobacco have declared a policy to diversify and to find means of distributing nicotine other than by smoking it. In 1991 they ran a publicity campaign for 'SNUS', a form of mouth tobacco sometimes referred to as 'WET SNUFF', which rests inside the mouth and is not chewed. They also happen to own 'PINKERTON' which makes chewing tobacco. If Nicorette gum and patches can be advertised as aids for quitting smoking, then why not 'SNUS' or chewing tobacco?

I now have a reply to my letter to the ITC. It informs me that their role is to ensure that television advertising is legal, honest, decent, and truthful. They make not one mention of the blatant lies in the advert which I have pointed out in my letter which make this particular advert dishonest, indecent and deceitful.

They assure me that, before being accepted for transmission, the advert was carefully scrutinised by an eminent, medical consultant of many years' experience. My letter consisted of six pages and I am now regarded as the leading expert on helping smokers to quit. Apart from the blatant lies, I think you will agree that I have made sufficient points for the ITC to at least question whether they made the correct decision, particularly as it appears to have been made on the recommendation of just one eminent consultant. Naturally they omit to name the consultant, or even to indicate in what field his specialised knowledge or experience applied. However, amazingly, the letter does not indicate that they have even passed on my comments to this consultant.

Surely it wouldn't be too much effort for these protectors of the public to seek a second opinion, let alone a third or fourth? But no, surprise, surprise! The really annoying factor is that they haven't actually dealt with any of the specific complaints raised in my letter, but merely dismiss them by detailing their raison d'etre and the procedures they go through. The fact that they have failed to fulfil their role and their procedure in this particular case was completely inadequate, seems to be irrelevant as far as they are concerned. They ended their whitewash with: "In the circumstances although we don't agree with your contentions, we will ask for your letter to be passed to the advertiser concerned." Thanks very much ITC. I've already spent the last 9 years sleeping with one eye open, now I'll try to do it with two. I'll continue the correspondence into the inevitable cul-de-sac.

It didn't take long, I received a letter dated 12th. May from Eve Salomon, Sponsorship & Advertising Officer, (strange title for someone dealing with complaints) to the effect that:

"I'm sorry that you remain dissatisfied with our reply but I feel we have nothing constructive to add to this debate beyond the comments in my previous letters."

I replied as follows:

"Although I find it strange that you should refer to our correspondence as a debate, it doesn't surprise me. The whole content and tone of your letters have been to treat this whole matter as just a hypothetical debate. We are talking about lying, deception, even smokers very lives. **YOU ARE SUPPOSED TO BE PROTECTING THE CONSUMER.**

I have made a genuine complaint. You have made not one constructive point in your previous letters. Why do you blatantly refuse even to attempt to answer the important points that I have raised? I can only assume that you have no constructive answer and that you have an ulterior motive for allowing this scandal to continue."

-o-o-o-o-

Have you ever started up a business on your own? If you have you will know that when you step back to admire the brand new sign that you have just erected, you will bump into a representative from Yellow Pages. Initially he or she will ask you under which heading you would like your free entry, shortly followed up by a pressure sale to get you to pay for a bigger entry. I've nothing against that. I'm all for aggressive marketing. That is where we fall short in Britain, we are far to modest to publicize our marvellous products.

Good old Yellow Pages. Let your fingers do the walking. Unless that is if you wish to know of a firm that will provide a guaranteed cure to Britain's No. 1 killer disease. Their representatives duly contacted us for both the Raynes Park and the Birmingham clinics:

"Under which classification would you like your free entry to appear?"

"Stopping Smoking."

The girl is attractive, has a very pleasant disposition and is sufficiently intelligent to see your point without undue fuss. She explains that there is at the moment no separate heading for 'Stopping Smoking' and that she has to refer us to the 'Index Classification Organiser'. Great, not like the ASA, this is private enterprise at its best. Immediately I'm put in touch with the person that has the authority to handle the situation. The conversation went something like this:

"Why don't you put it under 'Hypnotherapists'?"

"Because that would be like a doctor specialising in brain surgery appearing under the heading of: 'Hypodermic Syringe Operator'. Hypnotherapy is just one of the tools that I use to achieve my specialised objective, which is helping smokers to quit. If I were to advertise under the heading of 'Hypnotherapists', I would receive a stream of calls from people requiring treatment for other phobias and problems. This would block my telephone line and cause annoyance and inconvenience to both myself and the callers."

"Ah, I've got the solution."

"Good, you'll start a classification for stopping smoking?"

"No, better than that, we'll put you under clinics."

"But that would be even more ridiculous."

"Look, (conversation now tending to become a little more heated on both sides) I assure you that a lot of thought goes into these classifications. The whole aspect has to be considered not only from your point of view but to help the people that are using the register."

"Exactly! We are so lucky to be in one of these situations in which we have absolutely no conflict of interest whatsoever. If people that want to stop smoking can find me easily, they'll be happy, I'll be happy, I am even prepared to pay for a larger advert, so Yellow Pages will be happy. Now let us apply a little thought to this case. Just put yourself in the position of someone that wants to stop smoking. They might not even know that some hypnotherapists treat this problem. Even if they do, they might not wish to use hypnotherapy. I cannot imagine one in a thousand looking under clinics. As far as I know my clinic is the only one that specialises in smoking and it only just opened. Now you have 14,000,000 smokers left in the UK the vast majority of whom want to stop smoking. I've put myself in their position and thought I would first look under smoking. Zilch! However, there is something under smokers. In fact, no less than six classifications, all for smoking requisites. There are over 20 classifications for advertising alternative medicines. I don't suppose that one person in ten has even heard of the ALEXANDER technique, yet it rates a separate classification. Understandably there is a separate classification for ALCOHOL abuse, which kills less than 4,000 a year in the UK. Do you not think that the 14 million smokers are entitled to just one? After all smoking is Britains No.1 killer disease."

NEEDLESS TO SAY HE DIDN'T

Why do these clones continue to blurt out this 'Gobbledegook'. They boldly state rational and sensible policies, then proceed to act in a manner that is completely inconsistent with them. It makes no difference if you point out that they have a separate classification for 'Almond Merchants'. Now be honest have you ever met anyone or even heard of anyone desperately fingering through Yellow Pages in search of an almond merchant? It should have read 'Almond Merchant', because there's only one in SW London and in case he thinks I'm picking on him unjustifiably, I'll give him a free plug. It's J.F.Renshaw Ltd. Locks Lane, Mitcham. O81 648 3005. (I'd like some commission if there's a sudden unexplained boost in your trade Mr.Renshaw). I suspect that there are classifications that have nobody under them but I haven't got time to search for them.

I find the most worrying thing about these conversations is that these people give every appearance of being endowed with intelligence, compassion, understanding and common sense. That is until they have to make the simplest of decisions. Then they transform into complete zombies, unable to understand the cause of your frustration. In the end they just write you off as an awkward customer and you are left doubting your own sanity. You can imagine the conversation when they get home to their wives:

"You wouldn't believe the weirdo I had on the phone today. He'd somehow got the notion in his mind that the lives of 14 million smokers were more important than almonds. He was on for over an hour wasting my time. I just couldn't seem to get through to him. He really ruined my day."

"Don't let him upset you dear, he was probably one of those cranks that has nothing better to do with his time."

I have discussed this refusal to include a separate heading for stopping smoking with dozens of people. Without exception they can see the logic of my argument. Why is it the only person that seems unable to see the point, is the one person whose job it is to allocate the headings? After all, you would expect that person to have a greater insight into these things. Can Yellow Pages really be that stupid, inefficient or callous, or is there a more sinister explanation for their attitude?

However, nothing would surprise me. I heard recently of a rumour that the manufacturers of a well-known brand of cat food include nicotine in the recipe.

A few years ago an employee in the chemical industry informed me that his company supplied regular and large amounts of nicotine to the tobacco companies. Now why would tobacco companies need nicotine? Tobacco already contains nicotine? Why would they need more nicotine?

Many older smokers will remember when the tobacco industry introduced cigarettes containing substitute tobaccos. They spent a fortune in research and development. But smokers who tried them found they could get no *pleasure or satisfaction* from them. Or to put it another way, they couldn't suffer the illusion of enjoying them. The tobacco companies dropped them almost overnight. Strangely, although the introduction of substitute tobaccos was supported by a massive publicity campaign, their withdrawal went almost unnoticed by the media. I wonder why? Surely because it must have then dawned on the tobacco industry that there is no pleasure in smoking for smoking's sake, and that the so-called 'smoking habit' was simply nicotine addiction!

Millions of smokers found a similar problem when they switched from non-tipped to tipped cigarettes and later when they switched to low tar brands. To begin with, there was no sense of satisfaction. They had to puff twice as hard and end up smoking twice as many.

It has yet to be proved that smoking causes lung cancer. However the statistical evidence is so high as to be irrefutable. But since we don't know exactly how smoking causes lung cancer, why is it that so much emphasis is placed on the tar, rather than the nicotine content of a particular brand? Particularly when nicotine is known to be a very powerful poison in its own right, and even more so when you realise that nicotine is the sole cause of the problem anyway. I understand the tobacco industry's need to divert attention from nicotine to the tars, but why does the medical profession and the government assist them? I sense the influence of one of those invisible tentacles!

Now the tobacco companies have a very tricky problem when manufacturing filter tips: how to filter the tars yet let the nicotine through. Because if they filter all the nicotine no one wants the cigarette. I wonder if they are actually adding nicotine to tobacco. That might be one reason why the chemical company was supplying nicotine to tobacco companies.

I could write a separate book on tobacco advertising. I'll go further, the subject could occupy a lifetime's study for one person. Come to think of it, it probably already occupies a lifetime's occupation for many.

The brand names are worth a separate study in themselves. I'm told that I have a vivid imagination. You might well conclude that some of the connections that I infer are merely the product of that imagination or just coincidence. My accountancy training taught me: when the odds against coincidences are so great as to be almost infinite, use your imagination to find the real reason.

Can it be just coincidence that most brand names, either sound very impressive, or imply that they will benefit you in some way? Examples of the latter are: 'Slims' no comment necessary or 'Consulate', slightly less obvious, but might they console you? It also happens to be a menthol brand. Have you noticed how many menthol brands are in green packets? This isn't coincidence. The implication is that they won't harm you. It's the fresh, clean outdoors. Don't be fooled, menthol cigarettes contain the same poisons. Smoking menthol cigarettes is like causing the cough and taking the cough mixture at the same time, or using a pine odour spray to hide a foul smell.

However, the vast majority of brand names are designed, not just to impress you by conveying an aura of prosperity and success, but by making you believe that you will convey a similar impression to other people. It is all part of same ritual of glossy packets, gold lighters and cigarette cases, just part of the massive brainwashing and confidence trick of camouflaging what is simply addiction to a filthy, disgusting, highly lethal poison with so much regalia, pomp and ceremony, that the addict is fooled into believing the ritual is not only necessary, but pleasurable.

Can it be just coincidence that no less than three brands are named after 5 star hotels: DORCHESTER, CARLTON and BERKELEY? Can it be just coincidence that two of the world's most macho, leading brands are WINSTON and MALBORO? (The Churchill family name). Do you remember CHURCHMANS, a very popular brand during Churchill's peak years. Did the brand name also imply that smoking was perfectly acceptable to church goers? Normally, brand names are not dropped without a reason. Did the decline in 'Churchmans' coincide with the decline in church attendance in England?

Other obvious examples of the connection between smoking and the upper crust are 'Regal', 'Royal', 'Parliament', 'Pall Mall', 'Embassy', to name but a few, 'Consulate' also falls into this category. Was 'Kensitas' derived from Kensington? Was 'Rothmans' Rothschild? Or is it all just coincidence? Whilst on the subject of Royalty, perhaps you do not agree that tobacco itself, or at least tobacco advertising should be made illegal, but surely it is ridiculous for British Royalty, not only to condone, but to actually promote this disgusting trade by allowing the likes of Benson & Hedges to display a crest denoting the Queen's patronage.

The different emphases that the individual tobacco companies employ to promote their particular brand, is another fascinating subject. I cannot but admire them for their ingenuity. In fact I thank them. I've studied their techniques and used them in my therapy. If only I had their massive resources.

I do not propose to go into all the various techniques of various tobacco companies. The technique I admire most is Benson & Hedges. At the same time it is the technique that I despise the most, because Benson and Hedges have discovered what I've discovered: the thing that keeps smokers smoking is **FEAR!**

In 'EASYWAY' I have described some of these adverts. The tobacco companies maintain that they do not direct their advertising at children. I believe this to be true in the main. In fact the only advert that I have seen which I believe was aimed directly at children was a B & H advert. B&H also directly target pregnant women. Even the MAFIA wouldn't stoop that low!

The medical profession tends to concentrate on lung cancer as the main incentive to persuade smokers to quit. Surprisingly, only about half the smokers that attend our clinics are aware that smoking not only can, but only too often does result in the amputation of limbs. However, Benson & Hedges cannot be accused of such an oversight, at least two of their adverts concentrate on the loss of limbs.

B & H are now actually using shock tactics on their main low tar brand: 'Silk Cut'. When the connection between lung cancer and smoking was first made, the tobacco companies were terrified that the news would not only be the death of the smoker, but also of the tobacco industry. Originally 'Silk Cut' was introduced as a counter to the cancer scares. The original advertising theme: "Low tar, smooth as silk, it won't harm you." The shrewd way in which B & H switched to shock tactics was almost as subtle as the nicotine trap itself.

The original adverts were just a piece of purple coloured silk with a scissor (or razor?) cut in it. What sinister implications could there possibly be? However, it wasn't a silk tie, blouse or shirt, but more reminiscent of the lining of a coffin (coughing). The cut was exactly where the heart would be. Surely this is just a coincidence, my prejudice is causing my imagination to go overboard. Then a black cat appears in the advert. Everyone knows that a black cat crossing your path is meant to bring luck. Surely B & H aren't trying to imply that you are lucky to be a smoker? Anyway, there's something rather sinister about this particular black cat and the cuts in the silk are no longer cuts, but the claw marks of a cat.

The campaign progressed. In later versions the cut in the silk was made by the dorsal fin of a shark, just when I thought it was safe to go back into the water. Then a really weird one appeared, a chain saw wrapped in purple (or mauve) silk. What possible connection could there be between a chain saw and smoking? Now, even with my vivid imagination, I can only think of one: **FEAR!** Have you ever used a chain saw? Did it have the same effect on you as it had on me? The thought that you're more likely to saw your leg than the tree? Did you see the 'Texas Chain saw Massacre'? I didn't but the reports were enough to terrify me. B & H's chain saw is even shaped like a locust. Locusts also create fear in the minds of most people. At the same time, the 'chain' implication engenders the introduction of another major cause of fear: that of being hooked. This effect is increased by the chain saw itself being tightly wrapped, or entrapped, in silk. No doubt you have seen pictures of a spider incarcerating a fly before storing it for a future meal? What effect did this have on you? A sense of being hopelessly trapped? A feeling of suffocation, of a slow, tortuous, living death? What did the spider use to imprison its victim? SILK!

You could attribute all of the above to a combination of my bias and my vivid imagination, but these aren't isolated examples. There is a progressive pattern. One advert depicts a very realistic Stanley knife, except that the blade is made of silk. Not so surprising. But the colour of the silk is not the normal mauve of the Silk Cut image, but pink. More like the colour of blood. If you've ever run your Stanley knife along your thumb instead of the object that you intended to cut, or if you've been unlucky enough to witness, or been more unlucky, to be the victim of an attack by Stanley knife, you will be well aware of the connection between a Stanley knife and fear. I understand it is now the preferred weapon of the football hooligan.

Some of these adverts do require the use of imagination. Others are so blatantly obvious they require no imagination whatsoever. There's one that merely displays strands of barbed wire. You get imprisoned by barbed wire, you get cut by barbed wire, you get hooked on barbed wire! Isn't it bad enough that we are imprisoned by this awful weed anyway? Do we really need Benson & Hedges to gloat over us? Isn't it sufficient for them to know that they've got us hooked? Why can't they be like the other tobacco companies and leave us with the illusion that we are tough or sophisticated, that we are in control, smoking purely because we choose to, for the abundant pleasure or prop that we get from smoking? Do B & H really need to extract the last vestige of our self-respect and dignity?

Why does the media give free publicity to events like 'Pipe-man of the year'? The sole qualification for receiving the award is to be a famous personality in order to convince existing pipe-smokers that they are macho and 'with it'. It is so obviously the result of one of the insidious, invisible tentacles. A few years ago Dave Lee Travis got the award. He was interviewed on TV expounding on the merits of smoking 'pure' tobacco. His 'pure' tobacco contains over 2,000 poisonous compounds! Obviously a disc jockey like DLT is bound to influence millions of admirers. Can you imagine the outcry if someone tried to organise an award for: 'Heroin Addict of the Year'?

Sometimes the adverts backfire. A client described a taxi drive from one of the New York airports into the City. He said there was hoarding after hoarding of 'Welcome to Marlboro Country'. Behind the hoardings was a massive cemetery.

I hear more stories connected with Marlboro than any other brand. Some amusing, some sinister, some no doubt fanciful. I merely repeat them and leave you to decide their credibility. That the tip contains a substance like fibreglass which accumulates in smokers' lungs causing a disease similar to silicosis (miners' disease). Fanciful? But if true, isn't it ironic when you consider the only object of the filter is to prevent disease?

A persistent rumour in recent years is that Malboro is owned by the Ku Klux Klan. Have you noticed the three K's on the packet? (Hard packs only). Frankly I never believed this rumour, but a later informant assured me that it was in fact true, what's more, if you opened up the glued parts of the packet, you would find the current number of members of the KKK listed there. I doubted it, and imagine my excitement when I found the numbers. I did the same to another brand and found similar secret graphics. It would be nice to believe that there was a connection between the Klan and Marlboro, however I suspect it's just a rumour and the real object of the graphics is something more mundane, like production control.

It is true that, having contracted lung cancer, one of the Marlboro cowboy models became an avid anti-smoking campaigner. Sadly, I've heard that he has since died. I hope that he persuaded as many smokers to quit as he helped to remain hooked.

I thought the 'Superman' anti-nicotine campaign was really effective, but I wonder how many children were influenced by those conspicuous bright-red Malboro vans featured in SUPERMAN 4. Do you think it was just coincidence that the film makers gave Marlboro *free publicity* or do you sense the influence of one of those invisible tentacles? Have you noticed how many comparatively recent films shown on TV fade-out a scene focusing on a cigarette packet? A Marlboro packet. Just this week I was informed by what the press would describe as: a very reliable source, that certain tobacco companies do pay some members of the acting profession to smoke whilst on screen.

Every time a man is about to be executed, what is his last request? A beautiful woman or a slap up meal? No way! A husband waits outside a maternity unit, always depicted, not just smoking, but chain-smoking. When the panic's over and the baby is born how does he celebrate? He hands the cigars around. What is the piece de resistance that culminates that really special, formal meal? The port? The Stilton? The liqueur? The brandy? No way! It's a cigar! So powerful is the brainwashing, that many non-smokers feel deprived unless they puff on one. Little do they realise that the more expensive and larger the cigar, the more frustrating it becomes to regular smokers, who can't wait to get back to their usual brand. Should we really wonder why our children still get hooked? The miracle is how any of them avoid it.

Many people find it difficult to understand why I don't support a total ban against tobacco advertising. There are two main reasons. The first is that I genuinely do not believe that tobacco advertising is effective in getting youngsters hooked. As far as I am concerned those millions of pounds are spent mainly in persuading nicotine addicts to smoke one brand as opposed to another. However, if such adverts were banned, it would merely serve to release those millions to be used in areas of promotion that does cause youngsters to become hooked.

There can be no doubt that macho sports like Formula 1 Grand Prix racing have an enormous effect on youngsters, particularly when the the car appears to be a replica of the brand of cigarettes being sponsored. Some of the incidents continually repeated on national television would appear to be more than just coincidence. A classic example is of Cliff Thorburn when he achieved the first televised maximum 147 snooker break. Understandably, his triumphant leap in the air has been repeated on numerous occasions. However such spontaneous gestures usually follow the release of tension after potting the black. Can it be just coincidence that Cliff makes his leap with cue in one hand and a packet of the sponsor's brand of cigarettes clearly displayed in the other?

The famous darts player Jocky Wilson would extract the darts from the board with the single motion of one hand. The same hand would be holding a cigarette and at times the sponsor's brand would even be discernible in the close-up. I'm obviously talking about the days when darts players were allowed to smoke on television. Could this have been mere coincidence? Most smoking dart players leave their cigarette in the ashtray when actually throwing the darts. Of those that don't, right-handed throwers normally hold the cigarette in their left hand. Was it Jocky's natural instinct to transfer the cigarette from the left hand to the hand which already had sufficient work to occupy it, or do you believe that his action was deliberate and that he was encouraged to do so?

You might well take the attitude that these are rather petty details which a normal, well-balanced individual wouldn't even notice, and that my obsession with smoking has left me paranoid. You would be wrong. To begin with, they are not isolated situations, but merely examples of hundreds that I could quote. Secondly, I admit to being obsessed, but I didn't even notice them. The real mystery is why I didn't notice them. How they'd been jumping up and biting me on the nose yet not until other people pointed them out to me did they become so blatantly obvious.

So if the particular examples that I have given appear to be insignificant and probably wouldn't even be noticed by more than one in a thousand, why do I even bother to mention them? If these tentacles are invisible, what possible harm can they do and how will this help you to stop smoking and to remain free the rest of your life? Electricity is invisible. It can still kill you! Your best protection is to be aware of it, to understand it and to respect it. You will then have no need to fear it.

The fact that your brain doesn't *consciously* register a point doesn't mean that it has missed the point. Your subconscious brain will certainly have taken the point. Remember the vast bulk of our views and opinions are formed by our subconscious minds. In order to dispel any conflict between your conscious and subconscious mind, you must first transfer the subconscious to the conscious. Only then are you in a position to assess all the relevant facts, and thus remove the anomalies, fallacies and misinformation from your conscious mind. That process in itself will remove them from your subconscious mind. The schizophrenia will be gone. Your whole brain will be in harmony, not just today and tomorrow, but for the rest of your life.

All smokers have been brainwashed from birth about *both* sides of the tug of war, not only the deadly killer, ruining our health, burning our money, dominating and controlling our very existence; but our little crutch, our friend, our pleasure, our courage, our confidence, our personality, our image, the lifelong companion that we can rely on during good times and bad. We are fully aware of the salient points on both sides of the tug of war before we start smoking, while we are hooked and after we have quit. However, once we become hooked, because for most of our smoking lives we either have no desire to stop, or when we do stop are miserable and want to start again, part of our natural defence mechanism is to block our minds to the bad side and to concentrate on all the marvellous advantages however illusory they might be. While we are in that frame of mind, the tobacco companies are our friends. They spend millions helping us to keep our head in the sand and to assist non-smokers, smokers and ex-smokers alike to regard each other as the enemy, and like modern Yugoslavs, we are so intent on attacking each other, we lose site of the real enemy:

THAT INSIDIOUS WEED

The publicity gives the impression, that it is not the tobacco industry that is evil. Indeed, it is not even tobacco itself that is the problem. Rather it is the unfortunate hazards inherent in the 'the habit' which are the true evils. The tobacco industry is on the side of the smoker. It feels just as badly as the smoker does about these hazards. It has gone to a lot of trouble to try to remove, or to alleviate the bad effects of these hazards by developing filter-tips and low-tar cigarettes. It makes no secret about the hazards, it even provides a warning on the packet. It has donated large sums to cancer research. It has spent large sums trying to discover less harmful products to smoke.

Stop kidding yourself! Take your head out of the sand! Don't judge the examples that I give as to whether they are insignificant or otherwise. Instead judge them as to whether you feel that they are natural or contrived. Think of and observe similar examples. They might also be insignificant, but if you believe they are also contrived, just think of the intricate machinations that the tobacco industry is prepared to employ to keep you enmeshed in its evil web.

I was recently on a TV programme with a professional non-smoker from FOREST accompanied by an equally glib non-smoking agent of some other 'freedom of individuals to make lifelong slaves of themselves' society. Fortunately, most smokers can instinctively sense that these people are phoney. In fact if there's anything that gets up smokers' noses more than non-smokers that try to force them to stop, it's non-smokers that try to force them to smoke. However some smokers are just too dumb or too frightened to appreciate the point. I had reached the stage in which these two characters were waffling in answer to questions like: "Would they encourage their children to smoke?" Or: "I presume you are in favour of legalising heroin?", when a third character came to their defense. A smoker who had announced on the programme that he would like to be allowed to smoke with impunity. He was rather smug and obviously felt safe with a majority of three to one. I wondered whether it even occurred to him that 3 of us considered him to be pathetic, that of the three, 2 were secretly laughing at him and that the only reason that the third wasn't secretly laughing was because he'd spent a third of a century in a similar state of stupidity and fear.

This is another reason why I don't want tobacco advertising banned. Smokers already have their heads in the sand and will keep them there without any help from tobacco advertising. However once they remove their heads from the sand, the adverts tend to backfire on the tobacco companies and have the complete opposite to the intended effect. The more you study those adverts and the psychology behind them, the more apparent it will become that the tobacco companies are merely patronising you, and laughing at you. They are preying on your fears and delusions, convinced that they have you by the 'short and curlies' and that their greatest ally is you! If you continue to keep your head in the sand:

THEY'LL BE RIGHT!

Why is it that I get tremendous verbal support from the

bureaucracy, the medical profession, the media and from private individuals, be they smokers, non-smokers or ex-smokers: "Power to your elbow Allen Carr, you're doing a grand job, keep up the good work." Yet all the codes, rules and regulations seem to hamper me and work in favour of the tobacco industry? Why is it that, apart from a small and loyal band of friends and associates, I keep coming up against a solid brick wall? There is only one logical explanation:

MONEY AND GREED!

There are 3 powerful institutions that make millions of pounds annually out of the misery of smokers. The prime evil is obviously the tobacco industry. Who do we have to protect us against this evil influence? Ironically, it is the other 2 great benefactors, the government and the media. Is it really surprising that this insidious, giant octopus continues to prosper?

The beautiful truth is that it is easy, not only to get free, but to stay free! However, it is not sufficient merely to reverse the brainwashing initially. There is one other thing that I need you to do. Shortly after you stop smoking you will feel completely free and you will lose your fear of becoming hooked. This is a danger and a serious one. Now, I don't want you to spend the rest of your life suffering the fear of getting hooked again. On the contrary, I want you to enjoy the same feeling of security that I do, knowing that I could never get hooked again. You don't need to fear, provided you don't get blasé. However, never lose respect, either for the subtlety and cleverness of the nicotine trap, or for the subtlety and cleverness of those employed in the tobacco industry. Once you stop smoking you are still being hit with massive advertising, not only from the tobacco companies, but from the media, other smokers and society generally. You need to be aware of it and to keep your guard up. Continue to search beneath the façade of the adverts, the names, and the glossy packets.

My method is based on reversing a lifetime's brainwashing, prior to extinguishing the final cigarette. I regard myself as the most counter brainwashed ex-smoker that ever lived. However, just as there is no such thing as 100% brainwashed, so there is no such thing as 100% counter brainwashed. I still have some of the brainwashing. Don't worry, I could never get hooked again, in fact, so confident am I of the fact, that I would take heroin to prove that I couldn't become addicted to it. However, if you said to me that one of your children will become addicted to a drug, you can decide whether you would rather it be heroin or nicotine. I would say, please let it be nicotine, even though my logical brain knows that nicotine is far worse than heroin, I'm still part victim to the brainwashing that I have been subjected to in relation to both drugs.

This counter brainwashing exercise must cover every aspect of smoking. Once you remove your head from the sand, it's easy to see the tobacco industry as the real enemy. However, it is much more difficult to see fellow smokers in their true light, and, as Dr. Miller found, to see the cigarette itself as it really is. However, it is absolutely essential that you do so.

Take a fresh cigarette from your packet now. Feel it. Observe it. The feel and appearance of a cigarette can be quite impressive, especially if it has been expertly manufactured, firmly packed, the tip nicely blending in with the rest of the cigarette rather than appearing to have been stuck on as an afterthought. The image can be enhanced by the brand name or by the addition of a gold band. Surely this isn't just brainwashing? An expertly manufactured cigarette is a genuine pleasure to feel and to touch! Would anyone deny that the pleasure of owning an automobile is not genuinely enhanced by immaculate styling, finishing and appearance. I for one wouldn't deny it, but that's enhancing the beauty of a genuine asset, as opposed to disguising a liability. I do not think that I would be unduly impressed with the appearance of a car that was about to run me over.

Now look at that cigarette again and imagine that it contains not tobacco, but arsenic. Would you still be impressed with the feel and appearance? Would you have the slightest temptation to imbibe the contents? If you are not convinced, imagine receiving a gift of a dead mouse. Would the fact that it had been beautifully gift-wrapped, reduce your feeling of repugnance? Of course not. If you are anything like me it would increase it.

Open your eyes! That cigarette contains not just one but umpteen poisonous compounds, including one in particular that is far more lethal than either arsenic or cyanide. Your chances of dying from arsenic or cyanide poisoning are almost infinitesimal. Nicotine is infinitely more lethal than any other poison known to mankind, because it possesses a special property. If you take it, you will have to take it again and again and again ad infinitum:

YOU WILL NEVER KNOW TRUE PEACE AGAIN

Think of the dead mouse. Packaging will only appear impressive if the contents are impressive. The feel and touch of cigarettes only ever appeared pleasant to us because we were deluded into believing that smoking is pleasant. There is no point in allowing the illusion of the packaging to perpetuate the illusion of the content. From today, whenever you look at a cigarette, stop looking at the wrapping, see the dead mouse inside. See it for what it really is:

A STICK OF DEADLY, ADDICTIVE POISON

You might well have formed the impression that I have an intense hatred of the 'weed' and of the industry that peddles it. If so, you have formed the correct impression. However, I must make it clear that I hold no animosity to the individuals employed within the industry. You might regard this as peculiar. In fact it has always struck me as curious that in war a doctor will try just as much to save the life of an injured enemy as that of an ally. Why should an army go to such pains to kill an enemy, almost succeed and then spend as much, if not more effort to reverse the process?

I now understand that attitude. In the early days of running the clinic from Raynes Park, I had a whole stream of employees from a large and famous brand leader, including the marketing and sales directors. The sales director was particularly on the defensive. He was expecting me to lecture him about the evils of smoking. While I am writing this book I can indulge in the luxury of moralising. I must avoid doing so during clinics. The first essential is to get the smokers feeling relaxed. Smokers will not feel relaxed if I attack, embarrass or insult them. Even if I wanted to allow personal views or prejudices to interfere, I could no more let them do so than I could stop myself from laughing if you tickled my toes. If Hitler were alive and a smoker, I couldn't help but try to cure him.

Actually this sales director was a very personable chap. He said:

"I come from a working class family and I was just a boy when I went into this business. In those days smoking was a prestigious industry. There were the mellow Virginia tobacco's, the Meerscham pipes, gold cigarette cases and lighters. I've worked hard to achieve my position, and I was proud of what I had achieved. Suddenly in the last few years everything has gone topsy turvey. I'm now regarded as a drug pusher. But what can I do? I know no other business, and at my time of life how could I possibly get another job. Anyway, what would be the point? If I did resign, there'd be someone a lot more enthusiastic than I am to take my place.

I know his argument would not have saved him at the Nuremburg trials. However, I do not feel that we are qualified to judge him unless we have been in a similar position. The real irony was, his reason for stopping was that he was the last member of the board that smoked, and his fellow directors were complaining that he was polluting the atmosphere.

Now let us deal with another group of people who on the surface are genuinely interested in your welfare. Yet, in spite of their attempts to be truthful, accurate and unbiassed, can ruin your attempts to succeed. I'm referring to:

THE CRITICS

CHAPTER 33

The Critics

Another powerful influence that can affect whether you get rid of all the brainwashing initially and remain free of it the rest of your life are the critics, whether they be critics of 'EASYWAY', this book or my method generally. Those critics can include acquaintances, other *so-called* experts or the professional book-reviewers of the media.

If those critics make comments in the nature of: "Read the book, follow all the instructions and you will already be a happy non-smoker and remain one the rest of your life." Believe them! Ignore all other comments they make. Often the critic will not even have read the book, or may only have part read it; but even if the critic has read the book several times, you must still follow my advice.

You have no doubt formed the impression that, for a man who appears to pull no punches in attacking the media, the medical profession and other experts, I can't take criticism. Isn't this typical? Those that are humble to the mighty are invariably mighty to the humble. Who curses the loudest at the driver that deliberately carries on when the lights change to red? None other than the driver who nearly collided with him because he jumped the same set of lights.

However you would be wrong. Some people try to endow me with special powers, like those of a medium or spiritual healer. As I have already explained, I have no need for special powers, like every other human being, I arrived on this earth already equipped with incredibly sophisticated powers. The reason that I know more about quitting smoking than anyone else is due to three main factors. The first two were pure chance. Because of the peculiar circumstances of my life, and in particular my own total capitulation to the 'weed', I did not have many of the normal illusions that make the whole subject of smoking so confusing.

The second element of chance was that I happen to have an analytical brain. To what extent I was born with it as opposed to it being developed by the cynical attitude of the accountancy profession that I loathed, I am not able to say. Those factors enabled me to understand the smoking trap completely and to escape from it myself. But they didn't automatically enable me to help others escape. To do that I needed the third attribute: imagination! I had to put myself in the same position as other smokers, to try to understand their exact position in the maze and then give them the correct directions to get free and at the same time try to make sure that they both understood and would follow the instructions.

I said there were three attributes. In fact there was a fourth without which the other three would have been wasted, and without which I do not believe anyone is capable of achieving a reasonable standard, let alone excellence, in any branch of life. That attribute is not just to be able to accept criticism, but to absolutely wallow in it, like a hippopotamus in mud. No matter whether that criticism be from a professional or layman, from a genius or an idiot. It doesn't even matter if the criticism is unconstructive, the recipient of the criticism has the choice to reject it, but if it happens to be valid, how can you benefit from it unless you hear it? Self-criticism is essential, but why limit your knowledge and expertise to your own experiences?

One of the most frustrating aspects of running the clinics is that I can't get enough feedback or criticism. The few failures that we get at our clinics say something like: "Thank you very much, you've tried your best, it worked for my friends but it doesn't seem to work for me." If only they weren't so polite and would attack me. If they would tell me exactly where it had gone wrong. I could then correct their misunderstanding and make them see just how easy it is to stop and how enjoyable it is to be a non-smoker. So much of the time I am having to judge for myself the effect, good or bad, of particular points that I make. It would be so nice to know the exact effect it had on each individual.

So, if I purport to wallow in criticism, be it good or bad, why am I so bigoted as to advise you to ignore any adverse criticisms about my method? I must admit that I have had some difficulty in justifying this attitude to myself. I have always had little sympathy for actors, authors, playwrights, entertainers or whatever that objected to the critics. Yet when the 'EASYWAY' was reviewed I soon learned to hate reading the reviews. Ironically, most of these reviews praised and recommended the book, but with just one exception, I found those reviews both frustrating and annoying, even when the reviewer had actually stopped smoking as a result of reading the book.

I now understand completely why I resented those critics and why I do not want a repetition with this book. I can best explain it to you by repeating the one review that caused me no frustration whatsoever. However, let me first repeat the one that, although I'm not normally a physically violent man, made me feel that I could have cheerfully wrung the neck of the particular chinless wonder that wrote it. Ironically he was the reviewer of the world's most famous daily: The London Times. 'The THUNDERER' which I hereby rename: 'The

WHISPERER'. The critic's name was Michael Grosvenor Myer. He writes

"Admirers of Bernard Levin will know that he is nearly always right about everything; but that, in the small number of cases in which he is wrong, he is so with the kind of purblind obtuseness which, if it were manifested by anyone equally stiff-necked about one of the things he is right about, would bring Levin's corrosive scorn down upon the offenders head.

Foremost among these few of his blind spots is his failure to recognize the absolute necessity to encourage as many smokers as possible to stop. The reasons for this necessity need not be rehearsed here: their force is known to all – even deep down, I am persuaded to Mr.Levin himself, who has pertinently written, "Who, enjoying in more than common measure something that is readily available, does not wish others to enjoy it too?"

I interrupt the narrative here, lest you suffer the same initial misconception that I had, i.e. that the book under review was written by Bernard Levin. In fact two books were under review, neither written by Mr. Levin, yet the above represents nearly half the narrative. I found myself wondering what relevance it had to the books under review. Does Mr.Myer have a love or hate relationship with Mr.Bernard Levin? Or perhaps you will get the feeling that I got, that Mr. Myer would rather be writing books than reviewing them. Are book critics like most sports critics, frustrated either because they never made it or because they have now passed it? The object of any written work is either to entertain or to communicate knowledge. In either case, the author is more likely to achieve the prime object if the work fulfils both objects. Myer and I write in order to communicate knowledge. Read his first sentence again. In order to qualify as an accountant, I had to read pages of unintelligible 'gobbledegook'. Nothing I have ever read remotely compares with that opening sentence. I had to read it six times before understanding it. I've yet to find someone that has managed in less than three. If I had communicated as successfully as Myers, I doubt whether a single smoker would have completed 'EASYWAY'. I have no doubt that had they done so, not a single smoker would have quit. How can any person capable of writing that opening sentence possibly be regarded as competent to criticise others? The narrative continues, words in brackets are my comments:

"In furtherance of the worthy aim of recruiting as many as possible to this enviable status, next Wednesday has been designated National Non-Smoking Day; and these two books have been rushed out for the occasion. A bit less rush might have been advantageous. Both Carr and Morgan are ex-smokers who are now professional encouragers of others to give up – as, respectively, a consultant and a tutor on the

Habitbreakers course. But neither, frankly, is much of a writer.

Time should have been found to edit out at least the worst of Carr's repetitions, tautologies, catachreses, inconsistencies in punctuation, irrelevant analogies, mixed metaphors and uncontrolled similes". (Of course, I see it all so clearly now, Myer is absolutely right, we should have postponed the book to the following year, what are the lives of another 100,000 UK citizens compared with the horror of a tautology, or a catchresis let alone an uncontrolled simile).

"These things matter, not just intrinsically, but also because they are liable to vitiate the book's most worthy message." (Yes but what is that message Myer? Why don't you tell us something about the message?)

"Carr's book is less structured. He deals in advantages and disadvantages in a tone supposed to be one of sweet reason. But, not least on account of its stylistic horrors, I was less convinced of his book's potential efficacy." (Now why couldn't I see that? The key to curing smokers isn't the content of the book, what really matters is the style. All they really need to do is to read 'Julius Caesar' or 'Twelfth Night' and they'd stop smoking just like that; and how could he possibly know what my tone was supposed to be? Surely he could only comment on what it was?)

"Doubtless, though, there are those who will find one or other of these books an encouragement to saying yes to freedom from their lives of slavery. If either succeeds in its purpose, then its faults won't matter a damn."

-o-o-o-o-

I have serious doubts as to whether Myer actually read my book. I'll give him the benefit of the doubt by assuming that he did. If so the man is a buffoon. He complains about repetition. He says my book deals with advantages and disadvantages. Yet the most common repetition by far, is that there are no advantages to smoking. The legendary Chapter 21 is devoted entirely to that subject and most readers find it to be the most poignant chapter of the book, yet somehow Myer managed to miss the point completely. No doubt he was so engrossed in the grammar and style that he missed that rather insignificant point, not once, but at least a dozen times. I'm not sure whether this proves Myer's point about repetitions or mine. If someone is too thick to grasp a point after two repetitions, they probably won't grasp it after twelve. On the other hand, had I repeated the point twenty times, perhaps even Myer might have grasped it.

I repeated the point a dozen times because, far from being insignificant, it is the most important myth to explode about smoking: THERE IS ABSOLUTELY NOTHING TO GIVE UP! It's the basic theme of my book and method. It's that knowledge Myer's readers might well have appreciated. I think he failed them miserably. I would also criticise his practice of including two seperate books within the same review. It is not only insulting to the authors, but must be confusing for his readers.

Incidentally I have taken Myer's point, even though he missed the point, so to speak. I'm not a writer, but I have learnt some of the tricks of the trade. Perhaps I can give Myers some advice. There's a word which means never use a long word when a short one will do. Unfortunately, I forget what the word is, but I do remember the point of it. I've no doubt that Myers knows the word, what a pity he has missed the point. A biology professor was asked by a student "Is it true that flies take off backwards?" After some considerable deliberation, The learned professor replied: "Flies take off in a direction inverse to the direction they were facing immediately before they took off." After a short pause the student said: "I believe the word that you were searching for was: YES!

The one review that caused me pleasure was by an Irishman, Pat Duffy, also of the Times: The Sligo Times:

"If you happen to be in Sligo on any weekday around midday you will see some of the loveliest girls in Ireland. They are schoolgirls on their way home to lunch. And as you pass by you are bound to notice the girls lovely clear skin and bright eyes. And seeing this your heart will rise on realising that Ireland still produces girls as beautiful as any in the world. But if you are a keen observer you will notice something else about those lovely girls which may cause you to be concerned for their future. About one in five of them will be smoking cigarettes! This will depress you because you will know, unless you've been on another planet for the past 20 years, that cigarette smoking is the biggest single cause of the world's major killer diseases – cancer – heart disease – and strokes.

Now it doesn't require a great imaginative effort to visualise what these cigarette-smoking girls will look like 10 years from now. By then they will probably have husbands or careers, or both. They will also have a car, children perhaps and the inevitable mortgage. Such responsibilities will weigh heavily on their minds and the nicotine intake will be increased to ease the tension. The once lovely clear skin will require ever increasing amounts of make-up to hide the blotches caused by damage to the circulatory system. The sparkle will have long gone from the once bright eyes. In all this one thing will remain the same and that will be the big myth, the myth about smoking easing tension, helping the concentration, relieving boredom and helping you to relax. Bunkum! The direct opposite is the case. Cigarette smoking is the chief cause of the problem it's said to relieve!

Don't take my word for this. I'm just an ex-smoker whose cigarette smoking habit led to a massive heart attack which I was lucky to survive, but which left me crippled for life while I was still in the prime of life. No don't take my word for it, instead buy 'The Easy Way To Stop Smoking' by Allen Carr. And if you haven't stopped smoking after reading it, then be prepared for the shock news that if you persist with your habit it will cost you a massive £30,000 during an average lifetime – assuming that you live an average lifetime!

Allen Carr's claim that he can get you off the fags if you follow his instructions is not a gimmick. No secret potion is involved. You just have to carry out his instructions from start to finish without skipping anything. Allen is a Chartered Accountant who used to smoke heavily until he discovered the method that enabled him to go from 100 cigarettes a day to zero. And he did this without the slightest ill-effects. In fact he says it was like 'Coming out of a twilight world into a world of sunshine and freedom'.

For the past 8 years Allen has been helping smokers to kick the habit and his success rate is, by any standard formidable. I could tell you Allen's cure but it wouldn't do you the slightest bit of good because you really have to read the book – all 110 pages of it – in order to get the message, as it were. Every chapter of Allen's book is vital to a correct understanding of what smokers are hooked on, and the popular notions about how to get off the weed – chewing gum, sweets, not carrying fags in your pocket/handbag – all this is rubbish, he argues, and I agree with him. By his method and logic you can kick the habit instantly with no ill-effects whatsoever.

I strongly recommend this book to all smokers. I recommend the book especially to my friends who are addicts so that I can enjoy the pleasure of their company without having to use my cap as a fan to protect my damaged heart from the deadly fumes of their cigarettes.

Of all the books I have reviewed – and recommended – over the years Allen Carr's book has given me the most pleasure because I'm convinced that it will do a great deal of good and may even save lives. If you are a smoker and you take his advice, you will be a healthier person and therefore a happier person. What more could you ask for?"

Reading the two reviews again it's difficult to realise that they were actually reviewing the same book. But why was it that two men, both obviously intelligent and cultured, should have such diametrically opposed versions? Perhaps you got the impression that one critic was not so much reviewing the book for the benefit of his readers, but more attempting to impress upon his readers what a clever reviewer he was. Had the book been an instruction on how to cure lung cancer, perhaps Myer would have realised that no one suffering from lung cancer would be the slightest bit interested in grammatical errors or even the style of the text. Their only consideration would be:

WILL IT CURE ME?

This is the only criteria on which 'EASYWAY' this book and my method can be judged. The problem with smoking is that because it is so commonplace, because smokers, ex-smokers and non-smokers alike can clearly see that smokers are idiots, because nobody forces smokers to smoke, because there are no terrible physical withdrawal pangs, all smokers should find it relatively easy to stop. Because everybody has this knowledge, everybody is equally expert on how to stop smoking. This is the great danger, this is why critics, professionals or laymen, even people that have never smoked feel qualified to give advice on how to stop, or to criticise the advice given by me.

Now, if I had written a book on the mating rituals of the quandiflori, a beetle found only in an area of 20 square miles of the southeastern region of the amazon rainforests, furthermore, had I devoted 33 years on site, observing that beetle and claimed to be the world's leading expert on it, who would dispute my claims or contradict me? A reviewer like Myer might criticise my style, he might enquire who is the slightest bit interested in the beetle anyway, and I would agree with him. The point is that millions of smokers are interested in how to stop. All these other experts know is that logically, smokers should be able to stop. What they don't know, is why smokers find it so difficult to stop. I do know! I also know:

HOW TO REMOVE THOSE DIFFICULTIES

Smoking might be very commonplace, it also happens to be very, very complex. If you are a critic and feel tempted to comment on my method, before you do so, ask yourself if you were reviewing Nick Faldo's book on how to improve your golf, would you contradict his advice? You surely wouldn't be arrogant enough, or stupid enough, to do so if you had never played golf. Even if you had played, you would be very reckless, unless you were someone like Jack Nicklaus. If you still feel competent to contradict me, first ask yourself how many smokers you have helped to quit. You might well think that it is quite easy to help smokers to quit. Before you assume it, try it! If you can achieve a quarter of the success rate I do, feel free to criticise my method. You'll still be wrong, but I'll forgive you.

The real difference between Myer and Pat Duffy, was that Pat had a tremendous advantage over Myer. He wasn't trying to impress his readers, he wasn't trying to assess whether what I was saying was intelligent, rational or otherwise. He didn't need to, he'd already been through the nightmare himself, had already had his health seriously affected by smoking, and could identify with what I was saying. He was like many other ex-smokers that having found it easy to quit after reading 'EASYWAY', had said to me: "It was as if I were reading not your story but mine. Thank you for helping me to see it so clearly."

Why did I resent Myer's review so much? Because he pricked my ego? Perhaps that was part of it. I have to admit to a wonderful feeling of gratification in being able to return his criticism. Or was it that I envied him his knowledge and command of the English language? Again perhaps I did, even though he seemed to make these assets appear to be liabilities. Was I envious because he had access to the minds of the influential readers of 'The Times'? Certainly! But these were all superficial matters that merely served to confuse the issue. I resented him, not because he had those advantages and privileges, but because he abused them. He was unable to find one word of praise for either book, but having devoted his total dialogue to denigrating both books, he concludes his review by stating that if either book achieved its object, then its faults wouldn't matter a damn.

I am pleased to inform Myer that 'EASYWAY' has been a best seller for all of the 7 years that it has been published, and is now printed in eight languages. It has already helped thousands of smokers to obtain freedom, but thanks to Myer, I doubt whether many were readers of 'The Times'. Had I been one, I would have appreciated at least some indication of the effectiveness of the cure. Perhaps Myer didn't feel qualified to comment on that aspect. If so he was absolutely right. So why did he? If I were still a smoker and had read Myer's review, I wouldn't have bought either book and as a result might well be dead now.

The reason that I resent Myer isn't because I envy him or his ilk. I was fortunate enough to discover a method that would help any smoker to find it easy to stop. I sweat enjoyable blood and tears perfecting that method. I sweat excruciating blood and tears attempting to transfer that knowledge to a written form. I resent Myer because he callously wrote off all that effort by denigrating my method without making the slightest effort himself to find out whether it was effective or otherwise. If all the reviews had been like Myer's, I doubt whether a single smoker would have benefited from my book.

Why did the majority of the other reviews frustrate me, even though they were complimentary? Because, no matter how well-intentioned they might have been, they made comments which were inaccurate or misleading.

Why did Pat Duffy's review cause me so much pleasure? Because he not only understood the essence of the message that I was trying to impart, he actually improved upon it. The grammatical errors must have been equally obvious to him, yet he found no need to mention them. I envied Pat Duffy. How shrewd he was to avoid starting his review, as so many smoking articles do, with the terrible effects smoking has on health. Had he done so, he would immediately have lost the bulk of his readers. Instead he used the beautiful colleens to ensure that his readers, male and female alike, were lured into reading the rest of his article. If all reviewers had been as shrewd as Pat, I'm convinced that my task would already be complete.

Myers is quite correct. I'm not a writer any more than I am an orator. I make no claim to be either. But I am aware of just how vital both forms of communication are in order to achieve my ambition. I am also well aware of my limitations in both departments. It would be nice if I had the skill of the bard combined with the eloquence of a Richard Burton. I do my best to learn from them, and from others like them. I envy Pat Duffy his insight and his writing skills. But I don't resent him. On the contrary I admire him. I am also grateful to him, as I am to Robin Hayley, to Roy Sheehan and literally thousands of other clients, friends, acquaintances and critics who have helped me to improve my method and to hone it and refine it to its present state.

I don't resent Myers because he criticised my work. I don't even resent him because his review was petty-minded, unimaginative and unconstructive. I don't even resent that he appeared to possess a less than average knowledge about the subject of smoking or that he failed to understand my method. I resent him because he misinformed his readers and as a result effectively prevented many of them from escaping the trap. It wouldn't have been quite so bad if I had had the right to reply. If a copy of that reply had immediately followed the review, at least I would have had the opportunity to reverse some of the effects of Myer's lack of imagination. That's the really frustrating thing about idiots like Myers, they callously pour out their pompous bilge, without fear of contradiction, oblivious to the damage that they inflict upon their readers.

For incompetence, Myer's review was head and shoulders above his nearest rival. There was however another which caused me infinitely more heartache. Ironically, it was the one that I looked forward to reading the most. In the early days at Raynes Park I had successfully helped the editor of a leading nursing journal to quit. He had been one of those smokers that had tried everything without success, and he was very impressed with my method, so much so that he sent me a letter to that effect and actually invited me to use the letter as a recommendation.

I was naturally looking forward to reading his journal's review of 'EASYWAY' safe in the knowledge that I would get at least one good review. It went something like:

"Mr. Carr's book contains some useful tips, but when it comes down to it, you have to use willpower."

You might not consider that to be unduly damaging, but to me it was inaccurate, misleading and a complete disaster. Partly because my method doesn't just give useful tips. It is a complete system that will enable any smoker to stop easily and permanently. But mainly because, if you tell smokers that they need to use willpower you are merely confirming what they already know. If they believe that they do not possess the necessary willpower, there is no point in trying the book, and if they believe that they possess sufficient willpower to stop, they don't need the book. Either way, there would be no point in them reading it.

I was deflated and phoned the editor:

"You didn't need willpower to stop when you used my method, why did you allow your reviewer to misrepresent it?"

"It is editorial policy. I have no power to influence or to interfere with the reviews."

I sympathise with the general principle. I even agree with it. However, like: 'IT IS FORBIDDEN TO SWIM IN THE BOATING LAKE', aren't there exceptions to these rules that could be applied with a modicum of common sense? You might quite sensibly lay down a rule in your home that hose-pipes should be confined to the garden. You would feel that your children were somewhat thick if in your absence, the living room caught fire and they failed to extinguish it because they weren't allowed to use the hose-pipe in the house.

Supposing the reviewer had been commenting on a new drug, but through misunderstanding, had omitted to mention that the drug would kill pregnant women and children under the age of ten. If that editor had been aware of this misinformation, would he really have applied the journal's non-interference rule? I like to think not. But what was the difference? He knew that my method didn't require willpower. He was in a much better position than his reviewer, he had actually tried the method, the reviewer was merely trying to assess it. What about all the smokers that have since died because they saw no point in reading my book after that review?

Now consider the domino effect if the review had been similar to the editor's letter. Nurses all over the country would have tried the method, found it worked and recommended it to their patients. Perhaps, even 'The Lancet' might have recognized its worth. Six years ago the BMA was rather harsh on alternative medicines. It is interesting to note that it has recently recommended a more open-minded attitude.

If the reviewer had indeed taken the trouble to read and try to understand the book, would it have been so much extra effort to telephone or write to me and say: "Look, you say that your method doesn't require the use of willpower. Now that would be marvellous if it were true, but having read your book, I don't believe it." At least I could have corrected the misunderstanding. For the lack of a nail the war was lost!

Please, please, if you are reviewing this book and wish to denigrate it, or contradict it in some way, I will respect your right and duty to do so. But please give me the opportunity to defend myself first. By not giving your readers incorrect or misleading information, you might well save their lives. Your readers have nothing to lose by buying the book anyway. If the book fails to fulfil its objects, I guarantee to refund the full purchase price, without inquisition, provided it's returned in a reasonable condition. A rash statement? It might appear so, but we've being doing this at the clinics for nearly ten years.

The truth is: **THE METHOD DOES WORK!** So why don't you help me to spread the message and help to save millions of lives?

CHAPTER 34

Women Smokers

All smokers smoke only because they have been brainwashed into believing that they get some benefit or crutch from smoking. Every smoker has his or her own individual brainwashing. But surely it is possible to subdivide smokers into various group types such as:

1. Cigarette, pipe or cigar smokers.
2. Taylor-mades or roll-ups.
3. Tipped or un-tipped.
4. Young, middle aged or old.
5. Casual, medium or heavy.
6. Social, stress, boredom, concentration or relaxation.
7. Inhalers and puffers.
8. Wealthy or poor.
9. Male or female.

If you confine the distinctions just to the nine points above, you already have over 5,000 different classifications of smoker. Add additional factors such as low, medium or high tar, or race, colour, religion or creed and you are soon into the millions. How can Allen Carr possibly relate to that great variety of circumstances? A possible answer is that, with the exception of two, I have experienced every one of the above nine possibilities at some time during my smoking life. One exception is that I never learned to inhale deeply.

It is true that my highest success rates are achieved with heavy, long-term smokers, those that were nearing the stage that I had reached 10 years ago. My lowest success rates are with teenage or casual smokers. This isn't because I am not able to relate to them. It might be partly that they don't believe that I can relate to them, or that they find it difficult to relate to me, but it is mainly due to the fact that they do not have the same need or desire to escape from the prison.

It is also true that my success rate with smokers, whose first language is not English, is lower than average. This applies even when such people speak far better English than I do. However the reason has nothing to do with race or colour, it is because such people are so obsessed in translation, they are apt to miss the point. I have no difficulty in understanding well-spoken French, but if it's a joke, I invariably fail to see the punch line.

The other exception to the circumstances in 1-9 above is that I have never been a woman. However, since the success rate with women is marginally higher than with men, the gender factor appears not to affect the situation. I admit to having had the same prejudices that most young boys have against girls. Whether this is natural, or I read too many 'William' books, I do not know. However Charles Chevalier helped me to overcome this block. Thank Heaven! They do indeed grow up in the nicest possible way.

It is a fact that in Britain and many other western countries, women smokers now outnumber the men. It is particularly disturbing to note how many teenage girls are hooked compared with boys. Many women believe that this is due to some inherent flaw a woman's make-up. Just as it is essential to realise that there is no such thing as an addictive personality, it is essential to know that it is just as easy for any woman to quit, as it is for any man. It is also necessary for you to understand exactly why there is currently a preponderance of female smokers.

Various reasons have been put forward by the so-called experts as to the reason for the reversal of the previous trend. Because in the old days smoking was not considered to be ladylike, there were more male smokers. Some experts maintain that the change is due to the women's lib movement: they not only have to wear trousers and take over our jobs, but they have to accentuate the point by adopting our disgusting habits. The number of female executives that find it necessary to use a preponderance of four-lettered words might lend credence to this view. However I do not believe that a smoker decides to become a smoker for any reason, any more than a fish decides to get hooked.

The chauvinists will tell you that it's not so much a matter that more women smoke than men, but that since smoking became anti-social, more men have succeeded in stopping. The obvious reason for this is that the stronger male has been able to exercise his greater willpower.

I'm sorry to disillusion you chaps, but the true reason that there are more female smokers today is the complete reverse. I do believe that the women's liberation movement has indirectly been the cause. Not because the woman wants to demonstrate her masculinity, but because, although woman's lib has achieved much to improve the rights and image of the modern day woman, it has at the same time created more stress in women's lives.

Any woman executive that is holding down what was traditionally regarded as a man's job will confirm that in order to be regarded as equal to a man doing the same job, she must be five times as good. In TV quiz or game shows, it's still always the male that presents the show, wittily quipping away with his carefully rehearsed ad-libs. The female role is still to appear half naked, with a permanent smile and to occasionally blurt out equally obviously rehearsed stupidities. Please do not think that I am complaining. I admire the beauty of the female body as much as the next man. But this image isn't very flattering to the female mind.

It upsets me deeply at the clinics, when we ask a woman her profession. Often the reply is: "I'm only a housewife." ONLY a housewife! How in this enlightened day can our society, not only denigrate housewives, but make housewives themselves feel subnormal? Okay, if we were back in the stone age when the man had to go out and risk life and limb to obtain food, and all the woman had to do was to sit in the cave and change the straw once a week, such an attitude might be excusable, but does this really apply today?

If you analyse most jobs you will discover that of housewife is one of the few genuinely stressful jobs. If she has young children to care for, their very lives can depend on her vigilance. Much of the housewife's work consists of mundane tasks, but that doesn't mean that the housewife herself is unintelligent. I used to think that my job as an accountant was highly responsible. It was stressful, but only because I hated it. The job I do now is far more responsible, peoples' very lives are dependent on me, but I don't find it stressful, on the contrary, I thrive on it.

I know that I will regret writing this, but my own situation is a classic example of the travesty of justice that many women still have to bear in this so-called enlightened age. I have received many compliments over the years for my knowledge about smoking and the ingenuity of my method. One of the main reasons for my success is that I have the luxury of being able to devote my time and thoughts to the battle against the 'weed' to the total exclusion of almost everything else. I regard myself as a very lucky man. However, my priveleged position doesn't depend on luck. On the contrary, it is entirely due to Joyce's incredible ability of being able to split her brain and energy into a thousand and one different avenues, and not only be able to handle them efficiently, but to remain cheerful.

I don't have to bother with paying the bills, cleaning the house, shopping, cooking, or answering the phone. In fact, when we ran Raynes Park together, I think she cured half the smokers that rang up before they even got to me. So efficient is she that she has almost undermined me. I'm now incapable of buying my own clothes. I've long since forgotten my neck size. Fortunately I'm still capable of dressing myself, but if she hasn't laid out the clothes that I wear each morning, I'm like a stranded whale! Yet who gets all the credit for this battle against the weed? Life can be so unjust. Behind every great man is a woman. I suspect in most cases, in front of every great woman is a rather mediocre man.

The main illusion about smoking is that it relieves stress. The reason that there are more female than male smokers today is because whether you like it or not, women generally have more stress in their lives than men. By encouraging women to stand up for their rights to obtain equality with men, the women's lib movement has made the woman's life more stressful. I am not criticizing the movement, on the contrary, they have not only my sympathy, but my support. I openly admit that women, in general, are not just equal, but superior to men. In fact, if you study nature, you realise that males are not really a separate gender, but merely an extention of the female gender, or mother nature's way to obtain a wider variation of the genes. It also has the added advantage of making the process of reproduction so much more enjoyable.

However just and worthwhile as that battle might be, the fact is, any battle increases stress. Many modern day women, in addition to the stress of having to compete with the male, still have the genuine stress of childbirth, motherhood, keeping the house clean, feeding and clothing their children. Very few modern men are capable of doing all that, even if they were prepared to try. It's not surprising that there are more women smokers than men.

A word of warning ladies. You might well conclude from what I have been saying, that it is more difficult for you to stop smoking, or even that you would be wise to continue to smoke. Not so! All that I am saying is that, whether it's just or otherwise, women tend to have more stress in their lives than men. That being so, they are more likely to fall into the smoking trap and to remain in it. Get it clearly into your mind, smoking doesn't relieve stress. It causes it! Indeed for most smokers it is not only the major cause of their stress, but it's their nicotine addiction which causes so many other aspects of their lives to appear so stressful.

I'm not just referring to the effect that the cumulative poisoning and financial cost has on physical and mental health, energy and self-respect, although all of these factors do increase the stress in our lives, but also the panic, empty, insecure feeling that nicotine creates. The combined effect on smokers, is to transform trivial, everyday set-backs, which non-smokers take in their stride, into great traumas.

Assume for a moment that cigarettes do relieve stress. You'd expect smokers to be relatively calm and laid-back compared to non-smokers. Is this the reality? Isn't it the smokers that seem to be uptight and restless, particularly when they aren't allowed to smoke? Isn't it the smokers that always need something to calm their nerves. If cigarettes do calm their nerves, why do smokers remain so nervous?

Your lives will be less stressful once you have stopped smoking and any smoker can find it easy to stop. In any event, mother nature has already equipped you to deal adequately with normal stress, but hasn't equipped you to deal with the evils of smoking. What she has done is to supply you with adequate warning signs not to smoke.

There are far too many pathetic aspects about smoking. It is difficult to decide which is the most pathetic, but high on the list is smoking when pregnant. It infuriates me that our society makes it so easy for young girls to get hooked. We almost force them into the trap. We wait for them to become pregnant, then, at what is probably the most stressful period in their lives to date and the time when they believe they most need their little friend, we subject them to massive pressure to quit. Should they fail, we treat them with the same contempt that we would a child molester.

From the medical profession, this attitude is understandable even though it's not particularly helpful to either the mother or the unborn child. But non-smokers, ex-smokers, relatives and strangers, feel justified and obliged to pour forth their abuse. Even the girl's smoking friends will join the witch-hunt: "I just can't understand you smoking now that you're pregnant, I'd definitely stop if it were me." That is until it is them, amazingly they are now able to sympathise with their friend.

Some girls are lucky. They find that just as nature alters their eating habits to benefit both mother and baby, so they just seem to lose the desire to smoke. Another example of the miraculous functioning of the human body. Other girls make a conscious decision to stop, but fail. Even if the baby is born healthy, their failure, which was really no fault of their own, leaves them with a guilty conscience for the rest of their lives. I dread to think what miseries they suffer if the baby is born with some defect. Some actually succeed, then after nine months of discomfort, fear, expectation and excitement, comes the most stressful period of their lives, the fear, pain, mental and physical exhaustion of the labour, culminating in the miracle of the birth.

If all is well with both mother and child, the fear has gone, the pain and exhaustion are momentarily forgotten. The mother is instantaneously lifted from the lowest of lows to the highest of highs. The two times in our lives that smokers' brains have been triggered to say: I NEED A CIGARETTE!

Some women that stopped for the major part of the pregnancy tell me that they lit up before the cord was cut or immediately after. Some survive the immediate impulse and are then caught out during the post birth depressions. Regrettably very few stop permanently because of pregnancy. Like all reasons for stopping, once the reason no longer applies, neither does the desire not to smoke.

Many pregnant girls either refuse to believe the adverse effects that smoking has on their unborn child, or justify them by saying: "I think I would do the baby more harm by attempting to stop at this stage." Some claim that their doctor actually forbade them to stop for this reason. I could write a separate book about the statements that doctors have purportedly made about smoking. No doubt some of them are true, but I think most of them are smokers quoting out of context, or using poetic license, or, another favourite ruse of the smoker, they've heard another smoker use the argument and think, if it applies to that smoker, it must also apply to me.

Many doctors, with the best of intentions, advise pregnant mothers to try to cut down if they cannot stop completely. The advice sounds logical, but as I will explain in Chapter 24, it is the worst of the three choices that the mother has. Instead of being subjected to the withdrawal from nicotine, whether it be mental or physical, for just a few days, she suffers the extra stress for the whole nine months. But the really terrible effect is to ingrain into the mother's mind the illusion of just how precious each cigarette is. After the birth the mother is in the same position as a dieter that can no longer sustain the feeling of deprivation. The dieter goes on a binge, the smoker goes on an orgy of smoking.

In the last few years more and more firms have sought our assistance in successfully instituting a no-smoking policy. This is an encouraging trend and will be a great influence in defeating the enemy. Most firms have no notion of the benefits that would ensue and were surprised to discover that the staff who most appreciate the policy were the smokers. That is provided the firm goes about it in the right way. Unfortunately most firms go about it the wrong way and it is at such occasions that I hear the most bizarre claims of: 'The doctor told me'.

At a recent seminar a young girl suffering from asthma said her doctor had told her that she had to smoke in order to relieve her asthma attacks. She made this statement in front of about 30 other smokers. I said: "But smoking is a major cause of asthma, I find it difficult to believe that your doctor actually gave you this advice." She confirmed that he had. I said: "That's scandalous, please give me the name of your doctor." She then amended her statement slightly: "Well he didn't actually say it, but I told him that when I had an asthma attack, a cigarette seemed to help me and he nodded". Had I not pursued the point 30 other smokers would have been able to claim that some doctors maintain that smoking relieves asthma.

Now I don't intend to go into details of the ways in which smoking can affect, injure or even kill an unborn child, partly because enough has already been written about it, but mainly because the last thing a pregnant woman wants to read about is the damage she is causing her baby. She knows that instinctively, if that was going to stop her she would already have stopped. What all these well intentioned people who vilify pregnant girls don't seem to realise is, that the person that is most aware of the damage is the girl herself. She might not admit it to you, and she might try to justify her actions, but she is merely doing what all smokers do throughout their lives. She already feels guilty.

The more guilty other people make her feel, the greater her need for the illusory crutch.

Apart from the pregnancy itself and the vilification that goes with it, pregnant girls are often hit by an additional shock at this time. Most smoking youngsters are convinced that they are in control and could stop if ever the need arose. Pregnancy is often the event that makes them realise that they are just another of the millions of nicotine 'junkies'!

There is one aspect about the effect smoking has on a baby's health that I do feel bound to mention. I have read that babies whose mothers are addicted to heroin, will themselves suffer withdrawal pangs. This seems to be perfectly logical, after all, the same blood courses through the veins of both mother and foetus. It follows that the same principle should apply to nicotine addiction. I did a survey of the babies in my own circle of relatives and friends to find out which babies were generally contented, or otherwise during the few weeks following birth.

Now I freely admit that this survey only covers about 20 babies. I also admit that it was carried out on a basis that would not stand up to a strictly scientific interrogation. A small proportion of the non-smoking mothers had discontented babies. Every one of the smoking mothers had discontented babies!

In most cases I was relying on observations made years before the time of my survey. You might conclude that my judgement was swayed by the results that I wanted to hear. You would be wrong. In fact the conclusions seemed to contradict my beliefs, so much so that it led me to question my convictions. I maintain that the physical discomfort from nicotine withdrawal is so slight as to be hardly noticeable and that what smokers suffer when they stop, is not the almost imperceptible itch itself, but not being able to scratch it. Therefore, even if a baby were suffering the physical discomfort from nicotine withdrawal, it cannot possibly know that a cigarette will relieve that feeling, so why should it get unduly disturbed?

I know that when I tried to stop when using the willpower method, I got very uptight because I wasn't allowed to have a cigarette. I also know that once I was aware that the empty feeling was actually being caused by the cigarette and that I knew it would soon go, it didn't bother me in the slightest. Now, I have only known those 2 situations. One in which I believed the cigarette relieved the empty feeling and the other in which I knew it caused it. I do not know what it is like to suffer the physical withdrawal discomfort from nicotine without relating it to cigarettes one way or the other. So how can I judge?

There is one useful guide we can use. I have said that the physical discomfort from nicotine withdrawal is identical to a hunger for food. I don't start to cry when I get hungry, but I did when I was a baby. Babies are programmed to cry when they are hungry, therefore a baby that is suffering the physical withdrawal effects from nicotine will feel permanently hungry and will keep crying, feeding it won't satisfy that feeling, on the contrary, the tired and confused mother will tend to overfeed it and by doing so will merely exacerbate the problem.

Another problem that has been brought to the fore since Anne Diamond lost her baby, is a connection between smoking and cot deaths. I am not clear as to the scientific basis for the connection, but I do know this: birth is the most stressful period that most creatures experience in their lives. I'm aware of the misery smokers undergo when using the willpower method. However, I was also aware that I could end that misery at any time that I wanted to by lighting a cigarette, and I was prepared to die rather than suffer that misery. Who knows what misery a baby suffers that doesn't even have the choice, that doesn't even have an illusory solution to a problem that it didn't create? Perhaps after the sheer trauma of being born, and still in a very vulnerable state, a baby's instinctive brain finds that not breathing is preferable to going through a trauma which might be a far greater trauma than stopping smoking by the normal willpower method.

It's an established fact that in western society, on average, women live longer than men. However, I gather that in recent years the gap has tended to close. Is this a direct result of the relationship between smoking and longevity?

Let's get back to the point. Be you male or female, be you pregnant or otherwise. I want you to stop smoking for the purely selfish reason that you will enjoy life so much more! Now I am not saying that there aren't genuine problems in life. If you have a genuine problem and you are able to do something about it, do it! If there is absolutely nothing that you can do about it, accept the fact – worrying about it won't help one iota. If you are a smoker, you do have a serious, genuine problem! Fortunately you are able to do something about it:

STOP SMOKING!

When you do you might well find, just as I and thousands of others have done, that those other problems that appeared to be so oppressive at the time, will suddenly evaporate. Either way, no matter what your problems or hang ups are, whether they be genuine or illusory, once you have escaped from the smoking trap, they won't feel nearly as bad as they do today.

There are two main reasons why smokers that successfully quit get hooked again. One is that they do not completely remove the brainwashing, there remains a slight, lingering sense of feeling deprived. Even when removed completely, the ex-smoker can still become trapped again by the second cause:

CASUAL SMOKERS

CHAPTER 35

Casual Smokers

"A little of what you fancy does you good."

"There's no real harm, provided it's in moderation."

Such advice might hold good for certain aspects of life, but when applied to smoking or any other form of drug addiction, it is equivalent to saying:

"It'll do you good to soak your feet in quicksand provided you don't go in above the knees."

"There's no real harm in going over Niagara Falls, but don't go down more than 3 feet."

Perhaps you think that they are not suitable analogies. They are! The only real difference between the first pair and the second, is that the results of the latter are obvious and quick, and the results of the former are subtle and comparatively slow. That's what makes the former so lethal. How many people do you know that have died from quicksand or from going over Niagara Falls?

Any smoker that has made several fruitless efforts to cut down, knows by trial and error that it will only work for a limited period. In 'Easyway' and at our clinics I go to great lengths to explain the actual mechanics of why casual smoking and cutting down cannot work. Yet in spite of this knowledge, backed by the proof of their own experience, the reason that smokers get hooked again is the belief that they can control their smoking, or can have an isolated or occasional cigarette. It is exactly this same reason that gets all smokers hooked in the first place.

Let me be quite clear. I am not saying that it is the only reason that smokers become hooked, or get hooked again. I am saying that, even if a smoker has many powerful reasons to light a cigarette, whether those reasons be illusory or genuine, that smoker would not light that cigarette if he or she knew that they would have to continue smoking the rest of his or her life, never, ever being allowed to stop. This means that if you can just get this one concept clear in your mind, you will never get hooked again.

Perhaps you doubt the concept. Let's first test it out with something that we know is pleasant. I loved the thought of playing golf long before I could afford the time or money to do so. I knew that I'd become hooked if I did play. However, if before I had played that first game you had said: "You can play this round of golf, but if you do, you will have to play golf all day, every day for the rest of your life," as much as I loved the idea of golf, there is no way that I would have accepted those conditions, and even had I have been stupid enough to do so, I know that I would have been utterly sick of the game within three months. Now, if you knew for certain that if you lit that first cigarette, you would have to smoke all day, every day, never ever being allowed to stop, it is inconceivable that a single person would light that first cigarette.

So why, in spite of knowing that logically we cannot have an occasional cigarette and in spite of having proved the fact to ourselves on several occasions, do we fall into the trap yet again? It's because part of the schizophrenia or brainwashing is still present, and this information is contradicting the conclusion of our logic and experience. This information is saying that it is possible to control your smoking or to have occasional cigarettes. Again, this information is incorrect, nevertheless it is essential to remove it. The main facts which tend to distort our beliefs are the following:

1. Not every youngster gets hooked after lighting their first cigarette. Therefore it is an unarguable fact that some people can have just one cigarette without getting hooked. Perhaps this time I'll be lucky.
2. Because I have found it easy to stop completely, it must be even easier to smoke just the occasional cigarette. Even if Allen Carr is right and I get hooked again, I can still use his method to stop again.
3. Allen Carr implies that all smokers become hooked and remain hooked for the rest of their lives. The truth is that many smokers quit when they cease to enjoy it and this is proved by the millions that have already quit.
4. In the early days, I used to be a casual smoker myself. I could take them or leave them, I only smoked the ones that I wanted to, so I know it can be done. That is another unarguable fact.
5. I know several one time heavy smokers that now happily smoke only a few cigarettes a day, or the occasional cigar. I've done it myself on several occasions for quite long periods. So I know that it can be done. Another unarguable fact.
6. I know several casual smokers that have been happy, casual smokers the whole of their lives. So I know it can be done. Another unarguable fact.

The above facts do indeed add up to powerful evidence that it is possible for some smokers, if not you or I, to remain happy, casual smokers the whole of their lives. I've yet to meet a smoker that doesn't envy casual smokers. Even most of those that have read 'EASYWAY' or attended the clinics still envy casual smokers. It proves my point: some of the brainwashing is still there. Most of the above is unarguable fact, but there is one very important exception: the use of the word 'happy'. There is no such thing as a happy smoker, casual or otherwise.

Let us get rid of these illusions once and for all. It is true that some youngsters do not get hooked when they try that first cigarette. This is really a red herring. You envy the lucky ones that don't get hooked, not for the actual process of smoking that one cigarette, but purely because: THEY DIDN'T BECOME SMOKERS! What is the point in lighting the first cigarette, if you're unlucky you get hooked. If you're lucky you remain a non-smoker. It's just like spinning a coin:

HEADS YOU GAIN NOTHING! TAILS YOU LOSE EVERYTHING!

It is time to explode the myth of the happy, casual smoker. Perhaps you believe there is this idyllic alternative to being either non-smoker or hooked for life? Since many such smokers obviously do exist, in theory it must be possible for you to become one. I can confirm that you actually can become one. Not just in theory but in practice. Now before you get too excited over the prospect, let's first examine why you are not already one, or if you are one of these happy casual smokers, why you are reading this book? Let's first establish whether you really want to be a casual smoker.

In my golfing analogy, I was not giving an unrealistic hypothesis. Obviously no one would want to play golf all day, every day for the rest of their life. But if it were once or twice a week, surely many golfers would jump at the opportunity? If I gave you the opportunity to smoke just 2 a day for the rest of your life. Would you accept it? Better still, suppose you were able to control your smoking so that you smoked, not habitually, but only when you really wanted to? Now, before you jump from the frying pan, I have very good news for you. That's exactly what you do now and what all smokers do throughout their smoking lives. You might question that statement, but has anyone ever forced you to light a cigarette? Every cigarette that you ever smoked, you did so because you wanted to smoke it. The fact that part of your brain wished that you didn't want to smoke them doesn't alter that fact.

Actually, it is not strictly true that all smokers smoke whenever they want to. It is true that every cigarette that you have ever smoked, you did so because you wanted to, but there are many times in all smokers' lives when they desperately want to smoke, but aren't allowed to, either because they have no cigarettes and can't afford them or obtain them, or because they are in a situation in which society forbids them to smoke, or because in the permanent tug of war in their own brain, the side that is saying: 'DON'T SMOKE' is temporarily in the ascendency. Therefore, if all smokers could smoke only when they wanted to, they would smoke more, not less than they do. In fact there would be absolutely nothing to restrict their smoking. They would all become chain-smokers as I was.

THAT IS THE NATURAL TENDENCY

So I take it that you'll settle for just the two cigarettes a day. Again I have good news for you. If that's what you want, you can do just that. Who's to stop you? In fact why didn't you just smoke two a day the whole of your smoking life if you envy casual smokers so much? Could it be that you wouldn't have been happy smoking just two a day? Well of course you wouldn't.

NEITHER WOULD ANY OTHER SMOKER!

Now, before you start envying casual smokers let's take a closer look at them. While we do, I want you to keep two facts clearly in your mind:

1. All smokers wish that they had never started.
2. All smokers lie. To other people, and to themselves.

In Chapter 25 of 'Easyway' I described the case of a man who rang me up late at night and opened the conversation: "Mr Carr I want to stop smoking before I die." He wasn't being flippant. There was clearly something wrong with his voice. He explained that he had cancer of the throat, that he just couldn't stop smoking by going 'cold turkey' and was doing it gradually trying to cut down. He had succeeded in cutting down from 40 tailor-mades to 5 roll-ups a day, but couldn't reduce it any further. I said: "You are doing the worst possible thing by trying to cut down. Just smoke whenever you want to for a few days and then come to see me."
This was during my early days of counselling and it never occurred to me that it had taken him a year of tremendous willpower and misery to cut down from 40 to 5. It had left him completely drained. He began to cry over the phone. I then made my second blunder. Instead of insisting that he follow my instructions, I agreed to see him the next day. In fact he needed two sessions and we were reduced to tears on each occasion. In fact it was the abject misery of this man that inspired me to write 'Easyway'.
As I have said, it is only fear that keeps people smoking and when

smokers have already crippled themselves as he had done, they are even more frightened. Cutting down merely reduces their desire to stop and at the same time increases the illusory pleasure of smoking. This all goes to increase the panic, which prevents the smoker from understanding what I am saying to them. This is one of the great frustrations that I suffer with smokers that have already crippled themselves. I know that they can find it easy to stop, but it's difficult to get them sufficiently relaxed, not only to hear, but also to understand what I am saying.

The first session was completely fruitless. I could tell I wasn't getting through to him. But the seeds I had planted began to germinate during the second. At one stage the fear left his countenance only to reappear a few moments later. Can you imagine someone falling out of a boat into a very murky lake. You make a grab for him but your hold is feeble. You daren't risk improving upon it lest you loose it completely. He has a look of horror on his face. Gradually he slips out of your fingers and disappears into the murk. That look of horror haunts you at various times during the rest of your life and you wonder what you might have done to save him. That's how I felt with this man, knowing I had the knowledge to help him escape from the maze, yet failing to enable him to absorb it. I thought, if I write it down, he can read it in his own good time as often as he wants. Perhaps that will enable him to understand.

Logically that man was exercising more control when smoking 5 a day than when he smoked 40. But that's only if you look at it from the distorted concept that the user controls the drug. Now look at the actual facts. When he was on 40 a day, he was not even conscious of smoking them, but on 5 a day his entire life is dominated by that evil weed. That's because:

THE DRUG CONTROLS THE USER

While he was on 40 a day he wasn't aware of it. He only became aware of it when he tried to escape. Ironically, had he been a heroin addict, he would also have been a criminal in law. Yet he could register under the National Health as a heroin addict and get free heroin and medical help. As a nicotine addict, he can't even buy his drug at cost. He has to pay the treasury 3 times the true value of the drug. Prior to seeking my assistance he had consulted his doctor. His doctor's advice was:

"You've got to stop. It's killing you."

"I know, that's why I'm seeking your help."

The doctor then prescribed chewing gum, which cost the man £11 in addition to the prescription fee, and that chewing gum actually contained the drug that he was trying to kick.

Now you might think that is an exceptional case and that you would never allow yourself to reach that stage. Take your blinkers off! **2,500,000 smokers reach that stage every year!** Do you think that they all just quietly pass away overnight in their sleep? He wasn't even dead yet, just on his way to the bottom of the pit:

JUST AS YOU ARE! UNLESS YOU STOP!

The point is that to his acquaintances, he was one of these happy 5 a day smokers. He wouldn't cry in their company and tell them the misery that he was going through. Like all smokers, while we still smoke we feel stupid. We have to conjure up phoney arguments to justify our stupidity. If only all smokers would take their head out of the sand and declare their hatred of smoking, like snuff-taking, it would be dead in no time. It's only this belief that everyone else is enjoying it that keeps us clinging to the illusion that there is some pleasure or crutch in smoking.

Now you probably know smokers like that man. Obviously, when you say that you would like to be a casual smoker, you don't mean people like him. You mean the happy, ones that haven't crippled themselves and only smoke about 5 a day or just the special ones. We have many such smokers at our clinics. The heavier smokers in the group stare at them in disbelief, thinking: "You must be mad, you've got it made, If only I could be like you."

In Chapter 25 of 'EASYWAY', I also described the classic case of a lady solicitor who rang up wanting a private session. In case you wonder why I repeat this case and certain other anecdotes contained in 'EASYWAY', it is because they were only included after about the 5th reprint. I explained that group sessions were just as effective but not nearly as expensive as private sessions. However the lady insisted on an individual session and was more than happy to pay the additional fee. You might think, well what is so unusual about that? Just this: that lady had been smoking for 12 years during which time she had smoked no more than 2 cigarettes a day.

Now most smokers would think: "That's every smokers dream. Just to be able to smoke 2 a day. Why did she want to pay all that money? I'd pay you double that if you could help me just to smoke 2 a day." But this is just part of the myth. We assume that these casual smokers are in control:

NO SMOKERS ARE IN CONTROL

In this lady's case, both her parents had died from lung cancer before she became hooked. Like me, she had a great fear of smoking before she became hooked. She too eventually succumbed to the immense pressure, tried an experimental cigarette, and found it repulsive. Unlike me, who capitulated to chain-smoking in no time at all, this lady fought it. Now she had every smoker's schizophrenia. Just like a hunger for food, the longer you go without it, the more precious it will appear, so the longer you crave a cigarette, the more precious it will appear when you finally satisfy that craving, and of course, the less you smoke, the less you cripple your health and your pocket, and the less you need to stop.

That lady was terrified to increase her intake lest she contracted lung cancer like her parents. But the less she smoked, the less likelihood of that happening, and the more precious her little crutch appeared to her. The nicotine trap has many subtleties: the more you take, the more you want to take: the less you take, the more you want to take! It's rather like that method of tying someone up, so that the slightest movement, no matter in what manner, merely tightens the rope around the victim's neck.

Now what was that lady's true position? Do you really believe that she was one of those happy cheerful casual smokers? If so why did she seek my help? The truth is, like the 40 down to 5 man, she was living a nightmare. For the whole of those 12 years her body craved nicotine, and her fear of contracting lung cancer inspired the immense willpower and discipline needed to resist that craving for all but 20 minutes a day. She was actually going through the process of quitting smoking for 23 hours and 20 minutes every day for the whole of those 12 years. Her friends and colleagues were so envious of her. But of course, she didn't tell them of the nightmare she was going through, she didn't want them to realise how stupid and weak she felt, any more than any other drug addict wants to.

That lady was an example of a rare type of casual smoker. One who hates and/or fears being a smoker, whose hatred and/or fear is insufficient to make them quit, but sufficient to keep them fighting it for most of their life. A much more common case is the smoker that seems to be able to take cigarettes or leave them, without having to struggle. These are usually smokers that are hooked, but do not have a great deal of stress in their lives. The problem is with such smokers, like Dr. Miller's wife, they get no particular pleasure or crutch from smoking, they just go through the motions to be part of the company. Remember we all started off like that. They are convinced that they will never become badly hooked. However should their lives suddenly become more stressful, they become heavy smokers. My mother-in-law was a classic example. She was one of these smokers who only smoked on social occasions. At the age of 60, she and her husband bought a public house. She was dead at the age of 65 smoking 60 cigarettes a day.

Many of these so-called happy casual smokers, are not genuine casual smokers, but are really going through a process of cutting down in order to quit completely, or have failed to quit completely and are cutting down as a form of compromise.

In the early days of counselling I had a typical example of a woman that was trying to quit by cutting down. She had been smoking 40 a day. One afternoon she screwed up her packet of cigarettes in disgust, and threw it into the dustbin. An hour later, she was wading through the potato peelings trying to find a cigarette. The next day she had the same revulsion to smoking. She was an intelligent lady and wasn't going to make the same mistake. So she smeared mustard over the cigarettes before banishing them to the dustbin. An hour later she was scraping potato peelings and mustard from those cigarettes. Most smokers have gone through a similar experience in their lives, yet some still insist they smoke only for the marvellous taste.

This lady then decided that there was no way that she could go 'cold turkey'. She thought: "I'll have to ease myself off of them. I'm smoking 40 a day. If I just cut out one cigarette each day, that shouldn't take too much willpower, in fact I probably won't even notice it, and provided I stick to it, I must end up a non-smoker."

We've probably all tried variations of this process at one or more times in our smoking lives It sounds perfectly logical and this lady reached the stage after about 6 weeks whereby she was down to just one cigarette a day. The trouble was, she couldn't bring herself to cut out that last cigarette. In fact she went another three months smoking just one cigarette a day. Then she sought my help and this is how she described her life: "I'd get my husband off to work and the children off to school. I would sit down and take that cigarette out of the packet, then put it back thinking - I'll do the washing-up first. After she had finished the washing-up, she would repeat the process with the ironing. All day she would be dangling the cigarette like a carrot under her own nose, but she wasn't even kidding herself. She knew that she wasn't going to smoke that cigarette until just before her children came home from school. Then she would sit down and smoke that cigarette. Having craved for it all day, can you imagine how enjoyable that cigarette must have appeared to her, and what she had to suffer to obtain that illusory pleasure? You might still argue that the pleasure was real. Not so, the cigarette tasted just as foul as it always did. Her pleasure was just the ending of the misery of the craving, and had that cigarette actually ended that misery, I would accept that the pleasure was real. Far from ending it, that cigarette merely caused her to suffer the same misery for the rest of her life.

Now that lady only smoked one cigarette a day. Supposing you had met that lady during the 3 months that she was on one a day. Just imagine the willpower and effort she had gone through, all to get free of the filthy weed. Do you think she went through that effort because she wanted to be a smoker, or because she desperately wanted to get free? If you had enquired how she was doing during that 3 months, bear in that at that stage she thinks that she is succeeding, what do you think her reply would be?: "Oh, I know that I am wasting my time, those cigarettes are so gorgeous, I don't even know why I am bothering to go through this trauma." Or do you think she would have said: "I'm doing great! I now only need one cigarette a day!" Your natural reaction would be to envy the lady, in fact you should pity her. Envying a casual smoker is equivalent to envying someone that is forced to spend the rest of their life on a permanent diet, with the added disadvantage, that the diet is not of food but poison.

Let us now look at the lady's true position. In her logical mind, she was just one cigarette away from being a non-smoker. But now for 23 hours every day, not only was her whole existence mentally dominated by thought of the next cigarette, but physically, the only pleasure in smoking, is ending the aggravation of the body craving nicotine. Just like a hunger for food, the longer you suffer it, the more marvellous it will appear when you relieve the suffering. That lady wasn't removing her illusory dependence on nicotine, merely ingraining into her mind that the only precious thing on earth is a cigarette. Was there any real difference between her and the 40 to 5 man, other than that he had already crippled himself?

You still don't believe me? You are still convinced that there are happy smokers, going through life in full control, enjoying each precious cigarette. How do you know they weren't just going through the temporary stage of cutting down? Let's look at what happened to you when you tried to cut down. I can't do that, but you can. What I can do is to describe traumas that I went through during my frequent attempts to cut down. I am aware from contacts with thousands of smokers at the clinics that they suffered similar experiences, and if you are honest with yourself, so have you.

Cutting down is really another form of casual smoking. In our early smoking days we try it as an alternative to stopping completely, or as a more acceptable method of stopping than going 'Cold Turkey'. In later years, we already know that cutting down doesn't work, and usually resort to it as a sort of compromise, after a failed attempt to stop completely. With the willpower method we initially build up in our mind all the terrible disadvantages of being a smoker and the marvellous gains we shall achieve if only we can succeed in stopping. This combined 'Stick and Carrot' effect gives us the initial incentive to put up with the irritability, depression and disorientation that we are suffering.

The problem is: **the moment you stop smoking, the massive, powerful reasons that forced you into the attempt, are beginning to lose their potency**. You no longer risk terrible diseases, you are not burning your money, you have more energy and no longer are you the pathetic slave of the weed. The facts about smoking haven't altered, but the effect of those facts on you have. Non-smokers don't have to worry about slavery, poverty, degradation and lung cancer. While the reasons for your desire to stop are gradually disappearing, on the other side of the tug of war, there is this little nicotine monster inside your body that hasn't had its fix. The feeling is no more painful than a mild cold, but we only know that feeling as 'I want a cigarette.' Why we want it, we don't know. But we can't have one. This causes us to feel deprived and miserable, and our need for that cigarette becomes even greater, this in turn increases the feeling of deprivation and misery.

A chain reaction has started which sooner or later can only end one way. Eventually we get fed up with being miserable, our initial resolve begins to weaken. We begin to doubt whether we will ever be completely happy again. We are between the devil and the deep blue sea. We don't want to give in. To do so is to lose self-respect and to admit that we are weak-willed and have once more failed to escape our slavery to the 'weed'. It also means that all the effort and misery have been wasted and the longer we lasted out and the greater the effort and misery, the more loath we are to throw it down the drain by giving in.

This is probably the most pathetic stage that any drug addict reaches, when the schizophrenia reaches its peak. Half of our brain desperately wants to surrender, the other half is determined not to. The irresistible force has met the immovable object. There can be only one outcome, a compromise:

"Surely one puff can't do any harm?" Or:

"I can't go 'cold turkey' I'll try cutting down gradually."

"I can't face the thought of never ever having another cigarette, I'll just smoke on those special occasions."

We have now switched from being a smoker who wanted to be a non-smoker, to a non-smoker who now wants to be a casual smoker. If you say: "I want a cigarette but I can't have one." Of course you will be miserable. If you say: "I want lung cancer but I can't have it." You will be miserable. Anything you crave but can't have will make you feel deprived. The fact that what you crave just happens to be the worst disease you'll ever suffer from, won't alter that feeling. Your feeling of depression and misery just gets worse and worse and eventually you will find some plausible excuse to allow you to smoke just one cigarette. But of course one isn't enough. Now you want another and another. You've fallen back into the trap that you fell into in the first place.

Just as I tried several methods to quit, so I experimented with various methods of cutting down. A very popular one is to cut out the habitual cigarettes and just smoke on social occasions. In no time at all I'd switched from visiting pubs about once a month, to drinking every night, just so that I could smoke. Not only didn't it cure my smoking, I was in danger of becoming an alcoholic!

I once hit upon the brilliant idea that, provided I stopped buying cigarettes, I must eventually end up a non-smoker. I am aware that the idea wasn't exactly unique. I'd heard of many smokers that had tried and failed by using this method. You've probably tried it yourself. The brilliance of my idea is that I had worked out in advance just why it hadn't worked for those other smokers. It was because they felt guilty accepting 'freemans' from their friends and that guilt would eventually force them to buy a packet. I avoided that trap by warning my acquaintances in advance, that if they offered me cigarettes, I'd accept them without feeling guilty or obligated to reciprocate.

The effect exceeded my expectations. People who had never previously offered their cigarettes began to do so. It was typical of all drug addiction. When you are hooked and desperately need a fix, no one will give you one. But once they sense you are trying to escape, they just keep blowing smoke in your face and sticking cigarettes under your nose. To begin with it was marvellous. I received a regular supply of cigarettes, and they were all free.

However, my benefactors began to realise the devilish cunning of my plan, and one by one they stopped offering them. Eventually, I had only one source of supply, my secretary. I had typical drug addict's schizophrenia. Half of my brain hated her for pushing the drug. The other half loved her because she was my lifeline. After a few weeks, guilt began to creep in. But I didn't give in. I stuck rigidly to my resolution and didn't buy cigarettes. However, my ingenious, addicted brain found a solution. I thought, she can't afford to keep giving me her precious cigarettes, so I'll buy a packet for her. After 3 months, I would buy her three packets of her brand every morning, a brand I did not particularly like, so that I could accept them back with a clear conscience, and still kid myself that I was stopping smoking.

I concluded there was nothing wrong with the basic theory of simply just never buying cigarettes. My mistake was that I had actually encouraged smokers to offer me cigarettes. However it was easily rectified, and after the usual period it took me to build up my resolution and reserves of courage after a failed attempt to stop, I put it to the test. This time, not only didn't I encourage my acquaintances to offer me cigarettes, I warned them that if they so much as breathed cigarette smoke in my direction, I would ram the filthy things down their throats. It's amazing just how reasonable people can be when you explain things clearly and politely to them. It had the desired effect. No one tried to tempt me. Now it was just a simple matter of not buying cigarettes and I would soon be free.

I survived about three weeks of misery. It was Saturday afternoon. England were playing Wales at Cardiff Arms Park. I sat alone at home watching TV, counting down the last, tedious, few minutes to the kick off. The atmosphere was electric and the excitement was getting through to me. I was desperate for a cigarette. Remember, I hadn't decided not to smoke again, but merely not to buy any more cigarettes. I started going through the pockets of my suits desperately searching for a dog-end.

I knew it was a waste of time. Hadn't I been through the same process several times during the previous three weeks, and any remaining dog-ends had long since been discovered. However, necessity is the mother of invention. Eventually I discovered one in the top pocket of an old sports jacket. Imagine my joy. It was over an inch long. True, it was obviously a very ancient dog-end, just how ancient I wasn't quite sure, but I hadn't worn the jacket for over ten years, and it was an un-tipped cigarette. I'd forgotten that I ever smoked un-tipped cigarettes, but what difference does muddy water make to a man dying of thirst?

In fact the tobacco was so dry, that when I tilted the dog-end slightly below the horizontal, all the tobacco poured out onto the carpet. I was down on my hands and knees stuffing a mixture of dry tobacco and carpet fibre back into the cigarette. When I lit it, it just burst into flames. Did I really believe that I could possibly have enjoyed that cigarette? Was I a happy, cheerful smoker? Or a miserable, pathetic drug addict? I also missed the first 10 minutes of the match. Do non-smokers have these problems?

Another classic attempt to cut down is the: "I'll restrict myself to 10 a day method." This one actually suited me fine, because although I chain-smoked during the day, I could quite happily go all evening without smoking. This meant that I could smoke just one cigarette each hour during the day. I had the best of all worlds, ten a day wouldn't kill me or strain my finances and I could still smoke.

Initially it was marvellous. Each hour of every day, I had a little reward to look forward to. I soon became a permanent clock-watcher. Each minute of my life would laboriously tick away. I was meticulously strict with myself. I would never light that cigarette until the minute hand had reached the twelve. Occasionally I would stand there with the cigarette in my mouth waiting whilst the second hand reached the vertical before I lit it. What a state to get into!

What we don't realise is that in order to do this we have to exercise willpower and discipline. Each cigarette lasts about ten minutes. Once it's finished, you have to wait 50 minutes for the next one. Eventually, you have one of those days when everything that can go wrong, does. You've exhausted your reserves of self discipline and are unable to restrict yourself. No problem, next day you will try again. But the spell is broken, you are now tired of the game, you cannot be bothered to apply the necessary restraint. You start to borrow next day's supply.

The Irish comedian Dave Allen summed up the inevitable result of trying to control your intake: "I have a very strict rule about smoking. I never smoke more than an average of ten cigarettes a day. Occasionally, I might borrow the odd cigarette from next day's quota, but I never, ever exceed the average of ten a day. The cigarette that I am now smoking is part of my quota for the fourth of July two thousand and forty-six!"

I didn't fall for the Dave Allen trap, in fact I would do the complete opposite, when the hour was up, instead of lighting the cigarette, I would go the whole of the next hour without one. Sometimes I would go the whole day and only smoke one or two. I was like a squirrel burying a reserve of nuts for the winter. But do you really believe that this was helping me to stop smoking? Was it making cigarettes less precious in my mind, or was I like the lady that was cutting out one cigarette each day. I remember the first time I built up 10 credits. I was like an excited child. I decided I would blow the lot next day. The sheer luxury of being able to smoke 20 whole cigarettes in a day. It was marvellous!

But the day after was murder. I'd blown my entire, hard-earned hoard in one day. Now I had to go back to the discipline of one an hour. Eventually my resistance ran out. There was no way I could survive with one cigarette an hour, so I tried one every half hour. 20 a day can't be that bad. But of course, the same thing happened. Wishing 2/3rds of your life away isn't much different from wishing 5/6th of your life away. They both add up to a miserable existence. In the end I decided that I couldn't be bothered restricting myself. I decided not to smoke during the day, but to save the whole 20 for when I got home. Again, it was great to start with. All day I would abstain and feel like a saint. On the exact stroke of 5.30, I would hurtle out of the office, rush home and immediately light up. Of course having waited all day, that first cigarette was marvellous. The next? Not quite as good. By the time I'd chain-smoked the fifth cigarette, I'd be thinking: **"WHY AM I DOING THIS?"**

An ingenious Russian solved this problem of disciplining yourself to 20 a day. He invented a solid steel cigarette case that worked on a time-lock principle. Once the 20 cigarettes had been placed in the case, there was no way that it could be opened. The case was designed to cough up one cigarette on the hour every hour. I've been trying, without success, to obtain one for my collection. Not surprisingly, most of them were opened by a sledgehammer within a week of being purchased.

Have you ever been in the situation in which you have to discuss a rather delicate matter, like asking the boss for a raise? You know it's his duty to keep costs down and expect strong resistance to your request. Like a chess grand-master, you try to anticipate his every argument and have prepared the necessary counter arguments. Finally, you pluck up enough courage. You take a deep breath, knock on his door, walk in as boldly as you can manage and croak: "I think I deserve a raise." He stares you straight in the eye for an interminable period, then replies: "So do I." You should be overjoyed. Strangely you are not. You feel those hours of preparation were wasted. You're almost tempted to say to your boss: "Come on, you can't give in just like that. Surely you're going to put up some sort of a fight. I've got all the answers anyway."

I went through a similar experience during the time that I was trying to limit my smoking to ten a day. I'd reached the stage when I was regularly failing to stick to just the 10, but still hadn't accepted that the attempt was doomed to failure. Each morning I would buy a packet of 10 from the nearest tobacconist. Two hours later I would be back buying another 10 and so on throughout the day. I began to worry whether the tobacconist might wonder why I didn't buy my day's requirements in one go. He must have worked out the true reason, it being the only possible explanation. He must think: "You weak-willed, lilly-livered jellyfish. You couldn't even make them last for 2 hours." I thought: "I'll show him!"

How did I show him? By sticking to just 10 a day? Not exactly. I took to walking a mile further in the opposite direction to buy the second packet, and to another tobacconist to buy the third. None of those tobacconists ever gave the slightest indication of even being aware of my existence. I truly thought of myself as a rational human being at the time, yet that evil 'weed' had reduced me to a state bordering on PARANOIA. Perhaps you already recognize the symptoms in yourself? If not, don't be too smug, it won't be long before you are playing similar games, unless that is, you have the sense to stop now.

Perhaps you still believe that there are some casual smokers that genuinely have the best of all worlds. Smokers that never desire more than 2 cigarettes a day, and what's more, really enjoy those 2 cigarettes. How can I convince you that such a situation is impossible? Just look at it logically. We know that there are smokers that can *discipline* themselves to just two cigarettes a day, but can you really believe that there is a single smoker living, that just happens to want or need just 2 cigarettes a day, every day, for the whole of their lives? Surely this would be stretching the bounds of coincidence too far. Now we have already established that the pleasure or crutch from smoking are really subtle illusions, but even while smokers are deluded into believing that they get genuine pleasure, or genuine relief from boredom or stress, or a genuine aid to relaxation or concentration, can you believe that there is a single smoker on the planet that goes through life receiving the necessary triggers no more and no less than twice every day of their smoking lives?

What about those casual smokers that aren't so regimented. The ones that can go days on end without smoking, that just fancy a cigarette every now and again? That sounds even better, just to need one on average say, once a week, or even better once a month, or even once a year. What's the point? Wouldn't it be even nicer to never need them? Assume for a moment that there is some genuine crutch or pleasure from smoking. Who wants to wait a year, or a month or even a day for that crutch or pleasure? Why should the smoker be denied that crutch in the meantime?

I heard of a pipe-smoker who decided to quit at the age of 40, on condition that he could smoke again when he retired. He deduced that in retirement he would need some pleasure to occupy his time, and that at the age of 65, the health aspect wouldn't particularly concern him. I'm not sure whether you would regard the end of the story as sad or happy. However, he overlooked one thing. I do him an injustice, he was obviously very meticulous and an extremely strong-willed character. More accurate to say that he was ignorant of just one fact: there is no pleasure in smoking. When the great day arrived, he found that no matter how hard he persisted, he just couldn't learn to enjoy his pipe. Not surprising really. It took me three months to learn to cope with a pipe, and that was when I was young and fit, already heavily addicted to nicotine and partially immune to the poisons.

Now it's bad enough when a smoker has to wait a couple of hours for the next smoke. Imagine the misery of waiting 25 years, only to discover that what you had been pining for all those years:

DIDN'T ACTUALLY EXIST!

My brother was one of these casual smokers for quite a long period. He stopped smoking long before I did. But whenever we went to a pub together, he would buy a 'Castella' I used to envy him. I tried something similar on one of my failed attempts to stop when using the willpower method. I say failed attempt, in fact I'd survived 3 weeks without a cigarette and was convinced that I had kicked it. I said to my wife: "I'll just have a Hamlet in the evening. It'll be something to look forward to during the day." I can still see the tortured expression on her face. Why is it that non-addicts can see it so clearly, yet the addicts who actually experience the misery, cannot? We have massive, powerful reasons to stop all of our lives, yet all we search for is any flimsy excuse for one more drag. Joyce said: "If you have genuinely kicked it, why play with fire?" But what does a non-smoker know about it? I knew better. In no time at all, I was chain-smoking 30 Hamlets a day!

As I said I used to envy my brother, but now I realise that he was still hooked. Originally he would buy the Castella when we reached the pub. Then I noticed that he took to carrying around a packet of 5 Castellas. The next stage was a nice leather cigar case. The gradual but relentless slide back into the depths of the pitcher plant was underway. He'd accepted that he was a regular smoker again, and whereas the heavy smokers were now using throwaway lighters and discarding the expensive cigarette cases, he was trying to create a nice aesthetic appearance to the addiction.

By even attempting to cut down or control their smoking in any way, casual smokers create several serious problems:

1. They keep their bodies physically addicted to nicotine. This creates an even bigger problem. It keeps their brains craving cigarettes.
2. They wish their whole lives away just waiting for their next fix.
3. Instead of lighting up whenever they want to and thereby partially relieving their withdrawal pangs, in addition to the normal stresses and strains of life, they now spend most of their lives suffering the withdrawal pangs from nicotine. If you observe casual smokers you'll find that they are almost permanently restless.

However there is a fourth evil about cutting down or casual smoking, which causes more damage than the other three combined. When you indulge yourself cigarette after cigarette, you lose the illusion of enjoying any of them. In fact even the lighting up becomes automatic and subconscious. You will find that those so-called special cigarettes, the ones that you really enjoy, always occur after a period of abstinence. Like the one after a meal, after sex, after exercise, after shopping or the first of the day. It's because there *is* no genuine pleasure or crutch whatsoever in smoking. All that any smoker ever enjoys when they light up, is not the cigarette itself, cigarettes are filthy, disgusting poison, but the ending of the aggravation of craving a cigarette, whether it be the almost imperceptible physical aggravation, or the far worse mental aggravation of not being allowed to scratch that physical itch for another hour or day or whatever.

This is why casual smoking or cutting down makes it infinitely more difficult to stop. What are you trying to achieve when you stop smoking? To go the rest of your life believing you are being deprived of a tremendous crutch or pleasure? If so, cutting down is guaranteed to ensure that you'll do just that. Or are you attempting to abstain for longer and longer periods, in the hope that you will eventually lose the desire smoke completely? If so you will find that cutting down achieves the complete opposite. It increases the illusion of pleasure and thus increases the desire to smoke. At the same time it reduces the adverse effects of smoking and thus reduces your desire to quit.

Now I can hear you saying: "If it increases the illusion of pleasure and reduces the bad effects, what's so bad about that? Just this: the pleasure *is* illusory! The pleasure is the ending of the aggravation of craving. The only way to increase the illusion, is to increase the aggravation. It is a pleasure to remove your hand from boiling water. The longer you leave your hand in the water, the greater the pleasure of removing it will appear. In reality when you cut down, on one side of the tug of war, you increase the misery not the pleasure. It's true that on the other side of the tug of war, you reduce the adverse effects. But you still have bad effects and no good effects on both sides. The whole object of this chapter is to make you realise from personal experience and case histories that casual smokers don't enjoy being smokers, and by explaining exactly how the drug operates, why it is impossible for any smoker to enjoy being a smoker. You should also remember that being a casual smoker is not a stable condition. The nature of the drug is to increase the intake, not to suffer the itch, but to scratch it.

Providing they are not at the stage where their smoking is seriously affecting their health or wealth, for most of their time, smokers are able to shut their minds to these effects, so although their lives are in fact permanently dominated by the weed, it is only occasionally that they are aware of the fact. However, casual smokers are almost permanently conscious of their smoking, and therefore in effect, their lives are also permanently dominated by the weed, but because they do exercise willpower and discipline, they suffer the illusion that it is they that dominate the weed. Many of them don't even realise that they are in a prison and without this realisation, escape is impossible.

Perhaps you feel that ignorance is bliss, and still envy casual smokers their blissfully ignorant state. There might well be circumstances when ignorance is bliss, but I assure you that smoking is definitely not one of them. Get it into your head, there is never any real pleasure or crutch, it is illusion. Let us dispel one of the doubts that I raised at the beginning of this chapter: we could take smoking or leave it when we first started, so what prevents us from returning to that blissful state?

To begin with, was it such a blissful state? Isn't the true reason that you find cigarettes so precious now, is not so much that they were so precious when you were allowed to smoke them, but that life seems to be miserable without them? If you are honest and have a good memory, you will remember that those first cigarettes tasted awful, that you had difficulty in learning to inhale or to feel the tough guy or the sophisticated lady. However, once you had learned to play the part, can you remember any particular desire, let alone need, to smoke a cigarette? That's because, although your body did suffer physical withdrawal from nicotine, and your subconscious brain knew that a cigarette would relieve the feeling temporarily, your conscious brain wasn't aware of that. Your conscious brain believed that you were in control, smoking each cigarette purely because you wanted to.

It is possible to remove all the illusions about smoking and to get back to the same frame of mind that you had about smoking before you became hooked, but it is impossible to remove just part of the illusion. No way can you go back to the stage when you only needed to smoke occasionally. Even if you could you wouldn't want to, because that supposedly blissful state, is also an illusion. You didn't actually enjoy being a smoker then. Do you ever remember thinking: "Yippee! I'm a smoker?" Get it clearly into your mind, at no stage in any smoker's life do they wish they were a smoker. The only reason that we ever think we do is because we get miserable without them. The only reason that you look back on those halcyon days when you only smoked occasionally is because you smoke far too many now. Even if I could transfer you back to those times, believe me:

YOU WOULDN'T LIKE IT

In Chapter 7 I listed various reasons why it is essential to understand the difference between habit and addiction. The most important reason of all is this: if smokers make the mistake of believing that smoking is a habit, they are quite justified in saying to themselves:

"I have got into the habit of smoking 20 cigarettes a day. If I can now train my body and brain to smoke only 5 a day or to just smoke the so-called special cigarettes, providing I persevere, I'll soon be in the habit of only wanting or needing 5 a day or the special cigarettes."

This all sounds very logical, and so it would be but for two very important points. One is that the blissful state that we are trying to return to:

NEVER ACTUALLY EXISTED

What is more, because of the nature of drug addiction:

IT IS IMPOSSIBLE FOR IT TO EXIST

The second important point is that:

SMOKING IS NOT HABIT! IT IS DRUG ADDICTION!

Your reasons for stopping might make you want to cut down, but it will never become a habit to do so. The nature of drug addiction is to try to relieve withdrawal pangs, not to suffer them. The reason that no

smoker, no matter how heavy or casual their smoking might be, can
ever enjoy being a smoker, is because of the nature of the drug. I know
many smokers genuinely believe that they enjoy it, and all smokers
believe that they enjoy some aspects of it at some period in their lives,
as I did, but the fact remains it is just a subtle illusion. Remember:

THE NATURAL TENDENCY IS TO CHAIN-SMOKE!

The moment that any smoker extinguishes a cigarette, the nicotine
starts to leave the body and part of that smoker's brain is saying:

**"I WANT ANOTHER ONE, NOT TOMORROW, NOT IN AN
HOUR, BUT NOW"**

Another part of the smokers brain will be saying:

**"YOU CAN'T HAVE ANOTHER ONE NOW!
IT WILL KILL YOU! IT WILL COST YOU A FORTUNE!"**

It's only the bad side of smoking that makes us attempt to control it.
Even to restrict your smoking to your present level, you would have to
exercise willpower and discipline for the rest of your life, because as
your body builds up a tolerance to the drug, it will want more and
more, not less and less. However, at the same time, the deterioration in
your physical health and finances caused by the cumulative effects of
the years you have been smoking, will be exacerbated by your ever-
increasing daily intake. You will become increasingly more irritable,
which in turn will increase your desire to cut down or quit!

However, the drug has also been gradually destroying your nervous
system, your courage and confidence. When you were a youngster,
you could take it or leave it, but now you are less able to resist the
intervals between each cigarette. One side of the tug of war desires
those intervals to be longer and longer. But in fact, they become shorter
and shorter. That is the logical progression of all drug addiction. When
you are not aware of your dependence on a drug, your conscious mind
sees no reason to be without it. Once you are aware of your
dependence, you believe that you cannot be without it, and if you
believe that, the fact that you *know* the drug is killing you won't make
the slightest difference.

Get it clearly into your mind: it will never become habit to restrict
your smoking to the level you are at, let alone reduce it. Why do you
think you got into the *habit* of increasing your intake in the first place?
You no more made a conscious decision to do so, than you did to get
hooked in the first place. Even to attempt to cut down would be like
the fly in the depths of the pitcher plant wishing to return to the rim.

The trap is designed to ensure that the fly can only travel in one direction: DOWN! Even if the fly could get back to the rim, it would only start to slide down again.

The nicotine trap is designed in exactly the same way. Smokers know from experience that if they do try to cut down or to control their intake, they too can only slide down. The only difference between the pitcher plant and the nicotine trap, is that although it might fool the fly, the pitcher plant is blatantly obvious to us, whereas the nicotine trap is infinitely more subtle and complex. However, the beautiful truth is that no one is dependent on nicotine and once you understand the trap completely, it takes no willpower to stop. Even if you did possess the massive willpower that it would take to discipline your intake for the rest of your life:

DO YOU REALLY WANT TO?

We have established that the only reason that any smoker lights a cigarette is to relieve the withdrawal pangs created by the previous cigarette, and that there is no genuine pleasure or crutch from smoking whatsoever. Surely I have contradicted myself. If the current cigarette is helping to relieve the withdrawal pangs of the previous one, even if the relief is only partial, surely that is genuine relief, after all the smoker does actually feel less nervous than before he or she lit the cigarette?

Smokers often use this argument as their excuse for failure: "The withdrawal symptoms were so bad, I just had to have the cigarette, I had no choice!" That may be so, but I still maintain that there is no genuine crutch or pleasure to smoking. The smoker does smoke to relieve the withdrawal pangs of the previous cigarette, but far from relieving them, the current cigarette actually causes them.

What is the total amount of the physical, withdrawal aggravation from just one cigarette? It's very, very slight and impossible to quantify, but, whatever it is, let us call it one NICOPAIN. As a smoker when you extinguish a cigarette, provided that you don't light another, you will suffer just one NICOPAIN. Now supposing you decide that you cannot suffer a whole NICOPAIN, and that after you have suffered half of it you feel obliged to light another. You have immediately relieved half a NICOPAIN. Or have you? Won't you now suffer a whole NICOPAIN when you extinguish that second cigarette? Far from relieving withdrawal aggravation, it has caused you to suffer an additional half NICOPAIN! Unless of course you light another cigarette. So let us examine the situation if you continue to *relieve* your withdrawal pangs.

Let us assume that you are a smoker that is lucky enough to survive 40 years of smoking an average of 20 a day. Let us assume that you light each cigarette after your body has suffered half the withdrawal aggravation caused by the previous cigarette. In your lifetime you will suffer a total of 300,000 half NICOPAINS. The first cigarette that you lit caused every one of those NICOPAINS, because if you don't light a first cigarette, you can't light another!

On the same basis the second cigarette will cause you to suffer 299,999 half NICOPAINS. Not so say you, each cigarette causes you but one NICOPAIN, because you don't have to light the one after. But we are talking about having to light the one after in order to *relieve* the withdrawal pangs of the previous one. If that is our policy we must keep the chain going until we die! However, perhaps we won't smoke the rest of our lives? But we will:

UNLESS WE STOP!

I often liken the pleasure from smoking to wearing tight shoes in order to get the pleasure of removing them. Perhaps you have heard the joke about the man who, ignoring the advice of the salesman, bought a pair of shoes which were obviously two sizes too small for him. The salesman happened upon the man two days later, hobbling down the street in considerable distress. He could not help but reprimand the man for failing to accept good advice. The man responded:

"Last week my house burned to the ground. Both house and contents were a complete write off. The insurance had expired the day before. Two days later my business partner absconded with the total assets including my wife. I have one remaining pleasure in life, to return to my lodgings each evening and remove these ruddy shoes!"

You might think the story is far-fetched, however that is what the smoking *pleasure* amounts to. But who do you think suffers the most, someone that can remove his tight shoes every half hour, or someone that has to keep them on all day? At least regular and heavy smokers are frequently relieving withdrawal pangs, casual smokers go through their whole lives suffering them.

Whether the withdrawal pangs be physical or mental, regular and heavy smokers only suffer them when they try to quit, or when they have run out of cigarettes or are in situations when they are not allowed to smoke. Casual smokers suffer them the bulk of their smoking lives. They are relieving their withdrawal pangs for about an hour of each day, the remaining 23 hours, they suffer them.

I emphasize that with my method there is no mental torture whatsoever, on the contrary, if you follow all the instructions, you will be in a permanently happy frame of mind about not having to smoke. You might have a slight feeling of tension, restlessness or emptiness for a few days. This is caused by the physical withdrawal from nicotine. However your happy mental state will ensure that you do not suffer. Perhaps you feel that it is not possible to have such feelings without suffering. Those are exactly the symptoms that a footballer has when awaiting the whistle to start the cup final. They don't suffer, on the contrary, they are on a complete high.

If for whatever reason, you are suffering and are tempted to *relieve* the situation with a cigarette. Ask yourself what will stop you needing the next and the one after. That cigarette won't relieve anything. On the contrary, that one cigarette will cause the withdrawal pains both mental and physical that you will suffer for the rest of your life. Also keep it clearly in your mind, if for any reason you are suffering withdrawal pangs, you're suffering, not because you've stopped smoking, but because you started. Non-smokers don't suffer withdrawal pangs from nicotine. It's only smokers that suffer withdrawal pangs from nicotine and they don't just suffer them when they attempt to quit. They suffer them practically every day:

THROUGHOUT THEIR SMOKING LIVES

Heavy smokers think that casual smokers have the best of all worlds. The truth is that they have the worst of all worlds, they can neither smoke when they want to, nor do they have the pleasure of being FREE!

With every cigarette that you smoke part of your brain will be saying: "I need it or want it." Another part of your brain is saying: "It's controlling me, it's costing me a fortune, it's filthy and disgusting." It's not too difficult to close your mind to that, but one thing you cannot close your mind to, the same drug that you need to relieve your withdrawal pangs, just happens to be the No.1 killer poison in western society. Every time that you try to relieve your withdrawal pangs, you will progressively poison your own body:

NOTHING WILL CHANGE THAT

There is another breed of smoker that are often envied by other smokers. They are not strictly casual smokers, but tend to be regarded in the same light. In fact, quite often, they are very, heavy smokers. I'm referring to the stoppers and starters. Most other smokers do not see them as unfortunates repeatedly falling back into a manhole, but as possessing the enviable ability to stop smoking and start again just whenever they choose to. Of course such smokers don't like to appear stupid any more than the rest of us do, so they tend to encourage the misconception.

Don't believe what these smokers tell you. Just look at the situation logically. If such smokers truly enjoy being smokers, why do they decide to stop? Surely they only decide to stop for the same reason that any other smoker does, because:

THEY DON'T ENJOY BEING SMOKERS!

Having successfully become non-smokers, why on earth do they change their minds and decide to become smokers again? There can be only one answer to that:

THEY DON'T ENJOY BEING NON-SMOKERS!

What peculiar people. Why can't they make up their minds? Peculiar they may be, but don't envy them. Like all casual smokers, they get not the best but the worst of all worlds. When they are smokers, they envy non-smokers. They go through the trauma of stopping using the willpower method, but never become *happy* non-smokers, so they start smoking again. Once they become hooked again, they remember why they stopped in the first place. They are permanently in a situation that they don't like. Their neighbour's grass is always green and their own is permanently brown. They do a house swap with the neighbour, and no sooner do they move in than their new lawn turns brown and their neighbour's turns green.

In fact there is nothing peculiar about them. Aren't they in exactly the same position that all smokers find themselves in the whole of their smoking lives? Whether they be casual or heavy, old or young, attempting to stop or otherwise. When we are allowed to smoke, we either take it for granted, or wish we didn't have to, only when we are not allowed to smoke do cigarettes become so precious. Just as if you mope for a cigarette, you are moping for an illusion, so if you envy other smokers, casual or otherwise, you are envying a situation that doesn't and cannot possibly exist.

Remember, to be a happy non-smoker for the rest of your life, you need to achieve a particular frame of mind. If you believe that there is some genuine crutch or pleasure in smoking, you might never smoke again, but you will suffer a feeling of deprivation no matter how rare or how slight that feeling might be. If you see just one puff on a cigarette as a crutch or pleasure, you will see a million puffs as a crutch or pleasure and feel deprived and vulnerable for the rest of your life. The real danger isn't actually smoking just one cigarette, it is desiring one. Because if you do desire one cigarette, what on earth will prevent you from wanting:

ANOTHER! AND ANOTHER! AND ANOTHER!

If you can see that there is and can be no genuine crutch or pleasure in smoking, then how even more ridiculous to mope for cigarettes or envy other smokers, because if you do that, there are only two things that can happen to you: you can either go through the rest of your life not smoking but feeling deprived and miserable, or you can go through the rest of your life smoking, and whether it be casual or otherwise:

YOU WILL FEEL EVEN MORE MISERABLE!

At the beginning of the chapter I listed six situations which would lead us to believe that it's possible to be a happy, casual smoker. I trust I've already convinced you that five of the situations are myths or illusions. But have I proved beyond any possible doubt that a happy, casual smoker is an impossibility? The answer to that must be no, for the simple reason that you cannot prove that something doesn't exist. For centuries man has failed to prove the existence of the Loch Ness monster. However, he hasn't even attempted to prove that it doesn't. Even if you emptied the loch and found nothing, who could prove that the monster isn't buried in the mud, or didn't escape overland?

If you are still not convinced, let me put the onus on you. If all these happy, casual smokers exist, it should be a simple matter for you to find one. What's that? You already know several. Are you absolutely sure? Have you really checked them out, or have you just taken their word for it and assumed that they were happy?

I used to believe that I knew several, even after Independence Day. It didn't dawn on me until much later that, because of the nature of nicotine addiction, it is impossible to be a happy smoker, casual or otherwise. Once I realised that and also that all smokers lie, not only to other people but to themselves, I observed them having first removed my rose-coloured spectacles.

I suggest you do the same. Ask them the same questions that I've been asking you in 'EASYWAY', in this book and particularly during the chapters on cutting down and casual smoking. Have you noticed how casual smokers actually brag about how little they smoke?" If you are a heavy smoker you might think the reason is obvious. But is it? With most pleasures or pastimes we feel the more we can partake of them the better off we are. You wouldn't hear a golf addict boasting that he only played once a year at Christmas and he wouldn't be a happy golfer if he did. Yes but smoking kills you, enslaves you and costs you a fortune. **EXACTLY!** The less you smoke, the happier you feel about it. The ideal is not to have to smoke at all. It is not just heavy smokers who wished that they smoked less, so do casual smokers. Why else would they boast about how little they smoked?

Why do casual smokers find it necessary to boast about the fact that they can go days without smoking, and it doesn't bother them in the slightest? Obviously a heavy smoker would love to be able to do that and would understandably envy such a smoker. I love lobster, I can go months, even years without it. As much as I love it, I can genuinely take it or leave it and it doesn't bother me in the slightest. But if the subject of lobster came up during our conversation, wouldn't you find it rather strange if I said: "Do you know, I really enjoy lobster, but I can go three weeks without one, and honestly, it doesn't bother me in the slightest."

I would only make such a statement if it did bother me, if I'd had to discipline myself to resist the temptation, and if I had succeeded in resisting it for three weeks, I would feel entitled to praise myself. If a casual smoker brags about how they can take them or leave them, it means they are trying to quit smoking, using the willpower method: **PERMANENTLY!** If they don't brag about it, and can genuinely take them or leave them, it means that they are in the same position as Dr. Miller's wife, far from enjoying them, they find them disgusting, but are literally:

PLAYING WITH FIRE

I said I've dealt with five out of the six situations. The one I haven't covered is: if Allen Carr's method makes it easy to quit, what possible danger can there be in smoking occasional cigarettes? Even if you do get hooked again, you merely use his method to quit again. You might have followed sufficient of my instructions to find it easy and even enjoyable to quit. However, if you retain or acquire a need or desire to take just one puff, you haven't understood my method completely. What possible purpose can be served by my helping you to escape from a prison, if you retain a desire to return to that prison?

My claim is that I can help you to find it easy and enjoyable both to quit smoking and to remain a happy non-smoker. I make no claim to be able to make you a happy smoker. On the contrary, I have gone to considerable lengths to explain exactly why it is impossible, and why casual smokers are more miserable than heavy smokers. It never seems to dawn on ex-smokers that it is quite possible to become a happy non-smoker, but if you take a single puff of a cigarette:

YOU ARE NO LONGER A NON-SMOKER AND WILL NO LONGER BE HAPPY!

It's easy to remain a smoker. It's just as easy to remain a non-smoker, but why should you assume that makes it easy to remain a casual smoker? That would be like believing that it was just as easy to remain balanced on a fence for the whole of your life rather than fall and remain on one side or the other. The whole object of my method and one of the main purposes of this book is to remove your need or desire to take even a single puff, and to make you see, that if you have a need or desire for one puff, you'll have a need or desire for a million puffs. You also need to realise that, even if you don't actually take that puff, but merely desire it, you will no longer be a happy non-smoker. You will feel deprived. You will have become:

A MISERABLE NON-SMOKER!

You will be miserable because you will be moping for something that doesn't exist. Eventually, when your resistance has been exhausted and you take that puff, you will cease to be a miserable non-smoker and become:

AN EVEN MORE MISERABLE SMOKER!

The most miserable smokers of all warrant a chapter to themselves. They are a special type of casual smoker:

SECRET SMOKERS

CHAPTER 36

Secret Smokers

There are many pathetic aspects to smoking. It is sometimes difficult to decide which is the worst. Watching smokers in the advanced stages of emphysema and finding yourself subconsciously trying to breathe for them rates very high. Listening to a smoker who has just had a leg removed and is trying to convinve you it had absolutely nothing to do with smoking is particularly disturbing. Equally pathetic are the smokers that have just discovered that they have contracted lung cancer and are trying to convince you, and themselves, that it was all worth it and that they enjoyed every precious cigarette.

Smoker do not realise that they are victims of an ingenious trap. They believe they continue to smoke because they are either stupid or weak-willed. They lie, not because they are basically dishonest by nature, but because self-deception enables them to retain a semblance of respect in their own eyes and other people's. In the main these lies are little white ones which help to sweeten the pill. Like understating the money we waste and the number we smoke each day. However, we'll unhesitantly tell whoppers if the need arises. Many teenage smokers will look their parents straight in the eye and deny that they are smokers.

Have you experienced that situation when you wanted to make a protest, but didn't have the nerve to say what you desperately wanted to say? You go through the rest of your life despising yourself. Fortunately I learned this lesson at a very young age. There are very few events in my life when I lacked the moral courage to say what I felt. I say moral courage. It wasn't really courage, more common sense. You weigh up the effect of appearing to be impolite, stupid or ridiculous if you make your protest, against going through the rest of your life despising yourself if you didn't. I find the former course to be less painful. A brave person dies but once, a coward dies a thousand deaths. When it comes to moral courage, I am not brave enough to be a coward.

However well I learned that lesson, it did not prevent me from becoming a secret smoker. To break a solemn promise to someone that you love and trust is bad enough, but then to compound that felony by lying to someone that loves and trusted you is the ultimate degradation. For me, secret smoking is the most pathetic of the many pathetic aspects of smoking. An otherwise honest person of integrity is reduced to lies and deception. In 'Easyway' I recorded how secret smoking almost caused a divorce. Ironically, the stories that we hear at the clinics about secret smoking, are at the same time, the most tragic and the most amusing.

One couple had a pact to quit. They were really determined. When they extinguished their final cigarette they threw out all the ashtrays and redecorated the house throughout. After about 3 months, the wife sensed that there was still a whiff of tobacco around the house. She accused her husband of having crafty puffs. He stared her straight in the eye and denied it point blank. A few nights later, she awoke in the middle of the night and discovered her husband missing. She crept downstairs only to find him kneeling in front of the fireplace exhaling smoke up the chimney. Fortunately the wife found the spectacle amusing and said: "If you enjoy smoking that much you might as well continue." But did he really enjoy leaving a nice warm bed in the middle of winter to kneel in a cold living room just to blow smoke up a chimney? He must have felt very stupid, weak and deceitful.

The story that I found most amusing was of a young housewife who stopped smoking because of the pressure that her 7 year old daughter was applying: "Mummy I don't want you to die." She had reached the usual stage when using the willpower method of abstaining for a few days, then falling for the compromise of just having one or two as a little reward in the evening. On this particular evening her child wouldn't go to sleep. She said: "I was getting annoyed with her, not because she wouldn't go to sleep, but because I was dying for a cigarette. Eventually she dropped off. I rushed down to the kitchen. No sooner had I lit up than a little voice behind me was saying - you're not smoking are you mummy?" She did manage to flick the cigarette unseen into the sink. The reason I found it so amusing was that when I was a boy, your parents would clip your ear if they caught you smoking, now it's the children that catch their parents out.

I suppose all smokers have slipped out to the garage for a crafty puff, but imagine the embarrassment of one of my clients who, visiting his non-smoking Canadian relatives, nipped out for a crafty puff in weather twenty degrees below zero, with the excuse that he needed a breath of fresh air. He returned in a state of panic. He smoked those awful little cigars which have their own plastic holder. The plastic had frozen to his lip. His little subterfuge came unstuck. Unfortunately the plastic hadn't. Such is the infinite pleasure of being a smoker.

My smoking often caused me to be the object of ridicule over the years. Yet curiously, the incident that caused me the most embarrassment happened to a complete stranger. It was during an internal, no-smoking flight in America. In the middle of the flight the routine calm was suddenly transformed into an air of panic. Four of the airline staff came charging up the aisle and started to hammer on the toilet door. I was convinced that we were involved in a highjacking, or at the very least, a bomb scare. In fact it was just that a lady was having a crafty puff in the toilets and had set off the smoke detectors. However the crew were somewhat over zealous and frightened the poor lady so much that it took them 20 minutes to persuade her to unlock the door.

Once they knew the true cause of the furore, the whole incident was an amusing distraction to the other passengers, including myself. That is until she eventually opened the door. She looked so embarrassed and forlorn, I'm convinced that had there been an escape door open, she would have leapt through it, regardless of having no parachute. The amused atmosphere was immediately replaced by a general feeling of sympathy towards her. I realised that but for the grace of God it could just as easily have been me standing there. I was very grateful that I was no longer in the prison.

To me signs like 'KEEP OFF THE GRASS' and 'WET PAINT' are completely irresistible. I think: "Who are these anonymous killjoys?" I can't resist slyly putting one foot on the grass, or lightly touching the paint, just to check whether it has dried. So the more society tries to force smokers to quit, the greater becomes the smoker's determination and ingenuity to defy and circumvent the ban. A pop star at our Birmingham clinic recently described how he had devised an apparatus that enabled him to smoke in aircraft toilets without setting off the smoke alarm. I couldn't understand the exact mechanics, but it involved kneeling down in front of the toilet and passing a plastic tube down the pan.

He was so proud of this gadget that he was actually thinking of patenting the idea, convinced that he would make a fortune. This is what happens when you try to force smokers to abstain. So intent are they on resisting the pressure, they lose sight of the real enemy. If only I could have shown that pop star a video of himself kneeling in front of a toilet pan in such a confined space, I'm sure he would have realised that by no stretch of the imagination could he have been enjoying that cigarette. Thank goodness non-smokers don't have to suffer that sort of indignity.

Many smokers believe they started because of this rebel attitude: "My parents were both non-smokers, I started smoking to rebel against them." Most parents are non-heroin addicts, I know of not one single heroin addict that became one in order to rebel against his parents. Wouldn't this whole attitude be rather like saying: "My parents had two legs so I had one of mine amputated to rebel against them?"

Now that smoking is generally accepted as anti-social, this rebel attitude has become the last line of resistance for many smokers: "I'm prepared to take the health risks and I'm not having other people telling me whether I can smoke or not." Some openly advertise the point by smoking the 'DEATH' brand of cigarettes referred to in Chapter 32. The fact that they are far more expensive than normal cigarettes doesn't deter them.

When you become a secret smoker, you are left with absolutely nothing. You can retain no semblance of dignity. You cannot even claim the somewhat dubious dignity of being a rebel. Rebels are proud of being rebels. They are prepared to stand up and be counted. You can no longer say: "I smoke because I choose to." You became a secret smoker because you are so utterly ashamed of what you are, that you do not wish other people to know that you are a smoker. You have lost every vestige of self-respect.

When you become a secret smoker, you sink about as low as any human being is capable of sinking. You begin to tell lies to the people who love you the most, and what's worse, to the people that you love the most. However, there is one saving grace to becoming a secret smoker. You might be deceiving people that you love, but:

YOU ARE NO LONGER DECEIVING YOURSELF!

You know you've reached the pits and that you smoke, not because you choose to or want to, but because you are:

A SLAVE! A MISERABLE, PATHETIC DRUG ADDICT!

Until you fully appreciate that fact, escape is impossible. Once you accept it, escape not only becomes possible, but if you follow all the instructions, it is guaranteed! Now let's remove one of the myths that makes smokers block their minds even to the thought of attempting to escape:

WILL I EVER ENJOY LIFE AGAIN?

CHAPTER 37

Will I Ever Enjoy Life Again?

Do you believe in coincidences? Sometimes the odds against them seem so infinitesimal that you feel that it cannot be just coincidence. Yesterday I attended the funeral of a very dear friend. He wasn't a saint, but one of those rare individuals that was loved by all and hated by none. He was the same age as me and a smoker. I am convinced that had he not been, he would be alive today and looking forward to many enjoyable years ahead of him. I feel low today, but I weep not for him, if this life is merely some sort of test to achieve a greater life, he will have passed with flying colours. Either way, his problems on this earth are over. If there is a heaven, he'll be a prince there just as he was here. I weep for the genuine void that he leaves, particularly with his family. They must be wondering whether they will ever enjoy life again.

He was a very special man. You won't find his name in 'Who's Who,' but had he been listed, his hobbies would have read: my family and my home. I wanted to pay him a special tribute, but as always seems to be the case at such times, the inspiration was lacking. The best I could think of was a wreath in the shape of the number of his home which was the focal meeting point of his many friends. After any social event he would say: "Let's go back to No. 37."

I felt too low to write yesterday. Today I thought the best way to lift my depression, would be to get stuck into this book. Is it possible that the number and title of this chapter are just coincidence?

If the belief that it is possible to have just one cigarette is the prime cause of getting smokers hooked, so the belief that you will never able completely to enjoy life, or be able to cope with stress again, is the main reason which makes smokers put off the evil day:

I'LL STOP ALRIGHT, BUT NOT TODAY, I'LL DO IT TOMORROW

The fear consists of two separate phases:

1. The initial period of misery and trauma, incorrectly referred to as

'The Withdrawal Period' and, assuming that we do in fact survive the initial trauma:

2. The rest of our lives. When our minds are no longer obsessed with smoking and we've proved that there is indeed a life after smoking.

Why do I refer to phase 2 as a fear? It is because we might have periods of sheer elation, overjoyed at our successful escape, bursting with energy, pitying other smokers, wondering why we found it necessary to smoke all those years and absolutely certain that we will never be tempted to smoke again, but, with the willpower method those periods are too few and too brief. They are punctuated by periods of doubt. We begin to envy smokers. We are still having to resist temptation. Most of the time there is neither elation nor temptation. We just get on with our lives. We're not consciously thinking about smoking, even so there is a sort of permanent void. In a way it is similar to the dark shadows that we try to block from our minds when we are smokers. But this is a lighter cloud, an awareness of something missing, that somehow life just isn't quite the same. It's as if for the rest of our lives we are waiting for something to happen.

We can never quite put our finger on the reason for that feeling. Is it because we sense that we are missing out, or is it that we are still not certain that we've kicked it and that we still fear failure?

Which is the worst of the two phases? The initial trauma, or the rest of your life as a non-smoker? The mere expression 'non-smoker' doesn't help. We talk of heroin addicts and ex-heroin addicts, but do we refer to people that have never been addicted to heroin as non-heroin addicts. 'Non' is negative. Like 'Giving Up', it implies that you non-smokers are missing out.

There is absolutely no doubt in my mind which is the worst of the two phases. I have described how I was reduced to tears on more than one occasion during the initial trauma. However, it wasn't the trauma itself that caused those tears, it was the belief that I could never be completely free.

When do you become a non-smoker? The answer is simplicity itself: every time you extinguish a cigarette. I really meant: when do you become a permanent non-smoker? Just as simple: when you extinguish your final cigarette! True, but how will you know it's your final cigarette? When you pass a driving test, you are no better a driver than you were the moment before you passed it, but you still have a wonderful sense of achievement: 'UREKA' I've passed! The really important question that you need to answer about stopping smoking is:

WHEN WILL YOU *KNOW* THAT YOU ARE A NON-SMOKER?

At the clinics, we get a variety of answers to this question. Such as:

"When I can go out drinking with my friends or enjoy a meal without wanting a cigarette." Yes, but the girl at the dinner party was still craving cigarettes after 8 years of abstinence. With all similar answers that depend on a specific occasion, smokers don't know how long they will have to wait.

"When I've managed to go a whole day without a cigarette." The time limits vary with the individual and usually range between anything from one day to a year, But how can any smoker possibly know in advance that their estimate will be accurate?

"When I feel like a non-smoker." We dealt with that one in Chapter 29.

The reason the driver can shout 'Ureka' is because he *knows* for certain that he has passed the test. With all of the above answers that I have quoted, the ex-smoker is feeling deprived. How can you possibly be certain that you will never smoke again, if you feel deprived. Even if you don't feel deprived, that is no guarantee that you are certain that you will never smoke again. To ensure success, it is not sufficient that you try, or hope, or even feel confident that you will succeed, but:

TO *KNOW FOR CERTAIN* THAT YOU WILL SUCCEED

Many smokers believe that they can never be completely free. For years I was one of those smokers. I didn't just believe it, I knew it. Smokers of my generation might remember a brand named 'STRAND'. If you remember the name you will also remember the slogan:

YOU ARE NEVER ALONE WITH A STRAND

I never smoked STRAND in my life, but as far as smoking was concerned, that slogan was my Achilles heel. That was my attitude to a packet of cigarettes. While I had a packet of cigarettes in my pocket, I didn't need any other companion. The cigarettes were not just my friend, but also my confidence, my courage, my very personality. I truly believed that if ever I stopped smoking, I would not only be losing a genuine companion, but the crutch that gave me my strength of character.

It never even occurred to me that it was the packet of cigarettes that was destroying my courage and confidence, that non-smokers don't feel insecure or get into a panic without cigarettes. Why didn't it occur to me that just one packet was no longer sufficient. In the early days we start to panic when we are down to our last 3 cigarettes. I started to panic when down to my last 3 packets.

The advertising experts inform me that the STRAND slogan was a commercial failure. I found that rather surprising, because I know that slogan had the same effect on many other smokers as it did on me. Perhaps it was one of those examples when the theme back-fired. In those days advertising emphasized the social advantages of being a smoker. Perhaps STRAND intended the slogan to convey: while you are passing round the STRAND you'll be surrounded by friends, and not: while I've got my packet of STRAND, I need no other friends. Perhaps smokers sensed that it was really an enemy, and resented STRAND for gloating over the fact that they had become dependent upon an enemy. Ironic that Strand should have spent so much money just to increase the turnover of its rivals.

The point is, if you believe that you can never be completely free:

YOU *WILL* NEVER BE COMPLETELY FREE

Imagine that you have reason to believe that you are HIV positive. You are tested and have to wait a week for the result. I don't suppose it would be the greatest week of your life. If you had to wait a month, or a year, it would be even worse. Now imagine having to wait the rest of your life and never actually receiving the result.

This is what happens to smokers that are not certain that they have 'kicked' it. Admittedly, it's not as bad as the example I have given, but the effect is the same. They are waiting for their certificate. They are waiting for the doubt to go. But while they have doubts, why should they ever go? They have to go through the rest of their lives to find out whether they succeed. In fact, they never know, because when you die, nobody sends you a letter saying: "Oh, by the way, just in case you are interested, congratulations, you actually succeeded in stopping."

They go through the rest of their lives hoping that they will never smoke again. I find it very frustrating waiting to see the world rid of the evil of smoking. But at least I have the satisfaction of knowing that I might live to see it happen. How many times more frustrating must it be, to wait for something that you hope will never happen? You can't look forward to something that you hope will never happen. You can only dread something you hope will never happen.

This is why smokers that use the willpower method are so miserable and whinging. They go through the rest of the lives waiting for **NOTHING** to happen. This is what creates the light cloud, the void, that feeling of 'something missing' that I referred to earlier. This is also a strong contributory cause that makes drug addicts believe that they have addictive personalities. This feeling that once hooked, you can never be completely free, or, once a smoker always a smoker.

Perhaps I am painting an over-pessimistic picture. The girl at the dinner party was still craving the odd cigarette, but she preferred to remain a non-smoker. However, I don't want you to feel that you will be in the same position as her. Fortunately you don't have to. You will be using my method. But why is it that all our smoking lives, we remain smokers despite knowing:

1. That we never made a conscious decision to become smokers for life.
2. That smokers are idiots.
3. That non-smokers are far better off than we are.
4. That we were quite able to enjoy life and to handle stress before we started smoking and that millions of ex-smokers have already proved that we will again once we stop.

The answer is that the first three points we know for certain, but with point 4, until we've actually proved it to ourselves, how *can* we be certain that we will indeed be able to enjoy life and cope with life without smoking? The schizophrenia is still there. This is the real problem. It's a sort of chicken and egg situation. In order to be certain that you have truly kicked the 'weed' always and forever, you need to have no doubts. But how can you possibly not have doubts, until you are certain?

It's not quite as bad as the chicken and egg situation. Take my case, the moment the hypnotherapist said to me: "Smoking is drug addiction, if you stop for long enough you will succeed." I knew that I would succeed. I was neither expecting it to be easy, nor was I expecting it to happen quickly. It never even occurred to me at the time, but I was already free the moment that I heard those words. Because I believed them, I was already certain that I too could succeed, my doubts were gone. It didn't occur to me until later that you become a non-smoker, not when you extinguish your final cigarette, but when you know that you will never have the desire or need to smoke another. With other methods of stopping smoking, you extinguish the final cigarette first and hope that the need or desire not to smoke will follow as a result. With mine, you do it the other way around.

To this day, I am unable to tell you why those particular words: 'IT'S DRUG ADDICTION' had the effect that they did have on me. I didn't fully understand either drug addiction or smoking at that time. I have tried to analyse why they had the effect. I know that the key was that I knew then that I was a smoker, not because of some basic flaw in my character or chemistry which I had no control over, but because of some evil, outside influence that I could fight and would defeat. Even if it took the rest of my life to do it.

The significance of the words to me was that they made me *certain* that I could succeed. I will never know why those particular words made it certain in my case, because to do so, I would have needed to have been able to understand the total effect of the information, true or false, that both my conscious and subconscious mind had accumulated about smoking over the years. All I can tell you, is that in my case:

'IT'S DRUG ADDICTION' had the desired effect.

So what are the magic words in your case, that can break the chicken and egg situation, that will make you realise that, not only won't you miss cigarettes, but that you'll enjoy life more and be better equipped to cope with stress? You don't actually need any magic words. The magic words in my case made it easy for me to stop, but the thing that guarantees that I could never get hooked again is my understanding of the nature of the beast. All we need to do is to make sure that you also completely understand its nature.

That's what we've been doing up until now. Many of you will be convinced that you already understand it completely. If you are one of those, avoid the mistake of jumping the gun. There are several sound reasons that I request smokers not to smoke their final cigarette until I ask them to. To do so would be to start your attempt on Everest before you have completed *all* your preparations.

You might be convinced that you are already sufficiently prepared to stop smoking forever. Perhaps you are correct. But there might just be something that you have overlooked, or might not even be aware of. It could be the difference between life and death once you are on the mountain. It might sound dramatic, but you are playing for exactly the same stakes and you have no need to gamble with your life. Remember, I have actually succeeded in stopping *permanently* and helped thousands of other smokers to do the same. If you had done it just once, you would have no need to read this book.

Perhaps you still suffer from the delusion that it is not possible for all smokers to stop easily and permanently. If so it is essential to remove your delusion. To do so you must understand why you believe what you do.

Isn't one of the main reasons that we are indoctrinated from birth into believing that it is difficult to stop? Don't we all know thousands of other smokers that have found it to be true? Most important of all, haven't we proved it to ourselves. We don't just *think* it's difficult to stop, we *know* it. That panic feeling when we ran out of cigarettes might well be illogical, but it was also very real, and so is the irritability and misery we suffered when we attempted to stop.

They were indeed real, but illogical they certainly were not. If you are locked in a confined cell with no ventilation or light. It is quite logical that you will suffer both fear and panic.

We know that smoking itself is illogical, but while we don't understand why we appear to be dependent on cigarettes, our feeling of panic and fear when being deprived of them, is perfectly logical. In Chapter 16 I described a typical, if somewhat exaggerated incident, of a man that had run out of cigarettes in a Spanish restaurant. If, as I maintain, cigarettes always taste filthy and disgusting, why do we get into such a panic at those times?

Let us suppose that his problem was not cigarettes, but that he had arrived at the restaurant ravenously hungry, but wasn't allowed to eat. There's the smell of this gorgeous food, everyone else was heartily tucking in except him. Now again, he wouldn't be undergoing any severe physical pain, but do you think he would be enjoying the evening? You might argue that his misery was due to the fact that he was being deprived of the taste of good food. I would argue that every time we are not eating, we are being deprived of the taste of good food, but that doesn't make us miserable. He would be miserable, not because he was being deprived of the taste of good food, but because he was not able to satisfy the aggravation of his hunger. That might appear to be the same thing. In fact it is important that you understand the difference.

His only problem was that he was addicted to nicotine. He had this empty, insecure feeling. Although he had no physical pain, the feeling was physical. It was also very unpleasant. He didn't understand the feeling, in fact he only knew the feeling as: "I want a cigarette." He didn't understand why he wanted a cigarette, any more than he understood how a cigarette would remove the empty, insecure feeling. He didn't need to know why, all he needed to know was that it would. But he wasn't allowed to have a cigarette and that was why he was so miserable and began to panic. There's no mystery, it was the natural thing to do.

However, in Chapter 28 we have already dealt with the panic that smokers suffer when they are either running low on cigarettes or attempting to stop by using the willpower method. That panic feeling is psychological. Once you understand that the cigarette, far from satisfying the empty feeling, actually causes it, you have already removed the cause of the panic. It will have the same effect as giving the key to the prisoner locked in the cell. If you have any doubts about this point, re-read Chapter 28.

You might argue that it is understandable for smokers running low to get into a panic. After all they have no intention of stopping and will naturally feel deprived and miserable if they are not allowed to smoke. However, if the physical withdrawal pangs from nicotine are truly almost imperceptible, why should smokers become so miserable when using the willpower method? They must have wanted to stop smoking, why else would they have decided to stop? So why should they feel deprived and miserable?

Did they in effect *want* to stop? Look back on your early attempts to stop. Did you really *want* to stop smoking? Was it not more that you were worried about the effects that smoking was having on your health and your pocket? Even today don't most smokers and even the so-called experts still talk about *'giving up'*? Part of your brain must have wanted to go on smoking, otherwise you would no longer be a smoker. Since you never understood *why* you got into a panic when you ran out of cigarettes, why on earth should you assume that the panic will go when you quit? Logically it should get worse. If we get into a panic because we are without cigarettes for a couple of hours at a restaurant, how much worse must it be to have to go the rest of our lives without one?

The truth is, that quite often when using the willpower method, we don't actually get into a panic during those vital first few days. So gunged up and fed up were we of being smokers, that we were quite happy to be free of them. Yet it is the first few days that the physical withdrawal pangs reach their peak. It is misleading to use the word peak, because it implies that those pangs are quite substantial. It's more correct to say: "After a few days the physical withdrawal pangs reach their least insignificant state." Even at their peak they are still insignificant.

You might find the last statement difficult to believe. Nevertheless, it is true. I believe that I switched from being the heaviest smoker in the world, to the heaviest passive smoker in the world. My body still suffers the aggravation from physical, nicotine withdrawal. After spending a whole day with heavy smokers in a confined space, I can actually feel the empty, tense feeling of the nicotine leaving my body. This worries some smokers. Ironically their fear is usually not: "Aren't you worried about your health?" Which I am, but: "Doesn't this make you want a cigarette?" No, it has the completely opposite effect. It makes me want to get out into the fresh air and get the filth and tension out of my body.

The truth is that the misery of stopping, even with the willpower method, only starts when doubt starts to creep in. Assume that we had sufficient courage to make the attempt. We might well start off with a feeling of panic. Not to worry. This time we are determined to see it through. If other smokers can do it, so can we. But no sooner have we launched ourselves than the little voice starts off again: "You want a cigarette." It's physical. It's real. We now find ourselves in an impossible situation. We are still absolutely determined to be a non-smoker, but part of our brain is saying I want a cigarette. Which is really saying: "I want to be a smoker." How can we possibly want to be a smoker and a non-smoker at one and the same time?

This simple fact doesn't seem to dawn on smokers. On the questionnaires at the clinics, some smokers will say: "I enjoy being a smoker, but I don't actually like smoking." Sometimes it's the complete reverse: "I enjoy smoking, but I don't like being a smoker." If you heard a golfer say: "I enjoy being a golfer, but I hate playing golf." You would advise him to get his head examined.

Such is the schizophrenic power caused by addiction to the weed, that smokers think that smoking and being a smoker are two different

377

things. Get it clearly into you mind: smokers are smokers for one reason and one reason alone: THEY SMOKE!   If you smoke: YOU ARE A SMOKER!   There is only one essential stipulation to being a non-smoker: YOU DON'T SMOKE! NOT EVER! That is not the *only* stipulation to be a *happy* non-smoker for *the rest of your life*, but bear in mind, it is also an *essential* stipulation to achieve the correct frame of mind.

Is it really so surprising that we get so confused, frightened, frustrated, irritable and miserable? The miracle would be if we didn't. In fact it's a tribute to our maker that we are able to survive the ordeal at all, let alone that some valiant souls actually succeed when using the willpower method.

However, we have already adequately covered part of the fear that prevents us from making the attempt to stop, that is the fear of the initial trauma. The prime object of this chapter is to remove the more subtle and greater fear: "Will I ever be able to enjoy life or handle stress again?"

I suppose by far the most common cigarette that smokers think they will miss is the one after a meal, particularly at a restaurant on holiday in the company of smoking friends. The case of one of our Raynes Park clients summed the whole thing up. He was intelligent, attentive and had a genuine desire to quit. His only real problem in life was his heavy smoking. In short, he was one of the types that normally find it easy to stop after just one session. After his fifth visit I was beginning to despair. Not only was he convinced that he understood the nature of the trap completely and had actually followed all the instructions, but so was I.

He hadn't smoked, in fact by the sixth visit he had gone nine months without a cigarette. He was not suffering terrible withdrawal pangs, but had that feeling of waiting for something to happen that I described earlier. I confess that I felt that the sixth visit would also prove to be abortive. It was purely a chance remark as we made our farewells that enabled me to put my finger on the problem. Easter was coming up and I mentioned that I would be doing a seminar in Paris. He said:

"I find it hard to accept that I will never be able to sit in the sunshine outside a cafe in Paris, listening to the accordions, glass of wine in one hand and a Gauloise in the other, just watching the crowds go by."

I would imagine that he had just described the archetypal situation for what many smokers would regard as their favourite cigarette. I said:

"Think back to the last time you did it, were you actually consciously puffing on that Gauloise thinking: 'This smoke going into my lungs is my idea of heaven'? The scenario that you described is a very pleasant one, and one that I plan to be enjoying myself this weekend, but the Gauloise didn't contribute to it one iota. I was convinced that I could never enjoy golf without smoking, now I find the thought of smoking on a golf course nothing less than obscene. You can still enjoy that pleasure whenever you want to. But if you tell yourself that you won't be able to enjoy it without a Gauloise, then you won't enjoy it without a Gauloise. Anyway you smoked Silk Cut, usually Silk Cut smokers can't stand Gauloise."

I was quite taken aback when he informed me that he had never smoked Gauloise or been to Paris. He had quite happily survived 50 years without feeling deprived because he hadn't experienced that situation, but there he was feeling deprived, because he would never experience it! Such is the power of the brainwashing, it didn't occur to him that he was moping for a myth.

Let us return for a moment to the lady at the dinner party that was still craving for a cigarette. What a ridiculous position to put herself in. She hadn't smoked for 8 years. In her own words she had no intention of ever smoking again. I've no idea the amount of willpower and self-discipline she had to apply over those 8 years, let alone the amount she'll require to abstain for the rest of her life, but she has spent 8 years and will spend the rest of her life craving for something that:

SHE HOPES SHE'LL NEVER HAVE

What is the point in craving for a myth, for something that doesn't actually exist? Let me make it quite clear, cigarettes exist, but it is a myth that they are some sort of crutch or pleasure, or that they improve meals. Even when we discover that highly desirable myths, like Aladdin's lamp or Santa Claus, are actually myths, we suffer no undue discomfort. However, what can possibly be more ridiculous than to crave for western society's No.1 killer disease? That does:

ABSOLUTELY NOTHING FOR YOU WHATSOEVER!

Just as society, epitomized by the STRAND slogan, had brainwashed me into believing that cigarettes were my crutch, so my Paris cafe client had been infected with an equally phoney image. You could argue that the girl at the dinner party was missing something that she did actually enjoy: the cigarette after a meal. In truth she was also moping for an equally phoney situation that she had never actually experienced.

If you still find that difficult to believe, just pause for a moment and think back over all those social functions that you've attended and all those meals. Of all those thousands of cigarettes that you have smoked in your life, how many times can you remember thinking: "What could possibly be more pleasant than breathing these fumes into my lungs?"

When I look back over those smoking years, I remember numerous occasions when those cigarettes tasted weird, stale or even obnoxious. I remember many more when I struggled for breath, or was convulsed with violent coughing fits. I also remember the embarrassment those fits caused me and how self-conscious I felt when non-smokers gave me that quizzical look. But of all the hundreds of thousands of cigarettes that I smoked, I cannot think of a single one when I sat there thinking: "This is my idea of heaven!" Or: "How lucky I am to be a smoker!" Oh I can remember meals and many other occasions when I was utterly miserable because I couldn't smoke and how relieved I was when I was eventually allowed to light up, but that isn't the same thing.

I have no doubt you can look back on many idyllic occasions in your life that you associate with smoking, like the man that was enjoying the evening of a lifetime at the Spanish restaurant. Was it the fact that he smoked that made it the evening of a lifetime? If so, he wasted his money. He might just as well have stayed at home and smoked. Do you think he was even aware that he was smoking while he had plenty of cigarettes? The truth is, what should have been the evening of a lifetime, turned into a complete disaster for one reason and one reason alone, not because he ran out of cigarettes, but because he was a smoker. Far from making his evening, cigarettes actually ruined it.

NON-SMOKERS DO NOT HAVE THAT PROBLEM

You've heard people say: "No, I'm not going out tonight, I'm looking forward to a relaxing evening at home just watching television." Of all the thousands of smokers that tell you they enjoy smoking, have you ever heard a single one say: "I have no need to go out tonight, nor to stay in and watch TV. I've bought a packet of my favourite brand of cigarettes and look forward to spending a thoroughly enjoyable evening doing nothing but smoking."

If you have been completely honest with yourself, you will find that the only occasions that you are ever aware of your smoking, are the occasions that you would dearly love a cigarette but cannot have one, or the times when you are smoking one, but wish you didn't have to.

The nicotine withdrawal creates the illusion but it is the brainwashing that addicts you. In Chapter 24 I described how by blocking out the cigarette on one of those pictures of people modelling cigarettes, it is easy to see that the cigarette does absolutely nothing for the model. It takes more imagination in order to achieve the same object in those real life situations in which you felt a cigarette is all important, because if you keep telling yourself that you cannot enjoy certain situations without a cigarette:

YOU GUARANTEE THAT YOU WON'T

My Paris cafe friend had in fact completely understood how the mechanics of nicotine addiction fools smokers into believing that they get some genuine crutch or pleasure from smoking, but what he had omitted to do was to relate those facts to his everyday smoking situations. He hadn't actually removed the brainwashing. It is imperative to do this. You need to analyse all of these situations, to ask yourself exactly why the cigarette appeared to enhance the situation, to realise that it actually made it worse, and instead of perpetuating the illusion by thinking: "I won't be able to enjoy such and such a situation without a cigarette." Do the complete opposite. Keep reminding yourself of the true situation:

HOW MUCH MORE ENJOYABLE THEY ARE FREE FROM THE SLAVERY

Now let us deal with the reverse situation:

HOW WILL I COPE WITH STRESS WITHOUT A CIGARETTE?

I am not just talking about the real traumas like the lady who lost her husband, but everyday annoyances that occur regularly in all of our lives. A typical one is a car break down. Okay, we're reasonable people and know that part of the price we must pay for the luxury of owning a car, is to accept that occasionally it will break down. But why does it only ever break down late at night, when it's raining cats and dogs? Why does it always break down on the most dangerous part of the road, 10 miles from the nearest telephone box, garage or village; and why, oh why do all the other drivers, instead of stopping to see if they can help, belt past at 80 miles an hour, splashing you with mud and blasting there horns as if you've stopped for a roadside pinic?

I have no doubt that at such times, if you were a smoker, you would quite understandably have lit up a cigarette. The problem arises the next time you suffer a similar situation after you have stopped smoking. What do non-smokers do at such times? They feel utterly miserable and do whatever they have to do to resolve the situation. What do ex-smokers do at such times? They also feel utterly miserable and think: "At times like this I would have smoked a cigarette."

They are absolutely right. But I would like you to now look back on the last time it, or some similar trauma, happened in your life. In all probability you have a clear recollection of the incident itself, but can you remember whether you were already smoking when it happened? Do you actually remember lighting that cigarette? I have no doubt that you would have remembered if you had run out. Did you just smoke the one special cigarette? But most important of all, did it solve your problem? Did you stand there happy as a sand boy thinking: "It doesn't matter that I'm cold, wet, miserable and late for the most important appointment of my life?" Or were you still utterly miserable?

It's exactly the same position as the social situations above and the concentration situations discussed in Chapter 25. Ex-smokers, when they experience these situations after they have stopped, start to mope for a cigarette. They forget that the cigarette, far from helping, actually made all of these situations worse. Accept that, just like non-smokers, you are going to have ups and downs when you quit, but if you start craving a cigarette at such times, you'll be moping for an illusion. The cigarette hasn't left a void in your life, cigarettes create voids, they do not fill them, but by moping for an illusion that does not and cannot ever exist, or by searching for a substitute that cannot exist,

YOU CREATE A VOID!

By doing so, all that you achieve is to turn good days into bad days and make bad days worse. Why not be nice to yourself? Do the complete opposite. If you are having a bad day say to yourself: "Okay, so today isn't so great, but at least I'm not the slave of that awful weed." If it's a good day, say: "It's great to be alive and so much nicer now that I'm no longer dependent on the weed." I'm not asking you to look at life through rose-coloured spectacles, merely not to wear the dark glasses which smokers tend to wear when they quit, and to see life as it really is.

Apart from cars that won't start, breakdowns and accidents, there are common danger situations which might trigger off the craving for a cigarette in the future. Rather than wait for these events to happen and hope that by the time they do, you will have forgotten all about smoking, it is far better to anticipate them and to prepare in advance what your mental reaction is going to be.

They might be social, stressful or boring situations including those which require concentration. Common examples are: house buying and particularly selling, Christmas, weddings, holidays and funerals. They might be situations that are peculiar to you. My greatest fear was: would I ever be able to play golf, let alone enjoy it, if I couldn't smoke? You need to ask yourself in advance what situations you feel might be a problem or a danger to you, and remove the brainwashing in advance.

Airports are places where ex-smokers are often tempted to try just one cigarette, or just one packet. You are anticipating your holiday with great excitement, and rushing around trying to ensure that nothing is forgotten. You got up in the middle of the night an hour earlier than you really needed to. Yet, for some reason you still don't manage to avoid that last minute panic, and arrive both late and flustered at the airport. Good news and bad news awaits you. The good news is that you haven't missed your flight. That's because it has been delayed. The bad news is that it has been delayed by about 8 hours.

You are tired, frustrated, disorientated and bored. Can it be just coincidence that you suddenly find that the only seat vacant in the airport lounge is smack opposite those duty frees? It might cross your mind that: "On just this one and only one occasion perhaps just one cigarette won't do any harm." Before you let the seed germinate, reminisce on those times you suffered a delayed flight when you were a smoker. Did you sit there thinking: "Yippee! I'm a smoker. Who cares if I've got to sit around here all day when I should be basking on some exotic beach? I've got packets and packets of these gorgeous cigarettes to smoke. I'll just sit here and smoke one after the other."

If you still have doubts, take a look at the smokers who are on the same flight. Do they appear even to be aware that they are smoking? Are they happy and cheerful? Or do they appear to be even more frustrated, bored and tired than you do. In all probability they will, because:

THAT'S THE REALITY OF BEING A SMOKER

There are two and only two occasions when cigarettes could possibly be regarded as relieving boredom. They are your initial experimental cigarettes as a youngster and the 'it's safe to smoke just one' cigarette after you have successfully stopped. That will distract you from your boredom for a few moments. For the reasons that we have already established, the price that you will pay is to have to continue to smoke the rest of your life. Why even tempt yourself?

I've been saying that the girl at the dinner party and the whinging ex-smokers like her are stupid to go on craving for a myth and for something that they hope they will never have. You might be thinking, stupid they may be, all smokers know that they are being stupid the whole of their lives, but, either you crave for nicotine, or a cigar, or a cigarette or you don't.

WHAT CHOICE DO YOU HAVE? AND WHEN WILL THE CRAVING GO?

Fortunately you do have a choice. There are two very important misconceptions that we will dispel in the next chapter:

1. That your body craves nicotine.
2. That there is a physical addiction to nicotine.

CHAPTER 38

When Will the Craving Go?

I have already referred to expressions used by the so-called experts in connection with drug addiction, which in themselves cause the addict problems. By far the most common misnomer is 'Give Up' which implies a permanent sacrifice, but even more damaging is the term 'DEPENDENCY' whether it is preceded by nicotine, alcohol, solvents or heroin. You are only dependent on something that you cannot survive without. Drug addicts are never, ever dependent on such substances, they only think they are, but when a doctor or other *expert* uses the word 'dependency' they merely confirm the addict's fears.

An addict is never dependent on any drug. A person might well be dependent on a drug for survival, such as a diabetic needing insulin, but such a person is not a drug addict. They have a rational reason for using the drug and are in control. Addiction means the complete opposite. It implies no rationality and lack of control. Addicts might suffer the illusion that they have rational reasons and that they are in fact in control, but I am now talking about the facts not the delusions. Since there are in fact no rational reasons for smoking, all smokers, no matter how casual, are nicotine addicts.

You are never *physically* or *chemically* addicted to any drug. Addiction is a mental delusion. That delusion might well have been caused by physical or chemical aggravation, nevertheless, it is 100% mental.

Earlier I said that if any smoker, at any time during their life, were to analyse objectively, the advantages and disadvantages of being a smoker, the answer would be a dozen times over: **YOU ARE A MUG!**

Cast your mind back to the time that you lit your very first cigarette. Assume you weren't contemplating whether or not to try just one cigarette, but whether you were going to be a smoker for the bulk of your life. You'd obviously give such an important decision very serious thought. Let's assume that you actually went through the exercise of weighting each factor. The result would be something like:

FOR SMOKING: 10 lbs
AGAINST SMOKING: 100 lbs

You can actually go through this exercise if you want to, but there is really no need to. Like the man who listed 60 good reasons to stop, it didn't matter whether he thought of 6 or 6,000 reasons, he was only going through the exercise to convince himself of what he already knew: THAT HE WAS A MUG!

Obviously, each individual will come up with a different total weight on each side of the scale. The factual answer is:

FOR SMOKING: ZILCH!

However only people that had no brainwashing would be aware of that. The 'against' answer would depend on the individual. But let's not quibble about detail, the result would still be heavily weighted in favour of being a non-smoker. So why did so many people choose to become smokers? They didn't! They were all lured into the trap.

Once we become hooked the ratio doesn't alter much. The 'for' side might go up a few pounds when our bodies learn to cope with the foul taste and the illusions of crutch and pleasure take effect. But the 'against' side soon more than compensates once the health, financial, filth and slavery influences become apparent. So why do we continue to smoke? After all, no one forces us to. One answer is that we close our minds to the rational facts. That is true. But that merely begs another question:

WHY DO WE CLOSE OUR MINDS?

If you accept that the rational tilt on the scales is something like 100 lbs against smoking and only 10 lbs in favour, what is this force which not only balances the scales, but tips them in favour of remaining a smoker? Whatever it is, it must be an exceptionally powerful force in order to counteract the combined effects of the health scares, the money, the slavery and the filth.

The logical answer is the little nicotine monster inside our body which is constantly telling us to light a cigarette. But Allen Carr maintains that the actual physical aggravation caused by that little monster is so slight as to be almost imperceptible.

I promise you that it is, but while you don't understand that monster, its effect on the quality of your life can be disastrous. While your brain interprets that slight aggravation as: **"I WANT A CIGARETTE"**, you will be very miserable if you cannot have one, and if you believe that you will always be miserable without cigarettes, that misery will lead to fear and panic. That is the powerful force that keeps us all smoking against our better judgment, and keeps us in the prison:

FEAR!!!

It might be purely mental, but while you don't understand it, it is quite rational and it is also very real. However, that fear ceases to be a powerful force once you realise that the cigarette, far from relieving it, is actually causing it. In fact it switches to the other side of the tug of war and becomes an additional powerful reason to quit.

Fortunately, being purely mental and caused by ignorance, that fear can be removed before you extinguish the final cigarette. Once you understand the nature of the trap completely, and *know* that you will enjoy life so much more as a non-smoker and that it *is* really easy for any smoker to quit, that fear is already removed.

As I explained in Chapter 18, we use the word ADDICTION to cover a situation in which some unknown force compels us to continue taking a drug against our rational judgement. An addict is not imprisoned by physical walls, but by ignorance and fear. Remove the ignorance and fear and the prison walls disintegrate and so does the addiction.

The very slight physical aggravation from nicotine withdrawal is a mere molehill, but when combined with the massive brainwashing, that molehill appears to be a mountain. Remove the fear and ignorance and the only force left on the 'carry on smoking' side of the tug of war is that molehill. However that slight physical aggravation is also caused by and not relieved by smoking. Accordingly it should also tranfer to the other side of the rope. We are now have a contest in which both teams are pulling in the same direction. The contest is over.

AND SO IS THE MISERY AND SLAVERY

Anyone that has been unfortunate enough to have been a heavy smoker and also to have been coerced into a tug of war team, as I once was, will know that there couldn't possibly be a better analogy for smoking than a tug of war. It is incorrectly described as a sport. Legalised torture is a more apt description. With other sports, the best contests arise when the combatants are equally matched.

There can be few more excruciating or boring spectacles than two equally matched tug of war teams. Both teams just dig in and lean motionless on the rope for what seems like hours to the spectators, and days to the leaners. You would think it would be mainly a contest of physical strength and endurance. Not so it is purely mental, and the main mental problem is that you have absolutely nothing to occupy your mind other than your aching muscles. It starts in the thighs and then gradually spreads over your whole body.

The worst possible position on the rope is at the front. You stare straight into the faces of the opposing team. They all have granite jaws and bulging muscles. But the most disconcerting thing is their eyes. They just stare blankly like zombies. You can tell that absolutely nothing is going on inside their heads, they are not suffering the same torture as you are. You scrutinise each one in turn desperately searching for some weakness. There is none. It is blatantly obvious that they could quite happily spend the rest of their lives leaning on that rope.

A tug of war contest ends when an individual in the team cracks. You desperately try to make sure that it isn't you. Everyone feels sympathy for the footballer that balloons the ball over the bar in a penalty shoot out. In the bar room inquest that follows every match, there are always a variety of incidents that can be the topic of conversation. But what is there to talk about after a tug of war contest? You cannot wax lyrical for twenty minutes on the quality of the refereeing, the colour of the rope or the state of the course. Only one incident actually happens in a tug of war contest, eventually the weakest link in the chain snaps.

Having convinced yourself that there is no weak link in the opposing team, you begin to wonder about your own team. The problem is that you cannot see them. At times you are deluded into believing that they have already gone off for a pint. The pain is so intense that you are convinced that you're resisting the opposing team alone. You realise that it is just delirium, but you know for sure that they are not putting anything like the effort in that you are. Then panic sets in. You feel the first spasms of cramp creeping in and know, that unless one of your team cracks soon, you will be the sole topic of conversation until the next contest.

You've read somewhere that witch doctors can kill purely with the power of their minds. You experiment briefly to see if you can induce a mild heart attack on one of your team mates. Then complete and utter bliss. One of them finally cracks. The rest of the team would secretly like to kiss him, instead we persecute him. Tug of war must be the only sport in the world in which the bliss of winning is equalled by the sheer bliss of losing, that is of course, provided that the weak link in the chain wasn't you. The final indignity is that when the link eventually breaks, you are unceremoniously dragged along the gravel by the other team. For some reason, it doesn't seem to occur to you to let go of the rope. Perhaps the scratches and bruises that you now incur provide a masochistic pleasure after the previous torture.

When you look back on your smoking years, you will also find it difficult to understand why you ever bothered. The only difference between smoking and tug of war is that you will deliberately break the chain and feel like the match winner.

Smokers phoning our clinics are both bemused and relieved when we advise them not to attempt to quit, or even to cut down, prior to their appointment. They are even more surprised, and just as relieved, when instructed to ensure that they bring along an ample supply of their favourite brand, and to make no attempt to quit or cut down, prior to the ritual of the last cigarette.

Some find that they smoke less than they normally would, however most find that they smoke much more. So much so that in the early days of group therapy, before we had installed adequate air conditioning, the room had the appearance of an opium den. Many clients were convinced that it was some form of aversion therapy. If aversion therapy had worked, I would have used it for that reason, but I have already explained why it doesn't.

Other smokers found it to be contradictory. Near the beginning of the therapy I would say:

"Smoking does absolutely nothing for you whatsoever."

"If that is true, why do you instruct us to continue until the ritual of the final cigarette?"

There are several important reasons. One obvious one is that the whole therapy is based on exploding the myths and misconceptions that all smokers have about their smoking, many of which can only be successfully removed whilst actually smoking a cigarette, e.g. the belief that they enjoy the taste of certain cigarettes.

Another is, that whether they like it or not, smokers are drug addicts. One of the great subtleties of any drug addiction that makes the trap so effective, is that when they are actually imbibing the drug, they either do it subconsciously, or wish they didn't have to do it. It is only when they are not smoking and the nicotine starts to leave their body, that for some reason unknown to them, they want a cigarette. If they aren't allowed to have one, they will begin to ponder the fact, become fidgety, lose their concentration and begin to panic.

Ah! So I've admitted it, smoking does help concentration. No it doesn't! The lack of concentration and panic is caused by the the fact that they started smoking, not because they are stopping. Non-smokers don't suffer it. However, I don't want to be talking to a drug addict in a state of panic, whether that panic be caused by their being deprived of the drug or for any other reason. If I did, even if they tried to listen to what I was saying, there is no way that they would absorb my message.

What chance of success do you believe I would have, if when trying to persuade a claustrophobic to enter a crowded lift or a person terrified of flying to board an aeroplane, I said:

"Okay, Get in the lift, or board the plane and I will remove your fear."

Anyone that has suffered either one of those phobias will confirm that I would be wasting my time. Unless I remove all or part of the fear first, in no way could I persuade you to enter the lift or board the plane. If I forcibly tried to make you do so, I would merely increase your fear and panic. That panic might make you kill me rather than submit. If you did so, you would be justified, it would be self defence.

Again we have this difficulty of definitions and the awful problems they can create. We use the word phobia to imply a fear when the sufferer has no logical reason for having the fear, e.g. my fear of spiders. If I had consulted a psychiatrist, and he'd described my fear as a phobia, it would have increased my fear, because I would have felt that there was some basic flaw in my make up. Since there are no poisonous spiders in England, there appears to be no logical reason for my fear of spiders. Australians have every reason to fear spiders like the funnel-web. Their very survival might depend on that fear. Perhaps my ancestors were plagued by poisonous spiders and that fear is built into my genes.

If I'd spent the whole of my life on an island with no natural or man-made feature higher than four feet from the ground, there would be no logical reason for a fear of heights, but do you believe that I would not possess one? The experience of using elevators or of flying involve several common fears:

1. Fear of heights should the lift cable break or the plane suffer mechanical or structural failure.
2. Fear of suffocation occasioned by any confined space.
3. Fear of being trapped.
4. Fear of not being in control, or of being dependent upon the skill, competence and expertise of unknown people and the efficiency of their machines.

Nowadays flying involves the additional risks of sabotage and highjacking. These fears are not phobias. They are natural and normal. All are genuine threats to our survival. It is people that are not aware of them that are abnormal, be it because they are stupid, ignorant or insensitive. However, if you can first remove the bulk of the fear, by explaining the back up systems, the fail-safe devices, the fact that the aircrew are just as anxious to stay alive as you are, and have such confidence in the systems, including their own ability, and that statistically, flying is so safe, they are prepared to spend a large proportion of their lives in the air, then you have a reasonable chance of removing the bulk of the fear and persuading the person to enter the plane.

It is just fear that prevents people from stopping smoking. The extinguishing of that final cigarette is the equivalent to boarding the aeroplane. There are however some important differences. Once the hatches on the plane have been closed and it has taken off, the fearful passenger cannot get off. This might increase his fear, but at least he completes the journey. When smokers extinguish what they hope will be their final cigarettes, they really have no need to get into a panic because they always have the choice of lighting up again if they want to. However, I have already explained why it is essential in order to remain free for the rest of your life, to be certain that you never will light up again. So if you start off with the attitude that you always have the choice, it might remove any cause for panic, but at the same time it will almost certainly guarantee failure sooner or later.

It is essential to start off with a frame of mind that it *is* certain, that there *is* no going back. This makes it equally essential to remove all the fear and panic first. Fortunately it is possible to do this. A fear of spiders, of lifts and aeroplanes are normal and natural. We can never eradicate them completely. It would be stupid to even attempt to do so. They are part of our protection. It would be dangerous to lose them completely. We would become complacent. Over 200 people died on the Herald of Free Enterprise because the crew became complacent about the danger. However, there is nothing normal or natural about the fear of stopping smoking. It's not built within our genes. No one has a fear of stopping smoking until they become hooked. Ironically it is only created by starting smoking. That fear isn't a protection for survival. On the contrary:

IT GUARANTEES OUR DESTRUCTION

It is a completely abnormal and unnecessary fear created by smoking. But the good news is that this being the case, it is possible to remove the fear completely before you extinguish that final cigarette. However, I won't be able to do that If I'm talking to the panicking mind of a drug addict. I need to be talking to a person with the same relaxed, rational and logical frame of mind with which you would approach any other subject. Only then will you be able to understand completely and permanently, and become a happy non-smoker the moment you extinguish that final cigarette, and remain one the rest of your life.

When I was a smoker, I suffered badly from a fear of flying, medical examinations, dental appointments, even just visiting hospitals. I still don't enjoy doing any of those things, but they no longer cause me distress. Could the reason be that the major part of my distress was that I wasn't allowed to smoke at those times? Elevators have never caused me the slightest anxiety, unless they are transparent and on the outside of a building. Could this be because I would smoke in an elevator, or even if I wasn't allowed to, the abstinence was very brief?

You become a non-smoker every time you extinguish a cigarette. You become a permanent non-smoker when you extinguish your last cigarette. How will you know that it's your last cigarette? You won't, unless you are a happy non-smoker. You become a happy non-smoker when you stop craving cigarettes and a permanent, happy non-smoker provided you never, ever crave cigarettes again.

In the previous chapter I described some of the confusion in smokers' minds about the question: when do you become a non-smoker? We established that if your object is to achieve something positive, like climbing Everest, no matter how difficult your task might be, at least you know when you have achieved it; but how do you know when you have achieved not doing something? Surely you can only ever claim that you haven't done it: 'Up until now.' We have eliminated some of the confusion by recognizing that we were asking the wrong question, and that the real mystery that we are trying to solve is:

WHEN WILL YOU KNOW YOU'LL BE A HAPPY NON-SMOKER PERMANENTLY?

Unfortunately, essential as it is to get the question right, the answer becomes infinitely more complex. How can any ex-smoker *know* for certain that they will be happy to remain an ex-smoker for the rest of their lives? The so-called experts merely confuse the matter further. ASH lay down the standard for success as abstinence for one year. How convenient that it happens to be one year. Do you believe in such coincidences? How do ASH explain people like me and the thousands that have used my method who knew they were free when, or even before, extinguishing their final cigarette? How do they explain the smokers that had already abstained for several years, yet still found themselves craving for cigarettes, and attended our clinics to end that craving?

Obviously abstention for one year is a purely arbitrary period. What is supposed to happen when the year is up? And how annoyed smokers that abstain for a year must be if they continue to crave cigarettes after a year. The actual guidelines that smokers themselves lay down are more logical than an arbitrary period of abstinence, but if the so-called experts cannot even tell you exactly what it is that you are actually trying to achieve:

WHAT POSSIBLE CHANCE CAN YOU HAVE OF ACHIEVING IT?

This is why the willpower method makes it virtually impossible to stop. It is based on a series of misconceptions viz:

1. That smoking is a habit and that all you need to do to break the habit is to abstain for an indefinite period. We have already established that it isn't habit but addiction.
2. That there's a sacrifice to be made. That the smoker has to 'give up' something. If you believe that smoking gives a genuine crutch or pleasure at the time you quit, why should you ever believe

otherwise, no matter after how many years you may have quit? It doesn't matter that the sacrifice is an illusion, the illusion will remain and absence from it will merely make the heart grow fonder.
3. That massive willpower is needed in order to succeed. Which is your strongest hand, the left or the right? Test it out. Clasp your hands together in front of your chest. Now pull outwards gradually increasing the pressure until the weaker hand is forced to yield. It never will because, although one hand is actually weaker than the other, the conflict isn't one hand against the other, but you against yourself. Nobody forces you to smoke. It is not lack of will that prevents smokers from quitting, but a conflict of will.
4. That a transitional period of trauma has to be undergone between extinguishing what smokers hope will be their final cigarette and becoming a successful non-smoker, without giving any logical indication of the length of the period, or even defining what criteria defines success.

In short, the willpower method is a cocktail of ignorance, uncertainty and fear. Little wonder that smokers rarely succeed when using it. However its main fault, which supersedes the combined effects of the other four, is that smokers using it start off in an impossible position. They start the attempt by saying: "I want to be a non-smoker." They then spend the next few days craving for a cigarette, which is really saying: "I want to be a smoker." It is true that they dearly wish that they didn't still crave cigarettes, but while they do, at one and the same time, they want to be both non-smokers and smokers.

We have already established that the one essential to achieve success is to remove all doubt. What more destructive doubt could you have than not having actually decided whether you wish to be non-smoker or smoker? The resulting trauma of the period of abstinence that follows invariably ends up with the ex-smoker deciding that being a smoker is the lesser of the two evils. Who can blame them? Certainly not me, that's why I remained one for so many years. Fortunately, you don't have to use the willpower method.

Perhaps you still believe that it is not possible to *know* for certain that something in your life will not happen. You can't know for certain that you won't be struck by a meteorite. I don't suppose the prospect unduly concerns you because of the incredible odds against it happening to you, but you still cannot be certain that it won't. So how can you possibly be certain that you will be happy to remain a non-smoker the rest of your life, when literally thousands of ex-smokers get hooked again every year?

Nevertheless I assure you that I know that I could never become hooked again. What's more any ex-smoker can enjoy the same guaranteed freedom. Although the odds against getting hooked again are far greater than being hit by a meteorite, ex-smokers have a considerable advantage: if a meteorite is going to hit you, there is absolutely nothing that you can do about it, whereas:

NO ONE CAN FORCE YOU TO SMOKE
THE MATTER IS COMPLETELY WITHIN YOUR CONTROL

So, the only person that you really need to worry about is yourself. Why does any one ever light a cigarette? There is only one answer to that question:

BECAUSE THEY WANT TO

There are thousands of triggers that can make a smoker want to light a cigarette, and it doesn't matter whether those triggers are conscious or not, or whether it be the aggravation caused by the little monster or the brainwashing. It doesn't matter one iota that at one and the same time the smoker's brain is saying: "I want a cigarette", another part of his brain is saying: "I wish I didn't." In fact that schizophrenia existed with every cigarette that has ever been smoked, and the fact that smokers are seldom consciously aware of it when actually smoking does not alter the reality.

So, all we have to do in order to make sure that you are never, ever again troubled by the thought of: "I want a cigarette" is to ensure that 3 really essential points are ingrained into your mind. One is to remove this concept of being able to smoke occasional cigarettes. Another is to understand why cigarettes do absolutely nothing for you whatsoever, so that if and when something should trigger off in your brain the thought of: "I want a cigarette," you immediately reverse that thought without any feeling of sacrifice or deprivation.

However, the third and most important point, is to remove this myth that craving is a hit or miss affair. This concept that when you extinguish what you hope will be your final cigarette, that you have to go through some transitional period of indeterminate length, erroneously referred to as the withdrawal period, before the craving dies completely, or dwindles to endurable levels.

Many people find it difficult to believe that craving is a matter with which they exercise a simple choice. They suffer the misconception that you either crave something or you don't. There are three main causes for this misconception. The first is that, whether we like it or not, the body will continue physically to crave nicotine for a few days at least. Imperceptible as that physical craving might be, it is still there and so are its undermining effects.

Up to now, for convenience, I have at times referred to 'the slight physical craving'. However, the beautiful truth is that the body is incapable of craving anything, be it drugs, food or anything else. Your body is capable of undergoing hunger, tiredness, aggravation and pain, but even those can only be experienced through your brain. If you are unconscious, you are not aware of them.

It is only your brain that is capable of craving. What's more, it is only your conscious brain that does the craving. Every person has it within their power to decide whether they are going to crave a cigarette or not. There might be subconscious illusions that can influence a person to crave a cigarette, nevertheless the craving itself is conscious and within the control of every smoker. What's more, it always has been.

The second cause that makes us believe that we have no control over our cravings, other than to deny ourselves with the use of willpower, is because when we attempt to stop smoking by using the willpower method, we try not to think about smoking and end up by being obsessed by the subject. Because we find it impossible *not* to think about a subject, we assume that it is equally impossible not to crave.

However, the third and main reason that we believe that we have no control over whether we crave cigarettes or not, is because practically every smoker that has ever quit, like the girl at the dinner party that hadn't smoked for 8 years, does have occasional cravings no matter how infrequent they might be. Just as we've been programmed to believe that smoking provides some sort of pleasure or crutch, so we are programmed to believe that we have to continue to crave cigarettes, at least for a transitional period, after we quit.

Imagine a child craving a cream bun that is actually made out of cardboard and soap. Would the child still crave that bun after sampling it? Of course not, particularly if the bun also contained cyanide. The child was craving for an illusion, and once enlightened, ceased to crave. The dinner party girl and the millions like her only continue to crave, because, although they have quit smoking, they havn't been enlightened. Perhaps she was being stupid by moping for something that she hoped she wouldn't have, but her attitude was understandable, she genuinely believed that cigarettes were enjoyable after a meal and that she had made a genuine sacrifice. She still believed that there's a genuine crutch or pleasure in smoking and understandably felt deprived.

You might well argue that, although the child would no longer crave the fake bun, the fake might well have got its taste buds craving for the genuine article. In which case, at least the child was able to satisfy its disappointment by eating a bona fide cream bun. This is the real trauma that confronts ex-smokers, they either continue to see cigarettes as the genuine article and feel deprived, or they see through the façade. But whereas there are genuine cream buns, all cigarettes are fakes and they have nothing to fill the void. It's like finding out that your best friend is really your worst enemy. You are pleased that you found out, but you are miserable because you have lost your best friend and gained an enemy.

In fact you haven't. That person never was your friend, you only thought they were. They were only your worst enemy because you put your trust in them and they abused that trust. Now that you know they are your enemy, they no longer have your trust and can no longer harm you. The true position is that you have lost an enemy.

I believe this to be the most suitable analogy of all to obtain a correct perception of the smoking trap. If you lose a close friend or relative, by lose I mean that they die, you have to go through a mourning process. Even when you get over the initial tragedy and life goes on again, you are left with a genuine void in your life that you can never completely fill. But it is a "fait accompli" there is nothing that you can do about it, you have no choice but to accept the situation and eventually you do.

Smokers, alcoholics, heroin and other drug addicts, when attempting to stop by using the willpower method, also feel that they have lost a friend. They know that they are making the correct decision, but there is still this feeling of sacrifice. Assume that they also survive the initial trauma and that life goes on again, but there is still this void in their lives. This isn't a genuine void, but if they believe it is genuine, the effect is the same. But the really significant difference, is that this particular *friend* ISN'T ACTUALLY DEAD! On the contrary, the tobacco industry, other smokers and society generally, ensure that those ex-smokers are subjected to the temptation of the ever-present forbidden fruit for the rest of their lives. It just takes one weak or inebriated moment to end up back in the pit.

However if you lose your mortal enemy, you don't have to go through an initial trauma. On the contrary you can rejoice and celebrate right from the start, and you can continue to rejoice and celebrate for the rest of your life. The beautiful truth is that cigarettes do absolutely nothing for you at all and there is nothing to give up.

We have established that, after your final cigarette, you will in all probability be thinking quite a lot about smoking to begin with. You will also think about smoking at various times during the rest of your life. We have also established that it is impossible deliberately not to think about something, and that to attempt to do so would create problems. Although you may have no choice about the subject matter, fortunately you do have a choice about your feelings and attitudes towards that subject matter.

You could spend the next few days, and possibly the rest of your life craving cigarettes, and wondering when the craving will go. But how can it ever go while you continue to crave? If you adopt that choice, you will feel deprived and miserable. Eventually you will end up smoking again and feel even more miserable.

Your second option is not to actually crave cigarettes, but just to see what happens. You won't be quite as miserable as the first option, neither will you be over elated. You'll have that white cloud hanging over your head, waiting for nothing to happen.

Fortunately, you have a far better option. That is, whenever you think about smoking, neither to crave a cigarette, nor to wait for nothing to happen, but to feel: "Yippee I'm a non-smoker."

IT IS ENTIRELY YOUR CHOICE

But what about the little monster that will be there for a few days, don't we know that feeling as: "I want a cigarette?" Yes, he'll be there for a few days and it is essential that you realise that he is there. However, you now understand the true nature of that monster. If you do get that feeling of "I want a cigarette." Instead of having one, or getting uptight because you musn't have one, pause for a moment. There is no need to panic. The feeling itself isn't that bad. It's what smokers suffer throughout their smoking lives. Re-programme your brain. Your brain only registered that feeling of: "I want a cigarette." because up until now it had every reason to believe that a cigarette would satisfy the empty, insecure feeling that you were suffering. But you now know, that far from relieving that feeling, the cigarette caused it. So just accept the feeling for what it really is. Remind yourself: "Non-smokers don't have this problem. This is what smokers suffer, and they suffer it throughout their smoking lives. Isn't it great! It will soon be gone and gone forever. Never to return!"

If you adopt that policy, even if you feel a little tense, it will be a moment of pleasure rather than misery. Incidentally you might well find that, particularly in the first few days, you'll forget that you have stopped smoking. It can happen any time, but it usually happens first thing in the morning during that period when you are half asleep and half awake. You think: "I'll get up and light a cigarette." You then remember you've quit smoking. Another common occurrence is when you are socialising. You are chatting away and suddenly there is a pack of cigarettes being thrust under your nose, you automatically reach for one, then remember that you cannot have one. Such times can be make or break, particularly if the *friend* who is offering the cigarette remembers before you do, and interrupts your monologue with: "I thought you had stopped?"

You stand arm suspended in midair. It can be very disconcerting. The smokers cannot hide their delight. To them the incident is certain proof that you haven't kicked it and they are convinced that you are dying for a cigarette. Unfortunately, it can have exactly the same effect on you. Unprepared, the effect is like a punch in the solar plexus delivered without warning. Before you've got your breath back, the smoker follows up with a cluster of blows:

"Oh I do enjoy my cigarettes, what would life be without our little pleasures?"

"I know they aren't doing my health any good, but who wants to live to ninety anyway! I'm sure I would already be dead from an ulcer if I didn't smoke."

"Sure they're expensive, but what's the point of being rich if you're miserable?"

Even though we know that those statements are false and illogical, at such times these arguments can appear to be perfectly logical and can be very damaging. Almost in an instant our whole preparation and effort can collapse like a house of cards. We begin to lose faith in ourselves. We start to think: "Am I just kidding myself? If I were really free, why would I have these moments?" That's when doubts begin to creep in and we begin to question our decision.

We have established that eating is not a habit but a physical need for survival, and that nicotine addiction is not habit but the illusion of a crutch or pleasure. However, just as our brains and bodies have been programmed to relieve our hunger at regular intervals, with varying types of food, so the smoker's brain is programmed to scratch the 'itch' at regular intervals. With both eating and smoking we learn to associate certain smells or situations with ending hunger or scratching the itch.

Obviously those triggers and responses don't cease completely the moment you finish your last cigarette. For a few days, your body will continue to 'itch'. Although that 'itch' is almost imperceptible, nevertheless it's still there. Even after the physical aggravation has gone, some of the mental associations linger on. This undermines the attempts of smokers that use the willpower method. In their minds they have built up a massive case against smoking and can see little or no logical argument in its favour. Yet in spite of this, a little voice keeps saying: "You want a cigarette." They don't understand why. So the tap begins to drip.

If you understand it, there is nothing to worry about. It is natural and only to be expected. However, it is imperative that you prepare yourself in advance to expect these situations. Whether they be first thing in the morning, or whether you be returning to an empty house from work or a shopping trip, whether you be alone or in the company of other smokers, accept these moments for what they really are: you'd momentarily forgotten that you no longer smoke. That isn't a bad thing. On the contrary, it's a very good sign. It is certain proof that your life is returning to the happy state you were in before you became hooked, when the thought of smoking or not smoking didn't dominate your whole existence. The only bad thing that happens, is not that you can't have a cigarette, but that you had momentarily forgotten:

THAT YOU NO LONGER NEED A CIGARETTE

Expecting these moments to happen and being prepared for them, means that you can't be caught off guard. You won't even need to duck those blows, you'll be wearing a suit of impenetrable armour. You have no need to question your decision, you know it's the correct one. This is the moment to remind yourself just how nice it is to be free. That momentary feeling of vulnerability will be immediately transformed into a feeling of strength, security and immense pleasure.

THE CHOICE IS YOURS

It will also help you at such times, not only to be expectant and prepared about your own reactions, but when other smokers are involved, as they so often tend to be at such times, to understand theirs. A permanent psychological battle rages between smokers and ex-smokers. In fact the ex-smokers have all the aces and all the trumps. However, during incidents like the one that I described above, if unprepared, the ex-smoker can be bluffed into believing that the reverse is true. **THE SMOKER NEVER CAN!** We will look at the situation from the smoker's point of view in Chapter 40.

These 'throwbacks' tend to be more disarming when they happen months, or even years, after you have long since felt that you have 'kicked' it. Only a few months ago I went to put my head out of my car window and before doing so, I tried to remove a non-existant dog-end from my lips. Had I have stopped by using the willpower method, this would have been a very discouraging experience. My reaction would have been: "Almost 10 years now, but I still haven't broken the habit!" My actual reaction was: "10 years ago I would have had that filthy dog-end stuck in my mouth. I'm so pleased that I'm no longer a slave!"

No doubt you will be thinking: "Have I got to wait ten years for that to happen?" No! That was my frame of mind from the moment I extinguished the final cigarette. I was inebriated with the nectar of my newly discovered freedom. While we are on the subject of inebriation, many failures slip up after having too much to drink and are worried that this will happen to them again. This happened to me on more than one occasion when using the willpower method. I used to claim that I wasn't even aware that I was smoking. However I think the true reason was that part of my brain still missed cigarettes and that my inebriated state was the excuse I needed to start smoking again. Why else would I have continued to smoke the following day?

To my amazement, it happened to me about 6 months after Independence Day. I was playing pool at a friend's house. I was suddenly aware that I had a burning cigarette in my hand. Where it came from, I do not know. It was the same friend that used to blow smoke in my face. I'm ashamed to admit that I suspected that he had planted it on me like a 'Mickey Finn'. If so, he must have been very disappointed in my reaction. It gave me great pleasure to be able to stub that cigarette out immediately, without the slightest feeling of temptation or deprivation.

Accept that it will take time for your brain and body to adjust. But don't worry about it. Nothing bad is happening, there is something marvellous happening. There is a transitional stage for any change that you make in your life. Even when that change is an improvement, there is an adjusting period. A better job, a better school, a better house or neighbourhood all necessitate an acclimatisation process. You might feel slightly disoriented for a short period, but you don't have to feel miserable.

Accept in advance that there will be moments when you are 'caught out'. The crucial factor is the moment immediately following. It can either be: "I can't or musn't have a cigarette" which is illogical and destructive, making you feel deprived and miserable. Alternatively it can be a moment of pleasure: "I'd forgotten, I'm free! I'm no longer the slave of these filthy things!" The choice is yours. Again, I emphasize that I am not asking you to see things through rose-coloured spectacles, but as they actually are.

In my younger days, it was shortage of money which triggered off my attempts to stop. In the latter years it was the debilitated state of my physical health and the fear of dying. Strangely, low as my state of physical health descended to, I received two greater gains from stopping, neither of which was I expecting, and both of which didn't occur to me until some months after I had stopped. One I mentioned earlier in this chapter: the 'STRAND' image. I had been convinced the cigarette was my crutch actually giving me courage and confidence. My biggest fear when considering quitting was: will I be able to cope without my crutch? I note that when writing 'EASYWAY', in the chapter about the fallacy of smoking relaxing and giving confidence, I found it necessary to write a mere half-page about this most important aspect of smoking. This was because, although it was a revelation to discover that the empty, insecure feeling of wanting a cigarette, far from being relieved by cigarettes, was actually caused by them, it hadn't dawned on me the extent to which smoking had destroyed my confidence in other aspects of my life. Smoking had taken away my strength. I emphasize that I am referring to mental and not physical strength. It might well be that the loss of my physical feeling of wellbeing contributed in part to the loss of mental strength. When I stopped smoking I regained that mental strength. Because of that strength, situations that would have appeared frightening or stressful were I still a smoker, no longer appear to be so. For that reason, I don't need to exercise courage. I'm in control! It was meeting a very mentally strong and famous nicotine addict that helped me fully to understand the situation.

People think of me nowadays as a seasoned radio and TV campaigner. I still find it a nerve-racking experience. Imagine my terror when my first appearance on national TV was to be interviewed by David Frost. I had watched and admired him over the years as he interviewed Presidents, Prime Ministers and other great people. I had never seen him flustered or out of control. My panic was counterbalanced by my burning desire to defeat smoking and this marvellous opportunity to spread my message.

Part of me was thinking: "Marvellous! He is the ideal vehicle to get my message across. He has this clinical type brain that can see through the cobwebs and cut through the red tape." The other part was thinking: "What if he starts to interrogate me? He's king of his profession. It would be like a flyweight in his first bout being matched against Mike Tyson.

I pride myself that I can tell whether someone is a smoker without actually seeing them smoke, purely from their complexion or mannerisms. I was fortunate that it wasn't until I appeared on the programme that I realised that David was himself a nicotine addict. How I had failed to notice the obvious symptoms previously, I do not know. I can only think that the excitement of getting onto the programme had blinkered me. He has the typical grey complexion and twitching hands of a confirmed nicotine addict.

Even during the programme, I only noticed those symptoms after he began to play devil's advocate. I thought: "Why is he doing this? Why is someone that normally argues so logically being so illogical?" It suddenly hit me. Hadn't I been listening to the same arguments nearly every day for the previous three years? I was listening to the weak, feeble excuses of a nicotine addict.

If I had known in advance that David was going to play devil's advocate, I do not believe that I would have had the courage to appear on the programme. Yet ironically, when it happened it had the opposite effect. I had pictured myself as the lamb being led to the slaughter. It suddenly dawned on me that I could have sat there all day without food or water, least of all nicotine. I looked at David's twitching hands. I was no longer looking at the king of the media, just another pathetic nicotine addict waiting for his next fix.

The incident that followed merely reinforced my impression. After the programme, David has a champagne breakfast. At the beginning of the breakfast he lit up a huge Havana cigar. The other people present couldn't stand the smell of this at the start of breakfast, no doubt they took the opportunity of my presence to give David some stick. He actually blushed, which I have never seen him do before or since, and in his embarrassment he turned to me and said: "By the way, I never inhale." I said: "In that case, you can save yourself a fortune by not lighting them." The other people at the table guffawed and David went bright pink. Just like the man on the yacht, he was a classic example of an otherwise physically and mentally very strong person being made to look like an idiot because he was addicted to nicotine.

In the next chapter, we will deal with the second great gain that I had not anticipated when I put out that final cigarette. The end of:

THE SLAVERY

CHAPTER 39

The Slavery

Health is by far the most common reason that smokers give for wanting to quit. Money comes a poor second. Occasionally a smoker will say: "I would like to be in control." This is something that annoyed and baffled me throughout my smoking years. I controlled every other aspect of my life. I hated the 'weed', yet still allowed it to control me. Even so, the extent of the slavery didn't sink in until months after I had quit. I was always aware of the feeling of dependence, but that was just annoyance because I couldn't quit. I'm now talking about how smoking tends to dominate and control practically every aspect of our lives, including our work, our hobbies, our eating habits, even the company we keep.

In fact I do not believe that health and money are even the greatest benefits that we receive from stopping smoking. I don't deny that those are the main reasons that motivate the majority of smokers, including me, to stop. I also wholeheartedly agree with those that believe that good health is the greatest of all assets.

I appear to have contradicted myself. How can I in one breath say that good health is the greatest of all assets and then in another say that it is not the main benefit from stopping smoking? The point is if the smoker is already healthy, and the majority of smokers believe that they are, what benefit do they gain by stopping?

Let me use myself as an example. Health and money were always my reason for stopping and usually in that order. But I hadn't actually contracted lung cancer or any other terminal disease, so it was only losing the fear of doing so that I gained by stopping. But, because of the 'blinkers' effect, I had no fear of contracting lung cancer anyway, so the gain was not apparent.

I was aware that I was wasting an enormous amount of money on cigarettes. However, money is only important to the quality of your life if you don't have enough to survive in reasonable comfort. If you have excess money, it not only can become a severe liability, but all too often actually does. The reason that many teenagers didn't get hooked on cigarettes is because they were lucky enough not to be able to afford them during that very vulnerable period in their lives. While you continue to see the cigarette as some sort of crutch or pleasure, you will regard the money as well spent. If you cannot afford to smoke, quitting can make the difference between a permanent financial struggle and living comfortably within your means plus a few luxuries, in which case the financial gain is both apparent and substantial.

It seems ludicrous for me, who spent over £100,000 in my lifetime on tobacco, to say that I got no financial advantage from stopping. I obviously did. But the fact is that I could afford those cigarettes and after I quit there was no great change in my life style. However, I get tremendous pleasure from being able to spend that money on genuine pleasures and to be rid of the self-despising that automatically went with knowing that I had been using it to destroy myself. The real sense of achievement, was not so much the improved health and wealth, which were great in themselves, but no longer having to regard myself as a mug or a slave.

The most incredible thing that I find about the smoking phenomenon, is that almost invariably, it defies normal logic. Logically, the great benefits I would obtain from stopping would be health and money in that order. Ironically the greatest benefits that I actually received were completely unexpected. Just like the child that would refuse to jump from the Empire State building, it is not possible to apportion points to each benefit. They are all interrelated. The extra energy is marvellous. So is the increase in my courage and confidence. The return of the 'joie de vivre'. From my mid-twenties I felt like an old man, now in my late fifties I feel like a young boy. What it all adds up to is an improved quality of life. Why even try to analyse it? Perhaps it does tend to create this feeling of 'Holier Than Thou', but don't knock it. It's a wonderful feeling! Sample it!

What more conspicuous and ridiculous sight is there than an ostrich, head stuck in the sand, believing that if it cannot see the danger, the danger doesn't exist. As intelligent human beings, we laugh at its stupidity and pity its ignorance. Yet that is exactly what we do as smokers. So intent are we on resisting all these people that are trying to make us quit, on searching for any flimsy excuse that will allow us to smoke just one more cigarette, that we just close our minds to the terrible evils of being a smoker as if they didn't exist. We cannot see the real enemy, we completely overlook what is probably the greatest evil of all:

THE SHEER SLAVERY!!

Have you noticed when smokers are questioned about why they smoke, their answers are usually negative. Not so much reasons why they do, but more often excuses of why they haven't stopped. Viz:

"I can afford it."

"It doesn't seem to affect my health."

"It's my only vice."

"You have to have some pleasures in life."

Now imagine you had received similar answers if you had asked the question: "Why do you play football?" I used to believe that if you could explode the myth of the flimsy excuses that smokers hid behind to justify their continued smoking, you could trigger them to want to stop. I remember a particular weekend before my friend Ronnie Stokes saw the light. He'd just survived a particularly severe bout of coughing. His friend, also a smoker, was commiserating with him:

"You'll get lung cancer the way you're going. Why don't you quit?"

"You're a smoker, why don't you quit?"

"I would if I had a cough like that."

I pointed out to the friend that the cough wasn't a disease, but merely the body's method of ejecting poison from the lungs, and that it was smokers that didn't cough that tended to get lung cancer. The look of horror on his face confirmed that he had understood the logic of my argument, however, the removal of his excuse didn't stop him smoking. But it did start him coughing.

The most extreme example was a chain-smoking member of my golf club. He was physically and mentally a very strong man and, even though well into his 60's, still one of the best golfers in the club. I cannot bear to watch the 'weed' destroying someone like that. I tried sowing little subtle seeds that would make him realise how nice it would be to be free of the weed. It had the reverse effect.

It was a typical example of Sod's law, just like courting a woman. You send flowers, you are attentive, courteous and respectful. She treats you like a doormat. The moment you take the hint and drop your attentions, she gives you the come-on. So it was with this man, no matter how subtle my approach, he sensed I was trying to get him to quit and on went the blinkers. No sooner had I given him up as a lost cause, than the situation reversed. Every time I visited the golf club, he would collar me and start telling me about the evils of smoking; as if *I* needed to know!

You have probably already surmised that I can no more resist trying to help smokers to quit, than a cat can resist purring when it's contented. I spend 90% of my waking life thinking about curing smokers, and the main reason that I visit my golf club nowadays, is not just to play golf, but to distract my mind from my obsession.

On this particular occasion he spent a good half hour telling me about the tribulations of being a smoker. At the time the last thing I wanted to talk about was smoking. I had already told the man on several previous occasions, that if he wanted help, all he needed to do was to book an appointment. I wasn't impolite. I patiently listened to all the points that he made against smoking, restricting my part in the dialogue to the occasional nod of agreement. Eventually he exhausted the subject and left my presence with the usual promise that he would visit me soon.

No sooner had he left than he returned. He said: "I've been thinking a lot about my smoking lately and I agree with everything that you say. It does absolutely nothing for me at all. The only consolation I have is that I smoke Truborg & Freyer. They might cost more than other cigarettes, but they are the best!" I said: "If I were a heroin addict and spent half an hour telling you of all the miseries of being a heroin addict, then concluded by saying that my only consolation was that I pay twice as much for my poison as anyone else, wouldn't you think of me as an even bigger idiot? He said: "You've taken away the last straw that I was clinging to."

I believed him, but he still didn't come to see me. The ending of the story has good news and bad news. The good news is that he has since stopped. The bad news is that he waited for a heart attack to provide the trigger and he looks a shadow of his former self. What's the moral of this story? It is that it's not enough to explode the myths and excuses that smokers use to justify their smoking. They do not continue to smoke because of the reasons that they give, it's the other way around, they merely concoct the reasons to justify the fact that they continue to smoke. Explode the particular myth that they were hiding behind, they will merely search for another. Explode all their myths, all you do is to strip them naked, it still won't stop them, they merely reach the stage that I reached:

I DON'T KNOW WHY I SMOKE! I'M A FOOL! I'M A JUNKY!

Some assessors of my system say: "Allen Carr logically reverses all the myths and excuses that smokers give to justify their smoking." That is true. But that doesn't in itself trigger smokers to want to stop. What triggers smokers to want to stop is the realisation that they need not be slaves to the weed, that they won't miss smoking. That they will enjoy life more and be better equipped to deal with stress, and that they don't have to go through some terrible trauma in order to escape.

For years I have been saying: "All smokers want to quit." Many people, both smokers and non-smokers alike dispute this fact. I have already explained why nicotine substitutes actually make it harder to stop. However, one of the interesting facts that emerged from the massive nicotine patch campaigns, was the number of smokers that were induced to try them. Where did they all suddenly appear from? If prior to the patch they had no intention of stopping, why should the patch have created such interest? Surely the only explanation is that they did in fact want to stop. That they were waiting for some magic pill that would enable them to get free, and that even though the nicotine patches turned out not to be the magic pill that smokers were all searching for, many smokers were prepared to risk hundreds of pounds in case it might be.

Ironically, that magic pill that smokers have been awaiting has been in existence almost ten years. But because they have been programmed to believe that it requires massive willpower to quit, and because they have failed to quit, they believe that they do not possess the necessary willpower. They are all searching for some magic pill or gimmick that will provide them with the boost that they need.

Do you remember the publicity that Boy George received a few years ago when he was attempting to quit heroin. He was being treated by a doctor who had invented a magic box that helped to relieve the withdrawal pangs. That doctor moved to America. I was very flattered to receive a letter from her telling me that she was using 'EASYWAY' to help smokers to quit. I was even more flattered when Boy George plugged 'EASYWAY' on British television sometime later.

At times I have wondered whether I slipped up with my method. It would have been a simple matter for me to have produced some electronic devise, or a harmless pill comprising a secret recipe that would miraculously remove the withdrawal pangs. I could have patented it and made millions. Far more than the purveyors of nicotine patches, because my system works and their's doesn't, and I would have had no competitors.

I didn't do that for one simple reason. We all have a magic pill or magic box that is a million times more potent and effective that anything any doctor or drug company has been able to devise. Do you know of a more effective weapon than the human brain? You don't need these gimmicks. My method combined with your brain will provide you with a magic pill a thousand times more effective than any of these other gimmicks even claim to be.

It didn't occur to me that I'd never enjoyed weddings as a smoker until months after I had quit. It was easily explained: weddings are a bore: the ceremony's always the same. "Doesn't the bride look absolutely beautiful?" And she does. No matter how plain and insignificant she is normally, she exudes warmth, beauty and personality. What's more, she is in complete control of the situation. Up until the wedding she was completely domineered by her mother. After the ceremony she firmly but politely instructs her mother to stop fussing and to shut up. Incredibly, she does!

For some strange reason, the ritual seems to have the complete opposite effect on the groom. Up until that point he has struck you as having unusual savoir-faire for one of such tender years. Now he appears to be a shy, inarticulate, awkward, clumsy wimp. You wonder what such a vivacious, young beauty can possibly see in him, and why you hadn't noticed his severe acne problem before now. As he promises to love and protect her you are convinced that it should be the other way around.

Nowadays, I love wedding ceremonies. They are exciting social occasions. Have wedding ceremonies changed? Of course they haven't. The only thing that has changed is that I don't now have to sit in the church thinking: "I'm not allowed to smoke. I can't wait to get out of here and light up." I'm no longer wishing half my life away suffering self-imposed penances just because I'm not allowed to smoke.

I reached a stage where, through lack of energy and oxygen, I would no longer swim. I would go to the Mediterranean with my friends and say: "Right, lets have a dip." After 5 minutes, I would say: "Okay, let's go back." My friends would say: "What's the rush? We've only been here 5 minutes." How could I explain to them that the rush was that I needed a cigarette and that I would feel stupid smoking in the sea? I'd return to the beach alone. Before I was even properly dry, the cigarette would be in my mouth, soggy and covered in sand. Such are the great pleasures of being a smoker.

You should bear in mind that this slavery aspect will get worse and worse. Every week the poor smoker is being attacked by some faction of society either trying to frighten them, humiliate them or just ban them from smoking. Both ostriches and smokers bury their heads in the sand out of fear. They are both faced with a threat that they feel incapable of handling. Their only answer is to pretend that the danger doesn't exist. Does the ostrich remove the danger by burying its head? Of course not. Does it even remove the fear? I don't know the answer to that, but I suspect it is no. After all, with its head buried in the sand, there cannot be much to take its mind off the fear. What I can tell you from personal experience, is that smokers remove neither the danger nor the fear by burying their heads.

Perhaps ostriches are not quite as stupid as we think they are. Perhaps their traditional enemy could outrun them but had poor eyesight and that the burying of the head was the ostrich's best form of defence. Perhaps smokers aren't quite as stupid as they appear to be either. Perhaps they close their minds to the horrors of nicotine addiction, not because of the horrors themselves, but in the belief that there is no escape from it. The nicotine patch campaign proved that if there is a chance of escape: smokers will make the attempt. It is a tragedy that once again they were hood-winked, and makes me more determined that they all find out about the method that will enable them to escape.

However, while smokers keep their heads in the sand, they guarantee their continued imprisonment. Their only real danger is their own ignorance. If they were but to take their head out of the sand, they would remove the ignorance, the addiction and the fear. Open your eyes! It's not people or society that creates your problem, it's the addiction to nicotine! Non-smokers don't have to worry whether they have sufficient cigarettes, or whether the aeroplane will be delayed on the runway, or whether the next person they meet is a smoker or a non-smoker. It's only the poor smokers that have this problem.

In a strange way smokers themselves are subconsciously beginning to fight the slavery. One of the anomalies of smoking is duty frees. The smoker would gladly take the quotient, plus the allocation of a non-smoker if they were lucky enough to obtain it. The smoker would sit there feeling smug: "I've saved at least £20." But another little voice would at the same time be saying: "Are you really going to put all that filth into your lungs? And, if you've saved £2O, what must they be costing you normally?" You think: "Never mind, after I have smoked these, I will definitely stop." They go far quicker than you thought they would. You think: "Well, I gave most of those away, I *will* stop, but now isn't the right time." And so the nightmare goes on.

Many smokers won't buy duty frees nowadays. They hope that they will have stopped before they'll smoke that many. This is the marvellous thing that is happening in society today. All smokers wish they hadn't started. It is not just attitudes and mannerisms that are changing, but the whole paraphernalia. Have you noticed how the expensive gold lighters are now being replaced by throwaways. When I was a boy, the standard 18th or 21st birthday present was an expensive cigarette case. Nowadays you rarely see them. All smokers are thinking short term. They hope that some day soon they'll wake up in the position that you will be in shortly:

FREE FROM THE WHOLE FILTHY NIGHTMARE

Every smoker is ashamed to be a smoker. They all wish that they had never started. Society generally regards smokers as weak-willed people. But the facts do not support this conclusion. On the contrary, smokers that persist tend to be dominant individuals, the type that do not like being controlled by other people. Neither do they like being controlled by a weed that they loathe and despise. I can't tell you how nice it is to be free from that slavery, that domination. To be able to look at other smokers, not with a feeling of envy or deprivation, but with a feeling of genuine pity, as you would look at any other drug addict. The greatest gain from being a non-smoker is not the health or money, but not to loathe and despise yourself, in other words:

TO BE FREE!

Smokers have many powerful reasons to stop throughout their smoking lives. In answer to the question: "Why do you want to quit?" They usually reply: "Health, money, dependency, filth or family." Ironically, the true reason that so many smokers have already quit and why the eventual death of smoking is guaranteed, is because smoking has now become anti-social. The only valid excuse we ever had to justify our smoking was:

IT'S A SOCIAL PROP

CHAPTER 40

It's A Social Prop

Nowadays most smokers themselves regard smoking as anti-social and often feel self-conscious smoking in the presence of non-smokers. However, how can I possibly rate the anti-social aspect above health as the main reason for the decline in smoking? Because although health is the main reason that we wish we didn't need to smoke, it doesn't help us to stop. It never seems to occur to the so-called experts, or to smokers themselves for that matter, that smokers do not smoke for reasons that they shouldn't smoke, but for the reasons that they do. If smokers stop for health reasons, they feel that they are being forced to *give up* their crutch or pleasure. This makes them feel deprived and merely increases the feeling of sacrifice. Sooner or later, they end up back in the trap.

"To be sociable" was often the reply that smokers gave when asked why they smoked. In fact it never was the reason, merely their excuse to justify behaviour they knew to be illogical. However, the reason that the anti-social aspect is so effective in the fight against the weed, is that it forces smokers to look at the right side of the tug of war. Not why we shouldn't smoke, but why we do smoke. It has made them realise that they no longer enjoy even those special cigarettes. They think they no longer enjoy them because it's now anti-social. In fact they never did enjoy them, the anti-social aspect just makes sure that whether they like it or not, from now on they can't even suffer the illusion of enjoying them. It has helped them to realise that they are and always were:

MISERABLE PATHETIC DRUG ADDICTS

We know that we shouldn't smoke and don't really understand why we have to. We just know that we do have to and therefore our main problem is to find some plausible excuse to justify our stupidity. The problem is that the usual reasons that we give do not stand up to even a cursory interrogation:

"I enjoy the taste."

"You mean that you actually eat them?"

410

"It gives me something to do with my hands."

"So why do you light it?"

"It's oral satisfaction."

"You mean you haven't been weaned yet? It's really just a dummy?"

However, a few years ago: "It's a social prop" was a very difficult excuse to contradict. After all in those days the cigarette was the badge of the tough guy or the sophisticated lady. Didn't we all get started anyway because our friends or colleagues smoked? To pass the cigarettes around, or offer a light, was a very useful social ice-breaker when meeting strangers.

The truth is that smoking never was a social prop. In fact it would be hard to conceive of a pastime more anti-social than smoking. But how on earth did we ever get to the stage where society actually considered there to be something remotely sociable in polluting the atmosphere with poisonous fumes? Even smokers themselves complain about the suffocating effects of a smoke-filled room. Non-smokers have always regarded that atmosphere, in addition to being anti-social, as unhealthy and extremely offensive.

If you were to emit a volley of farts in a restaurant, the most lenient of poetic licenses would not allow you to interpret that as sociable behaviour, whether it be before, during or after the meal. If the emissions were deliberate, you would be asked to leave. Even if they were accidental it would be regarded as exceedingly bad manners. Apart from a group of schoolboys, I can only think of one possible scenario whereby polite, sensitive and considerate adults would regard continual farting in a public place as sociable behaviour: if they had insufficient control over their bodily functions, or found that they just could not enjoy the meal unless they were allowed to fart.

No, even then it would be regarded as extremely anti-social. However, supposing the majority of the population had exactly the same problem? Supposing it became the norm, the acceptable behaviour? Is it possible that the non-farters could be regarded as weirdos, even anti-social? After all, in certain societies it is regarded as being impolite to your host unless you emit a large belch after the meal. Even so, it takes some imagination to visualise farting in a restaurant as ever possibly being regarded as sociable behaviour.

Future generations will find it equally difficult to visualise that smoking could ever possibly have been regarded as sociable behaviour. Just as I find it difficult to imagine how snuff-taking was once regarded as sociable. My only memory of it was of my maternal granny, in fact it is the only vivid memory that I still retain of her, unfortunately it is not a very pleasant one.

Genuine sociable behaviour involves people meeting, either for the pleasure of social intercourse for its own sake, or because they share similar interests. Music lovers will visit concerts together to enhance their mutual pleasure. Anglers and golfers will plan outings to picturesque locations for the same reason. Smokers might huddle together because they feel less stupid, but can you imagine someone within a group of smokers saying: "Tell you what, why don't we have a day out at Brighton? It really is a super town to have a smoke."

Heroin addicts regard it as 'sociable' to share a syringe, in spite of the fact that they often catch very 'unsociable' diseases by so doing. The real meaning of sociable behaviour is promoting companionship. Golfers, anglers and similar people of like interests might band together to form clubs and societies in order to enhance the enjoyment of their pleasure or pastime, but, apart from FOREST which is phoney, and opium dens which are insidious, have you ever heard of a band of smokers organising smoking parties? The reason drug addicts tend to stick together is the same reason that all people sharing the same problems stick together: they don't feel quite so isolated if there are others on the sinking ship. A problem shared is a problem halved.

Have you ever been to a social function where someone has tried to persuade you not to drink? I'm not referring to those occasions when your spouse, or anyone else for that matter, is trying to convince you that you've already drunk enough. I mean has a complete stranger ever approached you and said: "Please don't drink any alcohol you'll be acting unsociably if you do?" I've never heard of a single occasion. But I've many times seen the reverse situation, when someone having politely refused an alcoholic drink, is then accused of being a 'party pooper' or of just being unsociable. It doesn't seem to matter if the person happens to be a teetotaller or an ex-alcoholic and that their whole future happiness, even their very life might depend on their not taking that drink. The pusher still looks at them in complete disbelief, as if it were they and not the pusher, that was acting in a completely irrational and unsociable way.

Why do otherwise intelligent, pleasant and rational human beings act in this way? It's because there is all the difference in the world between acting stupidly and feeling stupid. Drinkers know that when they've had too much to drink, they'll start acting stupidly. So what? Providing everyone else is acting stupidly, it doesn't matter. But if there's just one sober person present, the inebriates will not only act stupidly, but will feel stupid. So it is with smoking. As smokers we know we are stupid. So what? We're all in it together. But the last thing we need in the company is one of those patronising non-smokers, secretly despising us, making us feel uncomfortable, making us feel stupid.

I have mentioned that I regarded non-smokers as a different breed. In hindsight, I can think of a few pleasant, interesting people that I would have developed a deeper friendship with had they been smokers. But I felt both stupid and unclean in their presence. To their credit, they gave no indication that they were secretly despising me. Whether they were or not is immaterial. I suspected that they were and felt uncomfortable in their presence. Was that their fault or mine? I suggest it was neither. The situation only arose because I was hooked on the weed.

Again, this unsociable aspect about smoking didn't occur to me until some time after I had quit. In fact it didn't occur to me until I started getting the same treatment from smoking friends. I am fortunate in having several lifelong friends. If you ask them, they'll confirm that I am not the most tolerable person they have ever met. Yet the friendship, for whatever reason, has withstood, not only the test of time, but whatever shortcomings that I possess.

Since I became a non-smoker, I have lost several friendships that I regarded as valuable. You will undoubtedly conclude that it was because I became one of those holier-than-thou ex-smokers. I assure you that is not the case. I know that the one certainty to keep a smoker smoking is to try to force them to stop. On the contrary, some non-smokers attack me because I encourage smokers to smoke in my company. Can it be just coincidence that the friends that I lost were all smokers? After all, if we are not capable of seeing ourselves as we really are as smokers, can we bear the thought of being seen by a friend as we really are?

Whenever I walk into my golf club, out of the corner of my eye I see about three people immediately stub out a cigarette. Now this isn't my problem, this is one of the problems that smokers suffer the whole of their lives. Didn't I suffer enough aggravation from personal inconvenience and persecution during all those years as a nicotine addict? Must I now be ostracized for the rest of my life because I am no longer one?

People often say to me: "Are there any disadvantages in stopping smoking?" I can reply hand over heart: "Absolutely none." But didn't I lose those friends because I stopped smoking? Definitely not! I confess unashamedly that I miss those friends, especially the dearest of them who has since died in his prime because he was a smoker. But I didn't lose those friends because I escaped from the pit, I lost them because they were still in it. The only thing that causes a divide between smokers and non-smokers is smoking. If there were no such thing as smoking:

THERE WOULD *BE* NO DIVIDE

Some so-called experts not only advise you to avoid smoking situations when you stop smoking, but to actually change your friends. Please don't do this. It's bad enough to have this evil in our society anyway, it's bad enough that smokers and non-smokers subconsciously avoid each other. It's bad enough that it takes our health, our money, our energy, our freedom, our dignity, even our very lives, but to take our friends as well? That is surely too high a price to pay!

Apart from the self-imposed segregation that smokers and non-smokers alike subject themselves to, they are now compulsorily segregated in restaurants and on buses and trains. Segregation and sociability are direct opposites. Even if smoking were not a filthy and disgusting pastime, to describe it as sociable behaviour, is about as sensible as describing apartheid as sociable behaviour.

Why is smoking now generally regarded as anti-social? What's actually changed? Smoking itself hasn't changed. If anything, the filters, other refinements and the higher proportion of non-smokers, has caused the accumulated offence of tobacco excretion to be far less than it used to be. Only one thing has changed, not smoking itself, but the attitude of our society. It has changed for one reason only: non-smokers are now the majority. No longer do they have to sit in silence feeling that they are abnormal. It is now the smokers who are the weirdos.

No longer is the cigarette the badge of the tough guy or the sophisticated lady. Today it is an open declaration of someone that has failed to stop, or is too frightened even to try. On his questionnaire, the man on the yacht gave his reason for stopping as health. But he knew that smoking was adversely affecting his health for years. What actually triggered his attempt to stop was the incident on the yacht. He felt humiliated. Just as Joyce enabled me to look at myself as non-smokers saw me, what triggered him, was not that the non-smoker saw him as pathetic, but he was enabled to see himself as pathetic.

Some of the most tragic and most amusing stories we hear at the clinics are those that trigger off an attempt to stop, some isolated incident that enables the smoker to see smoking in its true light. The one that I found the most pathetic was of a young man who was doing the modern thing by being present at his child's birth:

"My wife was having an awful time in labour. After about two hours I couldn't take any more. I had to nip out for a smoke. She pleaded with me not to leave her, but you know how it is. The only place you were allowed to smoke in this hospital was a sort of circular stairwell at the back. I don't know whether it was hospital policy not to clean them up, but the floor was ankle deep in dog-ends. I was puffing away, feeling guilty and pretty low, when I heard this woman come panting up the stairs. She was struggling to breathe and clearly due to give birth any day. Yet she had this cigarette stuck in her mouth and looked the typical 'Fag Ash Lil'. I was disgusted. Then it hit me. There was my wife going through the most terrifying experience of her life, all because of me, and at the time she most needed me, what was I doing? To think I had the gall to be despising this other woman. I made up my mind there and then to come and see you."

Another classic case was of a man attending a parent/teachers association meeting:

"I had virtually no education, but I was so proud when my lad was accepted at this particular school. In fact I do two jobs to afford to keep him there. There were about 50 of us seated close together in this classroom. I was the only smoker there, and needless to say, there were no ashtrays. The meeting seemed endless, and when I finally got outside and lit up, my wife asked me what I thought of the various suggestions. It suddenly dawned on me that I had been so obsessed with not being able to smoke, that I hadn't taken in a word of what had been said."

In all probability, there were several other smokers at that meeting, all believing that they were the only smoker present, all going through the same experience. Another incredible incident was of a smoker that got on a London underground train in a non-smoking compartment. This was in the days when there was just one smoking compartment on the train. He said:

"At each stop I gradually worked my way down to the smokers compartment. When I finally reached it there were very few people in the compartment. I struck up a conversation with a very pleasant old lady who must have been over 80. I offered her a cigarette which she declined explaining she was a non-smoker. The floor was covered in dog-ends and even I was feeling a bit nauseated by the smell of stale tobacco. I asked her why on earth she sat in the smokers' compartment? She explained that it was the only carriage in which she could get a seat! It suddenly dawned on me that the other compartments had been very crowded and that even the smokers couldn't stand the filth and stench of the smokers compartment!"

It was probably not so much the filth and stench that the smokers couldn't stand, as having to admit that they were part of a dying breed. That isolated smokers' compartment made them feel that, even if they're not exactly in a condemned cell, they were certainly in a miniature leper colony.

A famous actress that sought my help told me that she had great difficulty in conceiving a child. After years of painful experimentation she produced a beautiful baby. She described how she was driving down the centre lane of a motorway. The baby sleeping securely in a back-seat harness. She threw a lighted dog-end out of the window. A few moments later the baby started to cry. She assumed that the baby had merely woken up. Then she saw flames flickering in the rear-view mirror. The baby's shawl was alight. She instinctively veered towards the hard shoulder. There was a screech of breaks, another car was nearly level with her in the nearside lane. Fortunately the driver reacted quickly and avoided a collision by following her into the hard shoulder. She quickly removed the baby's shawl, the baby's burns were superficial. The fire had been caused by the dog-end.

I enquired whether it was that incident that triggered off her decision to consult me. She explained that she thought the incident itself would have been sufficient to stop her smoking, but the incredible thing was, that when the crisis was over, the first thing she did was to light a cigarette. In fact there was nothing unusual about it, any smoker would have done the same in those circumstances. She said: "I decided that if that incident didn't make me quit, I must be beyond redemption, and frankly, I don't see how you can help me." I can sympathise with that lady, I *knew* I would die from smoking, but that didn't stop me.

I've said that I've yet to meet a smoker who thought they were more hooked than I was. I never smoked in the bath, although I have heard of many smokers that regard a smoke in the bath with a glass of champagne as the height of luxury. A recent client told me he actually smoked in the shower with a protective hand held over the cigarette. A tall story perhaps, but knowing smokers as I do, I believe him.

Ironically,the medical profession can take credit for planting the seed that eventually made society see what it had previously regarded as social behaviour, as highly anti-social. Just as the 'DON'T DRINK AND DRIVE' campaign changed society's attitude to forcing alcoholic drinks onto people that didn't really want them, so it was the link between smoking and lung cancer that changed society's attitude towards smoking.

Up until the cancer scares, smokers knew that they were mugs, that it made them lethargic and breathless. However, provided they were not literally gasping for breath or couldn't afford to smoke, they were quite prepared to put up with that, together with all the other disadvantages of being a smoker, for the greater crutch or pleasure that they thought they were getting.

But 'LUNG CANCER'! The words still send shivers down my spine. From that point on, all smokers wished that they had never started and made a conscious decision to stop in the not too distant future. Many smokers stopped there and then. It was probably the ones that had already reached the depth of degradation that I finally descended to. Like me, they probably already knew that it was killing them, the 'lung cancer' revelation was merely the 'Jump Start' that triggered them to make the attempt.

However, I and the vast majority of smokers had not reached that stage. Even years later, when I watched my father finally released from the misery of that dreaded disease, it still didn't sink in. I made a firm vow that I would never smoke again. That vow was broken the moment I left the hospital. The same vow was broken on numerous subsequent occasions until I finally saw the light.

Although the cancer scares had no more effect on most smokers than telling teenagers that motor cycles can kill them, it did have the effect of changing society's attitude towards smoking from a perfectly sociable pleasure or crutch, albeit one that it was filthy, expensive and debilitating, to the cause of an horrendous disease. The important effect was for the first time to make smokers want to stop. Unfortunately, the scare itself was insufficient to stop most of them, but now a real flaw appeared in what had previously been a flawless trap. Up to that point the whole trap had been designed to ensure that smokers blocked their minds to reasons that they shouldn't smoke, and concentrated exclusively on the reasons that they should.

The great effect of the cancer scares was to make many smokers remove the rose-coloured spectacles and to start seeing smoking as it actually was. Not only is this social aspect important because it was the only, or appeared to be the only, genuine advantage of being a smoker, but it is also important in obtaining the necessary frame of mind to remain a happy non-smoker for the rest of your life. Start observing and listening to smokers objectively. I don't just mean at the times when they are coughing and spluttering, but also on those really special occasions when they are supposed to be enjoying those cigarettes.

Consider this conversation between two of my companions in a recent golf match:

"Why do you smoke?"

"I don't smoke much."

"You've been chain-smoking cigars throughout the round. You even keep it in your mouth when you play your shot."

"Cigars aren't nearly as bad as cigarettes. Anyway, I can go months at a time without smoking at all."

It took enormous restraint for me to stay out of the conversation. The non-smoker seemed satisfied with the replies. I was pleased about this because I was sympathising with the smoker. Ten years ago it could have been me giving the illogical replies. To his credit, he didn't visibly squirm, but I knew what was going on in his mind.

The point is, had I stopped by using the willpower method, far from feeling sorry for that smoker, I would have been envying him. My thoughts would have been: "You lucky so and so. You can smoke during this round of golf but I'm not allowed to, and you can actually go for months without smoking at all? Some people have everything."

My actual silent thoughts were:

"Why do you say you don't smoke much when you are clearly a chain-smoker?"

"Why do you never answer the question that you've been asked?"

417

"Why did you say cigars are less harmful than cigarettes? Wasn't it like replying to a question: why do you keep banging your head on the floorboards? – It's much less painful than banging it on the wall!"

"Why do you boast that you can go months without smoking at all? You didn't seem to be unduly proud of the fact that you could also go months smoking. If you believe that going months without smoking is something to be proud of, why do you smoke?"

"Why do you smoke?" was the original question. The most frustrating song that was ever written is: 'There's a hole in my bucket'. It's obvious from the second line that it will be impossible to repair the hole without obtaining water, and that it is impossible to obtain water while you have a hole in your bucket, but still you have to go through the whole monotonous, cumbersome cycle. You'll go round the same interminable cycle if you ask smokers why they smoke.

I was in a restaurant about 4 Christmases ago. It was midnight and everyone had finished eating. Not one person was smoking. I couldn't believe it. I asked the waiter: "Is this a non-smoking restaurant?" He said: "No". A few minutes later, someone at a corner table lit up. Like a series of beacons, smokers at other tables began to light up. They had all been sitting there hoping that someone would pluck up enough courage to be the first.

Have you noticed how smokers' behaviour has changed in restaurants in recent years? Many now don't smoke between courses. When they do light up, they not only apologise to non-smokers on the same table, but cast furtive glances around the restaurant to make sure that as least one other person is smoking.

Another common smoking situation that forces smokers to take their heads out of the sand is flying. They have the dubious choice between not being allowed to smoke, or having to declare to everyone within earshot that they are nicotine junkies. Many smokers find abstinence the lesser of the two evils. Even if you are prepared to go through the hassle of trying to obtain a smoking seat in the first place, you find that the poor smoker is being crammed further and further towards the back of the aircraft. They have those ridiculous little ashtrays, and even if they aren't full of toffee papers, unless you're double-jointed, it's impossible to use them without breaking your wrists. There are never sufficient smokers' seats, yet the latest state of the art computer always manages to allocate one of those precious seats to a non-smoker. What's more, it's always the seat next to yours. Just as cats instinctively make a beeline for the lap of a person that is allergic to them, so, no matter how much you fiddle with the air-flow knob, the smoke from your cigarette shoots straight up the nostrils of the non-smoker. He stares straight at you while trying to flap the smoke away with his hand. But he doesn't complain. That's the most infuriating part of all. The lifetime's accumulated frustration caused by the indignities that you have had to suffer in silence over the years from all those previous supercilious non-smokers like him, is building up inside you like a volcano about to erupt. This time you are within your rights. You have all the arguments ready. You are dying to vent all that frustration on him, willing him to say just one word.

But he is far too shrewd for that. His ears are still ringing from the last time he was rude enough to complain about being legally gassed. So what do you do? You make out that you haven't even noticed him. You sit staring fixedly ahead, as if the back of the seat in front of you is more fascinating than the ceiling of the Sistine Chapel. You tolerate the situation, stubbornly believing that you are obtaining some genuine pleasure. Then comes the moment you really need a cigarette, be it take off or landing: "Please extinguish your cigarette." It's typical, if you are allowed to smoke you wish you didn't, and when you really need to, you are not allowed to.

The great mystery about smoking when you do get free and look back over your smoking life is: where was all the great pleasure? In fact there is none, it's just a lifetime of slavery, embarrassment, persecution, degradation and deprivation. It's a mistake to assume that smokers enjoy smoking even the so-called special cigarettes. Notice that they only appear to be happy and cheerful when they are not conscious that they are smoking, and that once they become aware of it, they tend to look uncomfortable and become apologetic.

Incidentally, social occasions are the times to observe casual smokers. These characters that assure you they only smoke about 5 a day. They'll chain smoke 5 while you are talking to them. You say: "I thought you only smoked 5 a day?" "Oh, I sometimes smoke more at social functions". Yes, don't we all. Observe how quickly the cigarette burns. No sooner do they light one than they are stubbing it out. Notice how quickly the smoker lights the next one and how even the process of lighting up appears to be subconscious. Observe that the moment the cigarette has been lit, the smoker is no longer aware of smoking it.

Even the mannerisms of smokers are changing nowadays. A few years ago you would find nine strapping young men in a pub, brazenly breathing clouds of cigarette smoke into the atmosphere. The tenth member of the group, a non-smoker, would appear the odd man out. Now the minority smokers have the cigarette cupped in their hand or behind their back. Lately, I have seen smokers flick ash into their hand, their matchbox, their pocket or even their trouser turn-up, because they were ashamed to ask for an ashtray.

I believe the whole anti-social trend was encapsulated at a party that I attended about a year ago. The host and hostess were both non-smokers. But they had done the proper thing and the house was liberally sprinkled with ashtrays. As each guest arrived I was trying to assess whether they were smokers or non-smokers. Half the guests had already arrived and strangely, none were smoking or even appeared to be smokers.

Eventually a lady arrived with her husband. She wasn't actually smoking, but had the agitated, hounded appearance which typifies smokers that are under attack. I discovered later that her husband was an HTT ex-smoker and was making her life a continual misery because he had quit and she hadn't. Her furrowed brow disappeared when she saw the ashtrays, only to reappear immediately when she realised that not a single person in the room was actually smoking.

As I discreetly observed this lady, she too began to examine each new arrival, desperately hoping that one would be a fellow smoker. For ages, she appeared to be the only smoker present, or if there were others, nobody wanted to be the first to light up. Eventually she cracked. She was standing in the centre of the room amongst a small group of people. She opened her handbag revealing a packet of Silk Cut. In the old days she would have asked if anybody smoked and probably half the packet would have disappeared in one offering. Instead she timidly proffered it without even taking it out of her bag. No one in the group accepted the offer. Then from about ten feet away, another lady suddenly appeared, how she even saw the offer I do not know. She said: "Thank goodness, I thought I was the only smoker here." She was a Marlboro smoker, but lit up the Silk Cut without hesitation.

They spent the rest of the evening glued together in the centre of the room, alternately offering and accepting each others cigarettes. Now Marlboro smokers will confirm that they would rather smoke cotton wool than Silk Cut. Equally, Silk Cut smokers would rather smoke camel dung than Marlboro. I presume that a combination of politeness and sheer gratitude in finding a fellow smoker superseded the choice. As it happened, all the ashtrays were situated on the outskirts of the room. Every few moments, one of these ladies would nip over to an ashtray. No sooner had she returned than her fellow conspirator would do the same. I would love to have been able to present them with a speeded up Benny Hill type video showing how they had actually spent their evening.

Another recently divorced client at our Birmingham clinic epitomised the whole situation:

"My matchmaking friend got all excited because at the previous night's party, I had spent practically the whole evening locked in conversation with a man that she had introduced me to. She was clearly piqued when I informed her that I found him boring, priggish and physically repulsive. 'Well no one forced you to monopolise him!' She was absolutely right. It puzzled me. Not only why I had in fact stayed with him, but why I hadn't asked myself that obvious question.

The conclusion that I came to frightened me. I stayed with him for one reason alone: he was a fellow smoker. He could have been Dr. Crippen, Dracula or Quasimodo! It wouldn't have mattered, just so long as he was a smoker!"

When you extinguish that final cigarette, you will find that your smoking friends and colleagues will fall into two distinct categories. The first I referred to earlier: the ones that blow smoke in your face, perpetually remind you of the pleasures of being a smoker and continue to offer you cigarettes in the pretence they have forgotten that you've quit. Why do even relatives and good friends become so unpleasant and vindictive in these circumstances?

The first thing that you need to realise is that you are dealing with the fear and panic of a drug addict. All aggression is based on fear. The great advantage of panic is that it enables us to place our own survival above all else. The great disadvantage of panic is that because we are oblivious to all else other than our own survival, we commit acts of which we are ashamed for the rest of our lives.

Those smokers aren't really being vindictive at such times. Their remarks aren't even aimed at you. They are merely trying to justify their own stupidity. Remember, all smokers lie. Let us examine more closely that situation I described in the previous chapter, when you automatically reach for the cigarette and your friend reminds you that you no longer smoke. Why was it that they only remembered that you had stopped smoking, not before they offered you the cigarette, not after you accepted it, but in the split second it took for you to reach out for it? Isn't this too much of a coincidence? That makes you feel even more annoyed, because you sense that they hadn't forgotten and deliberately set you up.

You are correct in sensing that they hadn't forgotten, but they were not guilty of deliberately trying to set you up. Look at the situation from the smoker's point of view. Smoking is now generally regarded as disgusting and unsociable. Today, the strong person is the one that has kicked it, that is no longer dependent on the weed, and the smoking ship is regarded more as a leper colony than a luxury cruise. Millions of smokers have already escaped from it. Smokers feel a little bit like the rats who remain on the sinking ship: terrified that they will soon be the only one left on board.

When you leave that sinking ship, your smoking friends and acquaintances will regard you as a deserter. They won't really blame you for that. They wish that they had the courage to join you. Nevertheless, you will have joined the millions that have already escaped and those remaining in the prison will feel even more stupid, isolated and vulnerable.

Not only are they feeling a little bit envious, but you haven't helped the situation by labouring the point of how nice it is to be a non-smoker and free. They were expecting you to be whining and miserable, instead you are happy and cheerful. They had probably resolved to support your effort by not smoking in your presence, but they are now beginning to suspect that you are gloating over them. Now this is one of the very situations when smokers most need a cigarette: the times when they can't have one.

They hang on until they can hold out no longer. They are desperate to light up, but are feeling weak and embarrassed because they failed to carry out their resolve and don't want to draw attention to themselves. So they wait until they sense that you have forgotten about the subject. To complete the delusion they have to pretend that they had forgotten as well and they offer you a cigarette just as they always do. Then their little ruse backfires on them. To their horror, you start to reach for it. They now suffer the typical drug addict's schizophrenia. Their choice is either to let you light that cigarette, in which case, they will have been the direct cause of your downfall, or to embarrass you by reminding you that you no longer smoke. Because they really love you, they choose the lesser of the two evils.

So why do they compound their felony by laughing at you and then telling you how much they enjoy their cigarettes? They are not laughing at you. You only think they are because you were momentarily caught out and felt embarrassed. But they feel far more embarrassed than you do. Their clever little subterfuge has backfired on them. That stupid grin on their face is occasioned by their own embarrassment, not yours, and their arguments about the pleasures of smoking are designed to justify their own stupidity and not to convince you: they know as well as you do that their arguments are phoney.

Once you can understand the fear that makes these otherwise pleasant people act as they do, they have completely the reverse effect on you. You sense that they are not normally unpleasant or vindictive people, and that the reason for their strange behaviour, is not that they are trying to harm you, but because they are frightened. The effect is actually to help you and make you feel even more grateful that you have left the sinking ship.

The dangerous smokers are the considerate ones. The type that knows the misery that you are going through and are doing everything within their power to help and encourage you. This type is considerate enough to actually succeed in not smoking in your presence. This can be exceedingly frustrating. You are dying for them to offer you a cigarette, so you can have the pleasure of saying: "I don't need them any more."

However, the most disarming thing of all, is that they're proving to you that they can take them or leave them. They are not like you, completely dependent on the drug. They are quite happy not to smoke in your presence. Have you noticed how many such smokers there are nowadays? "I wouldn't dream of smoking in the company of non-smokers." Why weren't they so considerate 10 years ago? But just as smokers say: "My favourite cigarette is the one after a meal" although it doesn't appear to make the slightest difference whether they smoke before or during the meal, so you need to question the smokers that claim they wouldn't dream of smoking in the presence of non-smokers. What they actually mean is: "I wouldn't dream of smoking in the presence of non-smokers, provided I am the only smoker there." Watch a situation in which you have 10 smokers and only one non-smoker. Not one of those smokers will give a damn whether the non-smoker finds it offensive or not.

The greatest help that non-smokers could give smokers when they politely enquire whether they object to their smoking, is not to say: "Please don't smoke. I find the smell offensive." But: "Thank you for enquiring. Yes I do find the smell offensive, but I am also aware that you are addicted to nicotine and really have no control over your smoking. So please feel free to smoke." You will find that there is no force on earth that will make that smoker smoke. Even if they don't have to prove to you they don't have to smoke, they will have to prove it to themselves.

Don't be hoodwinked by these smokers that convince you that they can take them or leave them. They say the biggest sucker to fall for a smooth-talking salesman, is another salesman. All smokers go through this process of convincing themselves and other people that they don't need to smoke. Remember the man on the yacht? He convinced his host and himself that he didn't need to smoke. Younger smokers will visit their unsuspecting parents for the whole weekend and not even think about lighting up. Smokers can sit throughout the entire performance at a theatre without smoking. They will go on a long-distance flight and not smoke. They will go into hospital for all of three weeks and not smoke. What's more, they always seem so surprised and pleased with themselves about such feats, that they find it necessary to boast about them.

I find no need to brag because I can abstain from lobster. So surely, their only reason for boasting is that they suspect that they are trapped, and that their short period of parole helps them to believe that they could stop, provided of course they really needed to, or wanted to. This is another subtlety of the trap that won't allow us to accept that we are really hooked: the fact that we are capable of going long periods of abstinance without undue aggravation, and, as we have shown, cigarettes appear to be more precious after a period of abstinence.

Does the fact we can go long periods of abstinence really prove that we are in control? We overlook the point that the only reason that we went through the period of abstinence, was not that we could take them or leave them, but because we weren't allowed to smoke during the period of abstinence. The fact that the ban was self-imposed doesn't alter the situation. What did the man on the yacht do the moment he left it? Why are the smoking theatre-goers in such a panic to reach the bar during the interval? What is the first thing smokers do when leaving their unsuspecting parents, or the hospital, or the flight or any other place where they aren't allowed to smoke? They immediately light a cigarette. Far from proving smokers are in control, these periods of abstinence merely demonstrate the complete opposite:

THAT THEY ARE DRUG ADDICTS

Now, back to these considerate smokers. The ones that don't try to tempt you, that make you feel that they can take it or leave it. Don't just take them on face value. They too are left on the sinking ship and feel just as vulnerable as the other type. In fact, because they are more subtle and intelligent than the other type, they are probably feeling even more vulnerable. Don't be fooled by them. They do not refrain from smoking in your presence to help you, but because they do feel so vulnerable. They are merely trying to prove to you, and to themselves, that they are in control and can take them or leave them.

In fact, there is no basic difference between the two types, the apparent difference was that the vindictive type cracked in your presence and the considerate type didn't. But if you understand and observe both types closely, you will realise that they are going through exactly the same nightmare. They will soon start to feel uncomfortable. They'll start to get the smoker's twitch. If they are really desperate, they will find some excuse to leave your presence. If they remain for any length of time they will begin to fiddle with the packet or their lighter. You might find that they keep forgetting and start to reach subconsciously for a cigarette.

Look for these signs. Say to them:

"Look, I really appreciate your not smoking in my company, and I fully understand your motives. But noble as they obviously are, it's completely uneccessary. It's me who has stopped smoking not you. Surely you wouldn't expect a non-smoker to feel obligated to smoke in your presence just because you did. So I don't expect you to stop smoking just because I have. If you smoke, it won't bother me in the slightest. I quit because I didn't enjoy being a smoker and I'm very happy to be a non-smoker, but I know how much you enjoy a cigarette, you have always smoked in my presence and you will embarrass me if you no longer do so."

You have now turned the tables. Instead of that smoker feeling that he or she was showing sympathy for, or consideration to you, the boot is on the other foot. Now those smokers find themselves in a very awkward position. By now they are really desperate for a cigarette, and since they enjoy smoking and you have made it quite clear that they are actually causing you embarrassment by not smoking, logically they should light up immediately. Yet strangely, they seem even more determined not to smoke and will try to pass it off with some comment like: "No, it really doesn't bother me, I can take them or leave them."

Continue to observe them. You'll find that they appear to be fascinated by your every word, as if you were the greatest wit since Oscar Wilde. In truth, they'll not be hearing a single word. Instead, they will be trying to figure out how to escape from the impasse that they find themselves in. They either light up and lose face, or they don't light up and feel utterly miserable. It's the same dilemma that all drug addicts suffer throughout their lives. That is, if they remain addicted. It's a case of:

HEADS THEY DON'T WIN! TAILS THEY LOSE!

Surely it's not *throughout* their addicted lives, but just at isolated times? No, it's throughout their addicted lives. Most of our smoking lives we are able to block our minds to it, the isolated times are the occasions that we find ourselves forced into facing up to our dilemma, but the black shadow is there throughout our smoking lives.

If you feel particularly vindictive towards your friend, continue to watch them squirm. When they believe that you are so absorbed with your dialogue that you won't notice, they will very, very slowly start to reach for a cigarette. Often they will ask questions at this stage. The object of the ploy is to distract your attention, hoping that you won't even notice. The snail's pace is a bit of insurance in case you have noticed. They are trying to give the impression that there is no panic, that the cigarette is of no real significance, the really important thing is your fascinating story.

For the same reason, they don't light the cigarette immediately. On the contrary, it often remains unlit for several minutes and is prominently displayed and actually used like an index finger to punctuate their conversation. You've possibly observed this same ritual being displayed in restaurants, or at social functions by the first smoker to light up. Why do smokers need to go through this ritual? After all, if you fancy a cigarette, why not just light up? Because in such situations, smokers find it necessary to display that they are in control. What they're really trying to convey to anyone present is: "Look, I'm not a junky, I can take these things or leave them, it must be obvious to you that I'm in no panic to light up." To the discerning observer, they merely confirm the reverse. It's all part of the slavery of being a drug addict. Once the cigarette has been lit, it ceases to be prominently displayed, in fact it often disappears under the table or behind the smoker's back.

If you do not have the stomach to watch your friend undergo this ritual, find an excuse to leave the room for a moment and give the smoker an opportunity to light up. If you have sadistic tendencies, after you have closed the door, count up to five then whip it open again and you will actually catch that smoker in the process of lighting up. However there will be no semblance of being laid-back about the ritual. On the contrary, there will be an air of panic. In fact if you count up to five, more times than not, the cigarette will already be lit when you open that door.

I'm not a particularly keen observer. I only know about most of these things because I was doing them myself for years. The trouble is, that while you remain in the trap, you so concentrate on being devious, that you lose sight of the fact that the only person that you actually fool is yourself.

Many so-called experts will advise you to avoid social functions for a period until you feel strong enough to resist the temptation. This is all part of the doom and gloom of the willpower method. Get it clearly into your mind, you are not giving up anything. You are ridding your mind and body of a terrible disease. What's more, you are achieving several substantial, positive gains. You have merely stopped smoking. That doesn't mean:

THAT YOU HAVE TO STOP LIVING!

Just the opposite. Life is marvellous and infinitely more so when you don't smoke. Attend social functions straight away. Remember social functions are happy occasions for smokers and non-smokers alike. Prove to yourself and to anyone else present that you can enjoy them immediately.

Do not be deterred even if you are the sole non-smoker at the event. Remember, it is not you who are being deprived, but those smokers. Every one of them will be wishing that they could be like you, free from the whole, filthy nightmare. Most of them won't admit it, any more than you would when you were still in the pit, but observe them. They can be the most powerful force of all to make you happy to be a non-smoker.

Don't just see them as smoking a cigarette. Observe what is really happening. Watch the smoker's twitch prior to lighting up. Think of that insecure feeling of nicotine withdrawal. Observe their need to tempt others to light up at the same time. See the relief of those first few drags. Notice how smokers do not appear to be aware that they are smoking. Watch what those smokers have to do to get the nicotine. Watch the filth that is exhaled from their mouths and nostrils. Imagine the accumulated filth left in their lungs. Be aware that they are only obtaining partial relief from the 'itch', even while they are smoking. But most of all, be aware that the moment that cigarette is extinguished, the nicotine will start to leave. Immediately the craving and twitching will start again. Observe their dull eyes and their grey complexions. Listen to the wheezing and coughing. Listen to their excuses and the illogical arguments they give to justify themselves. Try to visualise the feeling of fear and insecurity behind the façade.

Observe this chain reaction not just at social functions, but remember that when those smokers leave your presence, their nightmare continues. The following morning, when their mouths resemble a cesspit, the next budget day, the next cancer scare, the next National No Smoking Day, the next time they have a cold, or flu, or asthma or bronchitis, the next time they are short of money, the next time their family gives them that haunted look, the next time they aren't allowed to smoke, or are the only smoker in a group of non-smokers. Try to visualise how stupid and unclean they will be feeling. Remember they'll have to go through the rest of their lives, spending a fortune, to risk horrendous diseases. They are sentenced to a lifetime of bad breath, stained teeth, shortage of energy and breath, of slavery and deprivation, of being despised by other people, but worst of all, they have to go through life despising themselves.

Why do they go through this nightmare? Because each cigarette gives them a boost? What does that boost consist of? A partial return to the state of peace and tranquillity that they had the whole of their lives before they lit the first cigarette and could have again, if only they didn't light the next. What do they get in return for this lifetime's aggravation?

ABSOLUTELY NOTHING!

As I explained, one of the problems when stopping smoking is that it appears to be negative. The cigarettes are handed around, the smokers are positively doing something, the non-smokers aren't. The actual situation is the complete reverse: the smokers wish that they didn't have to smoke, but negatively, they can't help themselves. The ex-smokers are positively in control, they no longer *have* to do something that they don't wish to.

It will help you to keep reminding yourself of this. If you're offered a cigarette at a social function, or anywhere else for that matter, instead of attacking the smoker or just politely refusing the offer, or, even if no one offers you a cigarette and you feel that you are being left out, say something like: "I used to have to do that, and I can't tell you how nice it is to be free from the domination of the weed. To be able to wake up each morning and to breathe fresh air into your lungs. You should give it a try." Perhaps you feel that if you said this, you would be employing the same sort of one-upmanship tactics that smokers use against ex-smokers? The smokers will be convinced that you are, and will in all probability resent your remarks. But there's a difference, you will be speaking the truth and trying to help them escape from a prison. They will be telling lies and trying to get you back into one. The typical addict's schizophrenia will start. Even with your family and best friends, part of their brain will be hoping that you succumb and remain on the sinking ship. Even if you don't light up, they'll be hoping that you will start to mope for a cigarette. This will reassure them that they were right to keep smoking. Part of their brain will loathe you for succeeding in escaping and actually finding it easy and enjoyable to do so.

However, you will actually be doing those smokers a great favour, because it is the whinging stoppers, like the girl at the dinner party that was still moping after 8 years, that keep the rest of us too frightened even to attempt to stop, convinced that we can never be free. When they see that you are happy and cheerful, you will give them hope. This is the marvellous thing that is happening in society today, the 'hypnotic' spell that nicotine held over smokers for so many years is broken. There is a huge breach in the prison wall. Millions of smokers have already poured through it, and every time another smoker like you escapes, that breach gets wider and wider. Like the Berlin Wall: once breached, it soon collapsed completely.

The important point is this: they'll expect you to be whinging and miserable, but when they see that you are genuinely happy and cheerful, it will not only give them hope and the trigger that they need to make the attempt, but they will regard you as Superman or Superwoman. Even more important:

YOU WILL BE FEELING LIKE SUPERMAN OR SUPERWOMAN!

The only difficulty in stopping smoking, is not the withdrawal pangs, but the feeling that you are missing out, that you are being deprived. Whenever you see any smoker light up in any situation, get it clearly into your mind, it's only the smoker that is being deprived, not the non-smoker! I choose to sit here day after day writing this book. I haven't chosen to spend the rest of my life doing it. Although I'm beginning to suspect that I might!

For whatever reason, smokers do choose to light their first cigarette. Ironically it tastes awful. But they don't choose to spend the rest of their lives smoking. Get it clearly into your mind, whenever you see any smoker light up a cigarette, cigar or pipe, no matter what the occasion is, they are not doing it because they choose to, or because they want to, they're doing it for one reason alone:

THEY ARE ADDICTED TO NICOTINE!

They have a little nicotine monster inside their body, which creates a huge monster inside their brain. It's not non-smokers who are deprived, it is smokers. They are deprived of their health, their money, their energy, their self-respect, their confidence, their concentration, their courage, their dignity, their peace of mind and their freedom. Don't envy poor smokers. Would you envy a heroin addict? Heroin kills less than 300 a year in this little country, smoking kills over 2,000 every week!

If you are still not convinced that you should quit now, bear this in mind: like all drug addiction, it won't get better. The nightmare just gets worse and worse as you sink deeper and deeper into the bottomless pit. Don't envy poor smokers:

PITY THEM

CHAPTER 41

Health

If you have understood and followed all of the instructions, by that I mean if you have opened your mind and removed the many illusions and misconceptions that society teaches us about smoking and smokers, particularly if you have observed other smokers and honestly examined your own smoking, you'll now be regarding all other smokers as rather pathetic individuals. Your attitude to quitting will no longer be: "I must give up because it's killing me and costing me a fortune" but rather: "I really have no desire to smoke any more."

If you do not have that frame of mind, it means that you have missed the point somewhere. In which case, try to establish the particular points which cause you concern and re-read the appropriate chapters. If you still have a fear of failure, don't worry. All you need to do is to follow the instructions and you must succeed. If you believe that you are different from the millions of other smokers in the world, as I once did, then you are being incredibly arrogant, and also incredibly stupid, as I once was.

However, assuming that you are in the right frame of mind, you have now done all the hard work. Your training and meticulous preparation are almost complete. You are fully equipped to succeed in a wonderful achievement, one which many ex-smokers, including myself, regard as the most important and significant of their lives. If you have understood everything that I have said, you will now have a feeling of impatience and excitement, rather like a dog straining at the leash. Shortly you'll be smoking your final cigarette.

I would however beg you to restrain yourself just a little longer. We have already reversed the bulk of the brainwashing with which society has bombarded us since birth. There is however some additional brainwashing that we must remove. A form of protective brainwashing that we have been forced to inflict upon ourselves. I'm talking about the effect that smoking has on our health.

When I mention the subject of smoking and health at the clinics, I suspect the smokers are thinking: "You promised that there would be no shock treatment." It is only shock treatment if you are using health as the main incentive to frighten a smoker into stopping. Such smokers are in a similar position to people trapped in the upper stories of a burning building. They have to choose between two fearfful alternatives. They can either jump from the building, or remain within it. Not an enviable choice, and one that I hope I never have to make. In both cases they risk serious injury or death.

In fact, they do not actually make a choice, their reactions are instinctive. While they can survive within the inferno they will remain. There is always the hope of rescue. Only when the heat and suffocation become unbearable, will they jump. It is a simple tug of war of fear. Only when the fear of burning or suffocating becomes more imminent than the fear of jumping will the person jump.

Smokers are in a similar position. There is the fear of contracting diseases like lung cancer and emphysema on one side, and the fear of stopping smoking on the other. To stop smoking now makes that fear an immediate reality. Just as the person in the building won't jump until it becomes absolutely essential, so smokers instinctively put off the evil day hoping that they too will be rescued before they contract one of those killer diseases.

The subtlety of the smoking trap puts the smoker at a distinct disadvantage to the person in the inferno in two separate ways. That person cannot close his mind to his predicament. The fear of remaining, although not immediate, is imminent within the next few minutes. Whereas the smoker's risk of dying from smoking is many years into the future. It might never even happen. There is no need to solve the problem today, consequently, the natural tendency is not to do so. Smokers can block their minds to the problem, and that is exactly what they do.

Non-smokers find it difficult to understand why smokers are prepared to take the tremendous risks that they do for the dubious pleasure of breathing foul fumes into their lungs. I couldn't understand why I continued to smoke after watching my father suffer a protracted, painful and degrading death from lung cancer. I realise now that it was exactly the same as if he had suffered a similar death from a road accident, it wouldn't have stopped me driving.

So, if we've already removed the desire to smoke, why do we now have to go through all the gory details about what smoking does to your health, and if we now have to, isn't Allen Carr now using shock treatment, and, as he says, haven't smokers already had a bellyful of the health risks and if it hasn't worked why should it work now? Anyway we already know about the health risks. You might well *know* about the location of a minefield. But that knowledge will be of no use to you whatsoever, unless you use it to avoid the minefield. If you intend to walk through the minefield anyway, you'll be much less miserable, if you don't know it's a minefield. Smokers were less miserable before they knew about the cancer scares. What is the point of you knowing about the health risks:

IF THAT KNOWLEDGE DOESN'T STOP YOU SMOKING?

Or perhaps you are one of those smokers that believe they have indeed faced up to the health risks and are prepared to accept them. If so, I admire your bravery. I wonder if you are brave enough to check it out? Have you seen 'THE DEER HUNTER'? Do you remember the scene when they play 'Russian Roulette'? How many smokers do you think there are that possess the combined courage and stupidity to play 'Russian Roulette'? One in a thousand? One in a million? Yet that is in effect what smokers do every day of their lives. In fact the chances of dying from 'Russian Roulette' are one in six. With smoking it's one in four!

Ah! But surely I'm not comparing like with like. With 'Russian Roulette' the odds are one in six with just one pull of the trigger, one in four smokers don't die every time they light just one cigarette. True, but 'Russian Roulette' isn't addictive, one pull on the trigger doesn't compel you to take another. In fact I should imagine that one pull on the trigger, whether it be a lucky one or not, would guarantee that you never took another. I'm talking actual facts, one in four smokers suffer deaths in an infinitely more prolonged and painful manner than 'Russian Roulette' directly as a result of their smoking.

Ah! But the difference is surely that with 'Russian Roulette' either way it's over quickly. With smoking, you can survive years before it kills you. Do you honestly believe that would make it easier? Imagine that when you put that revolver to your head, that the odds were 150,000 to one against there being a bullet in the chamber, but that on the hour for 20 hours of every day of your life, you had to put that barrel to your head and pull the trigger. How long do you think it would be before you ended up in a lunatic asylum? That is what every smoker does every time they light a cigarette. Do you really believe they could do it if they were aware of the fact, if they hadn't blocked their minds to it?

Do you remember that tragic train crash near Clapham Junction? If you had known that the crash was going to happen, would you have boarded that train? Supposing I had tried to persuade you: "Look, the chances of your being injured are ten times less than your chances of dying from smoking, and I'll pay you £30,000 if you'll take the risk." How many people do you think would have the combined courage and stupidity to take that risk? Perhaps one in a thousand? Maybe, but that one wouldn't be me. Supposing I ammended the terms: "You pay me £30,000 and I'll let you ride that train." Do you think one single person in the history of the human race would accept that offer? Yet that's what the average smoker pays to run a ten times greater risk, every day of their smoking lives, and what benefits do they receive?

ABSOLUTELY NONE!

Do you believe that smokers would continue to perpetuate that situation if they were constantly aware of the facts? Of course not! That's why they have to close their minds to them. Because we feel that either we can't stop, or our fear of stopping is greater than our fear of contracting lung cancer, as a self-protect exercise, we have trained our minds to ignore the health risks. We do this by kidding ourselves that it won't happen to us, or that we'll stop before it does, and then when it does: "What's the point in stopping now? It's too late!" This is why we are not even aware of the bulk of the cigarettes that we smoke and think of it as just a habit. Most heavy smokers think that they only enjoy about two of the cigarettes that they smoke each day. In fact they don't enjoy any of them. The only reason that they think that they do is because they assume that they wouldn't smoke at all if they didn't enjoy them. Even when we block our minds to the evils of being a smoker we feel stupid. Imagine how much more stupid you'd feel if you had to be consciously aware of every cigarette that you smoked? The effect would be:

"Why am I breathing this filth into my lungs? There is nothing particularly pleasant about it."

"If I smoke this cigarette, what will stop me from smoking the next one? This cigarette will cost me £30,000."

"I've got away with it up to now, but this might just be the one to trigger off cancer in my lungs."

If you had to suffer that thought process every time you smoked a cigarette, even the illusion of pleasure would be gone. It's not difficult for smokers to block their minds to lung cancer, but what I found it impossible to understand, and still find it difficult to understand, is how a smoker can still fail to stop after a doctor has said to them: "If you don't stop, you will lose your toes."

Now, like the fire, the threat is imminent. Surely no smoker would rather lose toes than stop smoking? However, perhaps they might think that the doctor was just bluffing in an attempt to frighten them into stopping. So they don't stop and lose their toes.

The doctor now says: "You haven't stopped, and unless you do, you'll lose your feet and possibly your legs. Have you seen those films where a passenger is trapped by the legs on a sinking ship, and the only way to prevent him from drowning, is to amputate his legs? I cannot watch those films. I cannot visualise anything worse than having your legs removed. Yet many smokers who find themselves in that predicament still don't stop. They now know that the doctor isn't bluffing, they've *already* lost their toes.

Perhaps you are now convinced that I'm saying this to frighten you into stopping. I promise you that I am not. I'm only saying it to get you to understand how any smoker can get to that stage and still not quit. No doubt you are convinced that, faced with that choice, you would stop. I need you to understand why you would not. This is the other advantage that the person trapped in an inferno has over smokers. The fear of jumping from the building will remain constant, whereas the fear of burning or suffocation will increase and eventually supersede the fear of jumping, enabling the person to at least have the possibility of survival. The fear of health risks to the smoker will also increase, but that increase will be more than matched by the smoker's fear of stopping.

Amazingly, about half the smokers who attend our clinics are unaware that smoking can be the direct cause of loss of limbs. I didn't realise it until several months after I had finally stopped, yet years before I had stopped, I remember hearing that Arthur Askey was warned that he would lose his legs if he continued to smoke. He didn't quit and eventually lost both of them. Now why did my brain not accept that knowledge. Was it that I didn't believe the medical profession? Perhaps I didn't, but if you told me that a bomb had been planted in a building that I occupied, even if I didn't believe you, the second thing that I would do would be to tell you so. First, I would leave the building.

I can remember wondering how anyone could possibly deliberately have their legs amputated rather than stop smoking. I thought of two possible explanations. I cannot remember Arthur Askey's age at the time, but to me he appeared to be very old. I thought: "At that age, are legs really essential?" "Oh no, legs aren't essential. You can survive without legs. But cigarettes, they are absolutely essential!" To my credit, I dismissed this as a possible explanation, but how could my warped mind have considered it as a possibility? Such is the effect of addiction on the brain.

I opted for the second explanation, that smokers like Arthur Askey were just fanatical, isolated cranks. Why didn't it even dawn on me that I was already one of those cranks. I was already expecting to lose my life, let alone my legs, yet I still hadn't stopped. All smokers are cranks! Parents say to their children:

"You idiot, you've seen the state I've got into, why don't you quit while you can?"

The child says to the parent:

"It's you that needs to quit not me. I would never let it get to that stage."

The subtlety of the trap ensures that any smoker that smokes the second cigarette is already a crank. We don't understand why we are smoking and in the early days we have no reason to stop. Once we have a reason to stop, those are the times that we are least able to do it, when we most need our little crutch. Oh bad health or lack of money might help you abstain for a period, but once you have quit, it is not long before you have good health and ample money, and while you still have a desire to smoke, sooner or later you will fall for the trap again.

Eventually, you reach the stage that I did, when the debilitating effect of the drug and the poisons have so dragged you down, both physically and mentally, that even though you know that smoking is killing you, you just become resigned to your fate. You think: "If this is life with my little pleasure or crutch, life cannot be worth living without it." It's blatantly obvious to non-smokers, and, as with the parent and child, it's blatantly obvious to smokers what it is doing to every other smoker, but the one smoker that we seem incapable of seeing in true perspective is ourselves.

What powerful force makes *every* smoker a crank, warps our minds, makes us bury our heads in the sand, persuades us that it is better to lose our limbs or our lives rather than quit? It is:

FEAR!!!

Let me make it quite clear, I'm not talking about the fear of lung cancer, or the fear of death. I'm talking about an even greater fear. A fear that makes us block our minds to these things. The fear that we cannot enjoy life or cope with life without cigarettes. Non-smokers don't suffer this fear. Nicotine doesn't relieve this fear, it actually causes it. The greatest gain you'll achieve by stopping is to be rid of that fear.

The fear of contracting lung cancer didn't stop me from smoking and, if it were going to stop you, you would already have stopped. While I believed that it was not possible for me to cope with life or enjoy life without cigarettes my instinctive reaction was to close my mind to cancer scares. However, once I realised that, not only could I enjoy life or cope with life without smoking, but would enjoy life more and be better equipped to cope with it, I no longer had to block my mind to the health scares, they became powerful bonuses of quitting.

I am not trying to underplay the effects of diseases like lung cancer, heart disease, arteriosclerosis, emphysema, angina, thrombosis, bronchitis and asthma. They are terrible diseases and it is an unpardonable crime that even today our society needlessly forces millions of smokers to suffer protracted, painful and premature deaths because of them, but the fact remains that shock treatment, for the reasons that I have explained, just doesn't work.

A person might be shocked into jumping from a burning building by the shock of being burned alive. They will not be shocked into jumping if there is an adequate fire escape. I provide smokers with a fire escape: an easy method of stopping. My treatment is not therefore shock treatment. However health is the main force which triggers off attempts to quit, and while smokers continue to block their minds to the health scares, they have insufficient incentive to use the fire escape.

It is therefore an essential instruction that you reverse this process of closing your mind to the health scares because it only helps to keep you a miserable smoker. Face up to these horrors. If you feel stupid being a smoker now, just think how a many times more stupid you will feel if you did contract lung cancer? Stop saying: "It won't happen to me." Thereby ensuring that it does! Use this information to help keep you a happy non-smoker. Start thinking: "It *will* happen to me."

THEREBY ENSURING THAT IT DOESN'T!

Another subtlety of the trap which enables us to block our minds to the killer diseases, is that we tend to regard them as hit or miss affairs. In other words, provided we don't actually contract one them, we get away with it completely. Okay, I knew that smoking made me short of breath, made me cough and congested my lungs. But these were not actual diseases. I wasn't actually ill. It was just that I wasn't as fit as I would have been as a non-smoker. So what? I didn't exercise as much as I used to, that didn't mean that I was ill. In 'EASYWAY' I describe smoking as a continuous chain reaction, like lighting a fuse and not knowing how long the fuse is, just knowing that every cigarette is one step nearer to the bomb exploding. I often compare smoking to walking through a minefield, you might step on a mine, on the other hand, you might be lucky and get away with it. However, once you have safely traversed the minefield, you can relax. With smoking you remain in the minefield the rest of your life.

How do smokers cope with that situation? They cope with it because life itself presents us with exactly the same problem. The only certainty in life is that sooner or later we all die. If we spent our lives worrying about it, we would be miserable. So we do the sensible thing, we get on with our lives and enjoy them as best we can. Smokers apply exactly the same logic to their smoking: "There's nothing I can do about it, so what's the point of worrying about it?" I suppose it is only to be expected that the medical authorities should concentrate on the horrific killer diseases, even so, that shock treatment didn't stop me. Some experts will try to stop you by showing you the colour of a smokers' lungs. But if the risk of lung cancer doesn't stop you, why should the colour of your lungs? Anyway, smokers must already be aware of the colour of their lungs. When non-tipped cigarettes were the vogue, badly nicotine-stained fingers, teeth, beards and moustaches were commonplace. In fact many people regarded that visual side effect of being a smoker as even more repulsive than the smell of a smoker's breath. However, those smokers must have realised that their lungs were being subjected to at least ten times more tobacco smoke than were their fingers. They must also have realised that, because they were never able to wash or scrub those stains from their lungs as they could from their fingers, the discolouration and gunging up of their lungs must be thousands of times worse. But this didn't stop them smoking!

Horrific as these killer diseases are and repulsive as the effects can be, I find another connection between health and smoking, though less dramatic, even more horrific. I once watched a nature film showing a huge toad being slowly swallowed legs first by a snake. Eventually, only part of its head remained in view, but it had this contented look on its face, as if it had found a nice, warm, comfortable resting place. The effect on me was much more sinister than watching a lion kill an antelope. I thought: "Surely it realises that its legs are already being digested and it won't be long before its head disappears completely?"

It was so sinister because the toad appeared to be oblivious to what was happening. That's what I find so sinister about the smoking trap. Another of its subtleties is that, like old age, the process is so gradual, the face we look at in the mirror each day is identical to the face we peered at the previous day. Not until we look at a photograph taken 10 years previously does the ageing process become obvious. So the deterioration of our physical and mental health caused by smoking is so gradual that we are assisted in our desire to close our minds to it. Even when we cannot help but notice it, we tend to blame it onto old age rather than smoking.

I'm convinced that if I could have seen what was happening inside my body, I would not have continued to smoke. I am now referring to this regular and progressive gunging up of our circulatory system. It wouldn't be quite so bad if we just starved every cell in our bodies of oxygen and other nutrients, but we actually replace that shortage with numerous poisonous compounds such as nicotine, carbon monoxide, tars and many others.

It's bad enough that this starvation process causes shortage of breath and a feeling of lethargy, but its most serious effect is that it prevents every organ and muscle of our bodies from operating efficiently. It has a similar effect to AIDS. It gradually destroys our immune system. Ironically, the medical profession has recently announced that smokers that are HIV positive contract full blown AIDS twice as quickly as non-smokers. Why does it take them so long to confirm what has been blatantly obvious for years?

Whether it be animal or vegetable, life on this planet is a constant battle for survival. This battle takes many different forms. Some are obvious, like one species preying on another for food, competing with a similar species for survival, or even one species competing with a member of the same species for food, territory or a mate. All species have to battle against the elements for survival. Some battles are not quite so obvious, such as the battle not to be eaten or overwhelmed by parasites.

The bulk of the human race has managed to solve most of the problems of survival. Our chief remaining adversaries are war, pollution and starvation. Apart from these threats, which remain only because of our own greed and stupidity, the only substantial threat that we still have to conquer is disease.

I believe that disease itself is mainly caused by pollution. As I explained in Chapter 6, wild animals can survive, and some of them survive longer than human beings, without the aid of doctors or processed food and shelter. A strong, healthy body is equipped to fight disease. Our most formidable weapon in the battle against disease is our immune system. The great damage that smoking does to our health, isn't directly causing diseases, but preventing our immune system from functioning properly to conquer them.

AIDS is a terrible disease, however, it has highlighted just how vital our immune system is. I'm sure that if I could have seen what smoking was actually doing to my body, I would have stopped in my teens. Because when we are youngsters, we can keep up with non-smokers, we convince ourselves that smoking cannot be affecting our health. It often comes as a revelation to smokers at our group clinics, when smoker after smoker suddenly remembers that they were not only just as good as non-smokers, but were actually outstanding at sports or athletics.

Perhaps the imperceptibility of the ageing processes is one of the many kindnesses of nature. Perhaps another was the non-violent and gradual process by which the snake swallowed the toad. It is conceivable that the toad felt genuinely contented. After all, ignorance is bliss, and there was nothing that the toad could do about it any more than we can prevent getting old. However, this subtlety isn't being kind to smokers, because there is something that they can do about it. Do you never check the oil level in your car? Do you never have it serviced, or change the oil filter or the oil itself? How long do you think the engine would last if you did none of these things? We've been talking about man's stupidity. Do you really believe that your car is more important than your body? Even if you were stupid enough to abuse your car, you can always buy another:

YOU ONLY GET ONE BODY!

Perhaps those that are lucky enough to have good health tend to take it for granted. Perhaps your health is not the most important thing in your life. Believe me, without it, what you regard as the important things will fade into insignificance.

Since there's nothing that we can do about it, we might be better off without the old photograph that prevents us from kidding ourselves that we haven't aged. But what a pity we are not able to examine a photograph of ourselves to reveal how we would look today if we hadn't fallen for the smoking trap. Even better, if only it were possible to transfer every smoker immediately to their state of mind and body as if they had not become a smoker; or even to give them a preview of how they would feel after just 3 weeks of abstinence, there would be no need for me to write this book. They'd think: "Will I really feel this great?" I emphasize that not only would a substantial improvement be felt in their physical health and energy, but also in their confidence and self-respect. What it actually amounts to is: "Did I really sink that low?"

The problem is, not only is the debilitating effect caused by smoking so gradual as to be imperceptible, but the return to normal health after stopping is also gradual and does not have the same dramatic effect as it would were it instantaneous. It is perceptible to most smokers using my method. However, many smokers when using the willpower method to stop, actually claim that they feel physically and mentally worse than when they smoked. This isn't really surprising. When using the willpower method, you feel deprived and miserable, and are obsessed with finding any flimsy excuse that will allow you to start smoking again. Whether you do actually feel physically worse off because of your depressed mental state, or whether it is merely the addict's ruse to find an excuse to start smoking again, I cannot say. It doesn't really matter, I can confirm from personal experience that the effect is the same.

Fortunately, there is a way that you can transfer your mind and body immediately to know how you will feel when you become a non-smoker. If you've ever owned a pet, you will know the frustration of not being able to communicate with it on certain occasions. Like when the pet is sick but cannot tell you what is wrong, or when you are going on holiday, knowing that your pet will be pining for you the whole time you are away, wondering if you'll ever return. If only you could talk to and understand each other at such times.

As human beings, we have two marvellous advantages over other species. We can communicate with each other. I am able to communicate to you in detail, not only my own experience, but the experiences of other smokers that thought they could never be free. You have the opportunity to associate with and to learn from those experiences. The other marvellous advantage that you have over other animals is that the human brain has the ability to imagine. You don't have to wait to actually undergo the experience. Just as it is possible for you not only to observe, but actually to share in the pressures, trials, tribulations and glory of Nick Faldo winning the Open Championship, so you are capable of assessing the level of physical and mental debilitation that you have sunk to, and anticipating the level that you will soon be achieving.

If you observe heavy smokers, alcoholics or heroin addicts, it is obvious to you that they get no true benefit from the drug. You can see so clearly that they would be so much better off without their *crutch*. Don't just write them off as fools. Instead use them to help you to see yourself in true perspective. Realise that you are being sucked into the depths of a pitcher plant. It doesn't matter how far down the pit you have already sunk, you will feel so much better when you are out of it. Stop thinking: "It couldn't happen to me." It's already happening! It started:

WHEN YOU LIT THE FIRST CIGARETTE

Many doctors are now relating all sorts of diseases to smoking, including diabetes, cervical cancer, and breast cancer. Several of the adverse effects that smoking had on my health, some of which I had been suffering from for years, did not become apparent to me until many years after I had stopped smoking.

While I was busy despising idiots and cranks like Athur Askey, it didn't even occur to me that for years I was on the way to arteriosclerosis myself. My almost permanently grey complexion I attributed to my natural colouring or to lack of exercise. It never occurred to me that it was really due to the blocking up of my capillaries. I had varicose veins in my thirties which have miraculously disappeared since I stopped smoking. I reached the stage about five years before I stopped when every night I would have this weird sensation in my legs. It wasn't a sharp pain or like pins and needles, just a sort of restless feeling. I would get Joyce to massage my legs every night. It didn't occur to me until at least a year after I had stopped that I no longer needed the massage.

About two years before I quit, I would occasionally get violent pains in my chest, which I feared must be lung cancer but now assume to have been angina. I haven't had a single attack since I quit.

When I was a child I would bleed profusely from cuts. This frightened me. No one explained to me that bleeding was in fact a natural and essential healing process and that the blood would clot when its healing purpose was completed. I suspected that I was a haemophiliac and feared that I might bleed to death. Later in life I would sustain quite deep cuts yet hardly bleed at all. This browny-red gunge would ooze from the cut.

The colour worried me. I knew that blood was meant to be bright red and I assumed that I had some sort of blood disease. However I was pleased about the consistency which meant that I no longer bled profusely. Not until after I had stopped smoking did I learn that smoking coagulated the blood and that the brownish colour was due to lack of oxygen. I was ignorant of the effect at the time, but in hindsight, it was this effect that smoking was having on my health that most fills me with horror. When I think of my poor heart trying to pump that gunge around restricted blood vessels, day in and day out, without missing a single beat, I find it a miracle that I didn't suffer a stroke or a heart attack. It made me realise, not how fragile our bodies are, but how strong and ingenious that incredible machine is!

I had liver spots on my hands in my forties. In case you don't know, liver spots are those brown or white spots that very old people have on their face and hands. I tried to ignore them, assuming that they were due to early senility caused by the hectic life style that I had led. It was only three years ago that a smoker at the Raynes Park clinic remarked that when he had stopped previously, his liver spots disappeared. I had forgotten about mine, to my amazement, they too had disappeared.

As long as I can remember, I had spots flashing in front of my eyes if ever I stood up too quickly, particularly if I were in a bath. I would feel dizzy as if I were about to blackout. I never related this to smoking. In fact I was convinced that it was quite normal and that everyone else had similar effects. Not until only two years ago, when an ex-smoker told me that he no longer had that sensation did it occur to me that I no longer had it either.

You might conclude that I am somewhat of a hypochondriac. I believe that I was when I was a smoker. One of the great evils about smoking, is that it fools us into believing that nicotine gives us courage, when in fact it gradually and imperceptibly dissipates it. I was shocked when I heard my father say that he had no wish to live to be fifty. Little did I realise that 20 years later I would have exactly the same lack of joie de vivre. You might conclude that this chapter has been one of necessary, or unnecessary, doom and gloom. I promise you it is the complete opposite. I used to fear death when I was a child. I used to believe that smoking removed that fear. Perhaps it did. If so, it replaced it with something infinitely worse:

A FEAR OF LIVING!

Now my fear of dying has returned. It does not bother me. I realise that it only exists because I now enjoy life so much. I don't brood over my fear of dying any more than I did when I was a child. I'm far too busy living my life to the full. The odds are against my living to a hundred, but I'll try to. I'll also try to enjoy every precious moment!

There were two other advantages on the health side that never occurred to me until I had stopped smoking. One was that I used to have repetitive nightmares every night. I would dream that I was being chased. I can only assume that these nightmares were the result of the body being deprived of nicotine throughout the night and the insecure feeling that would result. Now the only nightmare that I have, is that I occasionally dream that I am smoking again. This is quite a common dream amongst ex-smokers. Some worry that it means that they are still subconsciously pining for a cigarette. Don't worry about it. The fact that it was a nightmare means that you are very pleased not to be a smoker. There is that twilight zone with any nightmare when you wake up and are not sure whether it is a genuine catastrophe, but isn't it marvellous when you realise that it was only a dream?

When I described being chased every night in a dream, I originally typed chaste. Perhaps this was just a 'Freudian slip', but it does give me a convenient lead into the second advantage. At clinics, when covering the effect that smoking has on concentration, I would sometimes say: "Which organ in your body has the greatest need of a good supply of blood?" The stupid grins, usually on the faces of the men, would indicate that they had missed the point. However, they were absolutely right. Being a somewhat shy Englishman, I find the subject rather embarrassing, and I have no intention of doing a miniature 'Kinsey' report by going into detail about the adverse effect that smoking had on my own sexual activity and enjoyment, or that of other ex-smokers with whom I have discussed the subject. Again, I was not aware of this effect until some time after I had stopped smoking and had attributed my sexual prowess and activity, or rather lack of it, to advancing years.

However, if you watch natural science films, you will be aware that the first rule of nature is survival, and that the second rule is survival of the species, or reproduction. Nature ensures that reproduction does not take place unless the partners feel physically healthy and know that they have secured a safe home, territory, supply of food and a suitable mate. Man's ingenuity has enabled him to bend these rules somewhat, however, I know for a fact that smoking can lead to impotency. I can also assure you, that when you feel fit and healthy, you'll enjoy sex much more and more often.

We are nearly there now. There is just one more important subject matter to discuss before you smoke that final cigarette:

TIMING

CHAPTER 42

Timing

As smokers we tend to pick two basic types of occasion to make our attempt to quit. To distinguish them, I need to refer back to the smoker's schizophrenia, and more specifically to the scales referred to in Chapter 38. Although the tilt on those scales is subject to continual fluctuation, for most of our smoking lives, no matter how irrational it might appear to our logical minds, they are tipped in favour of remaining a smoker. The first type of occasion is when an event in our lives tips the scales and triggers off an attempt to stop. Examples are: worrying about our health due to an asthma attack, or no longer being able to afford to smoke because you've been made redundant.

The second type is what I refer to as meaningless days. These are days like New Year's Day, National No Smoking Day or birthdays. I describe them as meaningless because they have absolutely no bearing on our smoking whatsoever. In other words they do not affect the weights on the scales. Their sole purpose is to provide smokers with a target day to stop. What's wrong with that? There would be nothing wrong with it at all, if it actually helped even a few smokers to stop. I don't deny that many smokers have actually stopped on meaningless days. But just as many smokers using the willpower method, succeeded in spite of it, and not because of it, so meaningless days made it harder for the ones that did succeed. The truth is that meaningless days cause immense harm for several reasons.

The first is that, because the meaningless day hasn't affected the scales, the smoker's schizophrenic brain is still tipped in favour of remaining a smoker. Any attempts to force them to 'give up' their crutch, whether they emanate from themselves or other people, merely increase the illusion of crutch or pleasure. The classic example is National No Smoking Day. The pressure from the do-gooders tends to make the hair stand up on the back of most smokers' necks. The result is that most of them refuse point blank to quit even for the day, let alone permanently. Because so few smokers even attempt to stop on NNSD, the bad effects are mitigated, but how tragic that so much effort is wasted on actually making it harder for smokers to quit!

By far the most popular meaningless day is New Year's Day. Ironically, it also happens to be by far the worst day in terms of success. This anomaly can best be explained by examining a typical attempt to quit at New Year. It will also help you to understand why all meaningless days are so counter-productive. In addition to the lack of commitment inherent in all meaningless days, the particular circumstances pertaining immediately before and after New Year, make failure practically certain.

It is not just coincidence that New Year is the most popular time to quit. Quite apart from being the traditional time for making resolutions anyway, we usually attend so many parties and smoke so many cigarettes around Christmas and New Year, that we awake each morning with a mouth resembling a cesspit. Another irony: it is these same cigarettes that we insist taste so good. By New Year's Eve our chests are so congested we're only too pleased to commit ourselves to a resolution.

After a few days of abstinence, the bulk of the gunge has left the body. The conditions that prompted the resolution in the first place are rapidly disappearing. At the same time the little monster inside the body hasn't been fed for a few days. It has reached the peak of its death throes and is crying out for nicotine. This void is increased by another void caused by the anti-climax that always follows a period of celebration. Even if we survive this, the real crunch has still to come: we have to return to work. The normal Monday morning feeling is bad enough, but the first day back at work after New Year is the daddy of them all.

Who could blame us if we accept one, only one mind you, of the cigarettes that our colleagues who have already broken their resolution, keep shoving under our nose? Oh how precious that cigarette seems. It isn't long before we try another, and another.

Meaningless days cannot possibly help you to quit, because they do absolutely nothing to affect the tilt on the schizophrenic scales inside your brain. While the tilt remains in favour of being a smoker, a smoker you will remain. Meaningless days do immense harm because they force us to go through the motions of a half-hearted attempt to quit, and all we succeed in doing is to suffer a period of penance and deprivation, the result of which is to ingrain further into our minds just how difficult it is to stop and that the most precious thing on earth is a cancer stick!

The great evil about any failed attempt to stop, is that smokers only fail because they feel deprived. They've been using willpower and they've exhausted their reserves. It will take them about two years before they build up the courage to make another attempt. It's rather like saying to a marathon runner that collapses 100 yards from the tape: "Don't get upset. Have a couple of hours rest then start from the beginning again. I'm sure you'll succeed this time." The marathon runner couldn't possibly succeed under those circumstances. Ironically, the smoker could if they used my method, but there's no way you could convince them to try!

Perhaps you still feel that meaningless days have one redeeming feature: that they force smokers into at least making an attempt. In fact, this is their greatest evil. All our lives as smokers, we desperately search for reasons to postpone the evil day. They merely provide us with a ready made excuse to postpone our attempt to quit until the next meaningless day, when we fail anyway!

If you had a painful thorn in your foot, would you decide not to extract it until New Year, or National Pulling Thorns out of Feet Day? If you were 20, would you wait until you were 40 before you extracted that thorn? We delay the evil day because we don't want to stop smoking today. So what happens on the meaningless day to change the situation? Just a feeling of deprivation and panic!

It is clear therefore that we should confine our attempts to stop to the first type of occasion, those times when some event tips the scales and triggers off an attempt to stop. Often it will be one of those events that we had always assured ourselves, that if they ever came, we would quit without compunction or hesitation. Events like pregnancy, or when it becomes blatantly obvious that, not only is smoking adversely affecting our health, but will kill us unless we stop. Ironically these are also the times that we find it most difficult to stop. This is yet another ingenuity about the smoking trap, no matter what day you pick, it always seems to be the wrong day.

Perhaps you think you would quit if you lost your job, or it became obvious that smoking was killing you. But aren't these the times when the need for our illusory crutch is at its height? If you think it's difficult to quit and that you'll feel miserable when you stop at normal times, do you really think it will become easier if you've just lost your job, or are about to have a multiple by-pass operation?

Sometimes clients say to me: "I followed your instructions and I'm grateful that I have stopped, but I can't seem to get the same excitement and joy that you obviously obtained." That's because I had no real problems. I honestly believed that I had and I was always waiting for a less stressful period in my life for the right time to stop. When I was a young accountant struggling to bring up a family, I thought I had all the pressures in the world. If my children did something wrong, I would go berserk, out of all proportion to the gravity of the offence. I truly believed that I had some serious defect in my character. I now realise that the irritability was not a defect in me, but was due to the empty, insecure feeling of the body craving nicotine. Even to this day I cannot explain this to my children because, every time they hear a smoker talk about smoking, they hear: "It calms me, it relaxes me."

It wasn't until I had quit that I realised that these other problems only appeared to be so great because of my physically and mentally debilitated state. If you are unemployed or about to have major surgery, you are obviously not going to be jumping with joy the moment you quit. But are unemployed smokers, or smokers about to have major surgery jumping for joy? Of course they aren't, any more than non-smokers would be in that position. The point is, you will be less miserable as a non-smoker. Like me, you might even find that these problems, real as they might be, cease to worry you as a non-smoker. The danger is, if you delay your decision to quit until after your problem is solved, be it financial or health, you automatically remove your reason to quit. Such is the subtlety of the trap. But we are going to be more subtle.

For several years, I have maintained that I know more about smoking than anyone on the planet. It is an unbelievably simple confidence trick, which society has transformed into an even more unbelievably intricate and complicated labyrinth of deception due to the lies, ignorance and misconceptions that smokers in particular and society in general have about smoking, including the so-called experts.

Because I understand both the simplicity and the intricacies, I am able to give clear and categoric advise on the best way to stop. Timing was the one aspect that I had doubts about when writing 'EASYWAY'. I advised that it would be a good idea for a businessman who smoked for the illusion of relief from stress to stop on his annual holiday. I can categorically state that the best time for such a person to quit, would be the most hectic, pressurised day in the year. Similarly, the best time for smokers whose really essential cigarettes are the social ones, would be the biggest and most exciting social event of the year.

Although I have absolutely no doubt that these would be the best times, I do have doubts as to whether to advise smokers to stop at such times. I will explain my quandary. Let's use the business executive as an example. Seemingly, if such a person were to quit while on holiday, they would obtain the following advantages:

1. The ex-smoker is happy, relaxed and better equipped to cope with the withdrawal pangs.
2 If he does suffer loss of concentration or irritability at least it's not affecting profits or upsetting the rest of the staff.
3. After 3 weeks abstinence, the ex-smoker will have got over any withdrawal problems, most of the gunge will now have left his body. Add to this the effect that the 3 weeks rest will have had and that ex-smoker will arrive back at the office, bursting with energy and confidence, forgetting that he ever smoked in the first place.

This is a distorted image of both of smoking and of holidays. The illusion is that you arrive back from holidays, fully rested, with the batteries recharged, just raring to conquer the business world. But what are the actual facts? For the few weeks prior to your holiday, you were rushing about like an ant after the top of the ant hill has been removed, making sure that everything is up to date and that the firm will survive in your absence. For the first few days of your holiday, you find it impossible to relax, you keep worrying if you remembered everything. Then you forget about the office you get caught up in the spirit of the holiday. Suddenly the things that you worried about appear to be so insignificant. You wonder how you could possibly have got so uptight about such petty matters? You promise yourself that when you return to the office, you'll see these insignificant details in their true perspective.

For 3 weeks you've been waited on, pampered and generally treated like visiting royalty. You've had no problems or responsibilities. You've been spending money as if there were no tomorrow. You've eaten and drunk too much. You've stayed up too late and in your inebriated state have exercised muscles that you'd forgotten you ever had. On top of all this, your flight home has been delayed by umpteen hours and you return a physical and mental wreck.

The truth is, the more you enjoy a holiday, the more miserable you feel when it's over. The fact that the holiday turned out to be twice as expensive as you had budgeted, and that you couldn't afford it in the first place doesn't help. Not to worry, perhaps there's something in the accumulated mail to cheer you up. In fact you've been very lucky. Amongst the usual circulars, bills and the even more depressing official brown envelopes, you have received not just one, but three letters assuring you that you have won a prize worth more than £250,000.

You've hardly had time to unpack before you find yourself, still utterly dejected, back at the office. Your colleagues are completely unsympathetic. They don't actually say so, but their attitude is unmistakably one of: "It's all right for you. While you've been away enjoying yourself, we've been stuck here doing your work for you." The truth is that you return to a 3 week backlog. Not one of those simple tasks that you took so much trouble to make sure would be carried out in your absence has been done. We are sympathetic if ex-smokers cannot resist the temptation of just one cigarette in such circumstances. However our sympathy will not help them:

THEY ARE STILL HOOKED AGAIN

The problem is if you pick what you consider to be an easy day to stop, you won't know whether you've succeeded until you come to

447

what you consider to be the real test: "Okay, I've proved that I can enjoy a holiday without smoking, but what happens when I get back to the office, or when my car breaks down, or when I play golf or cards and my friends light up? What about the next wedding, Christmas, or when the cigars go round at the next official dinner?" You have to continue to prove yourself in several different circumstances and on different occasions. Which means that you will still have doubt and uncertainty.

However, if you quit at what you consider to be the most difficult time for you, whether it be a stress, relaxing, social, boring or concentration situation, you are able to prove to yourself immediately that you can enjoy life, or handle life without a cigarette right from the start. You will then know that you can also do so in any other situation. In other words, if you try to jump a two foot fence and succeed, you will still not know whether you are capable of jumping a four foot fence, or of succeeding in your ultimate ambition, which is to jump a six foot fence. If you jump the six foot fence first, you have no need to bother with the other two.

So if I can categorically say that the best time to quit is the time that you feel will be the most difficult, where is the quandary? Why don't I just advise you to do that? Okay, I will. But will you have the courage and confidence to do it at that time? If you attempt the six foot fence first, perhaps you'll fail and shatter your confidence, whereas, if you succeed first with the two, four and five foot fences, you will obtain sufficient confidence and expertise to succeed in jumping the six foot fence.

There are other problems with selecting what you feel will be the most difficult time for you to stop. Even if you can appreciate why that would in fact be the easiest time, and even if you believe that you will have the courage to do it at that time, how will you know that when the time comes, you won't back down? After all isn't this what we spend our lives as smokers doing? Just finding any reason to put off the evil day?

Even if you understand the principle and are convinced that you won't back down, supposing you are genuinely convinced that the most difficult time for you is some event months or even years into the future, does that mean that I am advising you not to quit until that time?

CERTAINLY NOT!

No doubt you feel that, far from clearing up any doubts, I'm just confusing the situation. Unfortunately the situation is confusing. Whilst you have the fear of the addicted brain, it is virtually impossible to know whether your decision is rational or otherwise. Fortunately, there is a very simple way to decide the best time for you to quit, and that is to follow the advise that you would give to another smoker.

Imagine that your child, father or mother were suffering from a disease that was slowly killing them. A disease for which there is an easy and simple cure. Would you advise them to wait until after their holiday, or until their lives became less stressful, or would you say: "Please stop now. I'm terrified that you are going to die. This disease won't get better. It will just get worse and worse and worse! **PLEASE STOP NOW! THEN YOU CAN REALLY ENJOY YOUR HOLIDAY THEN LIFE WON'T APPEAR SO STRESSFUL."**

I have explained why planned days in the future, whether they be meaningless days or otherwise, will always be wrong. There is no real mystery about it, in fact what could possibly be clearer. They must be wrong, because there can only be one correct time to quit:

NOW! TODAY!

There is really no decision to be made about timing. After all, there are no valid reasons for delaying and there are several good reasons why now is the only time to quit. Let's examine them:

1. Having reached this stage in the book, you have gone through an elaborate process of preparing and training your brain to make it easy to quit. Like the boxer about to take his shot at the title, or the climber about to make his attempt on Everest, you are at your peak NOW!
2. There is absolutely no logical reason why you should delay your attempt. If you do so, it means that you have not completely understood the nature of the trap. BEWARE! If you have failed to understand today, you'll go through the rest of your life failing to understand. Before you decide to delay, either re-read the book, discuss the matter with a friend, ring our help line or consult one of our clinics.
3. What purpose is served by delaying? Why should you even want to delay? Nothing bad is happening. You are giving up nothing. On the contrary, you are getting rid of a terrible disease and achieving marvellous positive gains. What's more, the process is painless. Unlike the boxer or mountaineer who, in addition to meticulous planning and preparation, have to endure considerable pain and hardship to reach their gaol, your meticulous planning and preparation has been to create a key to the door of your prison. That door will open the moment you extinguish the final cigarette!

There is no reason to delay! There is no reason to be miserable or even apprehensive! Rejoice in the fact that the ever-increasing dark cloud at the back of your mind will soon be gone!

ENJOY YOUR ESCAPE!!

REJOICE IN YOUR FREEDOM!!!

CHAPTER 43

The Final Cigarette

The mere phrase: 'The Final Cigarette' will strike terror into the hearts of most smokers. Perhaps it still generates a feeling of foreboding, fear, apprehension or even out and out panic within you? Or perhaps, like the 'Wet Paint' sign it brings out the rebel in you. Perhaps, even after all the counter-brainwashing, you still find the thought of never, ever smoking another cigarette, cigar or pipe difficult to accept. If so don't worry about it, it's just a part of the brainwashing. Nevertheless it's essential to remove it.

At the clinics, some smokers arrive in an obvious state of panic. We gradually break down this fear and convert it to a feeling of confidence, then elation at the thought of being free. Occasionally a smoker will immediately revert to panic when we come to the ritual of the last cigarette. Usually they are intelligent, rational people that genuinely want to quit and have understood my method clearly. It's almost as if it hasn't dawned on them that they are never actually going to smoke again; and that's exactly the problem, it hasn't.

Older golfers will remember Henry Longhurst with fond nostalgia. He was the predecessor and mentor of Peter Allis, and I'm sure Peter will agree, Henry is widely accepted as the best writer and commentator on golf of all time. There are two deadly diseases inherent in the sport of golf. Ironically, the better the golfer you are, the more vulnerable you become to them. One is so horrific that it is regarded as bad form in golfing circles even to mention it. It is referred to as 'The Unmentionables'. I'll respect the golfing code and say no more about it, except that it is highly contagious and if you catch it, as I once did, your best friends will treat you like a leper.

The second disease affects putting and has several names, the two most common being the 'twitch' and the 'yips'. If ever you have wondered why some golfers, whose swings compare favourably with the beauty and grace of a ballerina, undergo grotesque contortions when attempting to putt, or adopt weird grips or peculiarly shaped putters, some about 8ft long which appear to screw into the chin or chest, wonder no more, they are merely attempting to avoid the yips.

Twitching usually starts with putts of about four feet. As you strike the ball, your subconscious brain creates a spasm in your right hand, which causes you to deflect the ball just to the left of the hole. As you become more adept at twitching, you find that you are able to miss putts of shorter and shorter lengths. Chronic sufferers can consistently miss putts as short as nine inches. You might think it a simple solution to allow for the twitch by aiming to the right of the hole. Thousands of golfers have tried this remedy, but there is not one single recorded case of a golfer actually twitching when using this ruse. You might find this surprising, but if you think about it, the only purpose that your subconscious mind has in causing you to twitch, is to make you miss the putt. Why should it make you twitch if you have already planned to miss on the right?

Non-golfers will be excused for believing that I am being flippant about the subject. I assure you that I am not. Ben Hogan, who rivals Jack Nicklaus as being regarded as the greatest golfer of all time, was actually forced to give up the game because of twitching. No doubt you have already surmised Henry Longhurst was a twitcher. His misery, along with thousands of twitchers like him, was relieved when someone had the brilliant idea of inventing the 'Mallet' putter. As its name implies, it enabled you to strike the ball in exactly the same manner as if you were striking a croquet ball. The manufacturers maintained that it was impossible to twitch with a mallet putter. This was not strictly true. For what it's worth, my one claim to golfing fame, was that I was skillful enough to twitch, even with a mallet putter.

However, Henry and his fellow twitchers reckoned without another disease that all sportsmen suffer from, far worse than the 'Unmentionables' and 'twitching' combined. I'm talking about the officials that run the sport. Those unselfish, dedicated people who are now either too old to play the sport, or were never good enough in the first place. The official body that runs golf in the UK is 'The Royal & Ancient'. It suddenly dawned on them that twitchers were now actually enjoying their Sunday morning round of golf. They thought: "We can't have this! Whatever next?" Now like all golf club officials, and all other sporting officials for that matter, they knew their solemn duty: it would be sacrilege to allow people to enjoy themselves. So in their wisdom, they banned the mallet putter. Sportsmen and women worldwide just don't appreciate how lucky they are to have these ancient, noble people protecting their interests.

While all this was happening, I was a young articled clerk, travelling daily to the city by tube, under conditions that would have made London Transport incur the wrath of the RSPCA had I been a battery hen. One of the things that made the experience remotely tolerable, was that I could immerse myself in Henry's fascinating articles. His reaction to the ban was typical of the man. He wrote: "My golf clubs are now in the loft where they will remain for ever." I felt sympathy for him, he was not only an excellent amateur golfer in his own right, but golf had been his life long obsession. At the same time I admired his gesture, to make such a sacrifice on a question of principle.

The very next day my opinion of him was shattered. He was my fallen idol. To me Henry Longhurst had encapsulated everything that was best in being British. Not only did he have a great knowledge and understanding about the game of golf, but he had this marvellous ability to open your eyes to facets that you would otherwise have missed. He was able to point out human frailties without denigrating the golfer involved. He had that rare quality of being able to convey strength and humility at one and the same time.

What caused me to lose faith in him? He wrote: "I cannot tell you the utter joy of the man who has finally given up golf!" Bear in mind that I had just taken up golf, that I was already a fanatic and thought it was the greatest game ever invented. I thought: "Henry, you're a phoney. How could you possibly be thinking like that about the game that you have devoted your life to, after just one day?" I put his article down to sour grapes.

It wasn't until I finally stopped smoking 30 years later that I realised that it wasn't sour grapes. Henry was merely being honest. Golf is a marvellous game. It also happens to be the most difficult game in the world. When you first start, you hit endless useless, sometimes humiliating shots. This doesn't worry you, you have no great expectations anyway and you're out in the fresh air working off all your pent up frustrations on that little white ball, or more accurately, on the ground that immediately surrounds it. Occasionally you make a shot of which a professional golfer would be proud. You get immense pleasure from those rare occasions and they inspire you to practice and improve.

You soon become reasonably proficient and learn to avoid those disaster shots, or most of them. But now you expect to hit good shots. You get no particular pleasure from them, they are the norm. However, when you now hit one of those bad shots, you are furious. Without your even being aware of it, the whole conception of the game has changed. When you start, it is positive, your bad shots do not bother and your good ones give you pleasure. You have nothing to lose and everything to gain. Once you become accomplished, it becomes negative, you get no joy from your good shots, just misery from your bad ones.

I can't imagine a more pleasant way to earn a living than travelling to the most picturesque and exotic places in the world and just hitting golf balls. Yet these players stomp around with faces like thunder as if they were wearing thumbscrews. Who looks the grimmest of all? The leader of the competition. Why does he look so miserable? Because he knows that any moment disaster can strike. The more tense he becomes the more certain the disaster becomes. He should be enjoying a pleasant round of golf at the peak of his skill. But you would be excused for believing that he was crossing Niagara falls on a tightrope. Not until he has safely completed the trial can he enjoy himself. That's assuming of course, that he doesn't blow it.

Far too many amateur golfers have fallen into the same trap on a lesser scale. Observe them. Listen to their expletives. They eventually fail to hit a golf ball more than a few yards, yet can throw a golf club distances that the olympic javelin champion has never even dreamed of achieving. They probably don't enjoy one round of golf in ten. But they are loath to give up their Sunday morning ritual. They cling to the thought of how it used to be. They are flogging a dead horse, not because golf is a less enjoyable game, but because they have the wrong mental attitude towards it. The point was, that rightly or wrongly Henry had been flogging a dead horse for years. The Royal & Ancient inadvertently did him a great favour. They forced him finally to abandon the tortuous ritual that he had been undergoing, but it was only after he had accepted the fact did the 'utter joy of the man that has finally given up golf' dawn on him.

You must be wondering, at this most crucial of all chapters, what this has to do with quitting smoking? I assure you it is very important. Do we not go through a similar ritual throughout our smoking lives? For years we block our minds to the reality in our desperation to find some excuse, no matter how feeble, to cling to our little crutch or pleasure. Yet, we didn't need to smoke before we started, non-smokers seem quite happy without them, even the millions of ex-smokers seem quite happy without them, what's so great about smoking anyway, where is all this supposed joy and pleasure? It suddenly hit me:

I DIDN'T ACTUALLY NEED TO DO IT

I CANNOT TELL YOU THE UTTER JOY OF THE PERSON THAT HAS FINALLY ACCEPTED THAT THEY DON'T NEED TO SMOKE ANY MORE!

The relief is unbelievable! No longer to have that insidious monkey on your back. It's like a huge dark shadow being removed from your mind: no longer having to despise yourself, or having to worry about all the money that you waste and what it's been doing to your health. No longer having to worry whether you have enough cigarettes, or whether you'll be be permitted to smoke, or whether the next person that you meet is a non-smoker. No longer having to feel weak, miserable, unclean, incomplete or guilty!

You will shortly be smoking your final cigarette and making a vow that you'll never smoke another. It is essential to first lay this bogey about never smoking another. To leave it there would be equivalent to working your way successfully to the exit of the maze, then finding some invisible barrier which prevented you from passing through it. It is the illusion that we get some genuine benefit from smoking that makes us build a resistance to accepting the fact that we can never, ever have another. This is reinforced by the fact that we have felt miserable and deprived when using the willpower method. We had what we thought were genuine reasons for building a barrier. We have already proved that these reasons were illusions, but in order to escape, we must also remove the barrier.

If you find the thought of never being allowed to smoke another cigarette difficult to accept, try to face up to the only alternative that you have:

TO SPEND THE REST OF YOUR LIFE NEVER BEING ALLOWED TO STOP!

That is the simple choice that you have to make. Perhaps this doesn't help you, that you consider that you are merely deciding between the lesser of two evils. If so, ask yourself these questions:

1. Does it unduly concern you that you might never, ever have flu again? Of course not! Flu is an evil. Okay, let's try something that's generally regarded as a delicacy.
2. Does the thought that you might never, ever eat caviar again bring you out into a cold sweat?
3. Does the thought that you might never suffer from AIDS, or never, ever be allowed to inject heroin into your veins cause you to have sleepless nights, or reduce you to a state of panic?

No? Then why on earth should it bother you that you will never again suffer from society's No.1 killer disease? I have promised you that it is ridiculously easy to stop smoking, providing you follow all of my instructions. The first instruction was to follow the rest. Your second instruction, is to stop even thinking in terms of: "I must never smoke again." You are stopping because you don't like being the slave of the 'Weed'. Start thinking:

ISN'T IT GREAT! NEVER AGAIN NEED I STICK THESE FILTHY THINGS IN MY MOUTH! I'M FREE!

It occurs to me that I might have led some golfers into believing that, like Henry, they would enjoy life more if they gave up golf. No! Golf and smoking are diametrically opposed pastimes. It's only our brainwashed minds that can make them appear to be similar. Golf is a marvellous game, anyone like me that is lucky enough to be a member of a golf club should forever be grateful. We create our own problems by taking the game and ourselves too seriously. We turn a pleasurable pastime into a penance. Smoking is the complete opposite. It is a deadly, killer evil that we are brainwashed into regarding as some sort of crutch or pleasure.

We need to remove *ALL* of the brainwashing. Just like a pilot goes through a check list before take off, we are going through a similar check list to ensure that your mission is safely accomplished. Your next instruction is not to pass on to the next item on the check list unless you are completely satisfied with the current item. If you have any doubt whatsoever, re-read the appropriate chapters or consult our help line or clinics. You are about to make an irrevocable decision. There is only one thing that can cause you to fail or be miserable, that is to doubt your decision either in the short or long term. There are two major factors that can cause you to doubt your decision.
They are:

1. The belief that you are making a genuine sacrifice. Get it clearly into your mind: THERE IS ABSOLUTELY NOTHING TO GIVE UP! By that, I do not mean that on balance you will be far better off as a non-smoker. I mean that smoking gives no genuine pleasure, crutch or advantage whatsoever. The fact that it appears to is just a subtle illusion. Of the many pathetic aspects about smoking, the most pathetic of all, is that the actual pleasure or crutch that smokers receive when they light up, the feeling that makes them block their minds to horrendous diseases, the money, the slavery, the filth and the humiliation, is the feeling non-smokers have their entire lives. Should you find this statement contradictory or confusing, let me to elaborate. It is relaxing to remove tight shoes. But what is the actual pleasure we obtain? It is no longer to suffer the aggravation of wearing tight shoes. In other words: to feel exactly the same as a non-wearer of tight shoes. We didn't need cigarettes before we started smoking. When nicotine leaves our bodies, we suffer an empty, insecure feeling. If we light another cigarette that aggravation is partly removed. The feeling of crutch, pleasure, relaxation or satisfaction is actually due to the partial removal of the aggravation. Therefore the actual pleasure we are experiencing is just to emulate someone that doesn't suffer that aggravation:

A NON-SMOKER!

The actual pleasure that a smoker gets when they light up is to return temporarily to the state of peace, confidence and tranquillity that non-smokers enjoy throughout their lives. Because each cigarette, far from relieving the aggravation, actually causes it, the pleasure or crutch is not genuine but illusion, and because the body becomes immune to the drug, even the illusory feeling of relaxation never takes the smoker back to the peak that non-smokers enjoy. Fortunately to return to that peak is simple:

QUIT

2. The second factor that can, and often does, cause you to doubt your decision, is the belief that it's possible to smoke occasional cigarettes without getting hooked. Remember the only essential in order to be a non-smoker for life, is never to smoke. In order to be a happy non-smoker for life, it is essential never to desire to smoke. If you have a desire to smoke one cigarette, you will have a desire to smoke another and another. You give yourself the choice of going through life desiring to smoke but not being allowed to, and being miserable, or of being allowed to and being even more miserable. Perhaps you find it sad that you cannot have occasional cigarettes, but once you accept the fact, it'll disturb you no more than the fact that you cannot occasionally inject heroin into your veins. Get it clearly into your mind:

IT HAS TO BE ALL OR NOTHING

There are three minor factors that can make you doubt your decision:

1. The belief that you are a confirmed smoker, or have an addictive personality or are in some way different to all other people.
2. The influence of other people. Remember it is other smokers that are being deprived, not you! If you have read and understood this book, you have infinitely more expertise on the subject than they. Ignore them. Better still give them the benefit of your expertise.
3. Sheer stupidity! From experience, I have no doubt that some of you will fail for that reason and like the others that did, you will feel miserable. Please don't let it be you!

Provided you are completely happy about the above points, we can now continue with the instructions. You are about to make a decision. Some people find it difficult to make any decisions. All people find it difficult to make some decisions. Some decisions are very difficult to make, like deciding what make of television or car to buy. Often the

457

price and quality of alternative products are so similar that it is virtually impossible to decide. It doesn't really matter if you normally find it easy or difficult to make decisions. Fortunately, the decision that you are about to make will be the easiest decision that you will ever make in your life. Not only because it will probably be the most important and beneficial decision that you'll ever make in terms of the length and quality of your future life, but also because, in weighing up the advantages and disadvantages of becoming a non-smoker, there are truly immense advantages and not a single disadvantage.

The scales are so heavily weighted on one side, that the correct decision isn't in doubt. That doesn't mean that you don't have to make the decision. The correct decision has never, ever been in doubt. But you didn't actually decide to become a smoker for life, you were lured into a trap. You just drifted into it. However, the trap isn't designed for you to drift out of. It is designed to keep you enslaved. Fortunately it is easy to escape from that trap. One of the essential instructions to make it easy, is for you shortly to smoke your final cigarette, and at the same time to make a solemn vow to yourself that, no matter what happens in your life from then on, come good times or bad, you will never smoke another!

Perhaps you feel that vow would have no substance because you have made it and broken it on one or even several previous occasions? If so, don't worry, so did I. We failed, not because we made the vow, but for other reasons. We have now dispelled those reasons, but it is still essential for you to make that solemn vow. As I have said, a major factor of failure is doubt. You must actually make the decision, otherwise you guarantee doubt.

When making that vow, don't just ritually chant the words, hoping that will automatically bring about the desired result. There is no need to speak the words aloud, but what you do need to do is to be aware that at the moment you are fired up with powerful reasons to stop. In a few days those reasons will fade. As the days, weeks and years slip by, your memory of how you were feeling about smoking today will dim. Implant those thoughts in your mind now, whilst they remain vivid, so that even if your memory of the details should diminish, your resolution never to smoke again doesn't.

Anticipate now that in a few months time, you'll find it difficult to believe that you once found it necessary to smoke cigarettes, let alone that they dominated your life. You will lose your fear of getting hooked again. This means **DANGER!** You will be vulnerable. Realise now, in advance that this will be a danger period, that you might have inebriated moments at social occasions surrounded by smokers, or it might be a trauma, when your guard will be down. Anticipate these situations now and make it part of your vow that, if and when they come, you are prepared, forewarned, so that there is no way that you will be fooled into lighting that cigarette.

In a moment I will ask you to smoke your final cigarette. Smoke it consciously. Be fully aware of the smell, the taste, the filth that you are breathing into your lungs. After the first puff, look at the filter tip. Observe that it's already discoloured by just one puff. Smoke the second puff through a clean, white tissue. Observe the stain on the tissue and be aware that the filter didn't completely fulfil its task. Be aware that the real filter that is accumulating the filth, not just of that one puff, but the combined effect of the millions of puffs, is your precious lungs. Be aware that you cannot change that filter.

Ask yourself what great pleasure you are obtaining? Use that final cigarette to cement clearly in your mind the whole lifetime's chain. Think of that little nicotine monster inside your body. The monster that you created when you lit that first cigarette. The monster that you have spent a large portion of your hard-earned money nurturing, hour after hour, day after day, year after year. A monster that has been slowly poisoning you. A monster that has been laughing at you, is still laughing, confident like the tobacco industry that manufactures it, that when you extinguish it, you will soon be lighting up another.

Do you remember the tale of Rumpelstiltskin? How for weeks he gloated over the princess, both of them knowing that she would never guess his name. Can you imagine how she felt on the final day when she'd discovered his name, but toyed with him, pretending she was still ignorant? Can you imagine the feeling of utter joy and confidence she had when their positions were suddenly reversed? Instead of being in the power of the insidious, little monster, she was now gloating over him.

That's exactly the position you are going to be in the moment you extinguish that final cigarette. That insidious little nicotine monster won't know it at the time, and neither will your friends and relatives:

BUT *YOU* WILL!

You will have cut off his lifeline as surely as if you had cut the air supply line of a deep sea diver. Extinguish that cigarette, not with a feeling of doom or gloom because you cannot smoke again, but with a feeling of elation, that you have already struck your mortal enemy his death blow. You have cut off his supply of nicotine. There is nothing more that you need to do. Nothing can now prevent his demise. Nothing that is, other than you worrying about his death throes.

For a few days those death throes will be there. However, far from worrying about them, you are going to revel in them. Those death throes can present themselves in a variety of contradictory ways: feeling irritable, bad tempered, insecure, disoriented, vague, lethargic, energetic or restless. It is the feeling that smokers suffer throughout their smoking lives, which they often encapsulate as:

I NEED SOMETHING TO DO WITH MY HANDS

The feeling is real, and it is physical. It is also rather elusive. However, if we examine it more closely, it can help to create a greater understanding of the trap. Why is it that smokers don't have the same need to do something with their feet? Why is it non-smokers never seem to have this problem, and that smokers didn't have it before they started smoking? Many will maintain that they did and that it was the reason they started smoking. You say: "Okay, I accept what you say. So let's assume that it is nothing do with smoking, that there's some basic flaw in your make up. If you genuinely needed something to do with your hands, could you not think of something less drastic, less expensive and more endurable than a cigarette? Wouldn't a pencil serve just as well? If your problem is genuinely needing something to do with your hands, why do you light it? Why breathe those lethal fumes into your lungs?"

Although that feeling of needing something to do with your hands is real, be aware that it is caused by the last cigarette and will not be relieved by the next one. Be particularly aware that it is only temporary. It will soon be gone forever. Also be aware that no great physical pain is involved, and provided you don't start to worry about it, or start craving a cigarette, you will suffer no undue aggravation. The fact that it is so slight is good news. It means that it is easy to quit. However, the very insignificance of the physical aggravation causes a problem for some smokers. They can only identify the feeling as:

I NEED OR WANT A CIGARETTE!

This can be very discouraging when they have followed my instructions to the letter, have patiently absorbed and believed everything that I have said and are convinced that they have removed all of the brainwashing. Why on earth should they still be needing or wanting a cigarette? This is why it is essential to understand fully the difference between the physical and the mental. The feeling of I need or want a cigarette is real and physical. Because for many years your brain has been programmed to interpret that physical feeling as I want a cigarette, it was fooled into believing that a cigarette would relieve the feeling. However, you now know that the cigarette actually causes that empty feeling. For a few days your body will continue to undergo that slight physical aggravation, that is the death throes which I referred to above. You might also find that it takes a little time to programme your brain to interpret that feeling as:

THIS IS WHAT SMOKERS SUFFER! ISN'T IT GREAT! I'M FREE!

However the feeling might manifest itself, your next instruction is to both expect and to accept that the feeling is there. That feeling might have absolutely nothing to do with the fact that you have stopped smoking. There are many other things in life that cause irritability, insecurity, restlessness or whatever. On the other hand it might be wholly or partially due to the actual physical aggravation caused by nicotine withdrawal. Either way, blame it on withdrawal.

Ask yourself what actual pain you are suffering. Remind yourself that any inconvenience that you might be suffering, is not because you've stopped smoking, but because you started. Also remind yourself, that this aggravation didn't just start when you extinguished your final cigarette. This is what smokers suffer throughout their smoking lives. Every time they run out of, or run low on cigarettes, every time they visit a library, hospital, cinema, theatre, museum, church, art gallery or any other public building. Every time they use public transport or visit a non-smoking friend or office. Even as they sleep at night, their conscious minds might not be aware of it, but their subconscious minds certainly will. The effect will be reflected both physically and mentally in their dreams and the quality of their sleep. In particular remember that another cigarette, far from relieving that aggravation, will ensure that you suffer it the rest of your unnatural life.

Remind yourself non-smokers don't suffer the physical and mental effects of nicotine withdrawal, that empty, insecure feeling, and it is that feeling that blocks smokers' minds to the health, the money, the slavery, the filth and stigma. So if and when that feeling should come during the next few days, instead of getting flustered, or bemoaning the fact that you can't have a cigarette, say to yourself: "Isn't it great, this little monster inside my body is dying." That way, even if you feel a little insecure or uptight, you will still be in a happy frame of mind.

Remember time is on your side. It's a bit like these Dennis Wheatley novels, in which the powers of darkness will get up to all sorts of tricks to persuade you to leave the protective circle. But the tricks are just clever illusions, provided you remain within the circle you are safe, and provided you know that, there is no need to fear or panic. Enjoy starving that little monster inside your body. Luxuriate in its death throes. No need to feel guilty about gloating over it, after all, it's been gloating over you for enough years and the only way it can ever gloat over you again is if you light another cigarette.

Often when we reach the ritual of the last cigarette at group clinics, one of the smokers will say: I don't really want another, is it absolutely essential to smoke that final cigarette?" Perhaps you have the same misgivings. It wouldn't be surprising, after all, the whole object of the exercise has been to remove your desire to smoke. However, loath as I am to suggest to anyone that they should smoke at any time, the ritual of the final cigarette is important for several reasons, not the least of which is, that this is a momentous occasion in your life, probably the most important decision that you will ever make. It is worthy of ritual, savour the moment. You will have something positive to relate back to should the memory dim. You are not only curing yourself of a horrible disease, but you're achieving a marvellous feat, one that all smokers would love to emulate, one that smokers and non-smokers alike will respect you for, and the person that will be most proud of you, is yourself!

You are about to escape from the most insidious, subtle, ingenious trap that was ever devised. I've said any smoker can find it easy to stop, that is true, but to go through the meticulous procedure in order to understand your own nature and the nature of the trap, to enable you to find it easy to stop, and to remain a happy non-smoker the rest of your life, requires considerable perseverance. It also takes courage to open your mind. I thrive on the praise that I receive from ex-smokers that have stopped with the aid of 'EASYWAY', my video or the clinics. I like to think that I am a good instructor, but I'm constantly aware that the greatest asset of a good teacher is a good pupil. Don't underplay your achievement.

However, the most important reason for the ritual of the last cigarette is this: the only difficulty in stopping smoking is not the physical aggravation caused by nicotine withdrawal, but the doubt, the uncertainty, the waiting to become a non-smoker. You declare your commitment to become a non-smoker when you make your vow. You actually become a non-smoker the moment that you extinguish the final cigarette. It's important to know when that moment is, to be able to stub out that last cigarette with a flourish, with a feeling of venom, of triumph, to be aware that at the same time you are effectively snuffing out that little nicotine monster, to be able say:

YIPPEE! I'M A NON-SMOKER NOW!

If of course you have already gone through this ritual, there is no need to repeat it. Or if you would still rather not smoke another cigarette, it isn't essential to do so. However, you must still go through the same mental processes. It is absolutely essential that you have accepted that you'll never smoker another. To hope that you won't will guarantee doubt and eventual failure. But how can you ever be certain that it will be your final cigarette? Easy, simply by following the rest of the instructions:

1. Be aware that you are already a non-smoker the moment you

extinguish that final cigarette. By cutting off the supply of nicotine you'll have completed the final act required to become a non-smoker. You will have unlocked the door of your prison. The rest of these instructions are designed to ensure that you start off a *happy* non-smoker and that you remain one for the rest of your life.

2. Don't wait:

> To become a non-smoker.
> For the physical withdrawal to go.
> For the 'Moment of Revelation'.

If you do, you will be creating a phobia. Instead just get on with your life. Remember, you don't have to wait until both your physical and mental health returns to normal, it will progressively improve the moment you cease the poisoning process. Expect good days and bad days, just as you did as a smoker, but realise that as your physical and mental health improves, the good days will be progressively better and the bad days not so bad. Realise and be aware that physically and mentally, a very important change is happening in your life. Like all major changes, including those for the better, it takes time for our bodies and minds to adjust. Expect to feel different for a few days. Those feelings can range from tension, insecurity and disorientation, to confidence and utter elation, and can switch from one to the other in an instant. Accept it and don't worry about it. If you do, you will be creating a phobia. Perhaps you do not think it is possible to feel tense and insecure, and yet feel happy at the same time. I promise you that you can when you know that the tension and feeling of insecurity are caused by a disease from which you are undergoing a certain cure.

3. Remember you've stopped smoking. You haven't stopped living. Do not change your life style purely because you have stopped smoking. By all means change it for the same selfish reason that you stopped smoking:

TO ENJOY IT MORE

4. Do not use substitutes. You don't need them!

5. You have made a very important decision in your life. If at any time in your life, you had rationally weighed up the advantages and disadvantages of being a smoker, the answer would always be a dozen times over: Don't do it! The conclusion is so heavily weighted in favour of being a non-smoker, we don't even need to go through the exercise. In fact it is so obvious, that smokers are even frightened to go through the exercise. You didn't need me to tell you that. All smokers know it throughout their lives, before

falling into the trap, while they remain in it and after they escape from it. What you do need me to tell you is this: having made what you have always known to be the correct decision, accept that nothing can ever possibly happen to alter that fact. Therefore never punish yourself by ever questioning or doubting that decision, neither in the next few days nor for the rest of your life. Because if you do question or doubt that decision, whether it be by craving for a cigarette, or bemoaning the fact you musn't have one, you will have put yourself into an impossible position, you will be miserable if you don't have one and even more miserable if you do. It is not only essential never to smoke a cigarette, the most IMPORTANT instruction of all is, having made what you know to be the correct decision:

NEVER, EVER DOUBT OR QUESTION THAT DECISION!

NEVER, EVER CRAVE A CIGARETTE!

I described how your vow should anticipate the danger of being tempted to smoke in the future when your memory dims. The actual lighting up is always preceded by the thought of lighting up. The temptation is usually to just smoke one cigarette, or one packet or just on this one occasion. Think of the misery and expense the first cigarette caused you. If you are never going to smoke after that just one, is there really any point in smoking it? Is it really worth taking that risk? Of course not! So get it clearly into your mind, if you are still tempted, the question that you are really considering is:

DO I WANT TO BE A SMOKER THE REST OF MY LIFE?

You don't need to even waste your time contemplating that one, and that's the whole key to staying stopped. Train your mind right from the start and for the rest of your life so that the moment the thought of just one cigarette or one puff, enters your mind, you crush it immediately. There's no point in dwelling upon it. In no time at all your brain will accept that it's trying to grow a tobacco seed on bright, stainless steel. You will be amazed how quickly it will learn that it is wasting its time. In no time at all even the thought of one puff will disappear.

6. Do not avoid smokers, or smoking situations, but do not keep cigarettes on your person, in your home, place of work or car. Many smokers that have successfully stopped when using the willpower method, recommend that you keep a packet of cigarettes with you. Indeed some ex-smokers attribute that one

point to the secret of their success. There are several useful conclusions to be drawn from 'The Man On The Yacht' story. You might argue that while he had no cigarettes, he was in a panic, and that once he had them, he was quite happy not to smoke them. It really proves my point that the problem is mainly mental. It wasn't the fact that he had cigarettes that prevented him from smoking them, it was the influence of the non-smoker. The moment he left the presence of the non-smoker he lit a cigarette. I accept that, if you are using the willpower method, keeping cigarettes on your person can help to remove the panic feeling. However, the willpower method is incredibly difficult and inefficient. Remember the story of the man that spent 6 months out-staring his packet of cigarettes? Surely you don't want to make it that difficult? With my method, we remove the panic first. You have no need to keep cigarettes with you. Look at it logically. The only difficulty in stopping, is the doubt, the waiting. If you are certain that you will never smoke again, why on earth do you need to keep cigarettes? If you do keep them, you guarantee that you start with doubt and you guarantee failure. Would you advise an ex-alcoholic to keep a bottle of whisky? If you do keep cigarettes with you, they will be taunting you and tempting you. You need just one weak moment, or some slight tragedy, and you will have failed. If you don't keep cigarettes with you, even if you do have a weak moment, by the time you've had the indignity of asking another smoker, or have reached the off-licence, that moment will have passed. It can make the difference between success and failure. So if I advise you not to keep cigarettes yourself, why don't I advise you to avoid the temptation of other smokers? Because once you can see smoking as it really is, it ceases to be temptation. Do you need to keep heroin on your person? Of course you don't! The very thought is anathema. Do you need to avoid heroin addicts because they might tempt you to start injecting heroin into your veins? Of course not, you would be repulsed by the sight. Start seeing smokers as they really are. You might have need to avoid them because they repulse you, but not because they tempt you.

7. Do not try to adopt techniques to take your mind off smoking, and most important of all, do not try **NOT** to think about smoking. As I say in my video: "Try not to think about **ELEPHANTS**." What are you thinking about now? It is impossible *not* to think about something deliberately. By even trying to, you create a phobia and make yourself miserable. Anyway, for the next few days, the death throes of that little monster inside your body will be reminding you. Even after its death rattle, smoking and smokers will still be around to remind you, as they have been since you

were born. Whether you like it or not, you cannot avoid smokers or avoid thinking about smoking. The point is, there is no need to avoid smokers. THERE IS NO NEED TO TRY:

NOT TO THINK ABOUT SMOKING

There is nothing bad happening. On the contrary, there is something marvellous happening! Thinking about smoking need not make you miserable. I think about smoking 90% of my life. It's what you are thinking that is important. If you are thinking: "I musn't have a cigarette." Or, "When will the craving go?" Of course you will be miserable. But if you are thinking:

GREAT! I'M A NON-SMOKER! YIPPEE! I'M FREE!

You will feel happy, and if those thoughts obsess your mind for a few days, or for the rest of your life:

YOU WILL BE OBSESSIVELY HAPPY

Your moment of triumph has finally arrived. Can you imagine how Hilary felt when he planted that flag on the peak of Everest or how the Count of Monte Christo felt when he finally escaped from that prison? You are about to achieve a similar goal. I would ask you now to smoke:

YOUR FINAL CIGARETTE

After the clinics some smokers worry that they cannot remember everything that has been said. Perhaps you have the same fear. Don't worry. I don't expect you to remember everything that you have read. I don't expect you to remember all the detailed instructions in this chapter. Fortunately, there is no need to. However, I will summarise those instructions in the next chapter and provide you with a code word which will help you to remember them.

CHAPTER 44

The Instructions

I have repeatedly assured you that, provided you follow all of the instructions, success is guaranteed. You might well have been tempted to cut corners by jumping straight to this chapter rather than reading the whole book. If so, far from shortening the procedure, you will merely succeed in short-circuiting it.

Often an interviewer, in an attempt to find the nub of the success of my method, will sum it up with: "It's really just plain common sense." Exactly, but all smokers know it's stupid to smoke, that knowledge doesn't free them. There's much more to my method than that.

If it were a question of just issuing simple instructions, the following would suffice:

1. Never, ever smoke again.
2. Whenever you think about smoking, think: "Yippee! I'm a non-smoker!"

Provided you followed those two simple instructions, you would be a happy non-smoker for the rest of your life. However, if you believed that smoking gave you some sort of crutch or pleasure, you might go through the motions of thinking: "Yippee! I'm a non-smoker!" But you wouldn't believe it. On the contrary, you would feel deprived and miserable, and sooner or later you would smoke again. Therefore it is essential, not only actually to follow all of the instructions, but also fully to understand the reasoning behind them and, most important of all:

TO BELIEVE IT

The real key to my method is first fully to understand the nature of the trap. To realise that there is nothing to give up and that the whole business of smoking is a subtle and insidious confidence trick on a gigantic scale. Having established that basic truth, we have RATIONALISED in order to reverse the massive and complex brainwashing that resulted from that confidence trick. The code word is:

RATIONALISED

If you have doubts now, or if in the future, doubts should begin to creep in, it means that you have forgotten to follow and/or to understand one or more of the instructions. This is your check list, go through each item, ask yourself: "Am I following it? Do I believe it?" If there is doubt, re-read the appropriate chapters.

R   **REJOICE:** THERE IS NOTHING TO GIVE UP!
A   **ADVICE:** IGNORE IT IF IT CONFLICTS WITH MINE.
T   **TIMING:** TODAY!
I   **IMMEDIATE:** YOU'RE FREE WHEN YOU STUB OUT THE LAST!
*O   **ONE CIGARETTE:** WILL COST YOU X POUNDS AND KILL YOU!
N   **NEVER** SMOKE OR EVEN CRAVE A CIGARETTE!
A   **ADDICTIVE PERSONALITY:** NO SUCH THING!
L   **LIFE STYLE:** DON'T CHANGE IT UNLESS YOU WANT TO.
I   **IMBIBE** NOTHING CONTAINING NICOTINE.
S   **SUBSTITUTES:** DON'T USE THEM.
E   **ELEPHANT:** DON'T TRY NOT TO THINK ABOUT SMOKING.
D   **DON'T DOUBT YOUR DECISION:**

   * To compute X pounds, smokers who average 20 a day should deduct their age from 55 and multiply the result by £750. Implant the result in your mind. Whenever you think about smoking in the future, remind yourself how much you've saved. If you are ever tempted to take just one puff, be aware how much that one puff will cost you. If you are over 55, you have no need to worry about the cost, if you continue to smoke, it is not likely that you will live long enough for the cost to be significant.

Should you have doubts about any of the above items, the following table will help you to locate the appropriate chapters to re-read:

CHAPTER NUMBERS:

	IN THIS BOOK:	IN EASYWAY:
R	14 16 23 35-37 39 40 43	6-21 29
A	20 24 30 32 33	1
T	42	28
I	28 29 38 43	33
O	35 36	16-17 23-26 34
N	35 36 38	23-26 33 34
A	21	
L	43	38
I	26	6
S	26 27	37
E	43	
D	38 43	

Do you ever find yourself querying whether the world is actually round? Of course you don't? You know it's round. If I spent a hundred years trying to convince you that it was flat, I couldn't do it. Yet 500 years ago it was a very controversial question. The only reason that it became a controversial question, is because someone, for whatever reason, found it necessary to question what the rest of the world regarded as undisputed fact. That person applied one of the shortest and yet the most important word in the English language:

WHY?

I have done exactly the same with the established and accepted facts about smoking. I have no doubt that in 500 years time, members of 'THE SMOKING SOCIETY' will be as rare as members of 'THE FLAT EARTH' society are today. I know it won't take 500 years. In fact I am still optimistic enough to believe that I will live to see it happen. I get many letters saying: "I can't possibly repay you for what you have done." You are not indebted to me, but if when you receive 'The Moment of Revelation' and feel a need to repay me, you can. Help spread the message, enable me to achieve my goal, and you will have more than repaid me.

All we are trying to achieve is a frame of mind, having achieved it, you no longer need to question it. You don't have to remember all the reasons why smokers are miserable, pathetic people. You knew before you started smoking that smokers were mugs. Your years as a smoker merely confirmed that fact. I have explained how otherwise intelligent

469

people are lured into the smoking trap in the belief that there is some genuine benefit to smoking. Having satisfied yourself of what you already instinctively knew, you have no more need to doubt the validity of your decision than to question whether the world is round. Indeed whether you be going through good times or bad, whenever the subject of smoking enters your mind, all you really need to remember is the letter: Y. It will serve 2 purposes. The first is to trigger that magic little word: **WHY?** This will remind you that you have answered all the whys about the subject of smoking and that there is nothing to be gained by dwelling on the subject. But I've said it's impossible not to think about smoking deliberately, so how can you help but dwell on the subject? You can't, and that's the second purpose of the letter: Y. It stands for: YIPPEE! It really is as simple as that. All you have to do over the next few hours, days and for the rest of your life, whenever the subject of smoking enters your head, is to think:

YIPPEE! AREN'T I LUCKY! I'M A NON-SMOKER!

DO THAT AND YOU'LL BE A HAPPY ONE FOR THE REST OF YOUR LIFE

CHAPTER 45

The Afterglow

I always thought it meant that wonderful feeling of warmth and complete satisfaction after sex. The 'Moment of Revelation' is very similar. To my surprise, my dictionary makes no reference whatsoever to the sexual connotation of the 'Afterglow'. I assume it's just part of this 'no sex please, we're British' syndrome. Yet strangely, the definition it gives is even more appropriate to stopping smoking: "The glow left after a light has disappeared." It's been 10 years since the light of my final cigarette was extinguished, but I have never lost the afterglow. I truly believed that I could never escape the slavery of the 'weed' and the achievement still fills me with a feeling of immense pleasure.

Escaping from the trap has brought enormous benefits to me. I don't just mean the obvious ones such as improved health, happiness, energy, courage, confidence, longevity, wealth, freedom and self-respect. It has brought a whole new meaning to life, a whole new philosophy. If you find that there is something missing in your life, it might help you to try it. However, before we get onto that, we need to deal with two things that can go wrong.

The first is that you might not receive the 'Moment of Revelation'. If that doesn't particularly bother you, and you are quite happy being a non-smoker, then why worry? Just get on with enjoying your life! If it does worry you, we must do something about it. Ex-smokers who do not receive the 'Moment of Revelation' are usually those who had no real intention of stopping, but merely went through the ritual to pacify a loved one. However, it is not always easy to establish whether these circumstances apply to any particular ex-smoker. As I have said: "All smokers want to stop, and all smokers want to smoke." This schizophrenia exists throughout our smoking lives. The situation is further confused because practically all smokers have some friend or relative who would dearly love them to quit. Take my own case. When I visited the hypnotherapist, I did so purely to appease my wife, with no expectations of stopping. But because I had a strong underlying desire to be free, I obtained freedom.

If you believe that your failure to receive the 'Moment of Revelation' is due to the fact that you were not sufficiently motivated to stop, you might be tempted to start smoking again. If so, first consider this: usually smokers that are not sufficiently motivated to quit, find some excuse, either not to read the book, or not to finish it. It is unlikely that you would have reached this far were you not genuinely motivated. If you still contemplate taking the drastic step of smoking again, before condemming yourself to death row, answer the following question as honestly as you can:

"If a doctor informed you that you would lose your legs unless you quit smoking, do you think you would succeed in quitting?"

If your answer is: "Yes, I believe I would succeed in quitting under those circumstances." It means that you have failed to understand one or more fundamental points. If re-reading the book doesn't alter the situation, you might be relying on the hope that some miracle cure will be invented to help you to quit. If so, take your head out of the sand, it *has* been invented! What you need to figure out, is why you don't want to use it! The most subtle of all the ingenious aspects of the nicotine trap, is that no matter at what stage you are at in your slide down the pitcher plant, the trap is designed to delude you into wanting to remain in it. I suggest you either ring our help line or contact one of our clinics. Details are inside the back cover.

Often smokers arrive at the clinics without the slightest intention of quitting. They might well believe that they are wasting our time, but we don't look at it that way. Much of our time is spent removing the blocks that prevent them from wanting to quit, before we explain how easy it is to do so. When I initially set up the Raynes Park clinic, I was fully aware of two important factors:

1. Although smokers themselves might not realise it, I knew that every smoker can find it easy to stop.
2. I also knew that I could convince some smokers of that fact within 10 minutes, and that with others, It might take me ten years.

Because I knew this, the fee charged at our clinics is not based on so much an hour or per visit, as with most therapists or consultants, but at a fixed price. This has a dual advantage. Smokers don't have to worry whether they can afford extra visits. In theory, they can attend a thousand sessions and it wouldn't cost them a penny over the fixed fee, and if we fail to cure them, even the fixed fee is refunded without inquisition. In practice the majority are successful after just one session, and the majority of the remainder after two or three visits.

It is the proud boast of the Royal Canadian Mounted Police that: "A Mountie always gets his man." I would dearly love to emulate them.

We try to achieve a 100% success rate, we know that we will never achieve perfection, but in our attempts to do so, we have managed to get fairly close to it. Occasionally smokers do give up on us, but we are just as proud as the Mounties about our boast: "That we have never given up on a single smoker." And I promise you, that while I remain in control, we never will.

I once had a car that had a particularly nauseating habit of starting effortlessly whenever I really didn't need it to, and not starting at all whenever it was absolutely essential that it did. Several reputable agents of the manufacturer failed to trace the fault. This was mainly because the car always started effortlessly in their presence. In desperation I phoned a part time mechanic who had advertised in the local paper. I said: "I'm terribly worried about my car." "You can stop worrying. You solved your problem when you called me. It is now my problem not yours."

It was the most confidence inspiring remark and I've tried to adopt the same principle in helping to cure smokers. Unfortunately, it is not possible for me to take over your smoking problem completely. While you remain in the trap, you still have a problem and I need your help to free you from it. However I also want you to know, that whilst you remain in the trap, I will also regard it as my problem. This is the other advantage of our price structure. It also takes the pressure off us. We don't have to worry whether an individual smoker can afford the sessions, or whether we are making a loss on any particular individual. The majority that find it easy subsidise the minority that need further sessions. We are then able to concentrate on getting through to each individual, regardless of the number of visits.

Occasionally ex-smokers that are desperate to quit fail to receive the 'Moment of Revelation'. In such cases it is because their desire to quit is so great, that it creates anxiety. This in turn causes them to fail to follow or to understand one of the instructions. The most common failings are:

1. Waiting for the 'Moment of Revelation' to happen.
2. Trying not to think about smoking.
3. Perpetuating the belief that certain situations can never be quite as enjoyable again.
4. Believing that stopping has left a void in your life.

Remember, if you follow the instructions, you must succeed! Don't just assume, that because you believe and understand them, this automatically means that you are following them. The last thing I tell myself before I strike a golf ball is: "Don't lift your head!" I'm sure I don't need to tell you the next thing I do. Go through each instruction meticulously. Ask yourself: "Am I actually following this instruction?"

473

Most important of all remember, all the instructions are designed to achieve just one thing:

THE CORRECT FRAME OF MIND!

If you have understood and followed all the instructions, yet still have a feeling of doom and gloom, you are like the prisoner, who having been given the key to freedom, neglects to use it. If that is your problem, you have absolutely no reason to have a feeling of doom and gloom. All you have to do is to turn the key. Replace it with a feeling of elation! This is within your power, provided you understand and believe the instructions.

Apart from not receiving the 'Moment of Revelation' the only other thing that can possibly go wrong, is that sooner or later after receiving it, doubt can creep in. Having emphasized that the most important thing of all is to remove doubt, and being fully aware of the power of suggestion, I'm loath even to put the thought into your mind that doubt might creep in. Let me make it quite clear, you have it within your power to ensure that it doesn't. However, there will be cases where for whatever reason, things either start off wrong, or start off fine, then begin to go wrong. If this happens to you, don't panic and don't despair. Above all, don't give up your attempt.

ANY SMOKER CAN FIND IT EASY TO STOP

If you are having problems, it can only be because you've either failed to understand, and/or failed to follow one or more of the instructions. Ask yourself what actual physical pain you are suffering. Having established the physical pain is either insignificant or non-existent, you now know that your real problem is mental and as such, it is within your power to remedy it.

Next go through the check list. See if you can analyse for yourself where the fault lies. If this doesn't solve the problem, re-read the description of the pill that I described towards the end of Chapter 26. Do you believe that you would be going through the same problem if it were those pills that you had been taking? If the answer is yes, it means that you are relating the pill to the cigarette. Do it the other way round. If the answer is no, try to work out why you see the cigarette as any different to the pill. Some people find it easier to relate to the analogy of the cold sore on your face and the magic ointment described in Chapter 14 of 'EASYWAY'.

Incidentally, the 'cold sore' analogy is useful to help dispel the theory that the government could easily cure the smoking problem, either by making tobacco illegal, or by raising the price of cigarettes to £5 a packet. If you believed that the ointment would cure the sore, you would pay £500 for a tube whether it were legal or not. That is understandable because the victim would believe that they were completely dependent on the ointment, even though that dependence is in fact an illusion. It's much harder to see with the nicotine trap, because most smokers don't believe that they are dependent on nicotine until they attempt to stop. Even when they fail to stop, most will still not accept it, because they can't understand it. But that doesn't prevent them from being effectively dependent on nicotine, even though, like the ointment, that dependence is an illusion. If cigarettes were still 50p a packet and you asked smokers: "If the price quadrupled, would you quit?" The majority would reply: "Yes." But the price has now quadrupled and still 13 million in the UK haven't quit.

Do you think heroin addicts worry about the price they pay for their heroin? Of course they do, just like smokers worry about the money they are burning, but the reality is that it doesn't prevent either heroin or nicotine addicts from coughing up.

"School days are the best of your life." Why is it that only adults make that statement? Do you remember one single child waxing lyrical about attending school? One of the many kindnesses of nature is that we tend to remember good things and forget the bad. This tends to sweeten the bitter pills of life, but with smoking it can, and all too often does, create disaster. I am fully aware that I have already laboured the point that I am about to make. I would also ask you to be aware that I consider the greatest crime that one individual can inflict on another, is not to insult them or to break their arm, but to bore them. So, if I run the risk of boring you now, please, please also be aware of the reason that I run that risk.

Parents think that their children are stupid to fall into the smoking trap. How many more times stupid is the adult, who having escaped the trap, falls into it again? Yet, in spite of all the warnings that I give, many smokers do. Never underestimate the ingenuity of the trap. I said there were two further matters with which I had to deal. The first was those ex-smokers that don't get the 'Moment of Revelation'. The second is far more serious. It deals with those that do. There is a great danger, and the easier you found it to stop, the greater is that danger.

I have already discussed this danger in some detail, and as I have already said, the real key is, having made what you know to be the correct decision, never, ever question that decision. However, I remember reading a book as a teenager. Chapter 1 was entitled: "Why a young lady should never accept an invitation to a young gentleman's bedroom, no matter how innocent the reason." Chapter 2 was entitled: "What to do when you get there!"

We live in the real world. It is necessary for you to be aware that the tobacco industry, motivated by greed for profits, together with existing addicts, motivated by fear and ignorance, are ingenious influences that will forever be trying to tempt you. I have already given advice and tips on how to cope with temptation should it ever arise. I am immune to that danger. If you haven't already immunised yourself against that danger, you need to do it now.

Have you heard the story of the nuclear holocaust that destroyed the earth and all livings things upon it, with the exception of a lone monkey? Years later, it was winter, he was wet, cold and hungry. He had roamed the earth in search of another living creature, but had long given up hope of ever finding one. He heard this voice: "Why don't you come into my cave? It is warm and cosy and I have plenty of food." He looked up at the most beautiful female monkey that he had ever laid eyes upon. He was sorely tempted, but strangely he hesitated, looked around at the desolation and said: "Thank you, but I think not, do we really want to start all this again?"

If I needed some form of insurance, that story would be it. When I think of my first cigarette and the years of slavery and misery that ensued from it, if I were tempted in the future to try just another, I would train myself to think: "Do I really want to start off that misery again?" Perhaps you can relate to that story. If not, you need to find some anchor that will support you should temptation come. But you need to do it now. If you wait for it to happen, it will be too late.

The real key is to realise that there is no such thing as one cigarette. If there were, what would be the point of smoking it anyway? Whether you are thinking of yourself smoking, or of some other smoker, stop seeing odd or occasional cigarettes, see it as it really is, the whole filthy lifetime's chain. If you do that, whenever you think about smoking, you can only think:

AREN'T I LUCKY! I'VE BROKEN THAT CHAIN!

Now, let's cast aside all thoughts of doom, gloom and failure and get on with my philosophy. Because I help to save lives, many people attribute to me altruistic and philanthropic motives to which I cannot honestly make claim. If you were expecting a philosophy based on this premise, I regret I must disappoint you. On the contrary, it is founded on the selfish belief that the god, intelligence or system that created us, intended us to enjoy life, and equipped all of us with an incredible machine to enable us to do so. That belief is not itself founded on hope or blind faith, but on observation, experience and fact.

Perhaps you have now jumped to the conlusion that my philosophy, far from being altruistic, is: "Screw you Jack, provided I'm alright." You'd be wrong. Whether we like it or not, the creator has given us a conscience. If we commit an act which we consider to be mean or nasty, even though it might bring us material gain, in effect we gain nothing, because we despise ourselves and feel miserable. On the other hand, do someone a favour, even though we might incur material loss, in effect we gain, because we feel great.

Christian standards, encapsulated by the Ten Commandments, are just a set of common sense rules, without which, no group of civilised people could live together in close community and harmony. Those that stick by the rules tend to be happy. Those that don't tend to be dissatisfied and miserable. Now I am not recommending that you cast aside all material comforts and possessions and give them to the needy, the poor, the starving or the disabled. The basic philosophy is to enjoy life. However, it's very difficult to enjoy life if you are surrounded by misery. Do you think you could enjoy eating a slap up meal if you were being watched by a person that was starving? Do you think you would be happier if you shared the meal with that person, or even gave it to them and went hungry yourself for a few hours? At Christmas we feel obliged to give presents and to give to charity. But we gain from that giving. It makes us feel good. Just think how much happier we would all be if we extended that policy to the whole of our lives.

No doubt you've heard of 'Einstein's Theory of Relativity'. My knowledge of it is vague, I believe that it is very complicated and has something to do with the speed of light. Frankly I have no desire to know anything more about it. However, I would like to tell you about Allen Carr's theory of relativity. It is basically to accept that life consists of a series of ups and downs. If it were just one straight line, it would be a complete and utter bore and we might just as well be vegetables.

A good day is a day that was better than the day before. A bad day is one that is worse than the day before. It doesn't particularly matter what your status is in the class structure, whatever it happens to be, you accept that as normal. As a young street urchin, I would envy the little Lord Fauntneroys, not until years later did it dawn on me how lucky I had been. If you start at the bottom, there is only one way to go and vice versa.

A few years ago I spent Christmas with friends at a hotel. The Christmas dinner was a typical eight course affair. I remember saying: "How on earth will I get through that lot?" Someone said: "Come on misery, it's Christmas, enter into the spirit of it." I did, but I didn't enjoy that meal. I ate nothing but indigestion tablets for the rest of the day and I was so bloated that I didn't enjoy another meal for a week. I was too wrapped up in my own problems at the time to think of it, but if 10 starving people had been allowed to share that one meal, it would have been a banquet for them.

Picture Papillon's horror when extracting a live cockroach from his first bowl of soup in prison. We've all had similar experiences in our lives and can sympathise with him. However, three months later

Papillon was trying to catch cockroaches for something to eat. How many of us can identify with that?

At the other end of the scale, there is the story of the man who won £100,000 on the football pools. The following week his best friend saw him looking so dejected:

"Jock, what on earth's the matter? I heard that you won a hundred thousand last week!"

"Aye, so I did."

"So why are you looking so miserable?"

"Because this week I didna win a penny!"

"Are all those begging letters depressing you?"

"Och no! I'm still sending them out!"

Now the key to the philosophy is to accept in advance that these ups and downs are an essential part of life. When you are on a high accept it. Rejoice in it! Sometimes the high will be caused by some pleasant chance of fate and you will understand the reason for it. Other times you won't know the reason for it, you'll just feel great to be alive. Either way, don't waste your time analysing the reasons. Just accept it, live for that moment and extract every ounce of pleasure that you can from it.

When you are on a low, you adopt the reverse tactics. Don't just accept it. Try to analyse why you are feeling down. Sometimes the reason will be obvious. Okay, perhaps fate has given you a body blow, but perhaps there is some positive action that you can take to lessen th effect, or to eliminate it completely, or even to turn it to your advantage. Either way, already you are starting an upward cycle. Perhaps it's one of those things, like a broken leg, that you can do absolutely nothing about. Even so, you don't have to get mentally depressed. From the moment you break the leg, it starts to heal. You are already on an upward cycle. Okay, you are forced to be inactive for a while, but isn't this a marvellous opportunity to read all those books that you've been promising yourself you would read, if only you had the time, or to learn to play that instrument, or chess or bridge or whatever?

Sometimes there is no positive action that you can take actually to lessen the blow. That is still no reason to get depressed. The bulk of the things that we tend to get uptight about in modern society aren't real problems at all. Before you buckle under the blow, ask yourself: "Is this really so bad?" Often we are worried about situations that might happen. If so, it is a good idea to assume that it will and to ask yourself: "Supposing it does? Is it the the end of the world? What is the worst possible thing that can happen?" Often the acceptance of the worst possible scenario is less frightening than the anticipation of the least.

This is a good time to look around and to compare yourself with people that are worse off than you are: "Okay, perhaps I have been made redundant, but I'm not like those poor Yugoslavs, at least I've still got my family and friends and I'm not going to starve.

Sometimes we cannot find the reason for our depression. We just wake up one morning feeling miserable and cannot understand why. Be sure that there is a reason. It might be that the moon is in the wrong position, or that our bio-rhythms are out of sync'. Or it might be one or more problems in our subconscious mind that we cannot put our finger on. Again, you don't have to accept this depressed state. Use your conscious mind to start counting your blessings. You might not reverse the situation, but at least you will negate the effect.

To sum up: if you are on a high, don't rock the boat, accept it. If you are on a low, rock the boat, question the situation, do what you can to eliminate the actual problem, or your mental approach to it. If you find that none of these techniques work, if you are having one of those days that we all have occasionally, when we are feeling down and there just seems nothing that we can do to rectify the situation, then accept it. Say to yourself:

"Okay, today I'm at rock bottom. Only two things can happen from now on. Either my position improves, in which case fine, or it gets worse, in which case, the chances of it improving the next day are even greater, eventually the cycle must start to go up."

The key is: when things are good, enjoy them, live for the present, extract every ounce of pleasure from them. When they are bad, fantasize, live for the future. Use the marvellous gift that human beings possess: IMAGINATION! Make sure that you have always planned something nice to look forward to. It doesn't have to be a luxurious holiday, it can be some little thing, like meeting a friend or your next meal. Even if you can find nothing positive to look forward to, then enjoy looking forward to the inevitable ending of the bad patch that you are going through.

In western society, we tend to be like a cork bobbing up and down in the fury of a spring tide. We rush from one panic to another, so absorbed in keeping our heads above the water, that we never seem to have time to sit down and to absorb the implications of the knowledge and experiences that we undergo, or indeed to reflect where we are going and whether we really want to get there. Certain societies do the complete opposite. These Bhuddist Gurus that spend their whole lives sitting on a rock, clad only in a loin cloth, consuming one glass of water and one bowl of rice each day. You think: "What sort of life is that?" But before you write them off without a further thought, ask yourself, do you really believe that they spend their lives just sitting on a rock? They are not on a rock, they are wherever their imagination chooses to take them. Who knows the delights that they experience? Also remember that their civilisation is thousands of years older than ours, don't knock them until you've checked it out.

In fact we all do this anyway. What are television, the cinema, the theatre or a football match but escapism? What's wrong with that? It works! On the rare occasions that I get depressed nowadays, I either play the Pavorotti, Domingo, Carreras world cup tape, or a video of the film 'It's a Wonderful Life'. It's one of those typical old tear-jerker films. James Stewart is the hero. He is seriously contemplating suicide because he believes that he is a failure and would be more valuable to his family dead. He is given the opportunity to see what would have happened had he never been born. This has the effect of making him realise how lucky we are to be born and just how precious life really is. It has exactly the same effect on me.

Some people make the mistake of trying to escape from their problems. That is a formula for disaster and misery. If you have a problem or a potential problem, first decide if there is some action that you can take to solve or avoid the problem, or to lessen its effect. If there is some positive action that you can take, then take it. If there is nothing that you can do about it, what is the point of worrying about it? Remember problems don't cause anxiety, worrying about them does.

If you adopt my philosophy, it will give you a different perspective on life. The highs will appear higher and more frequent than before, and the lows will appear less low and less frequent. This will be partly factual and partly your new perspective. Perspective is another tool that the incredible machine has been provided with. Tools can be used for good or evil, why not use them all to enable you to enjoy rather than destroy your life? By now you will already have solved one major problem, your smoking problem. Because of this, in a few days, you will actually be feeling physically and mentally stronger and this will be a great positive start to your new life!

Just in case there should be any possible doubt, let me make it quite clear that when I refer to a 'high' I am not talking about the sensation that drug addicts and inebriates refer to when they are 'stoned' out of their minds. A genuine 'high' is just feeling great to be alive. I have no doubt that many people believe that alcohol and certain other drugs will provide a genuine high. I will explain in the next chapter why this is just illusion. In fact they do the complete opposite!

CHAPTER 46

Alcohol, Heroin & Other Drugs

I believe the great fear that parents had about their children smoking pot, was not so much the pot itself, but that the so-called experts on drug addiction claimed that pot was the thin edge of the wedge that would lead to hard drugs like heroin. Pot might well have been part of the wedge, but it certainly wasn't the thinnest end of it.

The thinnest end was in all probability this practice of buying our children a bag of sweets. Apart from ruining their appetite and their teeth, this caused no great harm, except that is, to start programming their minds into expecting little, regular and phony rewards. When they reach adolescence, they tend to regard sweets as both childish and fattening. The natural tendency is to seek a substitute. They have already been brainwashed to believe that smoking provides regular rewards and they are already partially addicted due to passive smoking.

Now the wedge has a strong purchase within the crack or void. As the smokers progressively become immune to the nicotine, they only partially relieve the withdrawal aggravation and now have a permanent void. In their search to fill that void, they are either lucky and turn to over-eating as I did, or they increase their consumption of alcohol, or they turn to what society refers to as heavier drugs. All three routes increase their rate of descent to the bottom of the pit, and needless to say, their nicotine intake goes up rather than down. The great evil isn't pot, it's:

NICOTINE

"I've been listening to you for the last half hour and I've never heard so much twaddle in my life. In fact you have made me want to start smoking again."

I occasionally get this reaction during phone-ins. Initially it would throw me. I'd understand such a reaction from smokers that, like myself had tried umpteen attempts when using the willpower method

481

convinced that it could not possibly be easy to stop, but why should it have that effect on an ex-smoker? I would rack my brains to think what I could possibly have said that would induce an ex-smoker to want to start smoking again. It seemed to me that everything that I had said should be music to the ears of an ex-smoker. Unfortunately, the individuals concerned were so irate that they were incoherent. Rather than explain to me the exact reason for their wrath, they were confined to generalisations like: "You're talking rubbish!"

Ironically, it was ex-alcoholics that gave me the clue. In 'EASYWAY' I remarked on the fact that practically all alcoholics or ex-alcoholics are or have been heavy smokers. In fact I suggested in that book that alcoholism might really be a smoking, rather than a drinking problem. I had not accumulated enough evidence to be more explicit at that stage. Now I have.

It never ceased to surprise me to discover at group clinics, how many were attended by ex-alcoholics, ex-heroin addicts etc. In fact many had been addicted to practically anything that was going, and had kicked the lot, but had still not been able to stop smoking. Now society had always taught me that the really impossible one to kick was heroin. But, when I listened to these people talking to each other, it began to occur to me that no matter which particular chemical they were referring to, it could just as easily have been nicotine. In other words, in each case the problem appeared to be basically the same:

1. Initially, the addict (I include alcoholics in this definition) took the chemical, not for basic need, but out of boredom, curiosity, daredevildom or because of peer pressure, and that the initial dose either tasted foul, or gave no feeling of pleasure, other than the psychological kick from playing with fire.
2. That the user continued to take the drug in the belief that they got some genuine pleasure or crutch from it, but believed that they were in control and could stop if ever the need arose.
3. That the addict decided to stop because they realised that they no longer got genuine pleasure from the drug, that it was adversely affecting them physically and/or financially and that they were now dependent on the drug.
4. That the true reason that they couldn't stop, was not due to the terrible physical withdrawal pains that they suffered, or that they needed the great pleasure that the drug provided, but that they just felt miserable and depressed without the drug.

Mind you, it wasn't always easy to extract the corn from the chaff, just as a smoker is left speechless when a child innocently asks: "Why do you smoke?", it was necessary to challenge the usual clichés and platitudes from which addicts and non-addicts alike suffer. The chief misconception portrayed in films was that it was during withdrawal that addicts suffer nightmare illusions, such as having spiders crawling all over them, whereas in fact it would appear to be when under the influence of the drug that such illusions actually occur.

No doubt it is the addicts themselves that have helped to foster most of the fallacies. Just as when I tried to stop smoking using the willpower method, I was undergoing no physical pain. My only problem was that I wanted a cigarette, but I wasn't allowed to have one, so I felt miserable and deprived. Far from easing the problem, time merely accentuated it. Sooner or later my resistance would weaken and I'd give in. I had no rational reason for starting again, my logical brain cried out: **"FOOL! IDIOT!"** So to justify my stupidity to my family, and to myself, I told two basic lies:

1. That I was undergoing terrible physical pain.
2. That I got genuine benefits from smoking.

Before I proceed further I should explain that the main reason that I now understand the smoking trap so comprehensively, is that I was in the pit for a third of a century, and I got as near to the bottom of it as I could without actually dying. That wasn't the only reason, but unless I had gone through that experience, I could never have unravelled the mysteries. I'm not saying a non-smoker is incapable of understanding the mysteries of the trap; in fact one of the things that surprised me in the early days, was that it is much easier to explain it to a non-smoker than a smoker, because non-smokers don't suffer from the illusions created by the addiction.

You would be quite justified therefore, in questioning how someone that has never smoked a puff of 'pot', let alone been a heroin addict or an alcoholic, can speak with authority or be taken seriously on such subjects? It is because:

1. What I write in this chapter isn't just the result of my own experiences or observations. It is the accumulated experience and knowledge of many ex-alcoholics and drug addicts that I've been in contact with. In particular, everything that I write here is endorsed by my main collaborator, Robin Hayley. A young man, an Oxford graduate and physically and mentally as capable as any person that I've met, as well as being dynamic and well-adjusted. If I were still in the rat race, I'd be terrified that he'd take over my job. It was a great surprise to learn that he was not only an ex-heroin addict, but at the age of 13, he was so overweight that he was forced to seek the help of 'Weight Watchers'.
2. So confident am I in my beliefs, I would be prepared to take heroin

to prove that I couldn't become addicted to it or any other chemical substance. You might regard that as a highly irresponsible attitude. On the other hand it could mean that I know what I'm talking about. It might help your decision to consider, that if I have never taken a comparatively mild drug like 'Pot' out of fear, I wouldn't touch heroin unless I was certain of my beliefs.

Imagine that I had been the first person to invent the boat. I demonstrate it to you on a pond. You're impressed, but sceptical: "This pond is only 3 feet deep, will it float in deeper water? Will it float on salt water? Will it float on ink or fruit juice?" Because I understand the principle which enables the boat to float, I don't need to test these things, I can assure you that it will. When I discovered my method, it never even occurred to me that it could be applied to anything other than smoking. It was only as a result of listening to other addicts that it dawned on me that just as it didn't make the slightest difference to the boat whether the liquid was water or ink, so the actual chemical that you happen to be addicted to is immaterial. My method is equally effective for any addiction.

That's all very well, but hardly scientific. The established medical profession couldn't possibly work on such a haphazard basis. Any new drug or technique has to be tried and tested for years before it can be launched on the public. They've just announced a marvellous new breakthrough to increase the effectiveness of the immune system to resist tumours. What wonderful news that must have been for the thousands who suffer from tumours. Just imagine their utter frustration then to be told that the cure won't be available for years! Surely the medical profession is more aware than any other, that a drowning man will clutch at any straw. His effort might be futile, but being his only chance of survival, it also happens to be very logical.

How do I know that my method will work for all addictions? Because it's obvious. In exactly the same way that I **KNEW** that my method would work for all smokers before I had tried it out on a single smoker. But, how can I be sure of that unless I've tried it? I have tried it and provided the addicts haven't attended AA or NA, they are easier to cure than smokers. I admit that I haven't had time to apply the techniques to as many other addicts as I have to thousands of smokers. I also admit that using the analogy of the boat, I might know that the boat will be more buoyant on salt water, but how will the waves affect it? I know that they can and will affect it.

There are 'waves' with alcohol and heroin that don't apply to nicotine. The 'waves' are the matters incidental to the illusion of chemical dependence itself. They include loss of job, home and family. Incidental they might be, insignificant they certainly are not. In fact with my method, the waves present the only difficulty. However, they can be overcome and do not detract from the basic principle. These waves are dealt with in a later chapter.

I hoped that I would quickly obtain general acceptance of my method for curing smokers, and then be free to concentrate on other drug addicts. However, I hopelessly underestimated the idiocy and obstinacy of the establishment in our society. I still haven't solved the smoking problem and I can wait no longer. Just as right from the beginning, the more imaginative and discriminating smokers could see that I had got the answer and gave me their support, so several ex-alcoholics and other drug addicts, without any prompting on my part, have suggested to me that my method would work for other drug addiction. Perhaps you will be able to see it too, and be in a position to do something about it. If you find yourself disconcerted by the fact that I am not a qualified medical practitioner, or that the method hasn't been subjected to umpteen years of field trials, please keep the following in mind:

1. The existing so-called experts on drug addiction have failed. Far from solving the problem, they've virtually given up the ghost. There surely can be no doubt that the drug barons are winning the battle.
2. My method doesn't have to be subjected to umpteen years of field trials. I'm not prescribing drugs. On the contrary, I am providing a simple effective cure for addiction to poisonous chemicals. What possible harm could I do? It's a no lose situation. The worst thing that can happen is that the addict remains an addict. But just think of the immense benefits if my system works?
3. We are regularly recommended and endorsed by the medical profession.

Occasionally, when discussing the subject of alcohol, I would be subjected to a vicious attack which appeared to be out of all proportion to anything that the remarks I had made warranted. Sometimes the person would declare that they had a drink problem, but the position was confused for me if they didn't. Initially I would just write them off as being somewhat cranky. It wasn't until one such person wrote to me after the session explaining that she had been dry for 20 years, and described to me the willpower that she had applied and was still having to apply in order to remain dry that I began to understand.

I cursed myself for not having the insight to see it before. How frustrating it must be for addicts, be they smokers, alcoholics, heroin addicts or whatever, to have the guts and willpower to fight the addiction, the misery, the temptation for umpteen years, and then have Allen Carr glibly say: "You didn't really need to go through all that,

It's easy!" It also explained the mystery of why I was occasionally subjected to vociferous attacks from ex-smokers at phone-ins. So now let's look at some facts, starting with:

ALCOHOL

CHAPTER 47

Alcohol

I believe there is no such illness as alcoholism or such a person as an alcoholic as society understands it. When I use either expression, I use them in the context of what society generally believes. When I refer to drinkers, or drinking, I am referring to drinks that contain alcohol unless the context is obviously otherwise.

Because Alcoholics Anonymous is widely accepted as the leading authority on alcoholism, it is impossible to discuss the subject without also discussing AA. I am aware that many of you reading this book will have had, or still have drink problems, and feel indebted to the Fellowship. Many of you will feel that you owe your very existence to the support you received from AA. Nevertheless, I am going to criticise AA. By now you would be excused for forming the impression that I am a frustrated old man, whose only pleasure in life, is to criticise other institutions. You would be correct with the frustrated aspect. With the pleasure aspect, it varies. I admit to receiving actual pleasure when criticising the pompous stuffed shirts, such as the managing director of Yellow Pages, the ITC, the BBC and suchlike. With the medical profession and certain parts of the media it causes pain rather than pleasure. With AA I feel unclean. Rather like a spy, that for the sake of Queen and country, has penetrated the rebel faction to become one of the group, and plays his role so convincingly, that he begins to feel like one of the group. Then comes the crunch, the time to decide where his loyalties really lie.

I have nothing but admiration for the Fellowship. The motives, the support, the complete absence of any hint of prejudice according to social standing, race, colour or religion. The respect shown by the entire meeting to whoever holds the floor, regardless of the length and quality of their language, content or delivery, and no matter how outlandish their views. However, admirable as their motives are, they tend to advocate to alcoholics, the equivalent of the willpower method for smokers. I believe that AA, far from ending the misery of the alcoholic, is the main contributor to the perpetuation of that misery!

If you find that the hairs on the back of your neck are rising, before you throw this book into the bin, consider these things:

1. Bill Wilson, the co-founder of AA kicked the booze, but died from the 'weed'!
2. Perhaps you succeeded in kicking the booze with the help of AA, just as many smokers have quit by using the willpower method, but it didn't help me or thousands of other smokers. By its own admission, AA has failed to cure a single alcoholic.
3. You are prejudging me. First consider the evidence. Fortunately everything that I will tell you about alcohol, or any similar chemical for that matter is good news. If you feel that I am talking nonsense, it is your privilege to discard what I say, but keep your mind open. You have listened to AA. Please allow me the same privilege.

In order to be completely fair to AA, I feel it necessary to point out that my impressions and comments were drawn from three main sources:

1. Discussions with members of the Fellowship, past and present.
2. Listening to members of the Fellowship at meetings that I attended.
3. The official booklets sent to me by AA.

I know from my own clinics that individuals will often misinterpret points that I make, whether it be inadvertently, negligently or deliberately. I'm aware that an organisation the size of AA undoubtedly suffers from similar distortions. Therefore any criticisms that I make are confined to the official booklets. However, I believe that it is the official booklets that are the main cause of the major misconceptions about alcohol.

The first booklet is entitled: 'A Newcomer Asks'. The first question the booklet deals with is: 'Am I an alcoholic?' I have no complaints about that. I'm sure that would be the prime question that any new member would require answering. My complaint is, that like every other so-called expert that we consult, whether it be accountant, solicitor or whatever, we seem completely unable to obtain a simple answer to a simple question. I once answered an advert for: 'A One-Armed Accountant'. I assure you that it was out of sheer curiosity, rather than trying to cheat a one armed accountant out of a job. On enquiring how any accountancy job necessitated just one arm, the reply was: "I'm sick of asking accountants questions and getting replies like – On the one hand you could do this, on the other hand..." I'm sure we've all suffered from the same problem many times.

AA's answer to the leading question couldn't be more vague:
"If you repeatedly drink more than you intend or want to, or if you get into trouble when you drink, you may be an alcoholic. Only you can decide. No one in AA will tell you whether you are or not."

Not a good start in my opinion. That answer wouldn't inspire confidence in me. If I asked my doctor whether I were a diabetic and got a similar answer, I would not only never consult him again, but I would wonder why I had paid so much in national insurance during my lifetime.

The second question is: 'What can I do if I am worried about my drinking?' The answer is: 'Seek help – AA can help'. Having already obtained the booklet, It would appear that the reader had already consulted AA, and the answer to the first question hasn't helped whatsoever!

Question three is: 'What is Alcoholics Anonymous?' 'We are a fellowship of men and women who have lost the ability to control our drinking and have found ourselves in various sorts of trouble because of drink. We attempt, most of us successfully, to create a satisfactory way of life without alcohol. For this we need the help and support of other alcoholics in AA'.

Other than creating doubt in the drinkers' minds, the first two answers haven't actually made the situation worse. In fact I was relieved to learn that it was a fellowship of people who had lost the ability to control their drinking rather than an inherent disease that they suffered from birth. But now really serious doubts are being put into my mind – 'We attempt', bear in mind that what I am about to ask you, is not a question, but a statement of fact. If I say to you: "In 1932 James Henry Frog-Morton attempted to walk the circumference of Lord's cricket ground on his hands in under twenty minutes." Would you believe that he succeeded or failed? As I am not asking a question, there is a very strong implication that he failed. If he indeed succeeded, I would have said: "succeeded in walking round." So the expression: 'we attempt' implies failure. When it is immediately followed by a reservation: 'most of us successfully', the negative implication is increased rather than removed. Okay, you could argue that I'm playing with words, the actual meaning is most drinkers do succeed. But what do they succeed in achieving? Only a *satisfactory* way of life? No wonder they all sound so miserable. Is that all they have to look forward to? No more joy or excitement, no more great pleasures. Already there is a very strong implication that you can't even expect to enjoy life without alcohol. From now on the best that you can hope for is "satisfactory." But even to obtain that dull ambition, they tell you that you will need the continued help and support of AA!

AA point out that they are not professional therapists and that their only qualifications for helping others to recover from alcoholism is that they've recovered themselves, and that problem drinkers coming to them know that recovery is possible because they see people who have done it. Now that read very well to me. For the first time there was something positive to cling to. It doesn't inspire the powerful effect that Patrick's 'Miss them? You've got to be joking' comment had on me, but at least now I know, if I am an alcoholic, and I don't know whether I am or not, but if I am, and if most of them do actually succeed, it means I at least have a better than 50% chance of recovery. Even if recovery means that life can only be satisfactory without alcohol, and even if it means that I need the support of AA for the rest of my life.

Then comes the real crunch question: "Why do you keep going to meetings after you are cured?" The answer: "We in the Fellowship of AA believe there is no such thing as a cure for alcoholism. We can never return to normal drinking...." Just a minute! What do they mean? You can recover but you can never be cured? What's the difference? Okay, I can accept that it might take time to recover fully, but surely, once you have fully recovered, you are cured? And what do they mean when they say that you can never return to normal drinking? What is *normal* drinking? Why should I want to return to it? Are they implying that I'm missing out? This would confirm my previous impression, that I could never expect better than a satisfactory way of life. There is even something depressing about the word satisfactory. It was the most common comment on school reports. Your parents would say: "Satisfactory? Surely you can do better than that!" You were secretly pleased, because your teachers hadn't commented on your true progress. It wasn't because they were feeling magnanimous, but because with five hundred grubby little morons to assess at the same time, they couldn't even remember who you were. I can't imagine anything more boring or mundane than satisfactory, if I couldn't be good, I'd prefer to be downright bad.

If, despite AA's rather vague guidelines, I had decided that I was in fact an alcoholic, I would have found 'A Newcomer Asks' rather depressing. It might however have left me with one ray of hope. Even if there were no cure to my alcoholism, at least it didn't confirm the rumours that I was abnormal because of some flaw in my chemical make-up, rather than because of the drinking habits that I had adopted. The second booklet however would have removed any vestiges of hope!

Entitled 'WHO ME?' It commences:

"The unhappiest person in the world is the chronic alcoholic who has an insistent yearning to enjoy life as he once knew it, but cannot picture life without alcohol. He has a heart-breaking obsession that by some miracle of control he will be able to do so."

The statement itself is rather confusing. Does it mean that he has to exercise a miracle of control to picture life without alcohol? If so, his chances of success must be rather slim! The other booklet has told me that there is no cure! Surely that means that I'll always be a chronic alcoholic! This in turn means that I'm doomed to remain the unhappiest person in the world for the rest of my life!

The next few pages include the following statements:

"Alcoholism is a progressive illness often of gradual onset."

"Alcoholism is a fatal illness for which there is no known medical cure, and many of its victims are forced to wage a losing battle."

"If we take any alcohol whatsoever something happens both physically and mentally...."

My worst fear has now been confirmed. It's not just mental it's also physical. In fact the booklet groups alcoholism with heart disease and lung cancer!

I am trying to imagine that I am back at rock bottom, and that it was caused by alcohol rather than nicotine. Eventually I become so desperate that I seek help, in spite of the fact that I am convinced that I am beyond help. I would have sought the assistance of AA believing that AA were the leading experts on the subject. I find it difficult to imagine the effect it would have had on me if I had been told: "You are suffering from a FATAL, PHYSICAL & MENTAL disease, which is PROGRESSIVE and for which there is **NO KNOWN MEDICAL CURE!**" Accepting that alcoholics are going to be pretty low before they seek help, I do not find it surprising that they become the most unhappy people in the world, and once AA had confirmed that to me, I would have seen little point in attending their sessions. In fact I believe I would have seen no further point in living.

Now, before you rush off and do something drastic, let me assure you that there is a known medical cure which is complete, easy and instantaneous. Now I know that there are many alcoholics that haven't touched a drop for years who will try to persuade you otherwise. However, I assure you that I speak the truth. I can understand why such alcoholics get annoyed when I make such statements and why they get even more annoyed when I claim that there is really no such thing as an alcoholic.

The booklets talk about normal drinkers who can control their intake, whereas alcoholics have a physical and mental illness that, should they allow just one drop of alcohol to pass their lips, are compelled to have another, then another ad infinitum. The booklet even refers to it as:

"Similar to the manifestation of an allergy. It's compounded by an overwhelming craving for the very thing that can only worsen the effects of physical suffering, irrational behaviour and increasing isolation."

I find that a strange comparison. People with allergies have an overwhelming desire not to get within a mile of the cause of the allergy. They certainly have no desire actually to imbibe it nonstop. Alcoholism seems to be much more comparable to nicotine or heroin addiction. However, I suppose the comparison with allergies does help to explain the physical abnormalities. The implication is quite astounding if you consider it. It means that the actual alcohol is really just a side issue, you can be an alcoholic without ever having imbibed alcohol in your life. Someone recently suggested that it was possible to establish whether a two year old is an alcoholic!

WHAT UTTER BILGE!

Why is it that the only alcoholics we ever actually meet, are those that are incapable of controlling their intake, or used to be. Forget alcohol for a moment. If you watched someone drowning. Would you think: "Ah, that's a drownaholic, they are drowning not because they have got into difficulties that any other human being could have got into, but because there is some basic flaw in their chemical make up, they were doomed to drown from birth." Such a theory would be laughed out of court.

Yet that is what many alcoholics claim. This is what I used to believe about my smoking. You don't hear of smokaholics. However there is a Smokers Anonymous. Unfortunately, it is based on exactly the same principles as Alcoholics Anonymous and is equally ineffective. For years I genuinely believed that I was different from other smokers. They could control it, take it or leave it, whereas with me I had to have it, I was completely dependent on it.

It was such a great revelation for me to learn that there was no basic flaw in my chemical or mental make-up, to realise that I was no different from all the other smokers, that the reason that I smoked more than they did was that physically my body could cope with a greater quantity of the poison, that I could afford to smoke more, and that my job never restricted me from smoking.

I mistakenly thought that alcoholics would rejoice at the suggestion that they were chemically quite normal and had no inherent flaw in their make up. So why did some of them get so uptight when I made such a suggestion? It was because of the dogma that AA has instilled into them, that normal people can have the occasional drink, but it would be fatal for an alcoholic to do so. I agree with AA in that respect. It would be fatal for an alcoholic to take one sip, just as it would have been fatal for me to take one puff when attempting to quit by using the willpower method.

So why is it that alcoholics cannot control their intake, but *normal* people can? There are two obvious explanations. Either:

"I'm so weak-willed, immature, idiotic and lilly-livered, that I become incapable of acting like a rational human being after just one drink." Or:
"I'm none of those things, but you see it really isn't my fault, I'm different to other people. I suffer from a disease called alcoholism. Alcohol just affects me differently to normal people."

Now if you had to choose between those two alternatives, which would leave you with some semblance of self-respect? Unfortunately, I never had that choice as a smoker. It was plain to see that many heavy drinkers had lost their jobs, homes, families and all semblance of self-respect because they were clearly the slave of alcohol. But smoking was more subtle, even chain-smokers were, and still are, regarded as pillars of society. Even those that had sunk to my depths and obviously killing themselves, were assumed to do so, not because they weren't in control, but because the crutch or pleasure of smoking far out-weighed the disadvantages.

Although 'smokaholics' didn't officially exist, I knew that I was one, because I knew I was a strong- willed person and because most of my family were heavy smokers, it was the only logical explanation. Therefore I, and the millions of smokaholics like me, were not able to hide behind that particular cop out. The only means left to us to retain self-respect was to continue the lie that we smoked because we enjoyed smoking. It's a great pity that smokaholics hadn't been invented, because it gave alcoholics a great advantage. One thing on which I agree wholeheartedly with AA, is that the first step to a cure is to accept that you have a problem. It's easier to accept that you're an alcoholic because the disease is known to exist, but how can you accept that you suffer from a disease that doesn't?

The reason that some alcoholics take offence when I suggest that there is no such thing as alcoholism, is because they know from bitter experience that just one drink would be fatal. They now have a logical reason why normal people can have occasional drinks, but alcoholics can't. That reason is their protection, the reason that they will never ever be tempted to take just one drink. By questioning the reason, I am effectively removing their protection, I'm now leaving them vulnerable to the possibility that perhaps they too can control it.

If I believe that, why do I rock the boat and put doubts into the minds of ex-alcoholics? Because they have arrived at the correct decision for the wrong reasons. If I can put doubt in the mind of an ex-alcoholic because those reasons are false, so can the powerful influences in society that profit from making people alcoholics. What's more they do. Many ex-alcoholics sense themselves that the reason is false and all too many fall back into the pit because of it.

I knew it would be fatal to have just one puff of nicotine, but that

The Only Way to Stop Smoking

didn't stop me. Sooner or later I would end up in the pit again. It wasn't until I knew the true reason why I couldn't have one puff, or more correctly, not why I *couldn't*, but why I didn't need to have one puff that I knew I was safe and that no force on earth could ever affect my protection. At the same time, I ceased to be a smokaholic, ex-smokaholic or recovering smokaholic. I knew I would be happy to remain a non-smoker for the rest of my life. I was already free.

I began to form the strong impression that, although AA had helped to save the lives and self-respect of thousands of alcoholics, they had not made it easy. They appeared to rely mainly on the willpower of the individual together with group support. I started attending AA meetings and was completely taken aback by the proceedings.

A popular misconception about all drug addiction, is that it is the dregs of society that fall into these traps. I do not dispute that those that fall into them often become the dregs of society, but generally, it is the cream of society that falls for the trap. I was expecting to meet a group of pathetic, inarticulate, underprivileged down and outs that had been reduced to drinking meths. This image was far from the reality. If they gave an impression of being pathetic, it was certainly not because they were down and outs, although many had obviously suffered severe financial and personal relationship knocks because of their drinking. Far from being inarticulate or underprivileged, they were in the main the complete opposite: well educated, articulate and very successful people that had everything going for them.

In turn each member would give a monologue, the first half of which would cover in vivid detail, their slide down the alcoholic pit. The general impression I formed was that their dependency on alcohol was more the result of the success of their lives than any traumas or failures. Each speaker appeared to have sunk lower than the previous speaker. If the scratch golfer is the hero of the golf club, I formed the impression that unless you had reached the pit bottom, you wouldn't rate at all in AA.

If you have formed the impression that I am being somewhat self-righteous, let me hasten to say that the reason that I found them so pathetic was that, substitute nicotine for alcohol, I was listening to a group of people each of whom could have been Allen Carr when he tried to stop smoking using the willpower method.

However it wasn't the first part of the discourse that I found so disturbing. You might well argue that Allen Carr boasts that he has yet to meet a worse nicotine addict than himself. It might sound like a boast, but I was certainly ashamed of the fact whilst I was in the pit. Today I'm neither ashamed nor proud of the fact. I regard myself as merely a victim of circumstances, and if I go into gory details about the depths to which I descended, I do it for the same sound reasons that members of AA do. You are less likely to fall into the pit again if you remember how vile it was. It also helps other victims that have yet to escape from the pit to know that they are not unique or alone, to know that there are others that sunk just as low, or even lower, yet escaped to enjoy life again.

'Escaped to enjoy life again?' This is where I disagree so vehemently with AA! The second half of the discourse, with the exception of just one isolated case, was a diatribe of doom, gloom and depression. These people would go into vivid detail about how evil alcohol was, how it had clearly been the cause of their ruin, they quite obviously got no prop or pleasure from their drinking, and most of them hadn't touched a drop for umpteen years, and had no intention of ever touching another drop.

Why were they still having to fight the battle? Why were some of them still having to attend AA meetings, several times a week, ten years after they had touched their last drop of alcohol? Why did they still retain this feeling of doom and gloom, of having to take one day at a time, or take each day as it comes? Why weren't they over the moon because they were no longer having their lives ruined by alcohol? Some explain this attitude away by saying: "It took many years to sink this low, obviously it's going to take a long time to recover." That sounds very logical, but like many of the clichés and platitudes about alcoholism and drug addiction, if you bother to question them, they are not logical.

Prolonged unemployment is another social evil that ruins peoples lives. But if those people are fortunate enough eventually to obtain a secure job, they are elated immediately. The effect of that unemployment might have cost them their homes and broken up their families. It could take years to return to their previous financial and domestic status, indeed they might never expect to do so. However their problem is solved the moment they get that job, the cycle starts to move upwards again and they are happy. So why aren't alcoholics looking forward to each new day of freedom when they solve their problem, which is when they decide not to touch another drop of alcohol?

Partly because obtaining a job is positive. Once you've got the job, your problem is ended. You know you've got it. You can know when you decide never to touch another drop of alcohol, but how do you know when you can celebrate? How do you know when you've succeeded? While you have doubt and uncertainty, you never know. It is also partly because if you obtain a job after a period of forced unemployment, you are in no doubt that your change is for the better. Alcoholics are schizophrenic, they don't like the idea of never again being allowed to touch a drop of alcohol. So the basic factors that affect the situation are:

1. It's negative.

2. The doubt and uncertainty.
3. Do I really want to be a teetotaller?

The real problem is not the individual effects of the above three items. If I believe that I might lose my house, then find out that I won't, that's negative. But I would be highly elated once I learned that the threat definitely no longer existed. However, suppose there was uncertainty. I wouldn't be elated until that doubt were finally removed. Even if the threat were finally removed without any doubt whatsoever, I wouldn't necessarily be elated. If I absolutely hated living in that house I don't see why I should be elated by having to go on living in it!

It's the inter-relation of the above three factors that alcoholics find so devastating. How can you possibly remove the doubt and uncertainty if you have doubt as to whether you want to be a teetotaller anyway? How can you ever be certain if you want to be a teetotaller, if you enjoy a drink and found you were miserable when you weren't allowed to have one on previous occasions? How can you not have doubts when you have already taken and broken the pledge on several previous occasions?

Fortunately, you can succeed, easily and immediately. But this is my main complaint against AA. Their dogma ensures that their adherents will never become free. Every speaker, some of whom hadn't touched a drop of alcohol for over 20 years, commenced their monologue with:

I AM AN ALCOHOLIC

It is essential to accept that you are an alcoholic in order to get free, just as it is essential to realise that you are in a prison in order to escape from it. Once you realise that you are in a prison, you at least have the possibility of escaping from it. An alcoholic is someone that believes that they are the slave of alcohol. It is just as essential to know:

WHEN THEY HAVE BEEN FREED FROM THAT SLAVERY

How can they ever escape from their prison if they believe that escape is impossible? That is what AA is effectively saying to alcoholics when they tell them that there is no cure to alcoholism. It is true that they might think they are giving that alcoholic some consolation: "You can't ever hope to escape from the prison, but once you accept that fact, you'll find that prison life can be quite satisfactory. NO IT CAN'T!

ANY FORM OF SLAVERY CAN ONLY BE INTOLERABLE!

This attitude is particularly harmful because it *is* possible to be free. That's exactly the same problem that I suffered when I tried to stop smoking by using the willpower method. It's as if you've struck your enemy a mortal blow, but you cannot find the body to prove it, so you go through the rest of your life vulnerable, worrying that some day that monster will again rear its ugly head.

The other major complaint I have against AA, is that by referring to '*normal* drinking', they ingrain into the alcoholics mind both the belief that they are being deprived of a pleasure or crutch and that they themselves are abnormal. However, even if you believe that alcoholism is a physiological, rather than a psychological disorder, or to use terms that I am more comfortable with, if you believe that it is a physical not a mental disease, it still doesn't explain why alcoholics have to go through the rest of their lives fighting it.

Let's use my smoking again. I truly believed that there was some flaw in my chemical make-up. So what? I knew it was killing me. I knew that I didn't enjoy being a smoker. I knew one puff would start me off again. I knew that I would be far better off as a non-smoker. No one was forcing me to smoke. So where was my problem? Simply this: I **WANTED** a cigarette, and I felt deprived and miserable if I couldn't have one. Let's make this clear. The alcoholics problem isn't that they can't drink with impunity, it is because they cannot have just **ONE!**

You are probably now thinking: "This is what AA have been saying for years: "If you have a desire to have just one drink, you'll have a desire for a million drinks." That's true. But AA don't solve your problem. They're really saying: "If you don't resist the temptation of actually drinking just one drink, you won't be able to resist the temptation of drinking a million." That is a very shrewd argument, that happens to be true. But it misses the point. It doesn't actually remove the problem. It hasn't actually removed the desire to have just one drink. It is merely a form of shock treatment. It threatens the alcoholic with the disastrous consequences of submitting to the temptation. The oldest lesson in the history of the human race, is the one way to guarantee temptation is to make it a 'forbidden fruit'.

The AA argument sounds logical, because all you have to do is to resist one drink. That would be fine if the temptation was thereby removed, but it's a fallacy. What's the difference between resisting the temptation of imbibing a million drinks, or of resisting imbibing just one drink a million times? The fact is that many alcoholics have to go through the rest of their lives resisting that one drink. I agree with AA better to do that than the alternative of remaining in the pit, just as it's infinitely better to stop smoking by using the willpower method than not at all. But with nicotine, alcohol and other drugs, many find that they cannot succeed. Fortunately there is another alternative which enables them to do so. It also enables those that would succeed using

497

the willpower method, to do so without aggravation, immediately and permanently.

Perhaps you still believe that alcoholism is a physical problem. Again, let us assume for a moment that it is. I am aware that I do have certain physical flaws in my make-up. I know that I musn't take arsenic because it will kill me. This doesn't bring out the defiant rebel in me. Strangely, the same man that will fearlessly defy signs like 'Wet Paint' or 'Keep Off The Grass', does not have the slightest desire to imbibe arsenic. Why not? It could be that arsenic isn't an addictive drug like heroin. But what difference should that make? If I'm only taking it because I'm not allowed to, does it matter whether it's addictive or otherwise? Heroin is an addictive drug, but I've no desire to take heroin either. Do smokers, alcoholics and drug addicts suffer from withdrawal pangs *before* they first sample the drug? Of course they don't. This means that any flaw is not inherent in their make-up, but exists because of:

THE NATURE OF THE DRUG NOT THE ADDICT

I have stated that alcoholism is purely a mental problem and has nothing to do with the physiology of certain individuals. In fact there is no such thing as an alcoholic. If I truly believe that, why have I frequently referred to alcholics and why do I continue to do so? Surely I'm contradicting myself? Not really, some people believe in ghosts, I don't, but I don't contradict myself because I use the word, I merely refer to what I regard as a misconception that certain other people labour under.

However, I haven't proved that there is no such thing as an alcoholic. True, and I have no intention of wasting my time or yours in attempting to do so. I have already explained why it is impossible to prove something doesn't exist, but I would ask you to weigh up the evidence. The reason that I do not believe in ghosts, is because the people that do have had generations to prove their point. They've failed to do so. If ghosts really existed, I believe someone would have produced irrefutable proof by now.

Now before you point out that it has been proved many times that alcoholics are physically different, even before they start taking alcohol, have you seen the proof for yourself, or are you relying on hearsay? Of all the thousands of alcoholics that I've discussed this matter with, not one has been able to offer me any evidence other than hearsay or what other so-called experts tell them.

So if the fact hasn't been proved either way, let's examine the evidence and decide which is more likely. If it were physical, why don't we test each child at the age of two and warn them if they are alcoholics. If it were purely physical, why is it so difficult to decide whether someone is an alcoholic or otherwise, and why can't AA tell you whether you are an alcoholic or not? Let me quote the comments of a very famous international physician: *(The words in brackets and italics are my comments)*

"The process of becoming an alcoholic can take anything from 2 to 60 years, *(What could be more vague? but surely, if it's physical, why isn't the effect immediate)* although 10 to 15 years is the average. *(I cannot see what possible significance averages serve in this case, but this means that the average alcoholic would have to actually imbibe alcohol for over 10 years before the physical defect that he was born with took effect! People that are allergic to bee stings usually find out the first time that they are stung!)* You may think you are immune, but do not be complacent. Ask yourself the following questions replying honestly.

Do you take a drink before facing up to a problem? *(Usually no, but I'm sure there are times when I have done)*

Do you drink for the taste or for the effect? *(Sometimes for the taste, sometimes for the effect, sometimes both and sometimes neither)*

Do you sneak away from work for a quickie before lunch? *(I have drunk before breakfast, let alone lunch, but sneak away? Never. If I had to sneak away for a drink, I wouldn't need to answer any other questions, I would know that I had a serious drinking problem.)*

Do you drink by yourself? *(Yes, whenever I feel like it)*

Do you have memory lapses after drinking? *(Yes, whenever I have too much to drink.)*

Do you find other people slow to finish their drinks? *(Sometimes, particularly when I've bought the first drink and the other person sits there all evening sipping that one drink. That's almost as annoying as the person that buys the first pint, gulps it down in one go, then expects me to get up and buy another before I've had the chance to take the head off of mine.)*

The questionnaire concludes: "Exercise extreme caution if you have answered 'yes' to one or more of these questions – it could mean that you are drinking too much. Seek medical advice. You may not necessarily have to stop drinking, but you would be well advised to control your drinking. The above are extracts from 'The Body Machine'. The cover gives no author. The only name mentioned thereon is Dr. Christian Barnard, Consultant Editor. I find it sad that such an eminent 'path-finder' should have endorsed such rubbish. The questionnaire would be more suited to a subject like: "Do the opposite sex find you attractive?"

I have answered 'yes' to 5 out of the 6 questions. I would suggest that any person that wasn't a teetotaller, couldn't possibly come up with less than 3 affirmatives if they were being completely honest. The logical conclusion would be that nearly every drinker in the world should seek the advice of their doctor, including of course, the vast majority of doctors. Supposing we did all seek medical advice. I wonder what help or advice we would actually receive? I strongly suspect it would be identical to the advice that the book gives if you answer yes to just one question:

CONTROL YOUR DRINKING

But isn't that what we do and have been doing the whole of our lives? Whenever we've felt like a drink, provided we could afford one and have been able to obtain one, haven't we had one? Okay, perhaps your drinking habits are not identical to what is considered to be normal. Perhaps you like to drink at different times, at different occasions, different types of alcohol at a different speed to what is considered to be normal. So what? That is your prerogative. I assume you don't try to force your drinking habits onto other people, so why do they try to force theirs onto you? As young men we'd be the envy of our pals if we could down 8 pints in one session. So why are eyebrows raised because someone drinks a whole bottle of wine with their meal in later life?

Why does society keep moving the goal posts? Why is the person, who takes his flask to the office and has crafty sips throughout the day, regarded as an alcoholic with a serious problem, even though his total consumtion is two large whiskeys; whereas the person who drinks 8 pints or 10 double whiskeys in an evening, arriving home completely incapable, is merely someone who enjoys a drink? Society leads us to believe that the important difference is:

CONTROL?

Alcoholics have to have alcohol. The only way they can possibly control their intake is to abstain completely, whereas heavy drinkers are in control.

BULLSHIT!

Have you ever seen a single drunk, alcoholic or otherwise, that was in control? It's a contradiction in terms. There's no such thing as 'using' drugs. It's the other way around:

DRUGS USE US!

This applies whether you be the advanced addict in the depths of the pitcher plant, or the teenager taking the first cigarette or shandy. If you do so, you have alighted on the rim of the plant. Both pitcher plant and drugs give their victims a genuine choice at this stage. The first choice is that they can either fly away or abstain. The alternative choice is to take a second dose. Both fly or human believe that they retain their choice, but part of the subtlety of both traps is, having fooled the victims into making the wrong choice, why should the victims even want to change their minds? The trap is already sprung. Once the victims reach the stage where it becomes obvious that they made the wrong choice, they are well and truly hooked. Both pitcher plant and drugs are so designed that once the trap is sprung, the victims can move in only one direction:

DOWN!

The real difference between the alcoholic and other drinkers, whether they be casual or heavy, is not that other drinkers are in control, and alcoholics are not, it's that the other drinkers don't *realise* that the alcohol is controlling them and has been since the second sampling. It's exactly the same with nicotine. In fact the alcohol and nicotine traps have many things in common.

Victims of both are brainwashed from birth into believing that smoking and drinking are natural and enjoyable sociable pastimes that provide genuine benefits. True in recent years society has begun to regard smoking as anti-social. However, not drinking at social events is still widely regarded as anti-social behaviour, unless the person has a valid excuse, such as having to drive.

Youngsters are not normally influenced by whether a pastime is sociable or otherwise, however both alcohol and nicotine are both still regarded by teenagers as 'forbidden fruits' and signs of maturity. As such they are irresistible.

Both taste awful to start with. Victims are convinced they could never become hooked. Both entrap you so slowly and gradually, you don't even realise that you are in a trap. Both are poisons, but to begin with, our intake is so small and irregular, that physically and financially, it's no problem.

But, most insidiously of all, both initially fool us into believing that we are imbibing them because they are genuinely enjoyable, the chemical effect of both is that as our brain and bodies become immune to the drug, we require increasingly larger doses. Without even realising it, we have become dependent on the drug. It doesn't matter whether we think we are taking it for taste or effect, the point is in certain situations we feel miserable without it.

I have said that I am in control of my drinking. I drink whenever I choose to drink. But isn't this exactly the same argument that I applied to my smoking, even when I had reached the stage that I knew that it was killing me? Obviously it is I that decide on any particular occasion whether I choose to drink or not. But how do I know on any occasion that I am choosing, not because I genuinely want to, but because I am addicted to, or am dependent on a drug?

I would suggest that there is a simple way to find the answer, and you don't need to ask yourself a variety of questions. Let me use myself as an example. A few years ago I attended Royal Ascot for the first time. It was a wonderful occasion and I vowed that it would be a permanent feature of the Carr social life. There were many highlights including champagne and lobster. If you said to me: "You can go to Ascot in future, but there will be no lobster." I would have no need to even think about it. I would go. However, if you said: "There'll be no champagne or any other alcoholic drink." Not only would I hesitate, but I believe my answer would be: "Stuff Ascot!"

Perhaps you would have the same attitude. However, If you asked me which I enjoyed the most, a lobster or a glass of champagne, again I could answer without hesitation: lobster. So why is it that I much prefer lobster to any form of alcohol, yet the thought that I could never eat lobster again is of no undue concern to me, but the thought that I could never imbibe alcohol again, has a similar effect on me as the thought of never being allowed to smoke again used to.

I don't regard myself as having a drink problem. I know that I am not an alcoholic. In fact I regard myself as an average drinking man. However, apart from the lobster/alcohol conundrum, there is another indisputable fact that I find it impossible to ignore. Just as throughout my smoking life, the variety of occasions that I chose to smoke tended to increase, and the quantity of cigarettes that I chose to smoke on those occasions increased, so I find that exactly the same pattern has taken place with my consumption of alcohol. True, I haven't reached anything like the depths of degradation that I did with smoking, but it's the same downward trend. For some reason, this doesn't seem to happen with lobsters.

However, my drinking is no real problem to me at the moment and why should I deny myself a pleasure, even if I know it's only illusion? This is the real evil of both traps and the real difference between the alcoholic and other drinkers, while we are able to cope with the poisonous effects and the drain on our finances, why should we even consider depriving ourselves of a pleasure or crutch?

As the accumulative adverse effects on your health and pocket begin to drag you down, so the greater your dependence on the *crutch* becomes. You start to lie to yourself and try to hide your dependence from your friends, relatives and colleagues. You deceive neither yourself nor them. They hate to see you destroying yourself. They can see more clearly than you can, that you receive neither pleasure nor crutch.

They know you'll resent their interference, but can no longer bear to watch your degradation. No matter how diplomatic they are in their attempts to make you see what you are doing to yourself, you resent them. Because you are either aware of the depths that you have reached and have been able to do nothing about it, in which case they merely make the situation worse, or they point out what you have begun to suspect for yourself, but haven't yet been able to accept. They don't ask you to abstain completely, merely to follow Dr. Barnard's excellent advice: "Could you not exercise more control? Do you have to drink quite so much? Is it really necessary to drink on such or such an occasion? Do you have to start drinking before such and such a time? Do you have to drink *every* day?"

Now you've really got problems! Up to now your only problem was that you drank too much. You still drink too much, you haven't solved that problem, but you now have an additional problem of not being allowed to drink enough! Alcohol ceased to be a 'forbidden fruit' once you established that you were grown up. But now the 'Wet Paint' syndrome is back again. Alcohol wasn't particularly precious when you were allowed to drink all that you wanted, however now it's become the most precious thing under the sun. More important than your wife, your children, your friends, your job, your home! More important than existence itself. You are now at the stage that all addicts eventually come to, provided they live long enough, at one and the same time you have the problem of drinking too much and of drinking too little, or not being allowed to drink whenever you want to, which amounts to the same thing. What's more, both problems will get worse!

You have now reached an impossible situation: when you are drinking, you have a guilty conscience because you drink too much, and when you are not drinking, you feel deprived and miserable. Increase your intake and the guilt and the adverse physical and financial effects get worse. Reduce your intake and you merely spend more time feeling deprived and miserable. You've reached the stage when even the illusion of getting some crutch or benefit from alcohol has gone. The actual fact is that you are miserable when you are drinking and you are miserable when you aren't drinking. Hence the AA doctrine: "One drink is too many and a thousand are never enough."

However, because we believe that we used to get a crutch or pleasure and because it appears illogical to drink too much yet not enough at one and the same time, we cannot accept the situation. So start the years of trying to compromise, to cut down, to control, and with it the consequent failure, loss of self-respect, the lying and the deceit. Eventually it dawns on us how futile it all is. By trial and error we come to the conclusion that AA came to:

IT HAS TO BE COMPLETE ABSTINENCE

No wonder alcoholics find that difficult to accept. To a person that has sacrificed job, home, family, friends and all semblance of self-respect, all for the sake of that *precious* nectar, to have already reached rock bottom and then to have to accept that they can never, ever touch a single drop! It's little wonder that they start off with a feeling of doom and gloom and that it takes many of them years to recover. But what can they do about it? They were born with the problem. It's part of their physiological make up. There's nothing they can do about it, because they are ALCOHOLICS.

BULLSHIT!

There *is* something that they can do about it. The first thing is to understand the nature of the beast. AA relate the 'one drink is too many' doctrine to alcoholics. The doctrine is absolutely true, but it should be related not to the victim, but to the drug. It is in the nature of drugs like nicotine, alcohol and heroin. They are poisons. The poisonous effects of one dose might well be insignificant, but one *is* too many because they are also addictive and as you become mentally dependent on them, and your body becomes immune to the illusory effects of crutch or pleasure, the tendency is that you will steadily need to increase your rate of intake. There is nothing illogical about this:

IT IS THE NATURE OF THE BEAST

The cumulative effects of the poisoning plus the ever increasing daily intake, will eventually create a counter desire to abstain, or at least cut down the rate, but that won't remove your illusory need for the drug, on the contrary, the more it knocks you down, the greater is your need for the illusory benefits.

I have been saying that there is no such thing as an alcoholic. What I mean is, the definition generally accepted by society, is false. My dictionary merely adds to the confusion. It gives two definitions of alcoholism:

1. Continual heavy consumption of alcoholic drink.
2. Physiological disorder resulting from this.

The Collins dictionary defines physiology as the branch of science concerned with the functioning of organisms. How can someone that hasn't touched a drop of liquor for 20 years fall within the first definition? The second definition implies that the disorder arose from the heavy drinking rather than some inherent chemical defect in the alcoholic. To suggest vice versa, is rather like tipping the winner, after the race. It's about as logical as saying: "All persons born on December 25th, do so because they are born on Christmas day."

Let me explain what an alcoholic really is. To do so, I need to go back to the pitcher plant. The fly is oblivious to the fact that gravity combined with the volume and direction of the hairs on the plant, are designed to make it move in one direction: **DOWN**. It is so entranced with the quality of the nectar that, not until it has had its fill and tries to fly away, does it realise that, not only has it been nourished by the goo, it has been trapped by the goo. The more it panics and struggles, the more goo it accumulates, the greater its rate of acceleration to the depths of the pit. The plant sides have become smooth and hairless. Hairs would now only impede the rate of descent. At least the plant allowed the fly to sample the nectar, but like all good confidence tricks, the plant gave nothing. It gained the fly and lost not a drop of its precious nectar.

At what stage did the fly lose control? When it tried to escape? No that was merely the time it realised that it had lost control. From the time the fly tasted the nectar, it was being controlled by the plant, it just didn't realise that it was. So it is with nicotine, alcohol and other drugs. You become a smokaholic, a drug addict, or an alcoholic the moment that you *realise* that you are no longer in control, and just like the fly, that realisation causes you to struggle, panic and become more entrapped. Up until that time you were just a smoker, a drinker or a drug user; casual or heavy, it makes no difference. The truth is, that the moment you took that first or second dose, you were like the honoured explorer being wined and dined by the natives. In the excitement of the preparations for the annual harvest festival, too late you discover that you are not the main guest, but the main course!

Once the fly realises it's trapped, it's too late. There *is* no escape. Fortunately, for alcoholics, smokers and drug addicts, there is an easy escape, provided they fully understand the nature of the trap. If you believe that you do understand the nature of the trap, but have decided to delay your escape until some future date, it means that you have missed the point and in all probability, you'll never escape.

One essential in order to escape from the trap, is to realise alcoholics are no different in their chemical make up from *normal* drinkers or teetotallers for that matter. If you still believe that alcoholism was something that you were born with, rather than a sinister subtle trap that you and millions of others fell into, then re-read Chapter 21 dealing with addictive personalities.

I have said that the alcohol trap is almost identical to the nicotine trap. However, their differences can cloud the issue. It's necessary first to analyse these differences in order to see the wood from the trees. I have said there is no genuine crutch or pleasure from imbibing nicotine or alcohol. It is difficult enough to convince smokers of this, even when it should be obvious that no genuine pleasure could be obtained from breathing poisonous fumes into their lungs. It's even more difficult to convince drinkers that they get no genuine pleasure from alcohol. A poison it might be, but it also happens to be a liquid. Surely liquids quench your thirst? How could anyone argue that quenching your thirst is not a genuine pleasure?

I agree that there are few pleasures greater than quenching your thirst. However, this is one of the many illusions about alcohol, it doesn't quench your thirst! On the contrary, it dehydrates you and actually causes you to be thirsty. This is why you tend to want to drink eight pints of beer, but rarely more than one glass of water. Am I really trying to imply that a pint of beer after a game of golf, cricket or rugby doesn't quench your thirst? Beer isn't 100% alcohol or anything like it, in fact we now have beers that contain no alcohol. The largest constituent of beer or wine for that matter is water. No one drinks neat spirits to quench their thirst. It is not necessary to add alcohol to any drink in order to quench your thirst. In fact, after we have been successfully weaned, mother nature provides us completely free of charge, with an abundant supply of the best thirst quencher of all. A drink that contains no calories and flows cool and fresh out of every mountain stream. At least it did before we polluted them. But we've been hyped into believing that water isn't good enough for us. It's too mundane. We need something more exciting. Something green or purple, that contains a pound of fruit, has its own little umbrella and costs a fortune. Just as in the case of nicotine, taste is a red herring, it has absolutely nothing to do with it. If you imbibe a drink that contains alcohol, you do so either because you have been hyped, or:

TO GET THE EFFECT

The main difference between alcohol and drugs like nicotine and heroin is that no physical empty, insecure feeling ensues when alcohol leaves the body. I now hear cries of outrage. Have I not heard of delirium tremens? Yes I have. I believe it to be a very real condition. But I do not believe that it is caused by physical withdrawal from alcohol. On the contrary, I believe it is caused by the poisonous effects of imbibing too much alcohol, combined with the mental panic of being deprived of alcohol. I used to get the shakes when I had no cigarettes, I now know that physical condition was caused by the mental panic of being deprived of my *crutch*, rather than by the physical itch. I am not saying that alcoholics do not get into a panic when deprived of alcohol, they obviously do, but that panic isn't caused by physical withdrawal symptoms. It is caused by exactly the same reason as nicotine or heroin, that the addict believes they are being deprived of a genuine crutch or pleasure.

With nicotine the illusion of a crutch is created because the drug appears to relieve the itch that the last dose created. With alcohol the illusion of a crutch is created because it causes inebriation. This is why it takes an average of 10 to 15 years for a drinker to become completely dependent on alcohol. With smoking, provided the smoker can afford to smoke, it can happen immediately from the first cigarette. This is also why, even though most smokers start off by only smoking at social functions, it is regarded as quite normal for smokers to have cigarettes with them permanently. Indeed it would be considered abnormal for a smoker not to do so. It's not even considered abnormal if a smoker's first act of the day is to light a cigarette, and whose last act of the day is to stub one out, having smoked regularly throughout the day. Smokers aren't even regarded as unusual if they wake up during the night and light up.

Smokers don't have to answer questionnaires like: do you ever light a cigarette before you face up to a problem? Do you ever smoke alone? Do you find other smokers don't smoke as many as you do? Do you ever sneak away from your non-smoking office for a quickie before lunch? The reason that they don't have to answer questions like that is because everyone knows that such behaviour is regarded as quite normal.

However, if the poor drinker keeps a flask permanently with him, or were immediately to down a shot of whisky the moment he awoke, or had to take a slug from his flask every time the phone rang, boy would he have problems, just one of those acts and he'd be branded an alcoholic. As I say, because smokers become dependent very quickly, they and their smoking habits are regarded as normal. Because it takes drinkers years to become totally dependent, they're in the minority and their behaviour is regarded as abnormal.

The other great difference between nicotine and alcohol, is that alcohol blows the mind. Drinkers that become completely dependent, lose their jobs, homes, friends and families. I was lucky, I was dependent on nicotine. You might argue that had I been dependent on alcohol, I would have controlled my drinking, so that I didn't lose my job or my home. I truly believed I would lose my life because of my smoking. If that wasn't sufficient incentive for me to stop, my job certainly wouldn't have done the trick. I'm the same beast whether I had fallen into the nicotine or the alcohol pit, it would have been a headlong slide to disaster either way. It's the differing nature of the chemicals and not the victims that makes the difference. You might argue that the differences between alcohol and nicotine are quite material, and that because I've never been an alcoholic and claim that there is no such thing as an alcoholic, how can I claim to be an expert on the subject?

True, I have never been an alcoholic, but I have been a drinker and

507

on occasions a heavy drinker. I also know that, but for the grace of God, I could have become what people refer to as an alcoholic. It is true that there are material differences between alcohol and nicotine, and heroin for that matter, so what? There are differences between various species of pitcher plant. You might also argue that the variations in the pitcher plant are designed to entrap insects with correspondingly different chemical make-ups. Again, so what? Fortunately, these differences make no difference to the effectiveness of the remedy. There are substantial differences between a tree and a house, but the same ladder will not only enable you to surmount both obstacles, but will enable all other human beings to do so, in spite of their differing physiques, characters and personalities.

As far as the cure is concerned, nicotine and alcohol are identical:

1. Before we imbibed either, our lives were complete.
2. We are lured into both traps as the result of massive brainwashing from birth.
3. We believe that we get some genuine crutch or pleasure from both, yet at the same time know that they both adversely affect us physically and financially.
4. We associate that crutch or pleasure with many events in our lives and believe that those events can never be enjoyable without them. Consequently, we feel deprived and miserable if we attempt to abstain, which confirms our belief that the crutch or pleasure is genuine.

The really important things that they have in common are that they are both mental prisons. Once you realise that in fact there *is* nothing to give up, that they do absolutely nothing for you at all and that not only will you be just as happy without them, but infinitely more so, then there is no feeling of deprivation, there is no feeling of doom and gloom, there is only elation! So, all we now have to do is to make you realise that alcohol brings you nothing but disaster and that there is no *genuine* crutch or pleasure whatsoever.

We have already dispelled the myth about quenching the thirst, but surely I'm not going to be stupid enough to suggest that no one ever enjoys the taste of alcohol? That is exactly what I am suggesting. If you do not believe me, try drinking pure alcohol. Yes, but surely blended with other liquids alcohol tastes good? No, alcohol is a poison, and like all poisons it tastes awful. The whole object of the mixers is to cover up the awful taste of the alcohol. But whole industries have been built up around the wonderful taste of certain alcoholic drinks. Why else 'The Real Ale' society? What about expert wine tasters?

The hype about alcoholic drinks is even more exaggerated than the hype about smoking. I'm sure most of us have been fooled into paying

$20 for a cigar or double for a pack of cigarettes that has different coloured papers and then justified our stupidity by talking about the superb quality. But very few of us have been sober at the time. Yet there are people who will pay hundreds of pounds for a bottle of wine! At least I hear stories of such people, I've never actually met one. Do you believe that the taste of any bottle of wine is worth hundreds of pounds? If you do, you are either a fool, or in the wine business and make your living from fools!

I have seen people go through much pomp and ceremony when paying £20 for a bottle of wine. Ironically, they were always people who were either scraping the barrel or had so much money that they were finding it difficult to use it up. I also admit that at times, I have joined in the ritual. Not wishing to be impolite, I have congratulated them on the quality of their selection, but at the same time been thinking: "I can buy better than this for £3 a bottle in my local supermarket." Perhaps you are sympathising with me for being the uncultured cretin that I am, not able to distinguish between a superior wine and vinegar. If so, remember that you are paying six times as much as I am for your alcohol. I despise the meths drinker, but I'm paying six times as much as he is!

We are persuaded that wines improve with maturity. What a clever marketing ploy, if dealers over buy, they don't have to dump it in a half-price sale at the year end, they merely let it collect dust and charge more. There are many vested interests that have tried to persuade me that wine does improve with age, and I believed them. With food it is easy to tell when it has gone off, because it tastes awful. But with wine how can you tell when it tastes awful to begin with? The ritual that caused me to question the claim that wine improves with age, is this hype about Nouveau Beaujolais. "It's absolutely essential to drink it within 24 hours of being bottled, even if it means chartering a special plane, you might just as well poor it down the drain otherwise!" Tell me a product improves with age, and I might be stupid enough to believe you. But if you tell me the same product deteriorates with age, it is you that is being stupid. You insult my intelligence!

Do you have problems persuading your weight conscious and thrifty wife or girlfriend to try a little fresh cream on her strawberries? Do you think you could persuade her to drink a small glass of fresh cream? It's easy! You can make her drink several glasses and pay ten times as much as the cream would normally cost. Just buy her a bottle of one of these popular liqueurs that contain cream. If you enjoy the sweet taste of a wine or liqueur, what you enjoy is the sugar additive, not the alcohol. The wine trade is a bit more subtle than the beer trade, the opposite to sweet is bitter, but the opposite to a sweet wine is a dry wine. How can any wine be dry? I have heard wines described as precocious, sombre, flippant or even mysterious! The only mystery is why we are stupid enough to fall for the hype.

On presentation nights at my golf club, the drinks arrive quicker than I can drink them. Occasionally I down what I believe to be the dregs of a gin and tonic which is actually neat gin. The effect is about as pleasant as sniffing ammonia. How often do you see whisky drinkers obliterate the taste with a mixer and complain that the bar didn't stock their favourite brand of whisky? When blindfold these so-called experts have difficullty in distinguishing between the taste of whisky and cold tea!

Now let's try to cut out all the hype and get down to some facts. I have yet to meet the youngster, that when he had his first pint of beer, wasn't secretly thinking: "Have I really got to drink this muck? I would much rather have a glass of lemonade." Of course he would, but only kids drink lemonade, *real* men drink beer. Bob Hope summed it up in a film called 'Paleface'. He walked into the saloon where all the tough cowboys were drinking 'Rot Gut' or 'Red Eye' straight out of the bottle, and said: "Gimmee a glass of milk." He got some peculiar looks, then snarled: "In a dirty glass."

Just like tobacco, if you persevere with any drink that contains alcohol, you will *acquire* the taste. In fact you don't *acquire* the taste. A taste doesn't change because you persist. What actually happens is that your brain and body get used to the foul taste. Start imbibing a different brand of beer, or whisky, whatever, to begin with it will taste foul or weird, persist and you will learn to *enjoy* it. How many times have you heard someone say: "This is a tasty drop of bitter." It's a contradiction. There's no such thing as a tasty drop of bitter. It's called bitter because it tastes bitter. Bitter means having or denoting an unpalatable harsh taste. The advertising geniuses have recently based a whole marketing campaign on a Canadian beer because it tastes awful: "You won't like it!" What tough, hard-drinking rugby player could resist the challenge?

Now can you honestly say to yourself, that when you drink your favourite tipple, be it beer, wine, spirit, liqueur or cocktail, that the social ritual, your thirst, or the alcoholic effect have absolutely nothing to do with it, you down pint after pint, or glass after glass, purely, because you cannot resist the taste? Or are you like me, your favourite wine is the one that you find is not too sweet, not too dry, not too fruity and has no unpleasant taste. In fact, do you find that your favourite wine is the one which you can imbibe reasonable quantities of alcohol, at as little cost as possible, without too much aggravation, and that it's not so much that your favourite wine tastes so much better than other wines, but that you find other wines distasteful, some less tolerable than others? Believe me, if taste had any bearing on the matter whatsoever, just like tobacco, no one would take the second alcoholic drink. If you are still convinced that you drink alcohol because of its marvellous taste, try sticking to pure alcohol!

The problem is, we are all brought up on these Lee Marvin type films. Let's have a great night on the town. It isn't regarded as a great night unless he downs 10 whiskies, creates a punch-up in some bar, which has to be wrecked in the process, then spends the next four days in a stupor recovering from the effects! Then we employ thousands of expert psychiatrists to explain to us why we have given our children everything, yet they grow up drunken hooligans.

THE ONLY MYSTERY IS WHY SO MANY OF THEM DON'T

So if we don't imbibe alcohol to quench our thirst, or for the marvellous taste, we must do it for the marvellous effect. What is so bad about that? It is an established fact that, providing it's in moderation and people don't get offensive, any social gathering is much more enjoyable and exciting with alcohol. Is it? Or is it like the smoking, that from birth we've been brainwashed to believe that it is so? That like smoking, we associate it with becoming an adult? That like smoking, we tend to start drinking only at social occasions, at times when we are thoroughly enjoying ourselves anyway?

AA is quite right, the chronic alcoholic has an insistent yearning to enjoy life as he once knew it, but, like the ex-smoker, is he in fact pining for a myth, for something that never actually existed? Let us examine the reality.

Can you honestly say that before you started drinking, you never enjoyed social occasions, birthdays, parties, weddings, Christmas etc? Just watch children at a birthday party. They arrive in their best clothes, shy and inhibited. Butter wouldn't melt in their innocent mouths. Five minutes later they are destroying the place. They're on a complete and utter 'high'. But they don't need nicotine, alcohol or any other drugs, a true 'high' is just feeling great to be alive. The problem is that because drugs like nicotine are initially imbibed at such times, they get the credit. Alcohol also creates the outward appearance of a true high. In fact it has the opposite effect. You might believe that alcohol greatly enhances social occasions, because it makes you happy and merry. The truth is that alcohol is a depressant. Don't take my word for it. Test it out. Try sitting alone in a room, doing nothing else but drinking the quantity of alcohol you would normally drink at a party. See if it makes you happy.

I remember when I first started drinking and tried to keep up with those idiots that would brag about how many pints they could down. I can remember being violently sick and reaching what Jasper Carrot describes as the 'RAH' stage. That's the stage when your stomach fails to realise that there is nothing left to bring up and continues to retch. The vomiting was bad enough, but ten times worse for me was the period when you finally got into a nice warm bed, closed your eyes, then the room began to spin. The only way to stop it spinning was to lie with your eyes open, but by now you were so tired that you couldn't keep your eyes open. As they involuntarily close so the spinning and RAHING would continue until you were relieved by oblivion.

The following day was always a write off during which I would vow that never again would I drink more than I could handle. The memory would keep me from doing so for about a year. Okay, perhaps I'm just remembering the extreme cases, obviously no one enjoys being drunk, but surely there's nothing wrong with *normal* sociable drinking? All I can say is, observe drinkers at social occasions, when you yourself have had no alcohol at all. You will find that either the drinkers become over emotional, or they begin to giggle and to act stupidly. What's wrong with that? I hear you say, surely that's a sign that alcohol is making them happy? But are they happy? The fact that someone is giggling and acting stupidly can mean that they are inebriated or stupefied, it doesn't necessarily mean that they are happy and enjoying themselves. Have you noticed how fragile that giggling, stupefied state is? How easily just an innocent comment or glance can be taken the wrong way, and in an instant, the giggling becomes vicious aggression.

For years I've justified alcohol consumption in moderation, because I genuinely believed that it did serve just one useful purpose. Alcohol inebriates, which helps to remove fear, shyness, inhibitions. My golden rule when entertaining, was to pour as much alcohol as I could into the glass of each guest, in order to get over that awkward period at the commencement of any social gathering, particularly when people are meeting for the first time. It doesn't even do that, you still get that initial awkward period, whether the guests drink alcohol or not.

Another factor that nicotine and alcohol have in common, is that they both create the illusion of giving courage. However they do so in different ways. With nicotine, fear is engendered when it leaves the body and the illusion is created when the smoker lights up and partially relieves the feeling. With alcohol, the illusion is created because it inebriates, and by so doing, removes fear and inhibitions. So how can I claim that alcohol, like smoking, does absolutely nothing for you at all? Because courage and the removal of fears and inhibitions are not the same thing. In fact an act cannot be courageous unless accompanied by fear. I am convinced that one of the major factors that heavy smokers turn to heavy drinking, is that nicotine creates fear and alcohol creates the oblivion to block it out.

In fact the greatest evil of alcohol is that the inebriation does remove fear and inhibitions. That fear and those inhibitions are a vital form of protection and are essential to our survival. Perhaps you find that difficult to believe, let's study some practical examples.

Perhaps you have observed that when young boys have an altercation, they do not immediately resort to fisticuffs. There is invariably a prior ritual of threats, gesticulations, puffing up of chests etc, rather like stags during the rutting season. This is perfectly natural, because the first rule of nature is survival. There is a natural instinct inherent within all creatures not to fight. To do so is to risk injury or death both of which are not conducive to survival.

I have no doubt that you can think of numerous examples both in the animal kingdom and with human beings where creatures seem to be naturally aggressive. However, if you study the circumstances, animals only become aggressive when their survival is threatened anyway, either because of hunger, a threat to their territory, or because of a threat from a predator. In most cases, you will find that human beings become aggressive for exactly the same reasons. This is why I say that all aggression is based on fear. However, I do believe that in recent years, television has been brainwashing youngsters to become violent, purely for the sake of violence.

The second rule of nature is survival of the species. It might appear to be unjust, but one of the great attributes of natural selection, is that only the strong survive to pass on their genes and thus ensure the continued strength and improvement of the species. With many species, this principle is extended so that only the strongest of the survivors actually procreates. Stags spend most of the year living together in harmony. During the season of the rut, they become aggressive towards each other. Creatures will kill in order to survive, but the object of the rut is to establish which stag is the strongest without actually killing off the remainder. The rituals are designed to decide which animal is the strongest while keeping the risk of death or injury to the minimum.

So it is with disputes amongst young boys. They are both on a loser to nothing. They obtain no real benefit by inflicting serious injury on their antagonist. But they are in big trouble if they should suffer serious injury themselves. At the same time, they musn't appear to be cowards, so they go through this chest puffing preamble, hoping that the other boy will back down, or that some outside influence will intervene before they actually come to blows.

However, if those boys are affected by alcohol, they lose that protective fear and two awful things happen. Each boy loses the fear of serious injury or death and is ready to fight, but even worse, each boy loses any inhibitions about the injury that he is prepared to inflict on his opponent. With normal fights, once superiority has been clearly established, the fight ends. When alcohol is involved, there are literally thousands of cases where youngsters have actually killed each other, not for any great principle or difference of opinion, but purely because they had been drinking.

Exactly the same thing happens when driving. Some drivers are still stupid enough to believe that a little alcohol improves their performance. The truth is it slows down their reactions. However, at the same time it removes their fear of having an accident, and the effects the accident might have on their own health or that of their passengers, pedestrians or other road users. The overall effect is to make them feel more relaxed and competent. It's just an illusion. The actual effect is to transform a safe responsible motorist into a lethal killer!

I cannot think of one really happy social occasion in my life, when the participants looked back with nostalgia and attributed the success of the occasion to the volume or quality of the drinks. I can think of many social occasions that were a complete and utter bore, in spite of the fact that there was no restriction in the quality or quantity of the drinks. I can think of numerous occasions, when a marvellous wedding or party has been completely ruined because one or more people had too much to drink.

Perhaps you still feel that drink does convey some benefit in helping certain people to overcome shyness and inhibitions. Again, look at the facts. Everyone has a brain and a mouth. Most people have a sort of check point between the brain and the mouth. There is a rare breed that has no check point. There's a direct connection between their brain and their mouths. A sort of verbal incontinence. Whatever thoughts enter their brains, no matter how boring, mundane, irrelevant, trivial, inaccurate, scatter-brained, insulting, ridiculous, inconsiderate or offensive they might be, they just come spurting straight out of their mouths. These people tend to be both unpopular and unhappy.

I am lucky. I do have a check point between my brain and my mouth, but only one. This sometimes gets me into trouble. Occasionally, it lets things pass onto my mouth that it really should have blocked. Some people have two or even more check points to ensure that they never say anything that might make them appear to be stupid, or could be possibly taken as being offensive. Alcohol has the effect of negating these check points. We've all seen these people that won't say boo to a goose when they are sober, but get a couple of drinks inside them and they'll take on the world!

Is anyone fooled by them? Do we look at them and say: "I never realised Ted was such a dominant person?" Or do we say: "That's just the drink talking?" If you are shy and have inhibitions and regard it as a problem, alcohol won't cure it, any more than an ostrich putting its head in the sand will remove the danger. Alcohol will just inebriate you. It won't solve your problem but merely stupefy you and make you forget about it for a while. You won't enjoy that stupefied condition, you can't because being stupefied means you are not even aware of your senses, whether the feelings be good or bad. Whilst you are in that state, you remain vulnerable, unprotected and with your head in the sand.

In that vulnerable state, you might be very lucky, you might only insult or offend a close relative or friend, or you might be less lucky and just write off your car or sustain only minor injuries or lose your licence for a few years. Why do I describe such things as lucky? Surely I mean unlucky? No I mean lucky, because such things are bound to happen sooner or later if you are inebriated. You actually put yourself in the position of someone who's both deaf and blind. In fact you are far worse off. The deaf and blind are aware of their disabilities, and their senses of fear, touch, smell, vulnerability, compassion, decency and consideration for themselves and others become heightened to compensate. Alcohol deadens the brain, so that every one of your senses becomes incapacitated.

Then again, you might be unlucky, driving in your inebriated state, you might kill an innocent child and wake up screaming every night of your life in a cold sweat reliving a nightmare that is real. Football, our national game, has been ruined by alcohol. It's undignified enough for a child to be caned in front of the school. We taught the world to play soccer, then suffered the unbelievable indignity of being banned from competing in Europe for eight years because of alcohol. The once mighty Great Britain being punished like a naughty schoolboy! Just think of all the evil that you have seen caused by alcohol. Can you think of a single occasion when it actually did some good? When you are inebriated, you lose all of your senses, you are completely naked, defenceless, vulnerable. Do you really believe that you are happy at such times? Do you really believe that an ostrich with its head in the sand is happy?

At one time I believed that the inebriating effect of alcohol was a genuine short-term benefit to ease the effect of traumas. If your girlfriend drops you, better to go on a bender for a few days than join the Foreign Legion. If business is getting on top of you, and you just cannot afford the time to get away for that much needed holiday, what harm is there in having a few drinks in the evening to get your mind away from your problems.

However, the inebriation won't have solved your problem. It wouldn't be quite so bad if it had the same effect as a good night's sleep. That wouldn't solve your problems, but at least it would leave you more refreshed and better able to solve them. However, once the effect of the alcohol has worn off, your problem will actually be greater, because the effects of the intoxication will be to make you physically, mentally, financially and socially worse off than before. You now have even more reason to inebriate yourself and just like nicotine, the more you take the more your brain and body becomes immune to the poison, the more you need. The greater your intake, the greater the adverse effects, the greater your need. The rapid descent to the bottom of the pitcher plant is inevitable. It's the nature of the beast.

But surely, if you just drink for social reasons, that can't possibly do any harm? That's would be like saying: "There's no harm in becoming HIV positive if you don't let it develop into full blown AIDS." Of course there's harm in becoming HIV positive, because the nature of that particular disease is that it *will* develop into full blown AIDS. If you start drinking purely for social reasons the nature of that beast is that it developes into drinking for all other sorts of reasons. In any case, do we ever really drink purely for social reasons? We may start off by only drinking at only social occasions, but aren't we really taking that drink to help solve a problem? Because we feel immature, or shy, or inhibited, or because we want to be accepted as one of the crowd? If you start imbibing alcohol for purely social reasons, you start on the inevitable down-slope that *will* develop into what AA describe as chronic alcoholism!

THAT IS THE NATURE OF THE BEAST

But there are people that can use alcohol, nicotine, even heroin, all their lives, that never become alcoholics or addicts. That is true, but that is purely because the nature of these drugs takes many years for the majority of victims to realise that they have become dependent on them. As with smoking, the rate that any particular individual descends to the depths of the pitcher plant depends on many different factors, such as their physical capacity to cope with the poison, their wealth, the amount of stress in their lives, the company they keep. It is true that once in skid row, wealth doesn't come into it, the addict will find the money, but just as many youngsters never started smoking purely because they couldn't afford to, so many drinkers remained casual drinkers because they couldn't afford to do otherwise. Obviously, many flies die of natural causes before they reach the depth of the pitcher plant. So, many smokers, drinkers and other drug addicts, quit or die before they descend to skid row.

Don't let the fact that many of these traps have subtle delays confuse the issue. You certainly wouldn't envy the poor mouse for the split second of euphoria between nibbling the cheese and that steel bar smashing down on his nose or neck. Would you envy a fly that had just landed on a pitcher plant and taken its first dose of the nectar? Would you envy a lover the euphoria of his moment of ejaculation, if you knew that he was about to contract syphilis at the same time, even though the effects might not become apparent until 20 years later?

This is where AA and society generally have got it wrong. They imply that there is some genuine pleasure in *normal* drinking. The terrible trauma that alcoholics suffer when they take the pledge, isn't physical, but the belief that they are abnormal and that they are being deprived. They actually envy what they consider to be normal drinkers. If you have a drink problem, whether you regard yourself as an alcoholic or not, cast your mind back to the time when you looked upon yourself as a normal drinker. Did you feel that there was anything particularly marvellous about being one? Before you became aware that you had a drink problem, when you could drink as little or as much as you chose to, did you envy people that drank less than you did? Did you envy people that drank more than you did? Or was it only when your drinking became a problem that you began to envy *normal* drinkers?

So what? Say you, I don't envy other people being able to breathe, but I certainly would if for some reason I suddenly couldn't. That's right, but there is an important difference, we have to breathe. It's essential to our survival and always had been. The fact that we took it for granted doesn't alter that fact. But alcohol was never essential to our survival. It is a great pity that we took our *normal* drinking for granted also. Had we have studied it more closely, we would have realised that it did:

ABSOLUTELY NOTHING FOR US AT ALL!

Just like the smoking, it's not until we are not allowed to imbibe, and we feel deprived, that alcohol appears to be so precious, and the longer you're not allowed to have it, the more precious it becomes. Of course it is difficult to establish that something isn't particularly pleasant if you are not allowed to try it, and if you do, you find yourself in the hopeless position that AA so aptly describe: "Similar to the manifestation of an allergy. It is compounded by an overwhelming craving for the very thing that can only worsen the effects of physical suffering, irrational behaviour and increasing isolation."

Alcoholics don't have this overwhelming craving because they are stupid, or because of a mysterious flaw in their genes. They have it for exactly the same reason that smokers spend a fortune to destroy themselves. Society has brainwashed them from birth, and continues to brainwash them into believing that they get some genuine benefit from the drug. The nature of the drug is such to confirm this illusion. Society has also brainwashed both smokers and heavy drinkers that it is difficult, if not impossible to get free. In fact AA, the accepted leading authority on alcoholism state categorically to those seeking their help:

THERE IS NO MEDICAL CURE!

The stupid thing is that alcoholics band together rather like lepers in a colony, because society in general and AA in particular have convinced them that they are suffering from an illness for which there is no medical cure. Ironically, alcoholics cease to suffer the illness, the moment they cease to imbibe alcohol. It is the normal drinkers that have the illness. Alcohol causes no more problems than cyanide, provided you don't imbibe it!

IT'S IMBIBING ALCOHOL THAT CAUSES THE ILLNESS

However society has created, and AA in particular has perpetuated a cruel confidence trick on people that imbibe alcohol:

AN OVERWHELMING CRAVING FOR SOMETHING THAT IS EVIL

As I explained in Chapter 38, craving isn't physical, it can only be mental. Fortunately, craving is within the control of the individual. Just like smoking, you can remove that craving before you consume your last drop of alcohol.

The cure is easy and immediate. First understand the nature of the illusion. Realise that alcohol does absolutely nothing for you at all. Don't envy other drinkers, whether it be the youngster taking the first drink of poison, or what you regard as the mature seasoned drinker in control. See them for what they really are:

FLIES AT DIFFERENT LEVELS IN THE PITCHER PLANT

Obviously they won't see it that way, unless they are reaching the stage when they realise that their drinking has become a problem, and if you are tempted to envy them because their ignorance is bliss and they might never realise that they do have a problem, remember their ignorance is not bliss for them. Just as you took your *normal* drinking years for granted, so are they. They're getting no pleasure or benefits whatsoever, and, whether they realise it or not, already they are undergoing physical, mental, financial and social disadvantages.

Although alcohol and nicotine have different effects on our bodies and minds, they create an identical problem: they both cause us considerable physical, mental and financial harm. They both do absolutely nothing for us whatsoever, but create the illusion that they do. Because of this illusion, we feel deprived and miserable when compelled to abstain.

Fortunately, the solution to the problem is identical: to understand how the illusion is created; to realise that there is absolutely nothing to give up, and to rejoice in having no need or desire to smoke or drink rather than be miserable because you are not allowed to.

518

Provided that you have clearly understood that alcohol conveys absolutely no genuine benefits to you at all, and that the problem is mental and not physical, then all you need do is read the remainder of this book and re-read Chapters 42 to 45 substituting drinking or alcohol for smoking or nicotine. Do exactly the same thing if you need to refer to previous chapters.

Another fact that hit me at AA meetings was the high percentage of members that not only smoked, but smoked heavily. This did not surprise me, on the contrary, it merely confirmed my suspicions. I've already explained why for many people, the slide from *normal* to heavy drinking is precipitated by the fact that smokers become part immune to nicotine and have a permanent void which they consciously or subconsciously attempt to fill with alcohol.

If your drinking does go out of control for whatever reason, it becomes blatantly obvious to everyone else and eventually to yourself, that drink is ruining your life. It is therefore quite natural and logical to solve that problem by abstaining. However, if an alcoholic finds it so difficult to keep the pledge, how much more difficult will it be if you say to that alcoholic: "It's no good just quitting the booze, you have to stop smoking as well?".

The reason I enjoy being a non-smoker, is not so much being rid of the bad health, but just feeling great to be alive. Isn't that the same thing? In my case it was because smoking alone was the cause of my bad health. But to continue smoking after abstaining from alcohol, is tantamount to bringing a drowning man to within two inches of the surface. Obviously ex-drinkers will feel less unhealthy as a result of their abstinence. But they will not enjoy the feeling of: 'it's great to be alive' while they continue to smoke. I believe one reason that many members of AA never feel completely cured, is because they continue to retain the void that got them into the heavy drinking in the first place. They will also remain more vulnerable to falling back into the alcohol trap.

I can imagine the despair of someone who has battled over a number of years to quit alcohol and found it impossible to do so. I can also imagine what a daunting prospect it must appear, when I tell that person they must quit smoking at the same time. It must appear that I'm asking them to perform two miracles at one and the same time, and that's exactly what I would be asking them to do if they retained the misconception that they were giving up some sort of crutch or pleasure. However try to imagine a situation in which I had forced you to imbibe both arsenic and cyanide, in doses sufficient to ensure that your health was permanently debilitated without actually killing you and that I had made you pay through the nose for your poison. Do you feel that you would have any difficulty in not taking those poisons if I stopped forcing them upon you? Perhaps you feel that is not a realistic analogy? Not only is it realistic:

THAT IS EXACTLY THE POSITION DRINKERS AND SMOKERS ARE IN!

They are regularly forced to pay through the nose in order to imbibe two powerful poisons that:

DO ABSOLUTELY NOTHING FOR THEM WHATSOEVER!

I said they are in exactly the same position as taking arsenic and cyanide. In fact their is just one important difference: the only person that forces them to poison themselves with alcohol and nicotine is themselves. The only reason that they force themselves to take those poisons is because society and the nature of those poisons has brainwashed them into believing that they get some genuine crutch or pleasure from them and that it's difficult to abstain.

However, first remove the brainwashing, then abstention is not only ridiculously easy, but enjoyable. There is immense pleasure in finding a cure to what you suspected was an incurable disease. That pleasure will be almost non-existent if you happen to be suffering at the same time from another incurable disease. Fortunately there is a simple and effective cure for both nicotine and alcohol dependency. It is simply:

1. To realise that your dependency is an illusion.
2. To stop forcing yourself to take the poisons.
3. To realise that you give up absolutely nothing and achieve many marvellous benefits.

With the correct frame of mind, quitting alcohol and nicotine at the same time, is easier and more enjoyable than doing so separately. However, if you are a smoker with a drink problem and you cannot bring yourself to quit both at the same time, it is advisable to quit smoking first, even if you feel that your smoking is not really a problem. If you are a smoker with a drink problem but have already signed the pledge and successfully abstained from alcohol for a reasonable period, whether you feel that you are cured or otherwise, **DO NOT, I REPEAT DO NOT** start drinking again so that you can first quit smoking, just quit smoking and you will soon be free of both.

I have heard people who are 'on the wagon' say that the problem with non-alcoholic drinks, is that you can only drink so many orange juices. Get it out of your mind that you have to drink *continually* at social events. Remember that the pleasure on such occasions is due to the pleasant company, not the drink. As with smoking, there is no need for substitutes. It is particularly important not to drink these non-alcoholic beers, they are the equivalent to herbal cigarettes. It's incredible when you think about it, society spends years brainwashing us to become impervious to the foul taste of beer, in order to obtain the effects of alcohol. Then they try to persuade us that the effects aren't so great after all, take away the alcohol and leave us stranded with the foul taste. If you feel it would be more manly to drink non-alcoholic beer rather than water or some other soft drink, grow up! It was that stupidity that got you hooked in the first place!

There are certain other bogeys to be laid about alcohol. I have argued that the reasons or excuses we make for imbibing alcohol - thirst, taste, effect, social, whatever – are fallacies. You might well argue that the chemicals required to produce stainless steel would be ineffective individually, but the combination is effective. Perhaps it's the combination of thirst, taste and effect that makes drinking so pleasurable, after all any mathematician will tell you that two minuses make a plus.

These sort of arguments are red herrings, nevertheless, they are difficult to dispel. However, if you imbibed a combination of arsenic and cyanide, do you think that they would negate each other, or kill you twice as quickly? When we mix chemicals to make stainless steel, we include constituents not because of any individual benefits, but purely to obtain a product which we know will benefit us. With alcohol, we justify it for the individual reasons, not the overall result. But each individual reason is a fallacy, we then try to justify it by saying: "Perhaps the combination will cause a genuine benefit?" The fact is it doesn't. We already know that the combination causes:

MISERY AND RUIN

If we weren't meant to imbibe alcohol, why is it that from time immemorial, every form of civilisation from the most primitive tribes to modern western society have produced and imbibed alcoholic beverages? So what? From time immemorial, people have drowned in rivers, streams and lakes, but does anyone suggest that was the object the creator had in mind for them? Alcohol has other purposes than self-destruction, the only relevant point is that from time immemorial, imbibing alcohol has only served to produce misery.

THAT IS FACT

If that is the case, why did the United States abandon prohibition? I'll answer that question, but first a more relevant question, why did the United States institute prohibition? Why does the Muslim religion forbid alcohol? Why are some abstentionists so vehement in their opinions? What right has anyone to be so fanatical when many of them have never even touched a drop of alcohol in their lives? What right have these people to try to force their prejudice and spoil the pleasure of others?

The United States instituted prohibition, for exactly the same reason that Mohammed did. Because it is blatantly obvious that the effects are evil. Certain teetotallers are so vehement because their childhood was ruined by alcohol. They saw their mothers beaten, their families broken up and their brothers and sisters starved and taken into care because of alcohol.

So why did prohibition fail? For exactly the same reason that the willpower method doesn't work, that AA make it harder for *alcoholics* to quit. Drug addicts cannot force themselves to quit and the more that society tries to force them do so, the more determined are the addicts to obtain their crutch and the less likely they are to realise that the crutch is their real enemy.

Now let us deal with other drugs and in particular with the one that still sends shivers down my spine:

HEROIN

CHAPTER 48

Heroin and Other Drugs

Before I had actually met any heroin, or ex-heroin addicts, I had two differing concepts of heroin addiction. Both were rather vague impressions formed mainly from watching Hollywood films. My 'eastern' concept was of smoke-filled opium dens, packed with permanently drugged Chinese, who spent their entire lives laying on mattresses until the drug finally killed them. Their outward appearance was somewhat similar to the image of the down and out meths drinker on skid row. However, the obvious squalor and short life were apparently more than compensated by the pleasure of the ecstatic hallucinations induced by the drug.

My 'western' concept was of prostitutes who seemed to spend the whole of their lives going through the terrible physical withdrawal pains, not because they were trying to kick the drug, but because it was the policy of their pimps to make them suffer. I was never quite sure whether the girls became heroin addicts first and went into prostitution to pay for their 'habit', or whether they became prostitutes first and were forced into addiction so their pimps could more easily control them.

Strangely, the opium smokers never seemed to suffer the terrible withdrawal pains and the prostitutes didn't seem to get the incredible highs. But both concepts made it clear, that once hooked on heroin, it is virtually impossible to get free. I was always curious to know why. Was it because the withdrawal pains were so long and hideous as to be unbearable? That seemed unlikely. I believed that no matter how bad or persistent those symptoms were, I would endure them in order to escape from that hellish nightmare. Or was it because the delights of the hallucinations were so pleasurable? It was certainly this aspect that created my morbid fear of heroin, that once tasted, those delights could never be resisted. Or was it a combination of both?

I was so pleased to have the opportunity to question ex-heroin addicts. However, no matter how erudite or articulate they were on other subjects, they seemed to be terribly vague about their own addiction. At first I doubted whether they had actually been addicted, or wondered whether they had no desire to discuss the subject. It

523

transpired that many of them had been very badly addicted, and were only too happy to discuss the subject. But they seemed as vague about the subject as I was. None of them seemed to get the marvellous highs. Some would say that the physical withdrawal pangs were horrendous. However, if you asked them exactly where it hurt, there was usually a pregnant pause followed by waffle.

Gradually it began to dawn on me, they sounded just like smokers:
"Why do you smoke?"
"Because I enjoy it so much."
"I've been watching you smoke. You don't even appear to be aware that you're smoking, what's so enjoyable about it?
"Unless you've been a smoker it's hard to describe."
"I have been a smoker, so describe it to me."
"If you've been a smoker, you'll know what I mean."
"I'm afraid I don't. I was as vague as you appear to be. But if you enjoy it so much, why did you try to quit?"
"Because it was affecting my health and costing a fortune."
"So why didn't you quit?"
"It was the terrible withdrawal pangs."
"Describe them to me."

Start up that sort of conversation with a smoker and he'll soon find an excuse to leave your company. However, ask a golf addict why he enjoys playing golf and it will be you looking for the excuse. He'll spend the rest of the evening telling you why provided you are prepared to listen to him.

I've just watched a programme about heroin addiction on Open University. The expert doctors and psychiatrists were trying to analyse the chemical effects and relate it to what they called 'conditioning'. The chief doctor admitted that he just couldn't understand why these addicts continued to suffer such ignominy by remaining hooked. Ironically, most of the people taking part in the programme, including some of the medical experts, were smoking. Could they explain to their patients or children why they suffered the ignominy of being slaves to nicotine?

It was a surprise to me when many ex-heroin addicts told me that they got no high whatsoever from the first dose. In fact, just like smoking, they found the first dose repulsive, and just like smoking, the trap was sprung: "No way could I ever get hooked on this stuff." If heroin gives a genuine high, why doesn't the 'user' receive it on the first dose?

I am aware that some heroin addicts believe that they received a genuine 'buzz' on the first intake. However, if you question them on what the 'buzz' actually consisted of, you realise that, like the first cigarette, it's the excitement, the novelty, the rebel, the daredevil, rather than any actual physical pleasure. They are the sort of people that would have seen Hans Christian Anderson's King, not in his altogether, but in a suit of the finest silks.

The expression 'buzz' is confusing. It means different things to different people. Youngsters say to me:

"I think I'm going to miss that buzz."

"What do you mean by that?"

"A dizzy feeling."

"Are you telling me that you enjoy feeling dizzy? I can't imagine anything worse!"

At school I remember a crowd of schoolboys sniffing at a bottle of stain remover. I was curious and tried it myself. After a few sniffs I began to feel faint. In no way could it be described as a pleasant experience, but I was fascinated by the effect. I remember feeling exactly the same fascination when sniffing smelling salts and that was decidedly unpleasant. These were the days when glue-sniffing was unheard of. I loved the smell of the glue that was supplied with model aircraft kits. In fact I still do. I didn't become a glue-sniffer, but I can understand how these things get started.

Any chemical that we imbibe, touch or inhale must have some effect on us. That effect might be good, bad, insignificant or otherwise. Heroin is a powerful anaesthetic and as such, it has a relaxing effect on the body. However, that effect is only desirable if you believe that removing the flashing oil-warning light from your car will solve your problem. In both cases, far from solving your problem, you have exacerbated it. Even to describe the anaesthetic effect of heroin as a 'high' is erroneous, because heroin is not a stimulant but a depressant.

As I will explain in a moment, whether we become hooked or not, isn't affected one iota if our first experience of the drug is pleasant or otherwise. Except that is, if the first experience is unpleasant or insignificant, our fear of becoming hooked is removed. By definition, it is essential to gain the confidence of the victim in order for a confidence trick to succeed. We know the dangers, so why do we even take the first dose of nicotine, pot, heroin, whatever? I would suggest that nine times out of ten, it is because of curiosity, the rebel instinct, peer pressure or just sheer boredom. I would also suggest, that with the exception of nicotine, the initial dose is usually taken when the victim is under the influence of alcohol.

The awful thing is that when we sample that first dose of the drug, it's not a particularly momentous occasion in our lives. After all, we little suspect that this seemingly insignificant act will soon dominate and ruin the rest of our lives, any more than the person who is about to be the victim of a fatal car accident realises it when they commence their journey. It's only when we *have* become hooked, or more accurately, *realise* that we have become hooked, that the first experience takes on significance. Now the addicts feel pretty stupid,

525

they are looking back at that first dose with hindsight. They tend to feel more stupid if they have to say: "It was repulsive, so I went on taking it." Far easier to say: "I must have got some sort of buzz or pleasure from it, why else would I have continued to take it?" Why else indeed? Any addict's recollection of their first *insignificant* experience should be taken with a pinch of salt.

Most smokers believe that they only actually enjoy one or two of the cigarettes that they smoke each day. The truth is that they don't enjoy any of them. Occasionally we get smokers at the clinics who believe that they get a genuine high from every cigarette that they smoke. It's not until we insist that they smoke one consciously and ask them to explain what the actual high or pleasure is, that it even occurs to them that there isn't one.

There is no doubt in my mind that it is not the great highs that keeps the heroin addict hooked, any more than it is the great highs that keep smokers hooked. Being an opiate, there is no doubt a similar effect as with alcohol. I'm all for pain killers used as a temporary relief to physical pain, as used by dentists or anaesthetists, but as a long term, or even medium term solution to depression, they are merely a guarantee for ever increasing depression.

Perhaps the real power of heroin is that it combines the properties of alcohol and nicotine. It both inebriates and causes physical aggravation from withdrawal. Perhaps you still see inebriation as some sort of advantage. But why should someone want to be inebriated? Doesn't that mean that they are not contented? That there is something missing in their lives? Inebriation merely creates temporary oblivion. In no way does it solve problems, on the contrary, it makes them worse. It wouldn't be quite so bad if you actually enjoyed the temorary oblivion. But how can you enjoy a situation when you are oblivious to it? Do you think that alcoholics are happy people? If so, just attend AA see the reality.

If heroin does combine the dual aspects of alcohol and nicotine, they are both enormous disadvantages and double reason never to get involved with heroin. But what we are concerned with here is what keeps the addict hooked, and how to break the addiction. Is it the great highs or the terrible withdrawal pangs?

I do not believe there is a tremendous high from taking heroin. But let us assume for a moment there is. There are marvellous highs in life: Christmas as a child, a nice holiday, a meeting with good friends that you haven't seen for a long time, watching a great sporting event, or film or play, or listening to your favourite music. You can enjoy those things at the time. You can enjoy anticipating them and reminiscing after them, but do you feel punished when you are not doing them? Do you feel deprived if you cannot do them every day or every hour of each day? That is the real test. It's pleasant to have a genuine high, but if you must have it, it's not a real pleasure, but a need. Non-heroin addicts don't need heroin. Only heroin addicts need it for exactly the same reason that nicotine addicts need nicotine, to try to end the empty insecure feeling that the last fix created.

It isn't the marvellous highs that keep heroin addicts hooked, but the awful effects of withdrawal. Let's now examine some facts about these pangs.

Another great misconception about heroin addiction which persists in this enlightened age, is that the physical withdrawal effects are so severe, that they will kill advanced addicts should they attempt to quit 'cold turkey'. Yet the worst any of these ex-addicts described it as was: "Rather like having flu". If you asked a thousand people "What is the worst experience that you have ever had in your life?" Do you think even one of them would say: "I can answer that without hesitation. It was flu." If you asked a million people: "You have a choice of either having flu, or being a heroin addict for the rest of your life?" Do you think that even one of them would plump for heroin addiction?

Perhaps you are still not convinced. Let us examine further evidence. The programme that I referred to on Open University also explained how heroin, and other drug addicts, could serve long prison sentences, deprived of their dependence, without any noticeable horrific physical effects. Yet when they left prison and went back to their old environment, they were soon back on the drug.

Even more remarkable, they described how American police posed as heroin addicts to infiltrate the system. They discovered what they were buying contained only a small proportion of heroin, in certain cases none at all. Yet the genuine addicts who were buying exactly the same concoctions appeared to be completely oblivious to the fact. If the withdrawal was purely physical, how could the placebo relieve it?

The programme also briefly referred to an earlier programme about an exceptionally high success rate in treating heroin addicts achieved at a monastery in Bangkok. I had seen this programme previously in more detail. At various times of the day the addicts had to drink a special concoction. The leading monk claimed that the brew would purge all traces of heroin from the addict's body. What the brew actually did was to make the addict violently sick. This wasn't really surprising, when chemically analysed, the main constituent of the brew proved to be our old friend nicotine. Isn't it amazing how nicotine always seems to be associated with other addictions, be it alcohol, marijuana, heroin or crack?

The ordeal the addicts went through was quite horrendous, when they weren't throwing up, they just lay on their bunks feeling sorry for themselves. Yet the success rate was exceptional and I believe it. The western experts spent many hours searching for 'magic' ingredients within the concoction, mystified as to why the method was so successful. The method did help to explode this myth that advanced heroin addicts cannot go 'cold turkey'. Not only did these addicts go 'cold turkey', they were half starved and forced to imbibe regular doses of poison at the same time, yet not only did they survive, most of them succeeded.

The misconception that it is physically impossible for advanced heroin addicts to go 'cold turkey' has lead the so-called experts on heroin addiction, more than with any other drug, to advocate a policy of gradual withdrawal and the use of substitutes. I have explained why such a policy will guarantee to make success difficult if not impossible for nicotine. Exactly the same principles apply for all drugs.

I can imagine few worse traumas than being permanently blinded, but someone born blind regards that situation as normal. One of the evils of drug addiction is that the slide to ruination is so slow and gradual that the addict is not aware of it. Non-addicts will regard a chronic alcoholic, or someone injecting heroin into their veins, or a smoker permanently coughing his lungs up, with absolute horror. However, to the addict, that situation is normal. So much so, even advanced addicts aren't quite sure that they really want to stop. Heroin addicts don't get any great pleasure from heroin any more than smokers or alcoholics do from tobacco or drink. Neither do they suffer unbearable physical pains when they abstain, any more than smokers or alcoholics do.

All that keeps any of them hooked, is that when they attempt to stop, they believe that they are being deprived of a genuine crutch or pleasure. Sooner or later, they decide that the misery of being an addict is less than the misery of feeling deprived, after all, in their minds, the problem wasn't that they used the drug, but that they couldn't control the level. They don't understand that they never did control the level and that to attempt to do so only gives them the worst of all worlds, they are now both addicted and deprived.

It is in fact easy to quit all drugs. The so-called experts know that the real problem is for addicts to stay off the drug. They attribute this to the fact that ex-addicts return to the same environment and drug-using friends and it is this influence that sooner or later gets them hooked again. That is rather like saying that smokers got hooked again because they walked into a tobacconist shop and enjoyed chatting with the owner. The ex-smoker walked into that shop for one reason only: TO GET THE DRUG. The reason that so many ex-drug addicts fall back into the pit is because, while they are merely being abstemious rather than cured, and while they retain a craving for the drug no matter how slight or occasional, they remain vulnerable, and because they have no great fear of the drug, eventually they succumb. They return to the old environment and seek out their old friends because they want the drug. Addicts will return to associate with people they loathe for one reason only:

TO GET THE DRUG!

The monk's method was really reverse shock treatment. Shock treatment is usually ineffective because, no matter how horrific it might be, addicts don't believe that it will happen. They can only actually experience it when it's too late. However, any addict subjected to the monk's cure, survived an actual experience 10 times more horrendous than the addiction itself. No way were they going to become addicted again, because no way were they going through that cure again!

I underwent a very similar experience after seeing those awful VD films during national service. They were so effective, that not only have I never been tempted to visit a brothel, but to this day I cannot bring myself to sit on the seat of a public toilet. I remember absolutely nothing about the diseases themselves, but the cure seemed horrendous. The thought of the catheter still sends shivers down my spine.

I am not advocating the monk's method, but explaining why it works. It has three major disadvantages:

1. The horrendous trauma the addicts have to go through.
2. It doesn't actually remove the basic problem of the craving, so the ex-addict remains feeling deprived and vulnerable, so that some not only get hooked again, but have to go through the horror of the cure again.
3. Far from solving the mysteries of addiction, it merely adds to the overall confusion.

Fortunately, there is no need to resort to such drastic tactics. The beautiful truth is that it is easy to kick any drug once you have established that it does nothing for you at all, you merely substitute whatever the drug is for nicotine when reading this book and 'EASYWAY'. How can I possibly group together drugs like alcohol, crack, nicotine, heroin, cocaine and the myriad of other drugs that are now on the market with all their differing effects on our minds and bodies? I do so for just that reason:

THEY DO HAVE AN EFFECT ON OUR MINDS AND BODIES

I am often accused of being overconfident, sometimes to the point of being arrogant. However, I am not arrogant enough to believe I know better than my creator. On the contrary the confidence and moral strength that I have is a direct result of the immense faith that I have in the intelligence of our creator. I'm not talking about blind faith, as if I had a guardian angel watching over me, although I am bound to admit that often in my life it has appeared that way. I'm talking about confidence and strength based on facts. The creator has produced this incredibly sophisticated and complicated machine. The more we learn about that machine, the more we realise how little we know. Is it not terribly arrogant and unbelievably stupid for any human being, even if he be the most learned and qualified physician on the planet, to say:

I KNOW BETTER THAN MY CREATOR!

I have already given many examples of how chemically affecting your mind and body, although it might superficially appear to be beneficial, is merely courting disaster. Doctors prescribe 'uppers' and 'downers' for their patients. Can we blame youngsters for thinking: "Where's the harm in taking an 'upper'? It gives me energy. With two or three I can dance all night." But that youngster wasn't meant to dance all night. Tiredness isn't an illness, like hunger or thirst, it is a flashing warning light. It is saying:

YOU NEED TO REST

That tiredness might be the result of an illness, or it might be the natural functioning of the body telling you that now is the time to rest. In either case, by popping a pill, that youngster does the complete opposite to what his creator advises. That pill, far from solving the problem, has merely removed a vital warning light. Do you really believe that any pill can actually take the place of rest? If so, we need never sleep or rest again, all we need to do is just keep popping pills. Unfortunately, all too many youngsters, and adults for that matter, believe that the pill does solve the problem. Who can blame them if a qualified doctor has prescribed the pill? All too often pill-popping ends up with the victim sleeping permanently. It is essential to distinguish between an illness and its symptoms. Far too much modern medicine is based on removing or covering up the symptoms rather than curing the illness. Symptoms are not only vital warning lights, but are also often a vital part of the cure.

Imagine that you are an airline pilot, completely dependent on your instruments, your compass, your fuel gauge, your altimeter etc. If your fuel gauge read zero, would you alter its calibration and happily fly on? Your body is also equipped with senses and warning lights, each one many times more sophisticated than the most modern aircraft, all designed to protect you and keep you happy, in fact all designed to achieve one object:

YOUR SURVIVAL

Start playing around with those instruments my friend, and you might as well be flying blindfold. You might well survive for a while, but no way will you be happy and eventually you'll smash into a mountain.

It's not only that all these drugs actually achieve the opposite to the object you take them for, but they all have unpleasant side effects, physical, mental, financial and social. What's more, those side effects are also accumulative.

What's wrong with a drug that makes you feel more secure? Your *feeling* of insecurity was your protection and thus your security. The drug merely reverses a situation of *feeling* insecure but *being* secure, to *feeling* secure but *being* insecure.

Apart from the 'waves' my main problem in treating heroin addicts is to persuade them that they cannot possibly be completely cured from heroin or any other drug addiction if they continue to smoke. Heroin addicts will often inhale tobacco smoke with the heroin while 'chasing the dragon'. This seems to increase the 'high'. All it really does is partially relieve two lows until withdrawal starts again. I have met only one person that could have been described as an alcoholic but never smoked. I've yet to meet a non-smoking heroin addict. However, as is the case with alcohol, ideally it is best to quit both heroin and nicotine at the same time. If this cannot be done, then it is advisable to quit the nicotine first. It is the empty feeling caused by nicotine withdrawal that creates the need for other drugs, while that remains, so does the need. Now let's deal with:

THE 'WAVES'

CHAPTER 49

The 'Waves'

I have said it is easy to kick any drug be it nicotine, alcohol or heroin. Although nicotine is in a class of its own in terms of the total physical carnage that it reaps, and even though the adverse physical effects in many cases is acute and obvious, even chain-smokers are able to function mentally, financially and socially; whereas chronic alcoholics and heroin addicts have often lost their jobs, their homes, their families and their self-respect, even their desire to live. Usually, the only friends that they are left with are people in the same boat who have no desire to help the addict escape. I refer to these side effects resulting from the illusion of being dependent upon a drug as the 'waves'.

Many, who were once respected pillars of our society, will have become thieves or even murderers, as a result of the mind-blowing or financial burden of their addiction. The addiction itself is easy to defeat. Most people have enough imagination to realise how much happier their lives will be once they are free from the addiction. However, how can people possibly be happy if they have no job, home, family, friends, self-respect or desire to live?

It is a complete waste of time trying to persuade chronic alcoholics or drug addicts to quit their drugs, unless you can remove the 'waves', or at least some of them at the same time. Indeed some people believe that it's not so much that alcohol or drug addiction disrupts people's lives, but that people with disrupted lives tend to turn to drugs.

Many experts dispute this argument on the basis that the majority of alcoholics, cocaine and heroin addicts are strong-willed and previously successful people. But we tend to use material wealth as our gauge of success. Does material wealth bring happiness? I suppose the classic example of the man that had everything by normal western society standards, was Richard Burton. Did he throw away everything he had and suffer an early death because he became an alcoholic? Or did he become an alcoholic because, although he appeared to have everything, whatever he had didn't make him happy? Perhaps there was a void in his life. If he was so deliriously happy, why did he throw it all away to become an alcoholic? What is so pleasant about being an alcoholic?

One theory is that in depressed communities with high unemployment, many addicts with no purpose in life, continue to take the drug because the addiction itself gives them a purpose. It provides a reason to get out of bed each day, a justification to beg or steal sufficient money in order to obtain the day's fix. Groups of friends gather to discuss the business of obtaining money to support their 'habit'.

Ironically, the addiction provides them with a double purpose in life. The battle against society to support their 'habit', and the battle against the addiction itself. The problem is, if they defeat the addiction by kicking the drug, they lose both of their purposes and are left with a drab, purposeless existence. Little wonder that they are sooner or later lured back into the pit.

I believe that there is much substance in this theory. In fact I'd go one stage further by suggesting that it was the purposeless existence that got them onto drugs in the first place. I believe that our intelligence and the rapid changes in human lifestyles resulting from the industrial revolution has left a void in most of our lives. In other words, if there were no such thing as nicotine, alcohol or other drugs, we'd have had to invent something. Perhaps that is what we actually did. The great variety of new drugs which regularly appear on the market would tend to support this theory. Just as it doesn't matter what brand of cigarettes you smoke provided you get your nicotine, the impression I get from youngsters nowadays is: it doesn't particularly matter what drug it is, just so long you have some sort of fix!

Many believe that it's a chicken and egg situation. Did the depressed life style create the need for the drug or did the drug create the depressed life style? The depressed life style must have come first. Even if it were only a temporary situation like Vietnam conscripts, or just a fraction of a second like youngsters needing a boost in their confidence at social occasions, or not having the strength to resist the pressure from their peers.

It's incredible when you pause to think about it, in their blissful ignorance, all other species on the planet are quite content with the vital essentials that our creator has provided. But the most intelligent species has provided a massive and expanding problem for itself:

A DEPENDENCE ON DRUGS

What can we do about it. In many individual cases it is possible to do something about it. Often the lost family, friends or job might not be irrecoverably lost. It isn't so much that the family, friends or employer disown the addict, but just as addicts themselves eventually lose their resistance to fighting the drug and accept their fate, so their family and friends also lose faith in the addict's ability to do so. They are sick of the lies and the deceit. Eventually they also accept, not only the addict's failure, but their own.

It is not always appreciated that the people that suffer most in these situations are not the chronic addicts themselves. As explained above the effect of the addiction is to partly anaesthetise them to the true horror of their situations and they believe that they cannot escape so merely close their minds to the situation. However, the people that love them have no immunization against the true horror of the situation. It is hard enough to lose someone that you dearly love because they die. How much more painful must it be to watch that person change from a happy, loving, gentle and considerate friend into a selfish, aggressive and vulgar monster! Especially when the cause of the change is so obvious to you, and yet you seem powerless to make that person see that the drug that they have become dependent on is the cause of their misery.

Just as the drug itself helps the addicts to block their minds to a problem that they cannot solve, the only way that the family and friends can cope with the problem, no matter how painful such a course of action might be to them, is eventually to disown the addict. However, if you can explain the whole confidence trick of drug addiction so that both the addicts and their families realise that an easy and permanent cure does exist, usually those friends are delighted to help resurrect someone that they believed was lost to them forever.

However, how can we help the addicts who only got hooked because their lives were so drab in the first place, or the ones whose friends and family cannot be persuaded to become involved? That solution isn't so simple, but I believe that it is solvable with the use of common sense and cooperation. I will discuss it in the concluding chapter.

CHAPTER 50

Conclusion

How can we rid this 20th century equivalent to the black plague from our society? Up to now we have failed even to check the rate of the expansion of drug addiction. To date there have been six basic approaches to the problem:

1. Shock treatment: massive publicity designed to inform addicts of what they already know far better than the people who are trying to inform them: **THAT THEY ARE FOOLS!** Not only has this approach failed to cure most addicts, it doesn't even prevent non-addicts from getting hooked.
2. The search for suitable substitutes: in Chapter 26 I explained why a suitable substitute is an impossibility and why the pointless search for them merely guarantees that ex-addicts retain the feeling of deprivation for the rest of their lives.
3. To alter the social and environmental conditions that make people turn to drugs: I'm all for doing that for its own sake, but alcohol, nicotine and heroin have proved there are no social or class barriers to drug addiction. To succeed, it would be necessary to remove all forms of stress from everyone's life. A nice thought, but hardly realistic.
4. The AA approach: which I consider to be the worst of all in that it implies that the fault lies in the addict rather than in the drug and society's attitude towards it.
5. To ban advertising: I believe that this has the same disadvantages as banning the product itself. I know in the countries in which advertising has been banned, statistics are produced to prove that the consumption of tobacco has gone down. I am a Chartered Accountant, statistics are my stock in trade. I know just how misleading they can be, particularly when presented by the authority whose decision is being judged, and especially when that authority is comprised of civil servants or politicians. A classic example is: "The rate of increase in inflation has gone down for the third month running." You might be excused for thinking that was good news, especially when announced in a

535

tone that implied that it was good news. It actually means that inflation has gone up for the third month running! Even if the statistics were correct and not presented in a misleading manner, how do they know it is the ban on advertising that has caused the drop in consumption? After all, there has been a considerable drop in the consumption of tobacco in the UK in recent years, but no advertising ban. The organisers of National No Smoking Day take credit for that drop without producing a shred of evidence to support their claim.

6. To wipe out the supply of the drugs, or what I refer to as the 'King Canute' approach: every week we hear that the authorities have busted a huge drugs ring and how they are winning the battle against the drug dealers, and yet at the same time drug addiction is on the increase. President Bush spent 7 billion dollars in an attempt to eliminate the supply. His 7 billion dollars has had about as much effect as a spit in the ocean. Can we learn nothing from history? The prohibition experiment provided us with certain valuable lessons. One was that laws should reflect the opinion of society and not the other way around, because unless they do, they will be flaunted. The most important lesson was that if there's a demand for a product, there will be a supply, illegal or otherwise.

Making alcohol illegal didn't solve the problem. On the contrary it merely created a far greater problem: organised crime. In fact the drug rings of today probably owe their success to the experience and training provided by the bootleggers. Even with heroin addiction, the authorities appear to attach more importance to the *crime* of dealing in the drug than to the misery suffered by the addicts.

All of these things would be excusable if they solved the problem, but whether you understand why or not, they haven't. It is blatantly obvious that you cannot remove stress or depression from the whole life of a single person, let alone the entire population. It is also obvious that, while people believe that drugs will solve, or even just alleviate their problems, they will take them, whether they be illegal, advertised, harmful or otherwise. There is only one alternative, that is to extend the solution that I have been advocating and proving to be successful for the last ten years.

It needs a massive counter-brainwashing exercise to educate society generally, not about the awful side effects of drug addiction, but of the two aspects about drugs that are not generally known:

1. That drugs not only fail to achieve the object for which they are taken, but succeed in achieving the complete opposite.
2. We don't need the drugs in the first place. We are already perfectly

equipped both to cope with life and to enjoy it.

If we can achieve that object, we have solved the problem, we have removed the desire for the drug. Any businessman will tell you that the one thing that will stop him manufacturing a product is for the demand to dry up. If that happens, he can advertise it until the cows come home, he can't even give it away.

However, there is one huge snag. I believe the creator has equipped us more than adequately with the tools that we need to survive, but I do not believe that we are equipped to handle the problems that we have created ourselves. The discovery of the wheel, how to control fire, to sew and cultivate seeds have led to incredible advances. I believe that people of my generation have been privileged to witness developments in technology that would have astounded the most imaginative visionaries such as H.G. Wells.

I'm basically an optimist. I want to live to be a hundred. So why do I have another black cloud looming at the back of my mind similar to the one I used to have as a smoker? This black cloud is not a fear for myself but for my children, and even more so for my grand-children. I'm not talking about the normal fears that parents have for the well-being of their offspring. I am talking about a fear of doom, a foreboding that we are in a headlong race to destroy our planet.

I know there are always people that will argue that the human race will survive because it has the ingenuity, sooner or later, to come up with the answer to any problem. What they really mean is: "So far we have survived, so why shouldn't we in the future?" They are no better than the ostrich with its head in the sand. Admirable as their optimism might be, they have about as much vision as the man, who having fallen from the roof of a skyscraper, as he passed the tenth floor, was overheard to say: "So far, so good!" It was the last remark he ever made.

Our domestic fire has now progressed to the creation of bombs that could create a holocaust a million times greater than any natural disaster like forest fires or volcanos. Our simple wheel has progressed through the Rolls Royce through Concorde to spacecraft which travel at speeds which defy the imagination. What's wrong with that? Nothing, providing we are in control and know where we are going. But where is it all leading? If you went back to the simple wheel and were travelling downhill with no brakes completely out of control, is that a desirable situation? Is that situation improved by making your vehicle a thousand times faster?

This is the reason for my foreboding. This terrible dichotomy. We have this incredible technology. But it has resulted mainly from war with the need to destroy your enemy in greater numbers and from the ambition of individuals or groups to obtain material wealth. This technology is out of control. It is being used not to improve our lot, or to make us happier, but to guarantee the destruction of our planet and blind us to generations of accumulated knowledge compiled by our ancestors on how to live in a civilised community in harmony and happiness.

Let's just briefly consider some of these problems: automation in theory should have been an asset. Organised properly, we should, all have a better standard of living and work only half the number of hours we did before. What's the actual result? 20% of the population have no job at all and most of them have little prospect of ever finding one. The ones that are lucky enough to have employment get ulcers and have heart attacks or mental break downs because they have to work twice as hard trying to keep up with the technology which enables them to produce the extra goods that few can now afford to buy. They have less leisure time to enjoy their hard-earned money, and when they try to spend it, they have a guilty conscience because so many people are either starving, or without employment or even hope for the future.

Unemployment is a main contributor to the increase in other problems like crime, violence and drugs. Could anybody possibly deny that these problems are not getting progressively worse? We send our experts to Yugoslavia to solve their problems. Have we forgotten that we've failed to solve our own problem in Ireland even after hundreds of years?

Modern, civilised medicine has progressed through prayer to spells, witchcraft, herbs, leaches, and scalpels. In other words, it's gone from praying that the disease will go, through to sucking it out, cutting it out, poisoning it or finding a magic pill that will cure it. During my lifetime the emphasis tended to move from the knife to a search for pills, poisons or drugs. There is no doubt in my mind that the medical profession is the prime cause of our present drug problems.

Now I must reiterate that I am not a doctor. So what right or qualifications have I to question their methods? Just this, for years I've listened to doctors giving advice about smoking, alcohol and drug addiction, which I know is the complete opposite to what it should have been. How do I know that they are not just as wrong about the other advice that they give with equal conviction?

Look at it another way. At each stage as medicine progressed from spells to pills, had I as a layman queried their advice, I would have received the same reaction as I do today about smoking: "They are qualified doctors, they know what they're doing."

Let's assume that you had a problem not with your body, but with your car. What would your reaction be if the only action of the mechanic that you had consulted was to say: "Let's kneel down and pray that your car will start."

We wouldn't use that mechanic because we know that there is just one remedy to cure a fault in a car and that is to find out the cause of it, and to rectify that cause. Doesn't this basic principle apply to any fault about every aspect in life? We can see that clearly with cars because man created them and understands how they work. But if it were possible to transport a stone age human into the 20th century, that mechanic would appear completely logical to him. That basic principle applies just as much to something going wrong with the human body, as to a car. The problem is, because we didn't create the human body and don't fully understand it, we have about as much chance of curing faults in it as a stone-age man would have of curing a fault in a modern car. The truth is, we stand a billion times less chance, because for all our modern technology, stone-age man isn't much less intelligent that we are, whereas the human body is a billion times more complicated than the most advanced car.

You might have noticed that the latest trend in the fight against disease, and the key to all of our problems lies in our DNA, or more specifically in our genes. It now seems that everything can be traced to our genes. Research has discovered that characteristics ranging from alcoholism, homosexuality and brain tumours can be traced in our genes.

The thing that I find most surprising is that surprise is registered when traits like homosexuality are traced in our genes. Surely the surprise should be if they weren't. How else can one species evolve into another? Take the computer that I'm using as an example. It is the DNA of the book. Thousands of copies will be printed from that basic DNA. Now supposing I change my mind, what's the only way I can reflect that change? By altering the DNA. The point I am making is that whether my views are right or wrong, correct or incorrect, they go into the computer because they are my views. They do not become my views because they are in the computer.

Suppose you were vetting the manuscript of my book and that you thought that there was a serious flaw in my argument. You could alter the computer to rectify that fault. It wouldn't do you the slightest bit of good because I would merely change it again when I read the proof. How do you know whether someone is homosexual because of the genes they were born with, or that their genes altered because they became homosexual?

Ignore homosexuality. Take disease. Change that gene and you've solved the problem. But isn't this exactly the same as researchers discovering 200 years ago that people who had the pox broke out in sores. Was the problem solved by cutting out the sores? The sores didn't cause the pox. The pox caused the sores.

Surely the first priority in solving any problem, be it disease or otherwise, is to ascertain the cause of the problem and to eradicate that cause. Any medical treatment or cure that does not do that should be treated with the utmost suspicion. To assume that disease is caused by our genes, is to assume our creator was not only unintelligent, but so thick as to actually programme disease into our genes.

I find this latest trend more terrifying than dabbling with hydrogen bombs. I'm all for knowledge, experimentation and progress. But we have numerous examples of the damage that can be caused when we play at being God. When we meddle in things that we don't understand. Until now the damage caused by the mistakes of the medical profession has been limited to the destruction of a few thousands or possibly millions of individuals. You can argue that if disease does register in our DNA, surely it would be sensible to remove it and not let it pass onto the next generation. I agree entirely, but we now have numerous examples of how man has interfered in what appeared to be relatively simple matters and created disaster. We introduced rabbits in Australia. They became a national disaster. The experts had a simple solution, there are no foxes in Australia. So they introduced foxes. Unfortunately the foxes were more intelligent than the experts. They saw no sense in wasting valuable energy chasing rabbits when the indigenous species were literally sitting ducks. Not only did the experts not solve the rabbit problem, but they created two extra problems.

Now sawing off the occasional limb when not strictly necessary is bad enough, but if we start messing around with something like DNA, something that we only recently discovered, we are really playing at being God. We are dabbling with the programme that produces the whole human species. Any mistake could be compounded a million times over. The fictional fear of Frankenstein's monster could easily become a reality in proportions that we never dreamed possible.

The awful thing is that just as we've been programmed to accept that activities like smoking nicotine and imbibing alcohol are natural, so we have been programmed to believe that disease is perfectly natural and normal, and that doctors can provide a magic pill to cure these diseases. For years, if I had a bad cold, my mother, or later my wife, would persuade me to go to the doctor. If I went, the doctor would prescribe pills, cough mixture and a few days in bed. At other times, for whatever reason, I couldn't afford the visit, the concoctions or the few days in bed. However, it didn't seem to matter much which process I went through, the length and extent of the aggravation appeared to be equal. Apart from the amazing Dr. Maisey, the most encouraging thing that has happened to me in recent years from a medical point of view, was the last time I had a bad cold. My doctor said: "No need to worry. There's a bug going round, you'll be fine in a few days." He prescribed no medication. That honest assessment did me far more good than any phoney placebos that he might have prescribed.

I accept that we are subject to attack from other living creatures on this planet. I also believe that, human beings, like elephants, are well equipped with an immune system that will survive such attacks. I cannot accept that the great variety of modern disease with which man and other creatures on this planet are inflicted with are the natural result of this battle for survival between viruses and man.

Are lung cancer and heart disease caused by viruses? Do you believe God created us just to endure these diseases? When I was a boy, man was discovering cures to killer diseases. Regrettably, I've lived to see the day when he now discovers diseases for which there is no cure. Why for countless generations has the survival of any species been dependent purely on climatic conditions and competition with other species? Isn't disease itself merely a product of man's civilisation, whether it be the black plague or AIDS. How did AIDS originate? Do you really believe that the creator was stupid enough to devise a system which required creatures to copulate in order to survive and at the same time would kill them if they copulated? Do you believe that the creator intended any creatures to wear condoms?

The evidence is overwhelming, these diseases can only be the result of the pollution and systematic rape of this planet by man, and by man dabbling in matters that he doesn't fully understand. The effect could be the reality of Frankenstein's monster in proportions that we could never have dreamed of. In fact it's already happening. But because it's in a form that is individually minute and hasn't yet permeated its full effect to creatures of our size, we choose to ignore it.

For generations peasants and farmers have passed on accumulated knowledge of how to gain the best from their precious land in order to support generation after generation from time immemorial to time immemorial. Now modern, intelligent man has learned that by the use of mass production techniques, chemicals, poisons and insecticides, we can produce sufficient yields to create an overpopulation problem today which will leave our grand-children struggling to feed a population twice the size of ours with a dust bowl inhabited by insects immune to poisons!

The incredible reality is, that most of these problems like pollution, destruction of the rain forests, overfishing or war, we already have a simple solution to. Merely: **TO CEASE DOING IT!**

Take war as an example. If you and I as neighbours were stupid enough to get into a punch-up because I insisted that the apples which fell my side of the fence from your apple tree were mine and not yours, we would both be condemned by the authorities. We would be instructed that if we hadn't the sense to grow up and settle such a petty problem like intelligent human beings, we should be civilised enough to settle it in court. But do these same authorities settle their problems in the same way? When the Argentinians landed in the

541

Falklands, they didn't kill or injure anybody. But did we let the United Nations arbitrate on the rights and wrongs of the matter? No, we just condemned innocent Argentinians and Britains to death to satisfy no greater objective than pride.

Let's take the running of the economy. If you or I were deliberately to accumulate debts out of all proportion to what we could possibly hope to repay, it would be a criminal offence. Yet as a country, we've been doing just this as deliberate policy for years. The stupid thing is that most of those debts have been created to finance wars that nobody wanted anyway, or in anticipation of wars that nobody wants.

These are some of the matters that lie at the root of my dark cloud. I take no credit for pointing out the potential disasters that face the human race. Indeed, it is thanks to the likes of David Bellamy, CND, and the Green party that we are aware of them. But all the talk and making people aware:

DOESN'T SOLVE THESE PROBLEMS

There are organisations like Green Peace whose members have risked and lost their lives saving a few whales, but they are a spit in the ocean. Their main enemies are the very governments whose population depends most heavily on the survival of the species. Let's go back to the man that fell from the skyscraper. Is he being stupid by saying: "So far so good?" Perhaps he isn't. It might be that he recognizes the fact that there's nothing he can do about it, and that he is merely putting on a brave face. The analogy would be more appropriate if he wore a parachute but hasn't yet pulled the ripcord. If he waits until he reaches the 10th floor, he's not being brave but stupid, because he has already left it too late:

HE'S DEAD!

I believe that is the exact position that we are in. Perhaps we have already left it to late. I'm still sufficiently optimistic to believe we can still do something about it. But it must be blatantly obvious to anyone with the smallest modicum of imagination, that unless we do something about it soon:

IT *WILL* BE TOO LATE!

As I have said, the problems are obvious and even the solutions are obvious and simple. The only problem is to get some coordinated actions to carry out these obvious and simple solutions. It doesn't take much thought to realise that the only people that have the power and authority to take effective action are our leaders, whether they be elected or otherwise.

The trouble is that our leaders seem to be the last people to understand what is blatantly obvious to the rest of the population. If you think about it, is this really surprising? Their jobs are dependent on obtaining our vote. In order to obtain our vote, they need to assess what the majority of people would like to happen. In theory we elect them to lead us, in practice we elect them to do what we want them to do. In that case, do we really need them? In their attempt to obtain our vote, both sides produce manifestos listing what they believe are the leading points that will catch our votes. The main ingredients tend to be matters like taxation, health, unemployment. Meanwhile our planet is being systematically destroyed. It's almost like planning your next holiday while your house burns down with you sitting in it.

I openly confess that years ago I lost faith in politicians. They seem incapable of solving any of the domestic problems like drugs, health, employment and crime. All of these matters seem to get progressively worse. Is that really surprising?

If you were about to have a brain operation, would you dream of allowing someone to operate on you who had never had a single day's training in medicine? Would you allow someone to extract or fill your teeth who had not a single day's instruction in dentistry? Yet amazingly, the most important job in the land, that of Prime Minister, requires no training or qualifications whatsoever. In fact we're prepared to entrust it to someone that hasn't even achieved the minimum qualifications to be even considered as being worthy to hold down a comparatively insignificant job like accountancy.

But this isn't really so bad, because that person can surround themselves with experts. Unfortunately these experts are equally ill-equipped and unqualified. We can't understand why the England football manager has the cream of league football to choose from, yet cannot produce a national side that would beat an average third division side. But if he'd never played football himself, we would need to look no further for the reason. How can we expect the National Health Service to run effectively, if the Minister of Health isn't even a doctor? These ministers hold down their jobs until they make a complete cockup. This usually results in a cabinet reshuffle. Sad really, because they are now moved from a job with which they had gained some knowledge or experience, to one they know absolutely nothing about. Unless of course their mistake is of such magnitude that it becomes obvious that they weren't fit to hold office in the first place. Then what do we do with them? Chop their heads off? Of course not. We don't live in a fantasy world like the Queen of Hearts. So do we just sack them? Don't be stupid, you only sack miners or train drivers for being incompetent. If a minister is hopelessly incompetent, you make them a Lord or a Lady!

I do politicians an injustice. I believe they do possess expert knowledge and competence in one walk of life: getting elected. Therein lies the problem. So much of their drive and energy is used up in getting elected that they are exhausted until the next election. I sense that most people nowadays feel the same way as I do about party politics and have no faith whatsoever in the ability of our leaders to solve our domestic problems, let alone those which would need the cooperation of the whole world.

Why is the United States of America the most powerful country in the world today? Does anyone seriously believe that it would be if it had remained 50 independent states? Would any one seriously suggest that the US revert to 50 separate units, all with their own separate languages, borders, currencies, laws and governments? I doubt whether one American in a thousand would even pause to contemplate such a retrograde suggestion.

So why do any of us even hesitate to go all out for a United Europe? I cannot think of one logical argument against it. I've heard what would appear to be logical arguments against it. Such as:

"We'll lose our national identity."

Will we? Have I lost my identity as a Londoner because I also happen to be an Englishman? Have the Scots or Welsh lost their national identity because they are also British. I would suggest that it has actually made them more aware of it.

"I don't want to be ruled by the Frogs or the Krauts."

It didn't seem to worry us being ruled by a Scot, a Welshman or a Yorkshireman. Surely the vast majority of us are only interested in whether the Prime Minister is competent or otherwise. If we were a United Europe, it wouldn't matter which part of Europe the Prime Minister came from. In any event Britain hasn't exactly excelled itself over the last 40 years. We might actually gain enormous benefits from being led by a German.

Sorry to harp back to golf, but there is already an outstanding example of the effect of a United Europe. I'm talking about the Ryder cup. When it was just Great Britain and Ireland, it was a non-event. The United European side have more than held their own against the Americans. When watching that match, are you any less supportive if the European happens to be a Spaniard, a Scot, a German, an Italian or a Swede? It makes not the slightest difference. It's been strongly hinted that, in spite of his poor form, Ballesteros should our next captain. I haven't heard the slightest suggestion of a protest, let alone howls of: "Have we already forgotten the Armada?"

I would suggest that our fears of a United Europe, are not so much fears of the successful achievement of it, but that the method by which we are trying to achieve it, makes the task a virtual impossibility.

Suppose you ran a competition to devise the most inefficient method to achieve a United Europe. Might I suggest that the following method would be odds on favourite to win first prize.

Each country elects 600 odd Members of Parliament. The contenders need have no other knowledge, experience or qualifications other than a burning ambition to have the power to make the world a better place to live in. In order to get elected, each candidate must represent the special interests of their own constituents. At the same time they must toe the party line. This creates a conflict of interests between their constituents their party and their own consciences which ensures that they will not survive unless they bend their principles somewhat. Every one of the 600 odd in each country has different views and interests anyway, but they all have one thing in common. They've all worked terribly hard to get elected to achieve power. Does anyone seriously believe that they are going to vote themselves out of a job by meekly handing over that power to a European Parliament? It doesn't take much imagination to work out why issues like 'Maastricht' are bound to end up as a complete farce.

Perhaps you are wondering what all this has to do with smoking and drug addiction? Just this, while the anxiety caused by these other matters continues, the soil remains fertile for the seeds of drug addiction to germinate and thrive. Although the solution to these problems is simple, those solutions cannot be achieved by individuals or groups, no matter how dedicated they might be. They cannot be achieved by individual countries. Even a country with the strength and power of the USA has failed to achieve them.

These problems are worldwide problems and will only be solved by cooperation on a worldwide basis. Perhaps you think that would be very difficult to achieve? I think it is ridiculously easy to achieve. After all if you said to every individual on the planet: "I can offer you, your children and your grand-children a life free of drugs, war, violence, hunger, pollution and insecurity." How many people on the planet do you think would refuse such an offer? Bear in mind, there are no strings attached. I'm not suggesting communism, regimentation or a form of George Orwell's 1984, but the complete opposite.

Perhaps you think that I have flipped. But just think about it. If the solutions to the actual problems are both obvious and simple, and we all want to solve those problems:

WHY ON EARTH SHOULD COOPERATION BE SO DIFFICULT?

Okay, if it's so simple, what is Allen Carr's simple solution? I promise you that I haven't flipped and that the solution is simple. However just as it is ridiculously easy to stop smoking, it takes me four hours to enable the average smoker to find it easy, so I cannot in just a few words explain why the solutions to these other problems are equally simple.

All I would ask you is this: if you have the same feeling of foreboding and also feel that our current politicians are incapable of solving our problems, please write and tell me so. I emphasize that I am not referring to any particular party. I mean all of them!

I also emphasize that I welcome comments, adverse or otherwise, on any matters contained in this book. If you would like to receive a reply, please enclose a stamped-addressed envelope.

Throughout this book I've been referring to you the reader, I now refer to and hope the establishment will allow Your Royal Highness to support me. Either way, I have the honour to remain sir,

Your Royal Highness's humble and obedient servant,

ALL CORRESPONDENCE SHOULD BE ADDRESSED TO:

ALLEN CARR,
THE EASY WAY TO STOP SMOKING,
1c AMITY GROVE,
RAYNES PARK,
LONDON, SW20 0LQ
TEL: 081 944 7761

HELP LINE 0891 664401

(48p per min. peak rate. 36p per min. off-peak)